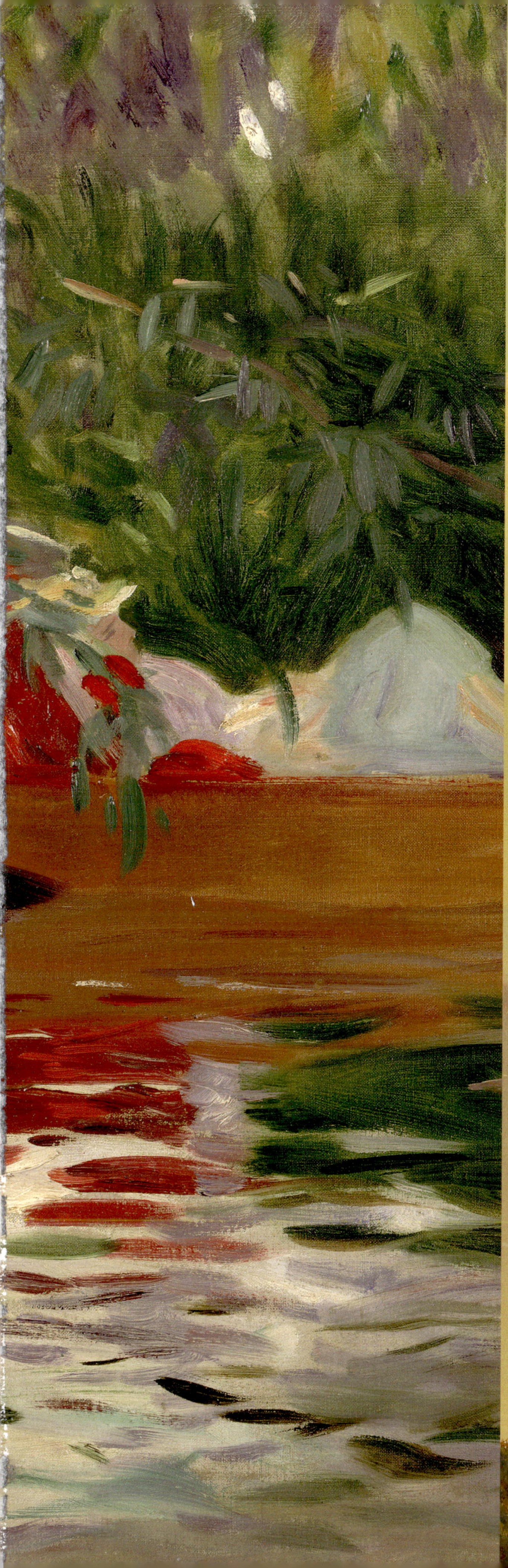
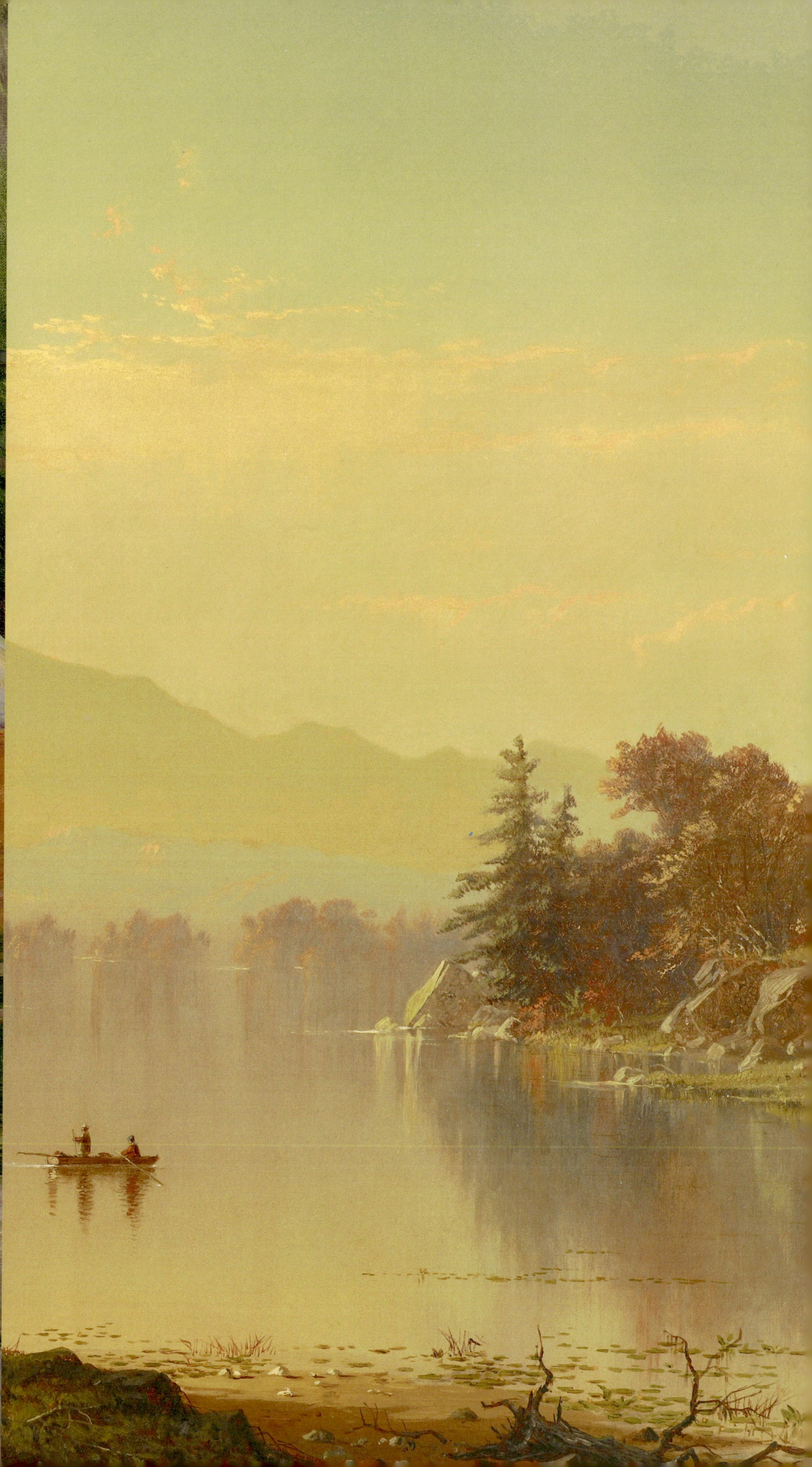

CELEBRATING THE AMERICAN SPIRIT

MASTERWORKS FROM CRYSTAL BRIDGES MUSEUM OF AMERICAN ART

Foreword by Don Bacigalupi

Christopher B. Crosman, *general editor*
Emily D. Shapiro, *managing editor*

with contributions by
William C. Agee
Don Bacigalupi
Carrie Rebora Barratt
Margaret C. Conrads
Christopher B. Crosman
Alison Demorotski
Anne Cohen DePietro
Stacey Epstein
Linda S. Ferber
Stephanie Mayer Heydt
Aaron W. Jones
Susan G. Larkin
Rebecca E. Lawton
Nancy Mowll Mathews
Alissa Walls Mazow
Leo G. Mazow
Linda Merrill
Emily D. Shapiro
Will South
Justin D. Spring
Niki Ciccotelli Stewart
Lisa Strong
Manuela Well-Off-Man
John Wilmerding

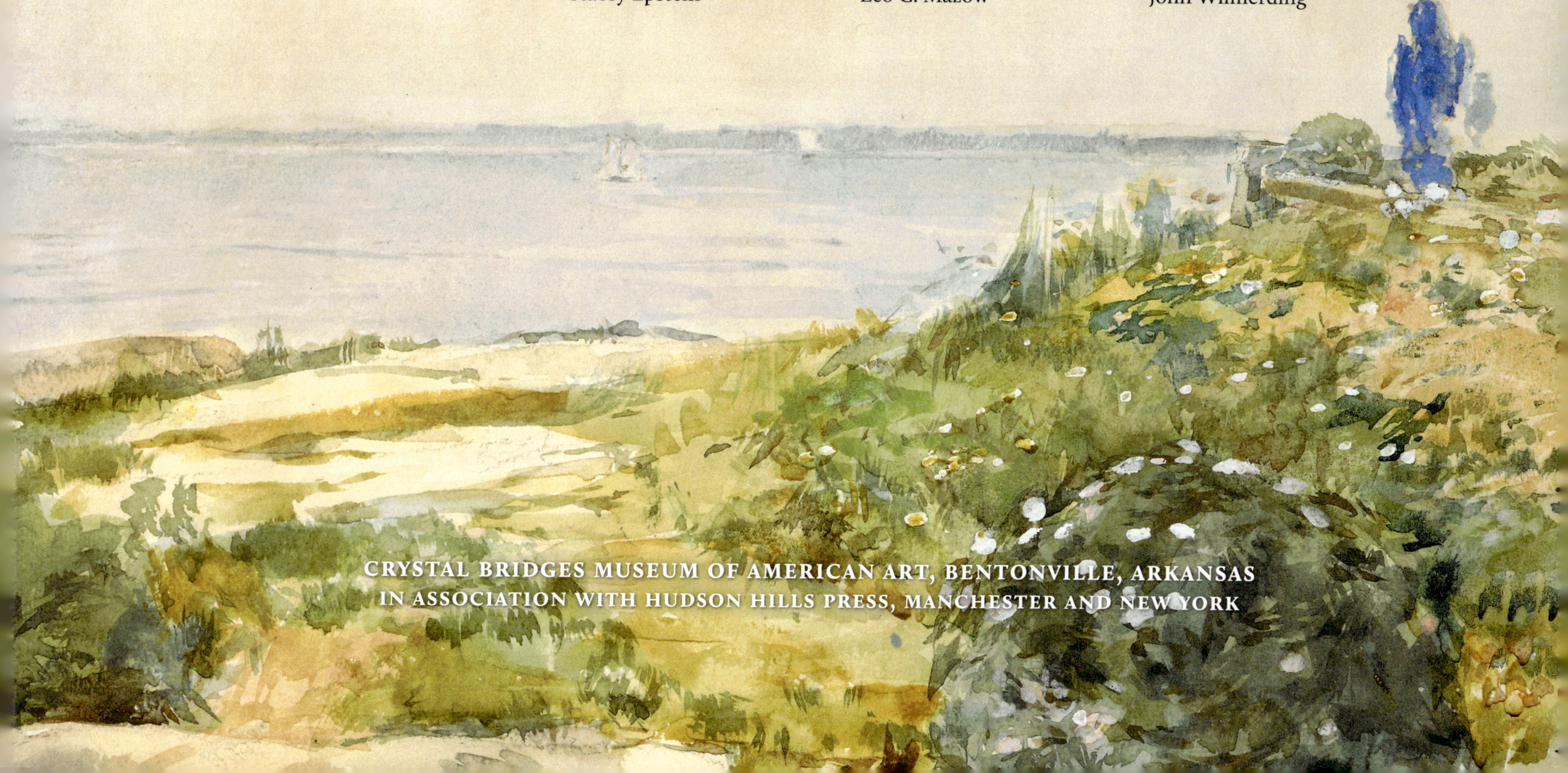

CRYSTAL BRIDGES MUSEUM OF AMERICAN ART, BENTONVILLE, ARKANSAS
IN ASSOCIATION WITH HUDSON HILLS PRESS, MANCHESTER AND NEW YORK

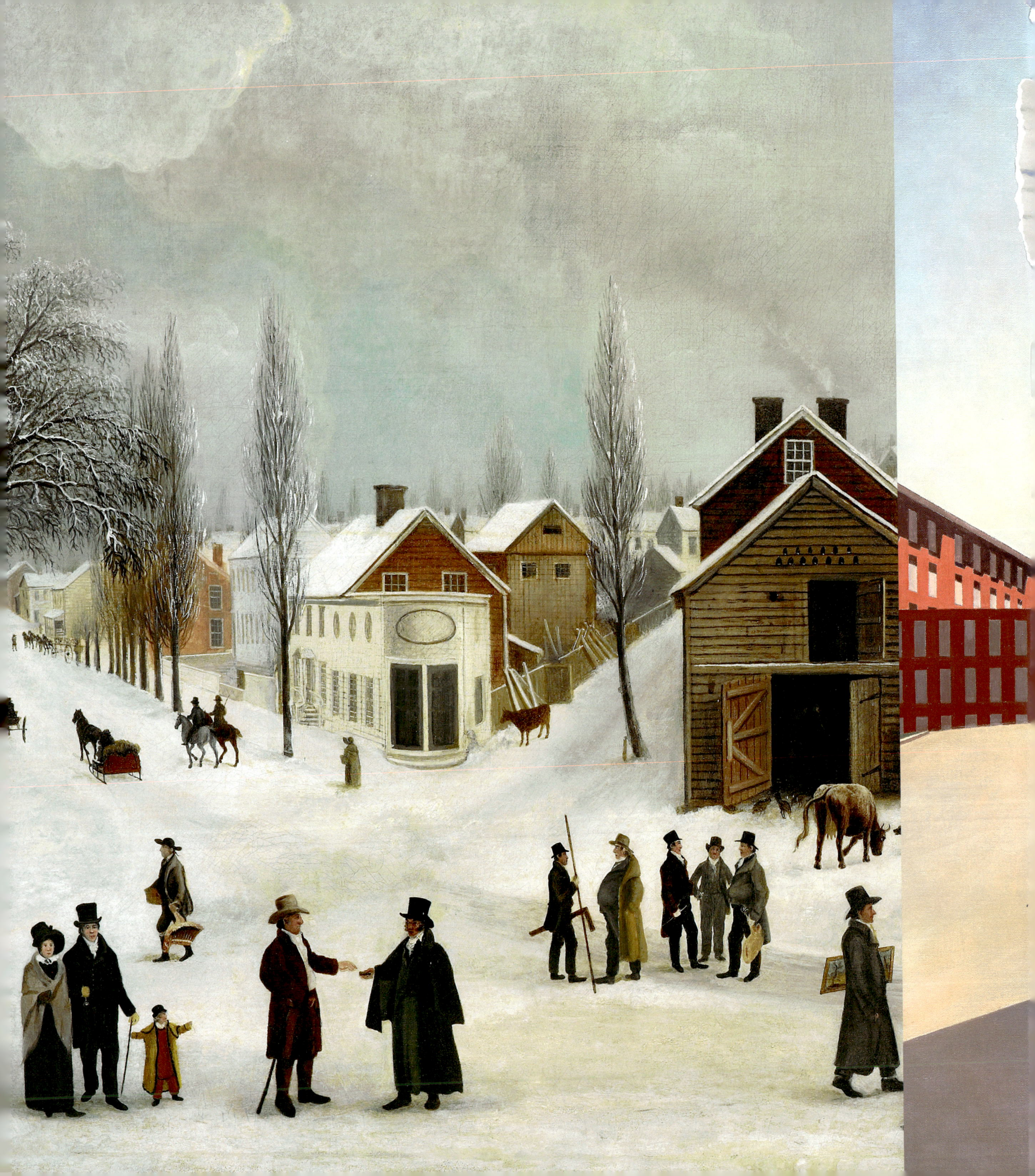

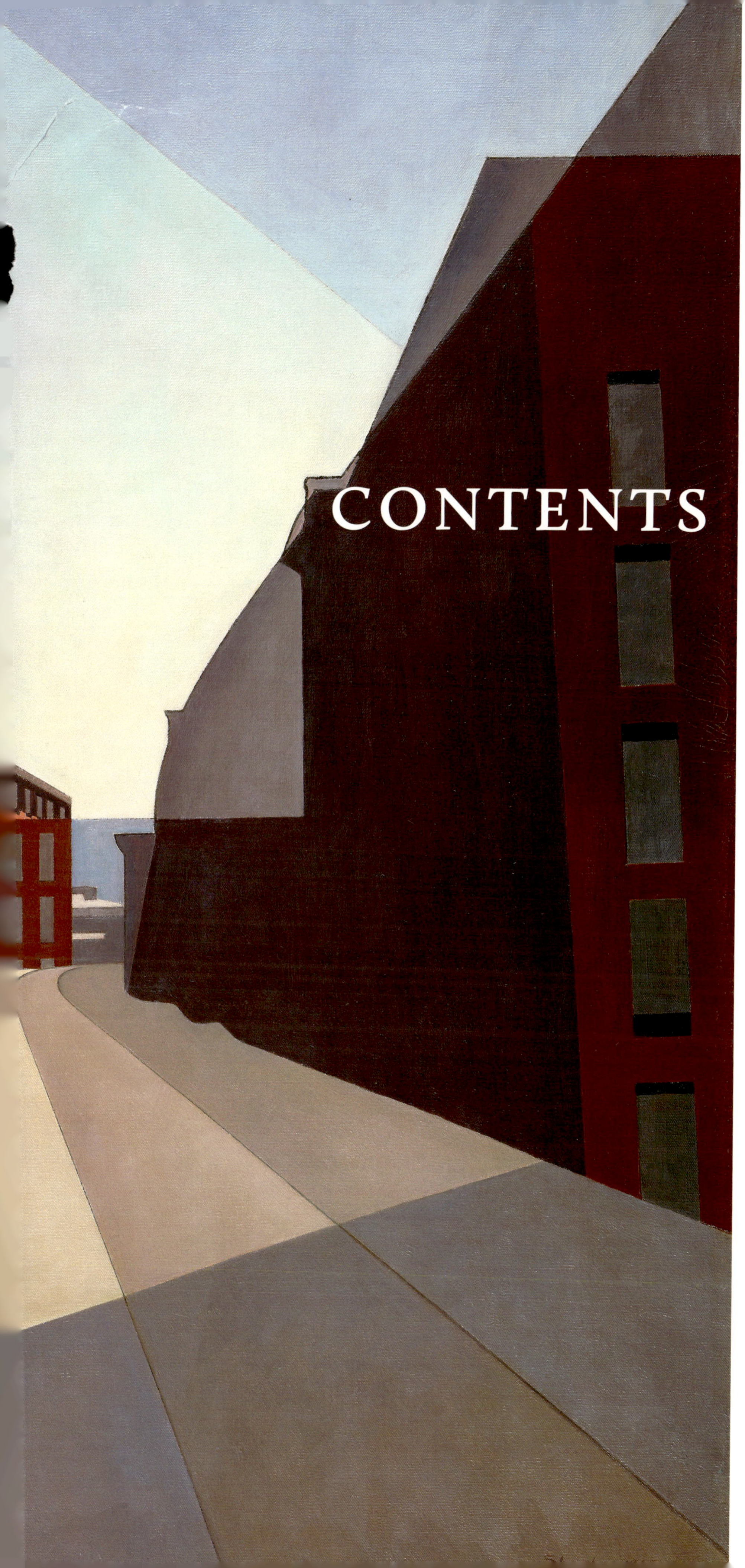

CONTENTS

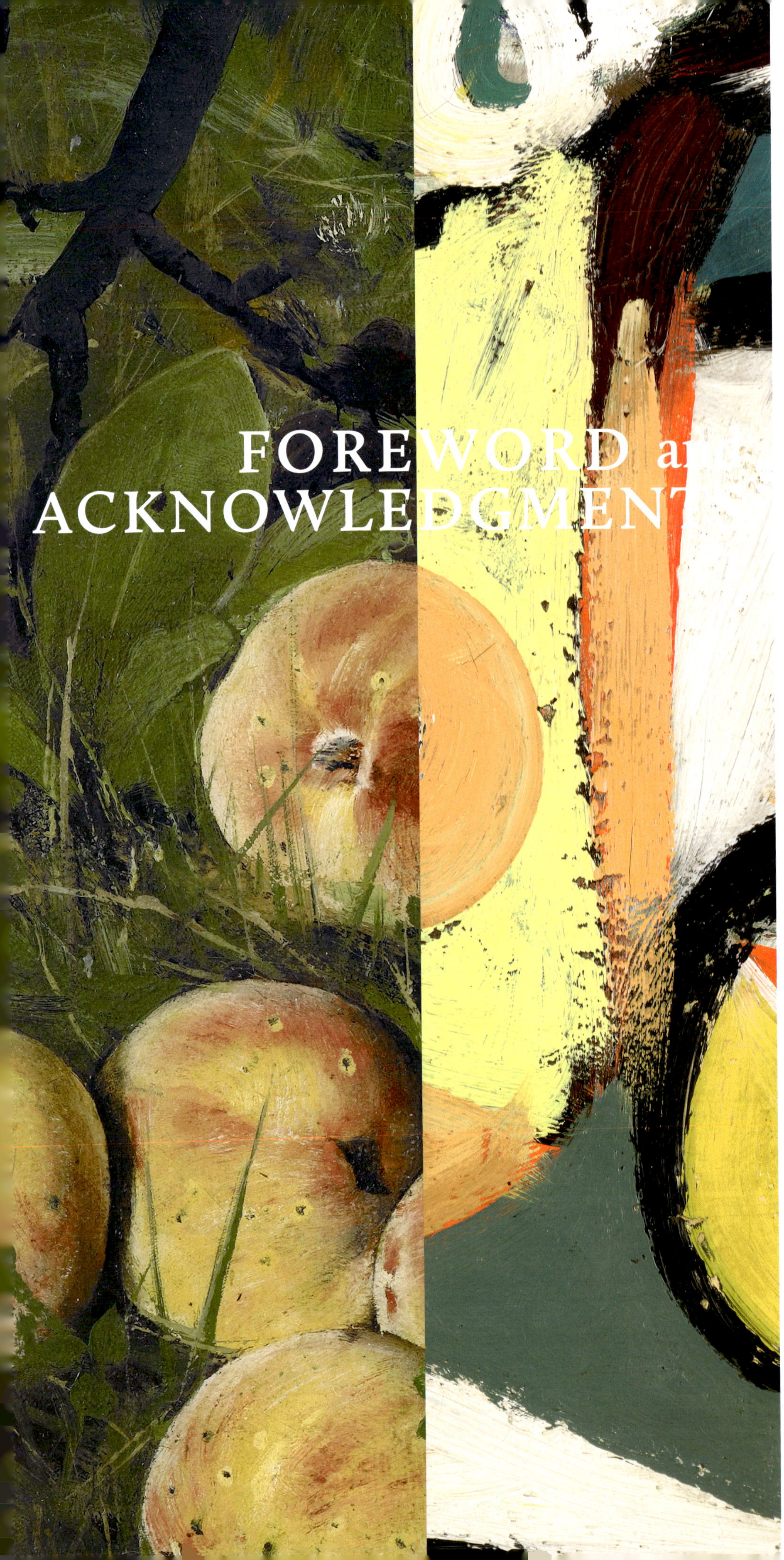

FOREWORD a ACKNOWLEDGMENT

Across America, great art museums adorn our cities, providing inspiration, education, and a unique sense of place. Encyclopedic museums like the Metropolitan Museum of Art in New York house massive collections encompassing the sweep of time and visual culture throughout world history. Increasingly, however, in our world of instant communication and constant connectivity, there is a need for places of respite—for more focused institutions scaled to and reminiscent of a walk around a town square, and where one can relax and linger.

Conceived as a series of discrete pavilions, the new facilities of Crystal Bridges Museum of American Art ring two ponds formed by the flow of a spring-fed stream, itself a metaphor for the slowing of our fast-paced lives. The rhythms of nature inform the visitor experience at Crystal Bridges through the dazzling glimpses of the natural surroundings that occur throughout the complex and along the

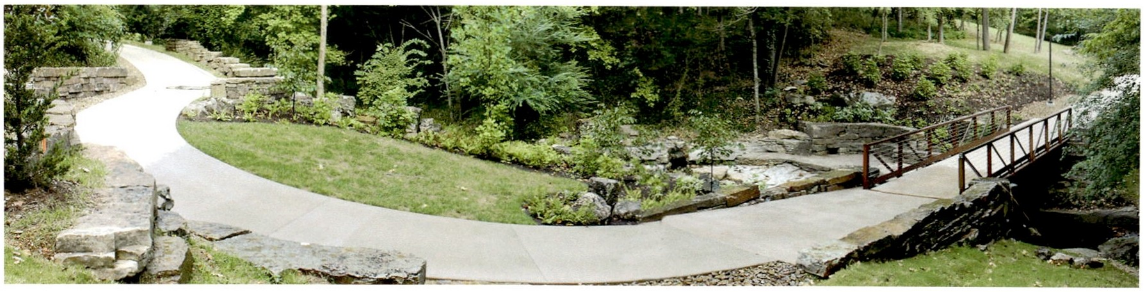

site's miles of trails and pathways (fig. 1). On several of these trails, outdoor sculptures encourage one to pause and reflect on art's place in the landscape and in our imagination.

The noted critic Robert Hughes once described the experience of visiting another museum founded by an extraordinary patron-collector, Duncan Phillips, as a "gift of intimacy and unhurried ease."[1] While we at Crystal Bridges welcome as many visitors as possible to this new museum nestled in the Ozark foothills, we want to ensure that the experience is like the gift that Hughes described: welcoming, special, and the opposite of rushed (figs. 2–3).

Conventional wisdom would suggest the impossibility of starting a new museum of American art from scratch in the twenty-first century. Conventional wisdom, however, has never deterred the Waltons, a family that embodies the "can-do" spirit that is a hallmark of their Northwest Arkansas region. This is a place where families like the Waltons, the Tysons, and the Hunts started small businesses that became international powerhouses. Alice Walton's vision to create a museum in Bentonville was as breathtakingly ambitious and exceptional as is the art it now contains.

Most museums were built to house existing collections, often acquired over decades or a lifetime. Many of America's most distinguished art museums began as private collections: the Isabella Stewart Gardner Museum in Boston; the Frick Collection in New York; the Huntington Library, Art Collections, and Botanical Gardens in San Marino, California; and the Phillips Collection in Washington, D.C., are among the best known and most beloved. The genesis of Crystal Bridges, however, differs from these inasmuch as the *idea* for the museum came first and the collection grew to fulfill the vision summarized in the title of this book—"Celebrating the American Spirit." As this volume goes to press, the Crystal Bridges collection is still forming. And while the museum structures steadily rising from the ground will soon be completed, the collection will continue to evolve for generations to come.

Collecting art is fundamentally and ideally fed by an insatiable appetite for seeing and learning. As this collection has developed and grown, its scope has pushed well beyond a mere survey of the grand and well-known achievements of historical American art to encompass artists whose work is only now finding audiences and acclaim. Alice Walton's own passion and curiosity has led to something quite rare in the world of collecting and philanthropy—a museum where the venerable landmarks of the past are in continual dialogue with the present. A portrait of a young artist by Thomas Eakins confronts a likeness of avant-garde composer John Cage by Nam June Paik; Asher Brown Durand's Hudson River School masterpiece *Kindred Spirits* resonates with James Turrell's Skyspace *The Way of Color;* Gilbert Stuart's oil portrait of George Washington meets Chuck Close's photographic triptych of Bill Clinton.

Alice Walton has also generously lent to the museum and to this publication a significant number of works that are promised gifts. It is a measure of this collector's generosity and her passion for sharing her delight in art that she has allowed her home to be stripped bare of most of the works she loves dearly (notably, Alfred Henry Maurer's raucous portrait of his favorite model, Jeanne, and Josef Albers's glowing, modernist *Homage to the Square: Joy*).

This publication, then, introduces a stunning array of American artists' achievements from the colonial period to the present,

FIG 1 View of the winding trails that surround and connect the Crystal Bridges museum site

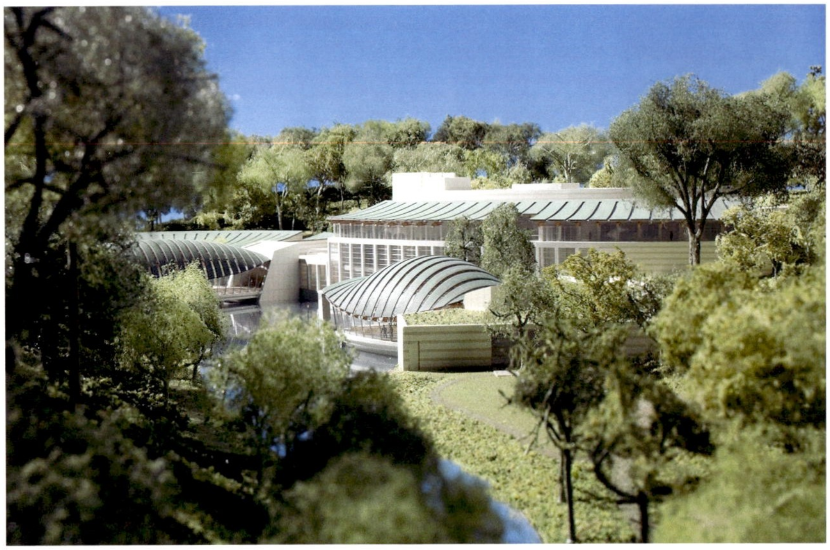

even as we continue to add to the collection. I am confident that as we open to the public for the first time, our curators and educators will be yet pondering how to adjust the galleries to make room for the latest acquisitions—disparate, complex, wonderful objects, each with a story to tell and each providing new insight into works already installed.

The success of this publication is a tribute to the agility and dedication of many people for whom this first outing of the museum's holdings has been a labor of love.

From the very conception of Crystal Bridges, John Wilmerding, trusted advisor and board member among his many other titles and affiliations, has been an invaluable friend to the museum and to Alice Walton. His 2009 interview with Alice, excerpted here (pp. 341–346), is a delightful conversation between good friends, and the mutual admiration conveyed in the text is both genuine and infectious.

Our burgeoning museum has also benefitted from the capable leadership of additional board members: Rick Chapman, Doug McMillon, Buddy Philpot, John Tyson, Ben Walton, and Tom Walton. Each of these leaders has contributed generously of his time and wisdom to bring the institution to this stage of existence.

We greatly appreciate the participation of our numerous guest authors, each at the forefront of advancing scholarship in the study of American art. The voices of these curators, educators, and scholars are as varied as their areas of expertise, and their crisp, accessible writing provides many new insights into our collection.

Managing editor Emily D. Shapiro, a freelance art historian, curator, and editor based in the Washington, D.C., area, has been a joy to work with. Emily's firm yet gentle command of wonderful but frantically busy and geographically scattered colleagues has been dazzling to watch.

Deputy director for museum relations Sandra Keiser Edwards and deputy director for operations and administration Rod Bigelow, along with executive assistant to administration Amy Jones, have all provided logistical expertise, financial acumen, and good common sense at crucial junctures. I also want to thank director of marketing Virginia Germann, whose knowledge of marketing and communications has informed key decisions related to the character of the book as well as its potential afterlife in online manifestations.

Director of education Niki Ciccotelli Stewart and interpretation manager Aaron W. Jones contributed catalogue entries on several works and provided much-needed research assistance and important guidance. Assistant curator Manuela Well-Off-Man and curatorial assistant Alison Demorotski ably supported the project, authoring entries and assisting with fact-checking and research queries. Alison's role as our in-house coordinator could not have been more critical or handled with more grace. Jeannie Whayne, the museum's adjunct curator of American history and professor of American history at the University of Arkansas, provided early support, and her extensive knowledge of Southern regional history has informed much of our ongoing research.

Registrar Elizabeth Weinman and her staff, including assistant registrars Jennifer De Martino and Aleesha Nissen and collections assistant Rachael Spiegel, coordinated conservation treatments and inspections that revealed new information about the objects' history, making, and meaning. Rachael's predecessor, Sarah Brutesco Vincent, was among our first staff members, and her duties

FIG 2 Model of Crystal Bridges Museum of American Art, view looking north, building design by Moshe Safdie (b. 1938)

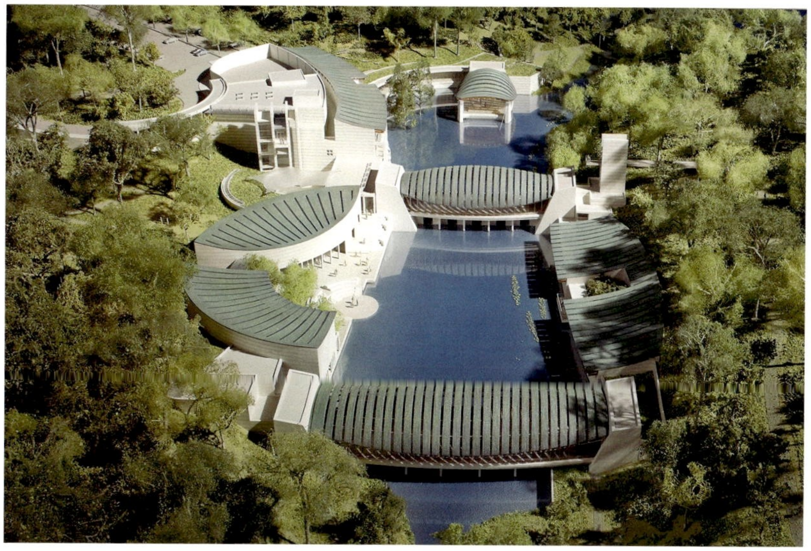

ranged from ad hoc librarian to digital gallery guru. Elizabeth and her team also provided mountains of data from the object and artist files to our authors. Jennifer De Martino coordinated in-house efforts to secure photography for the book, an extremely complex task since the collection was not readily accessible.

We were fortunate to have Dwight Primiano, a talented freelance photographer specializing in museum collections, provide much of the original photography, especially in the early stages of the project. We also greatly appreciate the work of Arkansas-based, internationally recognized photographer Timothy Hursley, who specializes in architectural subjects. Tim provided photographs of our James Turrell Skyspace that truly capture its magic and presence. Gina Glascock-Broze, a picture researcher based in Seattle, Washington, assisted in securing often hard-to-trace image rights.

With the arrival of library director Catherine Petersen and library cataloguer and technical services librarian Jason W. Dean, fact-checking and access to research materials and tools have been greatly facilitated. They are also beginning to research and catalogue the museum's special collections, including important holdings of colorplates by Karl Bodmer, and Thomas L. McKenney and James Hall.

Ed Marquand at Marquand Books provided astute guidance in the overall development of the publication, from production schedules to marketing and design. For the latter, Jeff Wincapaw and Zach Hooker deserve our appreciation for a unique design that emphasizes the primacy of the artworks as well as a sense of connectivity across time. At Marquand Books we also thank managing editor Brynn Warriner, whose editorial oversight was much appreciated; media manager Sara Billups, who assisted with images for the book; and managing director Adrian Lucia, who coordinated production and distribution.

In short, the process of putting together this first collection publication has been a foundation-building project that has touched and involved the entire Crystal Bridges team at many levels. Far from comprehensive, this book nevertheless sets the bar high for the in-depth research and publications that inevitably will follow. For initiating this important groundwork, I wish to extend my appreciation to founding curator of the collection, Chris Crosman. From the outset Chris has ably led this highly collaborative effort, one that grew in complexity and size as the collection itself was continually enriched by new discoveries in every area of American art.

Like many other celebrated American institutions, Crystal Bridges is the result of that rare but powerful alignment of individual vision and generosity of spirit. The museum's presence in Northwest Arkansas is Alice Walton and her family's gift, not only to the region and its people but also to the nation and the world. For this remarkable new museum, appropriately and lovingly set into the rolling countryside of America's heartland, Alice deserves our profound admiration and enduring thanks. This book, and the efforts of all of us involved, are dedicated to her.

DON BACIGALUPI, PH.D.
Executive Director, Crystal Bridges Museum of American Art

1. Robert Hughes, "Art and Intimacy," in *The Eye of Duncan Phillips: A Collection in the Making*, ed. Erika D. Passantino and David W. Scott (New Haven: Yale University Press, in association with the Phillips Collection, Washington, 1999), 1.

FIG 3 Model of Crystal Bridges Museum of American Art, view looking south, building design by Moshe Safdie (b. 1938)

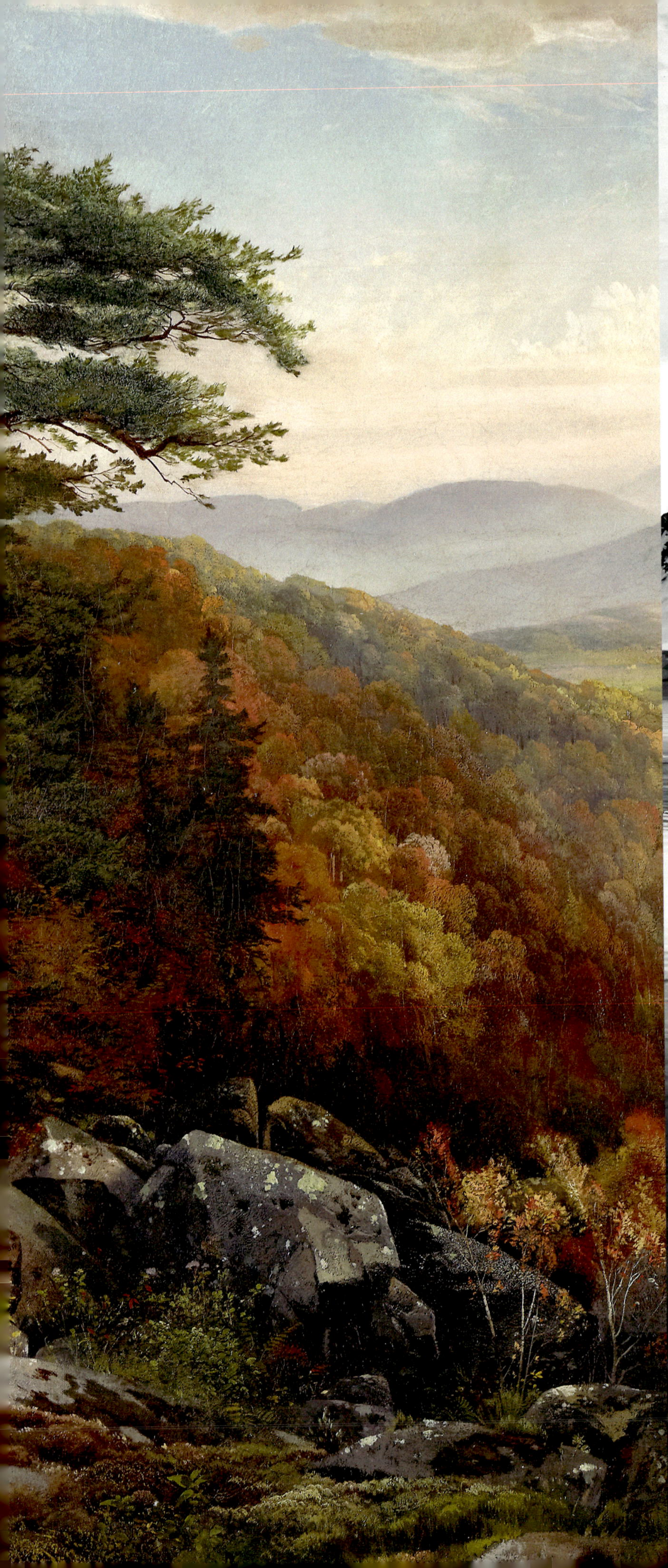
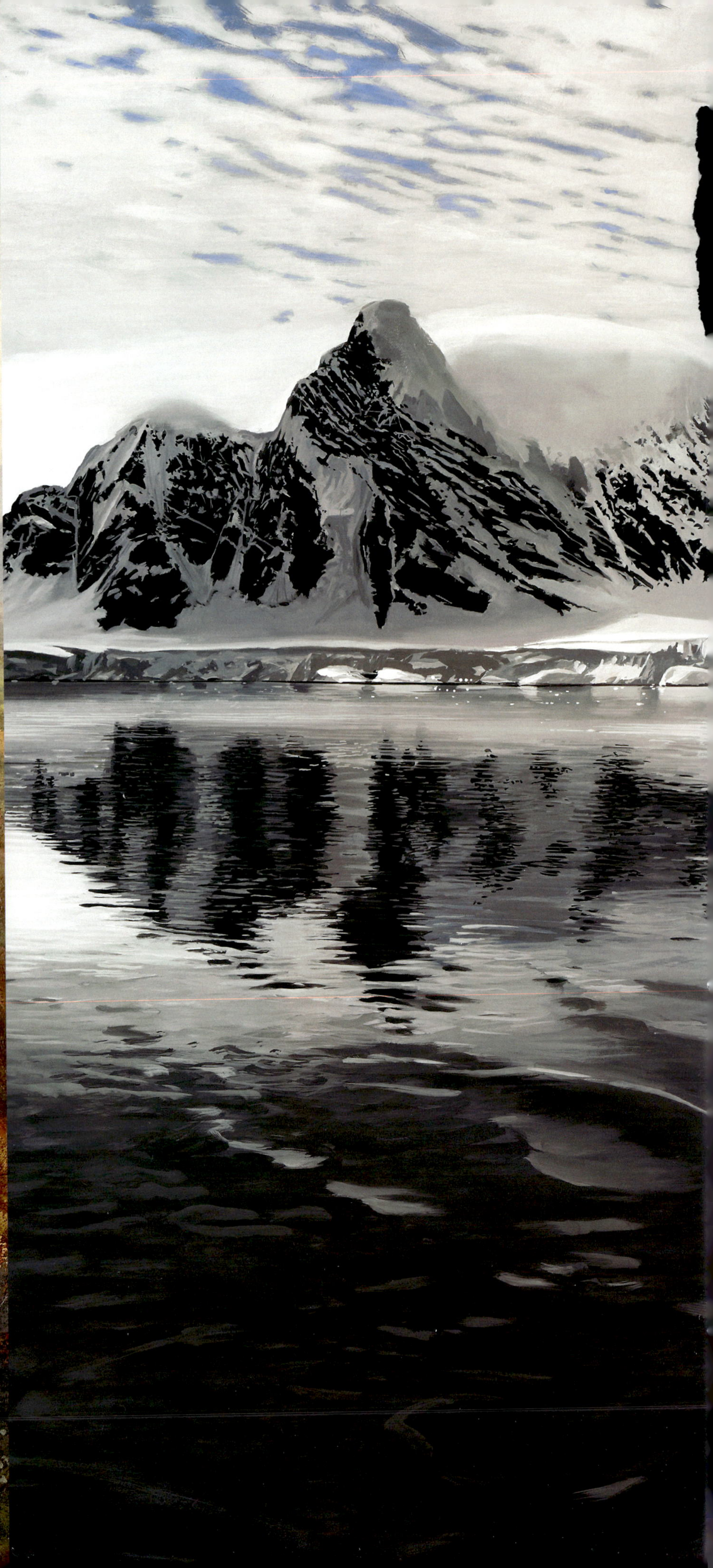

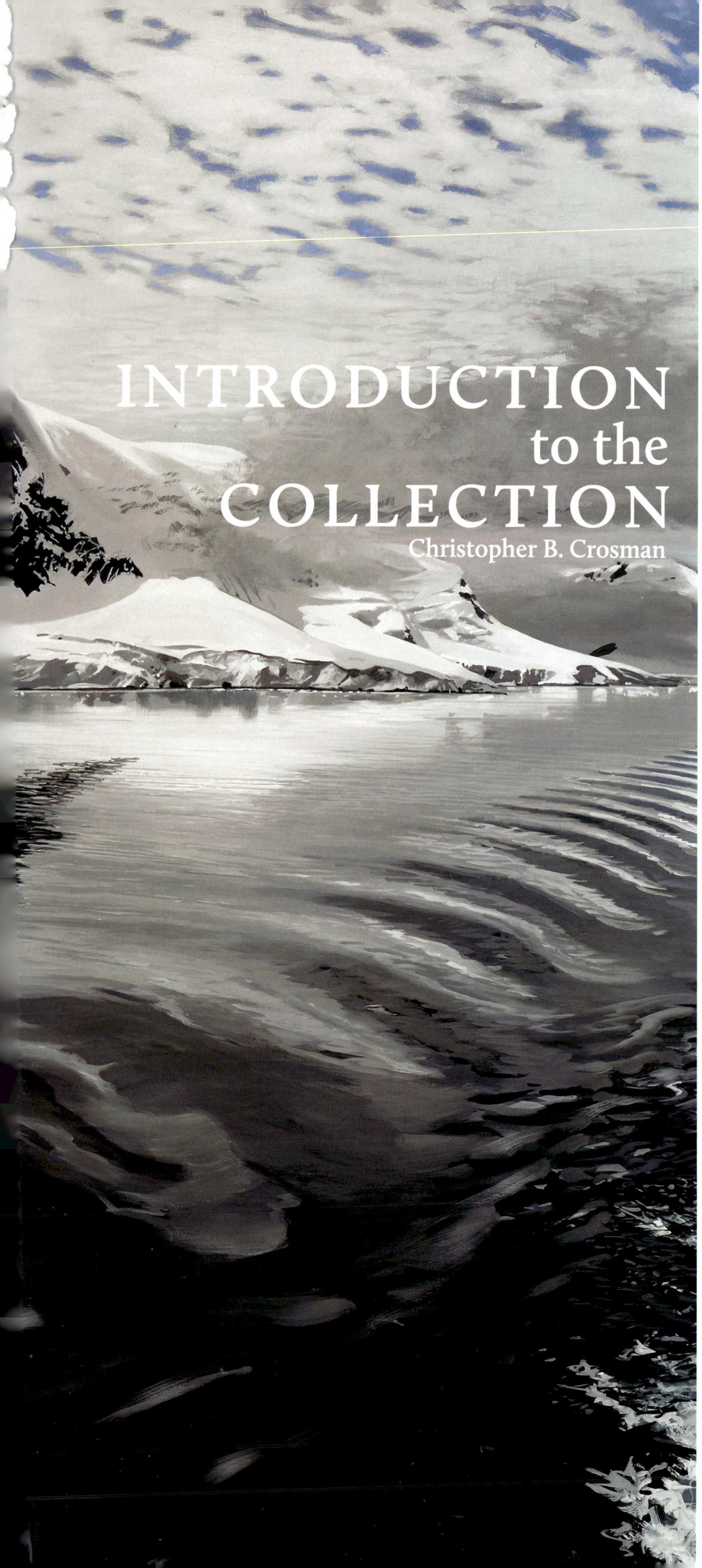

INTRODUCTION to the COLLECTION

Christopher B. Crosman

This inaugural publication for Crystal Bridges Museum of American Art is neither comprehensive collection handbook nor exhibition catalogue. Rather, it offers select views of a rich and diverse group of works that has been carefully assembled over a period of years for the purpose of establishing a new museum eager to take its place among those institutions advancing knowledge about and understanding of American art, past and present. The museum's simple but vital purpose is to tell the unfolding story of the United States through the lens of its visual arts: to probe its collections for insight into our national ideals and aspirations, our tragedies and triumphs, our broadly defining characteristics and idiosyncratic traits. As with most museums, but perhaps more so as an institution in its infancy, Crystal Bridges' collection is a work in progress. The 151 objects represented in this volume by brief entries penned by 23 leading American art scholars reflect a developing body of work that is in the process of becoming whole, if never complete. When the museum opens in late 2011, it will be installed with nearly the entire collection, supplemented by a few key loans.

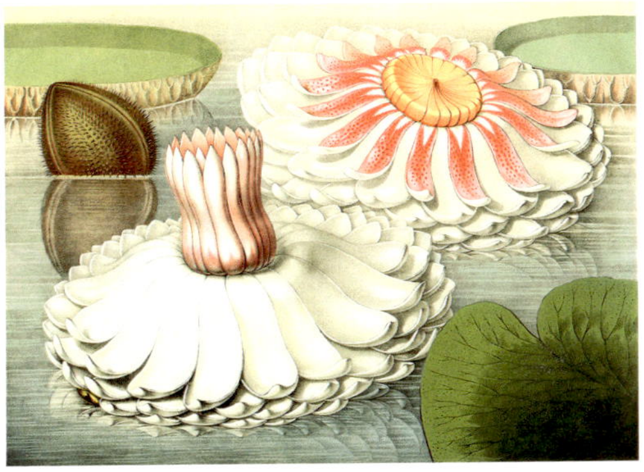

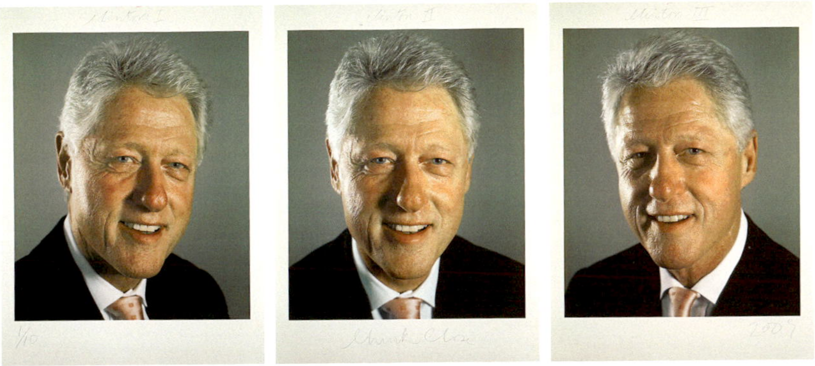

It is important to note that this publication focuses on paintings and works of art on paper. As such, it is an abbreviated survey of Crystal Bridges' varied holdings. Space and time constraints allowed for little more than a passing reference to the museum's growing sculpture collection (pp. 334–340), the chronological scope of which roughly parallels that of the institution's two-dimensional artwork. As these objects emerge from storage and are installed in the galleries alongside examples in other media, as well as outdoors, within the site's extensive parkland and gardens, close physical examination and scholarly research will doubtless provide the basis for a publication devoted to current and future sculpture acquisitions.

In this early stage of its development, Crystal Bridges' print holdings focus on examples by individuals already represented in the collection by paintings, sculpture, or unique works on paper. Other artists will be added in due course and as museum-quality objects become available. Crystal Bridges will likely also acquire prints by artists whose work in other media is unobtainable due to rarity.

The museum's American colorplate book collection—among the most comprehensive in the world—includes Thomas L. McKenney and James Hall's three-volume *History of the Indian Tribes of North America* (1838–44), with 120 hand-colored lithographs based on original paintings by Charles Bird King (p. 50) and others; Karl Bodmer's illustrations of Native Americans for *Maximilian, Prince of Wied's Travels in the Interior of North America, 1832–34* (1839–43); and John Fisk Allen's *Victoria Regia; or, The Great Water Lily of America* (1854, fig. 1), the first large-format chromolithographic book printed in the United States.[1] This visually stunning assemblage of books in which images amplify, clarify, and enhance the printed word graphically describes and documents nearly every avenue of nineteenth-century American intellectual curiosity. These volumes offer insight into broader cultural contexts, providing added texture to the Crystal Bridges collection as a whole. A related enterprise—the contemporary artist's book—is a wide-open field that the museum has begun to pursue with the recent acquisition of graphic novels by Sandow Birk and a newly compiled (2010) edition of Lynd Ward's pioneering graphic novels edited by Art Spiegelman.

In addition to Edward Sheriff Curtis's multivolume portfolio of over two thousand photogravures depicting Native American tribes (1907–30, p. 168), the museum has also judiciously acquired vintage early landscape photographs of the American West by Carleton E. Watkins and William Henry Jackson. The nascent contemporary photography collection includes examples of work by distinguished practitioners Gregory Crewdson and Chuck Close (fig. 2). While Crystal Bridges will likely expand its conventional photography holdings, we are aware that new digital formats for making and viewing pictures are changing how museums collect, present, and even define the medium. The manner of Crystal Bridges' involvement with performance, installation, site-specific, and new media formats has yet to be determined, but we embrace the opportunity to engage with contemporary artists' ever adaptable and elastic toolkits.

FIG 1 William Sharp (1803–1875), *Intermediate Stages of Bloom*, from *Victoria Regia; or, The Great Water Lily of America* by John Fisk Allen (Boston, 1854). Chromolithographic plate, 15 × 21 in. (38.1 × 53.3 cm); broadsheet, 21¾ × 28⅛ in. (55.2 × 71.4 cm)

FIG 2 Chuck Close (b. 1940), *Clinton Triptych*, 2009. Pigment prints on Crane portfolio rag paper, 3 panels, 46 × 35 in. (116.8 × 88.9 cm) each

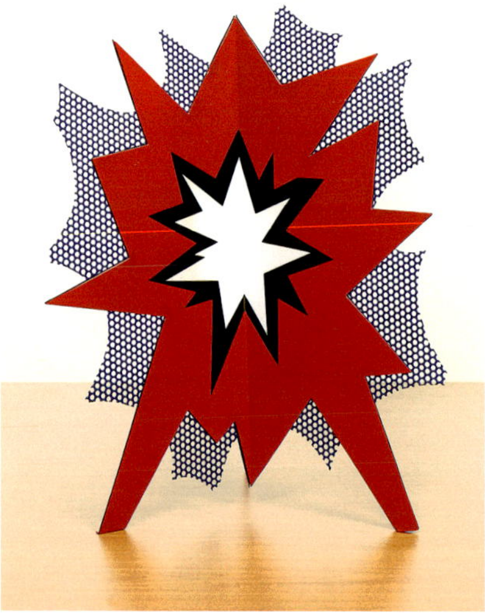

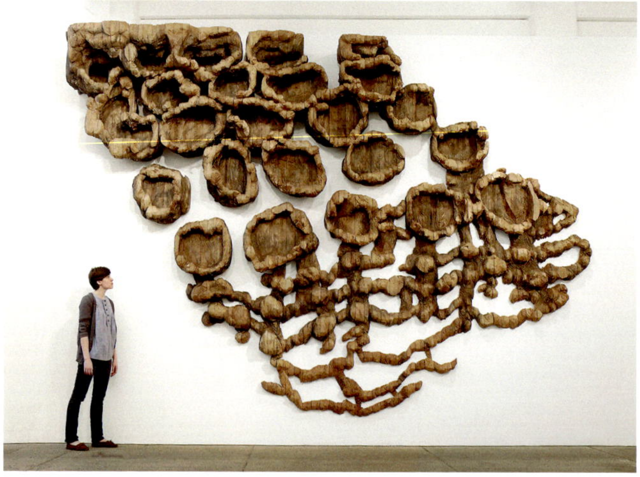

Although the foundation of Crystal Bridges' collection is historical American art, and we continue to acquire works from the colonial era through the first half of the twentieth century, holdings dating from the second half of the twentieth century and the first decade of the twenty-first are expanding at a particularly rapid clip—much faster than the necessarily measured pace of research and writing. Outstanding examples in varied media and materials by artists including Hale Aspacio Woodruff, Morris Graves, Theodoros Stamos, Roy Lichtenstein (fig. 3), Marisol (fig. 8 in Sculpture at Crystal Bridges), Jim Dine, Alvin Loving, Lynda Benglis (fig. 9 in Sculpture at Crystal Bridges), Frederick Eversley, Ursula von Rydingsvard (fig. 4), and Devorah Sperber—to name only a few—were too recently acquired to be featured in this volume. As transformative digital technologies change how many of us access images and information, long lead time print publications such as this one may soon be rendered obsolete in favor of formats that allow for the real-time posting of updates and addenda, perhaps only a touch screen away.

Crystal Bridges is a brand-new institution with a new collection enhanced by loans from Alice Walton, the museum's founder and principal patron. Aesthetic quality is, of course, paramount, but acquisition considerations also include relevance to other works in the collection; whether the object builds on an existing strength or fills a gap; or, as is often the case, whether it points in a new, perhaps wholly different direction that nevertheless broadens understanding and enjoyment. Indeed, in building the collection, there was no formal acquisitions blueprint nor was there an established list of "must have" artists. Yet the museum's holdings have evolved to reflect several overarching themes or tendencies that give the collection its particular character.

First and foremost among these is its rootedness in place. The theme of landscape seems entirely appropriate and "natural," as it were, for an institution located in "The Natural State," official state nickname of Arkansas. Crystal Bridges nestles into a series of intersecting ravines and hills cut into a high plateau to the west of the lower Mississippi floodplain that were formed by millennia of erosion. Museum architect Moshe Safdie's interconnected pavilions rhyme with the terrain in their undulating, organic contours. As the concrete, copper, and wood of these structures weather to gray, brown, green, and other earth tones, the entire complex will gradually settle into the surrounding hillsides and vegetation, their forms abstractly reflected in the adjacent pools, springs, and streams. In fact, the name for the museum—Crystal Bridges—derives from the adjacent Crystal Spring, which is the principal water source for the Town Branch stream. This small waterway flows into and through the museum complex before returning to its natural course, where it joins Little Sugar Creek a few hundred yards to the north.

The over 120 acres surrounding the museum have national historic significance. Traces of Native American cultures have been found in the area, along with artifacts left by retreating Confederate soldiers following the Battle of Pea Ridge, which was fought just a few miles to the east in 1862.[2] A long overgrown cut through the forest made by Kansas City & Bentonville

FIG 3 Roy Lichtenstein (1923–1997), *Standing Explosion (Red)*, 1966. Porcelain enamel on steel, 38 × 25 × 30 in. (96.5 × 63.5 × 76.2 cm)

FIG 4 Ursula von Rydingsvard (b. 1942), *Unraveling*, 2007. Cedar and graphite, 138 × 222 × 29 in. (350.5 × 563.9 × 73.7 cm)

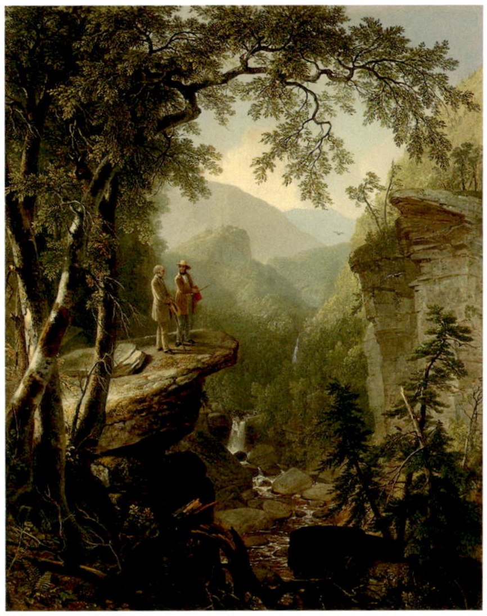

Southeastern Railway engineers in 1891 for what would have become the town's first rail depot now provides the breathtaking Rock Ledge Trail running through the surrounding grounds.[3] Along this and other trails on the museum campus are several State Champion specimens of flora, and museum visitors and staff have spotted deer, horned owls, and a vast array of other native animals. A heroic effort was made during the construction phase to mitigate the intrusion of the hardscape and buildings so that the forest remains undisturbed within only a few feet of massive concrete walls. Indeed, visitors experience something of a "Brigadoon" moment as they approach the complex, whether on foot or along the tree-lined entrance drive. The museum suddenly reveals itself, seeming to spring from the very earth upon which it was built.

Americans' attitudes toward, and encounters with, the natural world fundamentally shape our national identity and experience. Perhaps nowhere is nature's defining role in American culture more evident within an art museum context than at Crystal Bridges. Asher Brown Durand's *Kindred Spirits* (1849, fig. 5 and p. 64)—among the most celebrated, essential works of the Hudson River School; indeed, of all of American landscape painting—is the centerpiece of an outstanding mid nineteenth-century landscape collection that also includes masterworks by Thomas Cole (pp. 60 and 62), John Frederick Kensett (p. 72), Frederic Edwin Church (p. 70), Jasper Francis Cropsey (p. 76), William Trost Richards (pp. 82 and 166), and Alfred Thompson Bricher (p. 96). As the century progressed, a new generation of American artists including John Singer Sargent (p. 146), Theodore Robinson (p. 154), William Merritt Chase (p. 158), Willard LeRoy Metcalf (p. 164), and Frank Weston Benson (p. 184) absorbed the lessons of French impressionism, working en plein air (outdoors) to capture the fleeting visual effects of light through short, dabbing brushstrokes of unmixed, pure color. These painters' common agenda led them to establish artist colonies in such places as Old Lyme, Connecticut; Southampton, Long Island; and the Isles of Shoals, Maine.

Around the turn of the twentieth century, James McNeill Whistler (p. 160), John La Farge (p. 150), Maria Oakey Dewing (p. 162), and Thomas Wilmer Dewing (p. 176), among others, presented nature filtered through the softly focused scrim of heightened aestheticism, while in the first half of the twentieth century, Marsden Hartley (pp. 198, 200, and 232), Arthur Garfield Dove (pp. 214 and 216), Georgia O'Keeffe (pp. 204 and 228), Stuart Davis (p. 224), and Charles Ephraim Burchfield (p. 246) drew from organic rhythms, forms, colors, and textures to evoke the abstract essence of nature's infinitude. Critical theory notwithstanding, much of the most abstract American painting since 1950, including Joan Mitchell's gestural poems in paint (p. 262) and even the rigorously formalist but spatially ambiguous circle paintings of Kenneth Noland (p. 268), affirm their origins in natural phenomena. As the first decade of the twenty-first century draws to a close, environmentally conscious artists represented in the collection such as Yvonne Jacquette, Tom Uttech (p. 308), James Turrell (fig. 3 in Sculpture at Crystal Bridges), Walton Ford (p. 306), and Roxy Paine (fig. 2 in Sculpture at Crystal Bridges) have increasingly become concerned

FIG 5 Asher Brown Durand (1796–1886), *Kindred Spirits*, 1849. Oil on canvas, 44 × 36 in. (111.8 × 91.4 cm)

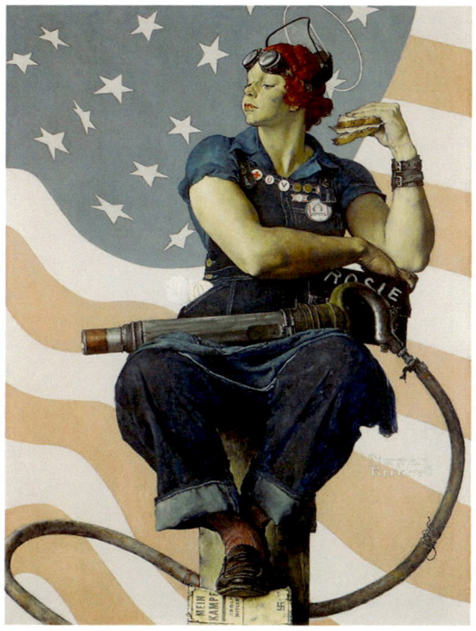

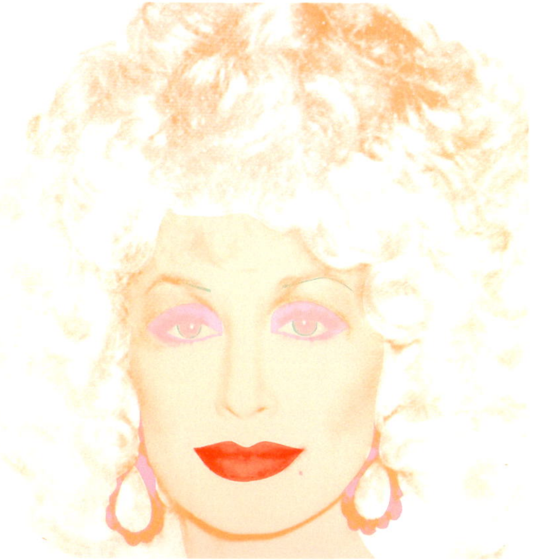

with nature's fragility. In their work, landscape becomes cautionary tale and urgent *cri de coeur*.

The socioeconomic history of Bentonville has also subtly informed collecting practices at Crystal Bridges. The museum is located just steps from a town square that once hosted an agrarian community of small farms and support businesses and now is home to the world's largest retail merchant. While the notion of an artistic agenda resembling a business plan might trouble some, the factors that contribute to artistic achievement are largely those required of any successful endeavor: passion, intelligence, independence, and invention. Art in the collection ranging from the multigenerational Levy-Franks portraits attributed to eighteenth-century New York commercial sign painter Gerardus Duyckinck I (ca. 1735, p. 24); to Norman Rockwell's *Rosie the Riveter* (1943, fig. 6 and p. 244), which reached millions of American homes on the cover of the *Saturday Evening Post*; to a portrait of Dolly Parton by Andy Warhol (1985, fig. 7 and p. 280), who, like his sitter, rose from humble beginnings to become a cultural icon, and who raised business acumen and entrepreneurship to its own art form, speaks to the time-honored American value of creative enterprise.

Indeed, innovation has long characterized the work of American artists. Take, for example, the insatiable curiosity of Charles Willson Peale (p. 34), who established the first American museum and its diverse collections of fine art, archaeological effects, and natural history specimens. In this regard one might also think of Thomas Eakins's interest in science and medicine, made manifest in his portrait of Dr. Benjamin Howard Rand (1874, p. 124); Robert Rauschenberg's engagement with commonplace imagery and commercial methods of picture making (p. 276); James Turrell's optical wizardry and artistic ambition in *The Way of Color* Skyspace (2009, fig. 3 in Sculpture at Crystal Bridges); and Nick Cave's clamorous, shape-shifting Soundsuits, assembled from such unlikely materials as vintage push toys, jack-in-the-boxes, and crocheted and beaded fabric (2010, fig. 12 in Sculpture at Crystal Bridges). These artists' left-brain thinking belongs to the same tradition of invention that yielded the cotton gin, the telegraph (conceived by the painter Samuel Finley Breese Morse, featured on p. 52), air travel, and the Internet. Sam Walton's hometown makes perfect sense as the location for a museum devoted to American art and its create-something-from-nothing spirit.

Still another subtheme in the collection, which both cuts through and binds elements of the others, is the presence of strong women both as maker and as subject. Crystal Bridges' holdings include a pastel portrait created by South Carolina native Henrietta Johnston around 1720 that is among the first extant fine art images attributed to an American woman (fig. 8). The landscape and nature paintings that form the core of Crystal Bridges' collection include Maria Oakey Dewing's masterful *Rose Garden* (1901, p. 162); nature-based painterly abstractions by Georgia O'Keeffe (pp. 204 and 228), Grace Hartigan (p. 266), Jane Wilson, and Joan Mitchell (p. 262); and one of Yvonne Jacquette's signature aerial views. While by no means achieving parity of numbers in the Crystal Bridges collection, female artists are increasingly

FIG 6 Norman Rockwell (1894–1978), *Rosie the Riveter*, 1943. Oil on canvas, 52 × 40 in. (132.1 × 101.6 cm)

FIG 7 Andy Warhol (1928–1987), *Dolly Parton*, 1985. Synthetic polymer paint and silkscreen ink on canvas, 42 × 42 in. (106.7 × 106.7 cm)

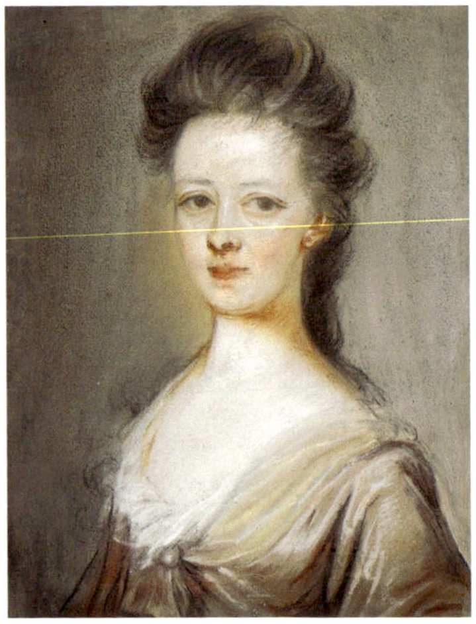

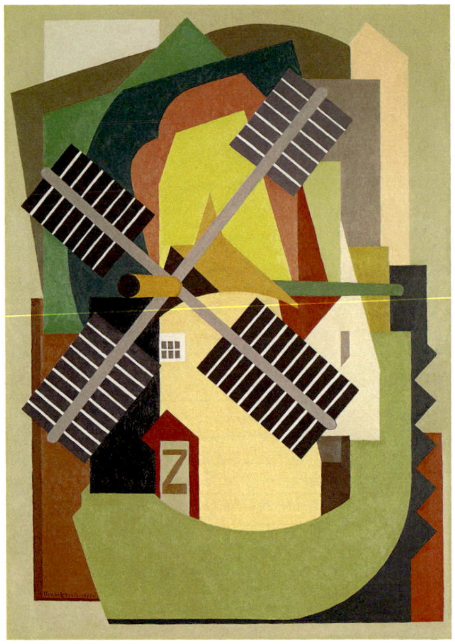

present. Among the museum's acquisitions since 2005 are works by Agnes Pelton, Helen Torr, Blanche Lazzell (fig. 9), Anni Albers, Louise Nevelson (fig. 10), Doris Lee, Elizabeth Catlett, Jackie Ferrara, Emma Amos, Jenny Holzer, and Karen LaMonte (fig. 11 in Sculpture at Crystal Bridges).

Images of strong women endowed with confidence, intelligence, determination, and power run throughout the collection, beginning with Duyckinck's portrait of Abigaill Levy Franks (p. 24), the literate, feisty matriarch of one of New York's earliest and most successful Jewish merchant families. The collection also includes John Singleton Copley's portrait of the youthful but already formidable Mrs. Theodore Atkinson Jr. (1765, p. 28) and Dennis Miller Bunker's likeness of Gilded Age Bostonian Anne Page (1887, p. 138), who represented a new type of beauty informed as much by her intellectual abilities as by her outward grace. Alfred Henry Maurer's full-length portrait of a favorite model brandishing her cigarette in defiance of the social conventions of her day (ca. 1904, p. 174) anticipates Rockwell's World War II–era heroine *Rosie the Riveter*, who thoroughly owns her pivotal new role in the theretofore all-male industrial workplace. Grace Hartigan's explosive canvas *Rough, Ain't It* (1949, p. 264) alludes to the struggles female artists have historically faced to be accepted as professionals. Tom Wesselmann's massive, in-your-face shaped canvas (1973, p. 282) presents a potent female presence that, however eroticized, is still a force to be reckoned with, and Dolly Parton's well-known rags-to-riches story renders futile any attempt to "frame" her image, even by the likes of Warhol.

A fourth major theme running through the collection is that of American artists performing on the world stage. Beginning in the late eighteenth century, with Pennsylvania native Benjamin West's (p. 32) ascent to the highest level of international prominence as president of London's Royal Academy and historical painter to King George III, American artists have always aspired to, and often achieved, international success and influence. This global perspective makes perfect sense for a nation founded by immigrants and that is still largely defined by its cultural heterogeneity. Many of the United States' most important artists have been first- or second-generation immigrants. Thomas Cole, founder of our first indigenous art movement, the Hudson River School, was born in England, and work by foreign-born Americans Arshile Gorky (p. 234), Yasuo Kuniyoshi (p. 220), and Josef Albers (p. 270) is central to the canon. The legacy of Albers's and Hans Hofmann's (p. 258) teaching has informed the work of generations of American artists. At the same time, nearly every distinguished artist born in the United States in the nineteenth century benefitted from training abroad, and the early twentieth-century European movements of cubism, expressionism, surrealism, and dada were formative influences on America's most innovative modernists, including Maurer (pp. 174 and 192), Stuart Davis (pp. 222 and 224), and Romare Bearden (p. 238).

The varied heritages and life experiences of the nation's diverse citizenry have produced a richly complex amalgam that now cross-fertilizes with contemporary art throughout the world. Indeed, the notion of a distinctly American art seems ever

FIG 8 Henrietta Johnston (ca. 1674–after 1729), *Portrait of a Young Woman*, ca. 1720. Pastel on paper, 10½ × 8½ in. (26.7 × 21.6 cm)

FIG 9 Blanche Lazzell (1878–1956), *Painting XI*, 1928. Oil on canvas, 50 × 36 in. (127 × 91.4 cm). Promised Gift

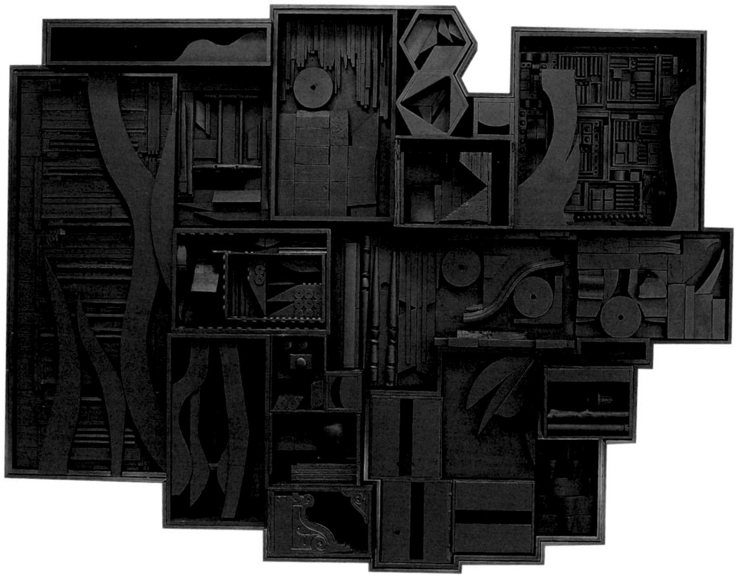

more complicated in the twenty-first century, as artists sell work, maintain studios, and stage exhibitions in multiple countries and on several continents simultaneously. So, too, does a single-voiced American art history seem inconsistent with the needs of an increasingly global society. Crystal Bridges is committed to exploring the United States' historic and continued dialogue with cultures worldwide; those of Europe, of course, but also the vibrant art scenes in Africa, India, China, Southeast Asia, the Pacific islands, the Middle East, and the America(s) to our north and south. The collage of identities that color and shape the work of American artists working in and outside of the United States is a topic we hope to examine more closely and one that will undoubtedly guide future acquisitions.

Unlike most art museums, Crystal Bridges assembled its collection almost exclusively through purchase, although several notable gifts have greatly enhanced the institution's holdings.[4] The collection has grown relatively slowly, and always selectively. With rare exceptions, acquisitions have come from private collections; many works recently acquired by Crystal Bridges have not been on public display for decades, or even generations. A critical goal of the museum's collecting program has been to bring little-seen works into public view and to provide permanent access to art that has national, and often international, resonance and significance. Thus, the acquisition of Eakins's portrait *Professor Benjamin Howard Rand*, a painting long tucked away in a locked alcove at Thomas Jefferson Medical College. At Crystal Bridges, this sensitive likeness of the distinguished chemist and respected professor is now available to a national audience, and especially to present and future generations of residents and visitors to Northwest Arkansas, who may be inspired by Rand's story as teacher and friend of the artist. One does not have to reside in Philadelphia to appreciate Dr. Rand's warmth or the gentleness of his demeanor, affirmed by his affectionate feline companion.

Some greeted with dismay Crystal Bridges' 2005 purchase of Durand's masterpiece *Kindred Spirits* from the New York Public Library. While the library has acquired a number of artworks over the course of its long history, the care, protection, display, and interpretation that art museums routinely provide their collections fall outside of the institution's core mission. An icon of the American landscape tradition—not just that of New York—the canvas now hangs among other prime examples of Hudson River School painting. *Kindred Spirits* is one of Crystal Bridges' signature works and has played a significant role in defining the overall direction and scope of the collection.

The museum's driving vision—its primary reason for existing—is a mandate to teach. Although still relatively small in size, the collection has been built with an eye toward education and, in particular, toward identifying and exploring moments of continuity and change in American art. For example, Jasper Francis Cropsey's sun-dappled pioneer landscape *The Backwoods of America* (1858, fig. 11 and p. 76) and Kerry James Marshall's dystopian view of suburbia entitled *Our Town* (1995, fig. 12 and p. 300) can be placed in productive dialogue. Marshall's pointedly political image of black youth in a traditionally white suburban landscape that

FIG 10 Louise Nevelson (1899–1988), *Night Zag Wall*, 1969–74. Wood painted black, 108 × 144 × 10½ in. (274.3 × 365.8 × 26.7 cm)

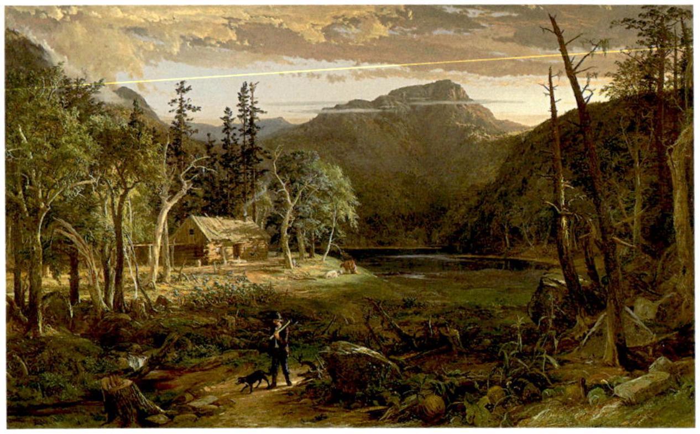

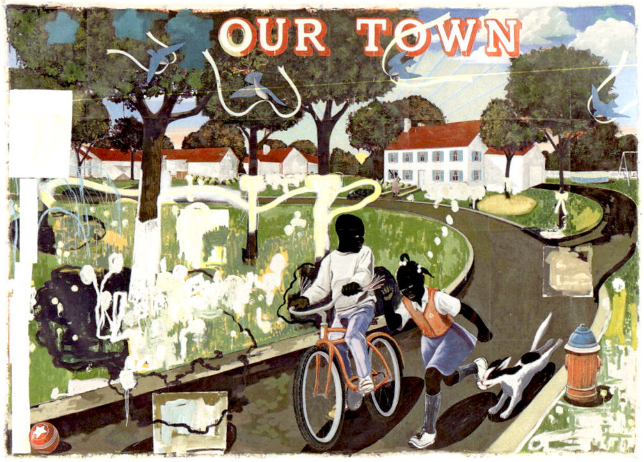

may say "Our Town," but really means "not yours," at first appears far removed from Cropsey's idealized family scene, in which children symbolize ever-brighter prospects through personal industry and nature's bounty. Indeed, Cropsey's vision of America, in which individual labor and collective family enterprise form the foundation for home and sustenance, seemingly stands in contrast to Marshall's interpretation of late twentieth-century suburbia, a place where the American dream is still only that for many citizens. Yet the fact that Cropsey painted his optimistic frontier scene on the eve of the Civil War, in a nation divided over the question of slavery, is relevant to *Our Town*, where the meaning of home remains an open wound.

Finally, Crystal Bridges' approach to collecting is unabashedly populist. While not every work will appeal to every visitor, the museum's democratic ethos accepts, celebrates, even promotes a certain unruliness and ambiguity, questioning and debate. Art is the product of individuals who have the capacity to make us see anew, or again, or better, or, simply, differently. More than a few times along this remarkable journey toward creating Crystal Bridges there have been moments when the usual tools of analysis, comparison, and reasoned discourse were discarded in favor of intuition. Something we have all learned, in large measure from Alice Walton herself, is to seek out works of art—regardless of medium, subject, style, artist's reputation, or critical consensus—that evoke a child's sense of enchantment, imagination, and wonder. Now, in the center of Bentonville, just off the town square, the museum opens its doors onto a landscape that was once Alice and her family's childhood playground. A joyful spirit of play and exploration has once again taken root in this ancient Ozark landscape. For the Walton family, Crystal Bridges is a gift of the heart.

FIG 11 Jasper Francis Cropsey (1823–1900), *The Backwoods of America*, 1858. Oil on canvas, 42 × 70¼ in. (106.7 × 178.4 cm)

FIG 12 Kerry James Marshall (b. 1955), *Our Town*, 1995. Acrylic and printed-paper collage on canvas, 100 × 142 in. (254 × 360.7 cm)

NOTES

1. Assembled over several decades by William Reese, antiquarian book dealer and the preeminent authority on American colorplate books, the collection was featured in a 2005 exhibition at the Amon Carter Museum of American Art. Subsequent to Crystal Bridges' acquisition of Reese's collection, the museum has continued to add volumes of colorplate books as appropriate and available.
2. Bentonville was also the western terminus for the Cherokee Trail of Tears. Quapaw and Osage Indians are believed to have hunted and lived throughout Northwest Arkansas, and local caves have glyph markings made by Quapaws and/or their antecedents. Native American signal trees (trees limbs bent to point in a particular direction) are also common in this region.
3. Tom Duggan, an expert on the history of Arkansas railroads, surmises that the rail line was never built because of unanticipated costs related to rail construction in the area's steep, inhospitable terrain and rocky, unstable soil. See Duggan, "Northwest Arkansas Railroad History—Ghost Train to Caverna," *Scrambler* [monthly newsletter of the National Railway Historical Society, Arkansas-Boston Mountains chapter] 15, no. 10 (June 2002): n.p.
4. The Cleveland Museum of Art's outstanding American art collection, comparable in scope, size, and quality to that of Crystal Bridges, was primarily acquired through purchases recommended by the professional staff, with the support of enlightened donors and trustees. See Henry Adams, *What's American about American Art?* (New York: Hudson Hills Press, 2007). Gifts to Crystal Bridges include a monumental metal sculpture by Seymour Lipton given by Barbara Palmer in memory of Clay Edwards; a pastel by Mary Cassatt donated by John Driscoll, in memory of Clayton "Clay" Edwards; Alfred Henry Maurer's *Midinette* (ca. 1902), a full-length portrait of favorite model Jeanne in the guise of a shop girl given by Donna and Arthur Hartman; and three oil paintings by Theodoros Stamos given by the Savas Private Collection, courtesy of the artist's sister Georgianna Stamatelos Savas.

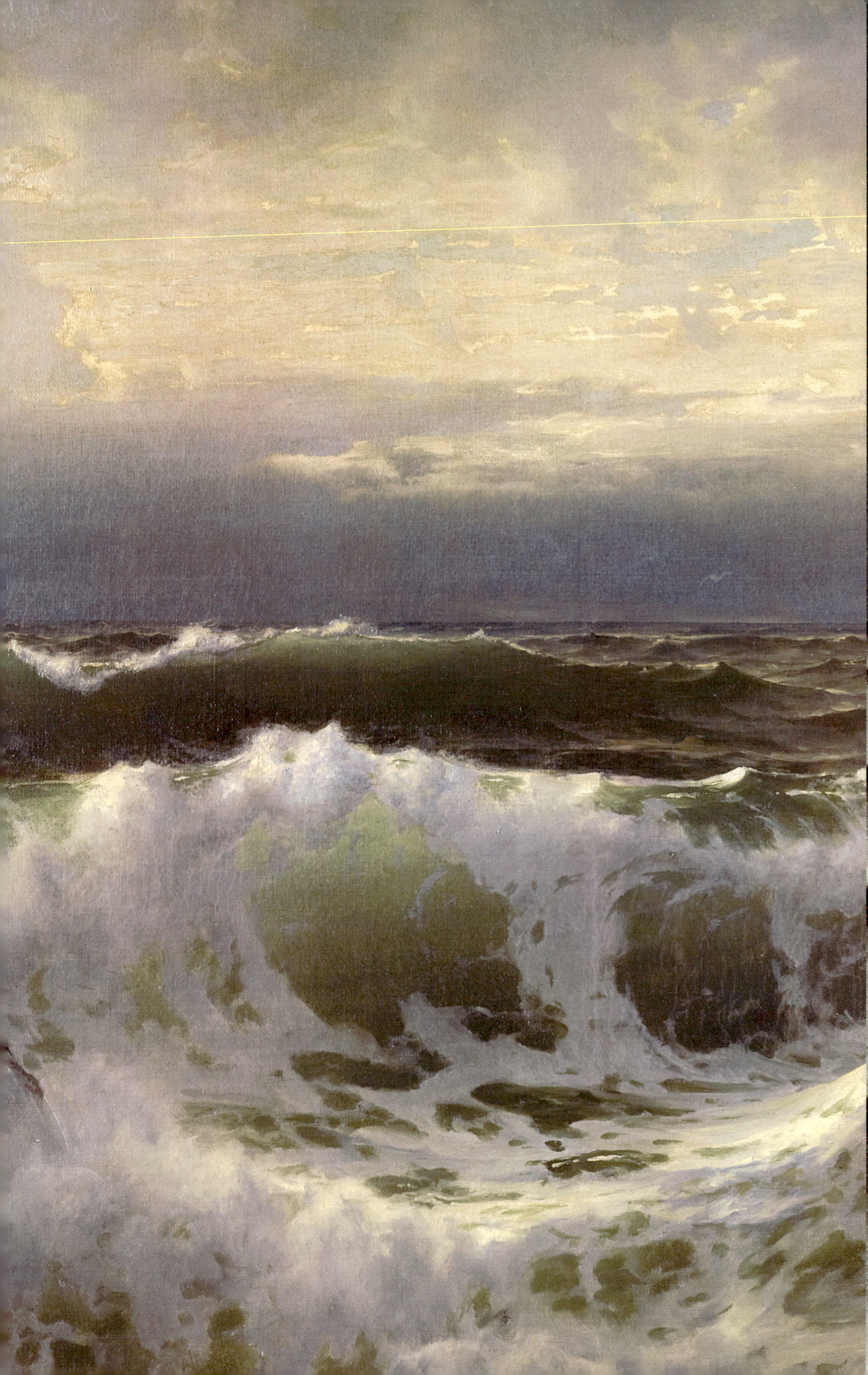
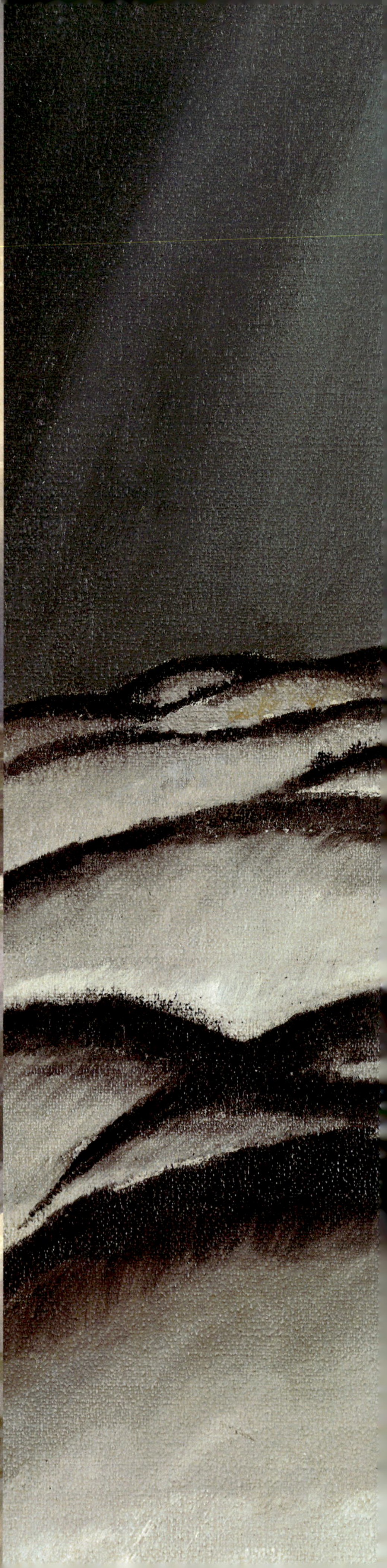

SELECTIONS from the COLLECTION

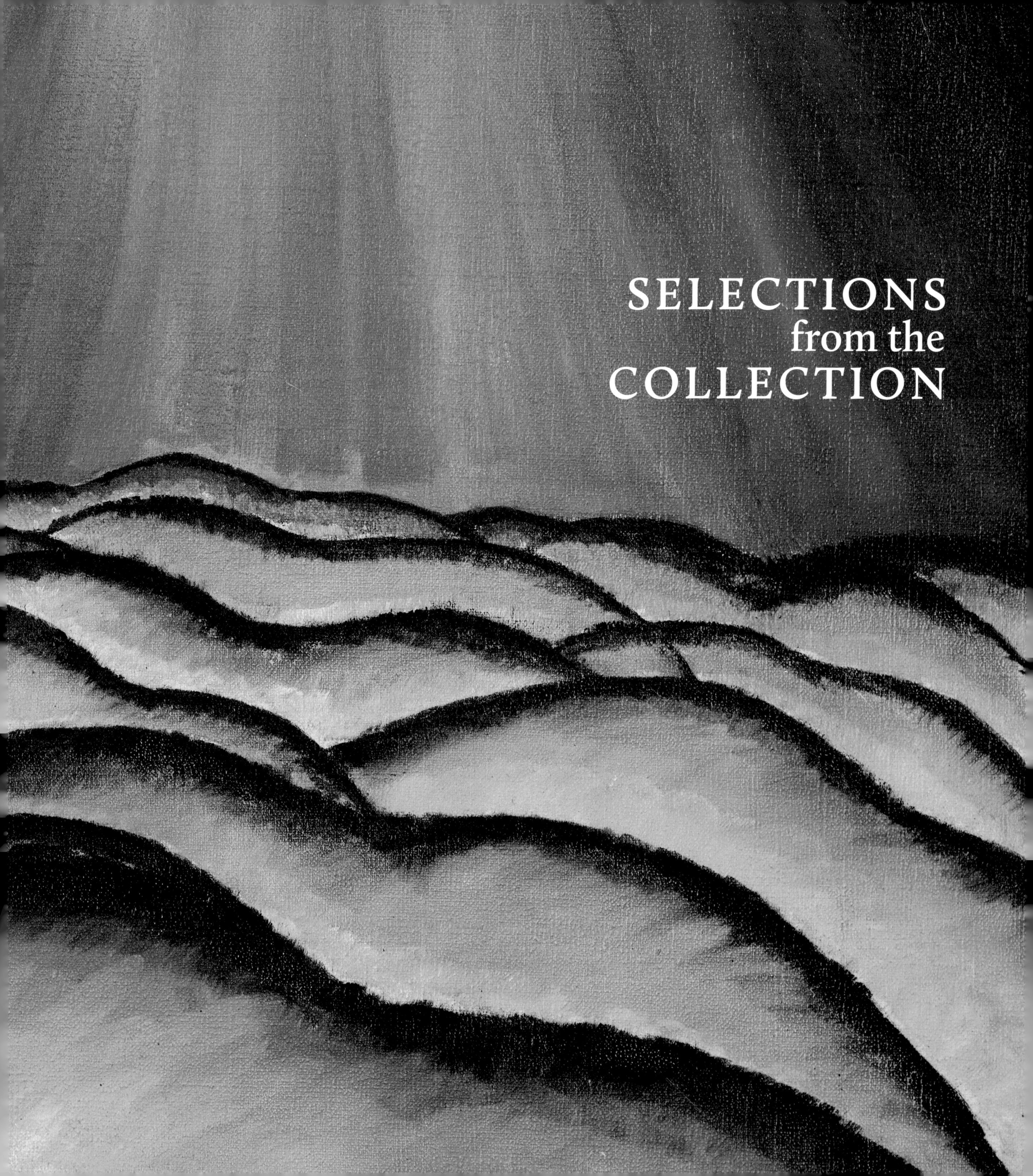

JAMES WOOLDRIDGE (CA. 1635–CA. 1695)

Indians of Virginia

ca. 1675
Oil on linen
29¾ × 42¾ in. (75.6 × 108.6 cm)

Three times removed from its source, James Wooldridge's painting of Carolina Algonquins from about 1675 is a composite of engravings published by Theodore de Bry in the first volume (1590) of his series *Grand Voyages*, a highly successful chronicle of early expeditions to the Americas. De Bry's engravings were, in turn, based on the watercolors of gentleman limner John White, who made five voyages to North America between 1584 and 1590 and is best known today as the governor of the vanished colony of Roanoke. In 1585, White was employed by Sir Walter Raleigh to make maps and paint promotional materials for investors in a potential settlement on Pamlico Sound, on land Raleigh had designated Virginia.[1] White's watercolors of the flora, fauna, and human inhabitants of what is now the outer banks of North Carolina offered spectacularly detailed imagery of a lush landscape abundant with fish and game and populated by friendly people.[2]

Wooldridge's painting includes the complete compositions of three plates from de Bry: "Their sitting at meate," included at lower left; "Their manner of praying with rattles about the fire," located at mid-left; and "The town of Pomeiooc," at mid-right. The remaining vignettes, as well as the square-shaped field opposite Pomeiooc, are parts of four other de Bry engravings. Wooldridge was faithful to de Bry on almost all points, including details of the architecture in Pomeiooc and the poses and clothing of the figures. Only small changes are apparent. The couple standing in the foreground of Wooldridge's image do not have body paint or tattoos on their upper arms, and the painter simplified and rearranged the objects on the reed mat at lower left, switching the placement of the stack of corncobs and the shell and removing a clay pipe, water vessel, and medicine bag.

Indians of Virginia is Wooldridge's only located canvas. Probably born in London in 1635, the artist was a member of the Guild of Painter-Stainers.[3] Court records indicate that he was involved in at least two large commissions for interior decorative programs in opulent homes.[4] One such commission, for Londoner Francis Holles Newman, included painted wainscoting and trim, for which Wooldridge was paid by the yard, as well as landscapes for the stairs and a hall, four paintings for the parlor, and "one picture in the bed Chamber [depicting] Venus & Adonis."[5] It is likely that *Indians of Virginia* resulted from a similar commission, this time for the Conway-Seymour family's ancestral home, Ragley Hall, in Warwickshire. Probably painted for Sir Edward Conway, the first Earl of Conway, *Indians of Virginia* may have been intended to commemorate Conway's grandfather, who was a shareholder in the 1609 Virginia Company.[6]

The painting was originally two separate works, each signed "J. Wooldrig" in the lower right, that were sewn together and retouched by Wooldridge shortly after their creation.[7] It was later restretched and reframed, probably in 1750, in association with the completion of a second Ragley Hall, construction of which began in 1680 but was not finished for another seventy years. The painting remained in the family until the twentieth century.[8] LS

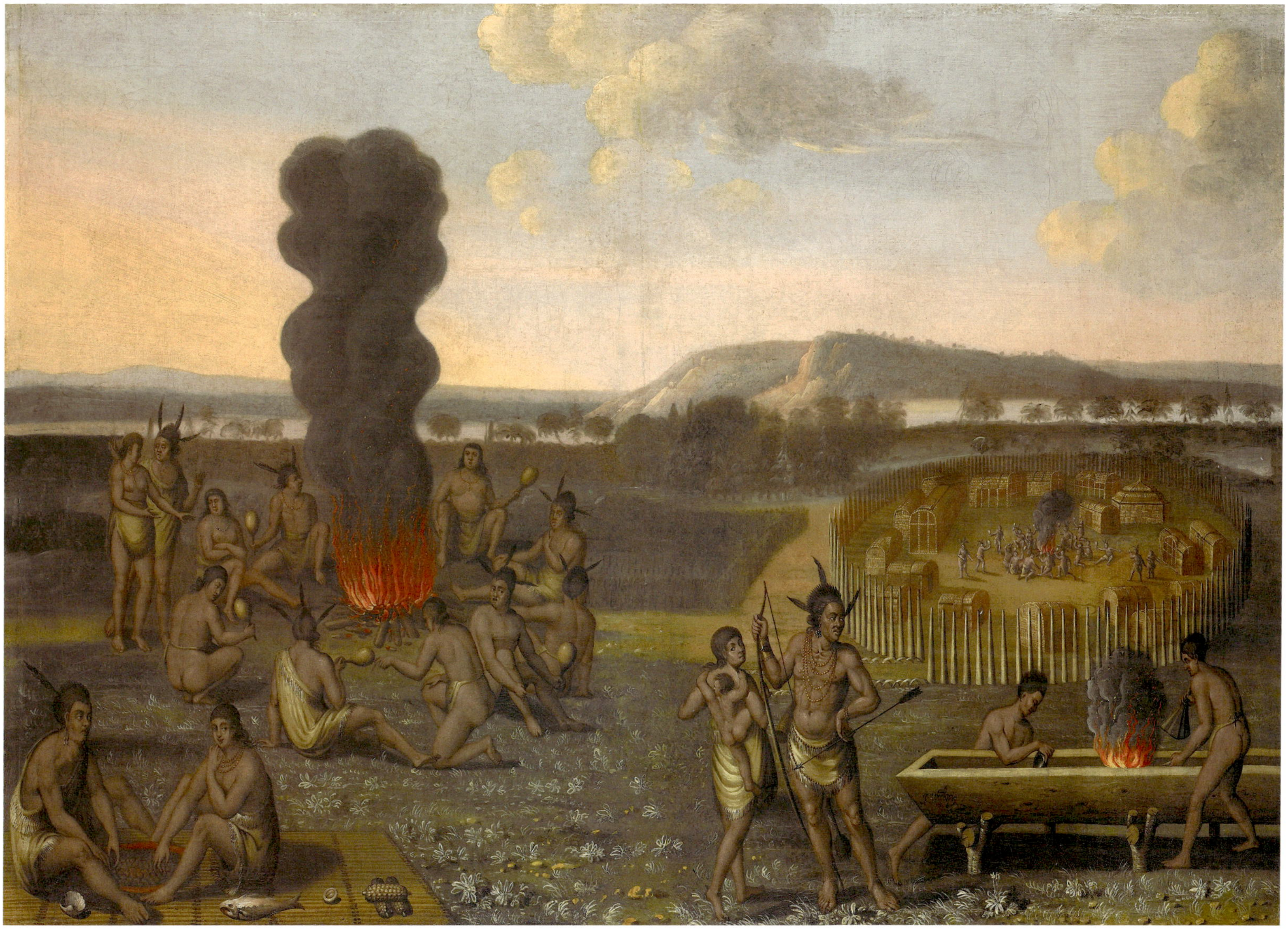

GERARDUS DUYCKINCK I *[attributed to]* (1695–1746)

Levy-Franks Portraits

ca. 1735
Oil on canvas
Multiple dimensions

This remarkable set of six portraits of a prestigious Jewish colonial American family, almost certainly painted by Gerardus Duyckinck, derives in style from the English tradition of Sir Godfrey Kneller, with a palette and iconography particular to the Dutch colonial taste prevalent in New York, even as it extends to an immigrant family of German descent. The only large set of early colonial family portraits to survive intact, this grouping has engaged generations of scholars, who have researched the identities of the sitters and artist and considered the central importance of the paintings to the story of Jewish life in the colonies.[1]

Abigaill Levy Franks was the eldest daughter of Moses Levy and his first wife, Richa Asher. A real estate broker and fleet owner, Moses immigrated to America from London in 1704, setting up business operations in Manhattan in the same year. Abigaill's future husband, Jacob Franks, who dealt principally in sugar, rice, guns, and diamonds, emigrated from London shortly thereafter. Both families were members of New York's prestigious Shearith Israel congregation. The marriage of Jacob and Abigaill in 1712, around the time of her sixteenth birthday, bonded New York's most prominent Anglo-German merchant families, a dynasty known and respected not only throughout the city but also in Philadelphia and London.[2]

The circumstances of this great portrait commission largely remain a mystery, although a series of letters from the mid-1730s between Abigaill and her son Naphtali shed some light on the possible impetus for the paintings as well as their dating. In this exchange, Abigaill expresses her pleasure in receiving a portrait of her brother-in-law Isaac Franks, with whom Naphtali was living in London, and discusses her efforts to have portraits made of her family in New York.[3] In 1959, Waldron Phoenix Belknap made the persuasive attribution of these paintings to Duyckinck based on style, composition, and the artist's close geographical proximity to the Levy-Franks family.[4]

Abigaill's portrait is the elegant linchpin of the Levy-Franks group that provides context for all the others. A typically Kneller-esque female portrait complete with uncorseted gown, flowing hair, landscape setting, and a pleasantly composed face, the painting defines the color scheme for the series, a vivid juxtaposition of crimson and indigo. Abigaill's fully frontal image is the centerpiece pendant to the likeness of her father, Moses, and her husband, Jacob. These two men, conservatively dressed in brown waistcoats and full bag wigs, each lean on a draped table and point inward, toward Abigaill, drawing attention to her beauty and privileged position in the family. The other three portraits in the series portray five of Abigaill and Jacob's nine children, with props of still life and costume that convey their beauty, composure, and wealth. The portrait of the couple's eldest daughter, Richa, is virtually her mother's image inverted, a red dress and blue wrap to her mother's blue dress and red wrap. As a group, the pictures comprise an iconographic program particularly suited to this family while respecting the portrait conventions of the time. The suite of portraits expresses an overall sense of familial well-being, prosperity, and pride without betraying specific details about any one individual. CRB

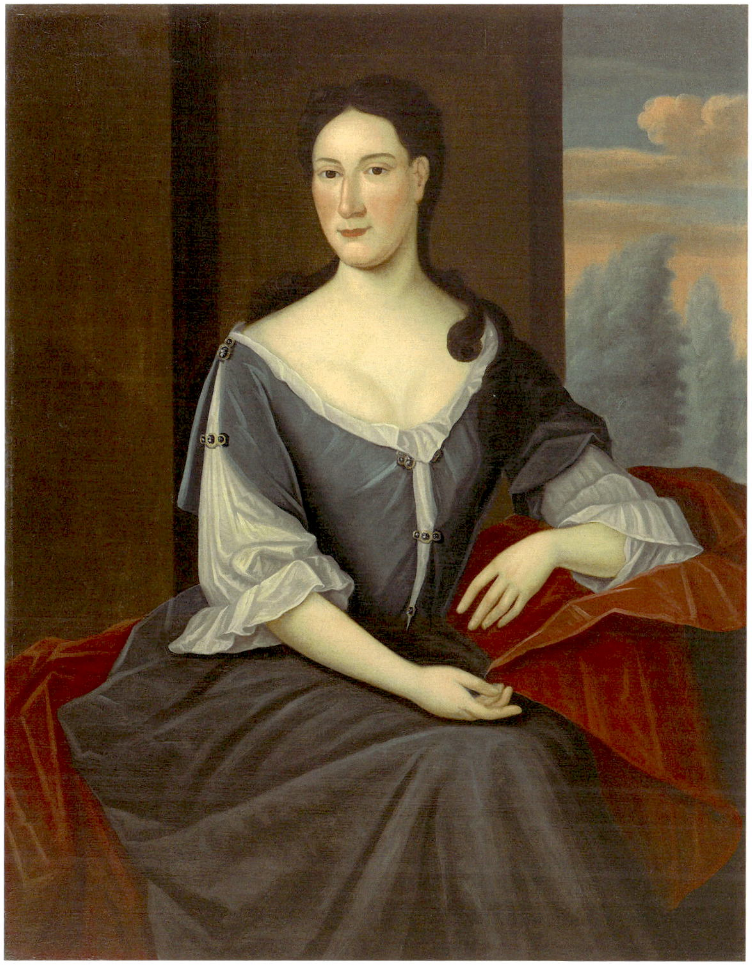

Abigaill Levy Franks
ca. 1735
Oil on canvas
45¼ × 35¹³⁄₁₆ in. (114.9 × 91 cm)

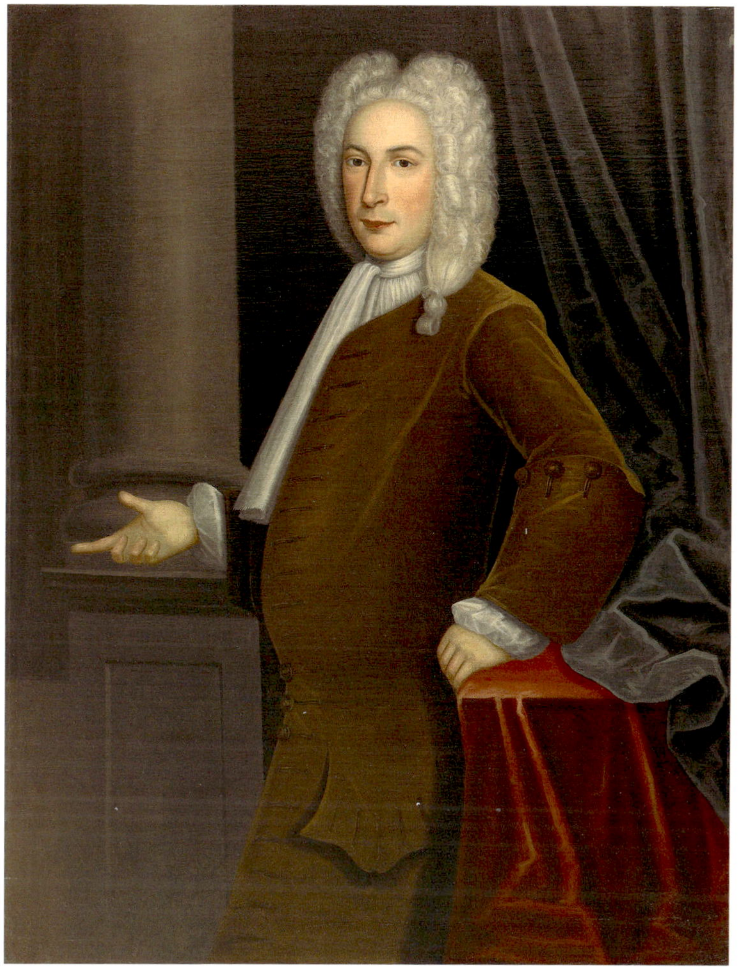

Jacob Franks
ca. 1735
Oil on canvas
45¾ × 35¹⁵⁄₁₆ in. (116.2 × 91.3 cm)

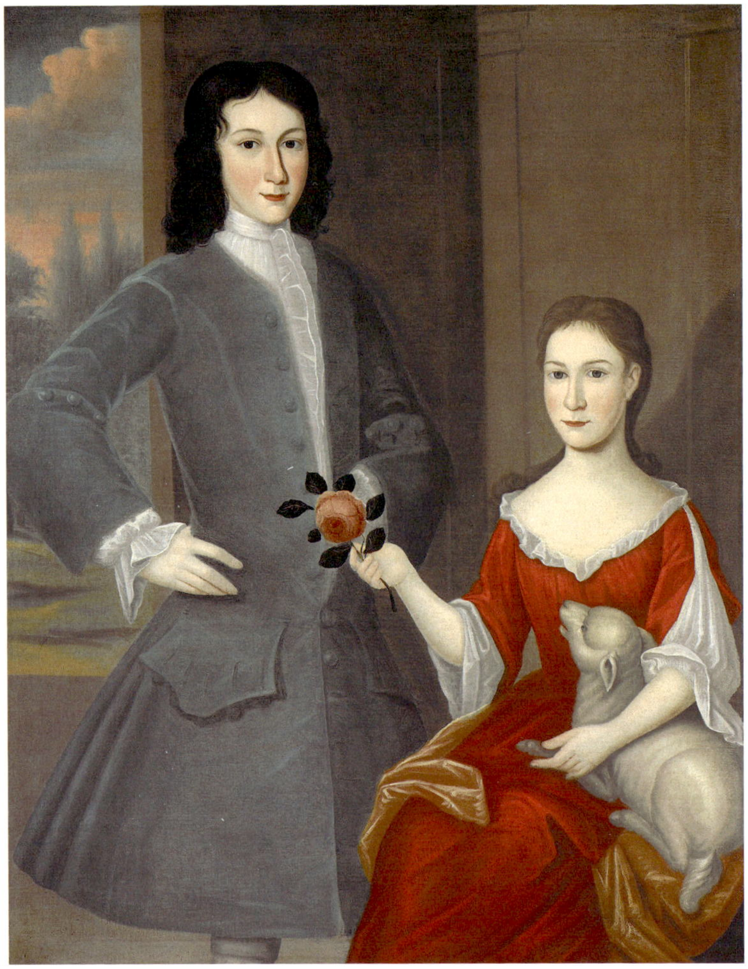

Franks Children with Lamb
ca. 1735
Oil on canvas
44½ × 35⅝ in. (113 × 90.5 cm)

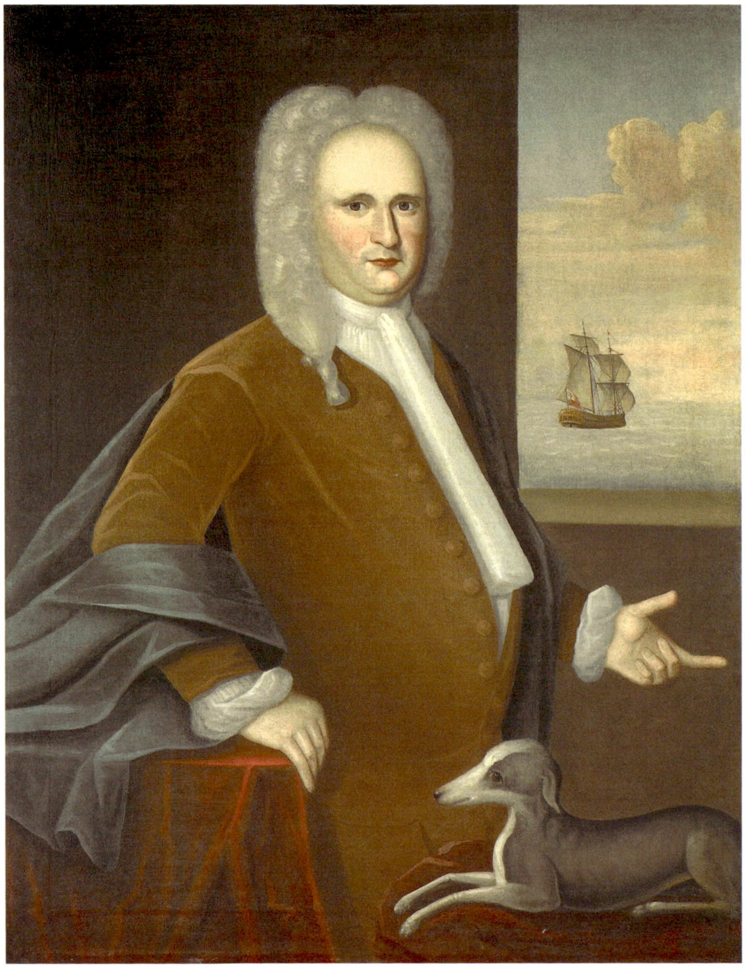

Moses Levy
ca. 1735
Oil on canvas
45⅛ × 35¾ in. (114.6 × 90.8 cm)

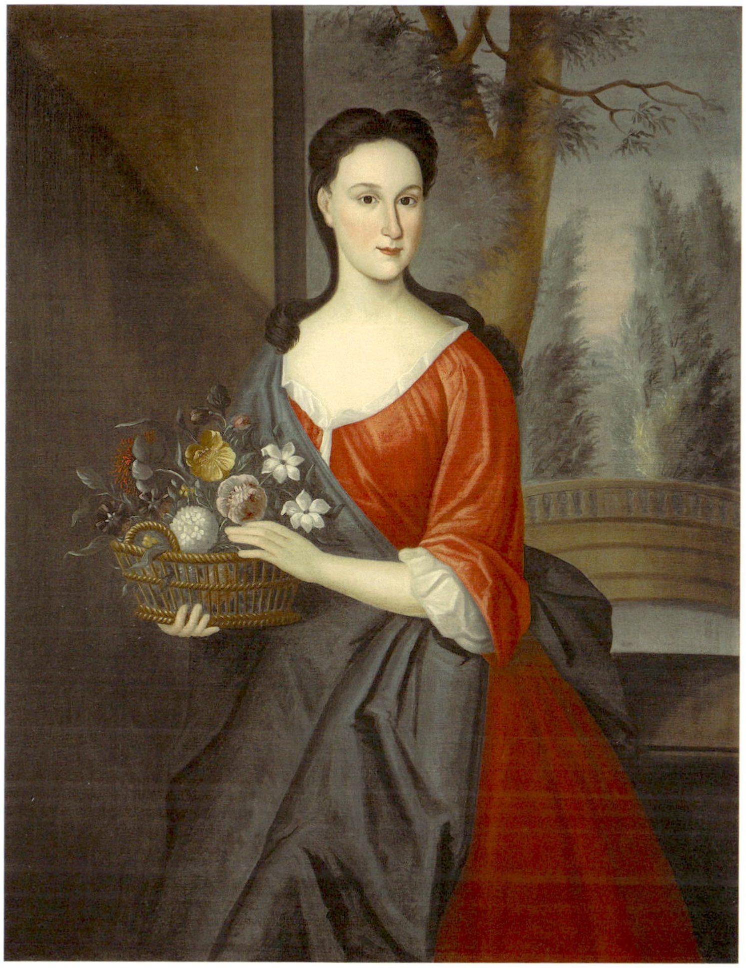

Richa Franks
ca. 1735
Oil on canvas
$44\frac{13}{16} \times 35\frac{11}{16}$ in. (113.8 × 90.6 cm)

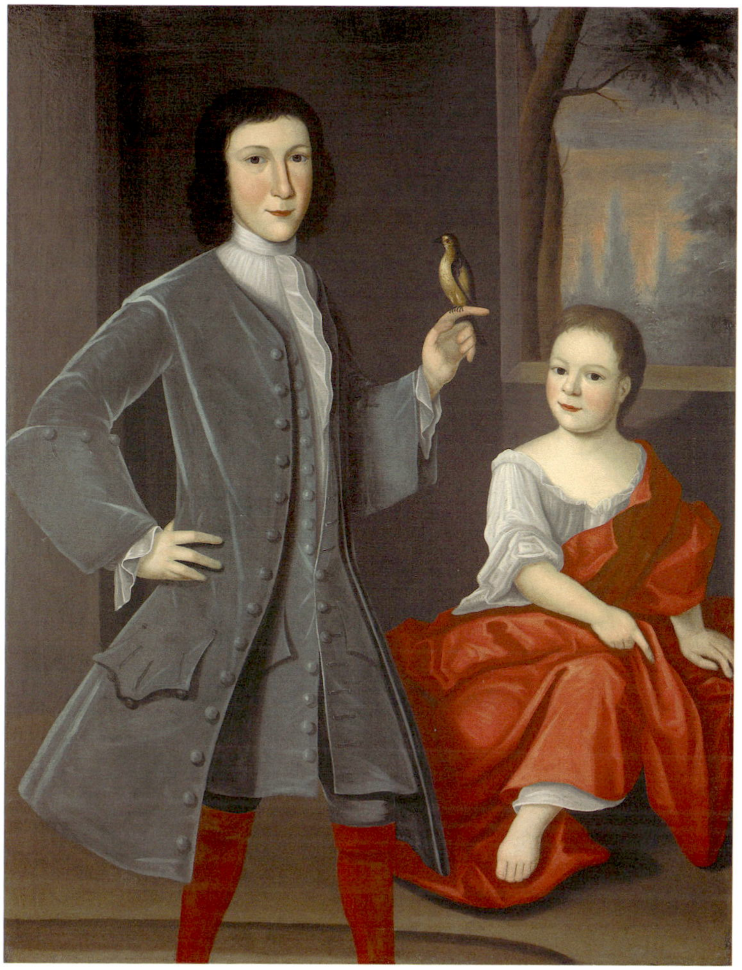

Franks Children with Bird
ca. 1735
Oil on canvas
$45\frac{1}{2} \times 35\frac{7}{8}$ in. (115.6 × 91.1 cm)

JOHN SINGLETON COPLEY (1738–1815)

Mrs. Theodore Atkinson Jr. (Frances Deering Wentworth)

1765
Oil on canvas
51 × 40 in. (129.5 × 101.6 cm)

The son of Irish immigrants Mary Singleton and Richard Copley, the foremost American artist of the eighteenth century grew up on the wharf in Boston, where his parents made a modest living selling tobacco. Copley's first exposure to the arts came after his widowed mother married Peter Pelham, an engraver who shared with his stepson his extensive collection of prints and encouraged him to explore his own talents in a variety of media. By the mid-1750s, Copley had tried his hand at drafting, printmaking, and miniature painting, but his true talents were revealed through his oil portraits, which even early on uncannily captured character and personality as well as accurate likeness. He honed his technique by studying portraits by the Scottish émigré artist John Smibert and successfully competed with the English painter Joseph Blackburn for clients. By about 1760, Copley had become the painter of choice for discerning and prestigious Bostonians, who appreciated his ability to convincingly render surface textures and to flatter his subjects with material possessions both real and imagined. He would paint over 350 portraits in New England before 1775, when he left Boston for London, never to return.[1]

Twenty-year-old Frances Deering, a Bostonian who married her cousin Theodore Atkinson Jr. in 1762, sat for Copley three years later. Her husband—the son and namesake of the President of the Council of New Hampshire—had posed for Copley in about 1757–58 (Rhode Island School of Design), perhaps on the occasion of his graduation from Harvard University. The fact that Copley's portraits of Theodore and Frances have different settings (his a landscape background and hers a warm interior) does not preclude the possibility that Theodore commissioned his wife's likeness as a pendant to his own, to be displayed together in the couple's Portsmouth home. The artist was known to select settings and poses to suit the specific needs and personalities of his varied clientele.

For Mrs. Atkinson, Copley used a seated format that foregrounds her great beauty and privileged societal position. She wears a corseted gown that accentuates her fine posture and demeanor, while the abundance of luxurious draped satin and velvet that surrounds her denotes her lofty status in Boston and Portsmouth. The rich mahogany table before which Mrs. Atkinson sits, a very fine piece of contemporary furniture, attests to her taste for the latest styles. The flying squirrel on a gold chain—a widely recognized symbol of a tamed character, a wild being turned sweet—was one of Copley's favorite themes in 1765, best known today in the artist's famous portrait of his half-brother, Henry Pelham (Museum of Fine Arts, Boston). Perhaps Copley deployed the iconography here knowing that the lively Frances had reportedly been involved in a love triangle in which she was courted by two cousins at once, ultimately choosing Theodore Atkinson over John Wentworth.[2] In his handsome portrait, she is depicted as a fine lady of grace and discipline.

CRB

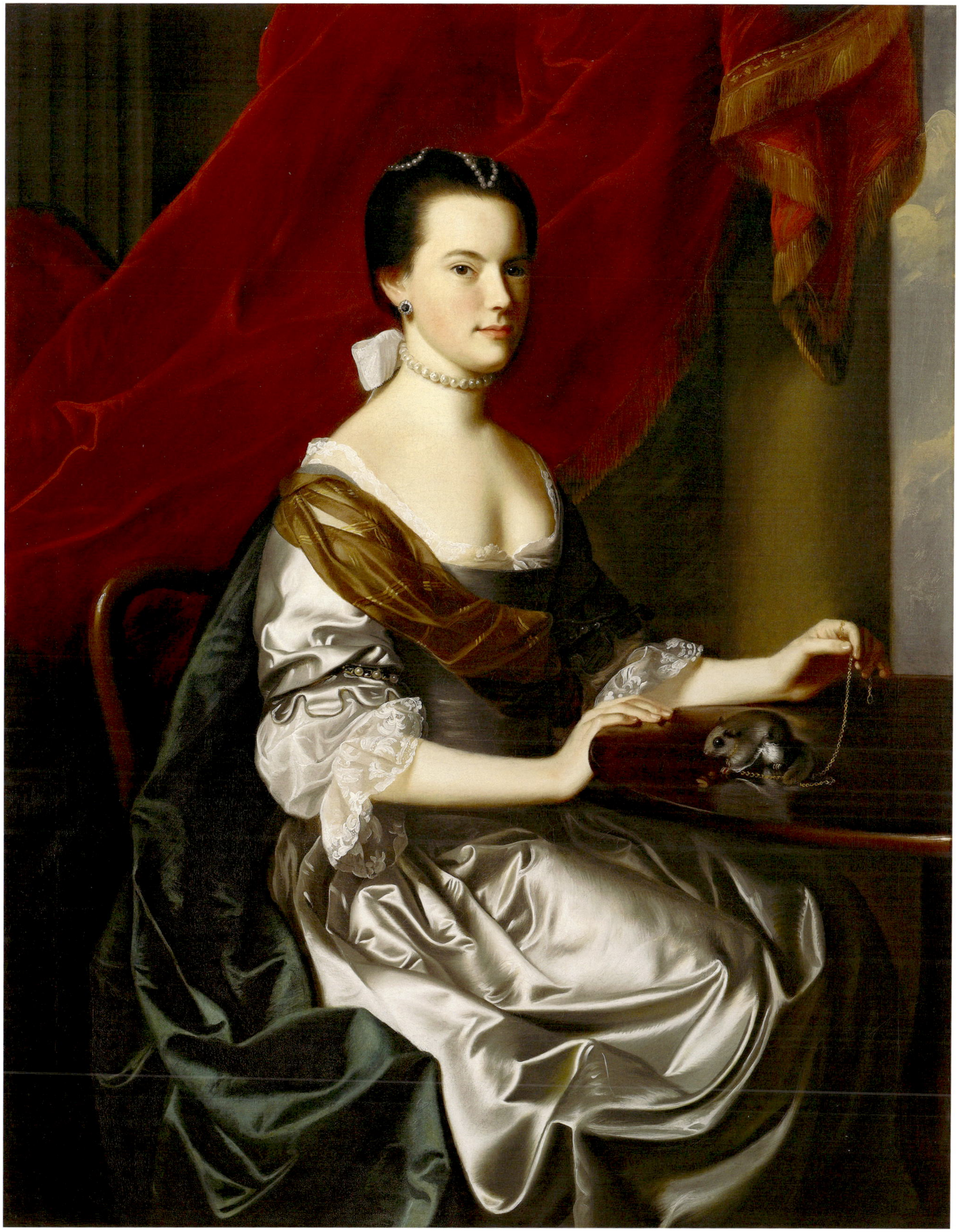

JAMES PEALE SR. (1749–1831)

The Ramsay-Polk Family at Carpenter's Point, Cecil County, Maryland

ca. 1793
Oil on canvas
49⅛ × 39⅜ in. (124.8 × 100 cm)

Over the course of his long and successful career, James Peale worked at the right hand of his older brother Charles on numerous replica portraits of George Washington (p. 34). But the artist also produced a significant independent body of work, including still-life paintings, miniature portraits, and conversation pieces, a traditional English portrait format in which the subjects engage in informal dialogue and activity.

Peale composed this large outdoor portrait of three members of his extended family on the spot, at Carpenter's Point, Maryland, on the northwest shore of the Chesapeake Bay. The artist had fled Philadelphia in 1793 in an effort to escape the yellow fever epidemic that was devastating his home city.[1] The specific site depicted in Peale's painting is the shad and herring fishery owned by Peale's brother-in-law Nathaniel Ramsay, a Maryland lawyer alongside whom the artist had fought during the American Revolution. The woman in pink at far right in the composition gesturing in the direction of the fishery is Charlotte Hall, whom Ramsay married shortly after Margaret Jane Peale's death in 1788. The woman on the left, dressed in a red-hued gown and seated on a painted settee from Baltimore, is Ruth Ellison Polk, the wife of James's nephew, the artist Charles Peale Polk. The woman in blue at center, standing behind the settee, is Mrs. Heath, Charlotte Hall Ramsay's sister.[2]

A tour de force for Peale, the painting fully deploys his artistic talents. The highly developed landscape setting, rare in his work, is specific and identifiable. At right, overhanging trees frame the three young women, while the shoreline features at left indicate a bustling fishing operation that supported the family's considerable wealth. Peale took advantage of his significant experience and skill as a miniature painter in rendering the women's individualized faces. Moreover, Peale revealed his knowledge of the history of art in composing the complex group. The three female figures make subtle reference to the Three Graces of Greek mythology—Aglaia (Beauty), Euphrosyne (Mirth), and Thalia (Abundance)—who were Aphrodite's handmaidens. As was typical of visual representations of the Graces, Peale's women stand in close proximity to one another, and each is seen from a different perspective (left profile, three-quarter view, frontal view). Peale's beautiful and charming Maryland Graces wear uncorseted silk dresses in keeping with the traditional English style of portrait painting derived from the tenets of Sir Joshua Reynolds.

CRB

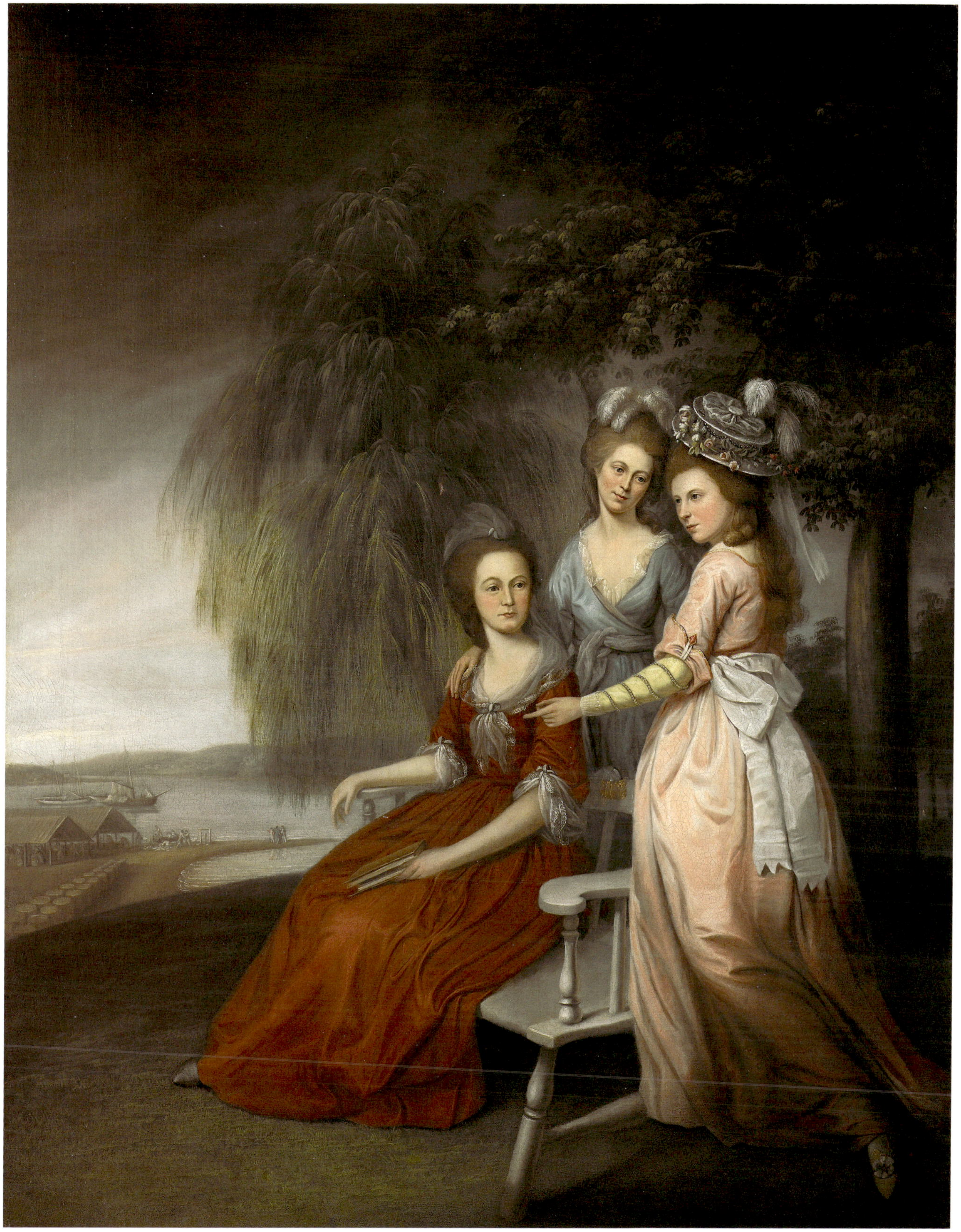

BENJAMIN WEST (1738–1820)

Cupid and Psyche

1808
Oil on canvas
54¼ × 56¼ in. (137.8 × 142.9 cm)

Benjamin West was the first artist born in the American colonies to attain international acclaim. Largely self-taught through years of studying and copying the old masters in Italy and France, the expatriate artist was appointed historical painter to England's King George by 1772, and in 1792 succeeded Sir Joshua Reynolds as president of London's Royal Academy. West taught and influenced such esteemed American artists as John Singleton Copley, Charles Willson Peale, Gilbert Stuart, and John Trumbull.

Cupid and Psyche is a relatively late work in West's long and distinguished career. The painting's mythological subject derives from Lucius Apuleius's second-century AD Roman text *The Golden Ass*, which chronicles the torrid love affair between Cupid, a god, and Psyche, a mortal princess. It is likely that West was familiar with Cupid and Psyche's story through a new translation of *The Golden Ass* published in London in 1799. While there is no passage in the novel that precisely corresponds to West's painting, it echoes the romantic and frankly erotic sensibility of Apuleius's text:

> With honied words, around his form
> With fond devotion now she twines,
> With rapt'rous kisses pressed and warm
> Each soothing, witching art combines.
>
> Forgetting his celestial race
> Unconscious of his own misdeeds
> He yields to her resistless grace—
> Who can resist when woman pleads?[1]

Leaving aside literary sources, West was surely aware of the many and varied interpretations of this mythological theme in the visual arts. He is known to have seen the Italian sculptor Antonio Canova's 1793 marble rendering of Cupid and Psyche (Louvre Museum) during an 1802 trip to Paris.[2] Much admired in his day for his ability to create the illusion of soft human flesh through stunning technical prowess and the use of milky white marble, Canova unquestionably provided a model for West's lovers, whose unblemished, iridescent bodies appear as if carved out of the dense shadow. Psyche's upraised arms are nearly a direct quote from the Canova sculpture, which in turn derives from an ancient painting of an embracing faun and bacchante published in 1773 as an engraving in the English edition of the landmark publication *Antiquities of Herculaneum*, which includes drawings of artifacts and architectural elements recovered from the ancient Roman city named for Hercules.[3]

While *Cupid and Psyche* can be tied to literary and artistic sources dating back as far as the Renaissance, the painting also neatly summarizes the main currents of European painting of its era: neoclassicism and romanticism. West's precise, nearly sculptural modeling of the two figures in the center foreground of the image stands in dramatic contrast to the more mysterious and loosely painted background, which features an airborne struggle between two doves and a larger, eagle-like bird, as well as cavorting putti and lions.[4] The trees and sky, rendered in muted mauves and adumbral greens and blues, pulse with movement; a small opening in the billowing clouds allows a glint of light to break on the distant horizon.

It is tempting to read into this allegory of youthful awakening, triumph over adversity, and, ultimately, familial reconciliation, something of West's latent sense of pride in the coming of age of the new American nation. In 1826 West's sons offered the painting to the United States government and, perhaps, this painter to King George III would have smiled upon the subtle irony of this belated valentine to America.[5]

CBC

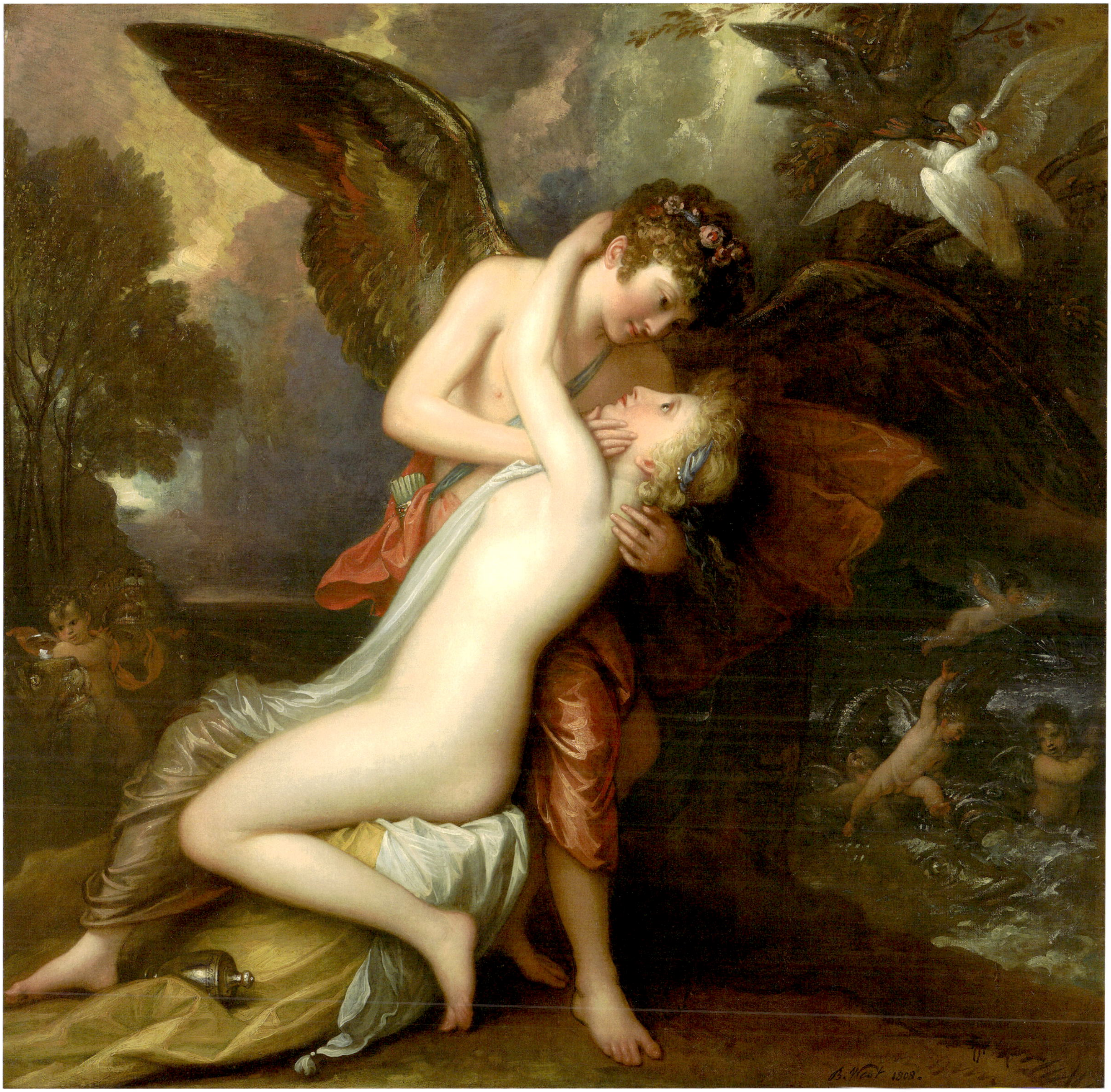
B. West 1808.

CHARLES WILLSON PEALE (1741–1827)

George Washington

ca. 1780–82
Oil on canvas
50 × 40 in. (127 × 101.6 cm)

The multiplicity of visual depictions of George Washington testifies to his persistence in American life and myth. Throughout history, most images of the commander in chief of the Continental Army and the nation's first president have derived from the work of two artists, both of whom enjoyed life sittings with the great man himself: Gilbert Stuart, who painted Washington during his presidency (p. 36), and Charles Willson Peale, for whom Washington sat an unprecedented seven times over the course of more than two decades.

Peale's 1772 portrait of Washington as a young Virginia colonel (Washington and Lee University) is the earliest known likeness of the sitter by any artist. At the time, Peale was the portraitist of choice in his hometown of Chestertown, Maryland; nearby Baltimore; and neighboring Philadelphia. He had traveled to London in 1767 to study with American expatriate Benjamin West but did not stay long, sensing that the established court traditions of formal English portraiture were unsuited to American tastes. Peale's unique approach to Grand Manner portraiture, which allowed his subjects a certain relaxed gentility, better suited the needs of the burgeoning new nation.

Within three years of entering the militia, Washington was named commander in chief of the Continental forces. On January 18, 1779, the Supreme Executive Council of Pennsylvania commissioned Peale to paint a portrait of General Washington for their meeting rooms. The original full-length likeness for Congressional Hall in Philadelphia (now in the Pennsylvania Academy of the Fine Arts), which depicts a victorious Washington at the Battle of Princeton, was a tremendous success. Peale completed numerous replicas and adaptations of the work for various governmental offices as well as for royal palaces abroad.[1]

Crystal Bridges' version was painted for François-Jean de Beauvoir, chevalier de Chastellux, an ally to the American cause who arrived in Newport, Rhode Island, on July 11, 1780. Bearing introductions from the marquis de Lafayette and the comte de Rochambeau, Chastellux developed a close friendship with the American general that involved not only diplomatic exchanges, but also gifts of claret and portraits and, as letters between them attest, a general patriotic bonhomie. Chastellux knew the full-length portrait of his friend, commenting in 1780 that the "handsomest ornament [in Congressional Hall] is the portrait of General Washington, larger than life: He is represented on foot, in that noble and easy attitude which is natural to him."[2] The Frenchman likely acquired his version of the painting directly from Peale in 1782, when he sat for his own likeness, although the picture may have been begun as early as 1780.[3] The version of the great portrait that Chastellux received—either by his own choice or, perhaps, as a gift from Washington himself—is one of only two that feature the Battle of Yorktown in the background, rather than Princeton.[4] The revised setting was fitting, as Chastellux was a major-general under the command of Rochambeau, whose French expeditionary army was instrumental in defeating the English in Virginia.

CRB

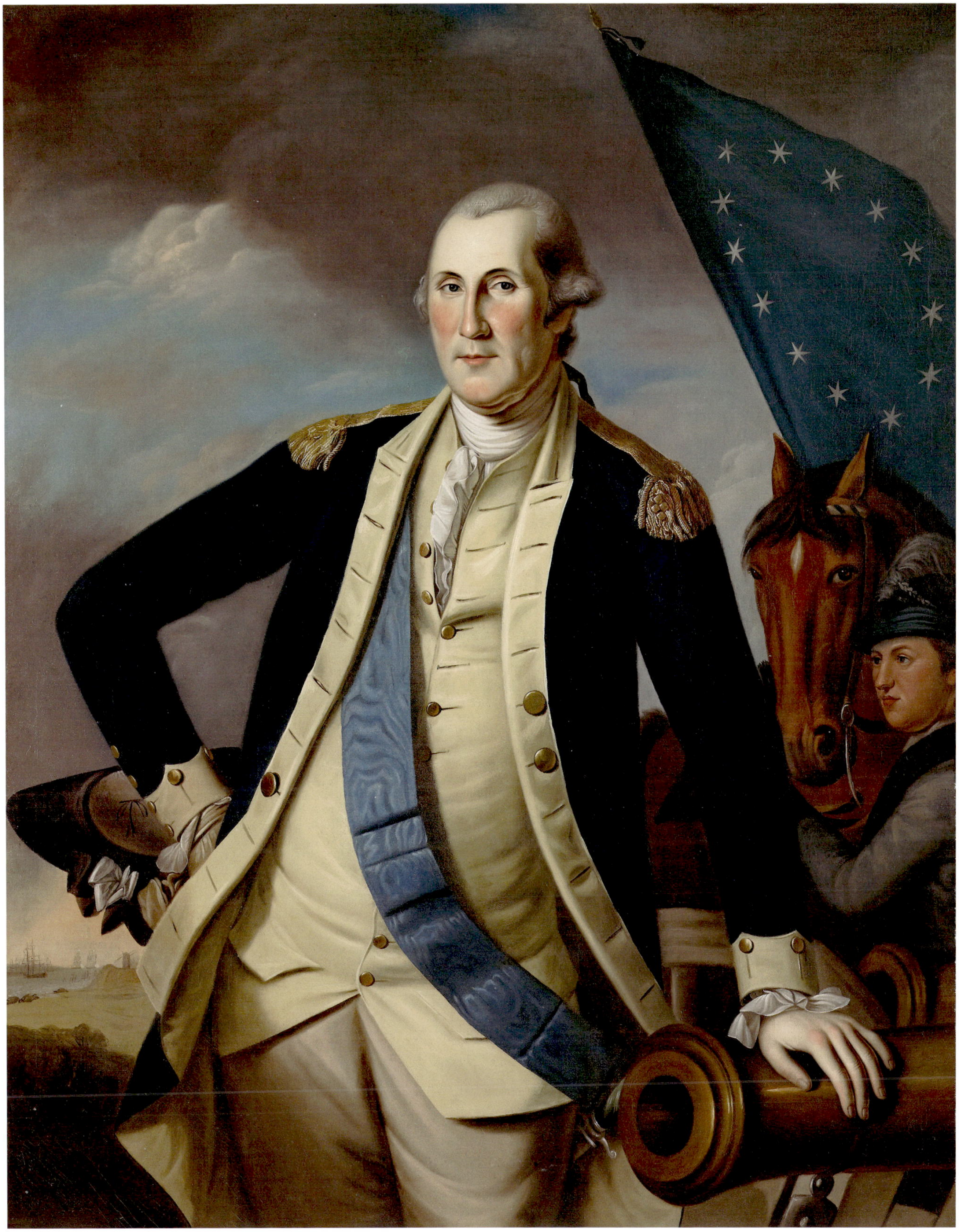

GILBERT STUART (1755–1828)

George Washington *[The Constable-Hamilton Portrait]*

1797
Oil on canvas
50 × 40 in. (127 × 101.6 cm)

When he first sat for Gilbert Stuart sometime in 1795, President George Washington was sixty-three years old and near the end of his second term of office. It took all of Stuart's colloquial powers to engage the famously reserved Washington in conversation so that the president's face would move and Stuart could fathom his character. His portraits of Washington were a success from the start. He was flooded with orders for replicas. In order to keep up with the volume of work, Stuart most often painted on relatively small canvases measuring about thirty by twenty-five inches, a standard size for English portraits. He developed three distinct portrait types for the president: the so-called Vaughan (showing the right side of Washington's face); the Athenaeum (showing the left side of his face); and the Lansdowne (full-length, showing the left side of his face). Over the next thirty years, Stuart painted at least one hundred versions of the different compositions, most of them based on the Athenaeum portrait.[1]

The Crystal Bridges likeness is a rare fifty by forty-inch, or half-length, derivation from the original Lansdowne version (National Portrait Gallery, Washington), the full-length portrait of Washington that Stuart painted for William Petty, first marquis of Lansdowne, as a gift from the Philadelphia merchant William Bingham. Like the Lansdowne, this portrait is characterized by formality, large scale, and an iconographic program suited to Washington's professional roles and accomplishments. The president's chair bears the seal of the United States; he holds a sword denoting his charge as commander in chief during the Revolution and a signed document suggesting a peaceful end to war and a laying down of arms. The seascape background, with a merchant ship flying an American flag, is unique among Stuart's portraits of Washington, an indication that the painting recognized American commercial interests. Ellen Miles has suggested that the Lansdowne portrait and this painting record Washington's support of the Jay Treaty, the resolution of peace and amicable trade between the United States and Great Britain negotiated in 1794 by the first Chief Justice of the Supreme Court, John Jay.[2]

This likeness of Washington is known as the Constable-Hamilton portrait in recognition of its purchaser and its first owner, respectively. In 1797 the merchant William Kerin Constable commissioned the work for his friend Alexander Hamilton, the New York financier who served as Secretary of the Treasury under Washington and authored the Jay Treaty. Constable was among Stuart's most avid patrons, having also commissioned from the artist a portrait of himself (The Metropolitan Museum of Art) and a full-length portrait of Washington (Brooklyn Museum).[3] CRB

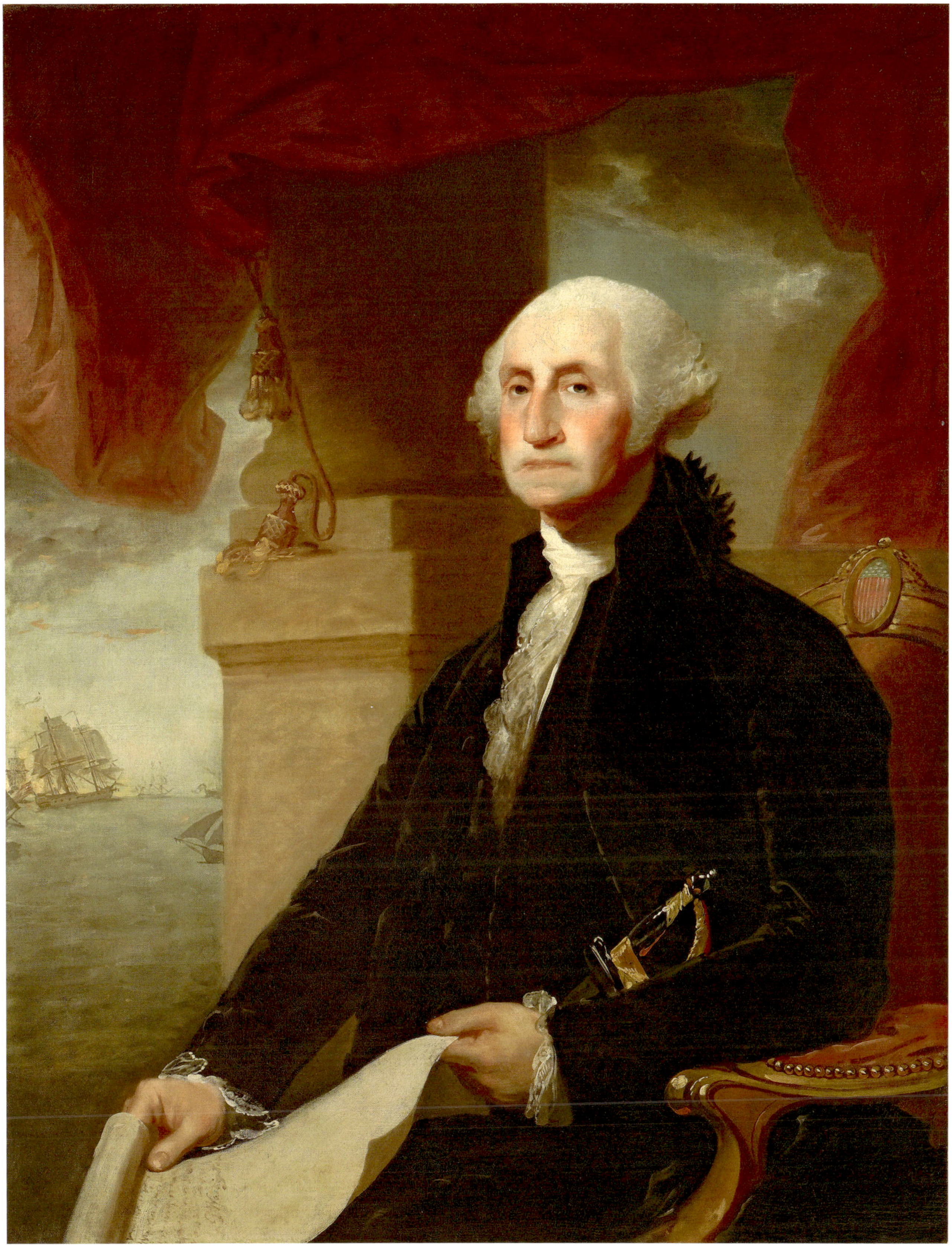

GILBERT STUART (1755–1828)

William Smith

ca. 1801–2
Oil on canvas
37 × 60 in. (94 × 152.4 cm)

The most successful and resourceful portraitist of America's early national period, Gilbert Stuart directed his enormous natural talent toward the representation of human likeness and character, bringing his witty manner to bear on each of his works. Stuart developed and maintained a distinctive portrait style, tailoring his portrayals to fit his diverse subjects. He proved his artistic skill in his hometown of Newport, Rhode Island, and mastered the techniques of late eighteenth-century Grand Manner portraiture—a traditional format for full-length likenesses developed for royalty and historical nobility—during eighteen years in London and Dublin (1775–93). Stuart returned to America with the specific goal of painting President Washington. The artist worked in New York for a year, making the key contacts that would get him to the president, then moved to Philadelphia, explaining to his uncle Joseph Anthony that he planned to stay just a short while: "The object of my journey is only to secure a picture of the President, & finish yours."[1] Stuart not only reached his goal of painting Washington (p. 36), but also received so many portrait commissions that he remained in the City of Brotherly Love for a decade, never to return to Europe.

Stuart met Dr. William Smith, the provost of the College of Philadelphia (now the University of Pennsylvania), early in Smith's tenure in Pennsylvania. The artist initially lived in a house owned by Smith's son, William Moore Smith, and when he moved to Germantown, it was to another house held by the Smith family.[2] The Aberdeen, Scotland-born teacher and clergyman sat for Stuart after his retirement from academia, sometime before 1803, when David Edwin engraved the portrait for inclusion in a posthumous publication of Smith's sermons.[3] Stuart captured a sensitive and realistic likeness of the aging educator, authoritative and respectful in dress and attentive to every line and crevice on the sitter's face. The unusual size and horizontal orientation of the canvas accommodated a composition richly filled with the details of Smith's life at the time.[4] The great waterway visible through the drawn red drape at left identifies the setting as Smith's home on the eastern banks of the Schuylkill River, while the plethora of objects in the foreground showcases his scientific interests and accomplishments.

Smith's scholar's robes with red hood denote his doctorate in divinity; the complex brass instrument before him is a theodolite, a surveying tool with telescope. The inclusion of such details of costume and prop was rare for Stuart, a master of bravura and swift completion. Many years later, Smith's grandson maintained that the artist had had help with the picture. "I believe," he wrote, "that the Books, Papers, Drapery, Table, Chair &c in this Picture, as well as the various ornamental portions . . . were designed and sketched by Samuel Blodget of Philad[a], who was a Son-in-law of Dr. Smith."[5] Ellen Miles's discovery of fine traced lines on the canvas suggests that the landscape background was transferred from a drawing; the theodolite, too, seems to have been based on an engraving or drawing, rather than an actual instrument.[6]

Regardless of authorship, Smith presumably liked his portrait. In February 1803 he offered Stuart payment in cash for a portrait of his son William, who was soon to leave for England; Smith died that spring without having heard from the painter. CRB

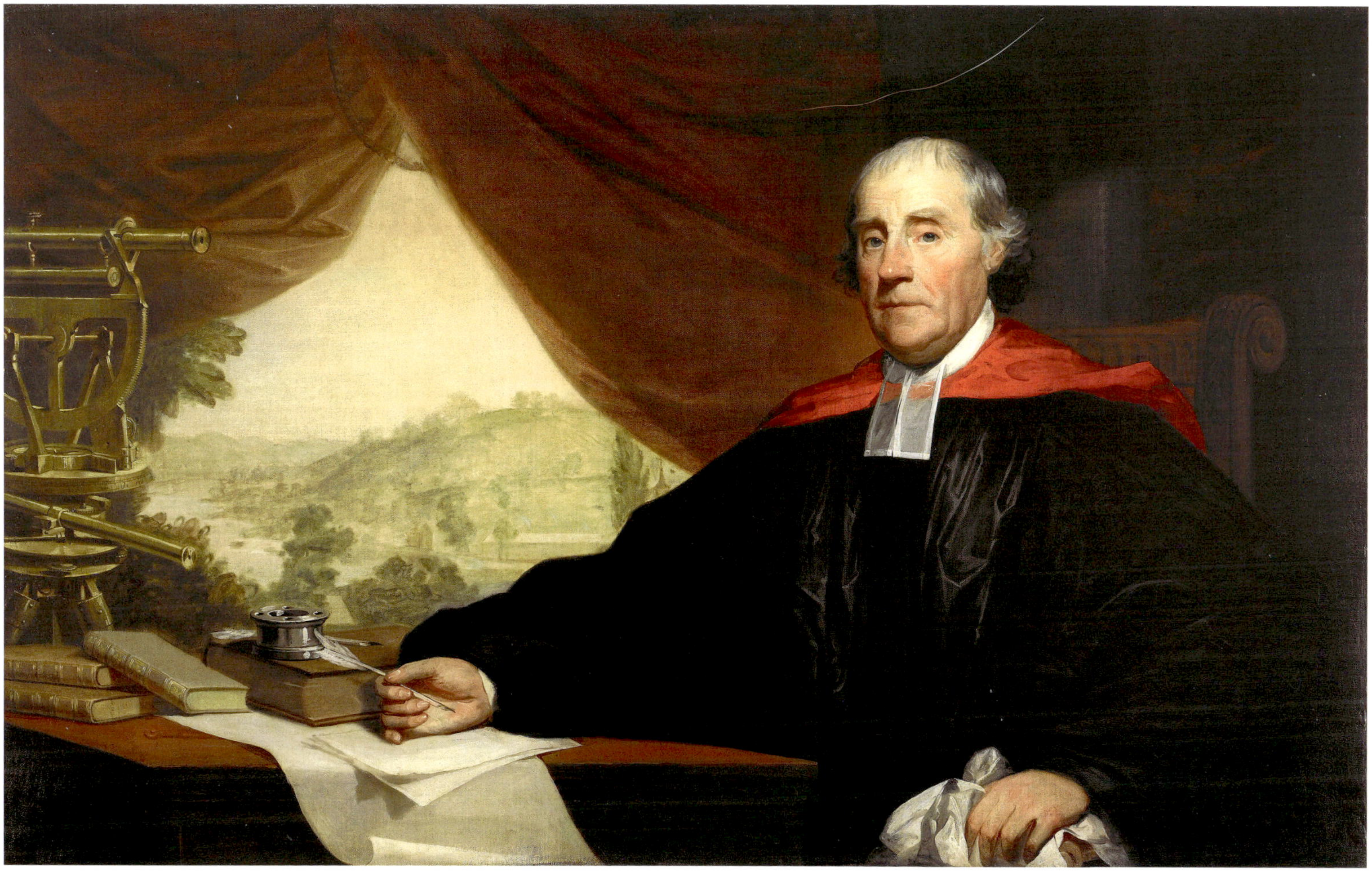

THOMAS SULLY (1783–1872)

Colonel Samuel Boyer Davis

1819
Oil on canvas
86 × 60 in. (218.4 × 152.4 cm)

The son of actors Matthew Sully and Sarah Chester, Thomas Sully was born in Horncastle, England, in 1783. The family immigrated to Richmond, Virginia, in 1792 and two years later settled in Charleston, South Carolina. Sully returned to his native England for study in 1809–10, and in that year his level of painterly accomplishment grew tenfold. Back home he was lauded as the "American Lawrence," in reference to the lauded English romantic painter Sir Thomas Lawrence. The finest portraitist in Philadelphia and one of the best in the country, Sully was flooded with commissions from the elite of Pennsylvania and Maryland society, and the affable and levelheaded artist admirably managed his professional affairs. He almost single-handedly created the vogue for full-length portraiture in Philadelphia, and his career soared on a trajectory that had him painting celebrated public figures as well as the most eminent and fashionable private citizens in the vicinity.[1]

Sully kept a detailed daybook documenting his work. He recorded painting his portrait of Samuel Boyer Davis between June 19 and July 15, 1819, on commission for the State of Delaware. He gave the picture a value of five hundred dollars, but it seems that the State of Delaware never collected the work, as it remained in Davis's family for nearly a century.[2] Davis sat for Sully shortly after resigning from a lengthy and distinguished career in the United States Army. A native of Lewes, Delaware, and remembered as "singularly handsome, fully six feet three inches in stature, with a most winning smile and graceful and courteous bearing," Davis had served as lieutenant colonel of the Thirty-second Regiment of the United States Infantry during the War of 1812.[3] He successfully led defenses in his hometown of Lewes; at Sandy Hook, New Jersey; and later at Fort Saint Phillip, one of the river defenses in the Battle of New Orleans. The waterfront setting in Sully's portrait of the military leader suggests that Davis is near Fort Saint Phillip, but could represent any one of his battles, all of which occurred near shore.

Full-length portraits by Sully are few and far between. The artist typically reserved this ambitious format for portraits intended for display in public spaces or for exhibition at the Pennsylvania Academy of Fine Arts, where Davis's likeness was shown in 1820. This large painting shows Sully and his sitter to best advantage: the artist demonstrated his firsthand knowledge and mastery of the graceful heroicism typical of English military portraiture by Lawrence and Sir Joshua Reynolds, and Davis comes across as distinguished and vital.

CRB

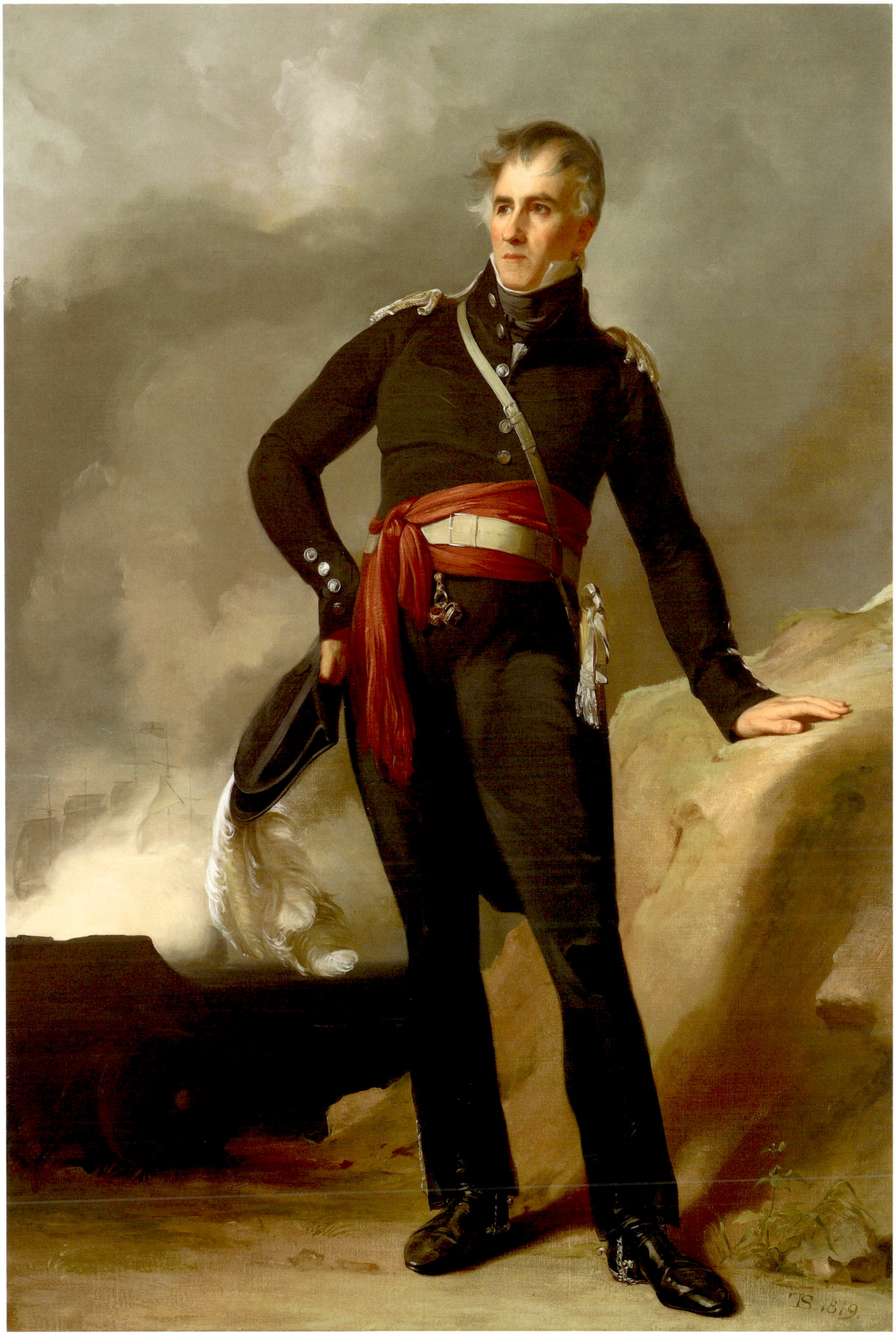
TS. 1819.

RAPHAELLE PEALE (1774–1825)

Corn and Cantaloupe

ca. 1813
Oil on panel
14½ × 19½ in. (36.8 × 49.5 cm)

Raphaelle Peale was America's first serious painter of still life. He began his career under the tutelage of his father, the artist Charles Willson Peale, and initially focused on the more lucrative genre of portraiture. Following a bout of debilitating illness—now thought to have been some form of chronic heavy metal poisoning—Peale shifted his attentions to still life. From 1812 until the end of his life, Peale created more than one hundred paintings of fruits, vegetables, cakes, and meats closely grouped on shallow ledges and set off against dark backgrounds. In this remarkable group of works Peale rethought the genre, casting humble, distinctly American produce in the place of European foodstuffs and infusing his subjects with an air of mystery and melancholy.

Corn and Cantaloupe juxtaposes a tall earthenware crock with a small, oblong sweet potato, barely big enough to serve one person; a short pickling cucumber; and half of a ripe, pale green melon. The fruit has been identified as an Anne Arundel melon, a delicate variety grown in southern Maryland and prized for its sweetness.[1] Propped up across the tops of this selection of produce is a large ear of corn, the husk of which has been cut away to reveal three well-formed rows of golden kernels and numerous tendrils of delicate silk. The silks cascading from the top of the ear cross a frond of the husk to form the loop of the letter P, more than likely a reference to the first letter of the artist's last name.[2] The shapes of the fruits and vegetables and the fullness and ripeness of their forms evoke human, as well as botanical, fecundity.[3] The perfectly ripe corn, a grain that loses its sweetness within hours of harvest, and the melon, whose glossy seeds slide toward its lip, also elicit the wistful sense of opportunities on the cusp of passing.

Peale's close scrutiny of the melon and sweet potato allow the viewer to identify the uniquely American produce. The Anne Arundel melon, today a popular heirloom plant in home gardens, appears in several of Peale's paintings from this period. Anne Arundel was the county of Peale's birth, so the fruit may have been a second autobiographical reference.[4]

Peale appears to have exhibited the oil in 1814 in Philadelphia, as *Corn and Cantelope* [*sic*], and likely held on to the work until 1820, when a painting trip to Maryland brought the artist into contact with an old family friend, Dr. Benjamin Lee. Peale may have given it to his friend at that time, as a token of friendship or in exchange for some hospitality. Lee was not an art collector; an estate inventory records that at the time of his death he owned only this one painting, which hung in the dining room of his plantation home, Oak Hill.[5] The fact that Lee grew corn and sweet potatoes at Oak Hill, and presumably consumed them in his dining room, would have made *Corn and Cantaloupe* a particularly appropriate gift.[6] LS

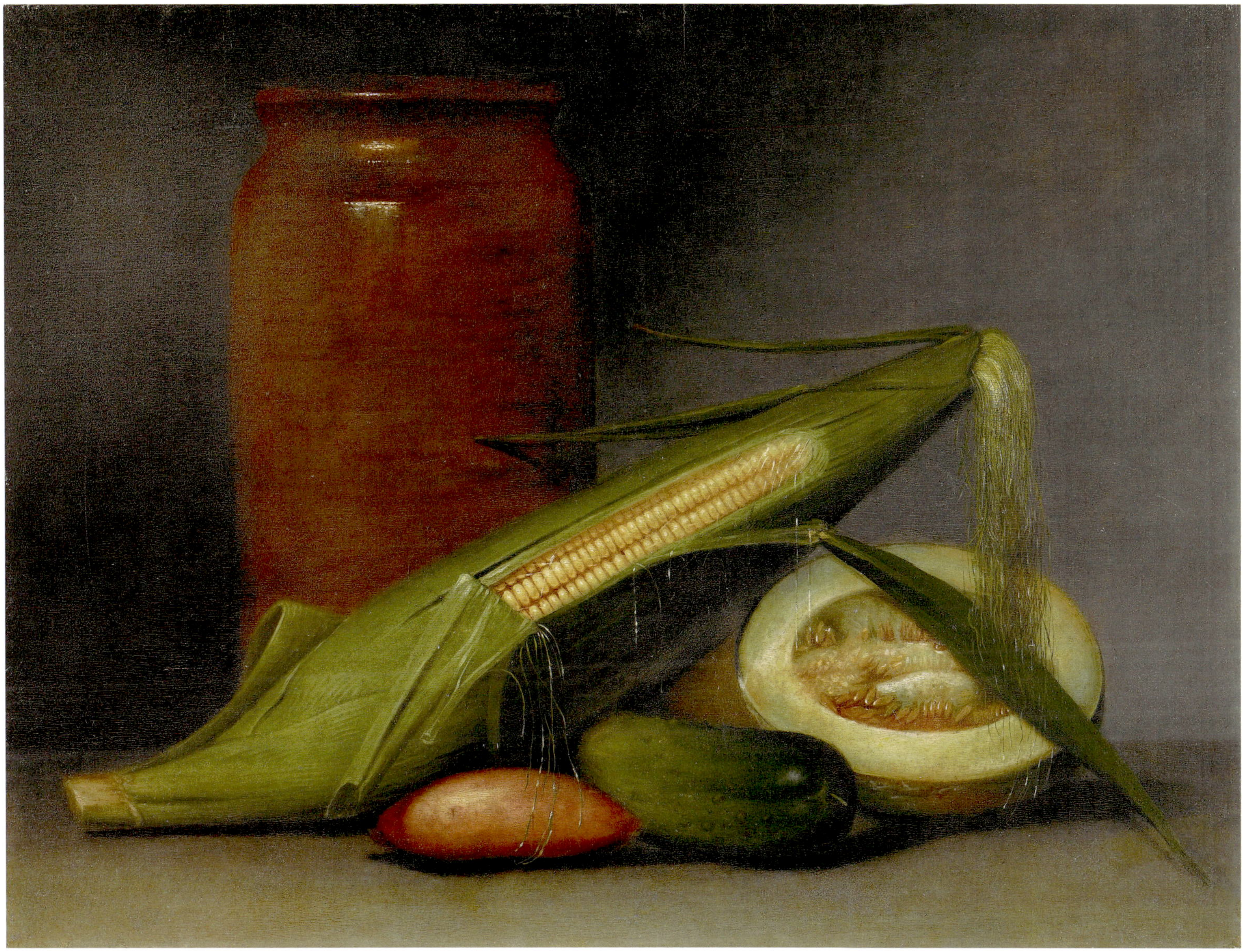

JOHN L. KRIMMEL (1786–1821)

The Village Politicians

ca. 1819
Oil on canvas
35½ × 48¼ in. (90.2 × 122.6 cm)

John L. Krimmel's *The Village Politicians*, which shows a group of men gathered around a table in a tavern arguing about politics, is a copy of a painting of the same name by David Wilkie, the most admired British painter of Krimmel's generation.[1] Krimmel, who came to be known as the "American Wilkie," immigrated to the United States from Germany in 1809 and dedicated himself to becoming an artist shortly after settling in Philadelphia.[2] The city was then a center for the arts in America, and Krimmel found numerous venues for study, including the newly formed Society of Artists of the United States, where he sketched from plaster casts and live models. As America's first documented painter of subjects from everyday life, another important source of instruction was British genre paintings available as engravings. Krimmel adapted numerous motifs from Wilkie and painted direct copies of at least two other of the British artist's best-known works.[3]

Wilkie first exhibited his *Village Politicians* in 1806, at London's Royal Academy, but Krimmel was not able to study the painting until Abraham Raimbach's engraving after the work was published in 1814. Although Krimmel was true to Wilkie's overall composition, he made small changes that both distinguish the later painting as American and imprint it with his own particular taste. As was often the case with his copies after Wilkie's work, Krimmel tidied up the interior, removing objects littering the floor and reducing the number of items arranged on shelves or tables. Krimmel also added a symmetrical arrangement of portraits to the chimney wall of his painting as a means of ordering the space. In this case, a small portrait engraving or sketch flanked by framed silhouettes decorates the wall above the fire. Most importantly, the artist changed the setting from Scotland to America. Krimmel replaced the metal tankard at the foot of the table in Wilkie's painting with a Philadelphia earthenware pitcher, and the newspaper in the hands of the elderly gentleman at the table is no longer Edinburgh's radical *Gazeteer* but the *National Intelligencer*, from Washington, D.C.[4] In Wilkie's painting, the presence of the *Gazeteer* has been interpreted as introducing an element of satire: common Scottish men have become upstart radicals in the wake of the French Revolution.[5] Krimmel's choice of a tamer, mainstream paper that supported the Monroe administration dulled Wilkie's satirical edge and rendered the American painting a representation of properly functioning democracy.

The Village Politicians was likely a commission from Commodore Alexander Murray, a naval officer during the Revolutionary War and the first superintendant of the Philadelphia Navy Yard who also owned two other Krimmel paintings indebted to Wilkie.[6] The painting may have been one of the last in the artist's tragically short career. Krimmel drowned in a friend's pond just two years later, leaving behind a scant twenty-four known works. LS

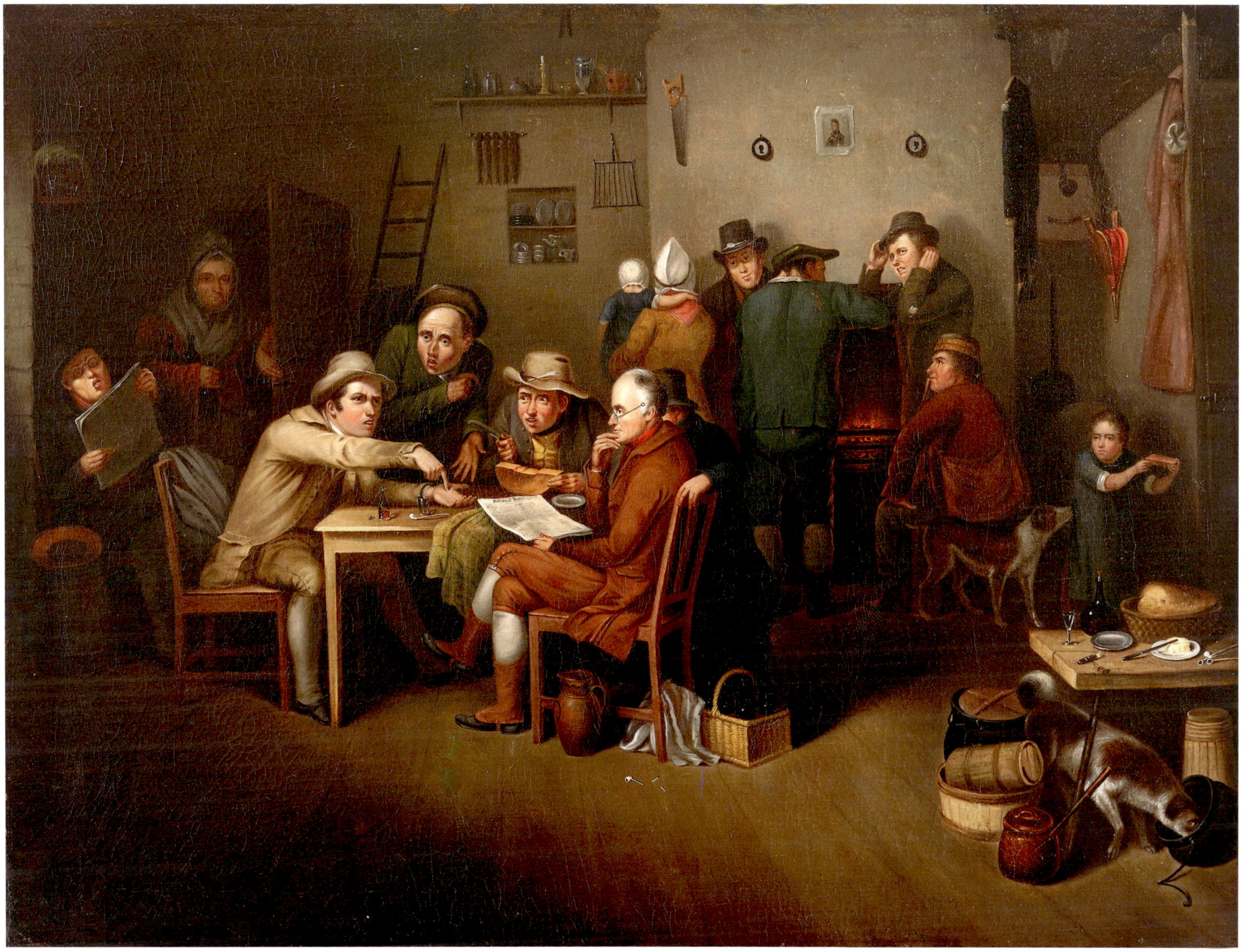

JOHN VANDERLYN (1775–1852)

Niagara and the Rapids

ca. 1801–2
Oil on paper on board
14½ × 46½ in. (36.8 × 118.1 cm)

Born in 1775, on the eve of the American Revolution, the New York painter John Vanderlyn would become one of the nation's earliest and most influential proponents of neoclassicism. Like most artists of his generation, Vanderlyn began his career painting portraits, an enterprise that acquainted him with numerous prominent and influential Americans. Impressed with his work, Senator Aaron Burr arranged an assistantship for the young artist under Gilbert Stuart and paid for his studies in Paris with the noted neoclassical painter François-André Vincent.[1] Upon his return to America, Vanderlyn received numerous commissions through his wealthy and politically powerful benefactor. Yet the artist desired to escape the constraints of portraiture and dedicate his talents to the loftier genre of history painting.

In an effort to earn the money needed to support his expanding artistic ambitions, Vanderlyn visited Niagara Falls during the fall of 1801. His intention was to produce a series of original oil paintings of the awe-inspiring cataract to be engraved, published, and sold.[2] Niagara Falls was widely recognized in early nineteenth-century America as a symbol of the young nation's strength, splendor, and natural abundance. Although the scenic natural wonder was familiar to a broad public, few had made the difficult journey to experience the falls in person. Most contemporary representations were copies of earlier prints or derived from oral or written descriptions, which often resulted in exaggerated and inaccurate accounts. Vanderlyn recognized the opportunity to capitalize on a well-known yet widely misrepresented subject.[3]

Niagara and the Rapids may be one of the studies of the majestic cataract that Vanderlyn created while on-site.[4] The composition emphasizes the falls' great breadth and extraordinary beauty. Too expansive a view to capture on a single sheet, Vanderlyn joined two pieces of paper in a horizontal orientation to paint the scene. The viewer's elevated vantage enhances the image's panoramic quality.[5] Despite the painting's grand, rather auspicious dimensions, Vanderlyn chose to depict an unconventional, peripheral view of the channel leading to Horseshoe Falls rather than focus on the powerful deluge itself.

Emulating the organic camber in nature, Vanderlyn's representation of the powerful Niagara River creates a visual flow through the composition. Within the straights of the waterway, the artist conveys depth through color. Along the shorelines, shades of blue and gray distinguish the shallows from the green and turquoise in the channel's deep recesses. Reflective, calm waters contrast with the torrent of rapids that approaches the edge of the falls. Thundering surges of white water roar from the rim of Niagara, a dense atmosphere of spray and mist emerging from the unseen chasm. Finally, a rainbow marks the focal point of the composition. Directing the gaze skyward, this multicolored refraction prevents the viewer from coursing over the falls. In the upper register, the fading arc unites the picture's two halves, implying a visual path back to the source of the falls and allowing the observer to visually experience the composition over and again.

Vanderlyn's carefully studied views of Niagara are among the first produced in oils by an artist who personally experienced the falls.[6] From the on-site studies he produced in 1801, the artist completed at least two finished paintings, both of which were engraved in London and subsequently published on both sides of the Atlantic.[7] Yet the prints did not produce the profits he expected. Vanderlyn's dogged pursuit of artistic and financial independence would continue throughout his career.

AWJ

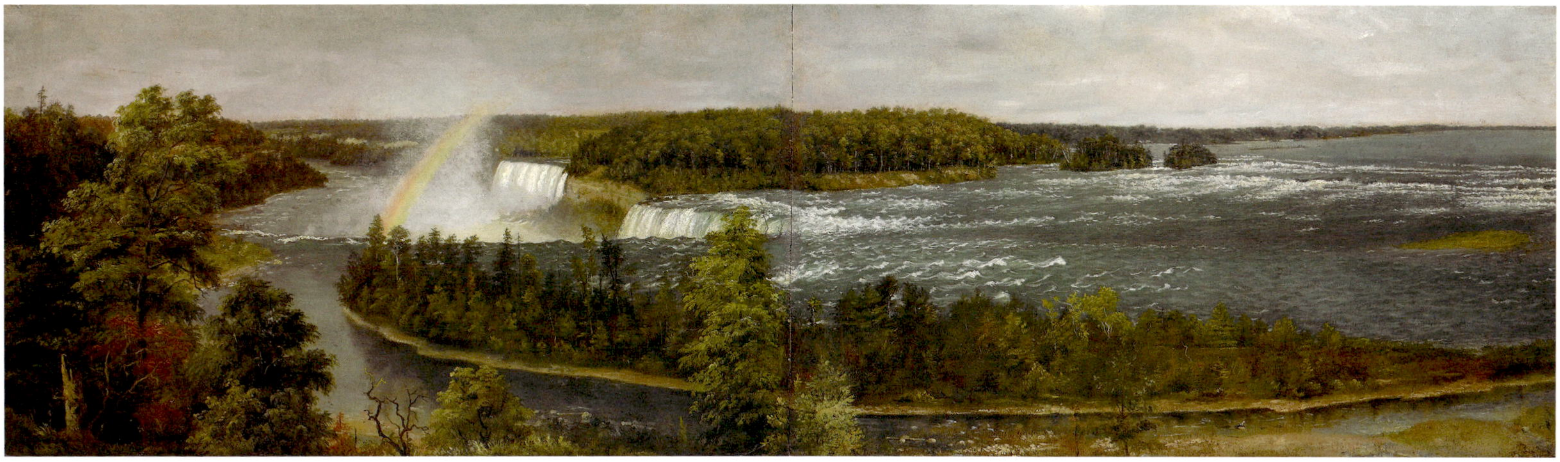

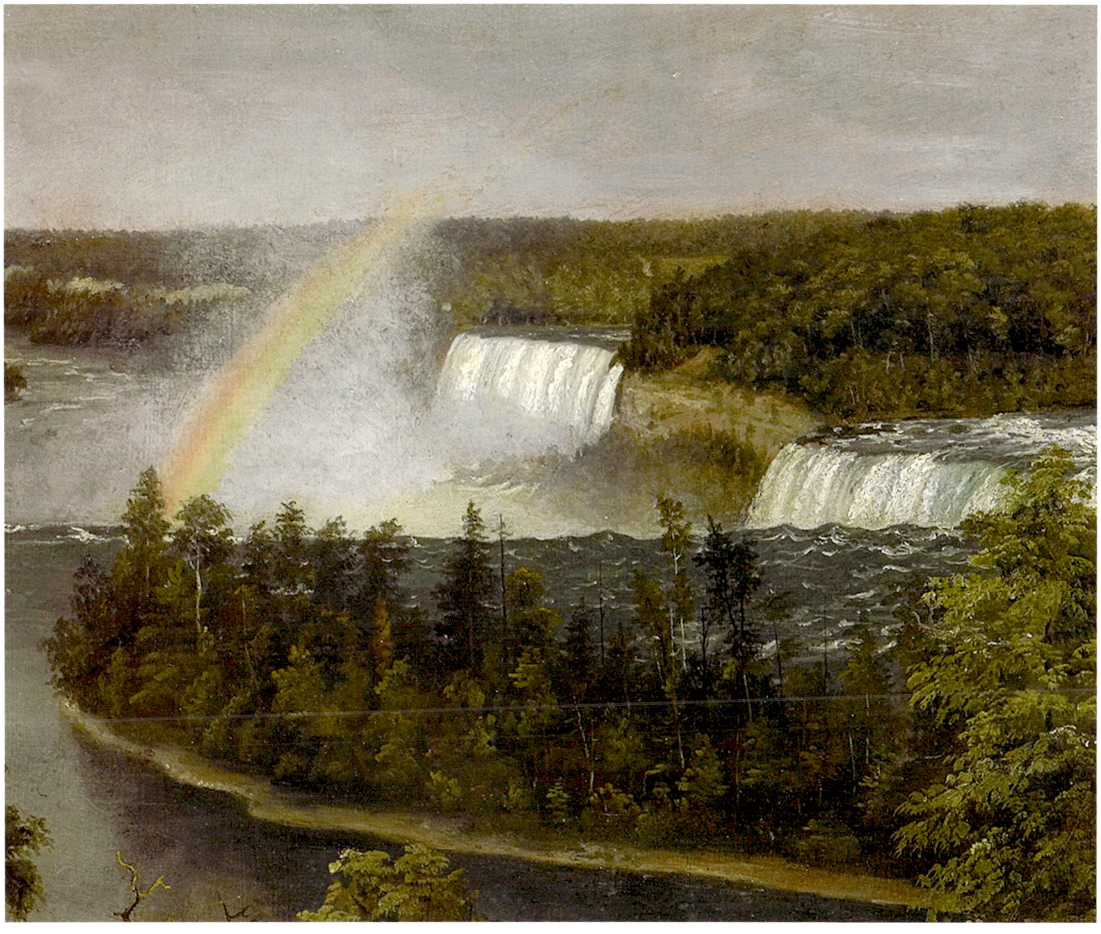

Detail

FRANCIS GUY (1760–1820)

Winter Scene in Brooklyn

1820
Oil on canvas
58 × 106 in. (147.3 × 269.2 cm)

Winter Scene in Brooklyn is one of five paintings Francis Guy made of the view from the second-story window of his home and studio in 1819–20.[1] Guy's intriguing panorama shows a snow-covered plaza at the busy intersection of Front, James, and Fulton Streets, now at the base of the Brooklyn Bridge. Under a dramatic blue sky filled with clouds and chimney smoke sit rows of meticulously rendered homes, shops, and offices set against the hills of Brooklyn Heights. In the center foreground an anonymous African American laborer cuts a large pile of wood while behind, dozens of his fellow Brooklynites, many of whom are identified in an engraving after the painting, mingle and chat in the street. Guy's close attention to his subjects offers up minute wonders, such as the square and measuring pole held by carpenter Benjamin Meeker at center left; the leg of mutton in the hands of Jacob Pachten, the "King of Butchers," at the head of Front Street; and the gilt-framed landscape painting tucked under the arm of an unidentified gentleman to the woodcutter's immediate left.[2]

Guy began his career in England, as a tailor and dyer. He immigrated to America in 1795 and eventually settled in Baltimore, Maryland, where he resided until his move to Brooklyn in 1818. While in Baltimore, he abandoned his work as a tailor and took up painting land- and cityscapes. He taught himself by studying engravings and paintings in significant Baltimore collections.[3] Guy also devised a method of tracing to help compose his views. He located a scene he wanted to depict, suspended a piece of black gauze in front of it, and traced the view in chalk. He then pressed the gauze against a canvas prepared with a dark ground and rubbed until the chalk lines appeared. Finally, he painted over these lines in oil.[4] The resulting works convey a striking topographical accuracy that was a source of astonishment and delight to his early nineteenth-century viewers. In *Winter Scene in Brooklyn* Guy took that accuracy to another level, recording not only the streets and architecture, but also his Brooklyn neighbors engaged in their daily routines. While at work on the painting Guy is said to have called out his window to his subjects, asking them to stop a moment and hold their poses for him.[5]

Winter Scene in Brooklyn is likely the second of Guy's views from his Front Street window. It is very close in composition and size to the first painting in the series, the 1819–20 *Brooklyn Snow Piece* (Brooklyn Museum), although *Winter Scene in Brooklyn* originally had a decorative balustrade running along its bottom edge that was removed during a restoration in the 1880s.[6] Based on the success he had enjoyed exhibiting *Brooklyn Snow Piece* in New York, Guy planned to exhibit, and probably sell, *Winter Scene in Brooklyn* in Baltimore. Illness slowed his progress on the work, however, and the painting never made it to Maryland.[7] A heavy drinker throughout his life, Guy is said to have stayed sober while at work on *Winter Scene in Brooklyn*. He relapsed upon its completion, however, and died shortly thereafter, following an alcoholic binge. LS

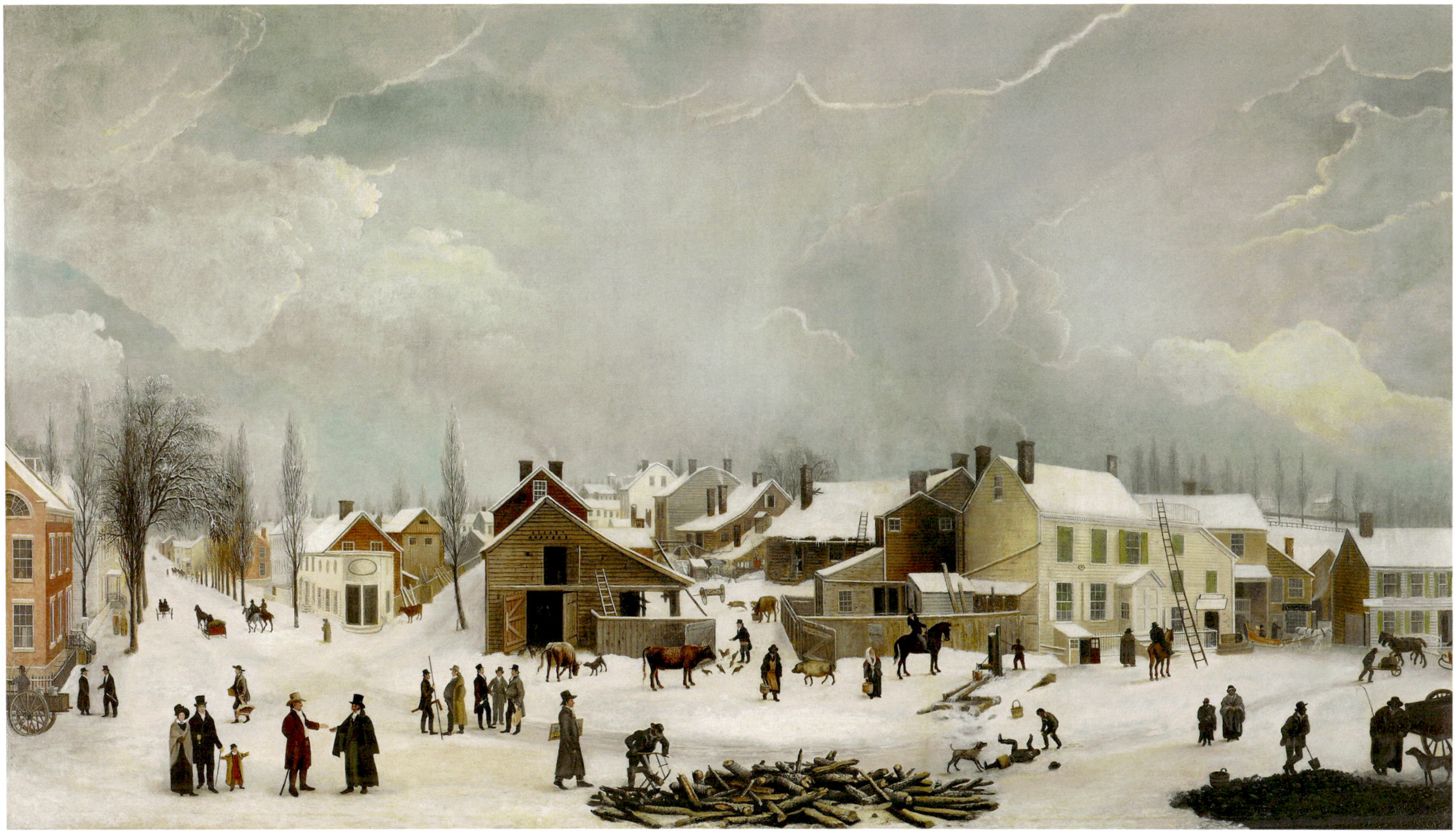

CHARLES BIRD KING (1785–1862)

Ottoe Half Chief, Husband of Eagle of Delight

ca. 1822
Oil on panel
18 × 14½ in. (45.7 × 36.8 cm)

Between 1821 and 1842, the United States government commissioned the Washington, D.C.–based artist Charles Bird King to paint a series of life portraits of prominent Native American leaders visiting the capital as part of treaty negotiations. In total, King produced likenesses of over one hundred Indian delegates from at least twenty tribes, a volume and diversity of images second only to George Catlin's Indian Gallery.[1] The first of these historic delegations consisted of a group of seventeen Kansa (Kaw), Missouri (Missouria), Omaha, Oto (Otoe), and Pawnee Indian chiefs who were brought to Washington by the Monroe administration in late 1821 in an effort to convince the tribal leaders to allow United States expansion into their territory.[2] The Indians' arrival was the source of much discussion in the local press. On November 20, 1821, the *National Intelligencer* newspaper enthusiastically described the exotic visitors as the "most remote tribes with which we have intercourse."[3]

Three of King's sitters, including Shaumonekusse, the subject of Crystal Bridges' painting, were members of the small Oto tribe, who lived with the remnants of the Missouri Indians near the mouth of the Platte River in Nebraska. As detailed by an inscription on the reverse of King's painting, Shaumonekusse was the "Ottoe [*sic*] Half Chief" at the time that he sat for his portrait; the Indian leader became head chief shortly thereafter, a position he held until his death in 1837.[4] The subtitle of King's painting identifies Shaumonekusse in relation to his wife Hayne Hudjihini, or, Eagle of Delight, who was the only female member of the 1821 delegation and also posed for King.

A fire at the Smithsonian Institution in January 1865 consumed nearly all of King's original oils, including his original image of Shaumonekusse, as well as numerous Indian portraits and genre scenes by the painter John Mix Stanley and Native American artifacts acquired by Congress in the course of treaty-making initiatives.[5] Crystal Bridges' painting is one of a number of replicas of these life portraits that King made for himself and others. Five copies of the Oto chief's likeness are known to exist today; King's identification of this version as "no. 2" on the verso inscription suggests that it was likely the second of the larger group.[6]

King's original images were also preserved for posterity in the form of large color lithographs in Thomas L. McKenney and James Hall's three-volume *History of the Indian Tribes of North America* (1838–44).[7] Shaumonekusse is described in volume one of this publication as "a daring, active, and successful warrior." In King's portrait, the distinguished Oto leader wears a bison-horn and horsehair headdress and a necklace of grisly bear claws, both of which reference his reputation as a great hunter.[8] The silver medallion bearing President Monroe's profile that hangs around Shaumonekusse's neck, suspended by a red ribbon, is an example of the so-called peace medals bestowed upon Native Americans by U.S. government officials as diplomatic gifts in their effort to facilitate the expansion of white settlement into tribal lands.[9]

EDS

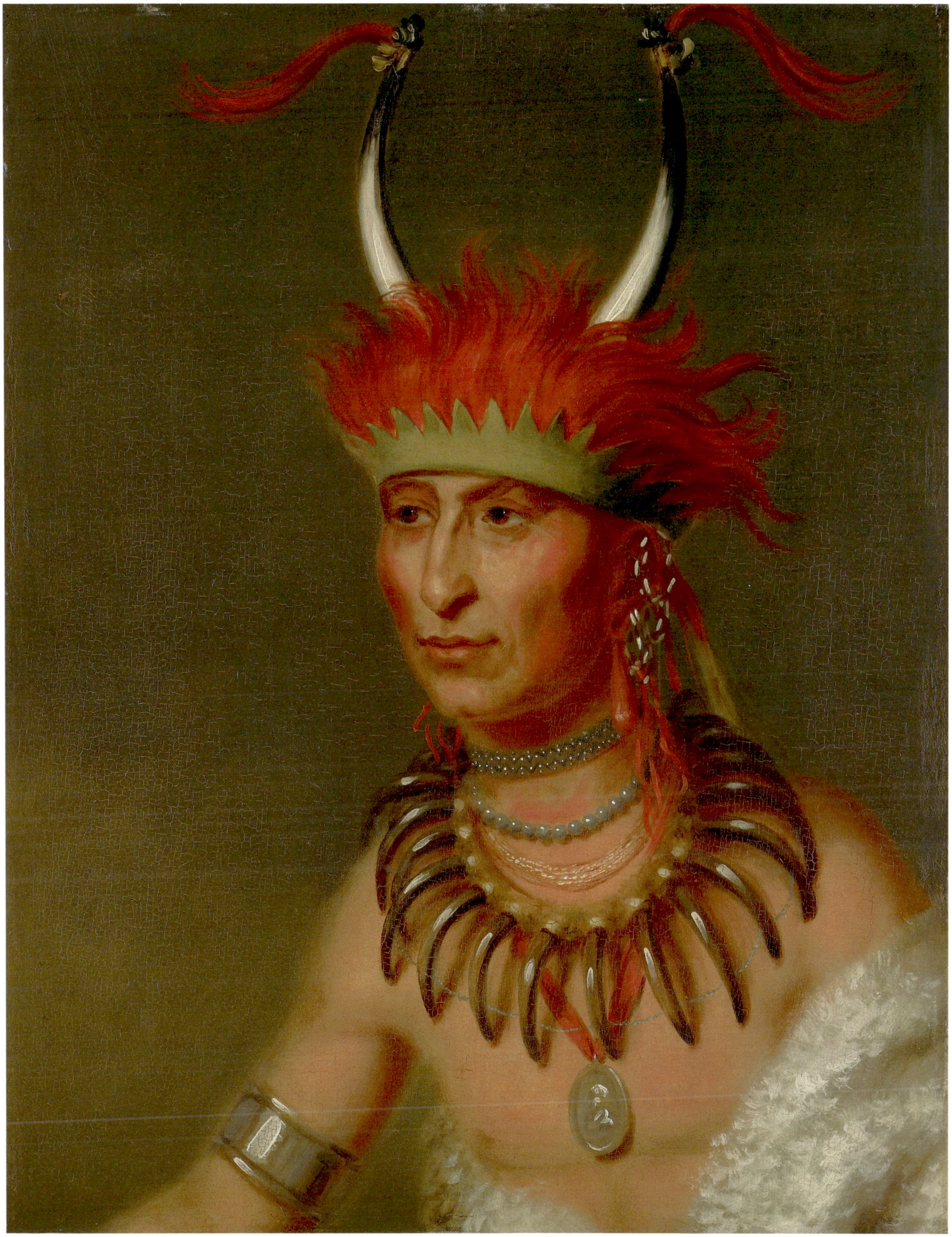

SAMUEL FINLEY BREESE MORSE (1791–1872)

Marquis de Lafayette

1825
Oil on canvas
29¾ × 24¾ in. (75.6 × 62.9 cm)

In the American Revolution, the French military officer Marie-Joseph Paul Yves Roch Gilbert du Motier, marquis de Lafayette, allied himself with the colonists' cause, serving as a general in the Continental Army under George Washington. Lafayette led his troops through key battles in the Brandywine River Valley and in Rhode Island before returning to France in 1788 to rally further support from his countrymen. As head of the Parisian National Guard, he sustained order during the storming of the Bastille; Lafayette subsequently sent the key to the infamous French prison to George Washington, whom he recognized as the father of liberty. Lafayette continued to lobby for French support of American independence, enjoying many fans abroad even as he sustained persecution at home. In honor of Lafayette's lifelong devotion to America, and in commemoration of the nation's twenty-fifth anniversary, President James Monroe invited him back to the United States in 1824. During this nearly yearlong visit, the Frenchman toured all twenty-four states in the union. Lavish banquets and parades were held in his honor, he witnessed the opening of the Erie Canal, and the Common Council of the City of New York requested that he sit for a portrait.[1]

Every portraitist of note in the surrounding area—including John Trumbull, John Vanderlyn, Charles Cromwell Ingham, Rembrandt Peale, John Wesley Jarvis, and Thomas Sully—competed for the commission.[2] Samuel Finley Breese Morse was a relative newcomer to New York, having settled there that very year following a successful early career painting near his hometown of Charlestown, Massachusetts; in London; and in Charleston, South Carolina. Better known today for inventing the first commercially viable electric telegraph and introducing to America the daguerreotype—the first practical form of photography—Morse received the coveted portrait commission based on his credentials of having painted likenesses of Presidents John Adams (1816, Brooklyn Museum) and James Monroe (1820, The White House), as well as a complex composition depicting the United States House of Representatives (1822–23, Corcoran Gallery of Art). At the time he was selected to paint Lafayette, Morse was in the process of founding the National Academy of Design, New York's first art school.

Morse traveled to Washington, D.C., in February 1825 for life sittings with Lafayette, and initially recorded the French general's distinguished visage in this oil study. After meeting him, Morse recorded having felt overwhelmed by the experience:

> My feelings were almost too powerful for me. . . . This is the man now before me . . . who took the oaths of the new constitution for so many millions, while the eyes of thousands were fixed upon him. . . . The very man who spent his youth, his fortune, and his time, to bring about (under Providence) our happy Revolution; the friend and companion of Washington, terror of tyrants, the firm and consistent supporter of liberty, the man whose beloved name has rung from one end of the continent to the other, whom all flock to see, whom all delight to honor.[3]

Morse finished the study during subsequent sittings with Lafayette in New York that summer. Over the next year, he used this dashing portrait bust as the basis for a grand full-length likeness of the man who had helped to establish a free and independent United States (New York City Hall).

CRB

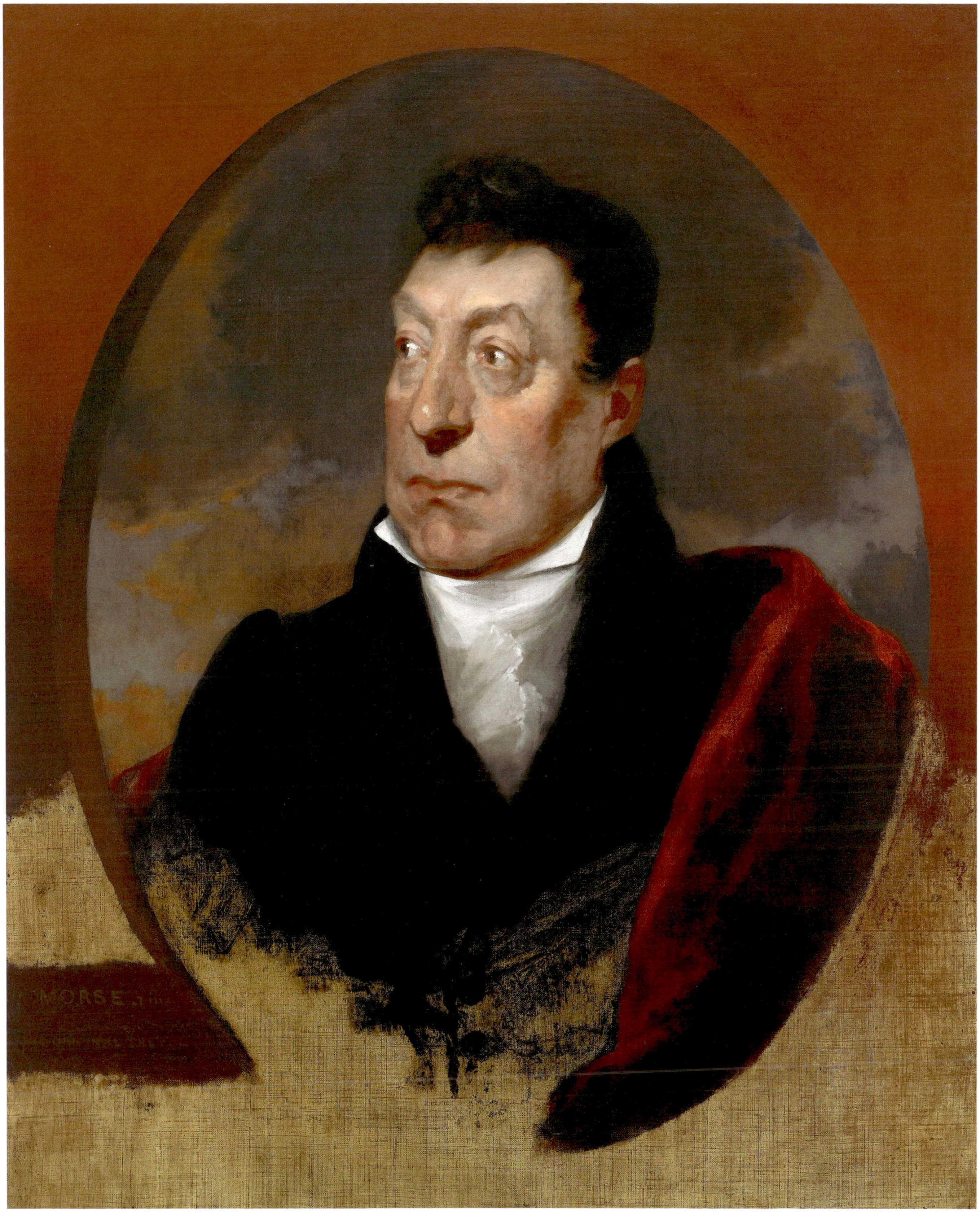
MORSE

EDWARD DALTON MARCHANT (1806–1887)

Samuel Beals Thomas, with His Wife, Sarah Kellogg Thomas, and Their Two Daughters, Abigail and Pauline

1830
Oil on canvas
40 × 48 in. (101.6 × 121.9 cm)

The little-known but perceptive and talented portraitist Edward Dalton Marchant began his career in Charleston, South Carolina, in 1827. Like many portraitists and miniature painters of the day, Marchant seems to have pursued an itinerancy in search of commissions, finding his way by 1829 to Worcester, Massachusetts. Of the four known canvases from his stay in Worcester, this is the only group portrait and by far the most ambitious work. With its plentiful interior details, lavish costumes and accoutrement, and carefully rendered faces, the painting was the commission of a lifetime for Marchant.[1]

The paterfamilias of the Thomas family was Samuel Beals Thomas, who owned and operated Thomas's Exchange Coffee House and Inn on Lincoln Square, in Worcester. His wife, Sarah Kellogg, hailed from Suffield, Connecticut. The couple had no surviving children of their own, but upon the death of Samuel's brother Orsamus they adopted his daughters, Abigail and Pauline. The highly decorated setting for this handsome group may be the parlor of the family inn. Replete with meticulously rendered prop and costume, the portrait recorded the family's proud image for posterity even as it showed hotel guests the fine taste and sophistication of their proprietor.[2]

At left, Samuel and Sarah sit together on a sofa upholstered in cut velvet; behind them, three heavily decorated alabaster urns rest on the mantelpiece. The objects associated with the two girls identify them as literate and skilled in domestic industry. Twenty-one-year-old Abigail stands at her adopted mother's side, an unfolded letter in her right hand. At right, nineteen-year-old Pauline rests her arm on a wooden sewing box upon which lie a spool of white thread, a thimble, and a pair of scissors. All four members of the Thomas family wear fine jewelry. Samuel dons green-tinted spectacles and has a chained pin on his shirt frill and a fob of accessories at his waistband. A portrait miniature is tucked into the folds of Sarah's lace wrap, and mother and daughters wear matching earrings, necklaces, and brooches. On the far wall behind the group is a framed engraving after Jeremiah Paul's esteemed painting of George Washington and his family (ca. 1800). Beautifully coiffed and dressed, set in the lap of the inn's luxury, and directly gazing out of the picture plane, the Thomases represent a proud, content, and successful early nineteenth-century merchant family. The portrait remained in the Thomas family for over 150 years after its completion, until the late 1980s. CRB

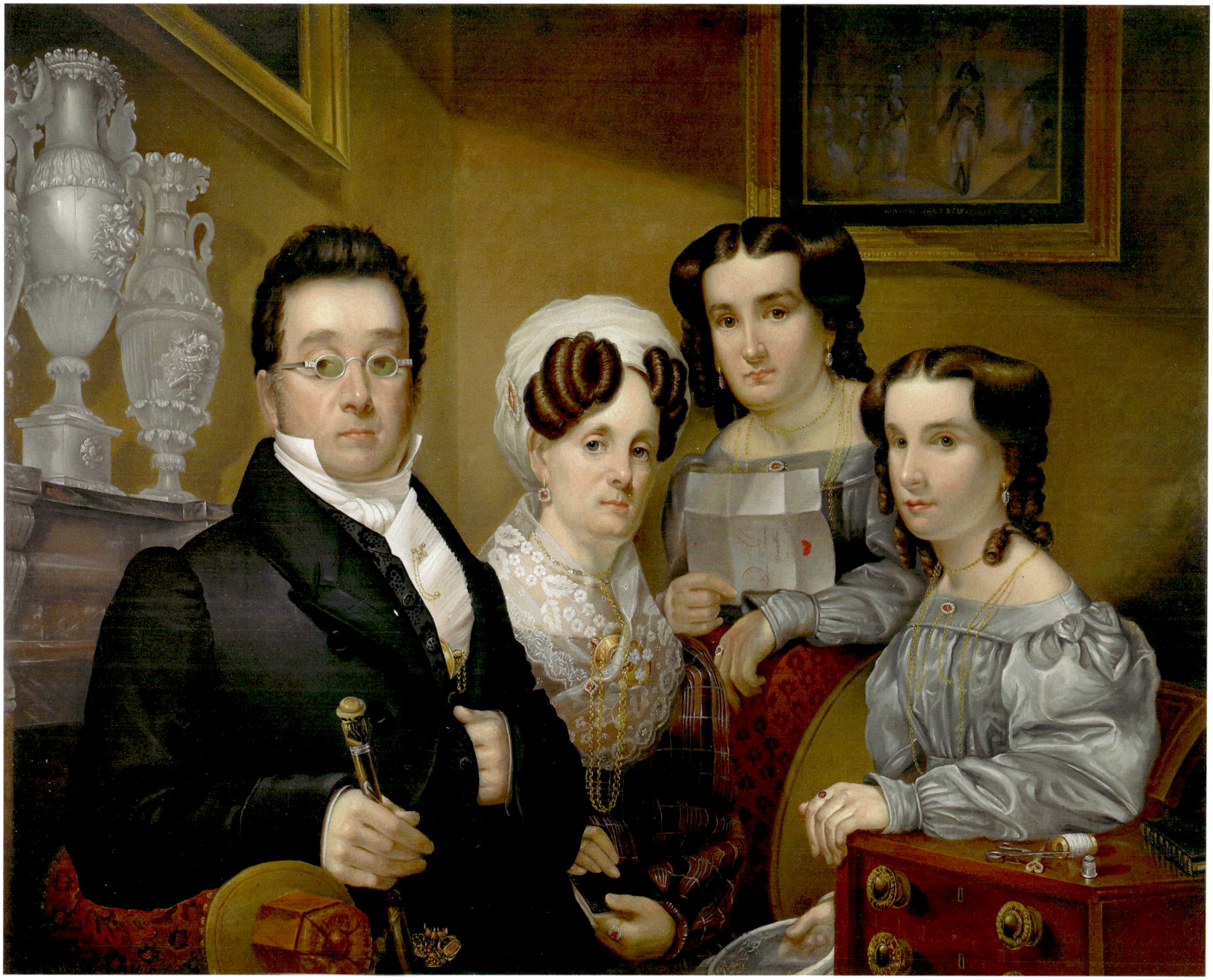

LEON POMAREDE (CA. 1807–1892)

View of St. Louis

ca. 1832–35
Oil on canvas
29 × 39 in. (73.7 × 99.1 cm)

Sometime after his arrival in St. Louis in 1832, Leon Pomarede painted this view of the city's bustling wharf from Illinois Town, on the opposite bank of the Mississippi River.[1] Visible across the water is Front Street, which had been paved the year before, enabling the construction of warehouses to serve the busy river trade.[2] Directly across from the ferry landing is Market Street, the city's main artery. The redbrick Market House on its corner was said to mark the spot where Pierre LaClede first landed, prior to founding the city.[3] A few blocks behind rise the spire of the newly constructed St. Louis Cathedral and the dome of the First Baptist Church; on the horizon is the dome of the First Presbyterian Church, of which prominent abolitionist Artemus Bullard was pastor.[4] Despite these grand edifices, no other buildings exceeded two stories in the downtown area of the developing city and there was still no public park, library, or hospital.[5]

Pomerade's *View of St. Louis* may be the first extant painting of the city. Although the back of the canvas bears the inscription, "View of Saint Louis by Leon de Pomarede, 1835," a lithograph of the work signed by the artist claims to be "A faithful copy of a painting of St. Louis made by me in the year 1832."[6] The only other canvas that rivals Pomarede's in date is George Catlin's 1832–33 *Saint Louis from the River Below* (Smithsonian American Art Museum), which notably does not depict the St. Louis Cathedral.[7] Since the cathedral was not completed until 1834, Catlin's may be the earlier painting. However, Pomarede could have added the spire after 1834 because of the cathedral's importance to his own biography (he first came to the city to paint its interior), as well as its prominence in the city and the region. Upon its completion, the St. Louis Cathedral was the tallest building west of the Mississippi, and it remained an important landmark throughout the nineteenth century.

Pomarede's painting succeeds in recording St. Louis's main features, but it also transcends the often-static genre of the cityscape to convey the spirit of the growing metropolis. The artist arranged his scene so that St. Louis appears a welcome destination for travelers coming from the east. The ramps of the ferryboat docked at the landing at the lower right of the composition extend outward into the viewer's space, unloading elegant travelers, stout cattle, and wagons filled with goods and making way for other passengers to board. At right, the boat's crew, who labor to moor the ferry, model the energetic work by which the city had rapidly grown from provincial town to urban center in the previous decade. The visual rhyming of the natural and the man-made—the steamboat's smoke meeting clouds overhead, the floating logs echoing the line of steamboats gliding across the glassy river—foreshadows the city's continued growth and lends it a sense of inevitability. In 1840, the city's directory would boast, "A city, situated as St. Louis is, when once it has attained the station of the principal mart of a great territory, must become, in spite of all adverse circumstances, a great emporium. That St. Louis will . . . assume that rank and station, no one, who contemplates her present condition and her exhaustless resources, feels a doubt."[8] LS

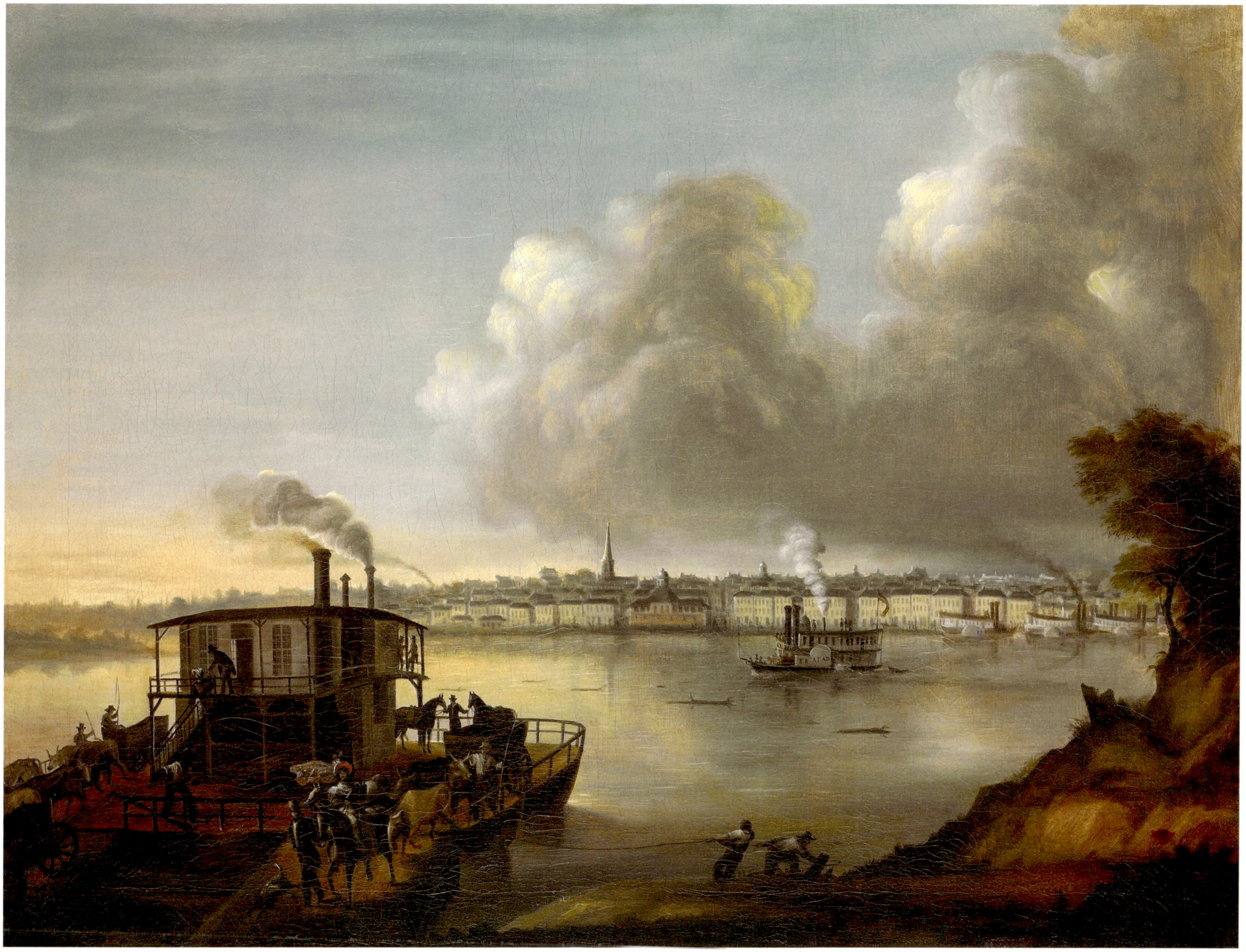

GEORGE CATLIN (1796–1872)

Indian Encampment

ca. 1852–68
Oil on canvas
19 × 26½ in. (48.3 × 67.3 cm)

In the early 1850s, after a series of personal and professional disappointments, the painter-naturalist George Catlin embarked on an extended trip to South America (1852–60). It was there that Catlin gathered inspiration for *Indian Encampment*, an image depicting the contented existence of an unidentified indigenous tribe living in a remote tropical wilderness.[1] In contrast to his work from North America, where he had often lived for periods of time among the peoples he painted, in South America Catlin typically made his studies at a comfortable distance, either from a boat or set back into the woods for unobtrusive observation. In *Indian Encampment*, men, women, and children perform the tasks of daily life, fishing, sleeping, and socializing under a dense forest canopy. Modest tents line the banks of a stream that may represent a tributary of the Paraná, Uruguay, or Amazon River. With generalized features of costume and geography specific to no one tribal group in this region, *Indian Encampment* is more of an artistic impression than it is a scientific document.[2]

Twenty years earlier, the largely self-taught Catlin had made his reputation through the images of North America's native populations that he painted based on a series of journeys to the nation's western frontier.[3] This ambitious, multiyear sketching project resulted in the two-volume illustrated book *Letters and Notes on the Manners, Customs, and Conditions of the North American Indians* (1841), as well as a popular traveling exhibition known as Catlin's Indian Gallery, which consisted of hundreds of portraits, landscapes, and genre scenes depicting indigenous cultures the artist had recorded on his expeditions. Catlin's paintings often resisted the popular tropes of the Indian as either noble savage or brute. Accompanying the touring pictures with staged re-creations of Native American rituals and impassioned lectures about America's "vanishing race," Catlin attempted to humanize his subjects for his largely white audience, presenting them as peaceful and sophisticated peoples that faced extinction at the hand of Anglo-American expansion.[4]

A number of Catlin's colleagues and competitors, including the prominent American ethnologist Henry Rowe Schoolcraft, questioned the veracity of his accounts of indigenous American cultures, and the artist's hopes of finding a permanent home for his collection in a national institution were quickly dashed.[5] Spiraling into debt, he toured the Indian Gallery in Europe in the 1840s. It was not a fortuitous trip: Catlin's wife and only son died abroad leaving him alone with three young daughters, and increased financial troubles forced him to release possession of the Indian Gallery to a private collector in exchange for debt relief.

South America offered the discouraged artist new hope. Although Catlin's written and painted accounts of his South American expedition are riddled with inaccuracies and vagaries, images such as *Indian Encampment* nevertheless served the artist's purposes perfectly well.[6] Combining the resources of the emerging field of ethnography and the traditions of artistic representation, Catlin's work brought to a Western audience further evidence of the humanity of troubled indigenous cultures. SMH

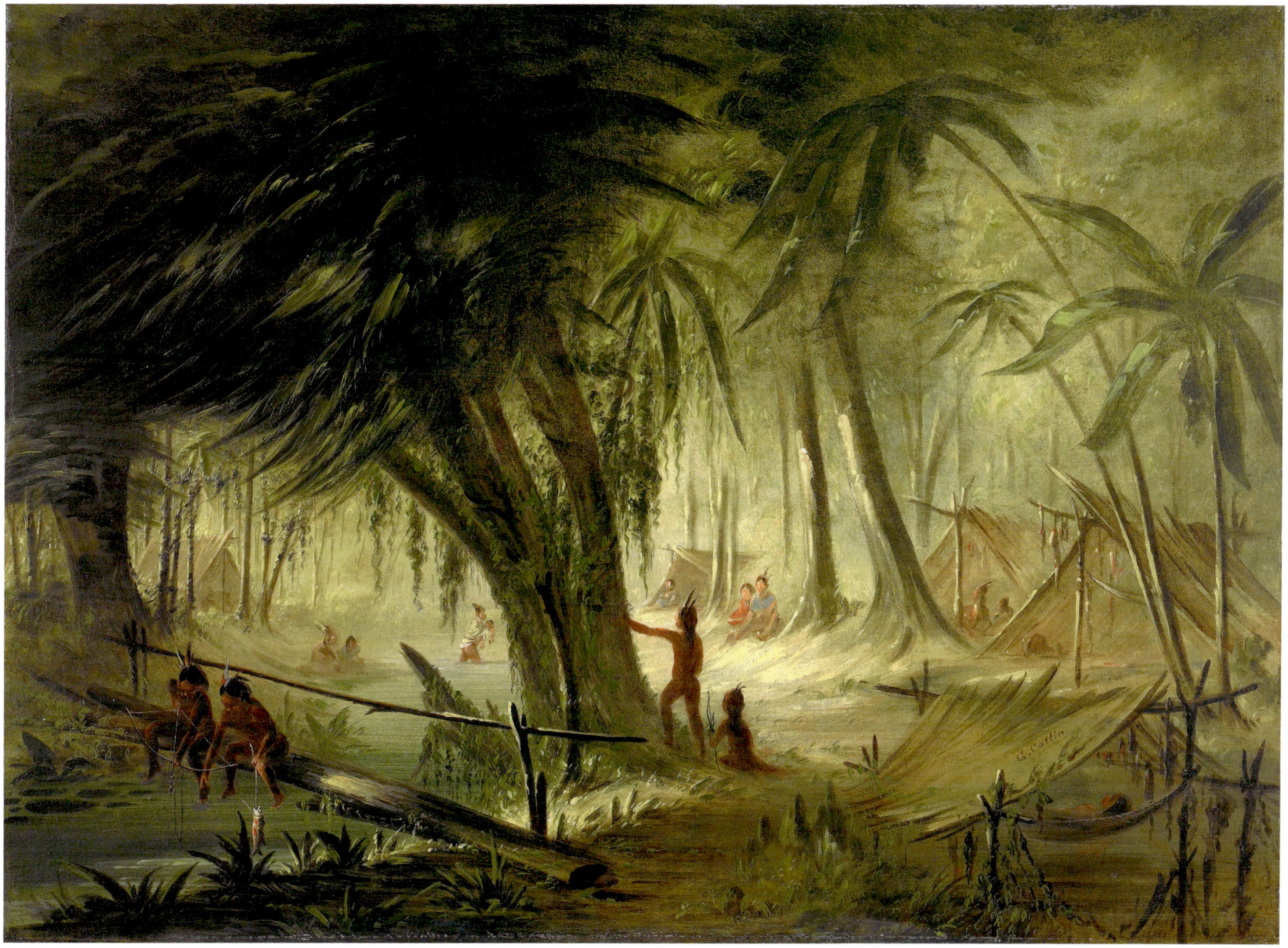
G. Catlin

THOMAS COLE (1801–1848)

View of Mount Etna

1842
Oil on canvas
32 × 48 in. (81.3 × 121.9 cm)

A young Thomas Cole emigrated from England with his family in 1818, making his debut as a painter of American landscape in New York, where his works were discovered by John Trumbull, William Dunlap, and Asher Brown Durand in 1825.[1] A decade later, in his famous "Essay on American Scenery," Cole enumerated the picturesque terrestrial features he believed deserved attention from American tourists and artists, beginning with mountains, "the most conspicuous objects in landscape."[2] Cole's own mountain experiences included visits to New York State's Catskills and Adirondacks as well as to the White Mountains of New Hampshire. However, the artist's interests (and those of his viewers) also included European ranges, especially the Alps, the Appenines, and the famous volcanoes of Italy: Vesuvius and Etna.[3]

Cole returned to Europe for two extended tours, in 1829–32 and 1841–42, to complete his artistic education and enrich his repertoire of subjects. Both of his Italian itineraries included excursions to the remote southernmost kingdom of Sicily. Cole's 1844 travelogue "Sicilian Scenery and Antiquities" indicates how deeply the rugged terrain and rich history of the island had impressed him. "A few months only have elapsed," he wrote, "since I traveled over the classic land of Sicily; and the impressions left on my mind by its picturesqueness, fertility, and the grandeur of its architectural remains, are more vivid and fraught with more sublime associations, than any I received during my late sojourn in Europe."[4] The artist communicated his responses to this landscape even more powerfully in a series of important paintings gleaned from the sketches and studies he made during his second Italian expedition, in the spring of 1842.[5]

View of Mount Etna is the earliest of these paintings, completed within months of Cole's return to New York. We are fortunate to have the artist's own account of the work: "The view is taken between Caltagirone and Lentini; the time just after sunrise.—Aetna, which is about forty miles distant, lifts its snowy head in the warm sunlight, while the base of the mountain is partly veiled in the vapoury atmosphere and the mists of the morning. On the left, and nearer than Aetna, is a range of broken hills. Upon the peak of one is seen a tower, which is said to have been occupied by Nero during an eruption of the Volcano. . . . The middle ground is composed of bean and grain fields, with groves of olive trees. On the left, in the foreground, is a large Caruba [carob] tree, and upon the right the remains of an aqueduct."[6]

Cole's panoramic view celebrates the beauty of a pastoral landscape enriched by the ruins of an ancient civilization. The majestic, brooding mass of Mount Etna, the life of which predates human history, looms above the broad horizon. A plume of vapor issuing from the great crater at Etna's summit reminds the viewer of the fiery forces contained within the snowcapped volcano and signals Cole's understanding of the ongoing geological processes forming the Sicilian landscape. A shepherd plays the flute among foreground ruins in a graceful reference to the Arcadian tradition of classical poetry. A "Letiga"—a traditional Sicilian carriage built to traverse mountainous passes—progresses along a roadway in the middle distance.[7] With this combination of visual references to the past and present playing out before the distant snowcapped volcano, the artist invites his viewers to reflect upon the mutability of human history.

LSF

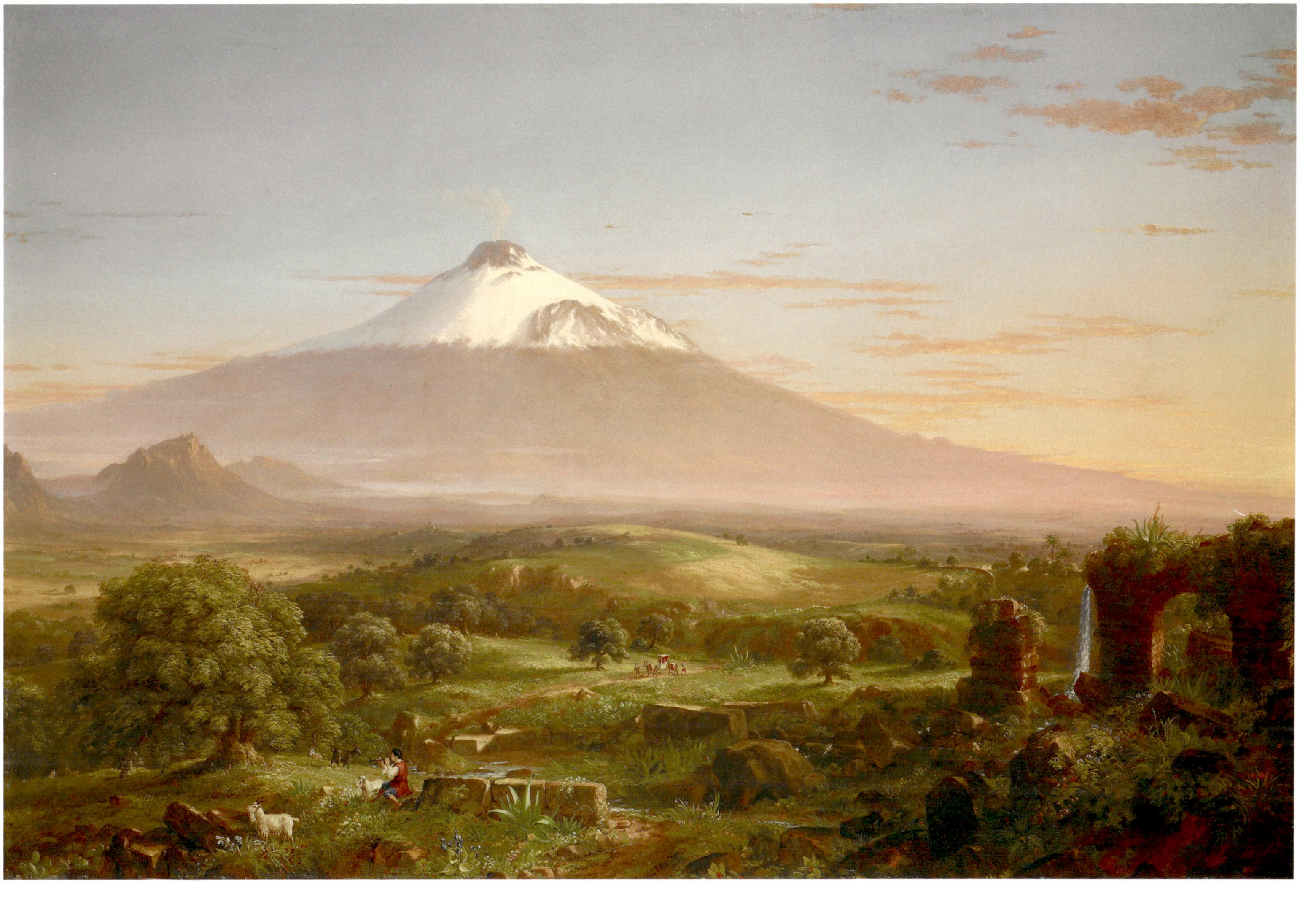

THOMAS COLE (1801–1848)

The Good Shepherd

1848
Oil on canvas on panel
32 × 48 in. (81.3 × 121.9 cm)

Although Thomas Cole was increasingly religious in his later years, biblical subjects from the Old and New Testaments had, in fact, appealed to him since the beginning of his career. Among his early masterworks are splendid landscape exercises in the beautiful and the sublime that portray *Saint John in the Wilderness* (1827, Wadsworth Atheneum); *The Expulsion* (1827–28, Museum of Fine Arts, Boston); *The Garden of Eden* (1828, Amon Carter Museum of American Art); and *The Subsiding of the Waters of the Deluge* (1829, Smithsonian American Art Museum). Cole conceived *The Good Shepherd*, which was painted in the last year of his life, as a bucolic landscape under a mild, late afternoon sky. The work presents a marked contrast to the elaborate allegorical rhetoric of the religious cycles that also occupied the artist during the final decade of his life: *The Voyage of Life* (1839–40, Munson-Williams-Proctor Arts Institute) and his final epic, *The Cross and the World* (1846–48, location unknown).[1]

Cole's appealing visualization of Psalm 23, painted while he was also at work on *The Cross and the World*, was commissioned by or for Mrs. Gideon Lee, the mother-in-law of Charles M. Leupp, a prominent New York art collector and Cole patron.[2] Described by Cole's biographer as "that most exquisite and most perfect of all his simple landscapes," *The Good Shepherd* was likely intended for Mrs. Lee's private devotions.[3] The composition draws upon Arcadian and Claudian landscape traditions as well as Christian iconography. The young shepherd leads a stray sheep, adorned with a small rose-colored cross, into a verdant terrestrial refuge, away from the barren, rockbound realm at the painting's borders. Shepherd and sheep return together to the flock seen grazing upon a sunny greensward in the distance, beyond the quiet pool that occupies the center of the image. The painting's religious narrative ("The Lord is my shepherd, I shall not want. He makes me lie down in green pastures; He leads me beside quiet waters"), which is reinforced by its title, is unmistakable.[4] Yet the message of personal salvation is carried as much by the comforting associations of the serene, parklike natural setting, with its gentle hills and stately trees beneath a radiant sky, as by the human and animal actors.

Adding a deeply poignant note to the theme is the fact that *The Good Shepherd* was the artist's last work, completed just before his sudden death early in 1848. Cole's minister, Louis L. Noble, probably spoke for many of the artist's contemporaries when he wrote of the painting as "the closing hymn to his whole artistic life. . . . The world's angry floods are crossed, its desert tracts all passed: a pastoral scene refreshes the sight: the flock is shepherded in the 'green pastures,' and by 'the still waters' of the heavenly Canaan."[5] Cole had also drawn the composition on a lithographic stone, from which a print was published posthumously. Mrs. Cole dedicated the lithograph "To the Artists of America," thereby invoking her late husband as the spiritual as well as the artistic leader of the American school.[6]

LSF

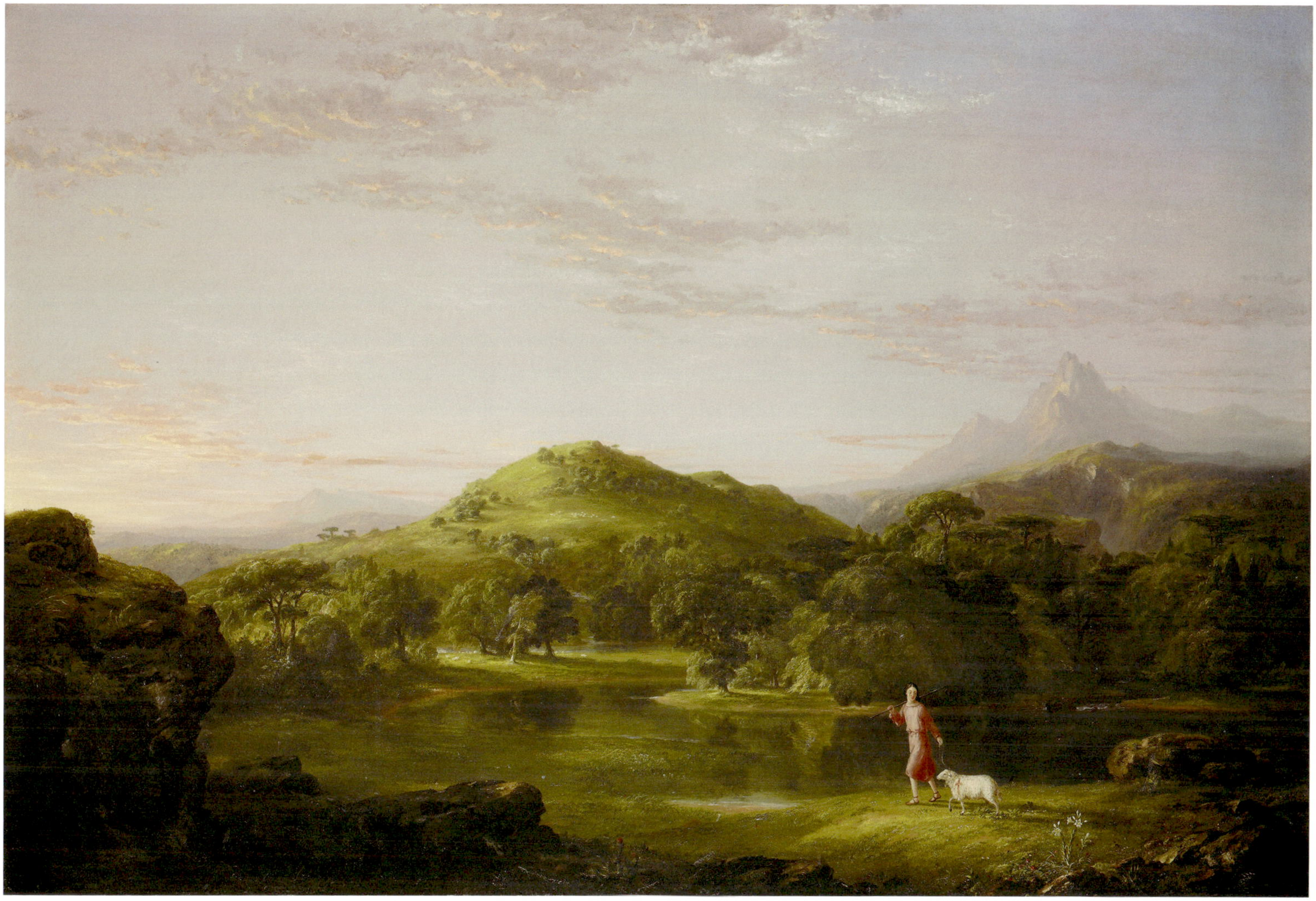

ASHER BROWN DURAND (1796–1886)

Kindred Spirits

1849
Oil on canvas
44 × 36 in. (111.8 × 91.4 cm)

Kindred Spirits is an outdoor double portrait of the painter Thomas Cole and the poet William Cullen Bryant. New York dry-goods merchant and art collector Jonathan Sturges commissioned it from Asher Brown Durand after Cole's sudden death from pneumonia early in 1848, which had been a shattering blow to the American art establishment. Sturges presented the work to Bryant in March 1849, a year after the poet eulogized Cole before the National Academy of Design. Mrs. Bryant recorded the unexpected delivery of the large draped canvas: "I . . . raised the cloth, and what should I find but a beautiful landscape. A scene among the mountains, a deep ravine with high hills covered with rocks and shrubs on each side, a little stream comes tumbling along cascade fashion, and on one side of the ravine is a large projecting rock on which are painted in full form, William & Cole the artist. . . . In the foreground are some large trees, and on one of these trees are cut the names, Bryant and Cole."[1] Durand's own name and the date of the painting appear as if incised into the rock upon which the two figures stand.

A note to Bryant from Sturges that accompanied the painting suggests that the project had been a collaborative one between patron and artist. Sturges claimed as his own the "thought" of a gift to Bryant, placing the imagery and "execution" in Durand's skilled hands.[2] A summary work that synthesized Durand's experience as a portrait, figure, and landscape painter, *Kindred Spirits* both demonstrated and consolidated the artist's new position as leader of the American landscape school. Cole's demise was recognized as a watershed; there was universal awareness that Durand had been passed the torch. The two artists' dual leadership positions had been acknowledged well before Cole's death, perhaps most succinctly a year earlier in Bryant's newspaper, the *Evening Post*: "It is now generally conceded, we believe, that Cole and Durand are the two most prominent landscape painters in this country.—They are indeed artists of superior ability, and will undoubtedly hereafter be looked upon as the founder of two American schools."[3] By the mid-1840s, the two painters had come to represent the poles of American landscape vision: Cole, the heroic and the sublime; and Durand, the domestic and the pastoral.

Durand memorialized Cole—his landscape mentor—standing in the deep Catskill gorge, sketch portfolio in one hand and flute or recorder in the other, in company with Bryant, their mutual friend and literary counterpart. Durand's own long friendship with Cole may well have inspired him to include a reference to their shared love of music, a bond reflected in Durand's fond description of their relationship as "'C. major'—D. flat."[4] The botanical precision of the dense mountain forest and foreground trees in *Kindred Spirits* marks the growing realism in Durand's work. The gorge and torrent embody geological process as well as sublime grandeur. The two figures might as easily be discussing their mutual fascination with the science of geology or meditating on the romantic sonnet by John Keats from which the painting takes its title.[5] LSF

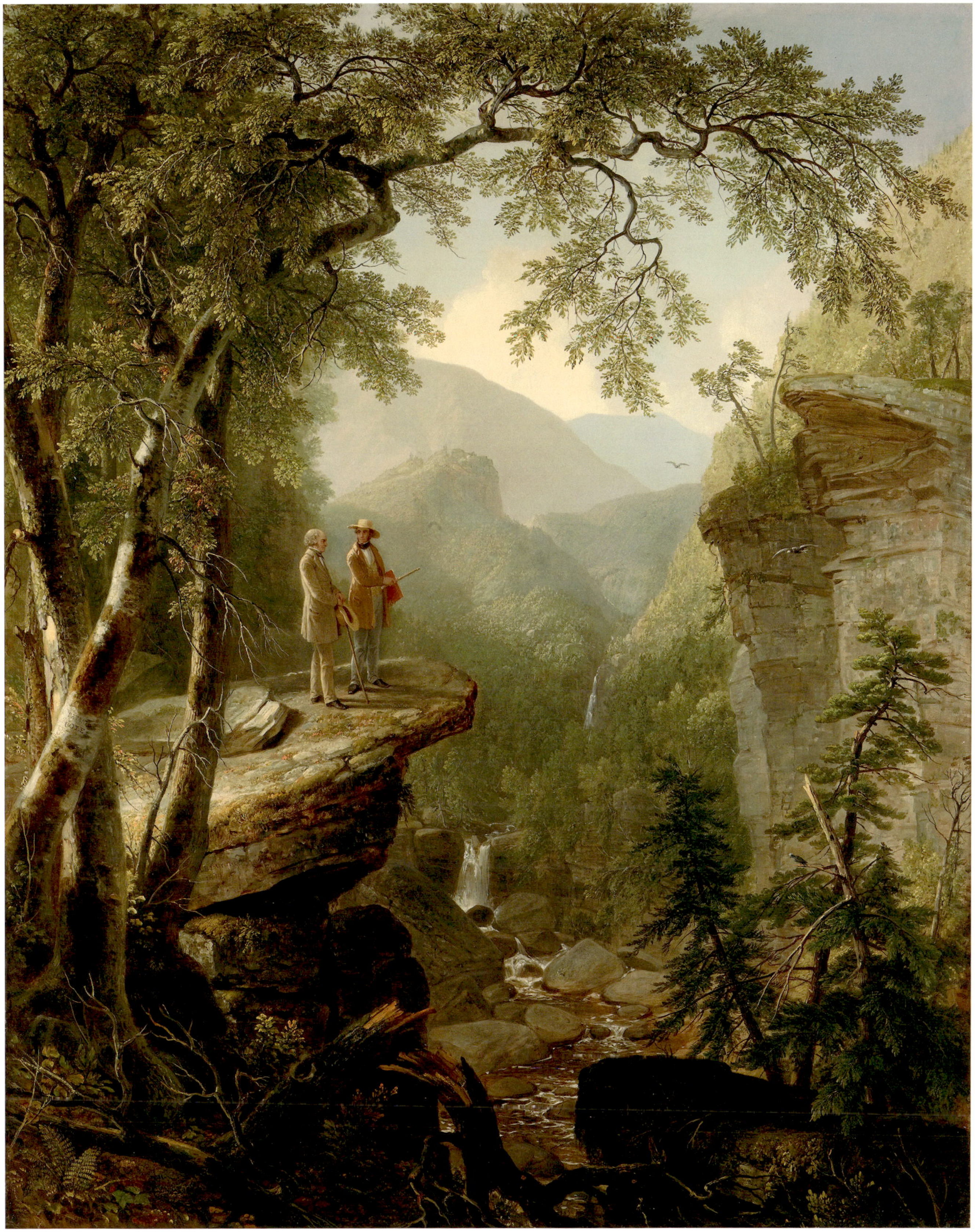

RICHARD CATON WOODVILLE (1825–1855)

War News from Mexico

1848
Oil on canvas
27 × 25 in. (68.6 × 63.5 cm)

The most popular and critically acclaimed painting of genre artist Richard Caton Woodville's short yet accomplished career, *War News from Mexico* addresses the promise, and the limits, of Jacksonian democracy. The canvas celebrates the increased freedoms afforded many mid nineteenth-century Americans by the creation of a broadened electorate, the development of mass media, and the expansion of the nation's geographic boundaries, all the while calling attention to those who remained on the margins of society.

A diverse group of eleven figures gather around the wooden portico of the symbolic "American Hotel" for an update on the United States' territorial conflict with Mexico. Gripping a sprawling newspaper with clenched fists, his eyebrows raised and mouth agape, the central character reads the paper's headline with rapt attention. Other hotel habitués lean in, straining to see the text of this "Extra" edition for themselves or to make sure they catch the narrator's every word. Recent advances in printing technologies coupled with an increasingly literate citizenry had resulted in the emergence of the penny press (cheap, mass-produced newspapers). For the first time, daily news was accessible to a broad American public. The Mexican-American War (1846–48) was the first U.S. war to be widely covered in newspapers, and it dominated their pages in the mid-1840s. A front-page story in the *New York Herald* in 1846 addressed the centrality of the conflict to contemporary political discourse, reporting: "Our relations with Mexico now absorb all other questions; it is the only question of the day."[1] Perhaps the news depicted in Woodville's 1848 painting was the signing of the Treaty of Guadalupe Hidalgo on February 2 of that year, which confirmed American title to Texas and ceded to the United States an enormous swath of land including California and much of the present-day Southwest.

Although the iconography of *War News from Mexico* promotes a unified body politic—the *Bulletin of the American Art-Union* boasted, "how well the individual peculiarities of each person represented are shown beneath the momentary feeling of common interest that animates them all!"—the spatial organization of the picture perpetuated long-standing social hierarchies.[2] White men—the category of Americans that was afforded universal suffrage during the Jacksonian era—sit and stand in the privileged space of the covered porch. The one white woman in the painting peers out of an open window at the far right of the composition, relegated to the confines of the domestic sphere, while the two persons of color are situated on a low step and on the ground, in positions of subservience. The African American man and child listen attentively to the war news, aware that the outcome of the military conflict has implications for the westward expansion of slavery.[3] Woodville scholar Justin Wolff has noted the perhaps purposeful irony of the artist having dressed this pair of politically and economically disenfranchised figures in a patriotic palette of red, white, and blue.[4] EDS

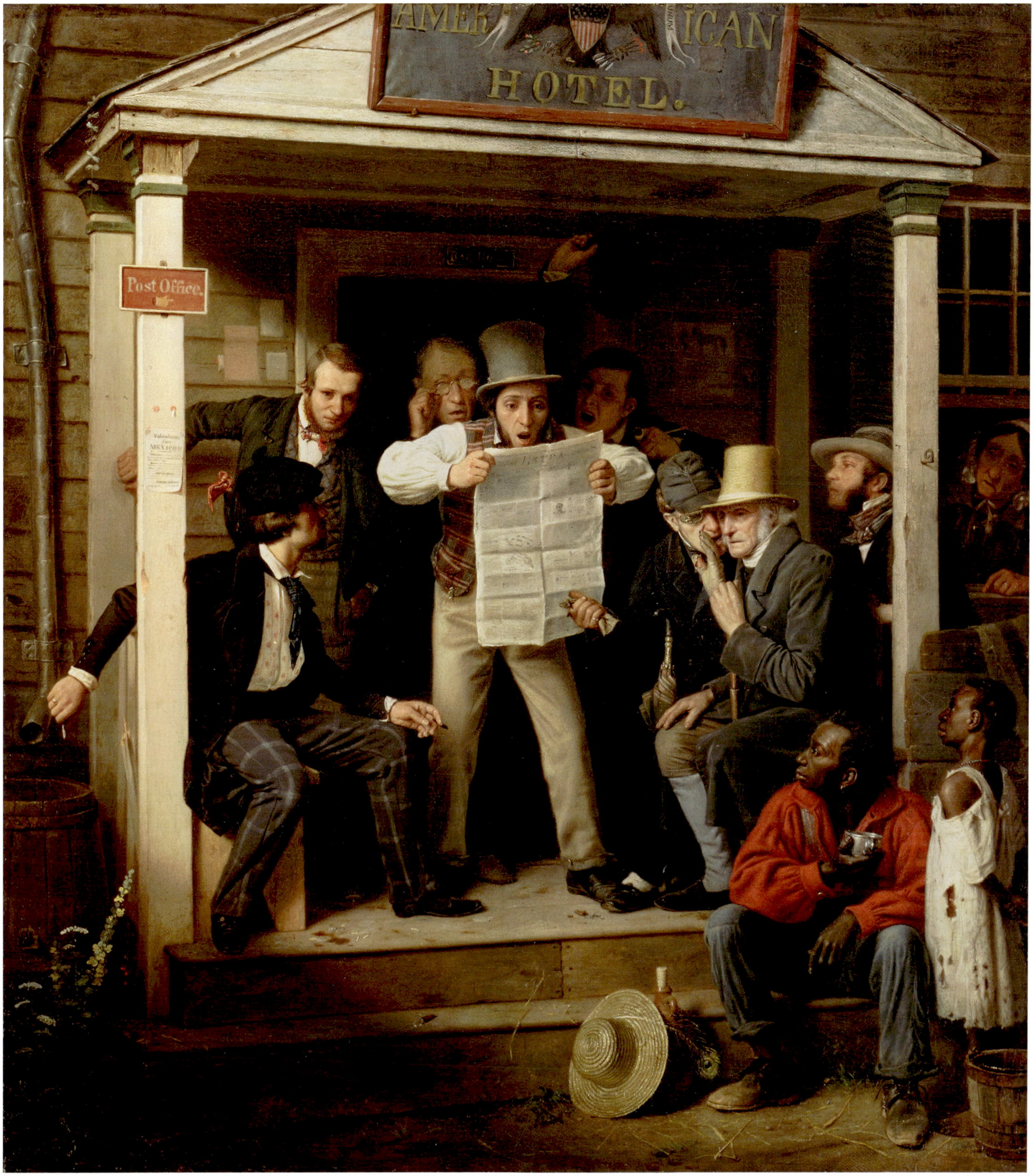
AMER ICAN
HOTEL.
Post Office.

FITZ HENRY LANE (1804–1865)

View of Camden Mountains from Penobscot Bay

ca. 1852
Oil on board
12 × 18 in. (30.5 × 45.7 cm)
Promised Gift

In 1851, Curtis Island Lighthouse (as it is known today) at the entrance to Camden Harbor, Maine, burned to the ground. Reconstruction began immediately and was completed by 1852. The inclusion of a construction derrick just to the left of the lighthouse in *View of Camden Mountains from Penobscot Bay*, by the noted nineteenth-century marine painter Fitz Henry Lane, confirms an approximate date for the work of 1852. Lane first came to Maine in 1848 at the invitation of his friend Joseph L. Stevens, whose home in Castine, on Deer Isle, became Lane's base for frequent painting excursions throughout Penobscot Bay and its island-dotted archipelago until his death in 1865. Here, at the intersection of human industry and natural beauty, Lane discovered a new kind of sublime defined by a quality of light and atmosphere that has come to be called luminism.[1]

Like many of Lane's best works, the tightly finished final painting simultaneously evokes natural grandeur and human intimacy. The visual scope of this relatively small image is panoramic, yet the foreground activity appears close enough for one to hear bits of the rowers' conversation and their oars slapping the water. The artist's precise rendering of detail, visible in the varied and type-specific ships' riggings, gives his painting an almost hyperreal intensity that is part of its mystery and appeal.

On the right, a sturdy, gaff-rigged fishing boat, its sail nearly slack in the dead-calm air, slowly makes its way toward the harbor just to the west, behind the sheltering island. At lower left, the two figures in the small open boat headed toward the island lead the eye further into the painting. It is tempting to see this smaller boat and its occupants as a kind of self-portrait of the artist and a reference to his creative process. Lane lost use of his legs as an infant through an unknown cause. With limited physical mobility, he relied on the assistance of his friend and patron Stevens, whose boat provided the painter with transportation to artistic vantage points along Penobscot Bay's indented shoreline as well as the coast of Massachusetts, especially Gloucester and Boston harbors.

More than simply a topographic representation of a particular place and time, Lane's gemlike painting set in the waning hours of daylight is a visual catalogue of all the essential characteristics of luminism: stillness, quietude, and the enveloping suffusion of light that unifies the pictorial space. Lane's *View of Camden Mountains* suggests "nature's infinitude" through a nearly cloudless sky dissolving into a distant horizon.[2] It is equally a view of *humanity's* infinitude and harmonious persistence within God's grand design, as, perhaps, the lighthouse construction derrick attests.

Today, Maine lighthouses have become something of a tourist art and photography cliché. But for Lane and other mid nineteenth-century Americans, who well understood the hazards and rigors of navigating the New England coast and especially Maine's treacherous, often barely submerged ledges, lighthouses played an instrumental role in facilitating travel, settlement, and commerce. In Lane's quiet, romantic worldview, lighthouses also provide spiritual succor and guidance. They are beacons in strange and unfamiliar realms, even at the farthest reaches of civilization and where the godhead may be seen to reside most clearly and reassuringly in the still air before a blazing, evanescent sunset. CBC

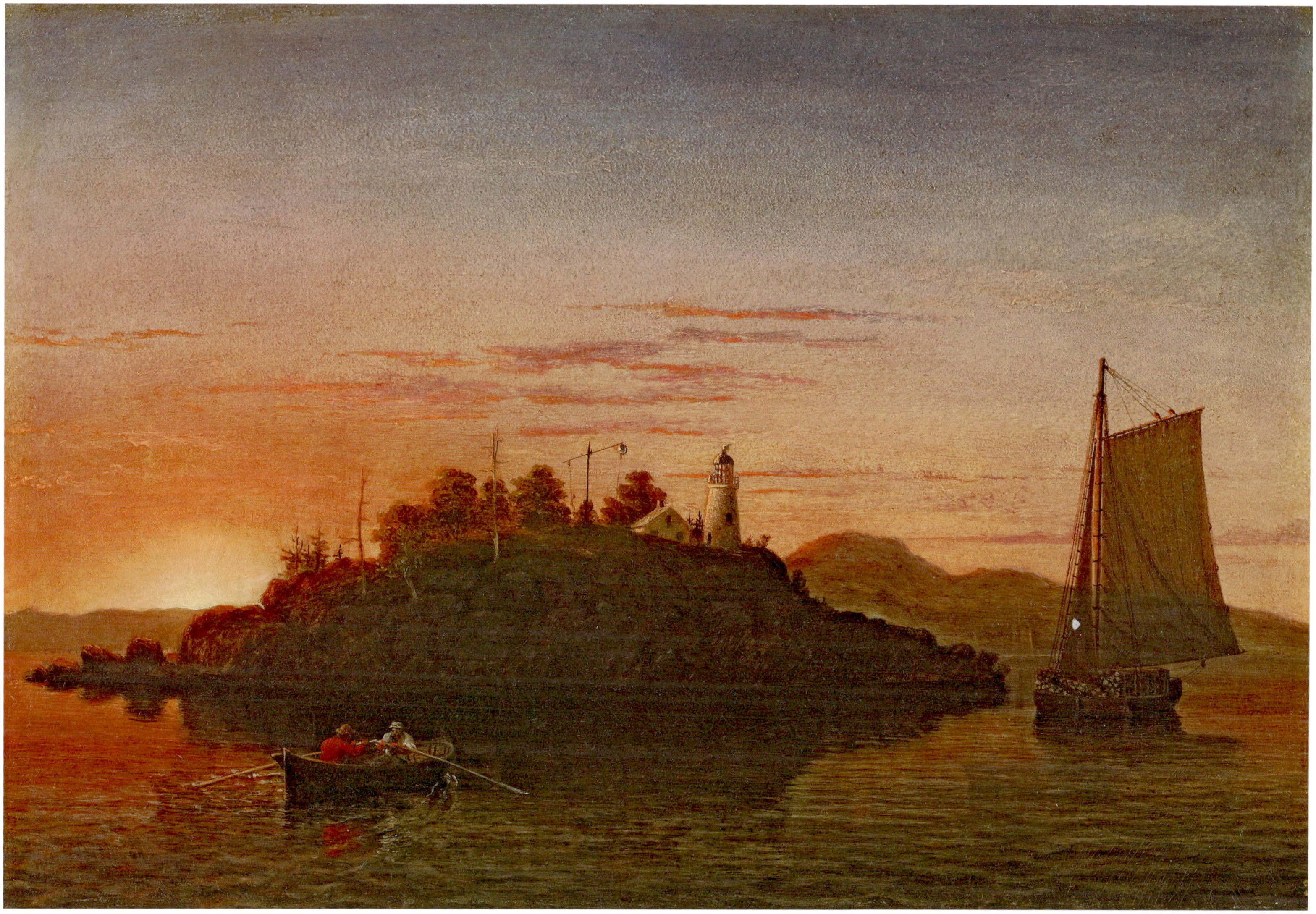

FREDERIC EDWIN CHURCH (1826–1900)

Home by the Lake

1852
Oil on canvas
31⅞ × 48¼ in. (81 × 122.6 cm)

When Frederic Edwin Church selected the American pioneer as a theme for his next major painting in 1852, the subject was timely. In 1846, negotiations had concluded with Great Britain settling the United States' control over the Oregon Territory and establishing borders between the United States and Canada. In 1848, Mexico ceded the whole of Texas as well as a large swath of western lands reaching to the Pacific Ocean; and with the discovery of gold in California the following year, hundreds of thousands of Americans traveled west to seek their fortunes. Populations were rapidly shifting. At mid-century, the United States was the land of the new frontier.

The frontier represented a thematic departure for Church. In the 1840s, the young landscape painter had gained his reputation as the talented protégé of Thomas Cole, the reigning force in American art celebrated for his romantic depictions of the wilderness of New York's Hudson River Valley. In addition to painting landmarks of the Northeast, Church—like Cole—created landscapes that drew from history, literature, and allegory.[1] In the early 1850s, however, the artist moved away from abstract allegorical concepts toward contemporary themes with wider appeal.

One of his earliest works to adopt this new approach, Church's *Home by the Lake* pays homage to the pioneer spirit.[2] A husband and wife tend to the chores of daily life at the far reaches of civilization. In the lower left, the woman carries a pail of water retrieved from the nearby basin back to her rustic home. In the lower right, her rifle-brandishing husband, a wild stag stowed in the stern of his small boat, takes aim at some distant target. The couple's modest log cabin, with its sunken, moss-covered roof and rickety lean-to for the farm's two cows, suggests the challenges of this austere frontier existence.

Yet the scene is not one of struggle and defeat. Bathed in the rosy glow of a day's end, this pastoral landscape reveals a fertile valley nestled among gently rolling hills and low mountain peaks. In the foreground, the rugged terrain simply awaits its purpose. The roughly cut tree stumps that dot the small grassy meadow evidence recent labors. More clearing will be required to establish working farmsteads like those visible in the distance. A dirt road bends past the cabin linking these various states of existence—from the productive farms of civilization to the rugged pioneer homestead to the as-yet-untamed wilderness.

Church was not the only artist to turn to the theme of the pioneer at mid-century, and within a few years westward expansion would become an exceedingly popular motif.[3] But in 1850 few had yet focused on the subject, a fact that inspired at least one critic to complain. "Is there any striking representation here," he questioned, "of one of the controlling passions and ideas of our own time and country? We are unable to find on these walls any expression of the American courage which seeks out at a day's notice a new home thousands of miles distant; of the self reliance which defies the wild beast and the savage, and plants a corn-field in the remote prairie."[4] With *Home by the Lake*, Church claimed his share of the frontier lore. Ultimately he built his reputation on it, seeking out ever more remote wildernesses for increasingly grander pictures that, by the late 1850s, audiences would line up to see.

SMH

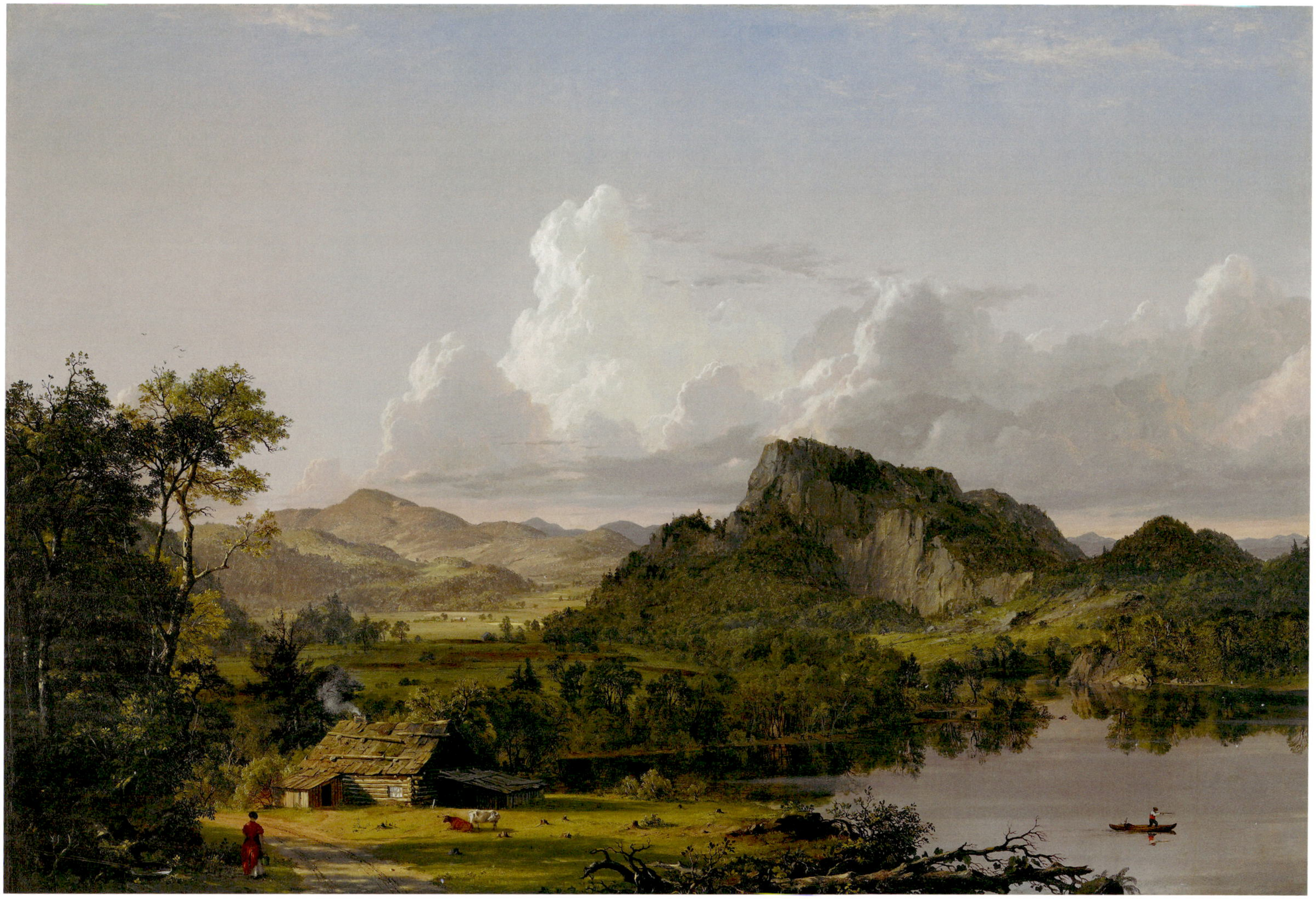

JOHN FREDERICK KENSETT (1816–1872)

View of Mount Washington

1852
Oil on canvas
30 × 45⅛ in. (76.2 × 114.6 cm)

John Frederick Kensett was a young engraver in New York City harboring landscape ambitions in 1835 when Thomas Cole delivered his famous "Essay on American Scenery," which celebrated the White Mountains as "a union of the picturesque, the sublime, and the magnificent."[1] Cole had first traveled to New Hampshire in the 1820s, producing dramatic paintings that established the region's legendary reputation as a sublime mountain wilderness with notches, peaks, and valleys more rugged and remote than those of the Catskills, or even the Adirondacks. The White Mountains also inspired Kensett, who made the transition from engraver to landscape painter while abroad in the early 1840s. In 1847, his artistic career quickly flourished as he rejoined his fellows at the sketching grounds of the American school in New York and New England. Kensett visited New Hampshire regularly from 1849, and his studies of the White Mountains from those excursions provided subjects for the paintings that would earn him early fame, including *View of Mount Washington*.[2]

By the time of Kensett's first expeditions, railroad access had facilitated the changing popular image of the White Mountains from forbidding wilderness to benign setting for human activity. The region's complex natural history also attracted attention in an era when geology and botany were popular pastimes. The valley of North Conway was developing as a destination for tourists as well as for writers and artists, inspiring paintings, novels, poems, and guidebooks.[3] The broad valley offered spectacular views of the Presidential Range dominated by Mount Washington. In 1850 Kensett summered there and made studies for the 1851 painting *The White Mountains—Mount Washington* (Wellesley College Museum), which was acquired by the American Art-Union and engraved for distribution to over thirteen thousand subscribers. This popular print established the signature mid-century image of the region as a picturesque, domesticated valley set among mountain peaks.[4] However, the bucolic vista depicted in this painting and print was by no means Kensett's only response to the region's majestic scenery, as we see in his *View of Mount Washington*, painted a year later. Here Kensett presents the eastern face of Mount Washington from Pinkham Notch, offering a clear view of the massive glacial scars of Tuckerman's Ravine on the shoulder of the mountain. Evoking Cole's sense of "savage grandeur" in its mood of somber isolation, a rugged foreground precipice replaces the easily accessible valley with its homesteads and steeples.[5]

Mount Washington is the highest mountain in the range whose peaks are named for the first five presidents. Together with Mounts Adams, Jefferson, Madison, and Monroe, Mount Washington represented nature's monument to the founding of the republic. In Kensett's painting, the once-dominant Native Americans gathered in the foreground acknowledge the continent's early, presettlement history. The pyramidal mass of Mount Washington rises in the distance, looming over uninhabited forests and foothills—a national symbol and a geological landmark presiding above all in remote splendor, under an exquisitely subtle sky. LSF

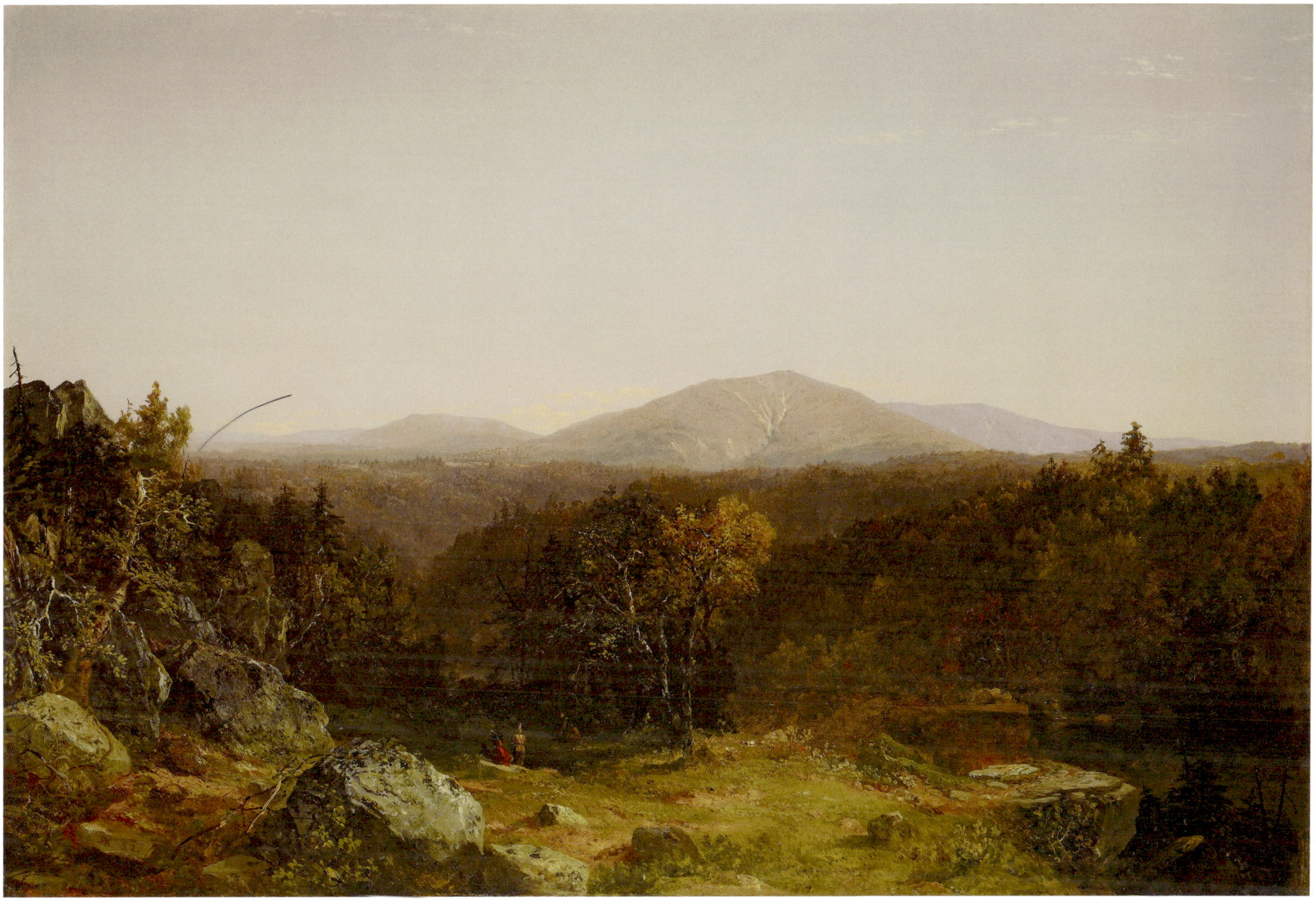

ARTHUR FITZWILLIAM TAIT (1819–1905)

The Life of a Hunter: A Tight Fix

1856
Oil on canvas
40 × 60 in. (101.6 × 152.4 cm)

Arthur Fitzwilliam Tait began submitting pictures of sporting adventures to the annual exhibitions held at the National Academy of Design in New York in 1852. The novelty of the subject bolstered the artist's reputation among a new class of patrons who enjoyed hunting as a leisure-time activity. In 1855, Tait presented *A Second Shot: Still Hunting on the First Snow in the Chateaugay Forest* (Adirondack Museum), a scene of two Adirondack deer hunters whose prowess in the backcountry is about to result in the swift felling of a second animal. The picture earned Tait critical acclaim and helped elect him an associate academician. But the increasing popularity of his sporting pictures did little to prepare the painter for the controversy that surrounded *The Life of a Hunter: A Tight Fix*, one of eight works he submitted to the 1858 academy exhibition.

Like *A Second Shot, The Life of a Hunter* is a winter scene of two outdoorsmen, but this time their adventure has led to a perilous encounter with a raging black bear. Based on the triumph of *A Second Shot*, Tait must have expected his newest composition to be greeted with an equal, if not greater, measure of approbation. Instead, the painting ignited a storm of negative criticism and the ensuing controversy surrounding its execution forced Tait to defend both his artistic skill and his reputation for honesty. The imbroglio began when an anonymous writer for the *New York Express* perceived "an incongruity of style between the landscape and the figures," and chided Tait for not acknowledging assistance from a fellow painter. The writer also denigrated the figures as "full of impossible attitudes."[1]

The criticism must have deeply wounded Tait, as did the implication that he had depicted a tall tale rather than an authentic account of bravery. A largely self-taught artist, Tait had developed his talent in his native England before immigrating to New York City in 1850. His boyhood pastimes of hunting and fishing were serious sport. Tait discovered the bounty of New York's Adirondacks in 1852, and spent nearly every season thereafter at one or another of the region's resorts. As an experienced outdoorsman, he knew well the dangers of bear hunting in the weeks leading up to hibernation. It seems unlikely that he would have mocked a sport he loved, or misjudged his patrons, who would have had little interest in hanging a large-scale caricature alongside their trophies.

Controversy aside, *The Life of a Hunter* is an engaging composition that offers multiple interpretations, all of which point to an unhappy ending for the bear. Tait accentuated the hunter's "tight fix" by providing a wealth of details for viewers to uncover. The hunter's rifle, tucked under the bear's right leg, has been rendered useless. Both combatants find themselves in compromised positions, and because their wounds appear superficial, the contest must escalate before reaching its deadly conclusion. The hunter's companion, with rifle ready, may not be able to risk the shot for fear of hitting his friend.

Scholars have speculated that at some point Tait made minor changes to the composition to render the contest more credible.[2] The artist created another version of the theme (location unknown) to serve as the basis for a lithograph issued by Currier and Ives in 1861. In the revised composition, Tait presented the knife-wielding hunter standing and lunging at the bear, his position more advantageous than in the original painting.

REL

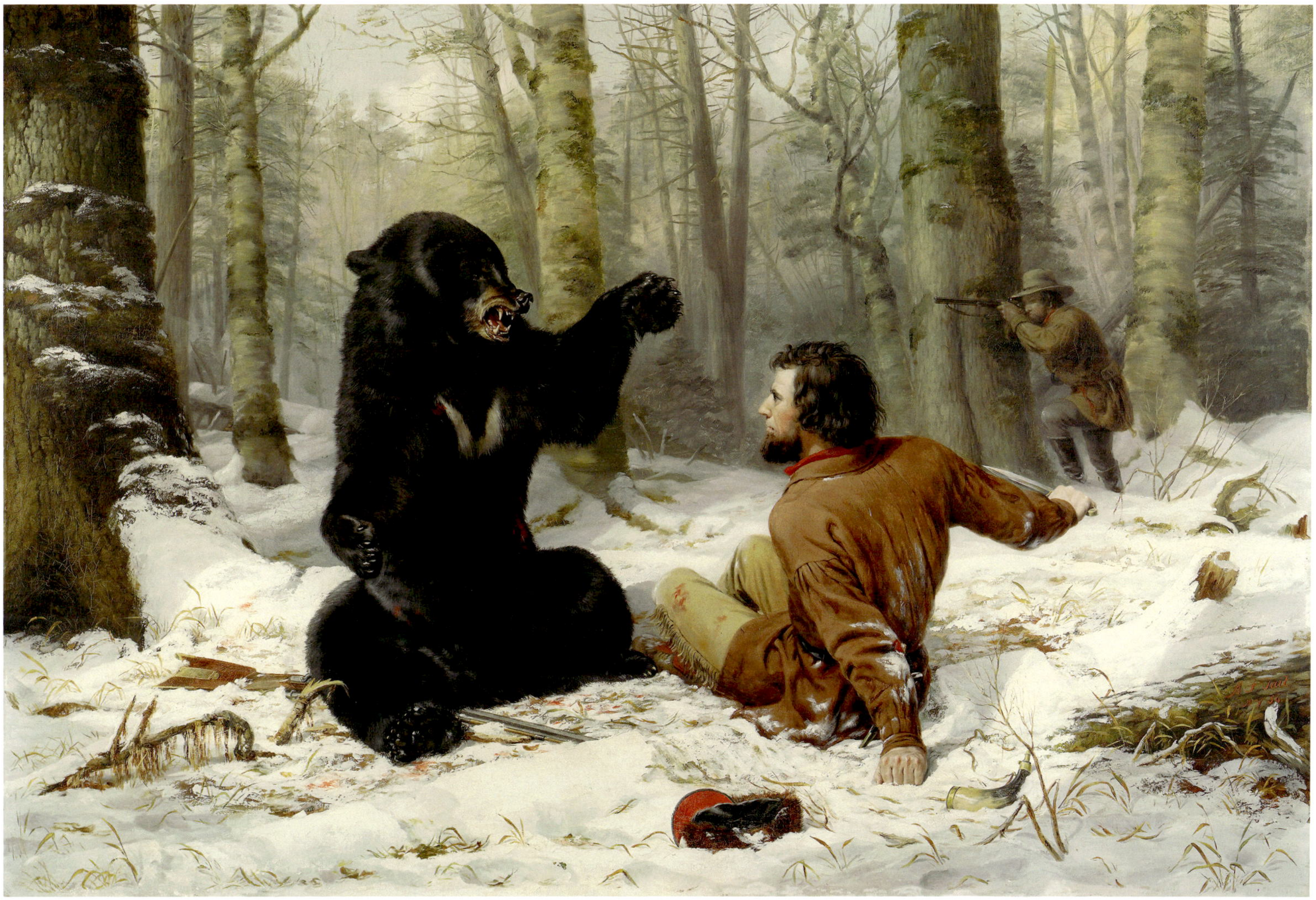

JASPER FRANCIS CROPSEY (1823–1900)

The Backwoods of America

1858
Oil on canvas
42 × 70¼ in. (106.7 × 178.4 cm)

On his second extended European excursion, the Hudson River School landscape painter Jasper Francis Cropsey discovered a foreign market for his distinctly American scenes. In London, where he lived between 1856 and 1862, Cropsey painted one of his most ambitious works: *The Backwoods of America*. The artist exhibited this grand-scale rendering of life on the fabled American frontier to positive reviews at the Royal Academy of Art in the summer of 1858. The following spring, a Scottish collector purchased *The Backwoods* for one of the highest prices the artist had yet received for a painting.[1]

Cropsey's canvas depicts a remote homestead nestled along the shore of a wilderness lake. As the sun breaks over the mountains, a pioneer family begins its day. In the left middle ground a woman stands in the doorway of a log cabin, her three young children playing nearby, while in the foreground her husband heads off into the woods, shouldering a long-handled broadax and accompanied by a dog.[2] In the distance, another man, perhaps an older son, launches a boat into the lake. Cows lull on the small grassy knoll near the water; a woman kneels by one of the animals to milk it. A rudimentary garden of hearty fall crops—cabbage, and the distinctly American pumpkin and cornstalk—grow in roughly cleared patches along the forest edge.

For Cropsey's foreign audience, the theme of the American pioneer—which had been widely popularized in recent years through literary and painterly description—had exotic appeal.[3] Yet *The Backwoods* also includes visual motifs that would have been familiar to an English viewing public. In his rendering of clouds, for example, Cropsey took inspiration from the painter J. M. W. Turner, who specialized in dramatic skies, as well as from British romantic poets. In an 1855 essay he authored on the poetic effects of clouds, Cropsey cited Percy Bysshe Shelley's description of a morning sky: "A multitude of dense, white, fleecy clouds / Were wandering in thick flocks among the mountains,/Shepherded by the slow, unwilling wind."[4] In *The Backwoods*, the sky is blushed with pink from the break of day, while a few clouds as white and fleecy as Shelley's flock hover just above the mountain at far left.

Although Cropsey's romantic aesthetic might suggest that his painting was a work of fiction, the canvas was rooted in reality. The painter's numerous trips to the wilds of rural New England resulted in sketches as well as written accounts that he later drew upon for inspiration.[5] In a journal entry documenting his August 1849 excursion to the White Mountains of New Hampshire, Cropsey recollected observing "some log houses, some garden patches about them [and] . . . pumpkin vines . . . growing and creeping around" from his perch in a passing coach.[6]

While Cropsey successfully marketed his pioneer landscapes as truthful documents of contemporary American life based on first-hand observation, he also appears to have forecast the imminent end of the frontier era. Land across the country was being acquired and developed at an unprecedented pace during this period. The artist signed his name in the lower right of *The Backwoods,* on a rock that resembles an old, tipped-over gravestone that soon will be covered by the cultivated pumpkin vines growing nearby. SMH

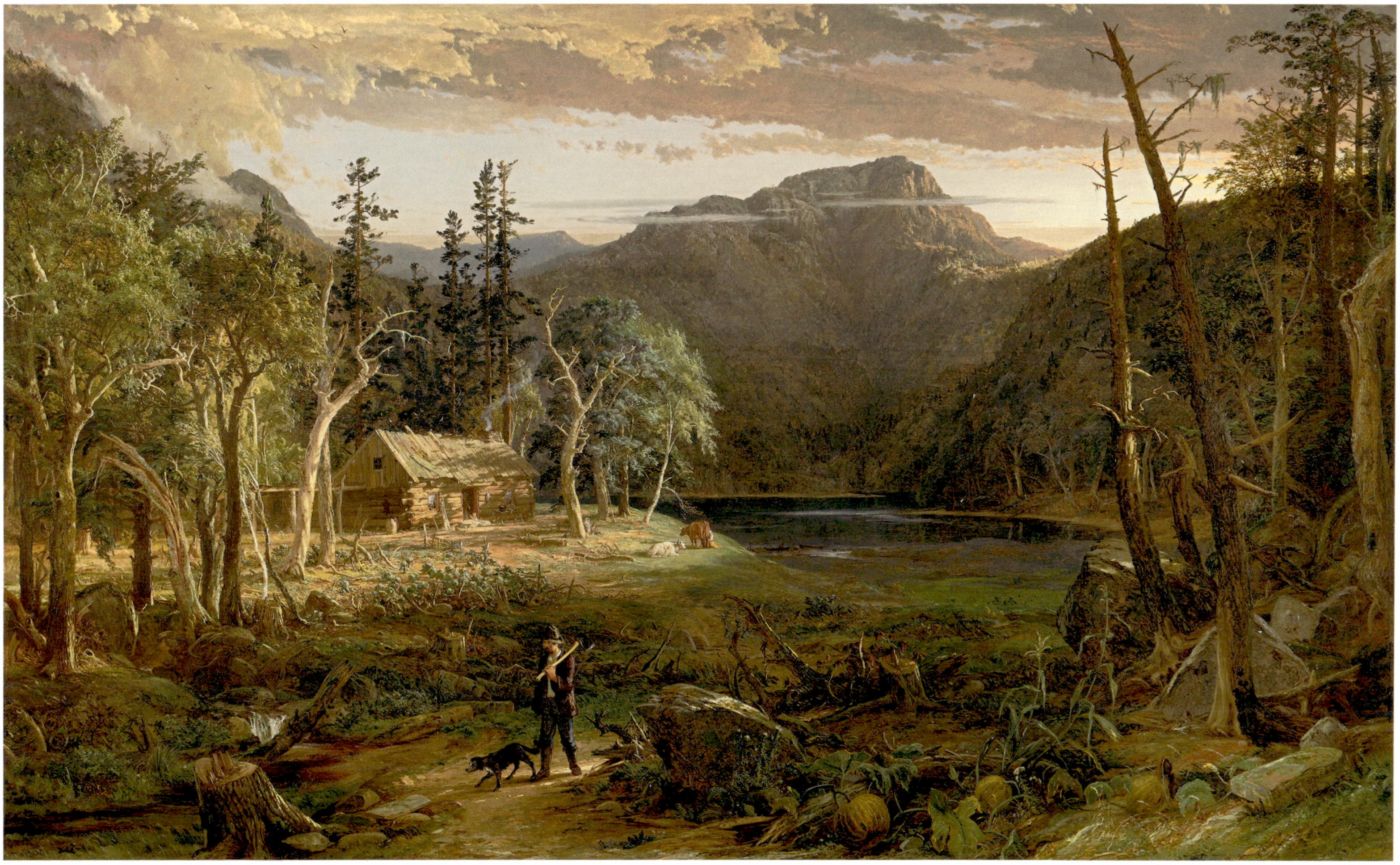

THOMAS MORAN (1837–1926)

Valley of the Catawissa in Autumn

ca. 1862
Oil on canvas
39¾ × 63½ in. (101 × 161.3 cm)

Thomas Moran is the best known of a talented quartet of English-born artist brothers who immigrated to the United States with their family in 1844, settling near Philadelphia. All were trained locally; Thomas, Edward, and Peter became painters, and John was a photographer.[1] In the spring of 1861, the Moran brothers went on a sketching and photography expedition to Catawissa, a small town on the Susquehanna River in the mountainous region of northeastern Pennsylvania. Thomas, who was also trained as an engraver, translated his sketches into illustrations for a travelogue published in *Harper's New Monthly* that extolled the Catawissa Railroad route as a picturesque touring itinerary.[2] He also mined his studies and, perhaps, John's photographs, to develop subjects for oil paintings of the region. In the spring of 1862, Thomas exhibited a work entitled *Valley of the Catawissa in Autumn*—a canvas that fits the description of Crystal Bridges' painting—at the Pennsylvania Academy of the Fine Arts.

In the 1862 travelogue, *Harper's New Monthly* invoked *Valley of the Catawissa* as a means of demonstrating the picturesque allure of the region's scenery for artists' excursions as well as for railway touring. "Back of the town of Catawissa," the author wrote, "from the top of the mountain looking due east, we have a most magnificent view of the Catawissa Valley, with the meandering course of the creek before us for fifteen miles, winding in the dim distance like a silver thread. This is another characteristic scene, and one that has attracted the attention of artists: a work of great merit, taken from this identical landscape, having been produced by the artist Moran, of Philadelphia, which attracted considerable attention and elicited the highest encomiums from connoisseurs at the recent artists' reception of Philadelphians."[3] Given that the Moran brothers had traveled to Catawissa in the spring, unless Thomas made a return visit in the fall of 1861, he took certain seasonal liberties with his painting. "The time seen in his picture," *Harper's* reported, "is the fall of the year—the forests tinged with gold and crimson—the first coloring of leaves by early frost, most beautifully delineated, greatly heightening the effect of the picture." The travelogue also extolled the picturesque qualities of the railroad itself: "The railroad, in sight all the way up the valley, furnishes, at times, the only lifelike object, when the train of cars with its engine and white, puffing steam ascending, gives something moving to relieve . . . so extended a view."[4] In his painting, however, Moran elected to omit the railroad in favor of a splendid panorama of autumnal mountain wilderness that demonstrates his early mastery of the American landscape vision.

LSF

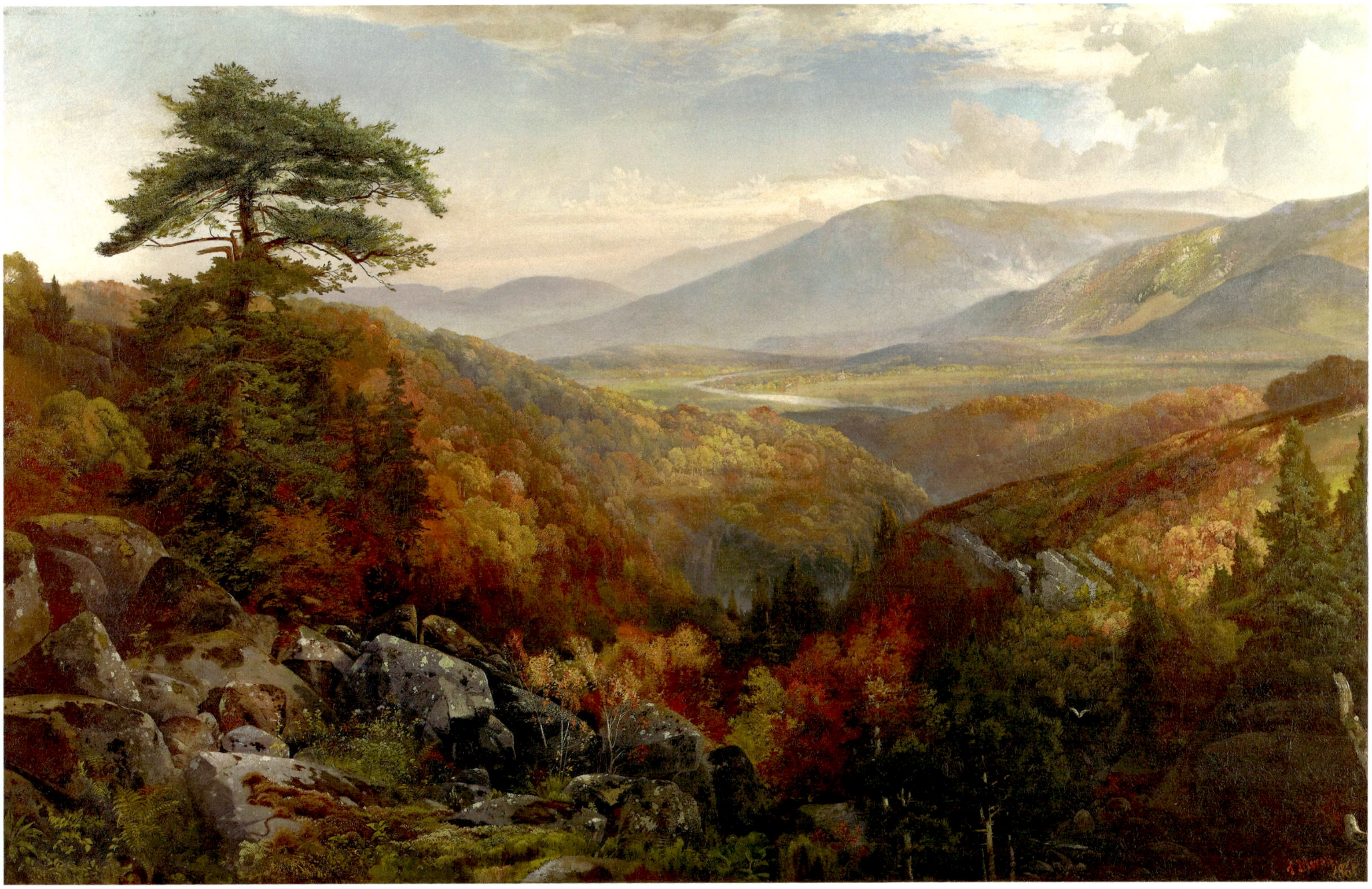

ALBERT BIERSTADT (1830–1902)

Indian Encampment

1862
Oil on canvas
20 × 28 in. (50.8 × 71.1 cm)

> *The manners and customs of the Indians are still as they were hundreds of years ago, and now is the time to paint them, for they are rapidly passing away.* —ALBERT BIERSTADT[1]

Albert Bierstadt gained international fame during his lifetime as the foremost painter of the American West. The artist directed his skilled hand and professional ambition toward producing grand, heroic pictures of the region's distinctive landscape and cultures. Characterized by a unique combination of carefully rendered details, theatrical atmospheric effects, and panoramic scope, these paintings offered armchair travelers vivid and inspiring views of America's frontier. Bierstadt's modestly sized 1862 canvas *Indian Encampment*, an intimate rendering of Native American life painted following his first journey west, presaged the mythic themes and arresting geography of monumental landscapes such as his 1863 masterwork *The Rocky Mountains, Lander's Peak* (The Metropolitan Museum of Art).

In April 1859, Bierstadt accompanied a government survey expedition to the Rocky Mountains. During this journey the artist documented his observations of the frontier landscape and its native inhabitants.[2] Painted upon returning to his New York City studio, *Indian Encampment* portrays a Native American community engaging in a peaceful moment of domestic activity at the end of the day, in the golden glow of dusk. A nostalgic and idealized representation of Indians as Bierstadt imagined they were prior to European contact, the painting depicts a noble civilization harmoniously coexisting with nature.

Yet the canvas may also be seen to offer a subtle political commentary on the contemporary plight of Native Americans. The dead and dying trees that flank Bierstadt's composition are conventional features of the romantic sublime as conceived by artists of the Hudson River School. The elegiac quality of these anthropomorphized trees may also serve a more specific symbolic purpose, however, alluding to the imperiled fate of the nation's indigenous peoples. Left to be absorbed into the landscape, its original placement and species forgotten, the uprooted trunk in the lower right offers a dark metaphor for the Indian Removal Acts and related United States government initiatives, which forced many native tribes to leave their homelands against their will. A group of three senior members of the encampment, who sit on the riverbank in the center of the composition, repeat the general shape, position, and direction of the felled tree. Likewise, the silhouette of the feathered headdress worn by the chieftan with his back to the camp mimics the rough and weathered roots at the felled tree's base, while the form of the pipe-smoking middle figure repeats the shape of the tree limb protruding upward from mid-trunk, the two feathers of his headdress recalling the bifurcated break of the limb. Finally, the resting left leg of the figure dressed in blue at the water's edge parallels the general position of the uprooted tree.

On the opposing bank, a hollowed-out oak with gnarled branches appears to announce its last season. The oak's silent scream resonates in the fading light, a further suggestion of the end of an era. However, a glimmer of hope exists in the presence of three Indian youths frolicking in the calm river waters. Perhaps the romanticism of Bierstadt's image was, at least in part, an aesthetic manifestation of the artist's hope that the tribal civilization represented therein might continue to survive and thrive. AWJ

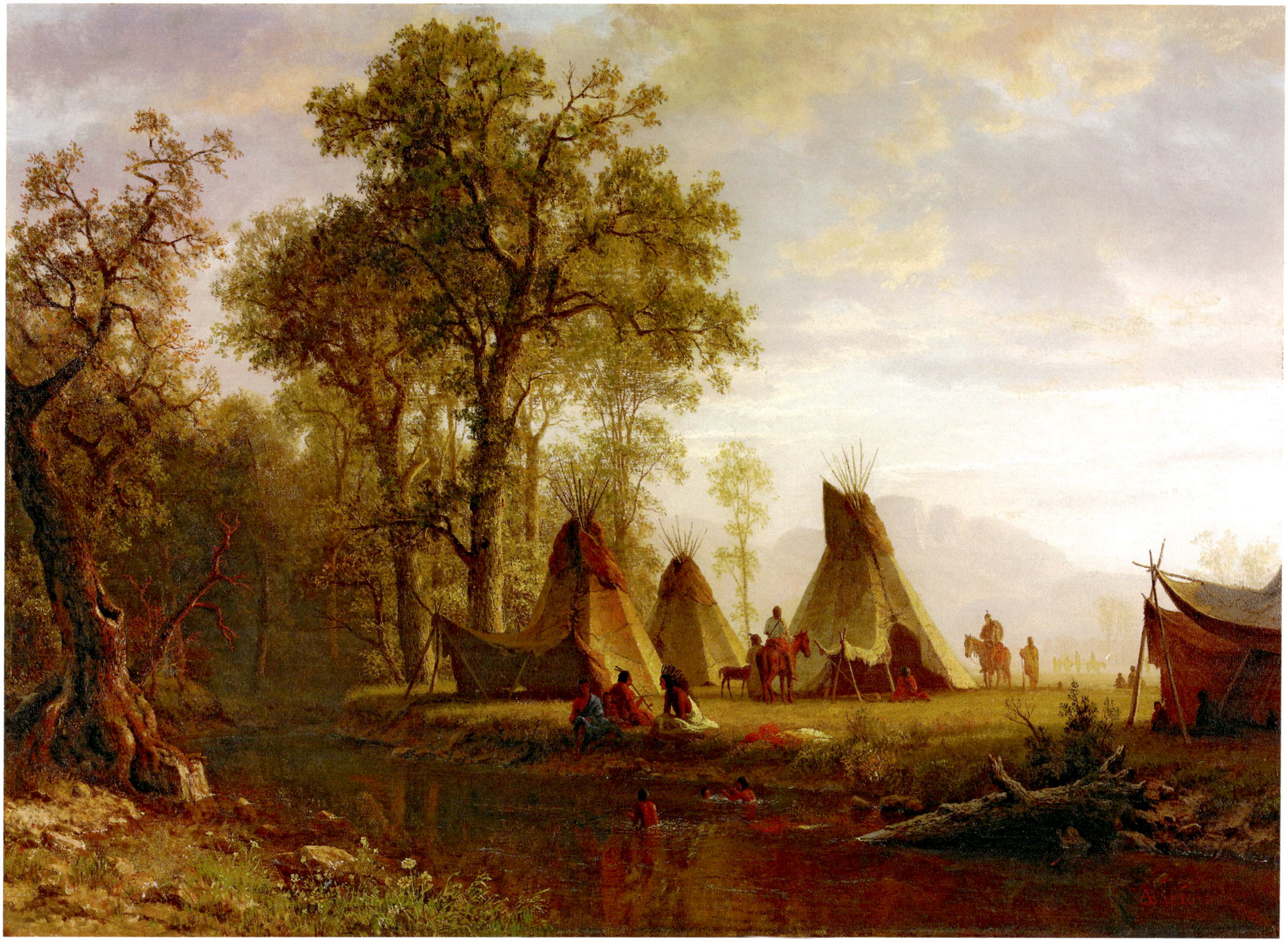

WILLIAM TROST RICHARDS (1833–1905)

Landscape

ca. 1863–64
Oil on canvas
23½ × 33½ in. (59.7 × 85.1 cm)

William Trost Richards was born and raised in Philadelphia and lived much of his adult life in nearby Germantown, Pennsylvania.[1] Already working full-time as a commercial draftsman in his teens, Richards studied informally with Paul Weber, an expatriate German landscape painter who also taught William Stanley Haseltine and Thomas Moran. As an aspiring landscape artist in the early 1850s, Richards' heroes were the luminaries of the Hudson River School: Thomas Cole, John Frederick Kensett, Jasper Francis Cropsey, and Frederic Edwin Church. However, beginning around 1858, Richards also experimented for a decade or more with John Ruskin's program of laborious study from nature, joining the English critic's New York followers, who were collectively known as the American Pre-Raphaelites.[2]

Under Ruskin's influence, Richards abruptly transformed his practice, abandoning his Hudson River School models for the intense, allover focus and brilliant color that characterize a remarkable series of landscapes painted during the 1860s. These canvases sparked controversy because of their amazing botanical exactitude. While one critic called them "miracles of special study," another complained, "Science takes the place of poetry."[3] All agreed that Richards was the foremost landscapist among the American Pre-Raphaelites.

Many of these jewel-like marvels of close study, including *Landscape*, were painted during the Civil War. In May 1864 a correspondent for the New York weekly the *Round Table* reported on a visit to the galleries of the Pennsylvania Academy of the Fine Arts, where he sought respite from a hot spring day in the city as well as from recent war news. Longing "for the green fields and budding woods now so enchanting in their wealth of vernal beauties," L. [the critic] spent his "leisure hours among the landscapes in the northeast gallery," where he commented at some length on *Landscape* as representative of Richards's Ruskinian "mood." L. described the painting as "a quiet brook, with overhanging rocks, some large dark oaks, and beyond, a sunny pasture—rendered with all fidelity, and without harshness." He also alluded to the critical debate about these landscapes: "I do not intend to discuss the right or wrong of Mr. Richards's manner; he endeavors to put upon his canvas the works of nature as he sees them, omitting nothing, generalizing nothing; and if we see nature differently, let us not pronounce him wrong, but try and look from his stand-point, and see if his pictures do not impress us as truthful renderings of their subjects. . . . The drawing is more beautiful even than Mr. Richards is wont to give us."[4]

In the context of current events, academy visitors and readers of the *Round Table* may well have joined L. in appreciating the masterful American pastoral presented by *Landscape* as a new kind of national narrative. Richards's bucolic image enlisted the healing forces of nature as a respite not only from the "heat and noise" of the city, but also from the "doubly heated" crisis of the Civil War, as the armies of Robert E. Lee and Ulysses S. Grant fought the terrible Battle of the Wilderness in Virginia.[5] LSF

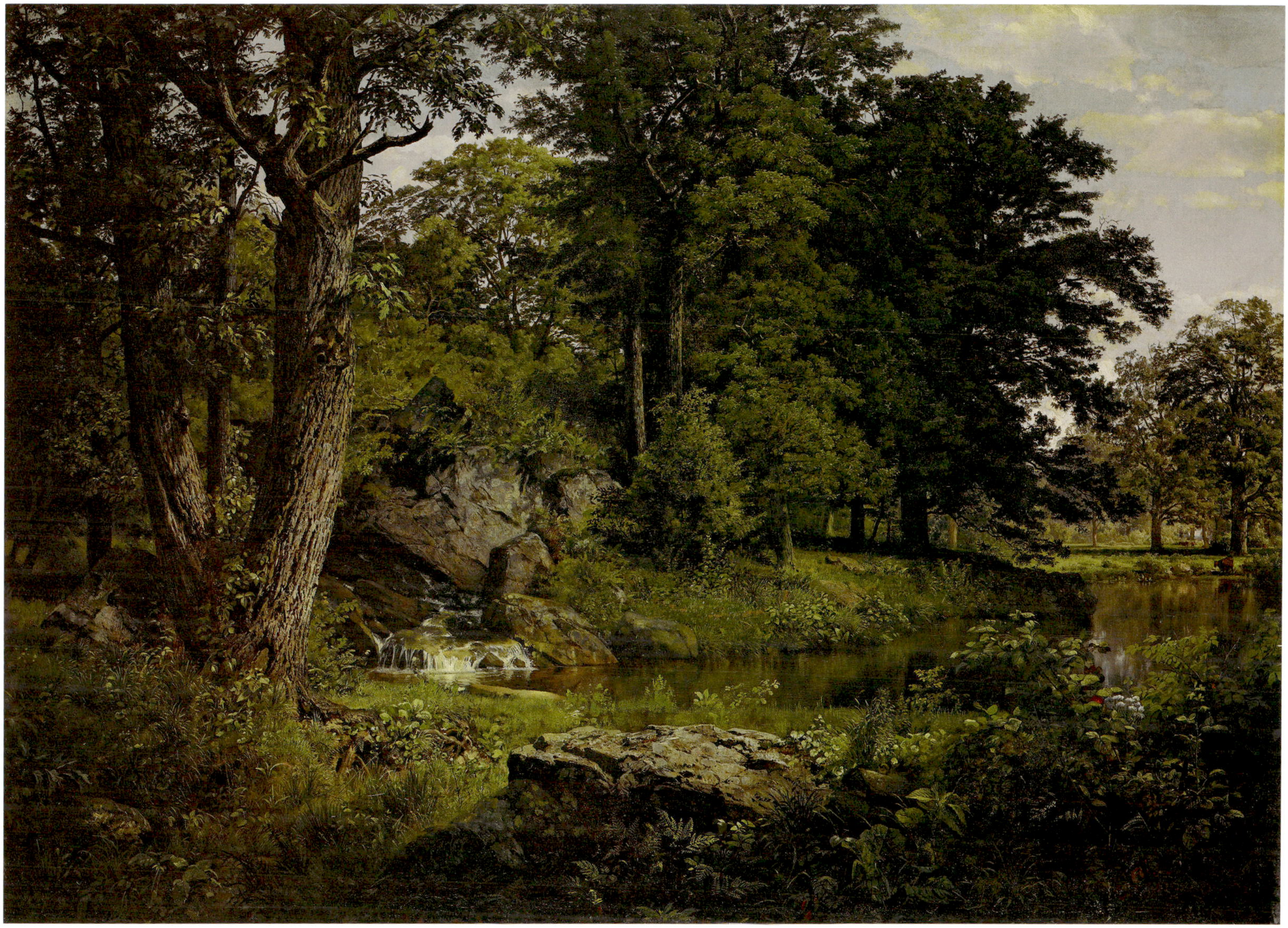

MARTIN JOHNSON HEADE (1819–1904)

The Gems of Brazil

ca. 1863–64
Oil on canvas
Multiple dimensions

In 1863, Martin Johnson Heade traveled to Brazil in pursuit of "the dream of his boyhood."[1] A self-described "monomaniac" on the subject of hummingbirds, Heade planned to combine his refined skills as an artist with his enthusiasm as an amateur naturalist to create the first artfully rendered, accurate portrayal of these birds in their native tropical setting. Heade would call the final result *The Gems of Brazil*, in reference to the popular association of hummingbirds with sparkling, precious jewels.[2]

The alluring little birds had recently captured the attention of American and British audiences through a series of popular publications. Yet Heade found the ornithological texts of John James Audubon and, above all, John Gould, whose five-volume illustrated tome had spurred the recent hummingbird sensation, to be lacking in two important ways. To Heade's mind, none had accurately captured the brilliant iridescence of the hummingbird's distinctive feathers and, perhaps more significantly, no ornithologist had ventured to the wilds of Brazil, the endemic habitat for a large majority of these birds. The artist's ambitious project would be the first on both counts.

Heade arrived in Rio de Janeiro in the fall of 1863 and quickly got to work. In addition to birds, he also spent time painting the landscape. Heade made at least thirteen finished landscapes in Brazil, including the 1864 exhibition piece *The Harbor at Rio de Janeiro* (p. 87). In contrast to the narrowly focused compositions of *The Gems*, this picture engages the traditional Claudian (after the baroque painter Claude Lorrain) format of a grand vista combined with rich atmospheric effects and anecdotal foreground detail. Heade also would have been aware of the previous successes of South American landscapes by his close friend Frederic Edwin Church, who had encouraged his initial travels to Brazil.[3] Yet his efforts to study and paint the Brazilian landscape were more likely driven by his desire to better understand the unique natural environment so essential to his winged protagonists in *The Gems*.

By early 1864 Heade had completed at least twelve of *The Gems*, which he exhibited to great acclaim alongside a few landscapes at the Academy of Fine Arts in Rio.[4] With this ambitious project, he appeared to be on the way to triumph. Yet for Heade, success was always elusive. The painter had tried his hand at a number of genres preceding his excursion to Brazil, and his lack of recognition was a constant source of discouragement.[5] Undoubtedly, Heade's ambition for *The Gems* was that it would propel him into a more central position in the art world. After completing a number of the canvases in Brazil, he arrived in London to have them engraved. The process proved untenable, however, as the nuance of Heade's brilliant portrayals of the jewel-like birds in their lush tropical settings was lost in translation to print. Heade finally abandoned the engraving project, frustrated by his efforts to alter the finished prints by hand.[6] Though regarded as a failure in the artist's lifetime, *The Gems* remain one of Heade's most ambitious and visually stunning endeavors.[7]

SMH

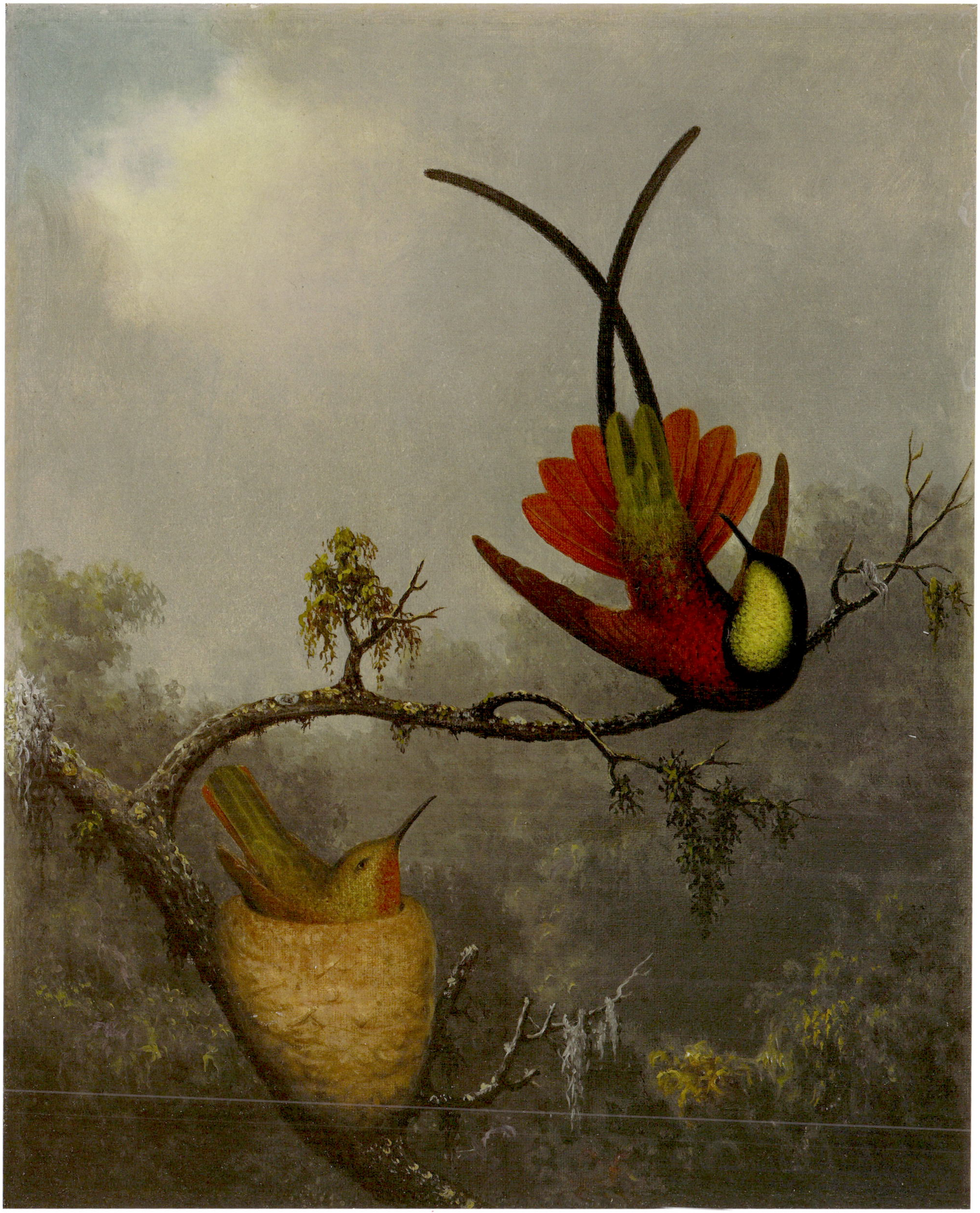

Crimson Topaz
ca. 1863–64
Oil on canvas
12¼ × 10 in. (31.1 × 25.4 cm)

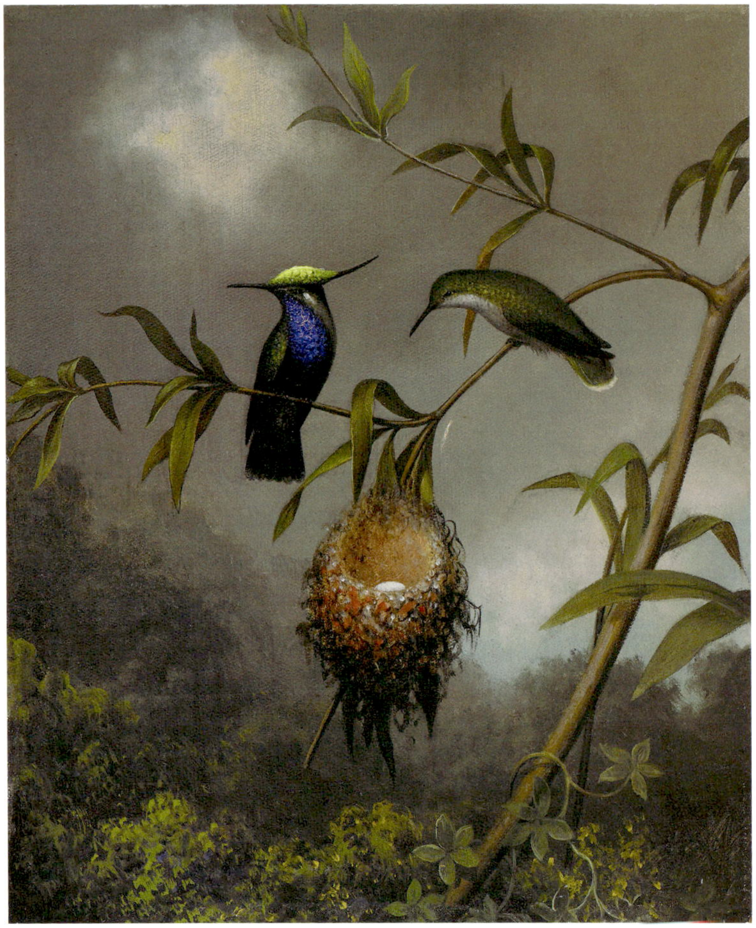

Black-breasted Plovercrest
ca. 1863–64
Oil on canvas
12¼ × 10 in. (31.1 × 25.4 cm)

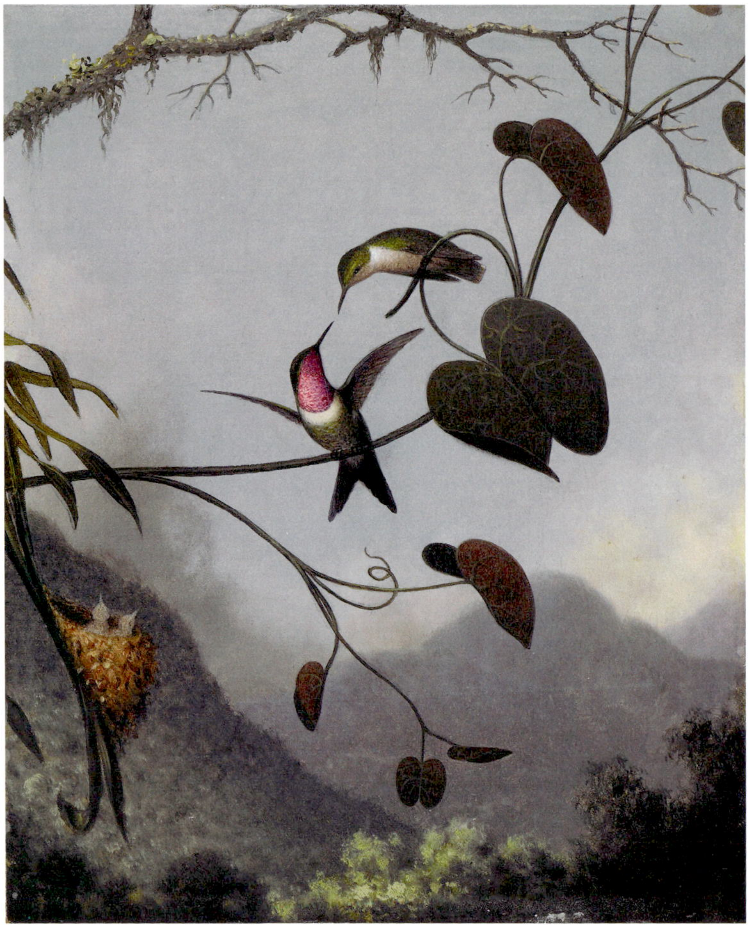

Amethyst Woodstar
ca. 1863–64
Oil on canvas
12¼ × 10 in. (31.1 × 25.4 cm)

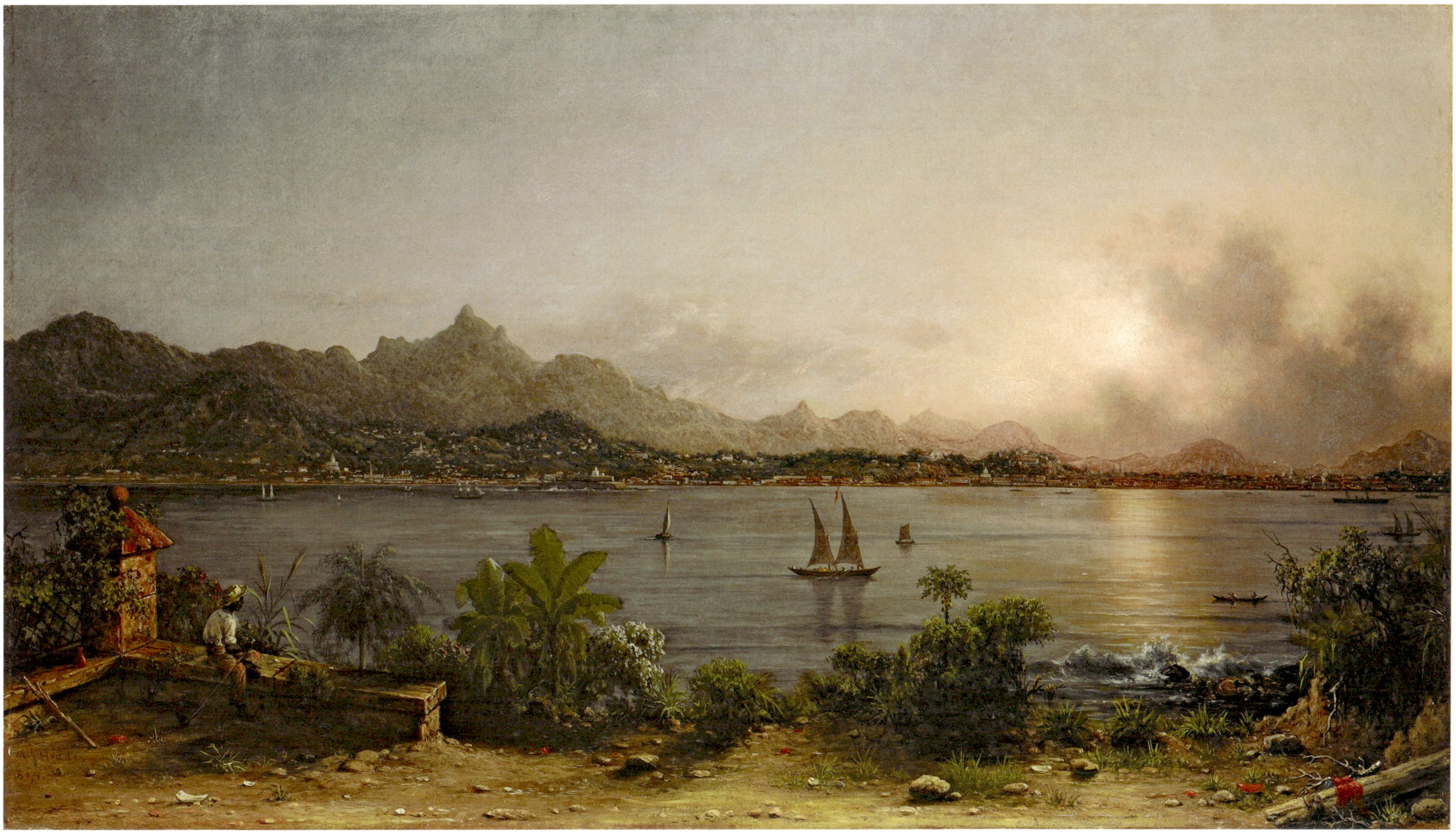

The Harbor at Rio de Janeiro
1864
Oil on canvas
19⅛ × 34⅛ in. (48.6 × 86.7 cm)

MARTIN JOHNSON HEADE (1819–1904)

Study of Pink Roses, Leaves, Heliotrope, a Carnation and an Orchid

ca. 1869
Oil and pencil on canvas
15¼ × 21¾ in. (38.7 × 55.2 cm)

Study of Varied Flowers with a Hummingbird

ca. 1870
Oil and pencil on canvas
17 × 21 in. (43.2 × 53.3 cm)

Martin Johnson Heade painted these two floral studies around 1870, after he had been working in the still-life genre for about a decade. Although Heade never exhibited the sketches, the painter repurposed their contents countless times. Individual flowers included in these compositions appear in numerous finished oils separated by years, and, in some cases, decades.

Study of Pink Roses, Leaves, Heliotrope, a Carnation and an Orchid, probably the earlier of the two paintings, includes three flowers that Heade used in the 1869 still life *Mixed Flowers with a Box and Pearls* (private collection) as well as other, later works.[1] The study features a selection of blooms that mostly derive from a northern climate. All but the pink *Cattleya* orchid at the far right would have been widely available in North America during the growing season, which suggests Heade's preference for naturalistic arrangements of native specimens. These images stood in contrast to lavish French and Dutch still-life paintings of the seventeenth and eighteenth centuries, which typically combined flowers grown in varying climates and at varying times of year.[2] Heade's devotion to orchids, which were known to the artist primarily through his South American travels, was the exception to his local and seasonal approach to flower painting. Rarely, though, did he include these tropical blooms in his interior floral arrangements; Heade typically depicted orchids in natural, outdoor settings, as if simply encountered on a deep forest path.

Heade's *Study of Varied Flowers with a Hummingbird* features the elegant *Dendrobium* orchid, which grows primarily in Indonesia, alongside several gladioli, a rubrum lily, and a rose. Heade's inclusion of a hummingbird in this flower study suggests that the artist likely painted it while working on his orchid and hummingbird compositions. Indeed, several of these flowers appear in exact form in finished paintings from the orchid series, which, even more so than his earlier *Gems of Brazil* (p. 84), dramatized the interactions of hummingbirds in lush settings abundant with wild orchids. Unlike flowers drawn from the gardens of northern climes, the orchid was a highly eroticized botanical specimen that at once intrigued and challenged the Victorians. Conspicuously absent from late nineteenth-century floral lexicons, the symbolic power of the orchid dates back to antiquity, where its root name derives from the Greek word for testicle. Heade took a calculated risk in selecting these blossoms as the central subject in a large number of his paintings, though their intrinsic beauty and mystique had inspired many wealthy Americans of his day to assemble the flowers in their hothouse collections.[3]

Heade painted dozens of flower studies over the course of his career, though relatively few survive.[4] In 1904, the aging painter gave a number of these works to a young art student in Florida, where he had resided since 1883. These two were among that group. SMH

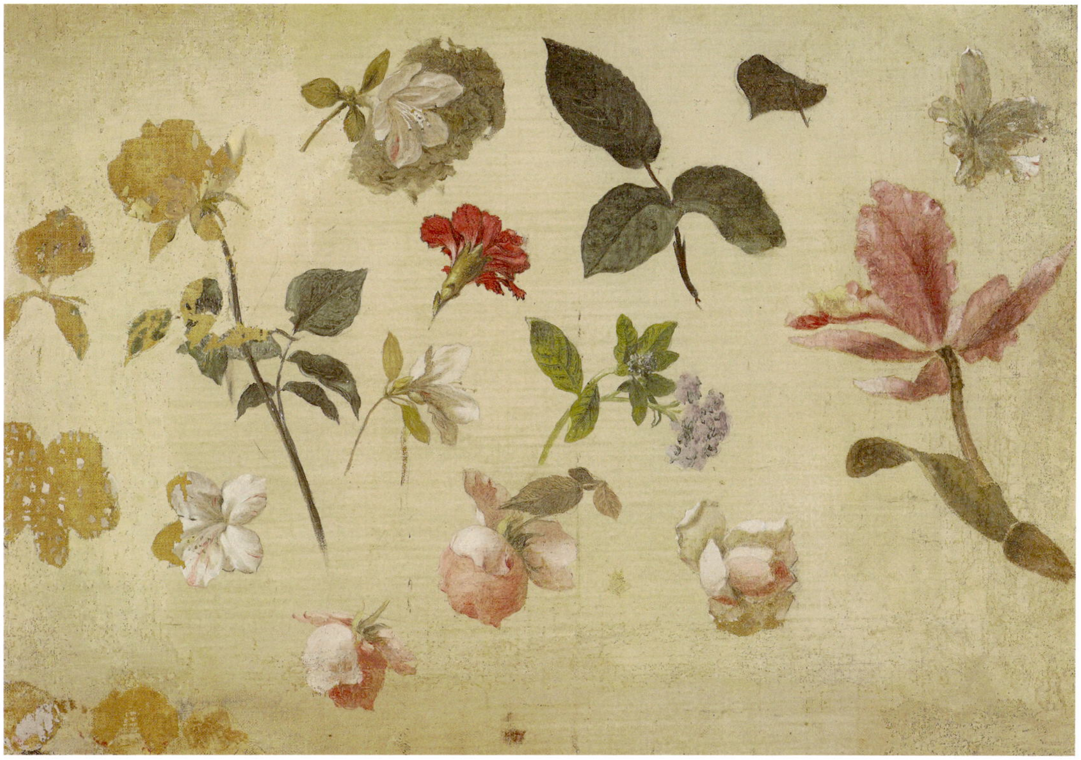

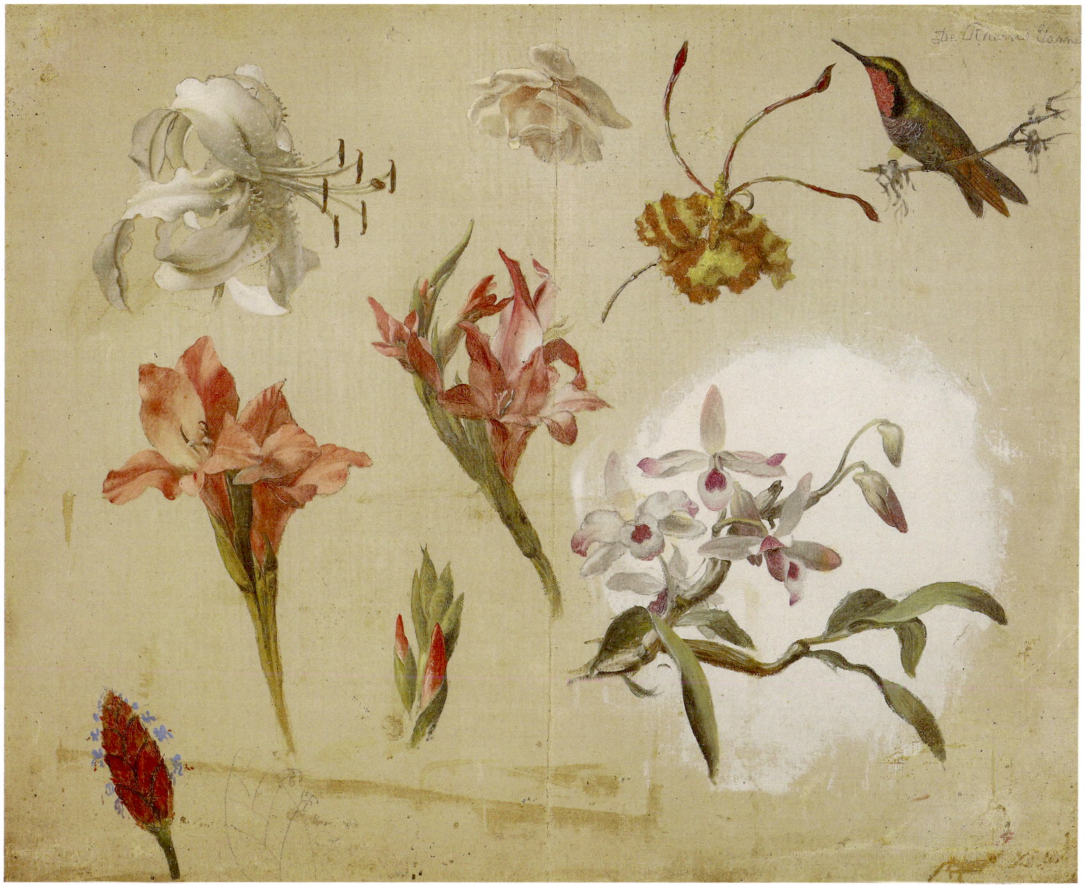

MARTIN JOHNSON HEADE (1819–1904)

Haystacks

1871–75
Oil on canvas
10 × 22 in. (25.4 × 55.9 cm)
Promised Gift

Over the course of his career, Martin Johnson Heade painted at least 120 marshland views. Before he turned to this theme Heade had tried his hand at a variety of genres. Early on he worked as portraitist, though he quickly abandoned that field of endeavor for landscape and still-life painting, including series of images depicting exotic hummingbirds, orchids, and passionflowers (p. 84). Of course landscape would have been a logical genre for Heade to pursue at mid-century, when Hudson River School painters such as Frederic Edwin Church and Albert Bierstadt were at the peak of their popularity. Most artists of ambition were in the business of painting picturesque and often dramatic vistas inspired by America's wild nature. But Heade neither settled entirely on landscape nor, in the case of those landscapes that he did produce, did he accept popular conventions of representation. While depictions of the nation's picturesque valleys and sublime mountains dominated the art world, Heade turned to the flat and humble salt marshes of the East Coast.[1] This subject would hold his attention off and on for nearly five decades.

Collectively the marsh scenes can be considered a series, although Heade made no effort to describe them as such. Generally small in scale and always oriented horizontally, these vistas onto the flat saltwater meadows of Massachusetts, New York, New Jersey, and Florida capture the subtle visual effects of changeable light and atmosphere. *Haystacks* shows Heade at the height of his artistic powers. A glowing view onto the marsh at dusk, this unpopulated scene features the outcome of the arduous labors of a recent harvest. Piles of hay dot the meadow, while a lone cow grazes near a tidal stream. Most likely painted in Newburyport, Massachusetts, where Heade spent time in the 1870s, *Haystacks* is undated and its specific location unrecorded.[2]

If Heade's hummingbirds and passionflowers reveal the artist's flair for the dazzling and the dramatic, his marsh scenes show his mastery of subtlety and restraint. Like many of his mature landscapes, the canvas masterfully captures the effects of light as it passes through the clouds, casting its warmth through dappled, diffuse reflection. Painted at least a decade before the French impressionist Claude Monet began his famous haystack series, these diminutive paintings are as much about light and atmosphere as they are about recording what Heade scholar Theodore E. Stebbins Jr. has called the "slower rhythms of a nature."[3] They celebrate a landscape rooted in a traditional agrarian lifestyle that had, by the mid-nineteenth century, been outpaced by technologies that cheaply transported better quality hay from inland farms to replace the salty product of the marshes.[4] SMH

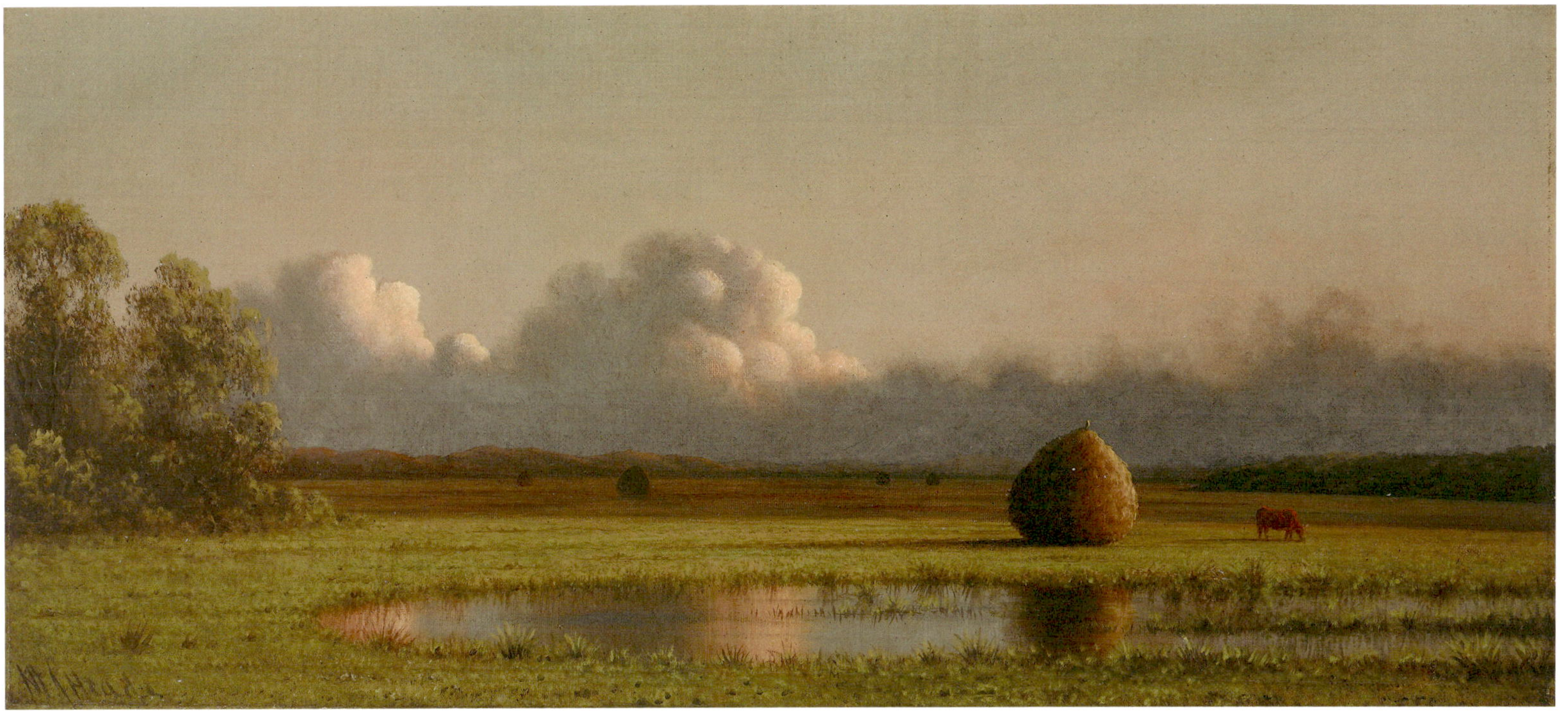

EASTMAN JOHNSON (1824–1906)

At the Camp—Spinning Yarns and Whittling

ca. 1864–66
Oil on board
19 × 23 in. (48.3 × 58.4 cm)

In July 1861, the *Knickerbocker* literary magazine appealed to American artists to embrace homegrown subject matter. "Honestly evolve the spirit, the 'genus [*sic*] loci' of the country in which you live," the author advised. "Be true to the indigenous poesy of the soil which cherishes you."[1] Eastman Johnson enthusiastically heeded that call. In fact, distinctly American themes already had been the focus of his work for some time. Following studies abroad in Düsseldorf, The Hague, and Paris in the early 1850s, Johnson had returned to the United States in 1857 to establish himself as a chronicler of native themes. He first traveled to Wisconsin, to paint the Anishinabe (Objibwe) Indians, but by 1858 had set up a New York City studio and begun to focus on the rural customs of northern New England. Nationalist in sentiment and ambitious in scope, Johnson's maple sugaring pictures, painted over a span of years that mirrored that of the Civil War (1861–65), are some of the most compelling works of the artist's career.

Early each spring during this period, Johnson made a pilgrimage to the sugaring camps in Fryeburg, Maine, to witness the siphoning of the sweet sap rising from the roots of maple trees and the communal festival during which this sap was boiled down into syrup.[2] Johnson set up a portable studio in the woods, where he sketched the harvest in all its local color and anecdotal detail.[3] His efforts resulted in nearly two dozen pictures ranging from single-figure studies to panoramic vistas encompassing more than forty men, women, and children.[4]

The protagonists in *At the Camp—Spinning Yarns and Whittling* appear in many of Johnson's wider-lens sugaring pictures, but this highly finished study stands on its own. Two men rest on a rough-hewn log bench. Behind them, a pair of wooden storage barrels used for transporting sap echo their forms. The modest structure to their right is the sugarhouse, where equipment and firewood was stored, and before it sits a large kettle filled with boiling sap. Johnson's figures are a study in contrasts. The gentleman "spinning his yarn" at right sits erect, his posture repeated by his rigid wooden cane. He wears the top hat and white beard associated with old-timers.[5] The younger, clean-shaven figure at left, who wears a soft cap more in keeping with current styles, straddles the bench and leans over his whittling. Yet the close physical proximity of the two men suggests an affinity that is enhanced by the fire-fueled kettle's evocation of the family hearth.[6]

The issue of unity was very much of the moment when Johnson painted *At the Camp*. A strong supporter of the Union cause, Johnson produced several overtly war-related paintings, including *A Ride for Liberty—The Fugitive Slaves* (ca. 1862, Brooklyn Museum). His sugaring images may also address the ongoing national conflict, if more obliquely. In mid nineteenth-century America, cane sugar was closely associated with the institution of slavery, since slave labor was largely responsible for its cultivation. Maple sugar, on the other hand, offered a "moral sweetener free of slavery's corruption."[7] Likewise, Johnson's contemporary viewers surely would have noted the physical resemblance between the artist's wooded sugaring camp and remote army outposts.[8] The quiet camaraderie of the two seemingly dissimilar figures in *At the Camp* offers the possibility of kinship in a time of unprecedented factionalism.[9] EDS

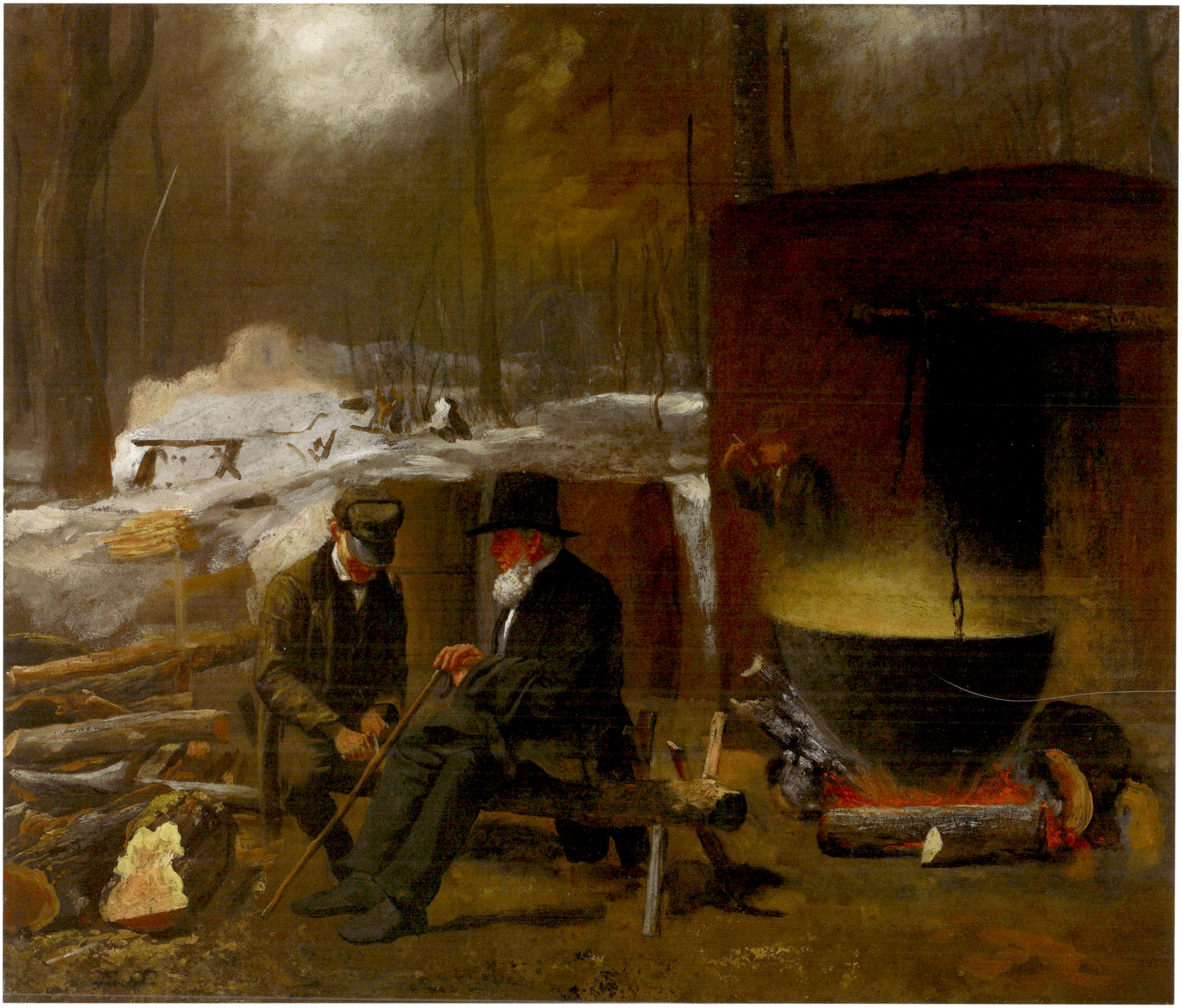

EASTMAN JOHNSON (1824–1906)

Cranberry Pickers, Nantucket

ca. 1879
Oil on canvas
19 × 43½ in. (48.3 × 110.5 cm)

After he returned to the United States from European studies in the late 1850s, the New York–based painter Eastman Johnson's artistic "sympathies" were, as a contemporary described them, "of the soil [of] his native land."[1] In the early 1860s Johnson produced many oil sketches of the annual maple sugaring celebration in Fryeburg, Maine (p. 92), although these pictures never resulted in a finished canvas. Nearly twenty years would pass before Johnson's *The Cranberry Harvest, Island of Nantucket* (1880, Timken Museum of Art) at last fulfilled his goal of creating an epic landscape that celebrated the picturesque folkways of rural New England. This project also showcased the artist's masterful ability to orchestrate light, color, and composition.

In late 1879, Johnson wrote to friend and fellow artist Jervis McEntee from his country retreat on Nantucket Island, where he and his wife had spent much of the year for nearly a decade. "I was taken with my cranberry fit as soon as I arrived," he explained, "I have done nothing else since I have been here, not a thing. . . . I have no finished picture at all, maybe further off than ever."[2] As he had done in developing his maple-sugaring theme, Johnson created numerous oil studies to observe color and character and to work through compositional challenges. *Cranberry Pickers, Nantucket* was likely one of his final studies for the finished painting.[3]

Johnson's insistently horizontal composition takes in the great breadth of a gold-and green-hued marshland on Nantucket's north shore.[4] The bog's wet and sandy terrain, which fills the entire surface of the picture save a thin band of cloudless blue sky, serves as the backdrop for the dozens of figures that dot the brilliantly sunny landscape, stooping or bending over to pick ripe fruit off of the cranberry vines. Punctuating the sweeping panorama is a statuesque female figure, seen in profile. This stately protagonist evokes the strong women who dominated contemporary New England local-color fiction in the immediate post–Civil War period, when the nation mourned the loss of one-fifth of its white male population.[5]

Shortly after its completion, Johnson exhibited the final version of his cranberry-picking scene at the National Academy of Design. Critics acknowledged the painting's appealing subject matter, but took particular note of Johnson's sensitive rendering of color and mood. A characteristic review called the work "an ambitious composition of very meritorious character," describing it as "cleverly arranged, interestingly suggestive, and harmoniously introduced into the well-painted landscape."[6] These aesthetic attributes are foretold in *Cranberry Pickers*. Lacking the detail of costume and landscape in the final canvas, this preparatory study highlights Johnson's concern with creating integrated compositions infused with "harmonious" color and palpable atmosphere.

Johnson's cranberry harvest paintings were his last outdoor, multifigural compositions.[7] A testament to the lasting impact of this subject, the final oil was exhibited at the World's Columbian Exposition in Chicago in 1893. In a tribute to the artist penned shortly after his death in 1906, painter James Carroll Beckwith wrote, "In telling the stories of our American people . . . he was never simply anecdotic. . . . The work of the *painter* was dominant. . . . One felt the merit of the man who handled the brush above the sentiment of the subject."[8]

EDS

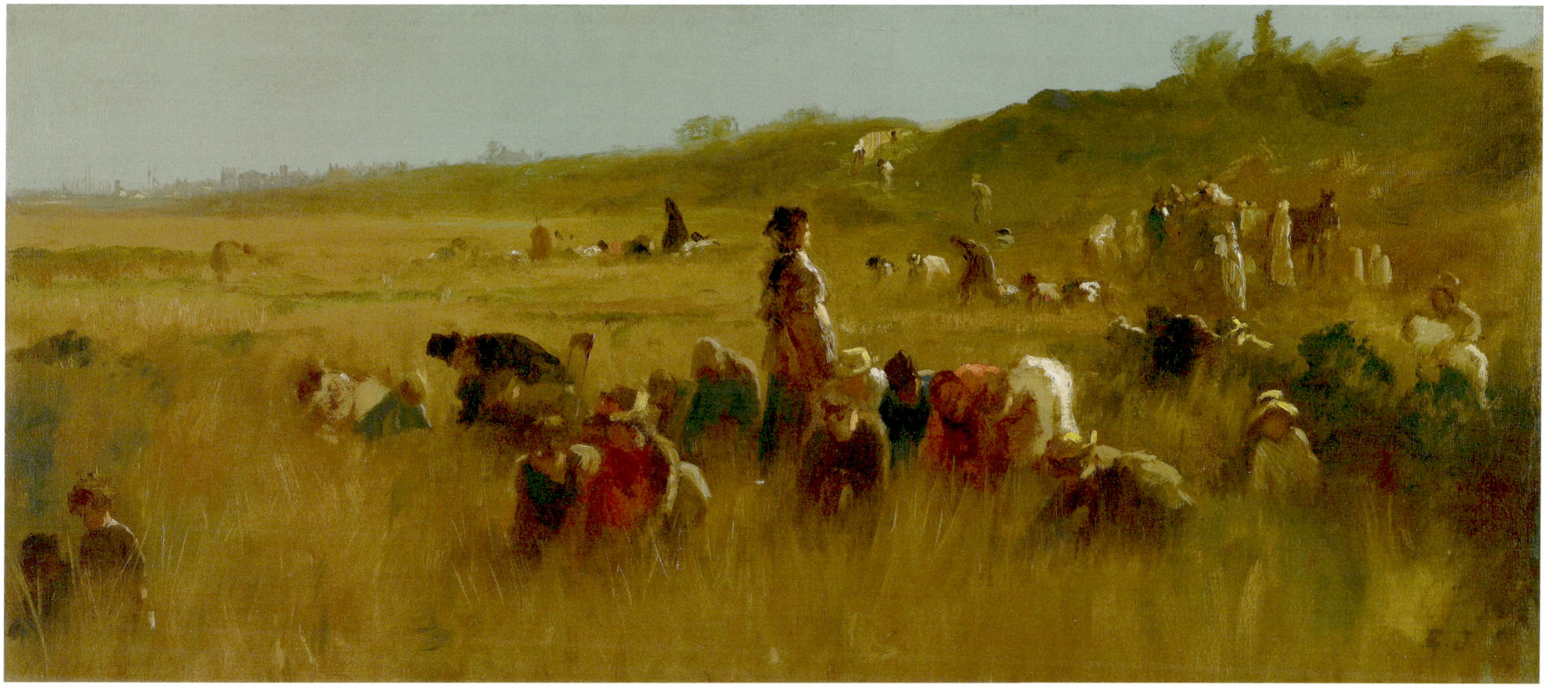

ALFRED THOMPSON BRICHER (1837–1908)

View of Mount Washington

1864
Oil on canvas
34 × 60 in. (86.4 × 152.4 cm)

Alfred Thompson Bricher was an aspiring young landscape artist when he painted this large and ambitious view of Mount Washington, the loftiest peak in New England. A native of New Hampshire, the White Mountains were home territory for Bricher. They were also a major tourist destination in the mid-nineteenth century, and one of the prime sketching grounds for American landscape painters. In 1860 Bricher had opened a studio in Boston, where his neighbor was fellow artist Martin Johnson Heade. His sketching itineraries included the New England coast as well as landscape sites in New York State and the mountains of New Hampshire. He first exhibited in Boston, in 1864, and in 1866 the noted commercial publishing firm L. Prang & Company produced the earliest in a series of chromolithographs after his landscape paintings. In 1868 the artist married and relocated to New York City, where he was active for several decades, gaining a reputation as a skilled interpreter of coastal scenery.[1] Bricher came to be celebrated for his sensitivity to luminous atmosphere, a characteristic already apparent in his early masterwork *View of Mount Washington*.

Bricher's expansive landscape invites comparison with John Frederick Kensett's *View of Mount Washington* (p. 72), a classic image of the iconic peak painted a dozen years earlier. Kensett's vigorous painting is steeped in the wilderness sublime vision of Thomas Cole, with a rugged foreground plateau populated by indigenous Americans. Bricher's canvas presents a more modern interpretation of the landscape, allied to the luminist interests of the 1860s. The artist chose a vantage point where the broad plain of the Saco River provides a quiet, light-filled foreground and middle distance for the viewer's vista of the distant peaks. Bricher also utilized the panoramic format then favored by landscape painters such as Kensett and Sanford Robinson Gifford, which emphasized the horizontality of the composition despite the mountainous subject matter.

While *View of Mount Washington* celebrates the New Hampshire wilderness, Bricher's painting also signals the region's appeal as a summer touring destination for city dwellers from Boston, New York, and Philadelphia. In this domesticated wilderness, Native Americans are no more; instead, a sportsman glides his canoe across the polished, reflective waters while a comrade waits on shore. Brilliant fall foliage glowing amid deep green conifers completes Bricher's poetic vision of the American wilderness in autumn. LSF

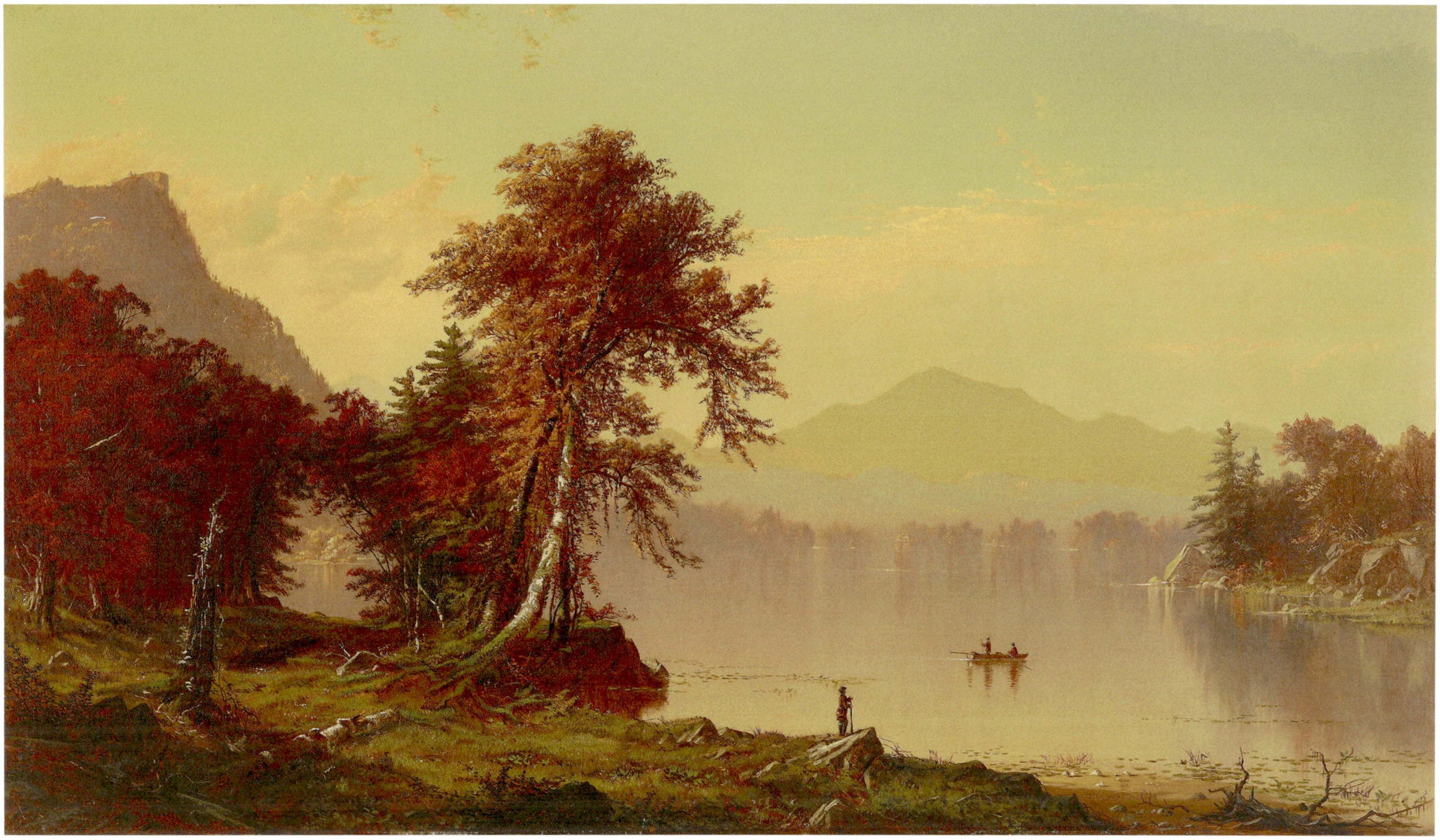

ROBERT SELDON DUNCANSON (1821–1872)

Landscape

1865
Oil on canvas
13 × 25 in. (33 × 63.5 cm)

Born in New York to mulatto parents descended from freed Virginia slaves, Robert Seldon Duncanson was among the nation's leading landscape painters in the mid-nineteenth century and the first African American artist to gain international renown. *Landscape* is one of a number of Canadian views he painted during a two-year sojourn in the modern-day province of Quebec between 1863 and 1865.

Duncanson was part of a talented group of mid-century American landscape painters, which also included William Louis Sonntag and Worthington Whittredge, who established themselves in the vicinity of Cincinnati, Ohio, an active commercial and cultural hub on the nation's western frontier. Cincinnati also was an abolitionist stronghold, which afforded the mixed-race painter supportive patrons for his ambitious artistic enterprise.[1] Primarily self-taught, Duncanson's work nevertheless demonstrates the influence of the Hudson River School and especially its unofficial leader, Thomas Cole, who spent some of his early career in Ohio. Like Cole, Duncanson's oeuvre encompassed imaginative outdoor scenes based on literary and historical sources as well as carefully studied descriptions of the natural world, such as *Landscape*. His artistic accomplishments were widely acclaimed by the late 1850s. The *Daily Cincinnati Gazette* reported in 1861 that Duncanson had "long enjoyed the enviable reputation as the best landscape painter in the West."[2]

Using Cincinnati as his home base, the peripatetic artist traveled extensively in search of picturesque scenery. It was political circumstances, however, that prompted Duncanson to cross the border into Canada in 1863. Two years into the American Civil War and with no end to the conflict in sight, the artist departed the United States in an effort to find a place "where his color did not prevent his association with other artists and his entrance into good society."[3] When Duncanson arrived in Montreal he was warmly received as an artist of repute, and he exhibited his works there to great acclaim.[4]

Strategically located on the Saint Lawrence River, Montreal was the center of the Canadian timber business in the mid-nineteenth century. During his two summers in Canada, Duncanson sketched numerous landscape views between his base, in Montreal, and Quebec City to the east, working up paintings in the fall for exhibition in the winter or spring. *Landscape*, which depicts loggers shepherding rafts down a watery channel, likely represents either an actual site or a composite of various locales along the Saint Lawrence.

Landscape is a rare extant Duncanson painting that depicts people at work. As detailed in the canvas, lumbermen typically transported their harvest from remote forests to the major markets in the form of simple rafts made by lashing together partially milled logs.[5] Yet the loggers' hard manual labor is ultimately subordinated to the quiet beauty of the landscape. Rendered as no more than a few small strokes of color from a fine-tipped brush, the floating figures are subsumed by their natural environment. The entire composition is bathed in the soft, golden glow of sunset, a visual effect that unifies the scene and recasts a mundane, workaday activity into pure poetry.

EDS

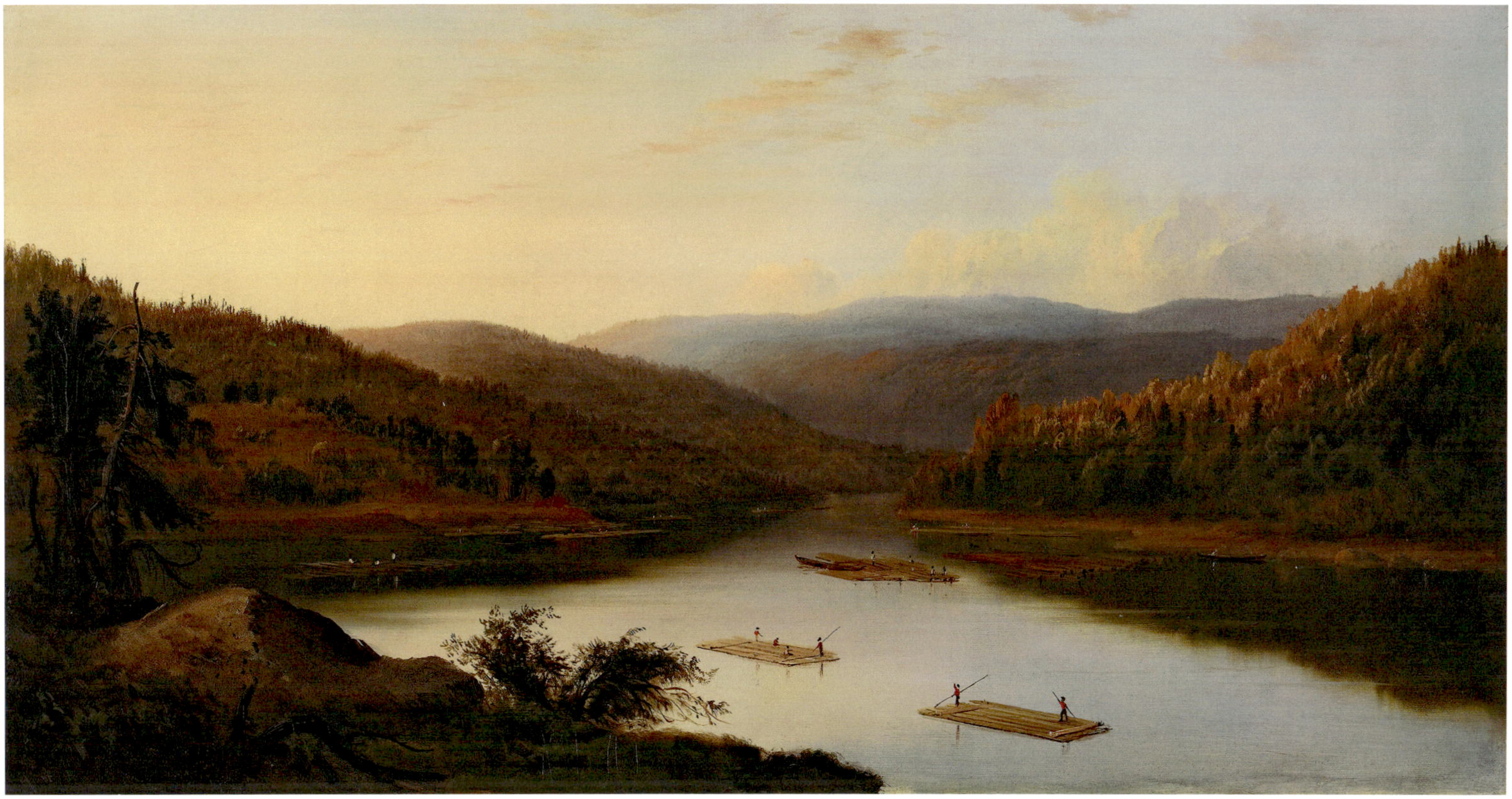

WORTHINGTON WHITTREDGE (1820–1910)

Twilight on the Plains, Platte River, Colorado

ca. 1866–67
Oil on canvas
14½ × 29 in. (36.8 × 73.7 cm)
Promised Gift

Worthington Whittredge made the first of three sketching trips west—to Colorado and New Mexico, with General John Pope—in the summer of 1866. At that point in his career, Whittredge was a well-established member of the Hudson River School with a studio in the prestigious Tenth Street Studio Building in New York City. Prior to his arrival in New York, he had spent ten years studying landscape painting in Europe. Although this training abroad was vital to his artistic development, upon his return to the United States Whittredge found it difficult to shed European conventions and look at his native landscape with fresh eyes. The arid, low-lying plains of the American West offered a type of scenery with little precedent in European art, allowing him to develop his own distinct vision of the land.[1]

Whittredge began sketches for *Twilight on the Plains, Platte River, Colorado* in late June, as Pope's party traveled along the South Platte River toward Denver.[2] Although the *Rocky Mountain News* recorded that the artist was "in ecsta[s]ies over our mountains and hopes to have a nearer view of them before he leaves," Whittredge claimed to prefer the scenery of the plains.[3] "I had never seen the plains or anything like them," he later wrote. "They impressed me deeply. I cared more for them than for the mountains, and very few of my western pictures have been produced from sketches made in the mountains. Whoever crossed the plains at that period . . . could hardly fail to be impressed with its vastness and silence and the appearance everywhere of an innocent, primitive existence."[4]

Whittredge's canvas, which is twice as wide as it is high, emphasizes the insistent horizontality of the plains landscape. His simple composition divides easily into four bands of color: silvery water, red plains, purple mountains, and a pink-tinged sky. The colors are close to one another in hue and intensity, lending harmony to the composition. The small row of trees at either edge of the canvas, the brilliant dots of white and red that compose the encampment of Ute Indians along the shore, and the lone rider on a black horse at the bank of the river form the only verticals. The Ute camp, though a subtle visual presence, plays an important role in the painting. It demonstrates not only the scale and habitability of the plains, but also the historic associations of Native American peoples with the primordial or arcadian landscape that the artist sought to portray.

Over the course of the next eleven years, Whittredge would paint more than forty western landscapes.[5] These scenes of quiet, open spaces contrast markedly with the densely wooded groves he recorded during his summer sketching tours in the East. They likewise differed from the dramatic, mountainous frontier images of Albert Bierstadt and Thomas Moran. Whittredge's western work helped the artist expand his pictorial repertoire and hone his skills while recording an often-overlooked feature of the American landscape.

LS

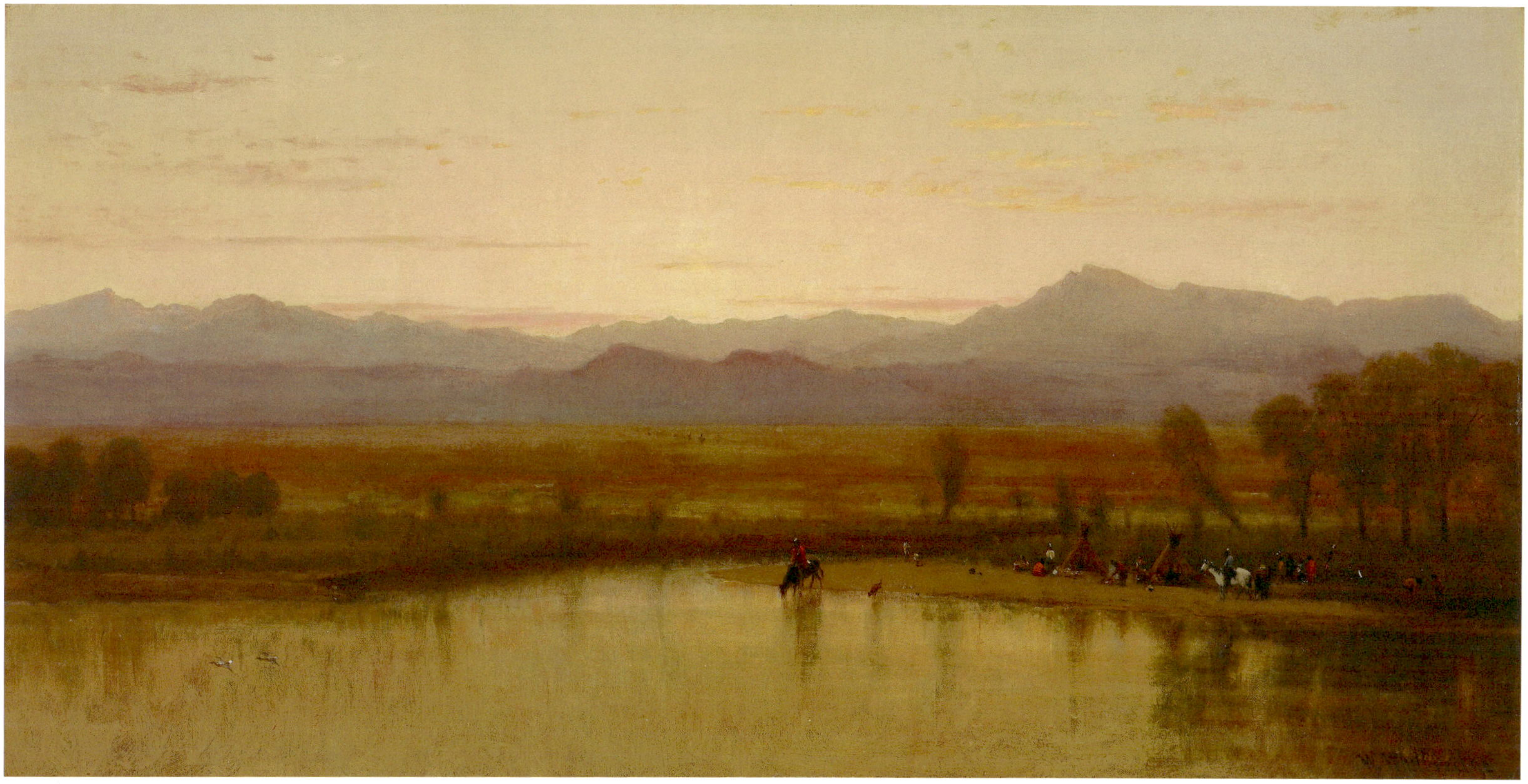

THOMAS MORAN (1837–1926)

Green River, Wyoming

1878
Oil on panel
11½ × 36 in. (29.2 × 91.4 cm)
Promised Gift

Thomas Moran quickly mastered the panoramic vision that dominated American landscape painting in the second half of the nineteenth century, as demonstrated by *Valley of the Catawissa in Autumn* (p. 78), his exciting depiction of the forests of northeastern Pennsylvania dating from about 1862. Moran's thorough knowledge of contemporary trends in landscape painting together with his early apprenticeship to a Philadelphia wood engraver and illustrator enabled him to flourish as an artist-illustrator, and these combined skills provided the turning point of his career. In 1871, a commission from *Scribner's Monthly* to improve the drawing in an amateur field surveyor's sketches of the Yellowstone region for publication in the popular illustrated periodical galvanized Moran to go west. He promptly applied for permission to accompany the surveying party of Ferdinand V. Hayden to the headwaters of the Yellowstone River, in the Wyoming Territory. The paintings that resulted from his 1871 journey not only earned Moran a national reputation as a visual interpreter of the American frontier, but also determined the course of his long and productive career.[1]

On this first trip west, Moran traveled to Yellowstone via the Green River Valley of Wyoming, then the western terminus of the Union Pacific Railroad. There he completed and carefully documented his "First Sketch Made in the West at Green River, Wyoming" (Gilcrease Museum), a watercolor study depicting the Citadel and Castle Rocks, the imposing, variegated buttes that rise high above the winding river. This small watercolor served as source material for the series of paintings, watercolors, and illustrations that established the Green River Valley, along with the sights of Yellowstone, as the artist's signature themes. Moran would visit the region again in 1879, fortifying his visual arsenal in preparation to create another series of Green River landscapes that extended into the twentieth century. The popularity of Moran's subject in its many variations over the decades signals the strong impression these natural landmarks made on his audience. The monumentality of the geological formations, whose architectonic forms were the result of prehistoric volcanic eruptions and whose multicolored striations were sculpted by millennia of erosion by wind and water, were as exotic and otherworldly as Yellowstone's amazing natural features.

In *Green River, Wyoming*, the powerful visual impact of these rock formations is reinforced by the monotony of the surrounding terrain. The buttes rise abruptly from the desert plain, the wide expanse of calm water mirroring their profiles as well as the turbulent sky above. The emphatic horizontality of Moran's composition and its illusion of depth present an extended topographical survey of the site, offering a sense of its open landscape. The viewer's somewhat elevated sightline is commanding and virtually unlimited. In an act of creative license, Moran edited out both the town and the Union Pacific railroad terminus along the riverside, substituting a graceful cavalcade of Native Americans on horseback that evokes the region's pre-settlement past. Although moderate in scale compared to other versions of this theme, Moran's *Green River, Wyoming* is romantically vast in scope, presenting a superb expression in its exaggerated panoramic format of aesthetically "possessing" the landscape, a visual thrill that is linked to the Anglo-American drive toward territorial expansion known as Manifest Destiny. LSF

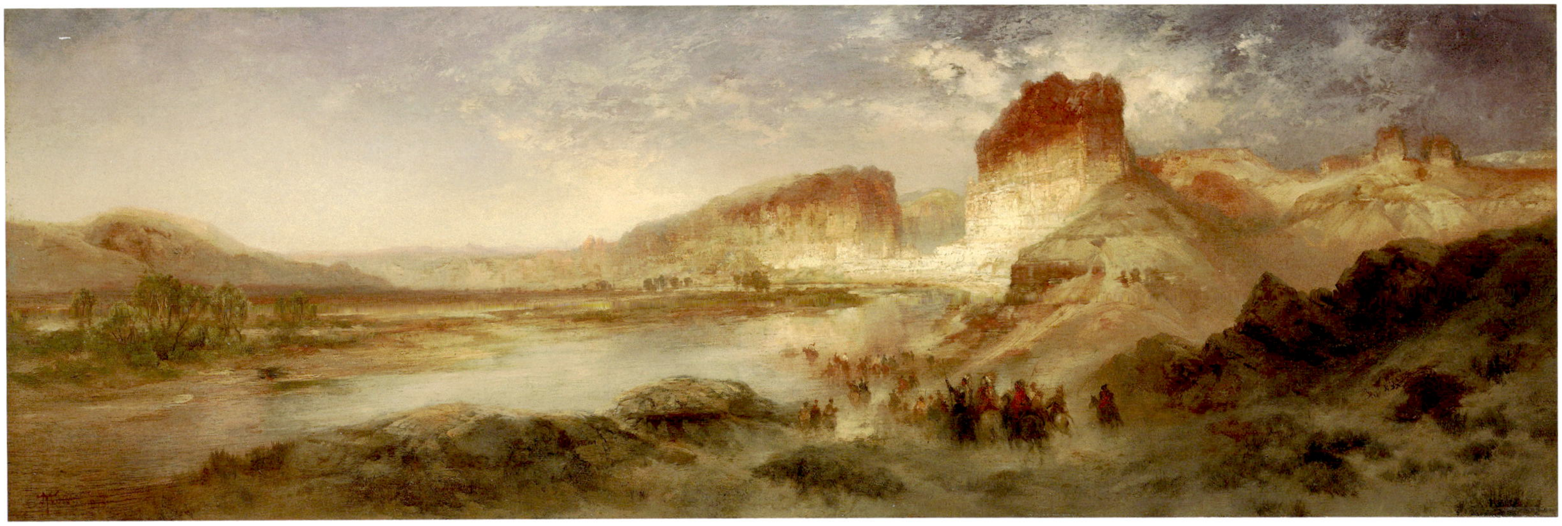

GEORGE INNESS (1825–1894)

Sunset on the River

1867
Oil on canvas
30½ × 45½ in. (77.5 × 115.6 cm)
Promised Gift

From 1863 through 1867, the landscape painter George Inness lived and worked as a drawing instructor at Eagleswood, an elite utopian community and military academy on the Raritan River, near Perth Amboy, New Jersey. As partial payment for his lodging there, Inness produced the monumental 1865 painting *Peace and Plenty* (The Metropolitan Museum of Art), which hung in the home of Marcus and Rebecca Buffum Spring, Eagleswood's proprietors. In the waning months of the seemingly interminable Civil War, Rebecca "daily . . . faced the picture of Peace and Plenty [and] prayed that peace might come soon." She was "enraptured" with the dark, majestic canvas, which represented "her dream of the Kingdom of God, with final peace and abundance on earth."[1]

During his Eagleswood years, Inness frequently took trips north, to the area around the hamlet of Leeds, in the Catskills. It was here, in upstate New York, where the artist drew preliminary sketches for a remarkable group of pastoral paintings.[2] Perhaps the most majestic of these works is *Sunset on the River*, a canvas that, like *Peace and Plenty*, elicits emotional responses by way of dramatic lighting and deep vistas rendered with painterly brushstrokes. While at Eagleswood, Inness immersed himself in the writings and philosophies of the eighteenth-century Swedish mystic Emanuel Swedenborg.[3] With the peaceful bovine kingdom in the foreground and the church steeple in the right middle ground, crowned by looming, wrathful thunderclouds that both illuminate and obscure myriad hues of green, brown, and yellow in the gently sloping meadow, *Sunset on the River* suggests something of the renewed spirituality in Inness's personal life and artistic practice. One might not pray to *Sunset on the River* as Rebecca Buffum Spring did to *Peace and Plenty*, but the artist nevertheless went to great lengths to locate archetypal nature as the site where celestial and terrestrial realms meet.

Sunset on the River is also highly significant as a visual expression of changing popular conceptions of nature in nineteenth-century America. Prior to his Eagleswood sojourn, Inness had adhered to the stylistic and thematic parameters of the so-called Hudson River School, which were exemplified by highly descriptive, halcyon idylls such as Thomas Cole's *View of Mount Etna* (p. 60) and Frederic Edwin Church's *Home by the Lake* (p. 70). Beginning in the late 1860s with *Sunset on the River* and related paintings, Inness increasingly used loosely applied brushstrokes and a vibrant palette to create painterly images in which broad planes of color subsume natural minutiae. Subtle and gradual as this stylistic shift was, it reflected the growing conviction among painters, authors, and philosophers of the day that the world was properly known not through precise vision but through generalized masses and ethereal forms. As Inness himself put the matter in 1878, "You must suggest to me reality, you can never show me reality."[4] Attending to the complex and idiosyncratic nature of human vision, *Sunset on the River* foreshadowed poetic works such as James McNeill Whistler's *Green and Violet: The Evening Walk* (p. 160) and anticipated the course of abstraction in late nineteenth- and early twentieth-century American landscape painting.

LGM

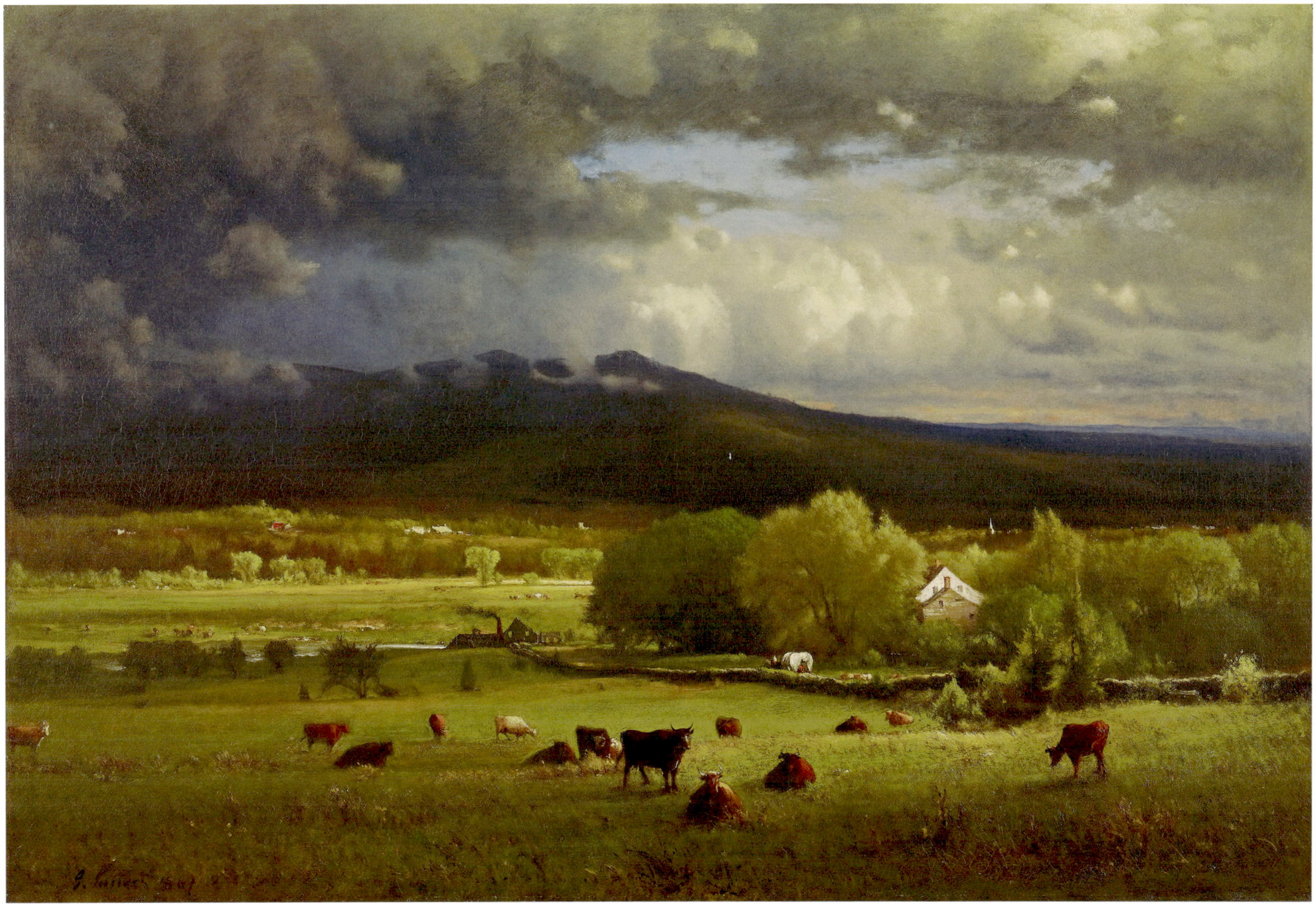

WINSLOW HOMER (1836–1910)

The Return of the Gleaner

1867
Oil on canvas
24 × 18 in. (61 × 45.7 cm)

Winslow Homer is best known for the epic seascapes he created in Maine after 1890. However, the largely self-taught Boston-area native devoted the initial thirty years of his career to narrative painting, centering his first oils on Civil War themes before devoting more than a decade primarily to images of women and children in rural settings. *The Return of the Gleaner*, one of about twenty paintings Homer completed during a ten-month stay in France in 1867, belongs to the group of works that chronicle the artist's transition from war-related subjects to rural genre scenes.[1]

Homer was thirty years old when he first traveled abroad, at the end of 1866. The selection of two of his paintings to represent the United States at the 1867 Exposition Universelle in Paris likely prompted his trip, but the artist had hoped to visit Europe since the early 1860s.[2] The delay, however, allowed him to arrive in Paris with a solid reputation as an illustrator and a first great artistic success with *Prisoners from the Front* (1866, The Metropolitan Museum of Art), which he had exhibited to great acclaim at the National Academy of Design earlier that year.

The Return of the Gleaner relates to agricultural subjects Homer had explored on native soil between 1864 and 1866, most notably *The Veteran in a New Field* (1865, The Metropolitan Museum of Art), which similarly depicts a single figure silhouetted against a wall of golden wheat. However, while Homer's painting of a recently returned war veteran is a highly symbolic work that is at once a poignant elegy on the nation's wrenching losses and an expression of its potential for regeneration, *The Return of the Gleaner* is primarily a formal exercise. Dressed in French peasant garb and carrying a common European hayfork of the day, Homer's gleaner reflects the American painter's admiration for Jean-François Millet and other Barbizon artists with whose work he had first become familiar in the mid-1850s, in Boston.[3]

Homer was sympathetic to the rural motifs of French artists like Millet and Jules Breton, but more importantly he embraced the Barbizon painters' simple yet striking compositions. Here, as in *Veteran in a New Field*, the artist appropriated the Barbizon strategy of placing a single standing figure against a background composed of horizontal bands of sky and earth, masterfully balancing figure and landscape to suggest the elemental relationship between man—or in this case, woman—and nature. Yet neither Homer's subject matter nor his style is wholly French. The artist's painterly technique in *The Return of the Gleaner*, characterized by the bold application of color in alternately broad and choppy strokes, predated his European sojourn. The gleaner's assertive, frontal pose, the strong diagonal of the two-pronged wooden hayfork she balances on her right shoulder, and the dramatic contrasts between light and shadow betray important lessons about compositional design Homer had learned during his early career as an illustrator. Moreover, the stalwart figure, with a stern gaze and ruddy complexion, suggests the increased self-assurance associated with young women in post–Civil War America more than a peasant girl in the French countryside.[4]

MCC

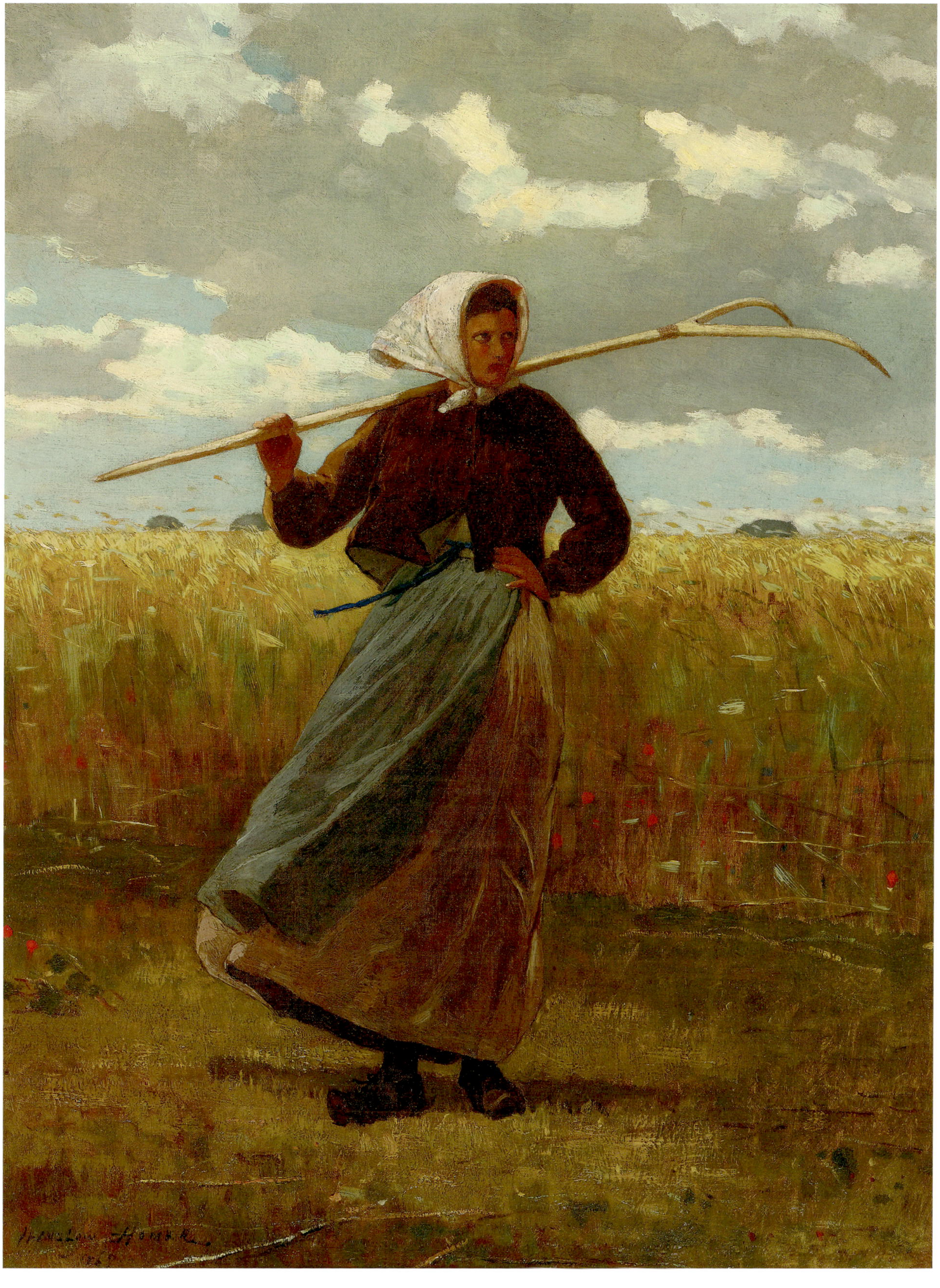

WINSLOW HOMER (1836–1910)

Spring

1878
Watercolor and pencil on paper
11¼ × 8¾ in. (28.6 × 22.2 cm)

Between 1859 and 1884, Winslow Homer often spent most of his summers and early autumns away from his primary residence in New York City. On these rural excursions he sketched, painted, and enjoyed his favorite pastime, fishing. In the summer of 1878, Homer traveled to Massachusetts and upstate New York, including Houghton Farm, the country home of his friend and patron Lawson Valentine. Over the course of several visits to the estate that year and the next, the artist created about fifty watercolors, including Crystal Bridges' *Spring.*[1]

Watercolor played an important role in Homer's art throughout his career. In the late 1850s and early 1860s, he frequently used thin, transparent washes to produce unified areas of monochromatic tone in the illustrations he created for *Harper's Weekly* and other magazines. Homer began his first concentrated work in watercolor in the summer of 1873. Over the next five years he explored the medium's expressive possibilities for a variety of subjects, from African Americans to women at leisure. The theme of children in rural settings, however, predominated in his art during the second half of 1878 and in 1879.

Although the identities of the children depicted in *Spring* are known—they were members of the Babcock family, farm squatters who lived near the Valentine property—such particulars were immaterial to Homer.[2] Indeed, the artist appears to have been most interested in conveying the light and color of the scene and creating an air of silence.[3] Silhouetted against a rural landscape with a high horizon, the girl and boy are posed to avoid eye contact with the viewer and each other. They inhabit separate spheres despite their pairing at the fence. Homer enhanced the image's pervading, if understated, tension by juxtaposing color harmonies such as the pink-purple of the girl's dress and the vibrant green of the field and foliage, and through an asymmetrical balance of form. These artistic strategies reflect Homer's interest in the color theories of French chemist Michel Eugène Chevreul and the unconventional compositions of Japanese prints.

In 1879, Homer exhibited *Spring* and twenty-eight other recent watercolors at the twelfth annual exhibition of the American Watercolor Society. These images captured the critics' attention as particularly original and American, especially in contrast to the nearly abstract works exhibited by Joseph Frank Currier, a young American just returned from Munich. If Currier's sheets were viewed as "arbitrary and capricious blots of color rudely splashed about the paper," Homer's contributions to the exhibition were applauded for their "naturalness," a quality that was viewed as uniquely American. Homer's farm children, noted William Laffan of the *New York Sun*, were "wholesome" and "hearty," and "full of that sense of dawning responsibility . . . that make[s] the seriousness of childhood so wholly inscrutable."[4]

Homer's great facility with the transparent medium also contributed significantly to these works' success. The suggestion of dewy, springlike moisture and the appearance of mottled light like that in the Crystal Bridges' sheet, the result of pigment particles settling on the high points of the textured paper, suggested a "peculiar lightness, brightness, and clearness" that the writer for *Frank Leslie's Illustrated Newspaper* and others found particular to the American landscape.[5] Indeed, the combination of subject and style evident in *Spring* brought all the critics in agreement with Laffan, who wrote that Homer's watercolors "should be considered apart . . . just as they stand in American art."[6]

MCC

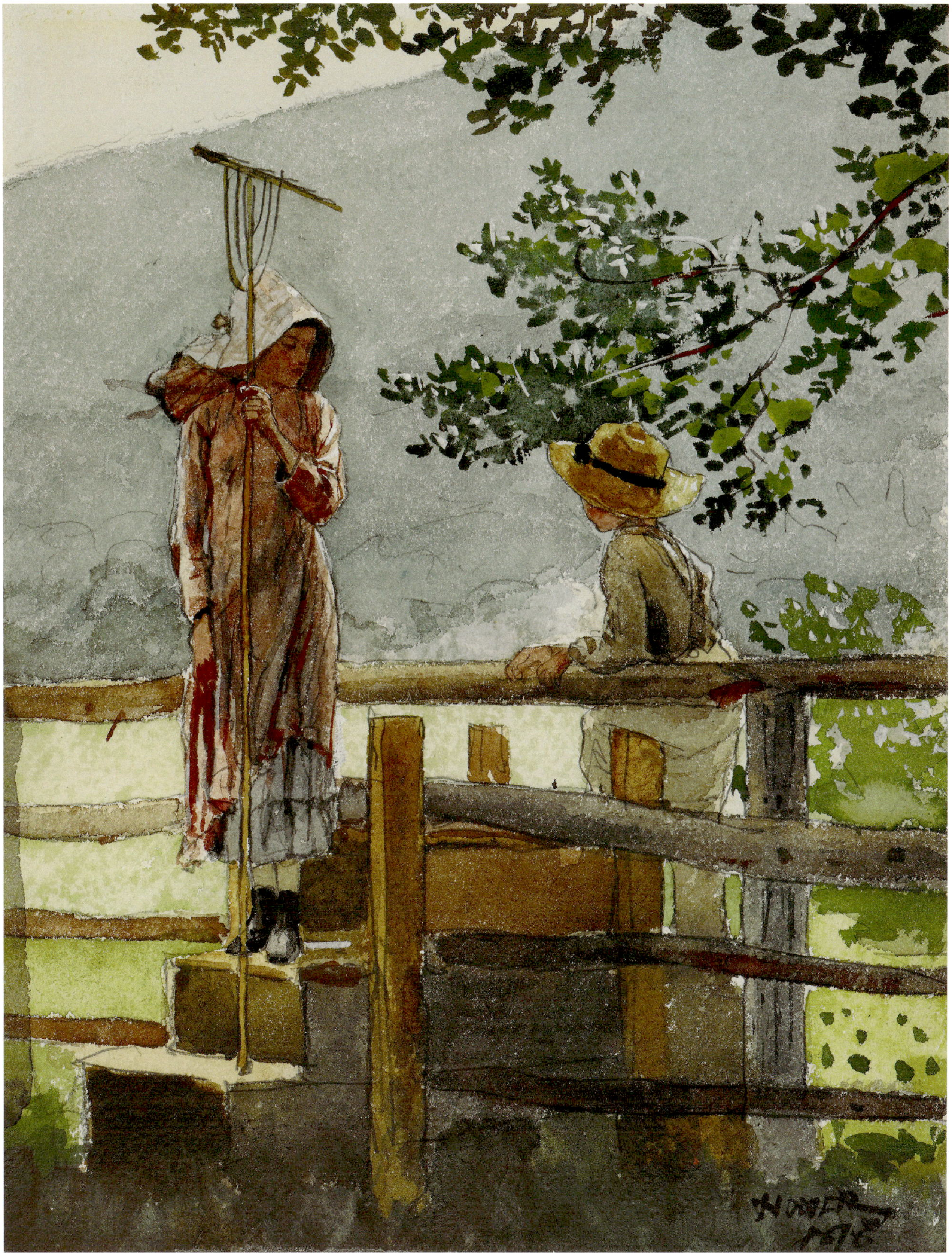
HOMER
1878

WINSLOW HOMER (1836–1910)

On the Beach, Tynemouth

1881
Watercolor and pencil on paper
13⅝ × 19¼ in. (34.6 × 48.9 cm)

In 1880, when Winslow Homer spent the summer in the seaport of Gloucester, Massachusetts, he was fully conversant with American art's increasingly cosmopolitan outlook. As he considered the next steps for his own art, he concentrated on marine subjects, experimenting with different watercolor techniques. In March 1881, just after his forty-fifth birthday and having received diverse responses to his past summer's work, he sailed for England for a twenty-month stay at Cullercoats, on the North Sea, a trip that scholars have long recognized as instrumental in his artistic development.[1]

Although he never divulged the reasons for this second and final trip abroad or his choice of destination, Homer knew a number of American painters who had lived in England or were current residents; he was also certainly aware of the Anglophilia sweeping the United States.[2] Landing in Liverpool, the artist first stopped in London before settling in Cullercoats, a village two miles from the town of Tynemouth, and less than ten miles from the bustling coal-mining and shipbuilding center of Newcastle-upon-Tyne. *On the Beach, Tynemouth* is one of 110 drawings and watercolors that resulted from this trip. Like the majority of these sheets, it chronicles the everyday lives of the local community's hardy fisherfolk.[3] Beautifully rendered in a palette of blues and browns accented with red details and bright white highlights, the Crystal Bridges sheet reflects Homer's three primary artistic concerns while in England: drawing the figure; honing his watercolor technique in the British tradition; and identifying subjects of significance on par with those he had created during the Civil War.

The two women and a child at the center of *On the Beach* fit together like puzzle pieces, anchoring the image's composition and theme. This carefully outlined, close massing of figures, a new trait common to many of Homer's Cullercoats compositions, may have been inspired by the artist's visits to London's British Museum, where the collection included ancient Greek sculpture and old master figure drawings by such artists as Michelangelo and Raphael.[4] The solid shape of each girl's body, created from a sophisticated weave of light and shade made of transparent wash and pencil outline, likewise may derive in part from the much-lauded watercolors of J. M. W. Turner, examples of which were available for study at the British Museum. The refined gradation of tone and color in *On the Beach*, evident especially in the wet sand in the foreground, suggests Homer's firsthand study of Turner's art.[5]

Although neither the physically largest of the Cullercoats sheets nor the most monumental in theme, *On the Beach* shares an increased gravity with most of Homer's 1881–82 subjects. The sky full of stormy clouds, its mottled appearance achieved by a blotting technique Homer may have learned from a popular English watercolor manual, suggests an ominous outcome for the girls and the absent fishermen for whom they appear to be scanning the sea.[6] The massive empty vessel against which the girls are partially silhouetted enhances their prominence, but through contrast of scale also suggests the figures' vulnerability. Indeed, this beached boat reminds viewers of those already returned to shore and heightens the sense of peril the stalwart fisherwomen and men of Cullercoats faced daily. With his Cullercoats pictures, Homer joined other late nineteenth-century realist painters on both sides of the Atlantic in honoring heroic laborers.[7] On the North Sea coast he also identified what would become the essence of his art for years to come—picturing the relationship between man and nature. MCC

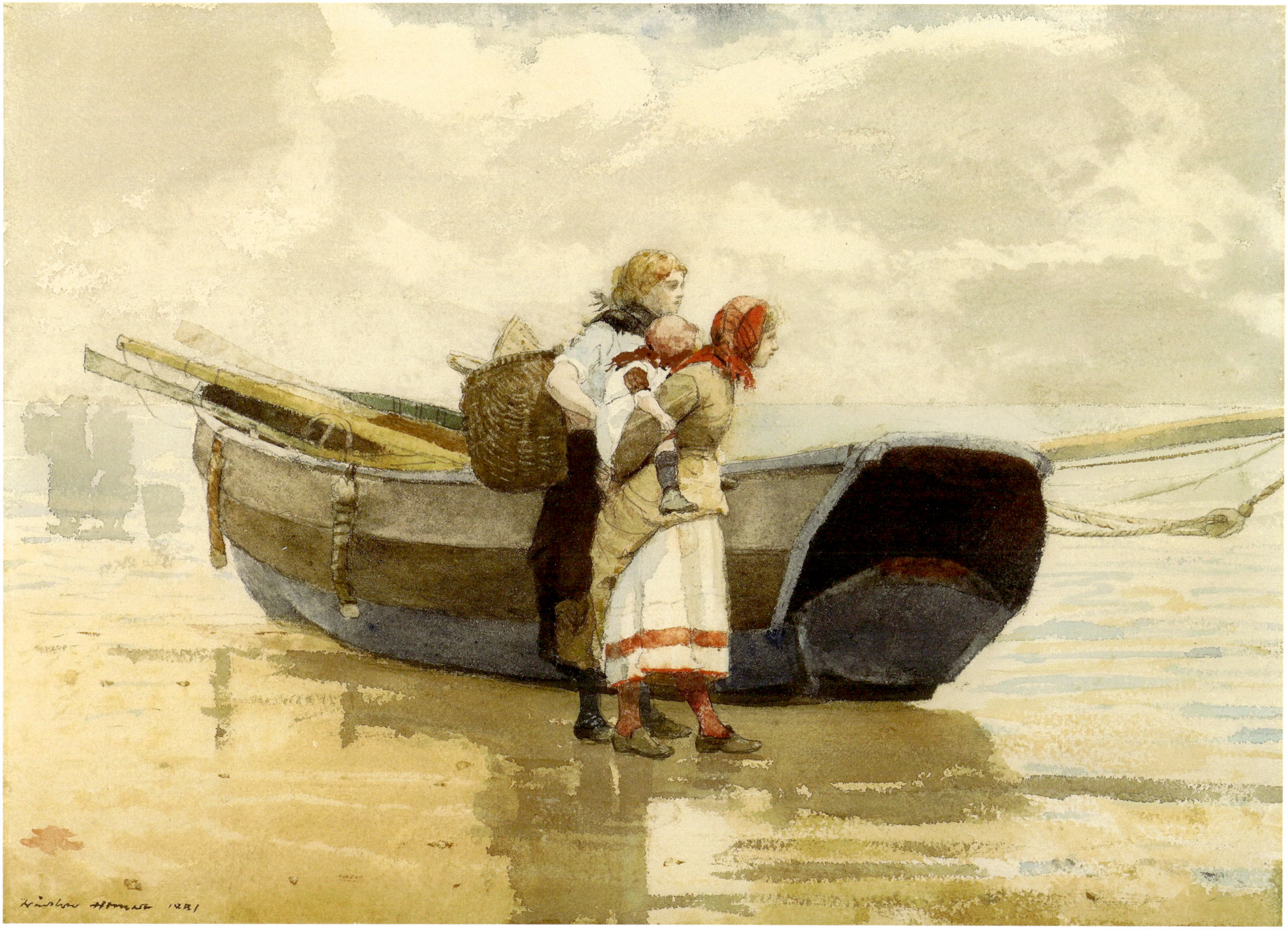

JOSEPH DECKER (1853–1924)

Basket of Peaches

ca. 1885
Oil on canvas
12 × 22 in. (30.5 × 55.9 cm)

The Brooklyn-based artist Joseph Decker brought an idiosyncratic eye to the centuries-old tradition of still-life painting with vividly realized images such as *Basket of Peaches*, from about 1885. Born in Württemberg, Germany, Decker immigrated to the United States as a teen. In young adulthood, he pursued training at the Royal Academy in Munich as well as at the National Academy of Design in New York, where he studied alongside William M. Harnett, who would become the premier still-life painter in late nineteenth-century America. Decker's career spanned three decades and included work in the modes of portraiture, landscape, genre painting, and especially still life, the last of which accounts for over half of his known images.[1] At the height of his renown, the artist exhibited at major American art venues including the National Academy of Design, Brooklyn Art Association, and Art Institute of Chicago.

Sweet edibles such as fruit and candy dominate Decker's still-life paintings. Yet the artist's approach to depicting these delicacies proved unpalatable to many viewers of his day. Critics readily acknowledged that the painter's subjects were "exquisitely drawn," but often complained that his fresh fruit and confections were "finished to the point of inanity."[2] Indeed, Decker's close-up, carefully observed, unsparingly truthful compositions seem to revel in imperfection. Unripe fruit—one critic described the artist as the "poet of green apples and greener pears"—and diseased specimens prevail.[3]

In *Basket of Peaches,* a number of the warm-hued stone fruits retain a tinge of green, suggesting they have not yet reached their peak of ripeness. Moreover, the fruit's soft flesh is marred by small, sunken, dark flecks ringed with yellow that suggest the presence of a disease known as bacterial spot. This image of an overturned basket of peaches is likely the painting Decker exhibited at the National Academy of Design in 1885 under the title *Upset*. The canvas elicited some of the artist's harshest criticism. A critic for *The Studio* lamented, "And what has got into Mr. Decker's head, with cholera coming on, to offer us his hard green pears, and harder peaches? What can be his ideas of the pictorial art, when he presents to us, as pictures, such unrelieved and impossible masses of raw green and rawer red?"[4]

Contemporary viewers' decidedly cool response to *Basket of Peaches* and other of Decker's meticulously painted still-life pictures may have been a visceral reaction to confounded expectations. The painter's diseased fruit flew in the face of artistic convention, in which the kitchen still life symbolized and celebrated nature's fecundity. Although material plenty is suggested by the sheer number of peaches spilling out of the wooden basket and the artist's close crop of the image so that the fruit fills nearly the whole canvas, the peaches' unripe and bacteria-infested condition compromises the promise of this bountiful offering. The stark contrast between the solidly rendered, highly descriptive fruit and the painterly, gestural foliage and grass that serve as a shallow backdrop underscores the contradictory nature of Decker's provocative pictures. EDS

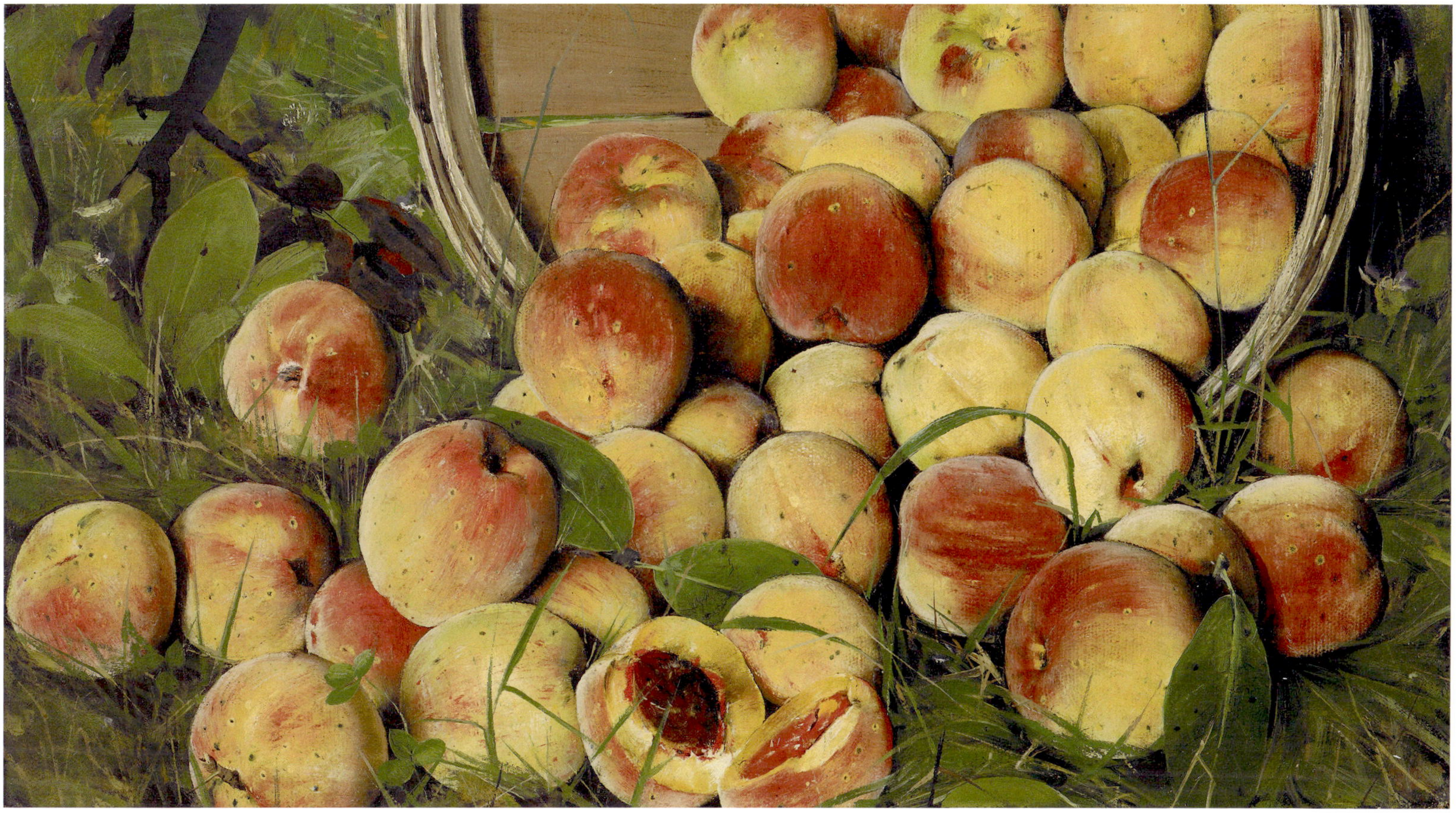

JOHN HABERLE (1856–1933)

Small Change

1887
Oil on canvas
9¼ × 7¼ in. (23.5 × 18.4 cm)

Interest in trompe l'oeil (fool the eye) paintings of money peaked in the United States during the last quarter of the nineteenth century, and John Haberle was among the genre's most successful practitioners. Haberle's precisely painted renderings of paper currency and coinage playfully dismantled the boundary between reality and illusion. The fact that they were greeted with both derision and delight offers an index to the cultural, social, and economic transformations of the post–Civil War period. For example, while a writer for the *Chicago Tribune* condescended that an artist as talented as Haberle would "waste time and ability upon such worthlesness [*sic*]," the painter did not lack for patrons, counting among the early purchasers of his work Thomas B. Clarke, the most prominent collector of American art of the period.[1] If the numerous accounts of bewildered spectators crowding before displays of illusionistic still-life paintings are any indication, the public found pictorial deceptions highly engaging entertainments.[2]

William Michael Harnett is credited with having invented the genre of the trompe l'oeil money picture, but he stopped producing paintings of currency in 1886 at the request of the Secret Service, who viewed them as illegal forgeries. Haberle reacted to his colleague's contretemps by producing a series of provocative pictures including *Small Change*, an inventive and witty composition involving a puzzling assortment of items arranged on a flat board. Replicated here are a well-worn one-cent copper coin depicting the figure of Liberty held in place by three tiny nails; a ten-cent bill featuring U.S. Secretary of the Treasury William M. Meredith and a torn and mended twenty-five-cent bill depicting George Washington (literally small change, the type of fractional paper certificates that were issued during the Civil War in lieu of metal coins); a tintype self-portrait; and a three-cent coin.[3] Are we confronting a visual game of association, or possibly decoding a riddle?

Haberle painted *Small Change* in 1887, the same year that he exhibited a similar picture, *Imitation* (National Gallery of Art, Washington), at the National Academy of Design in New York.[4] Reportedly, the bills portrayed in *Imitation* were so accurately painted that the Secret Service also issued Haberle a warning to stop painting currency.[5] Despite their different formats, there are several strong formal similarities between *Small Change* and *Imitation*. Both are spare, carefully balanced compositions, with objects set against a dark, wood-grained background. Haberle's meticulous, highly polished technique depended on minute, nearly indecipherable brushstrokes to render objects illusionistically. Compounding the treachery, Haberle used layers of gesso to build up the surface of his coins and paper currency, thereby adding a dimensional verisimilitude to the optical deception.

Haberle's irreverent attitude toward counterfeiting is evident in his prankish method for impressing his identity, and thus culpability, into his currency pictures. Besides including a photographic self-portrait in *Small Change*, he also added an inscription bearing his signature, "J Haberle," the date, "1887," and his hometown, "New Haven Ct," in the upper right corner. Below the faux-carved inscription is a dancing stick figure, perhaps a caricature of the artist, whose palm supports the word "New," a clever pun about the replication of old money.

REL

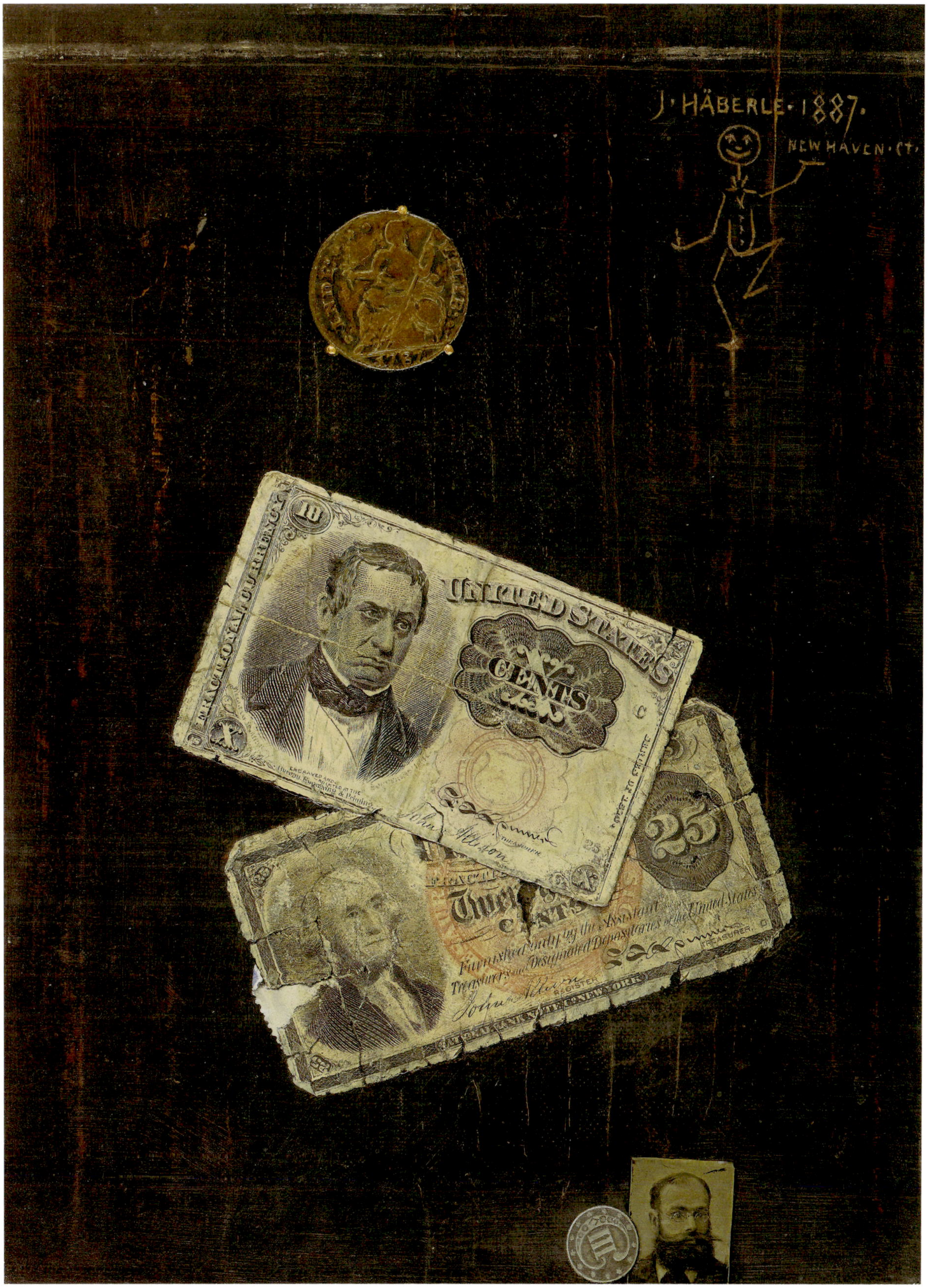
J·HÄBERLE·1887·
NEW HAVEN·CT·
UNITED STATES
CENTS
25

ALBERT PINKHAM RYDER (1847–1917)

Misty Moonlight

ca. 1885
Oil on canvas on panel
11¼ × 11¾ in. (28.6 × 29.8 cm)

> *The artist should fear to become the slave of detail. He should strive to express his thought and not the surface of it. What avails a storm cloud accurate in form and color if the storm is not therein?* —ALBERT PINKHAM RYDER[1]

Recognized for his romantic nocturnes, marine subjects, and allegorical themes, Albert Pinkham Ryder prioritized aesthetic vision over literal representation. The pioneering artist's lyrical images, often rendered by means of a unique and unorthodox painting technique, anticipated modernist trends in their nearly abstract forms as well as their emphasis on process over subject matter.

In Ryder's *Misty Moonlight*, from about 1885, a lone vessel quietly sails on the calm waters of a moonlit sea. A mélange of somber shades including olive, umber, and ochre creates a dense atmosphere. Veiled by the obscure firmament, the moon appears as a glowing orb, faintly penetrating the haze. The darkness looming overhead threatens to envelop the isolated sailboat. The sky's solemn hues graze the crests of the waves in the middle ground of the composition, reflecting the bleak sentiment and threatening intentions of the heavens. Full sails, an undulating aquatic horizon, and the highlighted peaks of rippled waves offer evidence of an unseen atmospheric element—wind—that will allow the small craft to escape the descending darkness.

Ryder's design for *Misty Moonlight* is as poetic as his subject. In an effort to express pure form and thought, the artist reduced the subject matter of his painting to its essentials, eliminating all extraneous detail. In focusing on the fundamentals (round moon, broad sky, full sails, and dark sea), Ryder was able to achieve a unified and harmonious composition unencumbered by specific iconographical associations. The painting's dense surface, which is composed of layer upon layer of dark pigments and varnish into which the artist blended unstable materials such as wax, further subdues the narrative elements of the composition in favor of conveying an overall mood.[2]

Misty Moonlight stands at the crossroads of fantasy and memory. The artist hailed from the New England coastal town of New Bedford, Massachusetts, and thus was intimately familiar with the ways of the sea. The highly atmospheric quality of his painting simultaneously evokes a dreamlike, otherworldly state and engages the senses as if in a reminiscence.

Notwithstanding Ryder's eccentric and somewhat reclusive nature, the rich surfaces, simplified forms, and strong designs of his idiosyncratic paintings inspired generations of younger American artists, including such notable figures as Arthur Bowen Davies, Marsden Hartley, and Jackson Pollock. Indeed, Ryder's protomodernist vision led to his participation in the famed Armory Show of 1913. The landmark exhibition featured ten works by the artist within its central galleries, a location reserved for legends who had challenged the academic tradition such as Jean-Auguste-Dominique Ingres, Eugène Delacroix, Francisco de Goya, Jean-Baptiste-Camille Corot, Paul Cézanne, and Vincent van Gogh.[3] Ryder was the sole American in the group.

AWJ

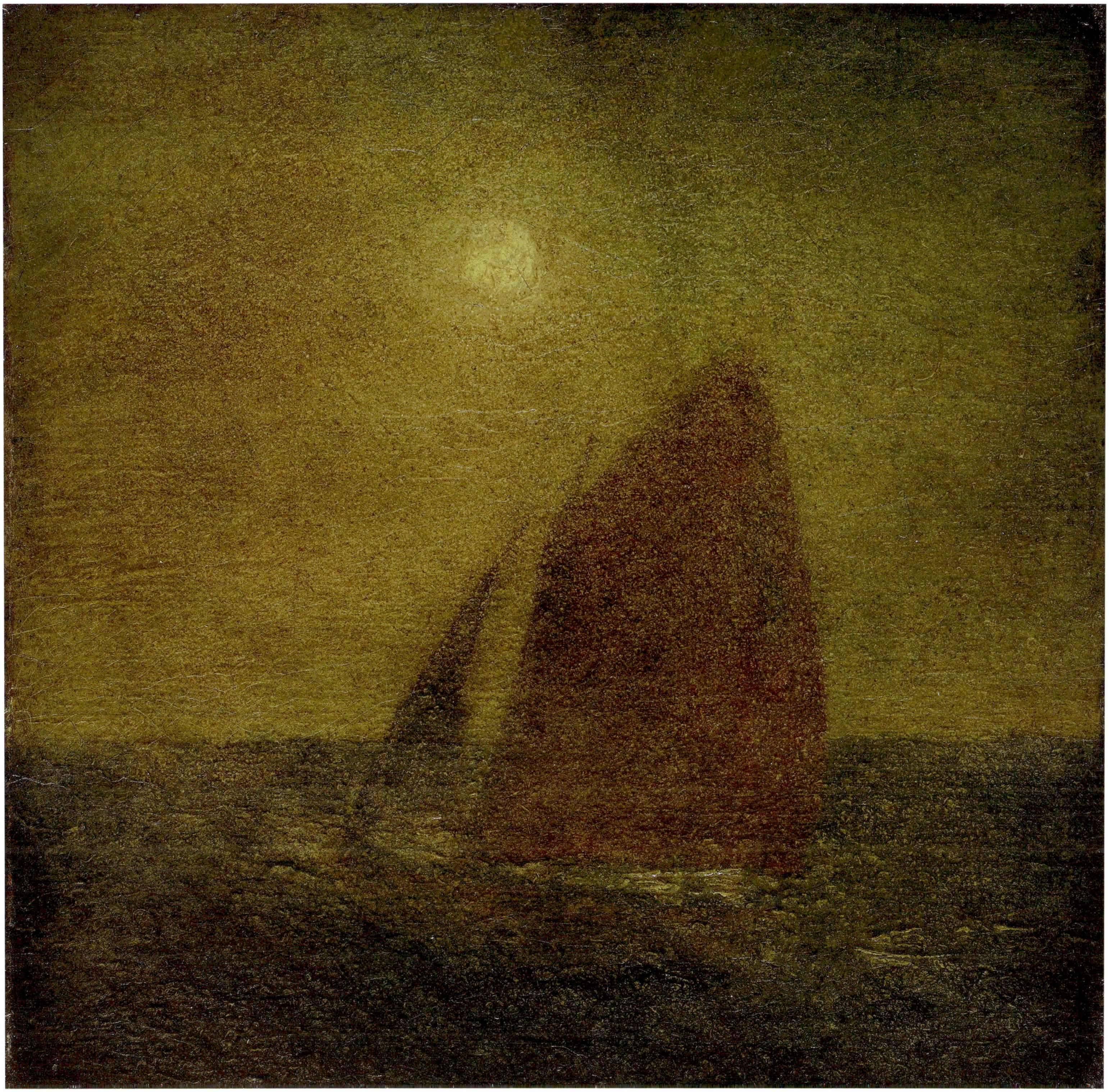

GEORGE HENRY SMILLIE (1840–1921)

Coastal Scene, New York

1885
Watercolor and pencil on paper
25 × 39 in. (63.5 × 99.1 cm)

George Henry Smillie's *Coastal Scene, New York* hails from the golden age of American watercolor—the decades around the turn of the twentieth century—when masters such as John Singer Sargent, Winslow Homer (pp. 108 and 110), and Thomas Moran were exploring the expressive possibilities of the medium in a variety of genres.[1] In the 1880s watercolors garnered as much attention as did oils, and critics often considered the watercolor offerings to be superior in quality.[2] The American Society for Painters in Water Colors (later the American Water Color Society), the governing institution for artists working in the aqueous medium, held an annual exhibition that, by 1900, rivaled in prestige that of the National Academy of Design.[3] Smillie's brother, James David, was an early member of the society; Smillie himself joined its ranks in 1868 and remained active in the organization throughout his career.[4]

One of the primary goals of the American Water Color Society was to promote the unique qualities of the medium and to encourage artists to exploit them by using medium-specific techniques. Because watercolor pigments are bound in gum arabic and suspended in water, individual layers of watercolor are semitransparent when dry. The society thus frowned upon the addition of thicker, opaque pigments, or "body color," which made watercolors behave more like oils. It also advocated direct painting, without underdrawing or sketching, in order to take advantage of the spontaneity watercolor offered.[5]

Smillie's *Coastal Scene* followed the society's recommendations. In light of the artist's chronology, the painting's inscription, "George H. Smillie—New York—1885" makes it likely the he depicted a beach in Westchester County, New York, looking out across the Long Island Sound. Smillie favored calm shoreline scenes and traveled up and down the New York and New England coasts throughout his career in search of picturesque views. In this image, nearly still, blue water dotted with sailboats is bound by a strip of white sand and a wider swath of shore composed of beach grass, low-lying shrubs, and broad, flat rocks. As was his habit, Smillie founded the composition on the juxtaposition of these clearly defined masses. "The silhouette is not everything; but it is by the silhouette that we must begin," he once advised. "Go first for broad and characteristic masses."[6]

Upon closer inspection, however, the painting's solidity gives way to a web of brushstrokes that create forms out of layers of semitransparent pigments. The foreground rocks are composed of a fluid olive wash dotted with charcoal gray, alternating with areas of light gray rubbed on with a dry brush. In keeping with the recommendations of the Water Color Society, Smillie forewent the use of a thickened white pigment, allowing reserved areas of the white page to create highlights. The thick beach grasses show greater technical complexity, with small pools of dried pigment over passages of long, bladelike brushstrokes in layers of brown, olive, gray, ochre, and green. Smillie's foreground reveals the artist working in watercolor directly on the page, with minimal use of thin, dark lines to define some of the rocks and branches. The resulting work captures the freshness and spontaneity one imagines the scene and the medium inspired.

LS

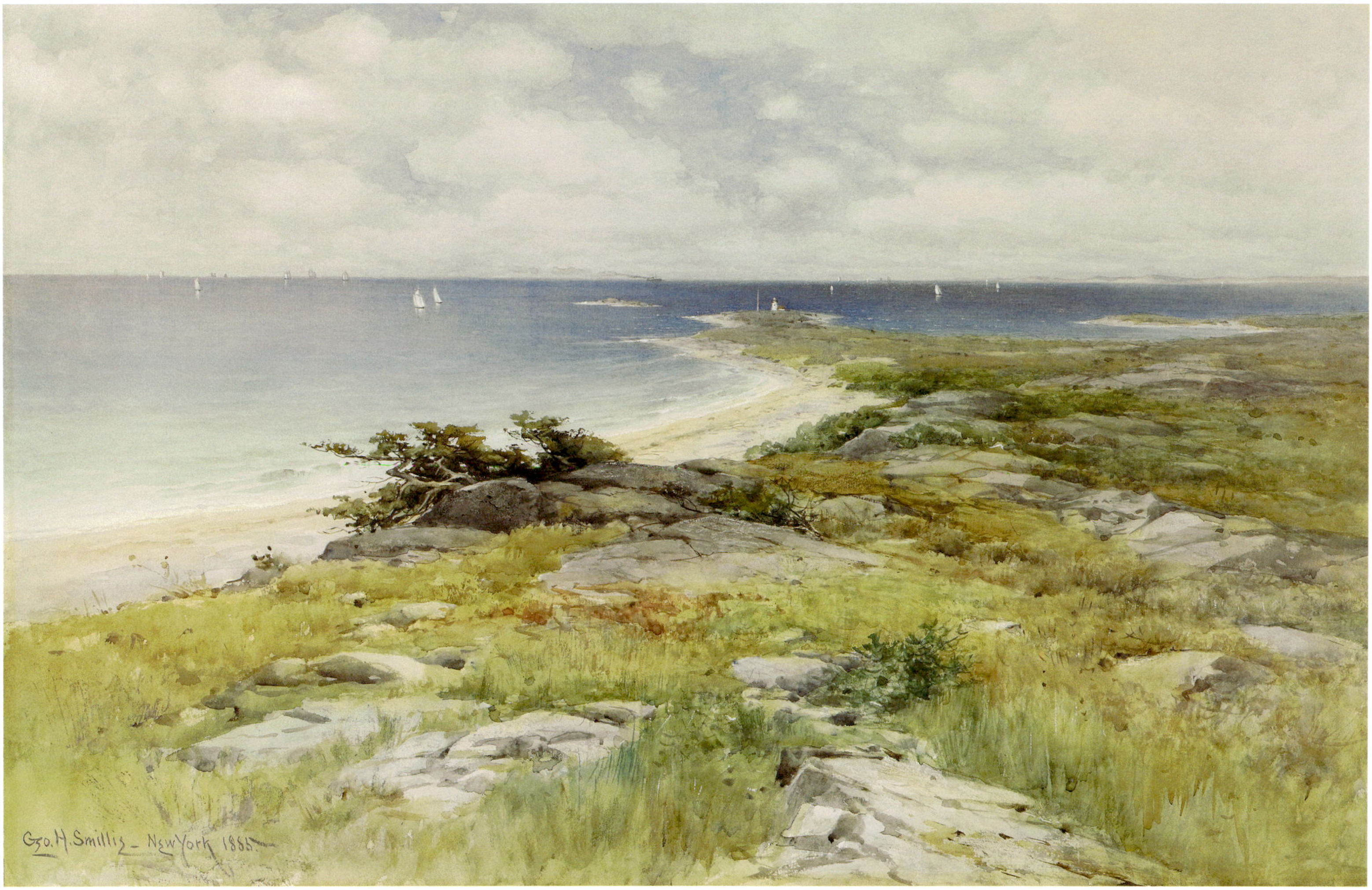
Geo. H. Smillie - New York 1885

CHILDE HASSAM (1859–1935)

Isles of Shoals

1886
Watercolor and gouache on paper
20¾ × 28¾ in. (52.7 × 73 cm)
Promised Gift

The 1886 watercolor *Isles of Shoals* and the 1887 oil *Paris at Twilight* (p. 123) are relatively early works by an artist who was just about to embrace impressionism, a movement born in Europe a decade earlier but still considered radical in the United States in the late 1880s. As these works appear to announce, two principal subjects and media would dominate Childe Hassam's long career: landscape and the urban scene, rendered in watercolors and oils.

The New England–based artist completed *Isles of Shoals* shortly before departing for his second trip to France in less than three years. Hassam studied at the conservative Académie Julian upon his arrival in Paris that fall, but soon thereafter was drawn to the circle of French impressionist painters including Claude Monet, Camille Pissarro, and Pierre-Auguste Renoir, whose former studio in Paris Hassam rented for a time. While *Isles of Shoals* predated this extended stay in France, it already contained the fundamental ingredients of the new movement. Using a transparent, inherently unpredictable medium well suited to plein air subjects and spontaneous, dabbing brushwork, Hassam ably evoked the shimmering, transitory effects of light on water and shoreline as filtered through the sea-saturated island atmosphere.

This watercolor originally belonged to the noted nature writer and poet Celia Thaxter, who likely received it from Hassam as a gift or in exchange for lodging at the Thaxter family's inn or her private cottage on Appledore Island in the Isles of Shoals, ten miles off the coast of Maine and New Hampshire. Thaxter's island retreat was one of the most popular artist colonies in late nineteenth-century America, hosting Ralph Waldo Emerson, Nathaniel Hawthorne, and William Morris Hunt, among other luminaries. An avid gardener, the flowers inside and outside of Thaxter's cottage as well as Appledore's native, coastal wildflowers—including brilliant blue

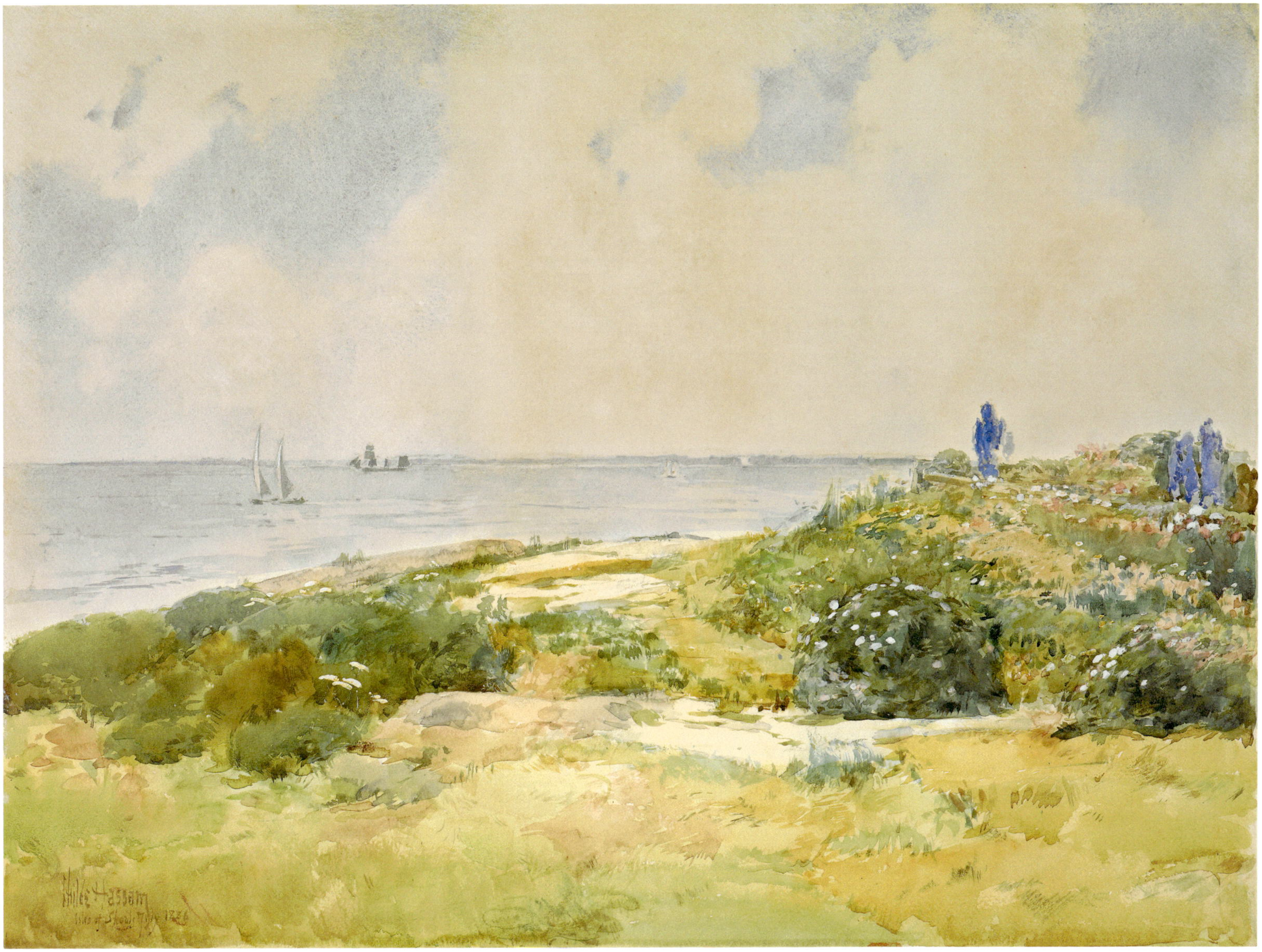
Childe Hassam

CHILDE HASSAM (1859–1935)

Paris at Twilight

1887
Oil on canvas
25½ × 21¼ in. (64.8 × 54 cm)

lupine, as seen in *Isles of Shoals*—were frequent subjects for Hassam's brush during the twenty summers he spent on the island.[1]

The oil painting *Paris at Twilight*, created the next year, reveals Hassam's innate grasp of impressionism's urban origins as well as the movement's fascination with the transitory textures and rhythms of everyday life in a modern world. Hassam's image of hansom coachmen huddling against their cabs on a wet evening while pedestrians pass by explores one aspect of this new urban scene.[2] Hassam saw Paris by way of Boston, where the new, wide, asphalt-paved Columbus and Commonwealth Avenues had been designed in 1869 in emulation of Baron Haussmann's grand boulevard system for the French capital.[3] Hassam embraced this new urban geography in terms of its modernity—the ways in which it enhanced and promoted commercial and leisure activities, opening ancient, dark, and twisting city streets to modern transportation, natural light, and long, sweeping vistas.

The artist's celebratory view of urban life evoked its essential vitality as well as its subtle poetry. The glow from within the café, at the far center right of the painting, provides an oasis of warmth on a chilly, damp evening. The painting is otherwise dimly illuminated by a crescent moon rendered with a single, quick brushstroke, the indistinct mass of multistory buildings barely discernible in the distance. Hassam's palette of dark earth tones, cool grays, and adumbral violet, as well as the dry autumn leaves littering the streets, suggests a city that is gradually waning and withdrawing into itself as it descends into the grayness of winter for which Paris is so well known.

CBC

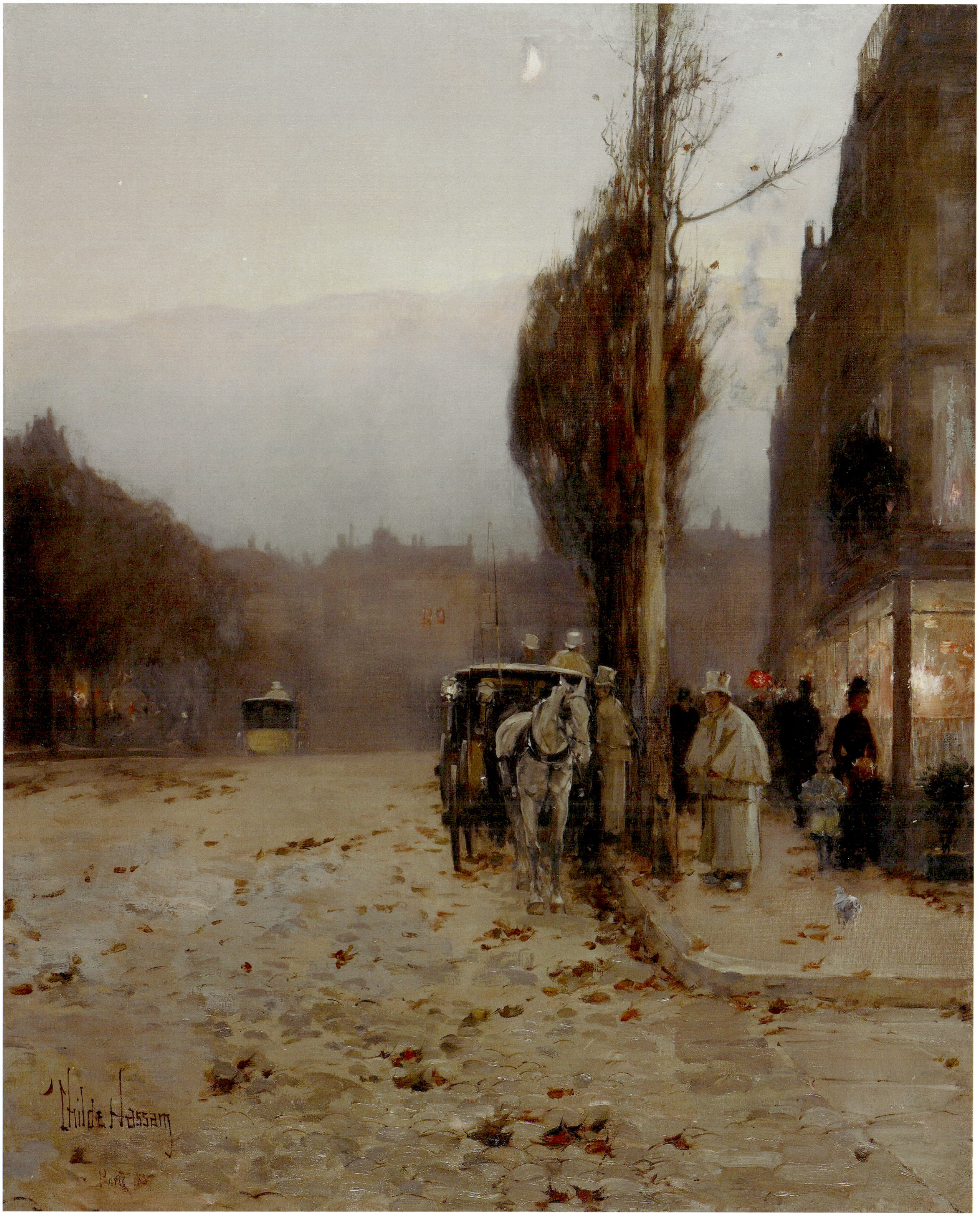
Childe Hassam

THOMAS EAKINS (1844–1916)

Professor Benjamin Howard Rand

1874
Oil on canvas
60 × 48 in. (152.4 × 121.9 cm)

Portraiture formed the core of realist painter Thomas Eakins's artistic production. Completed more than fifteen years apart, Eakins's likenesses of Benjamin Howard Rand and James Wright (p. 127) demonstrate the shifts as well as the continuities in the artist's work in this genre over the course of his lengthy career.

For Eakins, portrait painting was an intensely personal enterprise. The artist's subjects derived almost exclusively from his home city of Philadelphia, and the majority of his images depict family members and close friends. *Professor Benjamin Howard Rand* is the first portrait in which Eakins ventured outside of his immediate social circle and the first in a long line of images depicting prominent local professionals. Rand was Eakins's chemistry teacher at Central High School in Philadelphia, and joined the faculty at Jefferson Medical College in 1864. It may have been he who encouraged the budding figure painter to attend anatomy lectures and surgical demonstrations at Jefferson, which Eakins did in 1864 and again in 1874, when he asked Rand to pose.[1]

In the portrait of Rand, professional and personal items clutter the interior of the distinguished professor's study. A shiny brass compound microscope, test tubes, and a red-hued graduated cylinder with spatula are visible at left; the objects at right include a brightly colored pink rose and shawl, crumpled tissue paper, and a gray cat that the chemist pets with one hand while the other holds his place in a book. This tender image depicting Rand as an individual graced with both intellect and feeling betrays Eakins's affinity for his subject. Although nearly a generation separated artist

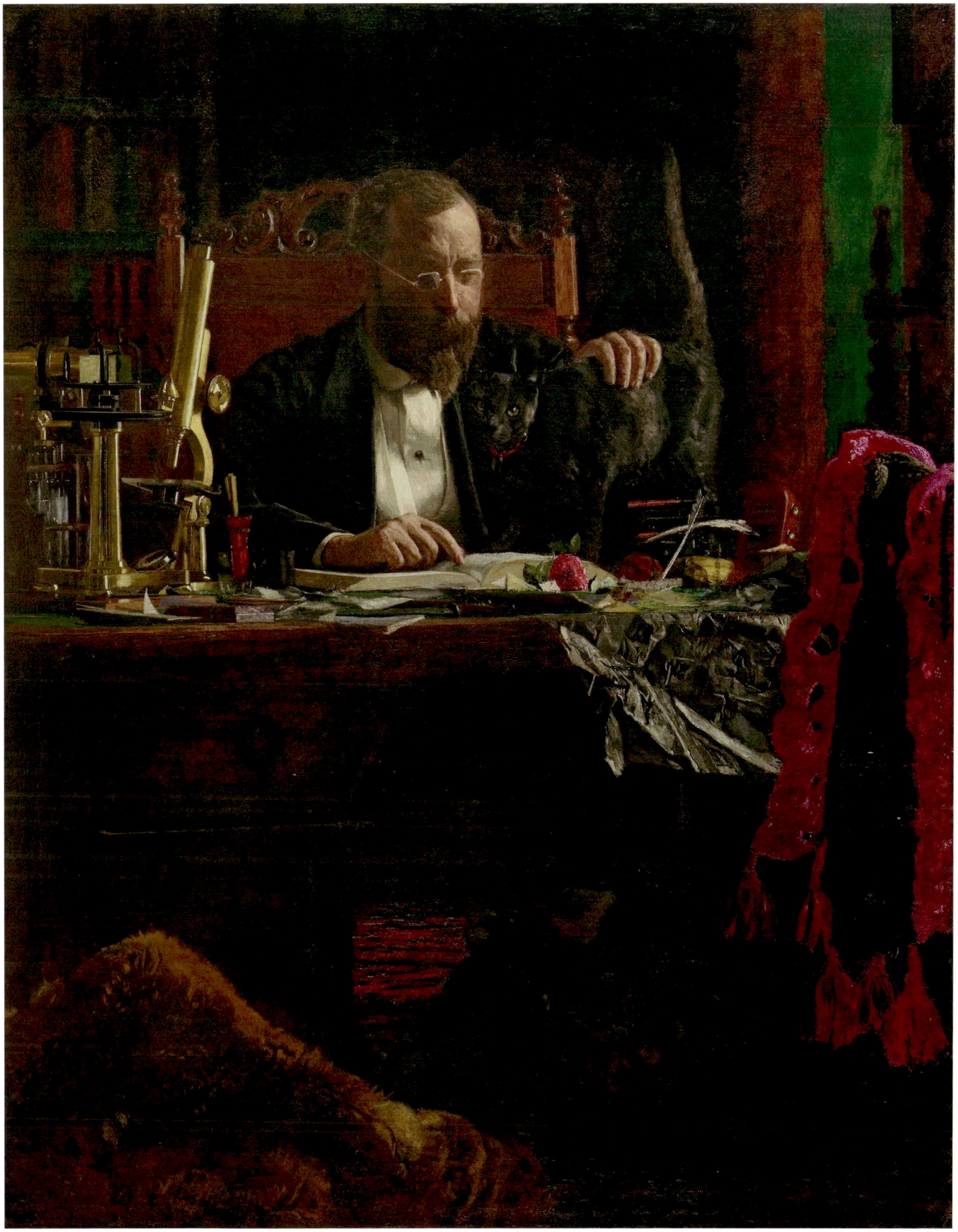

THOMAS EAKINS (1844–1916)

The Art Student [James Wright]

1890
Oil on canvas
42 × 32 in. (106.7 × 81.3 cm)

and model, both were avid recreational rowers and both of their fathers were writing masters.[2] Eakins had begun teaching in 1874, which perhaps heightened his appreciation for his former chemistry instructor.[3]

In *The Art Student*, an 1890 likeness of the artist James Wright, the mature Eakins shifted his attention from a mentor to a disciple. The portrait is one of a number Eakins created of pupils at the Art Students' League in Philadelphia, an organization established by loyal followers upon his dismissal in 1886 from the faculty of the Pennsylvania Academy of the Fine Arts for teaching from nude models. This series of uncommissioned likenesses attests to Eakins's dedication to these developing artists, whom he taught for free.[4]

By titling his painting *The Art Student*, Eakins prioritized his subject's professional role over his personal identity. Yet the likeness of Wright was by no means a conventional *portrait d'apparat*, in which the subject is surrounded by objects associated with his occupation. As was typical of Eakins's late work, and in dramatic contrast to his 1874 portrait of Rand, *The Art Student* offers little in the way of setting or props. The closely cropped image of a seated figure in a dark, nondescript setting sharply focuses attention on the sitter. The strong light on Wright's hands, and especially on his slightly downturned face, produce an intensely psychological study. The square of bright red fabric tucked into the left breast pocket of Wright's jacket is the only vestige of the vibrant still-life detail that embellished Eakins's early portraits. This vivid detail reminds the viewer that for Eakins, the most admirable of all pursuits—art making most assuredly among them—were those that engaged the head, hand, and heart.

EDS

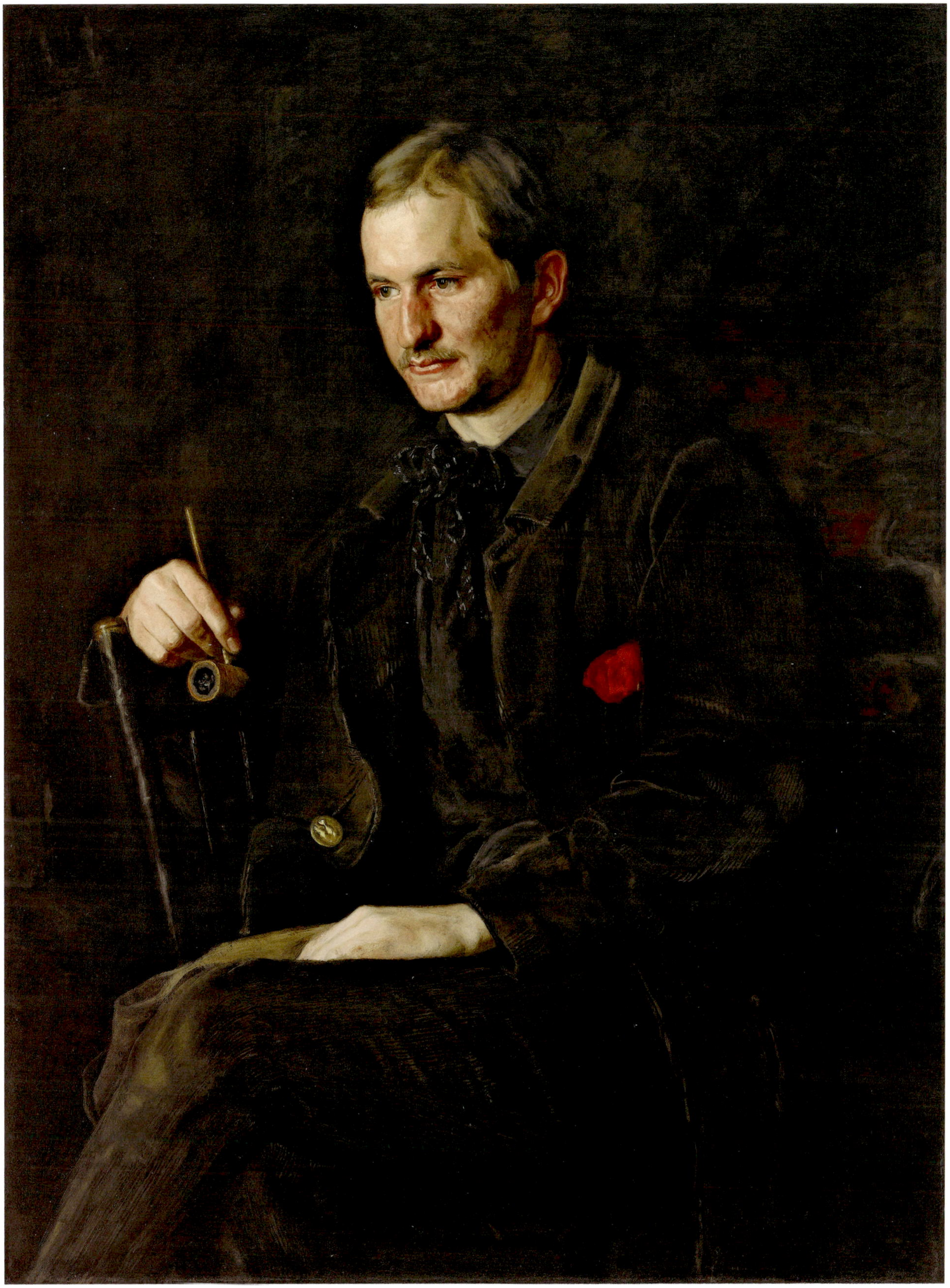

CHARLES FREDERIC ULRICH (1858–1908)

The Glass Engraver

1883
Oil on panel
11¾ × 16 in. (29.8 × 40.6 cm)

The Glass Engraver is one of a number of carefully observed images of men and women engaged in skilled manual labor that the New York artist Charles Frederic Ulrich painted during the 1880s. These works, which also include representations of an etcher, a spinner, a typesetter, and a group of glassblowers, received considerable attention in the fine art and popular presses.[1] The Munich-trained Ulrich's decision to focus his attention on laborers may have been influenced by Wilhelm Leibl, the noted German realist painter of peasant life. Yet the sociopolitical conditions of late nineteenth-century America surely also informed his choice of theme. Ulrich was one of a number of genre painters who applied their brushes to the depiction of craftspeople at work during this era, perhaps as a means of retreating from the rapidly industrializing workplace. These meticulously rendered images offered a vivid contrast to the realities of modern manufacture, wherein the factory and unapprenticed machine-tenders were supplanting the workshop and skilled artisans.[2]

A visual delight, Ulrich's small panel painting is energized by the diligent work of its subject and the plethora of still-life details that fill his urban interior. The craftsman sits at a green worktable, bathed in the light of the mid-afternoon sun (the clock on the wall to his right reads 2:35). He engages in the art of copper wheel engraving, a traditional method of incising glass in which copper disks of varying width, diameter, and profile rotate on a belt-driven lathe, allowing the adept artisan to create numerous types of textures and line effects. Holding the bowl of a clear glass goblet against a thumbnail-sized disk, Ulrich's engraver turns the vessel to make the necessary cuts. At left, a sampling of his finished handiwork with ornamentation ranging from simple horizontal banding to intricate floral and botanical designs demonstrates the extent and variety of his decorative repertoire.

The detail-oriented work of glass engraving required a steady hand and an exacting eye, traits that Ulrich shared with his sitter. Utilizing the smooth surface of the wood panel that served as his support, Ulrich convincingly depicted the wide range of materials in the engraver's shop, from metal to paper to glass. Contemporary critics often commented on the painter's "careful brush-work," and specifically commended *The Glass Engraver* for its "cunning rendering of details."[3] A white clay pipe interspersed among the pile of tools and equipment to the engraver's right further aligns painter and subject. An 1884 newspaper article identifying Ulrich as one of a select group of "Noted American Artists" described the painter as "the best judge of pipes and lager beer among the artists of New York," an allusion to his German ancestry.[4] German immigrants dominated the artisan class in New York in the 1880s, so it is likely that Ulrich perceived his engraver as a cultural comrade.[5] EDS

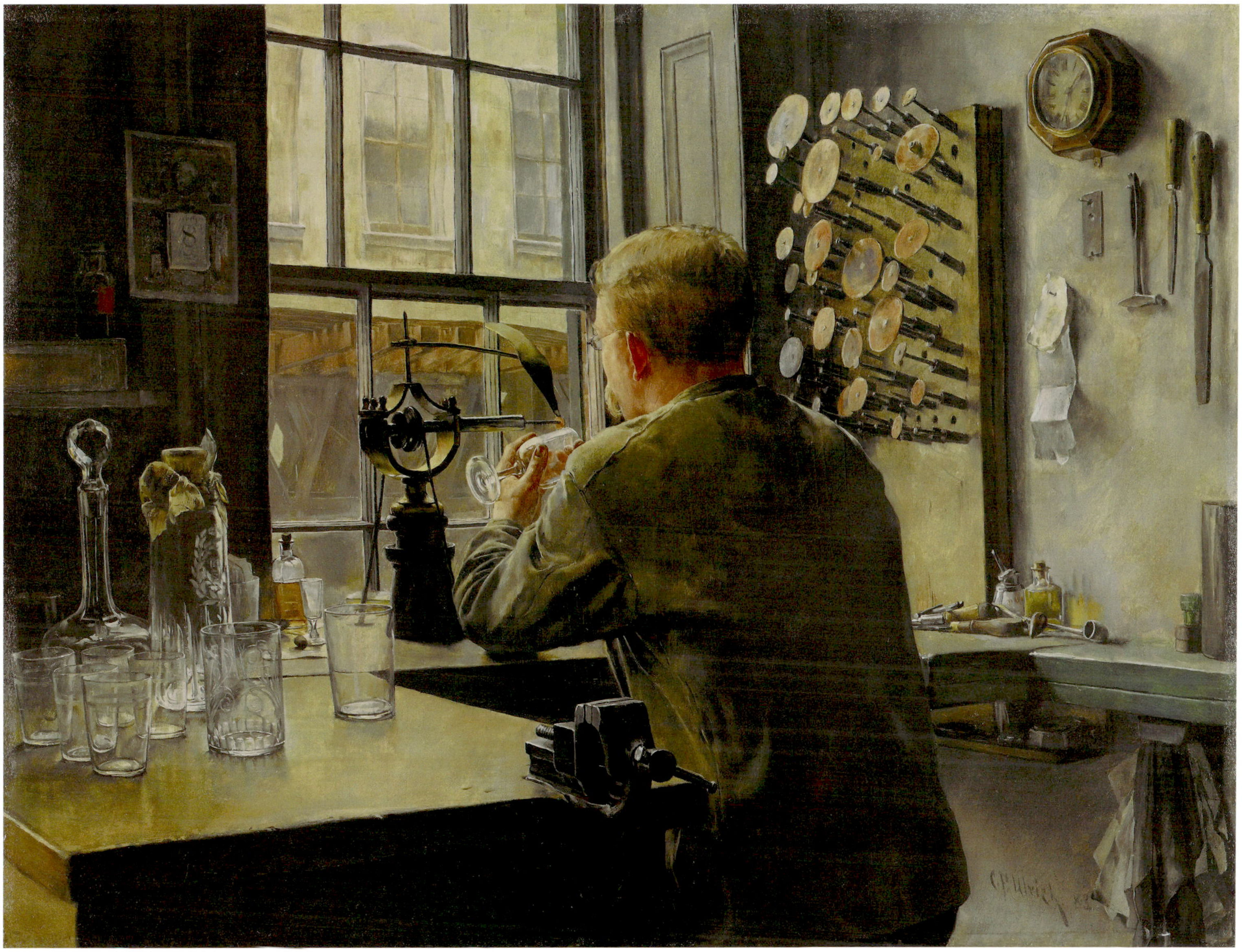

JAMES HENRY BEARD (1812–1893)

"It is Very Queer, Isn't It?"

1885
Oil on canvas
32½ × 26¼ in. (82.6 × 66.7 cm)

"It is Very Queer, Isn't It?" was one of animal painter James Henry Beard's most popular works during the artist's lifetime.[1] The canvas shows a chimpanzee sitting upright in a chair, chin in hand, as he presumably ponders Darwin's theory of human evolution.[2] Dangling from his other hand is a booklet with the title "Darwin's Descent of Man." On the floor to the chimp's left is a book with a human skull atop it; to his right, the skull of a primate sits on a tabletop. Beard, who began as a self-taught portraitist in Cincinnati and later made his reputation painting humorous scenes of anthropomorphized animals, surely intended to lampoon Darwin's theories. The book resting under the table, titled "Pythagoras' Theory of Metempsychosis," concerns the ancient Greek philosopher and mystic's theory of the transmigration of the soul from humans to animals. Beard may have included this text in his composition to suggest that Darwin's theory was as spurious as Pythagoras's. Or he may have meant to suggest that Darwin's soul (the scientist had died three years earlier) now resided in the body of the chimp. Like many of his era, Beard questioned whether humans were, in fact, descended from apes. But he did not fail to find humor in anthropomorphizing his subject, nor did he hesitate to play with the idea of ambiguities between the species.

Beard took as his model for *"It is Very Queer, Isn't It?"* a chimpanzee named Mr. Crowley, one of the most beloved and popular exhibits at the Central Park Zoo.[3] Mr. Crowley's uncanny human abilities—he was trained, for instance, to eat with a knife and fork—led one writer to tease, "after going to see 'Mr. Crowley,' one is almost ready to admit that we are really *descended* from monkeys."[4] Over the course of his sketching sessions, Beard concluded Mr. Crowley had "a mental ability that came very near to reason."[5] The artist recalled that upon finishing the painting, he leaned it against a wall facing the ape's cage. When Mr. Crowley saw the canvas, he supposedly took it for another chimpanzee, flew into a rage, and threw wet sawdust at it. After Beard spoke to the animal at length, Mr. Crowley reportedly became contrite and reached his arm through the bars to shake the artist's hand.

In a review of the painting during its exhibition at the National Academy of Design in 1885, a critic noted that Beard's chimpanzee "holds onto the lower rung of the chair in which he sits by his nether hands, but he is not a monkey; neither is he a man." The reviewer attributed this species ambiguity not to any arguments about evolution, but to Beard's unconventional and humorous artistic conventions. The chimpanzee "fits squarely with those animal humans or human beasts with which Mr. Beard delights his thousands and tens of thousands," the writer explained.[6] The humanlike qualities and apparent mental ability of Beard's anthropomorphized ape may nevertheless have introduced an unsettling challenge to evolutionary skeptics, even as the artist made light of Darwin's theory. LS

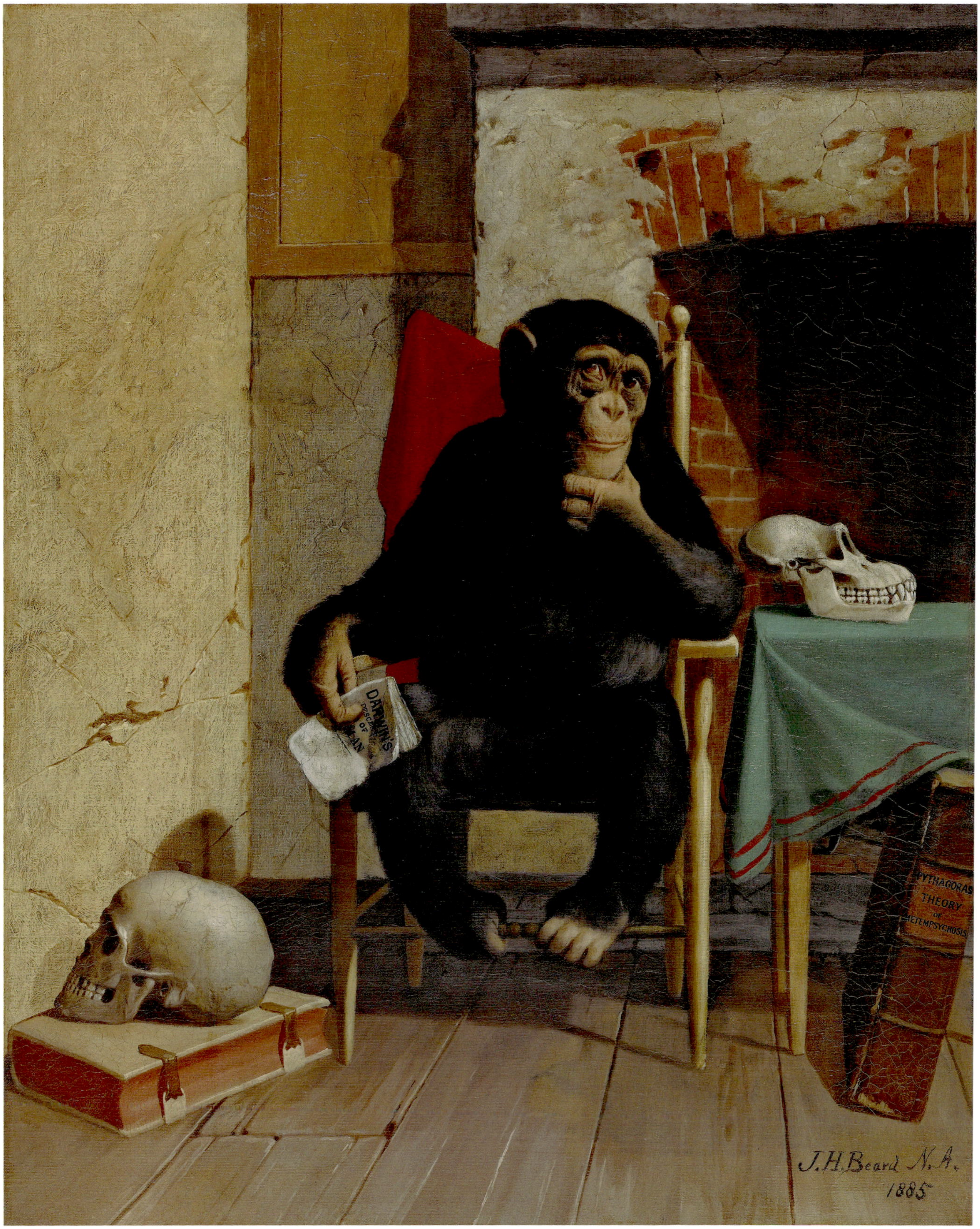
DARWIN'S
PYTHAGORAS
THEORY
OF
METEMPSYCHOSIS
J.H.Beard N.A.
1885

WILLIAM HOLBROOK BEARD (1824–1900)

School Rules

1887
Oil on canvas
18 × 24 in. (45.7 × 61 cm)
Promised Gift

William Holbrook Beard was the younger brother of artist James Henry Beard (p. 130). He began his career as a portrait and genre painter in Buffalo, New York, and studied in Europe in 1856–58. In 1860 he settled in New York City and, like his brother, began painting humorous scenes of anthropomorphized animals.[1] While James focused on mildly satirical scenes, usually featuring dogs, the younger Beard's work generally offered more pointed satires of Victorian culture and more overt moralizing using a wider range of species. William often portrayed his farm animals, apes, camels, and various birds in human scenarios: clothed in contemporary fashions, standing upright, and indoors.

School Rules, painted late in the artist's career, is a tale in the spirit of Aesop's fables.[2] Beard used various animals' characteristic attributes to personify his protagonists. An ape schoolmaster sits before his row of students. The industrious squirrel, who stands slightly apart from his classmates at the far right of the composition, appears to be answering a question, perhaps from the book in the master's hand. The squirrel's prominent pocket watch and neat, elegant clothing characterize his work ethic and foreshadow his future success. His composed demeanor contrasts with that of the slovenly hog beside him, who stands with shirt unbuttoned, pieces of a half-eaten apple littering the floor. Further down the row, a sly fox glances at the answer in his primer while the cat and dog beside him bicker rather than pay attention. The schoolmaster looks upward, perhaps toward the clock, but he is not oblivious to the misbehavior of his students. Holding a switch behind his back, the ape is ready to mete out punishments guaranteed by the "Rules" listed on the sheet hanging prominently on the back wall. Beard appears to have made at least one other painting that depicts the same cast of characters. His undated *Bent Pin* (unlocated) shows the same primate teacher standing at the head of the class and holding out the offending item accusatorily. Before him sit the natty squirrel in his velvet suit and ruff, as well as the hog, fox, cat, and dog.[3]

Although Beard's animals often bear the brunt of his jokes, he expressed a deeply felt appreciation for them and made careful studies in preparation for his paintings. In his 1893 instructional text, *Action in Art*, Beard described at length the nuances of squirrel tail position and what it could communicate. "Of all quadrupeds," he advised, "the squirrel makes the most expressive use of his tail, and with . . . knowledge and feeling perfected by study, this beautiful little animal may be brought into service to add interest to the landscape when larger animals would prove obtrusive."[4]

Although Beard has received scant attention from modern art historians, he was among the most prominent and successful artists of his time. An academician of the National Academy of Design and a member of the prestigious Century Club, he kept a studio in the Tenth Street Studio Building in New York City for almost thirty years.[5] His works sold well, and he received many critical notices, mostly positive, in the national press.[6] Toward the end of his life, the *New York World* praised him for his role as mentor and advisor to younger artists, referring to him as the "Nestor of American Art."[7] Beard's use of social satire, together with his mastery of animal genre, placed him at the forefront of artists of his generation.

LS

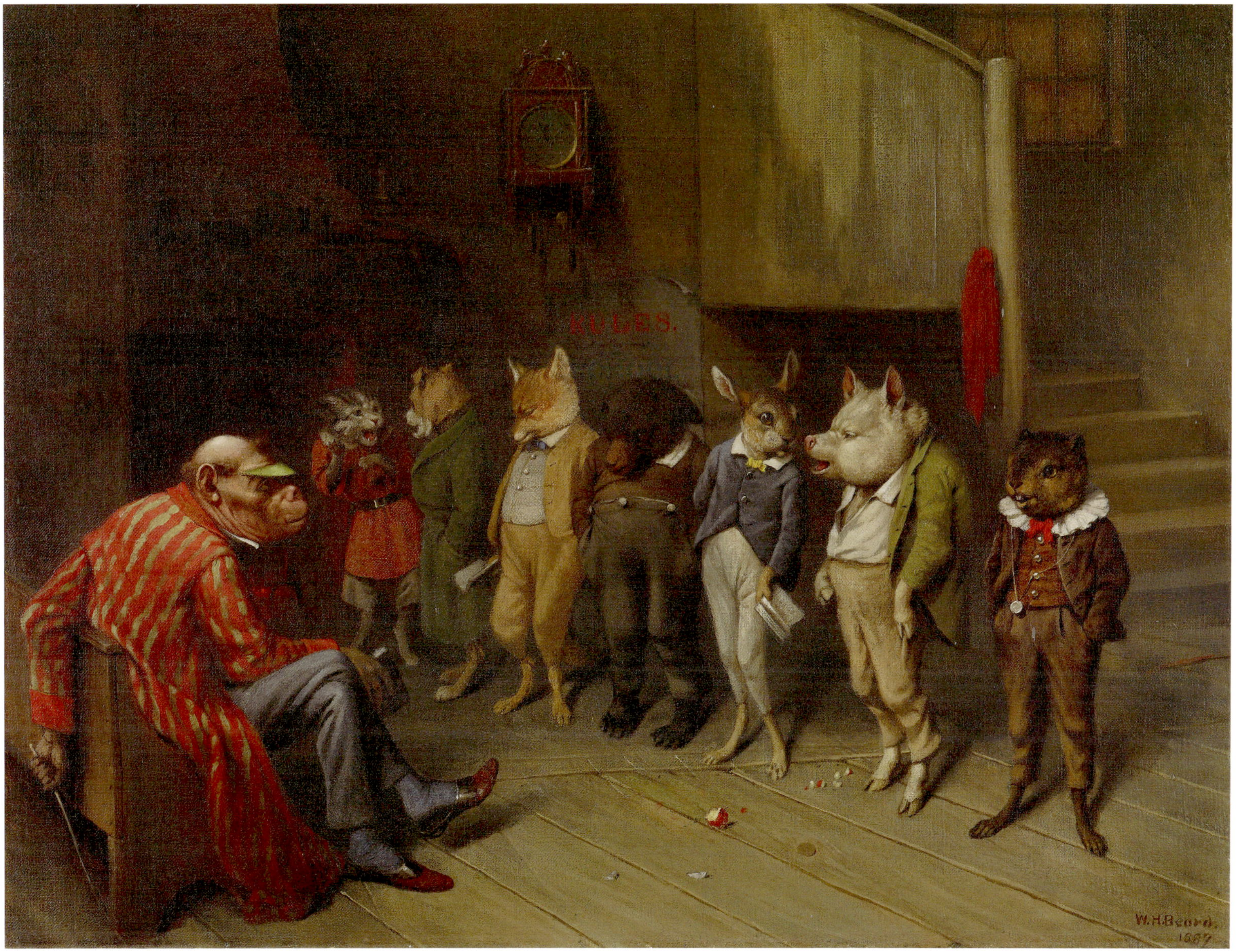
RULES.
W.H.Beard.

JOHN SINGER SARGENT (1856–1925)

Robert Louis Stevenson and His Wife

1885
Oil on canvas
20¼ × 24¼ in. (51.4 × 61.6 cm)

Robert Louis Stevenson and His Wife may be the most thoroughly discussed of all John Singer Sargent's likenesses of well-known figures.[1] The double portrait presents the distinguished Scottish author and his American wife, Fanny Osbourne, at opposite ends of their drawing room at Skerryvore, their home in Bournemouth, on the south coast of England. Stevenson stands to the left, looking outward, while Fanny sits to the far right, facing away from her husband. Between them, an open door offers a glimpse of the home's staircase and entrance hall. Alert and in mid-stride, Stevenson twists his mustache as if engaged in conversation with the viewer; Fanny lounges languidly, barefoot and bedecked in an exotic costume of glittering veils. Not surprisingly, Sargent's contemporaries found the portrait puzzling, but it is now regarded as among his most accomplished and incisive.

Painted in 1885, *Robert Louis Stevenson and His Wife* is the second of Sargent's three likenesses of the famed author.[2] It belongs to a group of informal portraits the artist began in the early 1880s that help define his impressionist period. By the time Sargent embarked on the Stevenson portrait, he had absorbed aspects of French and English modern art. Moreover, his circle of friends and acquaintances had broadened considerably in the past few years to include a wide array of artistic and literary talents, including Claude Monet, John Everett Millais, Edward Burne-Jones, Laurence Alma-Tadema, Edwin Austin Abbey, Oscar Wilde, and Henry James, among many others. Within this heady atmosphere, Sargent developed distinctly modern compositional strategies for plein air painting and for portraiture. He designated portraits like *Robert Louis Stevenson and His Wife* as "sketches," not only to differentiate them from his commissioned work, but also to denote their status as experimental canvases. In these paintings, Sargent grappled with the challenge of presenting modern genre subjects, searching for the technical means to bring his sitters to life through vivid characterization. The seemingly casual composition of the Stevenson portrait has the spontaneity of a snapshot, and its fluid brushwork and warm palette lend a sense of intimacy that reflects the affection Sargent felt for his sitters: the painter called Stevenson "the most intense creature I had ever met."[3]

Initially the Stevensons were ambivalent about the portrait, but they came to treasure it and even took the canvas with them when they moved to Samoa in 1890. Stevenson considered the painting "excellent, but . . . too eccentric to be exhibited."[4] Fanny commented, "[it] is lovely, but has a rather insane appearance."[5] Even Sargent expressed hesitation over his success. Referring to the portrait as "the picture of the caged animal lecturing about the foreign specimen in the corner," he acknowledged, "it is unlucky that I did not cut it down to a single figure."[6] REL

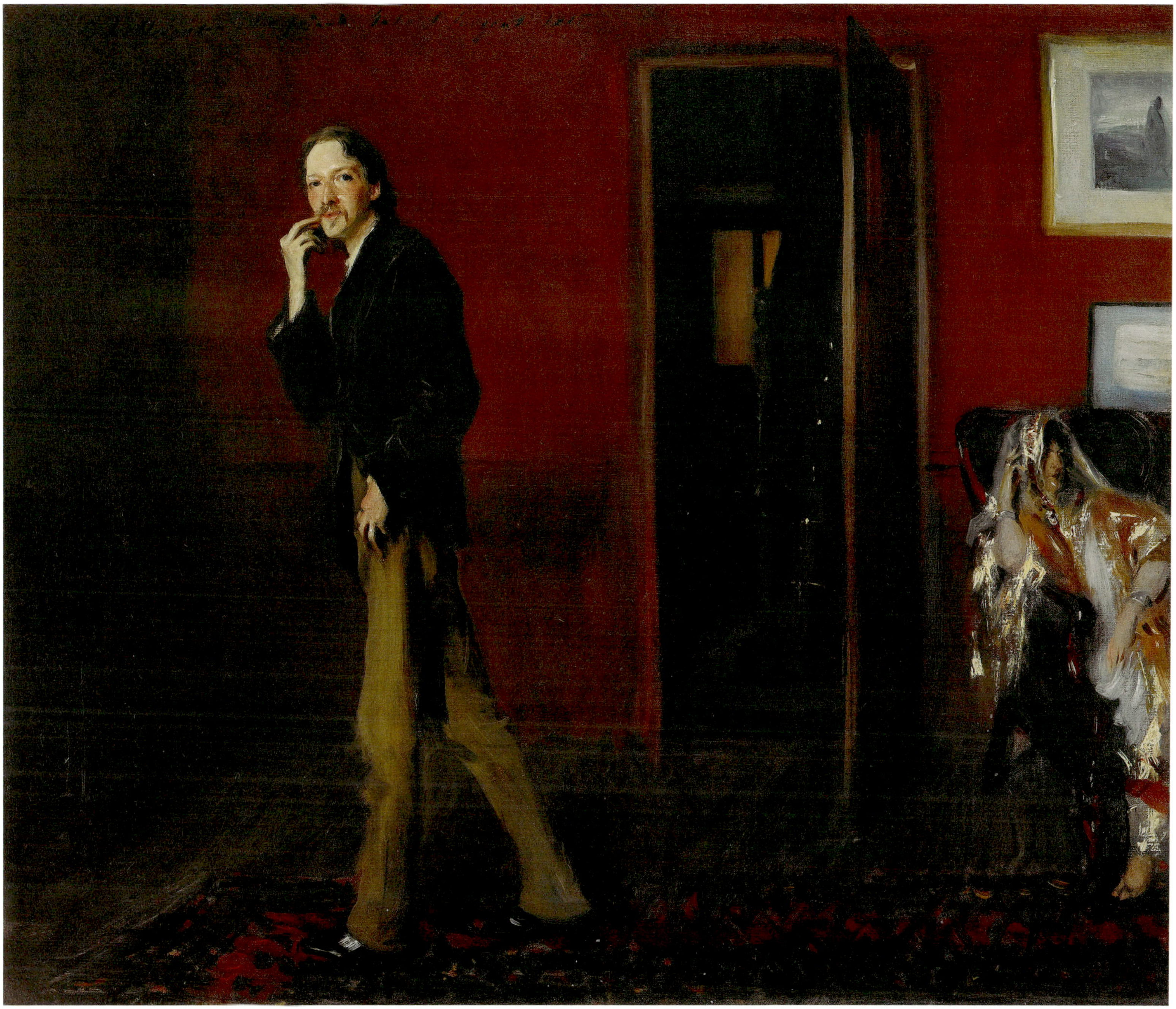

GEORGE DE FOREST BRUSH (1855–1941)

The Indian and the Lily

1887
Oil on canvas
21 × 20 in. (53.3 × 50.8 cm)

"I am going to make a desperate effort to secure again some commissions to go to Florida," the New England–based painter George de Forest Brush wrote to a friend in January 1887. "The Apaches are removed to the old fort at St. Augustine and it is a great opportunity for me to study them in winter."[1] Throughout the 1880s, Brush devoted his attention to painting Native American subjects. *The Indian and the Lily*, a product of the artist's trip to Florida in the spring of 1887, epitomizes the idealized, classically inspired renderings of indigenous American peoples with which the painter made his name.

The characteristic flora and fauna of coastal northeastern Florida provides the setting for *The Indian and the Lily*. Situated in a dark marshland against a backdrop of dense mangroves, Brush's lithe yet muscular protagonist kneels down at the water's edge, grasping a vine in his right hand to steady himself and extending his left arm toward a delicate water lily floating on the glassy surface of the pond. In contrast to the prevailing period image of the indigenous American as a violent and uncivilized savage, Brush depicts his subject as a refined individual with a keen aesthetic sensibility. The Indian wears a pair of intricately embroidered yellow leggings, a vibrant and carefully rendered detail of costume that references the painter's admiration for Native American artisanry.[2] The figure has set down his hunting bow to appreciate the quiet beauty of the lily, a symbol of purity and eloquence in the Victorian language of flowers.[3]

Brush's interest in Native American subjects transcended the specifics of history and ethnology. In an 1885 essay in *Century* magazine, he explained: "I do not paint [Indians] from the historian's or the antiquary's point of view. . . . I am interested in those habits and deeds in which we have feelings in common."[4] Three years later, a critic lauded *The Indian and the Lily* for achieving just this aim, remarking that the painting portrayed "an action that humanizes the savage, and it humanizes us, to regard him as a brother."[5] By depicting the Indian hunter as a nature lover whose senses are finely attuned to the beauty around him, Brush suggested a kinship between himself and his subject.

Yet the white-and-pink-hued bird slung over the hunter's shoulder reminds the viewer of the fundamental inequity in status between Anglo and Native Americans during the Gilded Age. This elegant creature appears to be a Roseate Spoonbill, a bird that was ruthlessly hunted in the service of the American fashion trade in the late nineteenth century, its handsome, pink-tinged plumes used to decorate ladies' hats and its wings sold as fans.[6] In pairing his indigenous subject with a local species of bird that had been reduced to near extinction, Brush called attention to the plight of Native peoples being systematically removed from their lands to U.S. government–run reservations. The water lily just out of the hunter's reach underscores the quiet tragedy of the Indian's plight. EDS

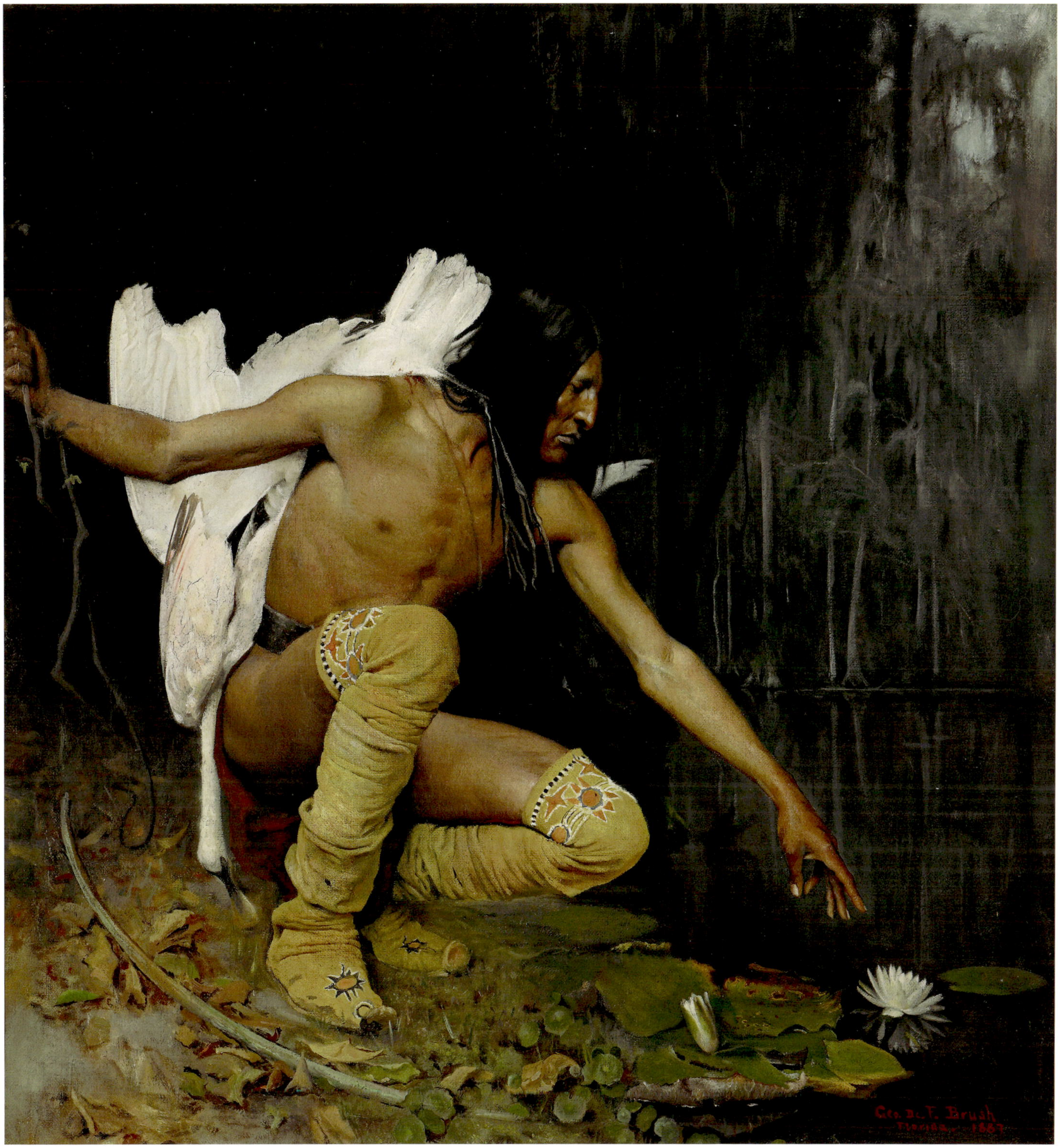
Geo. De F. Brush
Florida. 1887

DENNIS MILLER BUNKER (1861–1890)

Anne Page

1887
Oil on canvas
42½ × 54 in. (108 × 137.2 cm)

Dennis Miller Bunker's *Anne Page* is exceptional for a number of reasons. Among these are the extraordinary elegance and sophistication of the composition, the impressive skill of the artist's technique, the haunting beauty of the sitter, the restrained yet deeply poetic symbolism of the still life, and the image's poignant expression of human fragility and affection. The painting is all the more notable for having been made by an artist just twenty-six years of age. Bunker's astonishing potential, as evidenced by this work alone, was never to be realized. He died of influenza in 1890, at the age of twenty-nine.

The immediate source for this spare and precise composition was James McNeill Whistler's famous 1871 painting *Arrangement in Grey and Black No. 1: The Painter's Mother*, known popularly as "Whistler's Mother" (Musée d'Orsay). Whistler's austere profile portrait, which depicts his elderly mother seated in a simple interior rendered in a narrow palette of neutral tones, was a compendium of aestheticism. It demonstrated that simplicity is a virtue, veils of subdued tonalities can be poetic, and the self-conscious search for the beauty in everything is a worthy pursuit. Bunker was a young art student in Paris in the early 1880s when aesthetic ideas were first being introduced to and embraced by American students.[1]

Back in Boston by 1885 and invigorated by his encounters with aestheticism abroad, Bunker wrote a letter the next year to Anne Page, a legendary beauty who was friend and model to a number of artists including Augustus Saint-Gaudens, who would sculpt her bust in 1895.[2] In this letter, Bunker appealed to Page to sit for him: "I want to paint you awfully much, but I tremble to ask you to let me, for I know it would take me a long time to do you as I want to and I should not care a bit to do you unless I could make my best work of it. . . . Last winter . . . you said that you would pose for me, but I'm afraid you tho't I only wanted to make a study for some picture—you see I'm thinking of making *you* the picture."[3] His final painting of the Boston beauty is a masterpiece of quiet elegance and expression. Bunker set Page against a dark, nondescript background, softly and evenly lighting her face and her delicate hands, which rest in her lap palm-side up. Immediately across from her, on a dressing table draped with a moss green cloth, is a cluster of pink and yellow roses, one of which rests precariously on the table's edge in a Caravaggesque intimation of beauty that will ultimately fade.

Not only was Page a stunning woman, but she was also an ideal model. She and Bunker became good friends while she posed for him, and after completing the painting in 1887 the artist wrote her the following expression of gratitude: "I never have succeeded in thanking you for sitting so long and so patiently for me—Perhaps I never could unless I took this means of doing so. But I can't have you think that I don't appreciate how great a kindness you have done me in helping me with your patience and beauty to make a picture that has been almost the only loving task of my life."[4] WS

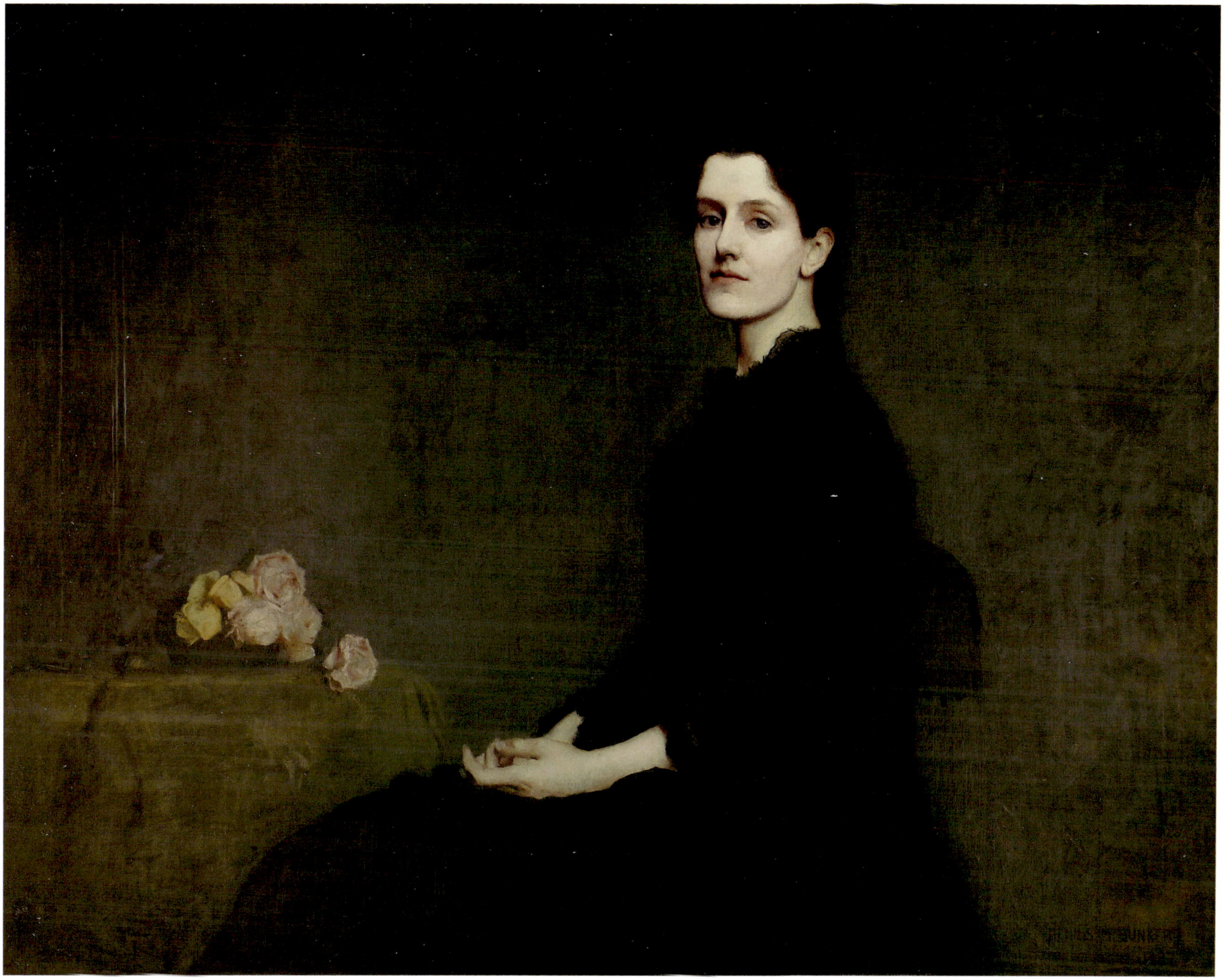

GARI MELCHERS (1860–1932)

The Embroideress [Portrait of Mrs. Hitchcock]

ca. 1889
Oil on canvas
35½ × 21¾ in. (90.2 × 55.2 cm)
Promised Gift

Internationally acclaimed in the late nineteenth century, Gari Melchers produced hundreds of paintings in a number of genres over the course of his lengthy career. Created at the height of Melchers's fame, *The Embroideress [Portrait of Mrs. Hitchcock]* is a signature work that references notable elements of his personal life and artistic development.

Melchers likely completed the painting in 1889, the year he was awarded a Grand Prize at the Exposition Universelle in Paris for a series of genre images depicting Dutch peasant life. The canvas marked the beginning of a new phase in his work during which Melchers expanded his repertoire to include portraiture. It also represents the earliest known appearance in the painter's oeuvre of Henriette Hitchcock, one of Melchers's primary models and the first wife of the painter's close friend and fellow artist George Hitchcock.[1] Many of Melchers's finest images were executed at the Hitchcocks' country estate in the Dutch fishing village of Egmond, where the two expatriate painters established a flourishing artist's colony.

During Melchers's lifetime, the Crystal Bridges canvas was often exhibited under the title *The Embroideress*, a moniker that aligns it with other full-length paintings in which the artist identified his subjects by vocation.[2] Indeed, the image may be the earliest example of this sub-genre of Melchers's work. In the lower right-hand corner of the predominantly dark composition is a handheld embroidery frame upon which a vibrant green and orange pattern has been stitched on a snow-white ground. The strand of orange fiber extending from the taut canvas to Mrs. Hitchcock's right hand suggests that she has just risen from her needlework.

Melchers's use of color and modeling is restrained yet masterful. The viewer follows the thin line of orange from the rectangular frame to the delicate pink flesh of the embroideress's hand, which is accented by a gold and turquoise ring on her ring finger. The light blue channels of her veins lead the viewer up to an elegant lace sleeve cuff and along the subtle curve of her arm to her head.[3] Mrs. Hitchcock's strong yet sensitive profile, which is bisected by a blue backdrop below and a framed painting above, testifies to the artist's rigorous academic training at the Royal Prussian Academy of Art in Düsseldorf.

Melchers exhibited *The Embroideress* to nearly universal acclaim. The *Chicago Daily News* lauded the work for providing "almost delicious harmony of color and a figure superbly drawn and modeled." The *Chicago Tribune* said it marked a turning point in his artistry, explaining: "He has acquired a superb technical equipment; now he begins with some diffidence to use it for the unfolding of thought." The *New York Evening Post* described the canvas as "remarkable for its quiet force in painting."[4]

Melchers and his early muse remained close even after the Hitchcocks divorced in 1905. In 1928, loyal friend and supporter Henriette (now remarried and known as Henriette Lewis-Hind) penned the foreword to the first Melchers monograph. In words that aptly describe *The Embroideress*, she lauded Melchers's images as "living, strong, human, fine in tone, often accentuated by a high note of colour, firm in impasto, 'fat' in the quality of the paint . . . [works of art] that hold their own without effort among masterpieces."[5]

EDS

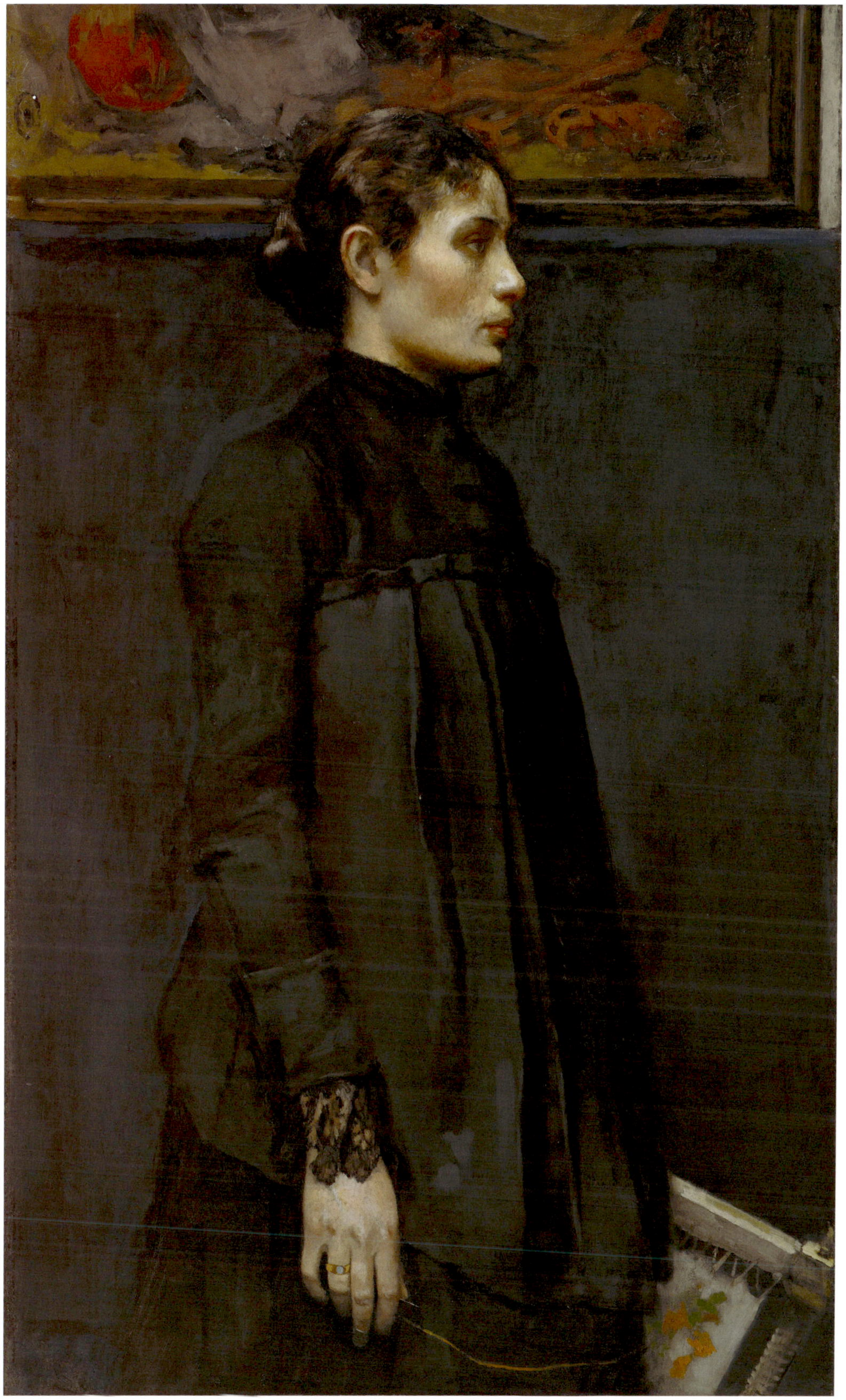

WILLIAM MERRITT CHASE (1849–1916)

Worthington Whittredge

ca. 1890
Oil on canvas
64½ × 53¼ in. (163.8 × 135.3 cm)

Although separated by nearly thirty years in age and a generation of change, William Merritt Chase and Worthington Whittredge had been acquainted for decades by the time this portrait was made—though perhaps not always under the best of circumstances. Chase returned to New York in 1878 from his studies abroad a leader among the "new men" who took America's art establishment by storm.[1] Whittredge, who had enjoyed a successful career as a landscape painter and served as president of the National Academy of Design from 1874 to 1877, was a central figure of the very establishment Chase and his contemporaries threatened to unhinge. Under Whittredge's watch the National Academy suffered through a series of offensive attacks in the mid-1870s. In 1875 a group of students left the academy to form a rival school, the Art Students League, much to Whittredge's dismay.

As Whittredge and his supporters lost ground to the rising tides of change, Chase arrived in New York to assume a teaching post at the controversial new school. Within a year, Chase further intensified the generational tensions by rallying with a group of young colleagues to form the Society of American Artists, which provided not only a new community but also an alternative exhibition venue for artists frustrated by the academy's limitations. By this point, Whittredge, along with the rest of New York, had undoubtedly taken notice of Chase.[2]

If these complex art world entanglements had not already facilitated an opportunity for the two to meet, Whittredge and Chase would certainly have encountered each other as neighbors at the Tenth Street Studio Building. One of the original occupants of the popular artists' complex, Whittredge established his studio there in 1859 alongside Hudson River School colleagues such as Frederic Edwin Church, Sanford Robinson Gifford, and Albert Bierstadt. In 1878 Chase moved into the building's largest studio, under the central atrium dome. The following year he expanded into the even larger room next door, a soaring space recently vacated by Bierstadt, who had used it to paint and display his massive landscape spectacles. Chase lavishly redecorated the studio with objets d'art and exotic bric-a-brac that complemented his fresh, bravura style inspired by contemporary European trends.[3] Chase's prominent presence in the Tenth Street Studios signaled the end of an era—Whittredge's era.

Yet Chase was anything but a rabble-rouser. While the ambitious painter was a major force in ushering in the next generation of artists, he also revered tradition. Chase joined as many art societies as existed in Gilded Age New York, including the National Academy. In 1890 he was elected an academician. The following year he exhibited a work there simply titled *Portrait*, which featured a distinguished older gentleman seated before an easel, brush and palette in hand. Although the sitter was not formally identified as Whittredge in the exhibition checklist, one critic described him as a "well-known artist," painted "with just the right twinkle and wise look combined."[4] An inscription in the upper right that reads, "To my friend Whittredge," confirms the subject's identity.[5] Whittredge had long since retired from his post as academy president, but for Chase and his contemporaries he remained a potent symbol of the venerated institution. A pleasing and stately likeness of the mature artist, Chase's portrait appeared as the frontispiece in a 1942 reprint of Whittredge's autobiography.[6]

SMH

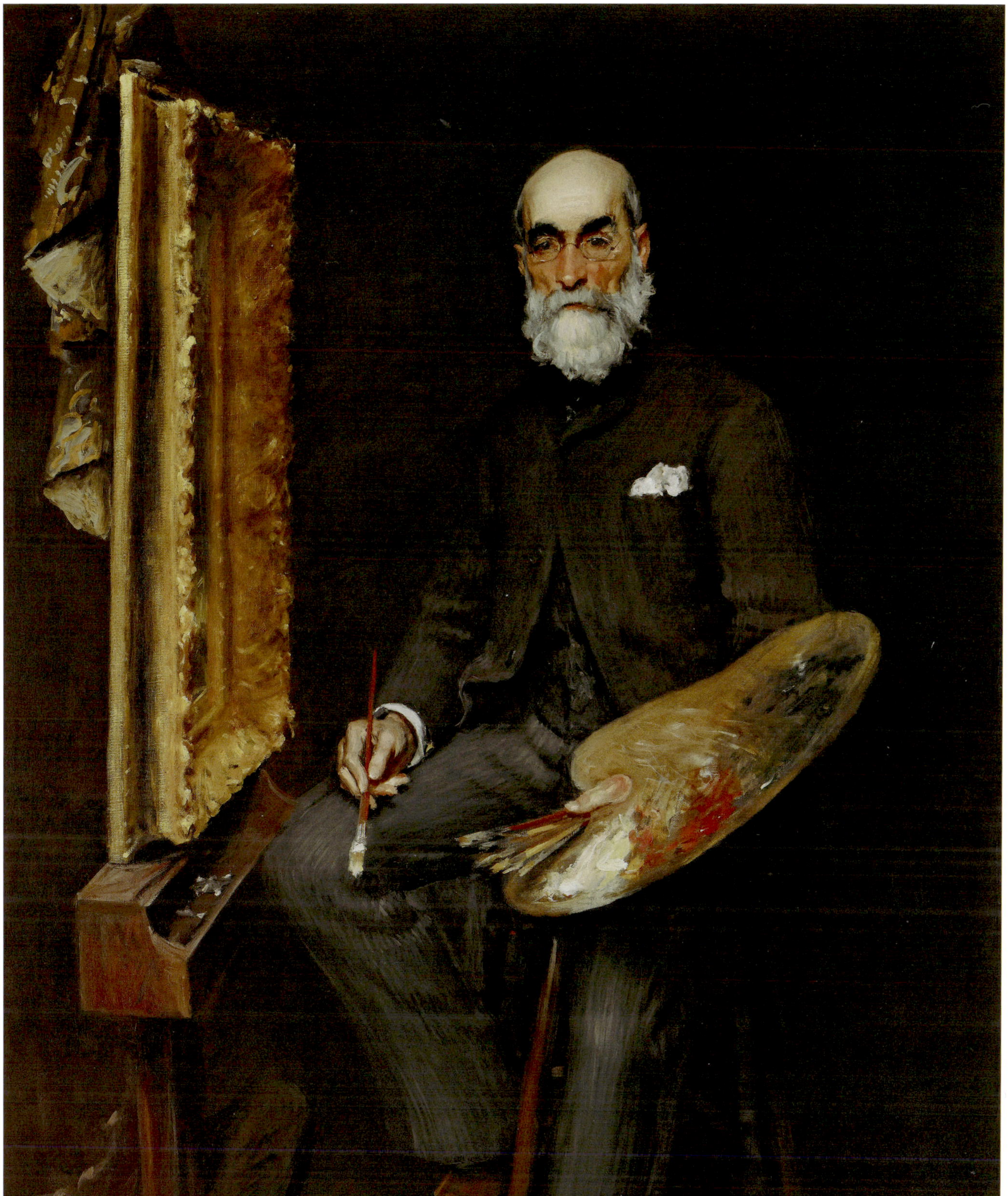

JOHN FREDERICK PETO (1854–1907)

Old Companions

1904
Oil on canvas
22 × 30 in. (55.9 × 76.2 cm)

Library-themed images were among trompe l'oeil (fool the eye) still-life painter John Frederick Peto's favorite subjects. His exploration of this motif culminated in a series of nearly life-size bookshelf compositions, of which *Old Companions* is a fine example. Completed late in the artist's life, this elegant assemblage of timeworn utilitarian objects—the type of arrangement Peto scholar Alfred Frankenstein has described as a "symphony of tatters, scuffs, frayings, and tears"—offers an appropriate "bookend" to a career devoted to revealing the poetry in the ordinary.[1]

Following in the footsteps of native sons Raphaelle Peale and John F. Francis, the Philadelphia-born and -trained Peto enjoyed a successful early career in still-life painting, exhibiting a number of his works at the Pennsylvania Academy of the Fine Arts in the 1880s. Peto and his new wife left the city in 1889 in favor of a quieter life in the resort community of Island Heights, on the New Jersey shore. Over the next twenty years, the artist dedicated himself to the solitary pursuit of painting in his home studio, selling the occasional canvas to a summer tourist. Like many of his works, *Old Companions* was still in Peto's possession at the time of his death.

Although the 1904 painting was assigned the title *Old Companions* posthumously, this name aptly describes Peto's relationship to his meticulously rendered objects. Period photographs of the interior of the artist's Island Heights home show tables and shelves heavily laden with old, often dilapidated artifacts.[2] The same props—Peto's "companions"—appear time and again in his images: the brass candlestick with bent collar at the center left of *Old Companions* features in numerous compositions ranging from library pictures to kitchen tabletop still lifes, and corncob pipes also repeatedly appear in the artist's work. The wooden shelf painted a deep green that figures in this and other of Peto's early twentieth-century compositions evokes the vibrant colors of the interior walls and trims in his beloved home.[3] In dogged pursuit of new and innovative compositions even at this late stage in his life, Peto used the shallow wall shelf to anchor varied formal arrangements of the same objects.[4]

Old Companions offers its viewers a glimpse into Peto's private world by documenting the contents of the spaces in which he lived and worked, but it is ultimately reclusive in nature. All of the books in the composition are closed and their titles obscured. The lard oil lamp hanging from the shelf at lower left and the candle above, to its right, have both been extinguished. The closely cropped image blocks out all signs of the outside world, and Peto's placement of the bookshelf in a dimly lit wall recess enhances this sense of retreat. The objects featured in the image—books, lamps, and writing tools—evoke reflection and introspection, appropriate themes for an ailing artist nearing the end of his career.

EDS

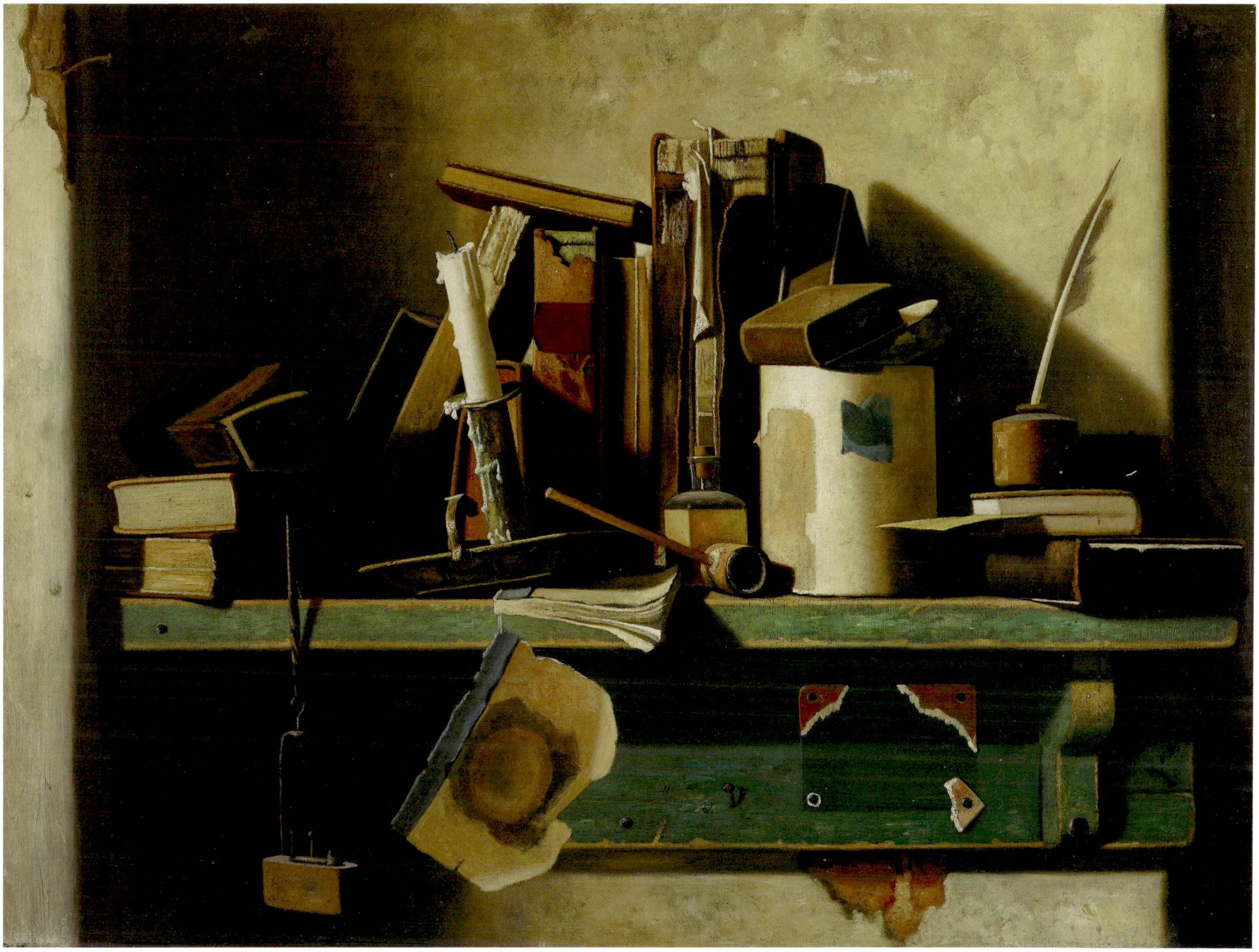

JOHN SINGER SARGENT (1856–1925)

Under the Willows

1887
Oil on canvas
27 × 22 in. (68.6 × 55.9 cm)
Promised Gift

The period of time the American expatriate artist John Singer Sargent spent in England between 1885 and 1889 was one of the most fruitful of his entire career. While residing in rural villages such as Broadway, Henley, Calcot, and Fladbury, the artist explored impressionism in a series of portrait sketches, landscapes, and still lifes. Sargent's traditional Beaux-Arts training did not thwart his interest in recent developments in French painting; he was keenly aware of the work of the French plein-air naturalists, as well as the impressionists, and likely attended the impressionist exhibitions while based in Paris in the later 1870s and early 1880s. It was his close association with Claude Monet, however, with whom he sketched out of doors at Giverny, that prompted Sargent to fully embrace the facture and brushwork of pure impressionism.

When Sargent visited Monet's home in Giverny during the summer of 1887, the lauded French painter was working from a *bateau atelier* (floating studio), using the low vantage point to depict family members afloat in punts. Monet's objective had long been to capture light reflected above and absorbed below the surface of the water. While working from his *bateau atelier* Monet was attuned to the motion of the water, and the physical and visual sensations he experienced afloat were carried out on canvas as he attempted to integrate figure and landscape. After visiting Monet, Sargent left for England, where he resided with Robert and Helen Harrison at Henley-on-Thames. For Sargent, the Harrison's riverfront home, Wargrave Hill, provided the ideal location to synthesize what he had observed working alongside the French master.[1]

Under the Willows is among the group of river views that Sargent executed while at Henley. The musician and opera singer George Henschel later described Sargent painting there en plein air, from his own *bateau-atelier,* and it is clear that *Under the Willows* was painted from just such a perch.[2] Like Monet, Sargent was interested in capturing the undulating motion of water and the reflection of light striking it. Here, a wooden punt is tucked against the riverbank, shaded by the cascading branches of a willow tree. A woman lying in the boat—later identified by Sargent as Helen Harrison—is barely visible among the shadows and flickering light.[3] The solid forms of the boat and tree trunk are embroidered within the loosely brushed water and shimmering willow leaves. Despite its vibrant palette of red, green, purple, and white and its active surface, the painting exudes a sense of relaxation, impressing us with its atmosphere of mossy coolness and warm sunlight. REL

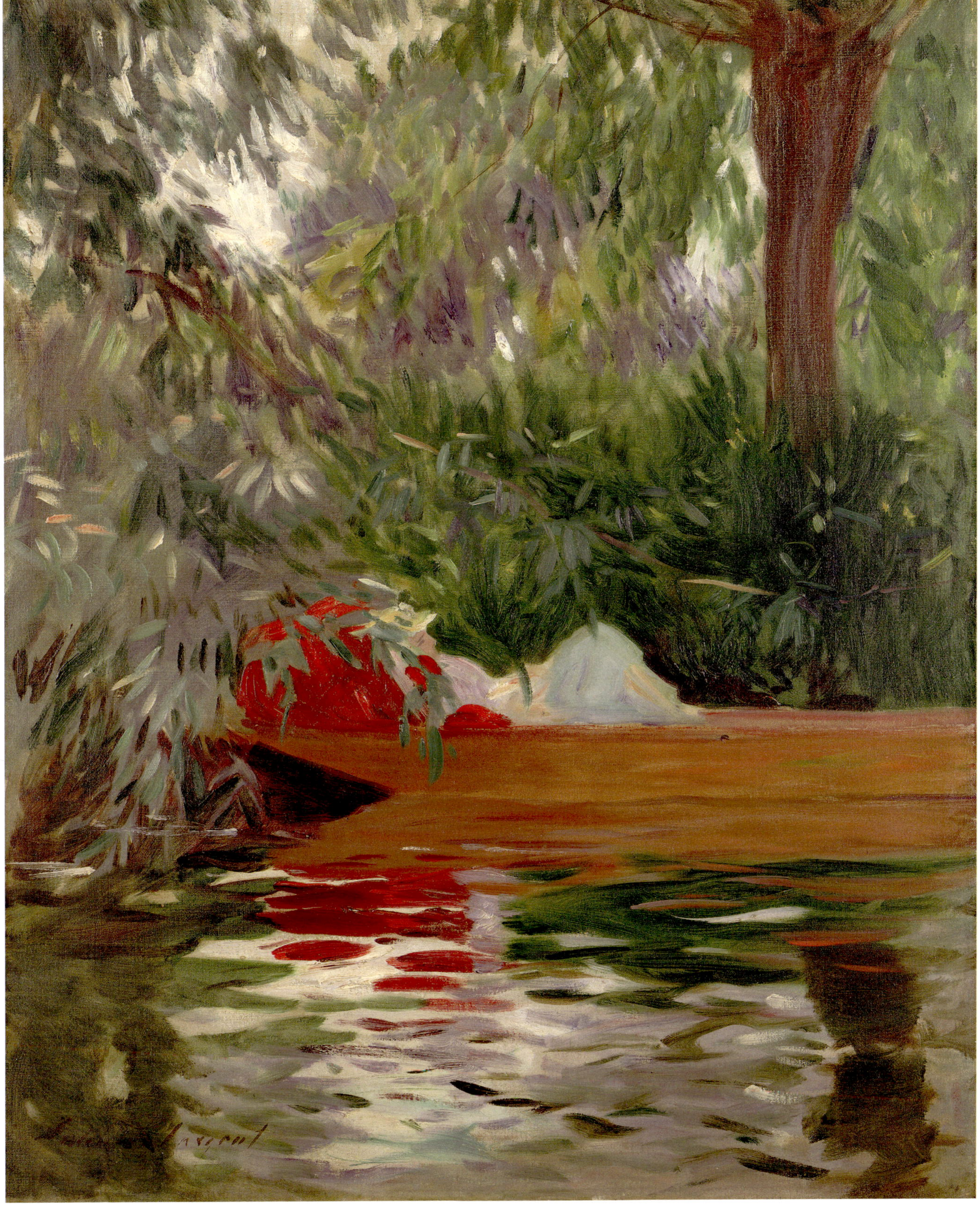

DENNIS MILLER BUNKER (1861–1890)

Wild Asters

1889
Oil on canvas
25 × 30 in. (63.5 × 76.2 cm)
Promised Gift

Dennis Miller Bunker's *Wild Asters* is a worthy impressionist counterpoint to the artist's magisterial *Anne Page* (p. 138), in that this landscape, like the 1887 portrait, portended a career of enormous achievement. That future would never materialize. The talented young artist died the year after he painted this fluid, lush view of a verdant Massachusetts meadow.

When Bunker painted Anne Page in Boston, John Singer Sargent was in the same city working on a portrait of the important art patron Isabella Stewart Gardner. In the summer of 1888, Bunker joined Sargent in Calcot, England, where the two painted the landscape en plein air (out of doors). Sargent, who had visited and painted with Claude Monet at the esteemed French impressionist's home in Giverny, France, the year before, was a master of the *alla prima* technique (direct painting, without underdrawing). This manner of painting, which imbued Sargent's landscapes with a sense of spontaneity, vitality, and atmosphere, had a profound influence on his traveling companion.

Indeed, Bunker's response to the aesthetic possibilities of impressionism was immediate, intelligent, and insightful. Upon his return to the United States in 1889 he painted a series of landscapes in Medfield, Massachusetts, that represent his command of the then radical style. *Wild Asters* is one of four intimate views recording the effects of transient light and the changing of the seasons on the same grassy meadow.[1] Critics considered these paintings colorful in the extreme: in writing about another work in the series, a commentator described Bunker as one of the "young men [who] have agreed to look at nature for a while through a blue glass."[2]

Indeed, the shimmering blue water in *Wild Asters* is in direct sunlight, painted with a startling combination of blue, red, and green strokes that flow in and out of one another yet retain their coloristic identity. This landscape is both landlocked and skyless, a tightly cropped view of the serpentine brook that bisects a field of green. The fresh, fast strokes of pinkish-white that form the asters lining the brook further enliven the scene. A comparison of *Wild Asters* and *Anne Page*, created just two years earlier, reveals 1889 to be a watershed moment in Bunker's artistic development. Where his spare, elegant portrait of Page honors academic traditions and conveys a hushed and solemn beauty, *Wild Asters* embraces transience and emotional intensity through its swirling rhythms, blurred edges, and flood of natural light. That Bunker so early in his abruptly ended life had mastered both academic and impressionist technique begs the difficult question of what course American art might have taken had he lived. In 1891, the year after his death, a memorial exhibition held at the St. Botolph Club recognized Bunker as a leader among Boston painters, a distinction we now extend to his position within the wider field of American painting. WS

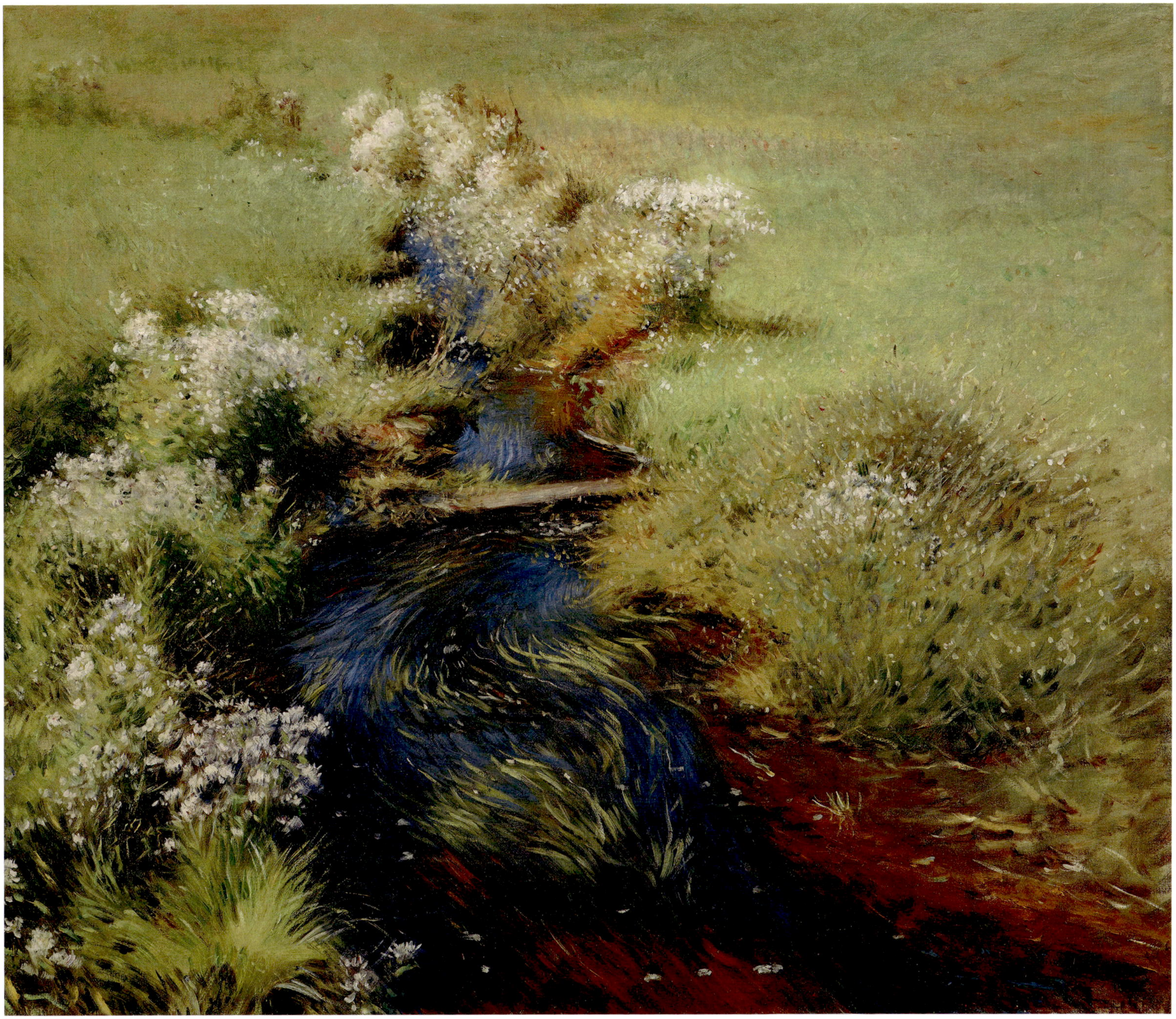

JOHN LA FARGE (1835–1910)

Peonies in a Breeze

1890
Watercolor and gouache on paper
37⅜ × 20½ in. (94.9 × 52.1 cm)
Promised Gift

An exceptionally versatile and innovative artist, John La Farge "strode over the whole field of art," his student Maria Oakey Dewing observed, "boldly adapting whatever he felt to be his own, till it was a wonder that one who so used others could be at the same time so undeniably original."[1] La Farge was born in New York City to French Catholic émigrés and raised in a prosperous, artistic household. At the age of six he learned watercolor techniques from his grandfather, and as a young man he studied briefly in the Paris studio of Thomas Couture. Impatient with the strictures of academic painting, La Farge embarked on a European tour, recording his favorite sites in architectural drawings. After his return to the United States, he sought out the artist William Morris Hunt—an American exponent of the Barbizon School—for further training, and soon launched his own career with landscape and still-life paintings. La Farge's remarkably early interest in Japanese art affected every aspect of his work, but most particularly his approach to floral subjects. In keeping with Japanese tradition, the artist frequently depicted flowers in their natural settings in order to portray their "spirit," as one critic put it, "rather than their botanical form."[2]

In the mid-1870s, the architect H. H. Richardson invited La Farge to develop a decorative program for the new Trinity Church in Boston. La Farge's eclectic scheme incorporated elements of Italian Renaissance and East Asian art and established his place as a leading figure in the decorative arts. The project also stimulated American enthusiasm for the almost lost art of stained glass, which La Farge went on to adapt for domestic use, especially in the opulent homes of Gilded Age millionaires. Around 1880 he produced a stained-glass window on a floral theme for the railroad magnate Henry G. Marquand (*Peonies Blown in the Wind*, The Metropolitan Museum of Art). He reprised that theme, with minor variations in border style and color scheme, at least six times, including in the watercolor *Peonies in a Breeze.*

La Farge had long relied on the translucency of watercolor to represent his ideas for art glass, but because *Peonies in a Breeze* is dated 1890, a full decade after the Marquand window, it must have been a "presentation piece" made to interest a potential patron rather than a preliminary sketch for a specific space. The composition and color scheme closely correspond to a window made in 1893 for the Washington, D.C., home of the statesman John Hay, which differs from the Marquand window mainly in its "kakemono borders" recalling the decorative mountings of a hanging scroll.[3] The watercolor's long, narrow format reinforces the reference to Japanese art, in which peonies are a traditional subject. Although scholars have long searched for an Asian prototype for this work, it seems unlikely that La Farge imitated a particular painting or print. As one of his contemporaries observed, La Farge took inspiration from the art of Japan, "but always in a spirit of free translation, strengthened by direct inspiration from nature."[4]

Beautiful as the peony windows are, the watercolor painting may ultimately be more aesthetically successful. Rendered in glass, the summer blossoms appear incongruously frozen in place, but the luminous, fluid washes of translucent watercolor convey the fragility of ink on silk, the better to capture an impression of full-blown flowers swaying in a breeze.

LM

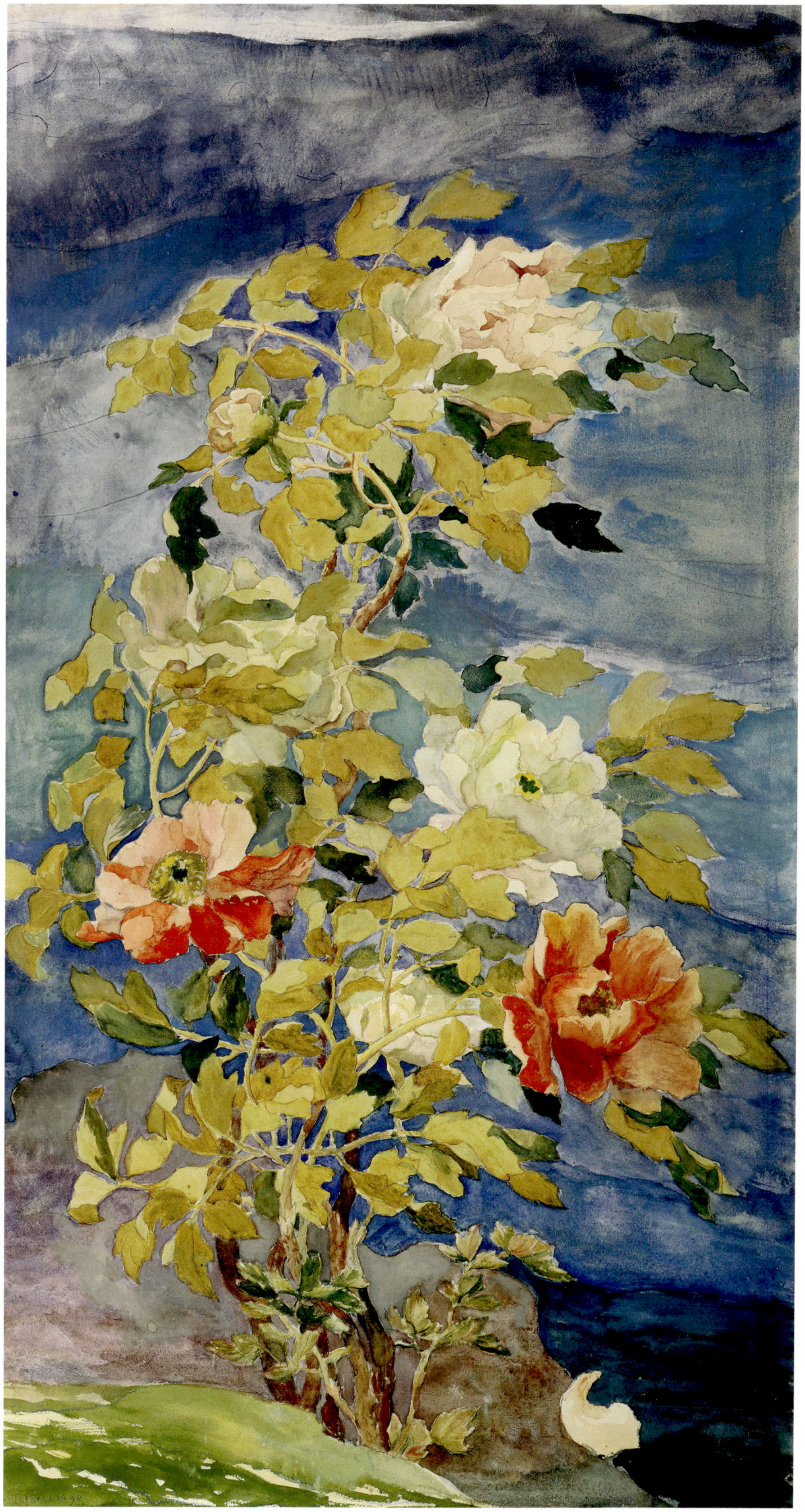

JOHN HENRY TWACHTMAN (1853–1902)

September Sunshine

ca. 1891–93
Oil on canvas
25 × 30 in. (63.5 × 76.2 cm)

"This is it!" John Henry Twachtman exclaimed at his first sight of the property in Greenwich, Connecticut, that would be his home for a productive decade. Twachtman and his oldest son, Alden, came upon the site while hiking along Horseneck Brook.[1] He probably rented the property beginning in 1889, before acquiring it in 1890.[2] Twachtman's homestead provided subject matter not only for him but also for his friends: "Mr. Twachtman's country place seems to be a regular rendezvous for Impressionists," a New York critic wrote in 1895.[3] Childe Hassam, Robert Reid, Theodore Robinson, Henry Fitch Taylor, and J. Alden Weir each painted occasionally at their friend's home, but for Twachtman the place was an unfailing source of inspiration. The brook, the cabbage patch, the poultry yard, the perennial borders, and the house itself moved him to put brush to canvas in all seasons.

The house was small and unattractive when Twachtman bought it, and his first impulse was to build a new one. In a letter to Weir, he sketched a gambrel-roofed mansion he planned to construct on the highest point of his land.[4] Financial realities and Twachtman's preference for the natural and understated soon eliminated that scheme. Instead, the proud homeowner embarked on a campaign of enlarging and enhancing his home, sensitively integrating it with the landscape. Because he rarely dated his paintings and he used the same titles repeatedly, the changing appearance of Twachtman's Connecticut property provides valuable clues to the sequence of his works.

September Sunshine portrays the house at an early stage of remodeling.[5] By then, Twachtman had added a dormer to the east (right in the painting); set balustrades in front of the two smaller dormers; removed the stairs leading to the porch; and semi-enclosed the porch with a half wall, clapboarded like the house itself. However, he had not yet replaced the porch roof with a grape arbor nor extended the house to the west, adding a second large dormer, front steps, and an entrance portico attributed to architect Stanford White. Those alterations began in the spring of 1894, when Robinson recorded in his diary that Twachtman was constructing a "trellis or porch for vines" and that Hassam was helping him lay the foundation for the addition.[6]

September Sunshine radiates the joy Twachtman took in his home. Framed on three sides by flickering golden leaves, the house rises from its stone foundation on a cushion of lawn like a gem presented on velvet. The foliage softens the edges of the house, disguises its small size, and shelters it, conveying a sense of intimacy and comfort. In the distance we glimpse the distinctive form of Round Hill, which gave its name to the road beside which Twachtman's house stood.

This may be the canvas that was shown as *September Sunlight* in the memorial exhibition of Twachtman's paintings in January 1905. A *New York Times* reviewer wrote, "Almost all these paintings are marked by an intense peacefulness and rest, characteristics which charm city folk because of the contrast with the movement and haste of town life. Perhaps the most restful of all is the view of his home near Greenwich called 'September Sunlight,' with its broad masses of building and trees, its cool sunshine and delicate gradation of values."[7]

SGL

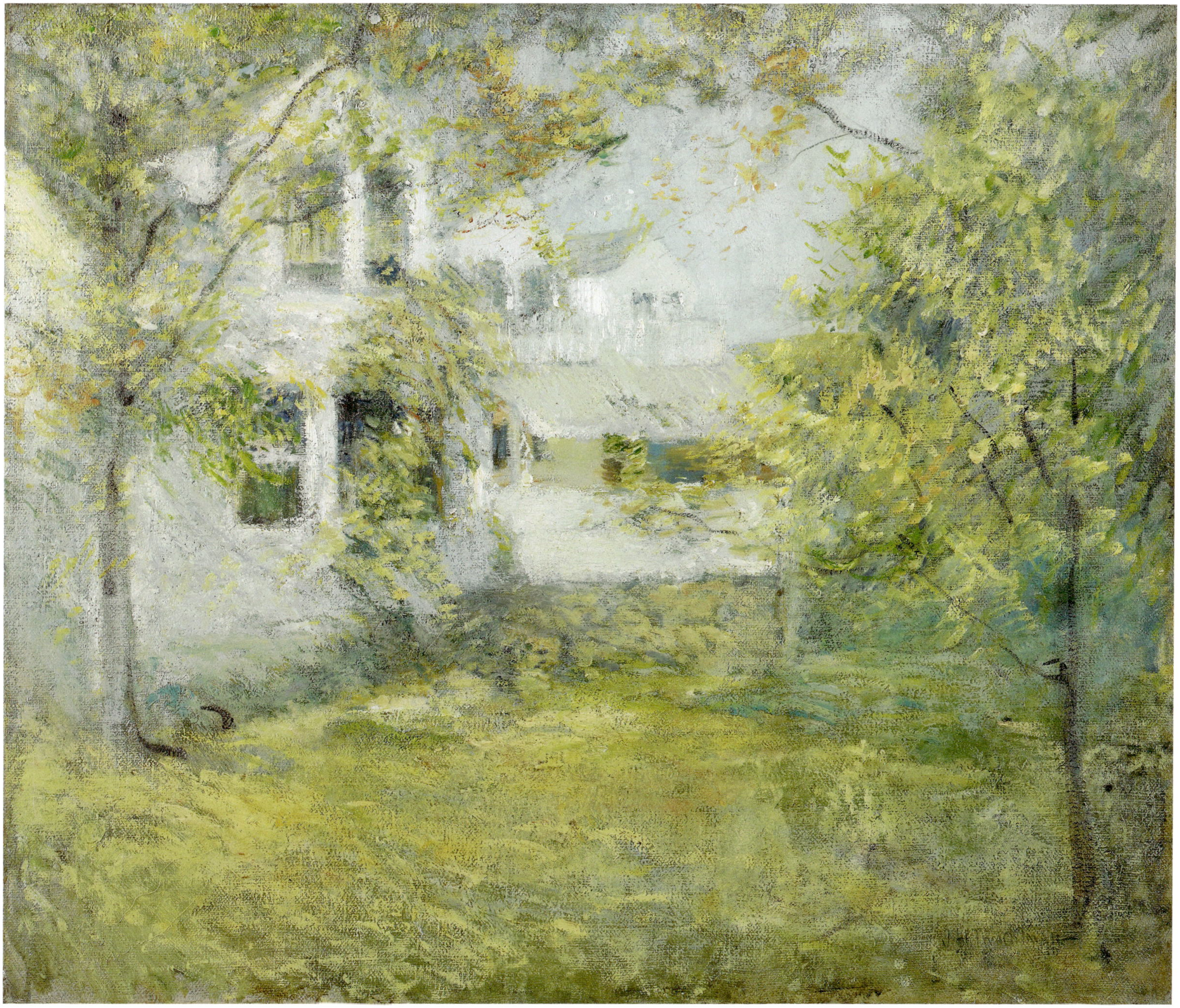

THEODORE ROBINSON (1852–1896)

World's Columbian Exposition

1894
Oil on canvas
25 × 30 in. (63.5 × 76.2 cm)

"One speaks a lot of the exhibition in Chicago—that they will do it on a very grand scale," the American painter Theodore Robinson wrote to the French impressionist master Claude Monet in 1892, adding, "One speaks a bit too much about the splendor of the buildings, which does not interest me very much."[1] The press-generated hyperbole regarding the World's Columbian Exposition—a massive spectacle conceived as a celebration of the 400-year anniversary of Columbus's voyage to the New World—did not impress Robinson, who preferred to paint subjects from nature. From 1887 through 1892, Robinson had spent his summers in the French village of Giverny, where he befriended Monet and immersed himself in the master's art.[2] Like Monet, Robinson frequently worked *sur le motif* (out of doors, directly in front of his subject) capturing the transitory effects of light and shadow as filtered through vibrant color and broken brushstrokes, often showing a subject's optical evolution over a series of paintings.[3]

Three of Robinson's works had been selected for display at the World's Columbian Exposition, and so it is not surprising that he visited the fairgrounds in Chicago, near the banks of Lake Michigan, shortly before the official opening in May of 1893.[4] Later that year, the painter-muralist Francis Davis Millet, who was the exposition's director of decoration, commissioned the present painting from Robinson for reproduction in a publication commemorating the international event.[5]

While Robinson surely drew from recollections of his time in the so-called White City in the early spring of 1893, he did not execute *World's Columbian Exposition sur le motif*. Rather, the artist based his composition on a published image of the grounds by the fair's official photographer.[6] The exposition's East Lagoon dominates the right side of Robinson's picture. At left, from background to foreground, are the mammoth, elongated Manufactures and Liberal Arts Building; the United States Government Building, with an American flag atop its cupola; and the red-roofed Fisheries Building, described by one historian as a "Spanish Romanesque design."[7] The exposition highlighted the industrial and cultural contributions of myriad nations and American states, and these monumental structures bespoke the scale and comprehensiveness of the larger project to catalogue five hundred years of contributions to humankind. The Manufactures and Liberal Arts Building alone showcased more exhibitors than had been featured in the entire 1876 Centennial Exhibition in Philadelphia.[8]

Robinson's letters document his frustration with the commission to paint the exposition, a subject that he believed stopped short of the lofty artistic goals prescribed by his French mentor. He wrote to Monet of the White City, "It is a bit shocking, the absence of modernity, of the new, it has the air of being made by good students of the Ecole des Beaux Arts, and one tells you with pride, 'it's very large, ten times larger than the exposition of . . .'"[9] Robinson applied a modern cast to his subject by interpreting the fair's highly classicized landscape through the au courant lens of impressionism, conceiving the grounds as an atmospheric tableau of cascading natural and man-made forms. With its pulsating hues, middle-class subject matter, and outdoor setting, *World's Columbian Exposition* certainly counts as a monument of American impressionism. LGM

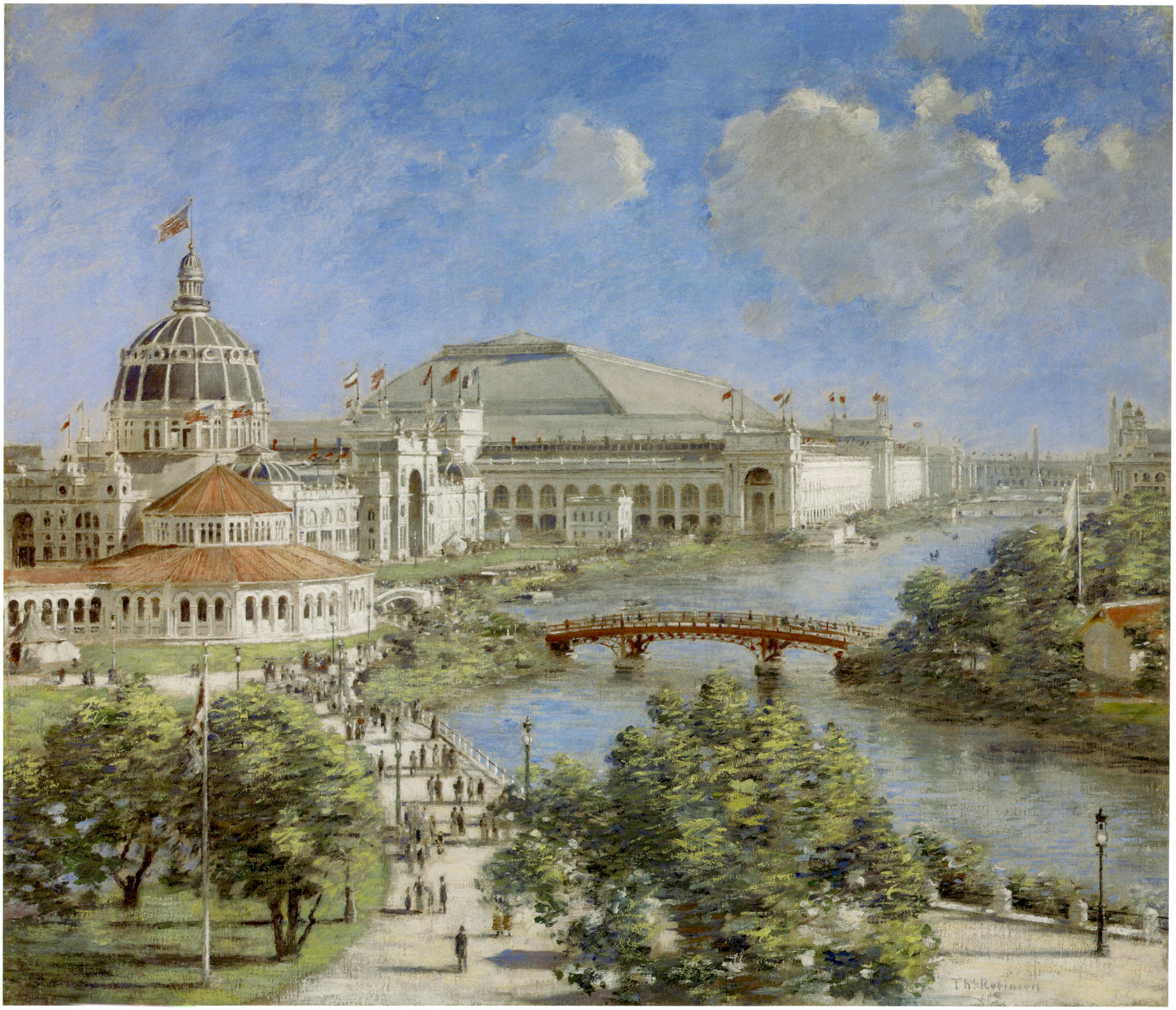

MAURICE BRAZIL PRENDERGAST (1858–1924)

People on the Beach: Revere Beach

ca. 1896–97
Watercolor on paper
13½ × 9¾ in. (34.3 × 24.8 cm)

When he painted *People on the Beach: Revere Beach* in the late 1890s, the Bostonian Maurice Brazil Prendergast was almost forty years old, having already spent two decades as a practicing artist. But it was work like this that suddenly established him as one of the most progressive artists of his day.

In 1891, after over fifteen years working in commercial art, Prendergast had finally gained enough patronage and money to travel to Paris, where he took classes at the Académie Julian and Académie Colarossi and made the switch to "fine" artist. Following in the footsteps of fellow Bostonian Childe Hassam, Prendergast quickly adopted the contemporary styles of Paris. He developed a version of impressionism that included scenes of both fashionable Parisians and peasant life on the French seacoast.[1]

When he returned to Boston in 1894, Prendergast found that the dichotomy between the urban and rural in his home town was being fundamentally challenged by the new ways that the city was growing. The famous landscape designer Frederick Law Olmsted had brought the country into the city by means of a string of urban parks and waterways called the Emerald Necklace. At the same time, much of the shoreline north and south of Boston was either incorporated into the city proper or made easily accessible to residents through the expansion of the electric railway. Prendergast was immediately drawn to the hustle and bustle of fashionable urban society in Boston's innovative new parks and in recently renovated nearby coastal resorts such as Revere Beach, which had opened to the public in 1896.[2]

Prendergast's *People on the Beach* makes the viewer feel as if he or she has happened upon "the place to be" on a summer afternoon. The electricity Prendergast created in his watercolor arises from the crowd—a mass of people in the distance so dense that the viewer can only discern fragments of hats and umbrellas. With large strides and billowing skirts, the men, women, and children in the foreground hasten to join the action, their outlines blurred against the tawny sand. The long, diagonal strokes of the figures' shadows are like pathways, showing their movements flash across the picture plane. These people are not here to bathe in the sun or the water. They are here to see and be seen: to stroll quickly, to stand and converse, and occasionally to sit on the benches provided for the people watchers with their backs toward Massachusetts Bay.

Prendergast's grasp of the fashionable modern beach was coupled with his quick adoption of abstract compositional devices newly proposed in the 1890s. One of the few artists to successfully translate the French impressionist style into watercolor, he used unfinished areas as abstract shapes, often allowing the white of the paper to show through. The tall, narrow format of the Crystal Bridges sheet and its flattened perspective echo the spatial construction of Japanese prints, which were held up by contemporary theorists such as Arthur Wesley Dow as a model for Western artists seeking an alternative approach to picture making.[3] Prendergast's openness to new ways of looking at the world and at art, which was widely recognized by critics, patrons, and exhibition juries in Boston and New York from the mid-1890s forward, made him a key figure in the unfolding of American modernism.

NMM

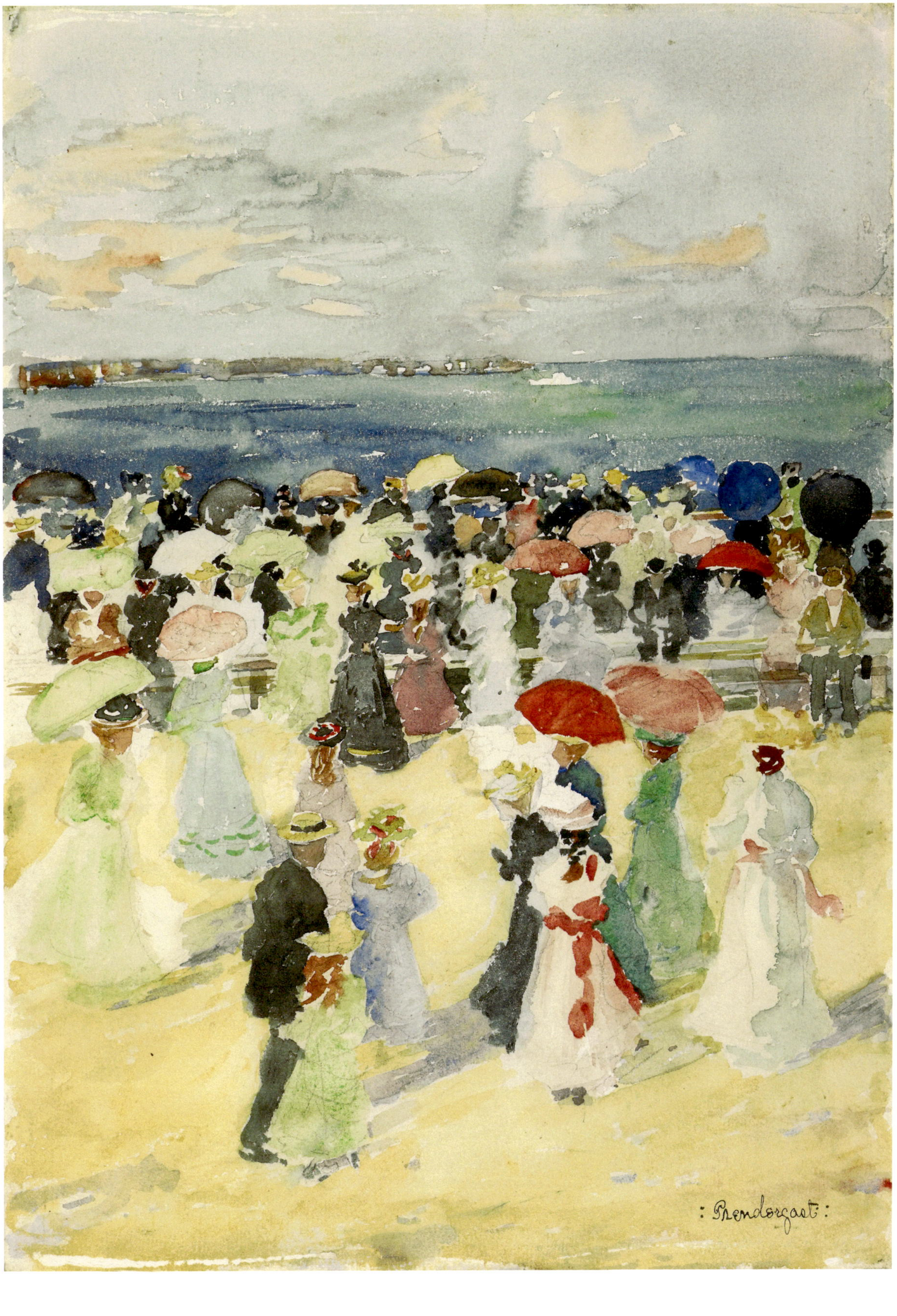
: Prendergast :

WILLIAM MERRITT CHASE (1849–1916)

Seaside Flowers

ca. 1897
Oil on canvas
29 × 38½ in. (73.7 × 97.8 cm)

In 1891, a small group of summer residents of Shinnecock Hills, Long Island, offered William Merritt Chase a tract of land on which to build a summer studio and art school.[1] Arrangements were quickly drawn up. The artist hired the fashionable architectural firm of McKim, Mead & White to design his home and the artists' village situated about three miles to its west. By the time he opened the Shinnecock Summer Art School in 1892, Chase had been teaching on and off for over a decade, first at the newly founded (1875) Art Students League in New York City and later at the Brooklyn Art School. Shinnecock was the artist's first independent teaching operation, and its success inspired him to open a year-round academy in New York, known as the Chase School, five years later. Although Chase sold his urban school after only two years in operation, Shinnecock remained active until 1902, when its founder decided to spend his summers traveling abroad with family and students.[2]

Chase enjoyed twelve productive summers in Shinnecock Hills. Although he spent much of his time there in the studio or teaching, his painting from this period reflects a wholly domestic focus, with numerous views of his family and friends enjoying the coastal setting. *Seaside Flowers* is among Chase's most ambitious paintings from the period. The large canvas features four of the artist's daughters picking wildflowers in a dunes landscape. His eldest, Alice Dieudonnée, as well as second- and third-born, Koto and Dorothy, are in the foreground, dressed in broad-brimmed hats and fresh summer whites. Chase made a number of paintings of these three engaged in outdoor leisure activities around the Shinnecock property. His wife, Alice, also dressed in summer whites, stands in the middle distance, holding hands with their young daughter Hazel and gesturing to a boy—probably the son of a neighboring family.[3]

Seaside Flowers combines Chase's flair for decorative formal arrangements with his staunchly modern dismissal of narrative. Although his family features prominently in the work, it is ultimately a painting about visual harmonies and compositional balance, not family leisure activities. With the horizon situated just above center, Chase stealthily avoided a static effect by interrupting the flat landscape with the dynamic diagonal of the sandy path at the far right. The shoreline loosely mimics the line of the path, and these two diagonals frame the central activity of Chase's daughters and wife. Figures dot across the landscape, lining up to form another implied diagonal gesture that leads the eye across the canvas. Chase obscures the girls' faces, further emphasizing their importance as formal devices meant to animate the composition. As Chase's daughters assemble their bouquets from the bounty of the grassy dunes, the painting's title begs the question of whether the seaside flowers to which the artist refers are, perhaps, the girls themselves.

SMH

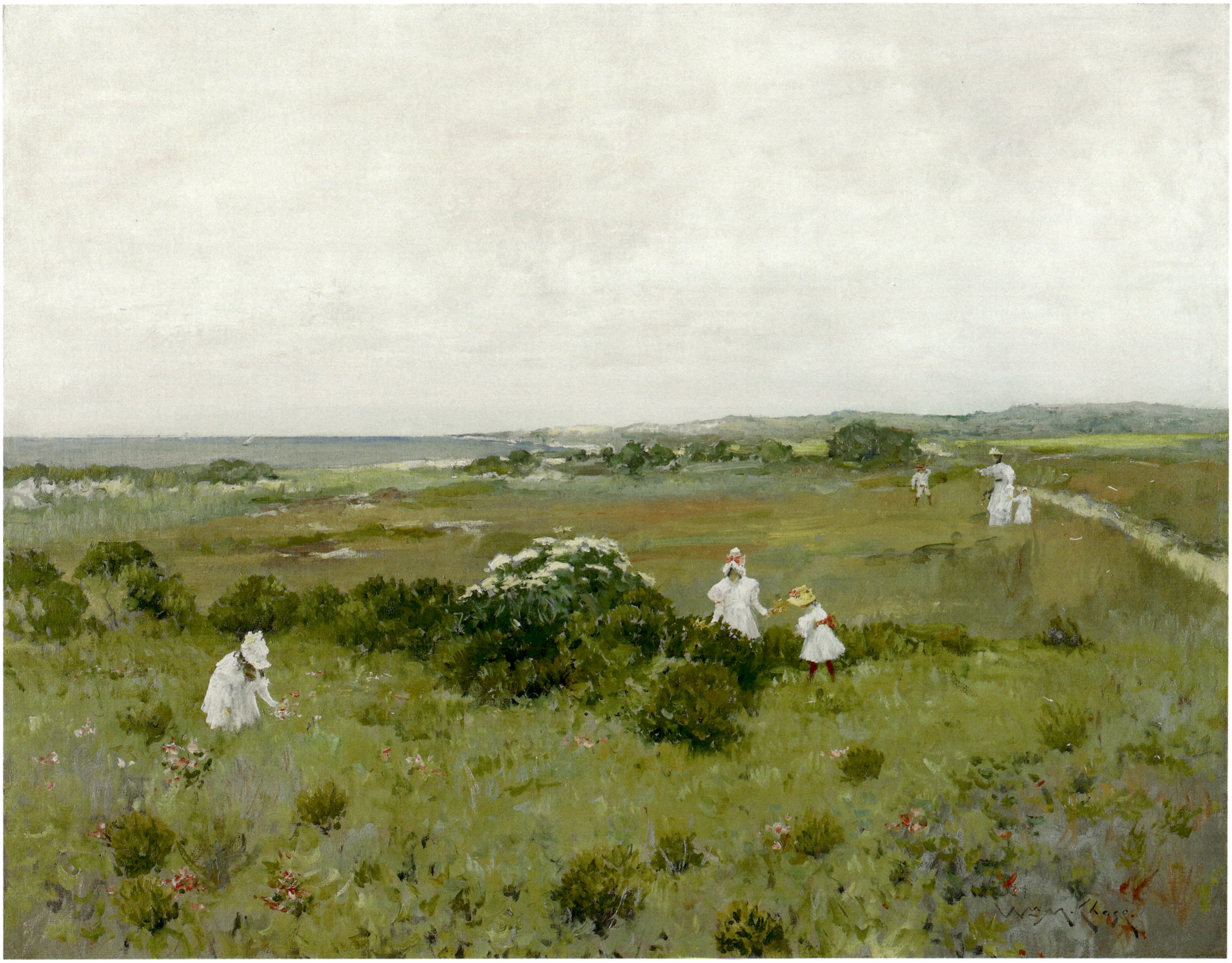

JAMES MCNEILL WHISTLER (1834–1903)

Green and Violet: The Evening Walk

1896
Oil on panel
5 × 8½ in. (12.7 × 21.6 cm)
Promised Gift

Born in Lowell, Massachusetts, James McNeill Whistler trained as an artist in Paris and spent the rest of his life abroad. As an American expatriate in London, Whistler countered the Victorian preference for eye-catching narrative pictures with works distinguished by their subtlety, understatement, and lack of a literary theme. In the 1880s, at the height of his career, Whistler contradicted another artistic convention—huge, pretentious canvases designed for public display—by painting on wood panels no bigger than the lid of a cigar box. To assert their status as important works of art despite their size, Whistler placed these diminutive oil paintings in proportionally large, gilded frames of his own design. He called them "Notes," choosing a word that implied both the spontaneity of a sketch and the fundamental elements of music—a useful analogy for Whistler's aesthetic compositions. Portable, affordable, and easy to enjoy, these little oils proved especially popular with American collectors.

Whistler painted a number of Notes in 1885 at the French port town of Dieppe, on the English Channel, in the company of his student Walter Sickert.[1] Some ten years later he returned to that seaside resort, this time under unhappy circumstances. After the death of his beloved wife, Beatrice, in May of 1896, Whistler had fallen into an incapacitating depression; that September he took a working holiday to France, hoping to escape from grief. *Green and Violet: The Evening Walk* is a rare souvenir of that journey, since bad weather conspired with low spirits to prevent Whistler from painting much at all. Indeed, the picture may only have been conceived in Dieppe and painted after the artist's return to London, when he threw himself determinedly into his work; in January 1897 *Green and Violet* was named among the many works "recently completed," and still to be found, in Whistler's studio.[2] The American poet Amy Lowell must have seen it when she called on Whistler there to purchase another of his Notes, *Blue and Silver: Dieppe* (New Britain Museum of American Art), even though its paint was not yet dry. The artist, to no avail, had tried to dissuade her by recommending a different painting of the same dimensions—most likely *Green and Violet*—that "he considered the better work."[3]

Broadly painted with pigments so diluted they resemble watercolor washes, *Green and Violet* is a charming picture with a melancholy air. The artist observed from a distance the calm, turquoise sea; faint suggestion of a pier; and sweeping, sandy pathway through a swath of grass. Although the water is still bright in the fading light of day, the sailboats have turned back to shore. A few hearty souls sit in deck chairs or stroll along the beach, but their summer parasols have been replaced with mournful black umbrellas. In Dieppe, Whistler seems to have found a landscape that expressed his mood: writing from there in late September, he observed that "a sea side place . . . after the season is like a theatre in the day time—there is an uncanny sort of loneliness about it."[4] LM

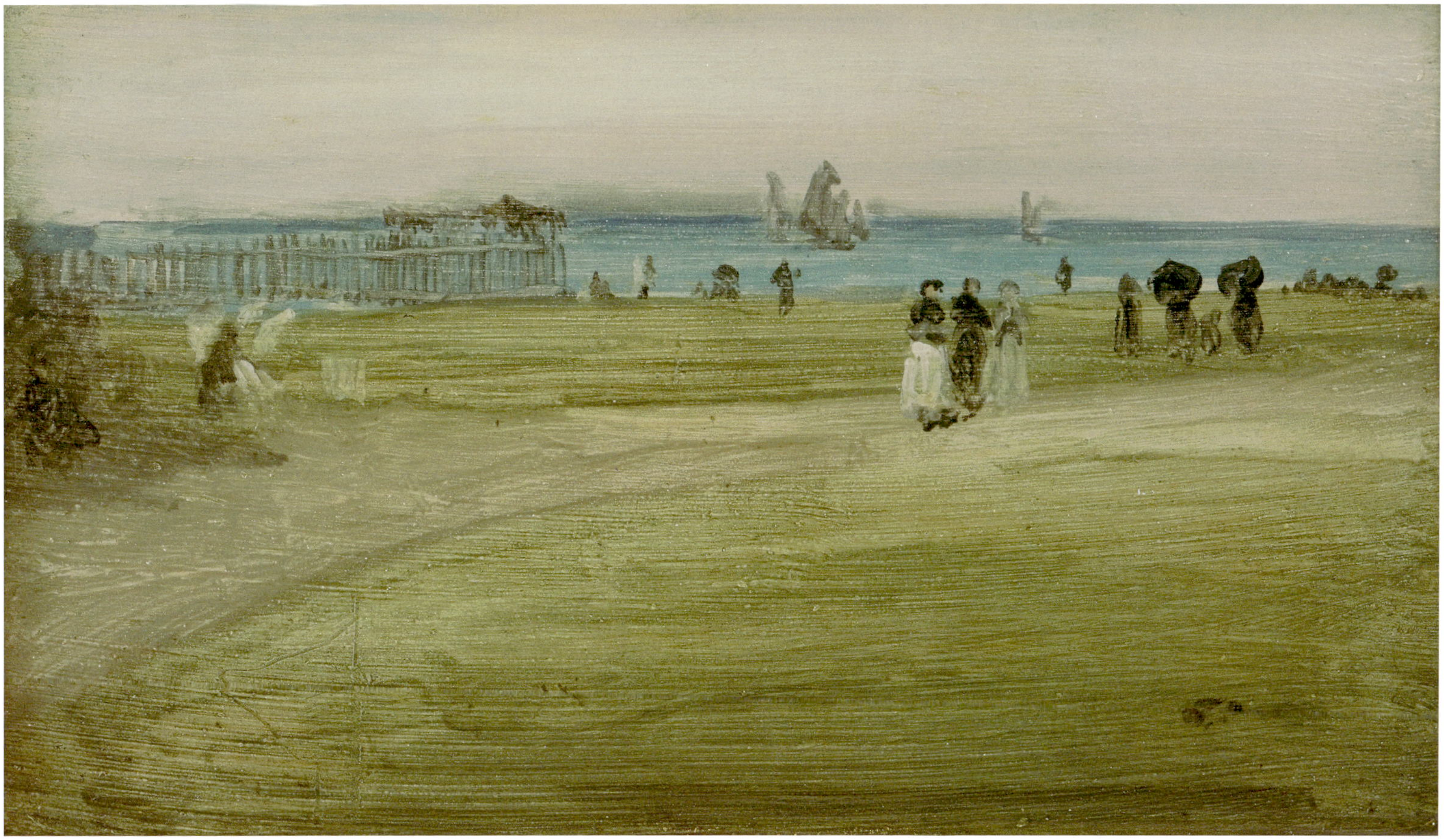

MARIA OAKEY DEWING (1845–1927)

Rose Garden

1901
Oil on canvas
24 × 40½ in. (61 × 102.9 cm)

Maria Oakey Dewing painted *Rose Garden* during one of her last summers in Cornish, New Hampshire, the rural enclave where she and her family had spent every summer for fifteen years. It was in Cornish that Dewing began the second phase of her artistic career, binding herself to what she described as "a long apprenticeship in the garden."[1]

Maria Richards Oakey's conventional education began in New York City, at the Cooper Union School of Design for Women, and continued at the National Academy of Design, where she studied with John La Farge. A founding member of the Art Students League in 1875, Oakey was among the first to join the progressive Society of American Artists in 1877, an action that helped establish her position in the vanguard of American painting. She also ventured into the decorative arts: the aesthete Oscar Wilde lavished praise on her design for a stage curtain, and when he asked her why she did not take up decoration exclusively, she replied, "Because I must paint pictures or die."[2]

By 1880, Oakey was being lauded in the press as "a young artist of talent [who] bids fair to occupy a high position in the art world."[3] The next year she married a slightly younger artist, Thomas Wilmer Dewing, who was not yet as well established in his career; their daughter, Elizabeth, was born four years later. Although Dewing continued to practice her profession, her attention shifted away from the portraits and figure paintings that had been her specialty to images of flowers—most of them produced (or at least begun) in the heady atmosphere of her Cornish garden. She referred to these outdoor works as "modern," distinguishing them from floral still lifes executed in the studio.[4] "Let not the student think that flower painting is the business of the amateur," Dewing wrote in 1915, as if to justify the dramatic change she made at the height of her career. "The flower offers a removed beauty that exists only for beauty, more abstract than it can be in the human being, even more exquisite."[5]

One Cornish acquaintance recalled that Dewing was "a true artist" who worked assiduously through the summers, and who failed to produce many paintings only because she "lingered so long over her large canvases."[6] Of those few, labor-intensive pictures, *Rose Garden* may be the most exuberant. A sinuous vine of morning glories weaves through an arabesque of roses looping across the verdant undergrowth in natural abandon. The leaves and woody stems, rendered with linear precision, are shiny and opaque, setting off by contrast the soft, semitransparent peony blossoms. An intimate view of an apparently boundless flower bed, the picture invites us to share this welter of color, texture, and fragrance, the garden that nourished Dewing's senses while she subordinated her professional aspirations to those of her husband.

Rose Garden occupied a special place in Dewing's affections. Many years after selling the painting she requested its loan for an exhibition, explaining to the owner that she considered it "highly representative of me"—syntax that suggests her identification with the painting, or perhaps with the garden it depicts. After the exhibition closed, *Rose Garden* remained in Dewing's studio for a few days; when at last she sent the painting back it was, she confessed, "with all the emotion of a mother in parting from a favorite child."[7] LM

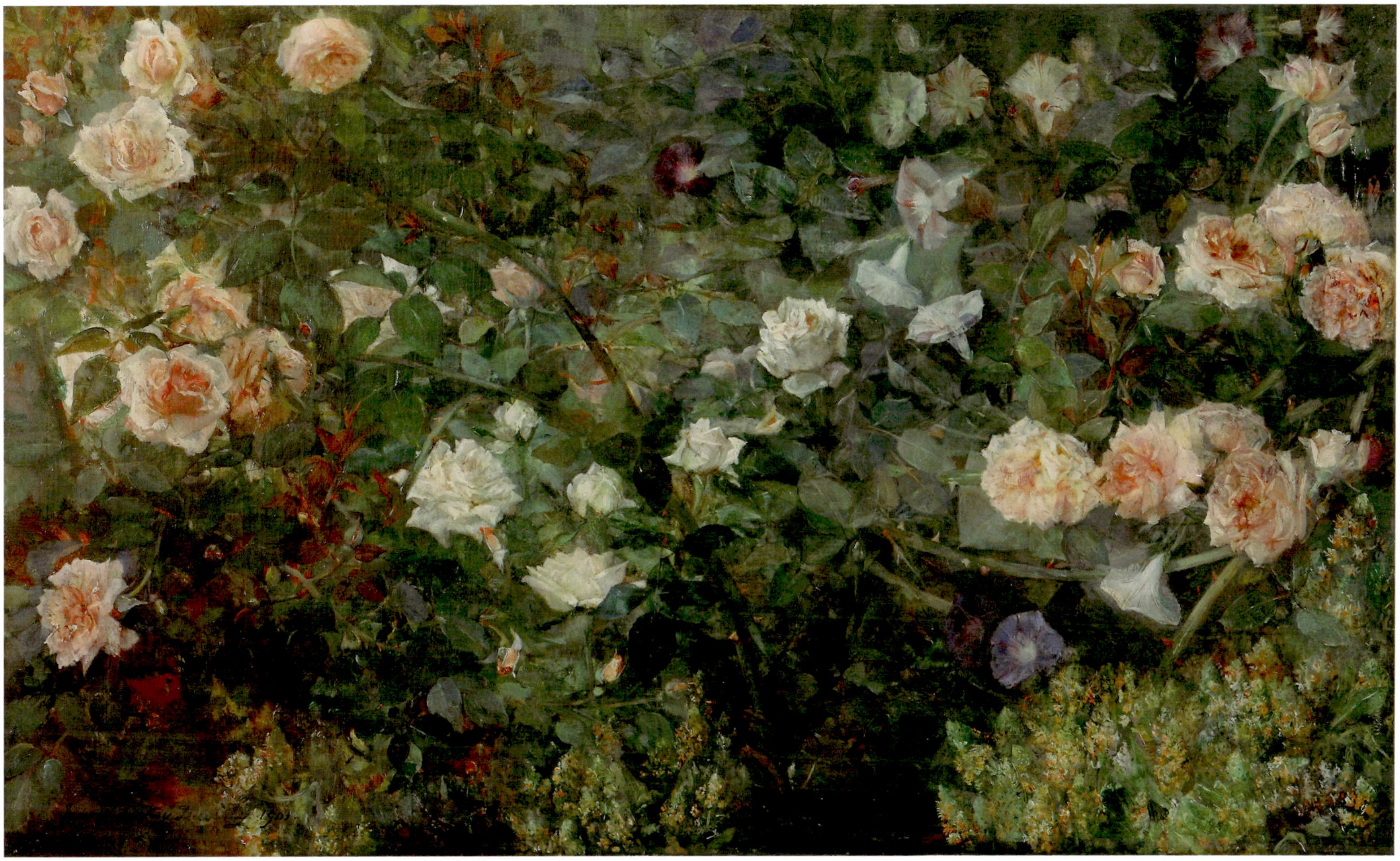

WILLARD LEROY METCALF (1858–1925)

The Pool

1904
Oil on canvas
36 × 36 in. (91.4 × 91.4 cm)
Promised Gift

Willard LeRoy Metcalf was destined to become an artist: a medium had told his mother so.[1] At an early age Metcalf was apprenticed to a landscape painter in Boston, and he became one of the first scholarship students at the new School of the Museum of Fine Arts. As an illustrator, he earned enough money to join the hundreds of Americans who were flocking to Paris in the 1880s to complete their artistic education. Metcalf studied for five years at the Académie Julian, spending his summer holidays in picturesque corners of England and France. He was among the first Americans to sojourn in Giverny, near the home of Claude Monet, though it would be many years before French impressionism significantly affected his own approach to painting.

Upon his return to the United States in 1889, Metcalf settled in New York, and despite some promising signs of professional success he had to teach to make a living. He was always an active figure in the art world, and in 1897 banded together with nine other European-trained painters to secede from the Society of American Artists and form an organization of their own. The works Metcalf showed in the first exhibitions of the Ten American Painters were mostly earlier paintings in the academic style—"trial flights," as one critic later recalled, "toward the consummation [*sic*] of the real work of his life."[2]

Metcalf's career stalled in 1903. Trained as a figure painter but naturally inclined to landscape, he was, at age forty-five, still uncertain what direction his professional life should take. Disheartened by indifferent reviews, Metcalf made the consequential decision to leave his wife in the city and live for a while with his parents at their modest home in eastern Maine. Rambling through the countryside and along the banks of the Damariscotta River, Metcalf set up his easel wherever he pleased, practicing impressionism in the open air. This retreat lasted just over a year, long enough for him to paint the landscape in every season. In the book of press clippings he began keeping around that time, Metcalf referred to this therapeutic period as "the Renaissance."[3]

Metcalf returned to New York at the beginning of 1905 with nearly two dozen paintings to represent his rehabilitation. In those landscapes, the critic Royal Cortissoz observed, the artist "may be said to have 'found himself,' producing a body of work broad in scope and rich in content."[4] The seemingly direct and unpretentious style of these compositions emanated Metcalf's renewed self-confidence, "as if expression were, with him, indeed, a condition following upon observation like the echo following speech in a vaulted chamber."[5] *The Pool* may be the most contemplative and satisfying of the Maine paintings. In the left foreground, a fallen tree trunk establishes a diagonal bridge into the picture space, leading the eye across the richly colored, placid pool to the gentle streams of water that cascade over the boulders on the far side. The painting reveals a private, protected, woodland oasis, emblematic of the peace the artist found in nature.

LM

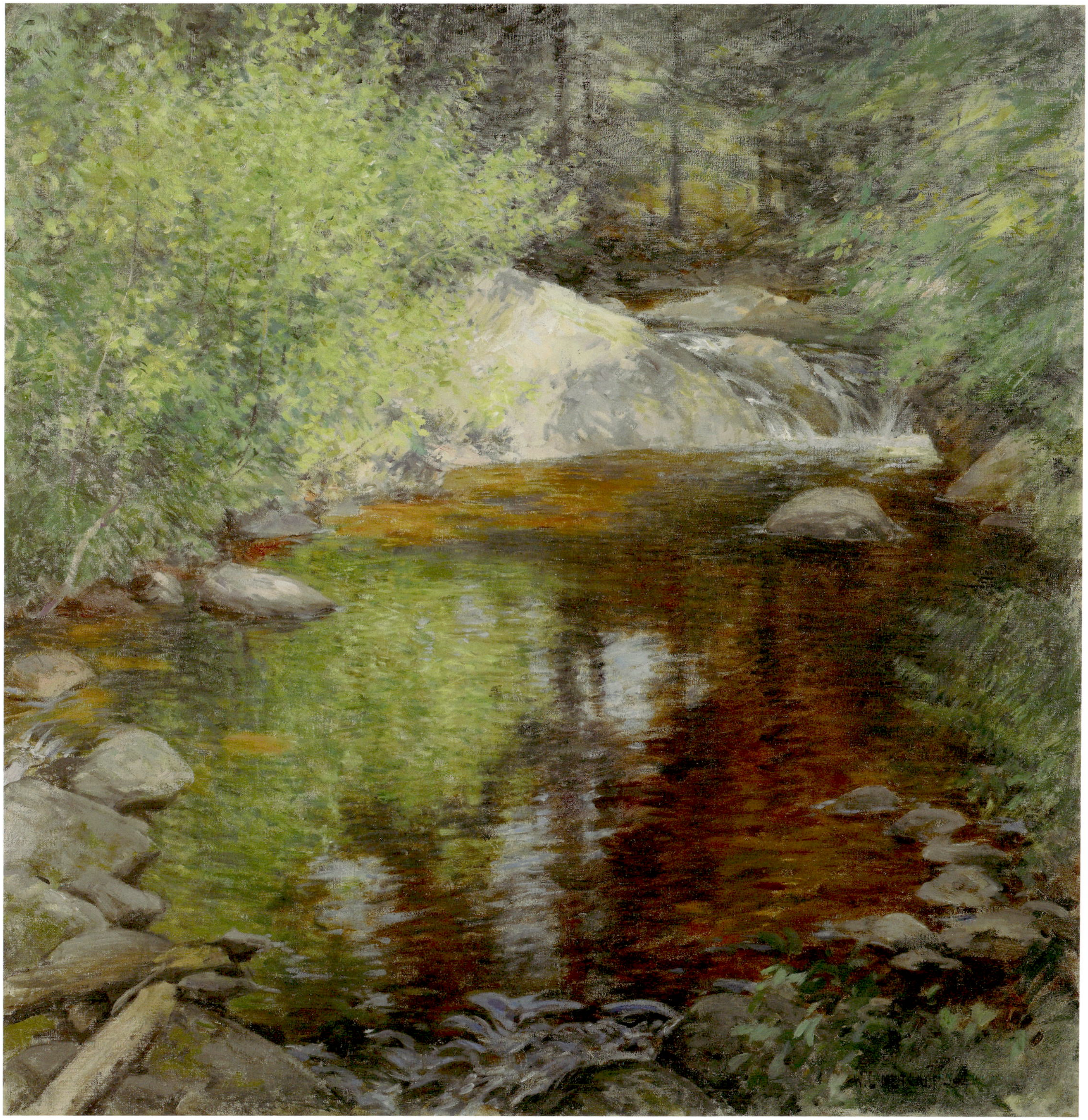

WILLIAM TROST RICHARDS (1833–1905)

Along the Shore

1903
Oil on canvas
39 3/16 × 78 1/2 in. (99.6 × 199.4 cm)

William Trost Richards was first drawn to coastal subjects during the 1860s, when he sketched and painted them on plein air expeditions along American shores from New Jersey to New England. By the early 1870s Richards was recognized among the growing cadre of artists like John Frederick Kensett, Sanford Robinson Gifford, and Alfred Thompson Bricher who were adept at portraying marine and seaside subjects as well as painting the American landscape. This increase in American artists' production of coastal paintings was met with great interest among critics and patrons, for whom Hudson River School landscapes had begun to lose their luster. The development of resort communities along the Atlantic seaboard after the Civil War also played an important role in the new popularity of coastal images. Historic seaside towns like Nantucket and Newport were promoted as therapeutic retreats for harried urban dwellers. Richards's selection of Newport as his summer residence by 1874 signaled his embrace of perhaps the most resonant site for picturesque and nostalgic subjects, as well as his pursuit of a population of socially and intellectually prominent patrons. The artist built a colonial revival summerhouse in Newport in 1882 and eventually relocated there year-round.[1]

As his reputation for marine subjects flourished, Richards spent two productive years (1878–80) in England, a mid-career sojourn driven by quests for new patronage and novel subjects. His artistic mission took him to Cornwall, Dorset, and Devon, where he recorded the dramatic British scenery that, along with the American coasts, would occupy him for decades to come. While Richards continued to paint landscapes during these years, by the 1880s his skill in rendering the age-old themes of sublime storm and marine disaster, as well as his ability to employ atmospheric effects as powerful narrative elements in their own right, earned him the enduring reputation as an artist who "has a skill all his own in painting the rocky coast of our Northern states and that of England."[2]

From about 1890, Richards concentrated on close-up images of surging breakers. These works were the culmination of a long campaign to master the representation of moving water that began in the 1860s with his minutely painted, serpentine rows of shining waves tipped with foam. By the mid-1880s the artist had developed a set of even more convincing pictorial conventions to portray the complexities of ocean waters. In these later paintings, such as the monumental *Along the Shore*, Richards employed a painterly touch that conveyed visual fact while also suggesting fluidity of motion. The stately cadence of waves in the earlier works gives way to openly violent forces, as massive swells rise in powerful crests to pound against the rocky Atlantic coast. The horizon is low and largely obscured by the mighty waves exploding in the foreground against equally turbulent skies. Richards's preoccupation with dramatic marine scenes up to the time of his death in 1905 demonstrates the lasting appetite for the subject among patrons and dealers. This exciting but somewhat melancholy motif appeared in contemporaneous works by Winslow Homer, Albert Bierstadt, and others, suggesting that the thrilling menace of the big wave may have been a resonant metaphor for fin de siècle cultural anxieties shared by artists and audiences alike. LSF

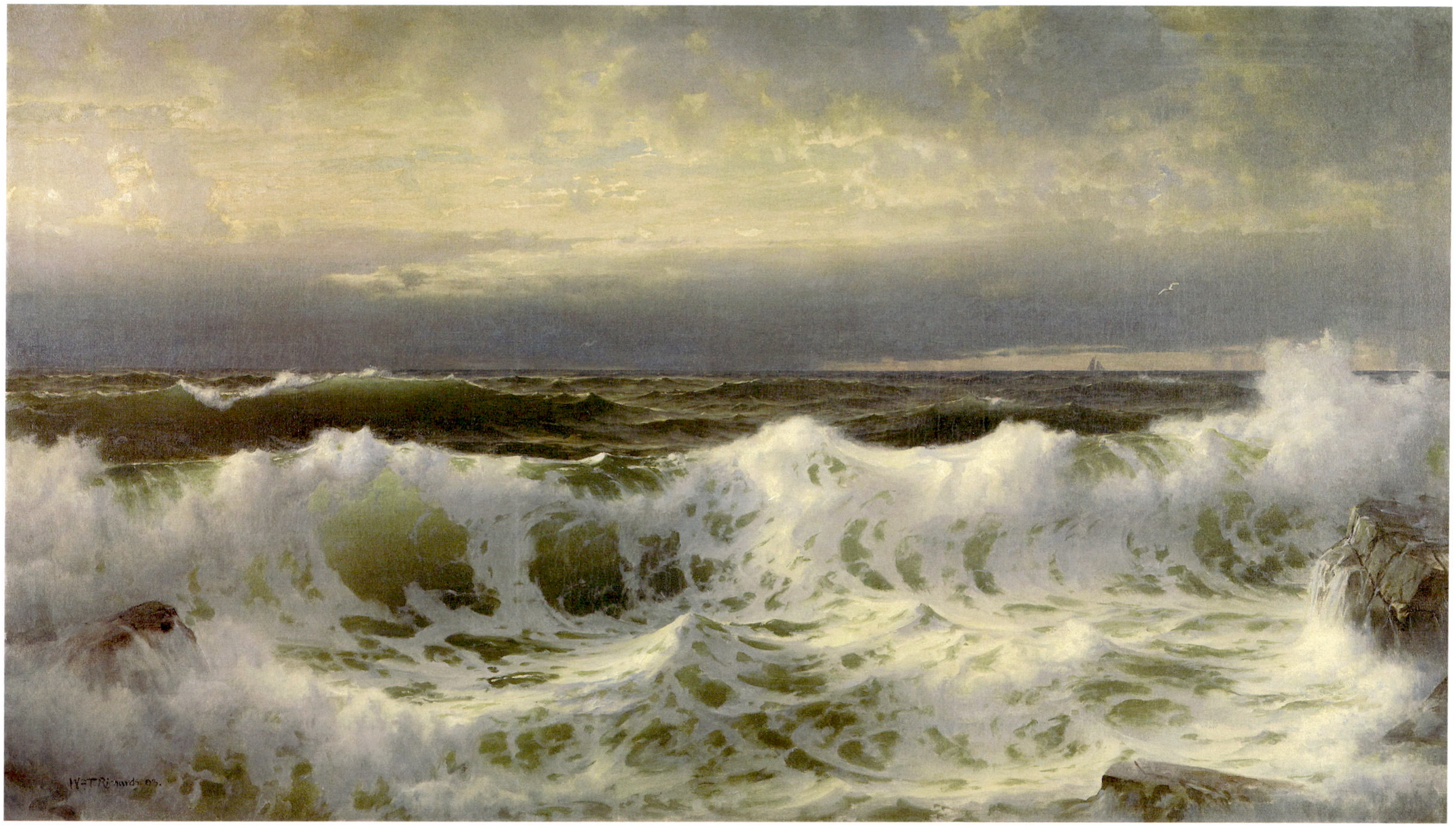

EDWARD SHERIFF CURTIS (1868–1952)

The Vanishing Race—Navaho

1904 (negative); 1907 (print)
Photogravure
Portfolio volume 1, plate 1 from *The North American Indian: Being a Series of Volumes Picturing and Describing the Indians of the United States, and Alaska*, 1907–30
14³⁄₁₆ × 17⁵⁄₁₆ in. (36 × 44 cm)

Edward Sheriff Curtis's masterwork, *The North American Indian*, is an expansive collection of twenty volumes of illustrated text and twenty corresponding volumes of larger, unbound portfolios. Combined, the complete series contains 2,228 photogravures documenting more than 80 Native American tribes that inhabited the lands west of the Mississippi and Missouri rivers in the early twentieth century.[1] A tribute to Curtis's talent and vision, the artist received political support for the project from Theodore Roosevelt and financial backing from John Pierpont Morgan.[2] The original agreement between Curtis and Morgan was to sell the limited edition, multivolume set on a subscription basis over the course of five years.[3] In the end, this labor of love occupied Curtis's attention for more than two decades, from 1907 to 1930.[4]

Curtis commenced his ambitious endeavor to document indigenous Americans in the late 1890s, after opening a photography studio in Seattle, Washington. In 1895 he photographed Princess Angeline, daughter of Chief Sealth, whose Duwamish tribe had lived in the Seattle area for generations and for whom the city was named.[5] Curtis soon began visiting nearby Indian reservations, and his field projects quickly took precedence over studio work. While Curtis had some small success publishing and exhibiting individual examples of this imagery, he aspired to create a more comprehensive picture of what was commonly, if erroneously, referred to as "the vanishing race."[6] His self-described aim in embarking on the massive undertaking was to create a "study of a people who are rapidly losing the traces of their aboriginal character and who are destined ultimately to become assimilated" into Anglo-American culture.[7]

Well versed in current artistic trends, Curtis employed the aesthetic of pictorialism throughout this remarkable series. In the tradition of noted fine arts photographers such as Alfred Stieglitz, Gertrude Käsebier, and Clarence White, Curtis created tonally subtle images with highly poetic resonances. For example, in *The Vanishing Race—Navaho*, the first image in the first portfolio, Curtis's masterful use of light and shadow emphasizes the symbolic period of darkness that he perceived contemporary indigenous Americans to be facing. The image depicts a line of Indians on horseback, represented as dim, faceless forms, as they move away from Curtis's view. The departing figures are consumed by a heavy gloom that suggests the uncertainty of their future and the potential disappearance of their traditional ways of life. The soft focus of the image enhances this sense of fading away.

In addition to applying his technical mastery to these photogravures, Curtis also shaped his purportedly documentary images by providing his sitters with traditional native costumes from his collection and eliminating other evidence of cultural assimilation. Although Curtis wished to capture his subjects' "Indianness" (as it was conceived by Anglo Americans) before it vanished, the process of acculturation had already begun.[8] Regardless of its romanticism and questionable authenticity as a document of Native American reality, *The North American Indian* is an elegant and thought-provoking portrayal of a turbulent time in the nation's rich culture and history.

AD

Plate 1

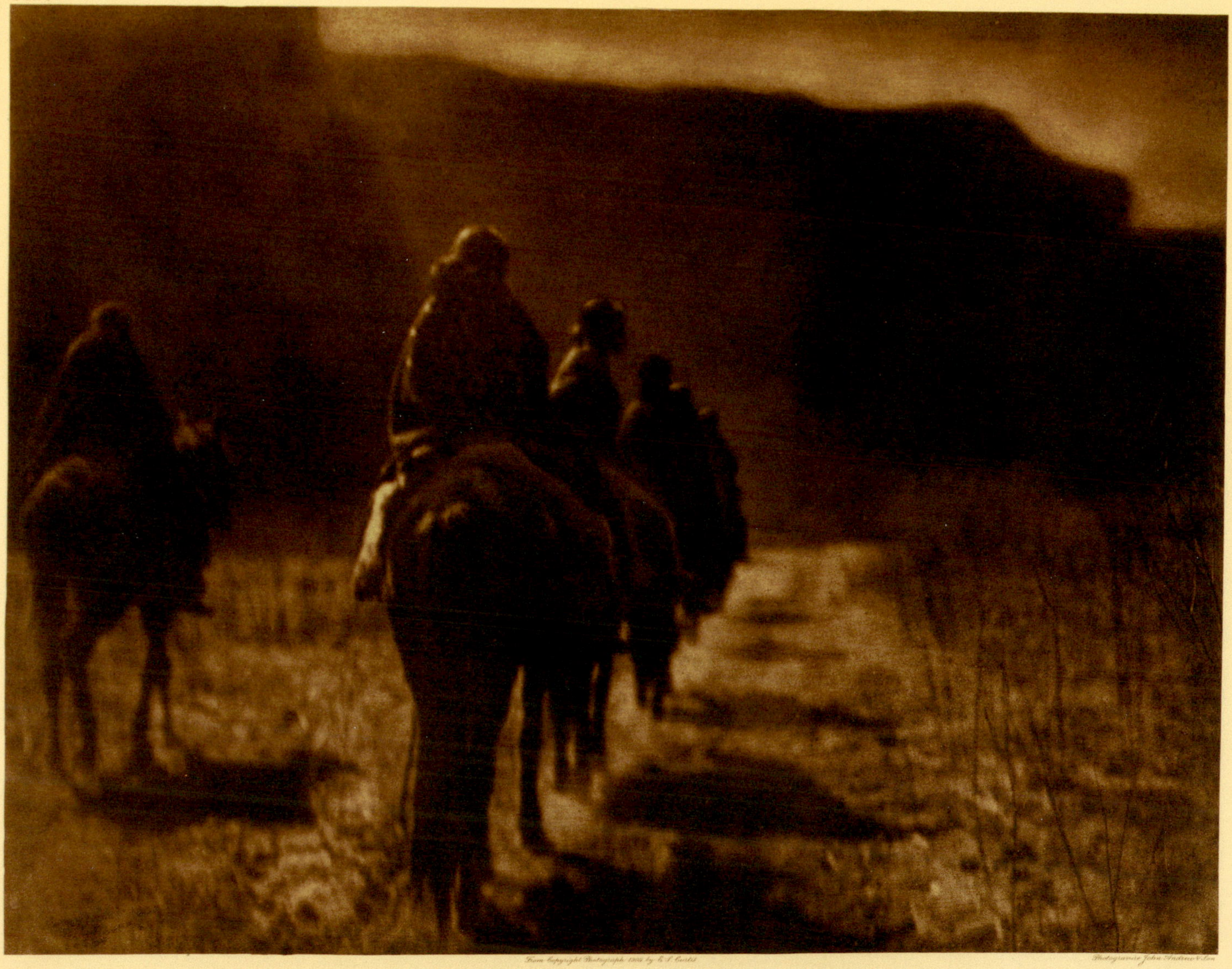

From Copyright Photograph 1904 by E. S. Curtis

Photogravure John Andrew & Son

THE VANISHING RACE – NAVAHO

FREDERIC REMINGTON (1861–1909)

Cowpuncher's Lullaby

1906
Oil on canvas
30 × 21 in. (76.2 × 53.3 cm)

Frederic Remington completed over seventy night scenes in the last decade of his life. Already established as the premier illustrator of the "Old West," Remington sought recognition as a fine artist, and his nighttime subjects were key to his success in this endeavor. Nocturnes had been growing in popularity since the eighteenth century, possibly in response to the increasing scarcity of darkness as towns and cities began to be illuminated at night by gaslights.[1] The genre had its heyday in the late nineteenth century, when artists such as James McNeill Whistler recognized that the nocturne's soft, ambiguous forms and close tonal range made it the perfect vehicle for exploring painting's formal aspects. Although he eschewed Whistler's radical embrace of form over content, Remington's choice of a genre closely associated with the avant-garde gave his paintings the imprimatur of fine art.[2] His interest in night scenes was also practical. Having worked for twenty years in black and white, the artist claimed to be flummoxed by color.[3] Remington's friend and colleague Childe Hassam suggested that nocturnes, with their limited hues, might provide a good entry point.[4] Indeed, one contemporary reviewer noted, "he takes the shades of night to help him to those tones of mystery which most of his previous pictures lacked."[5]

Cowpuncher's Lullaby, exhibited to critical acclaim at the prominent New York gallery Knoedler's in December 1906, is a mark of all that Remington had achieved in his first five years of earnest painting. Reviews praised the eleven works Remington exhibited that winter for having "softness and almost delicacy of color" that nevertheless "belongs to the West, that is . . . inevitably of the prairies, and foothills, and desert."[6] Remington rendered the rich range of green, buff, and brown that composes the lower half of *Cowpuncher's Lullaby* in a mixture of opaque and transparent pigments that provide visual interest as well as compositional stability. The horse, grass, and cows coalesce into a field of brown out of which the cowboy emerges, his black jacket barely distinguishable from the row of dark trees behind him. His white face draws the viewer's eye upward to the bright bursts of stars overhead, as if to suggest the loftiness of his poetic aspirations as he sings out into a resolutely material—and apparently indifferent—natural world.

For all his technical achievement, critics continued to praise Remington primarily for his western subject matter and sought to deduce his paintings' narratives. *Cowpuncher's Lullaby*, wrote one critic, "tells the story of the herd lying at rest under the stars, while a gaunt cowboy sings to them lest they lose their quiet and perhaps stampede away from his control."[7] The reviewer's interest in finding a story behind the scene points up Remington's most important contribution to the nocturne. In paintings like *Cowpuncher's Lullaby*, Remington discovered a means of instilling narrative into a theretofore aesthetically oriented genre. In so doing, he preserved the subject matter on which he staked his fame even as he sought a higher realm of achievement in the fine arts. LS

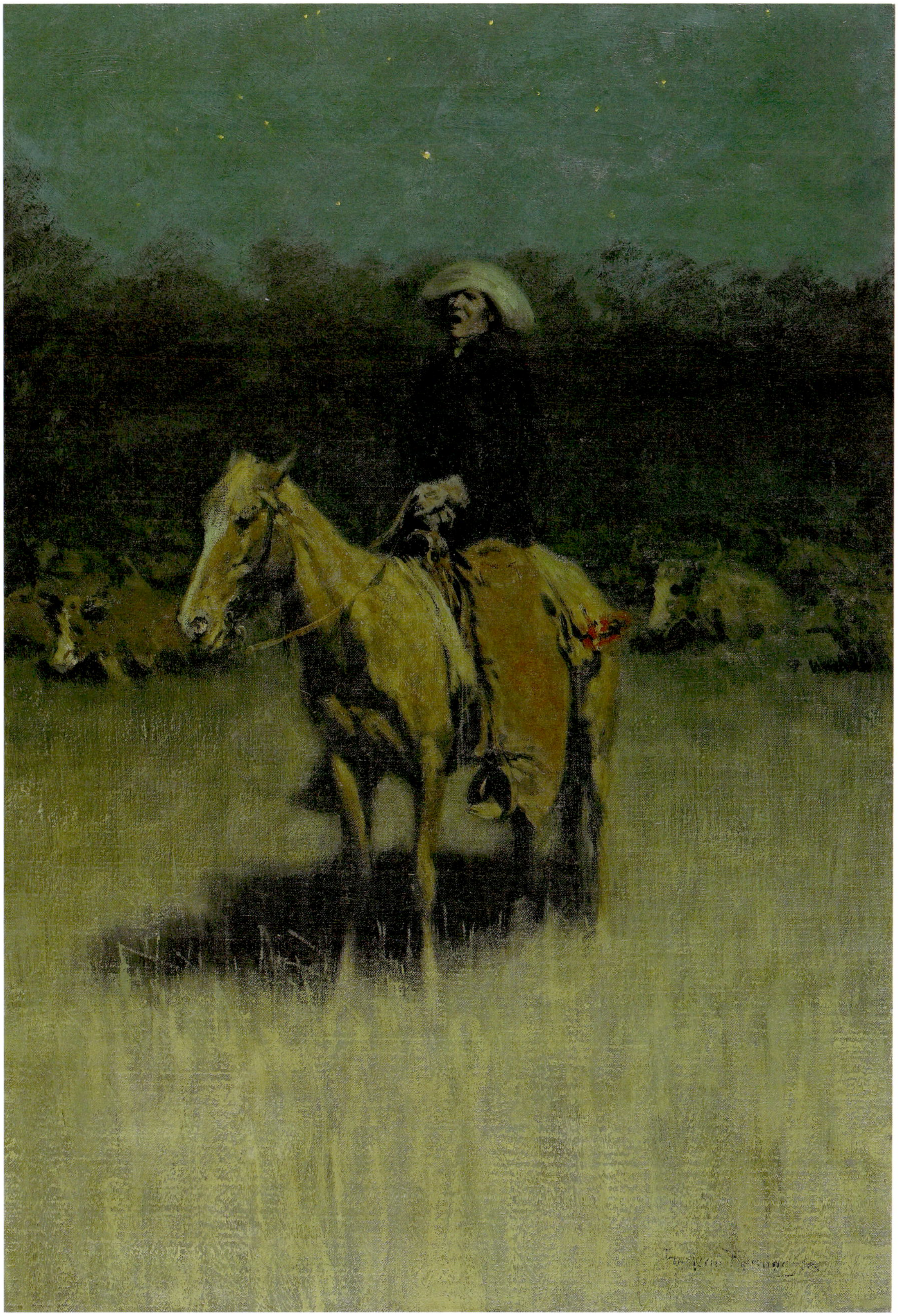

WILLIAM MERRITT CHASE (1849–1916)

The Song

1907
Oil on canvas
28 × 28 in. (71.1 × 71.1 cm)
Promised Gift

In 1907, William Merritt Chase spent a long summer in Italy. Landing in Rome, he traveled to Venice, central Italy, and Sicily, concluding the tour in Florence, where he established himself in the lofty fifteenth-century Villa Silli. Chase was warmly welcomed to the Tuscan city, and shortly after his arrival he was commissioned to add his self-portrait to the collection of the centuries-old Florentine museum the Ufizzi Gallery.[1] Chase's trip was an extension of the famous art teacher's annual summer academy, which he offered in varying locales over the years—first at his Shinnecock, Long Island, home (p. 158) and, after 1903, at destinations in England, Spain, and Holland. For the next five years he returned to Florence annually with students, ultimately buying the villa where he had based his summer studio.

Chase painted *The Song* during this first summer at Villa Silli. With his wife and family at home in New York, it was likely students who posed for this elegant composition, staged in the villa's sparsely furnished grand hall.[2] Like many of his contemporaries, who prioritized the decorative qualities of a composition above all else, Chase tended to avoid narrative.[3] This painting's title, however, helps guide the viewer's understanding of the scene. It briefly leads the eye to the musical source—the young woman seated at the piano in the center background, mouth open in song. With her face in shadow and her activity at the instrument obscured, Chase clearly did not intend the singing figure to be the work's central attraction. Rather, the subject is the music she generates, which is powerfully expressed through the outwardly emotive pose of the singer's companion, who sits in the foreground. Chase suggests the listener's complete absorption in the music through his positioning of her body—she bends forward as if suddenly interrupted from rising from her seat, resting her head in her right hand as her left arm drapes limply on the chair.

The theme of women and music has fascinated visual artists for centuries. Chase undoubtedly would have encountered numerous examples of this iconographical tradition during his European travels.[4] Paired with instruments and other symbols of culture, the female form came to embody the refinements of civilized society. In his own work, women often played the role of muse. Posed in the opulent interiors of his studios, Chase's women look, reflect, and listen—all the while surrounded by prints, paintings, exotica, and other objets d'art. The painter's women are not only consumers of culture, but as in *The Song*, visible expressions of it. As one woman creates music, the other articulates its presence, her immersion in the activity of listening lending a visual counterpart to the invisible melody that fills the air.

SMH

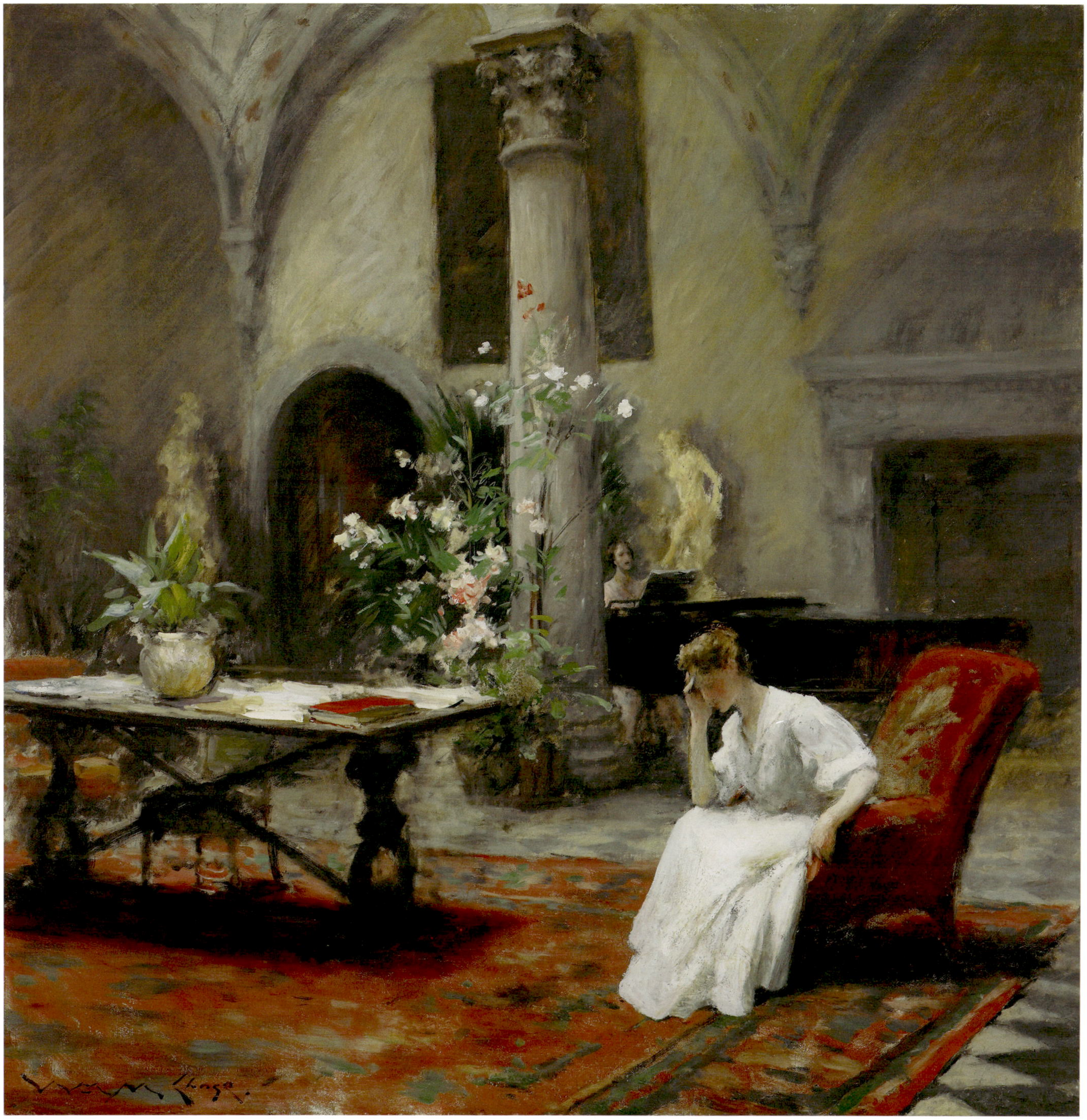

ALFRED HENRY MAURER (1868–1932)

Jeanne

ca. 1904
Oil on canvas
74¾ × 39⅜ in. (189.9 × 100 cm)
Promised Gift

The crowning achievement of Alfred Henry Maurer's early career as a figure painter, *Jeanne* is the artist's most sharply defined early character study. Rendered with liberal wit, this bold painting, which was exhibited to great acclaim during Maurer's lifetime, breaks with his earlier Whistlerian imagery and epitomizes the artist's mature sensibilities as a realist painter.[1]

In the first years of the twentieth century Maurer embraced a new candor in his work. Along with his American realist peers in the circle of Robert Henri, the artist shifted his focus from refined subjects rendered in an urbane style to unidealized sitters painted with vigor and immediacy. The idea of rarified beauty held little appeal; as his friend the artist Mahonri Young recalled, Maurer preferred "the girls who had a squint in the eye; were slightly cross-eyed or wall-eyed or had some distinguishing mark."[2]

Maurer's affection for unabashed subjects is nowhere more apparent than in *Jeanne*, a brazen depiction that challenges the very sanctity of the traditional portrait of a female figure. This painting features French model Jeanne Blazy, who had posed for James McNeill Whistler and Frederick Carl Frieseke, as well as for the sculptor Frederick MacMonnies's enormously popular figural group *Bacchante and Infant Faun* (1893–94, The Metropolitan Museum of Art). Jeanne modeled regularly for Maurer and was one of the artist's favorite subjects during his Parisian years (1897–1914). This arresting composition represents Maurer's most radical portrayal of Blazy.[3]

Rendered in the classic full-length format popular among society depictions, *Jeanne* reads like a caricature of grand manner portraiture. Though not necessarily intended as a moralizing social statement, the work nevertheless appears to mock the more gracious figurative imagery that was prevalent at European and American salons. Although Maurer painted Blazy in the studio, he convincingly transformed his model into a denizen of café culture. *Jeanne* becomes Maurer's answer to the French impressionists' call for paintings of modern life—works that exposed and explored the rich social and cultural disjunctions of contemporary Paris. *Jeanne* is also an important link to Maurer's contemporaneous vignettes of Parisian nightlife, which portrayed the dizzying spectacle of the city's noisy cabarets, lively dance halls, and colorful characters.[4]

A comedy of manners and larger than life, *Jeanne* depicts its subject posed as much for the visual delight of the artist as for that of his audience. With dazzling brushwork, she is rendered coquettish, risqué; in a word, unforgettable. Dressed and accessorized in garments from Maurer's costume trunk, she dons a feather boa and a straw hat ornamented with a taxidermied white bird.[5] Like the working-class women who populate Maurer's café and dance hall pictures, Jeanne seems a daring prototype of the "liberated" female. Emancipated from social mores, she sneers, teeth exposed between painted lips, communicating her vulgar presence without a word. The cigarette she holds in her right hand underscores her deviant disposition. It was common knowledge at the time that women who smoked publicly were typically prostitutes, lesbians, and others on the fringes of society.[6] Maurer's biographer Elizabeth McCausland has noted, "from the time Southworth and Hawes photographed the famous [dancer and courtesan] Lola Montez before the Civil War with cigarette in hand, to Maurer, perhaps no one had portrayed more engagingly a woman smoking. Jeanne is what the Victorians could only have called a minx, alluring as a kitten and as pettable."[7]

SE

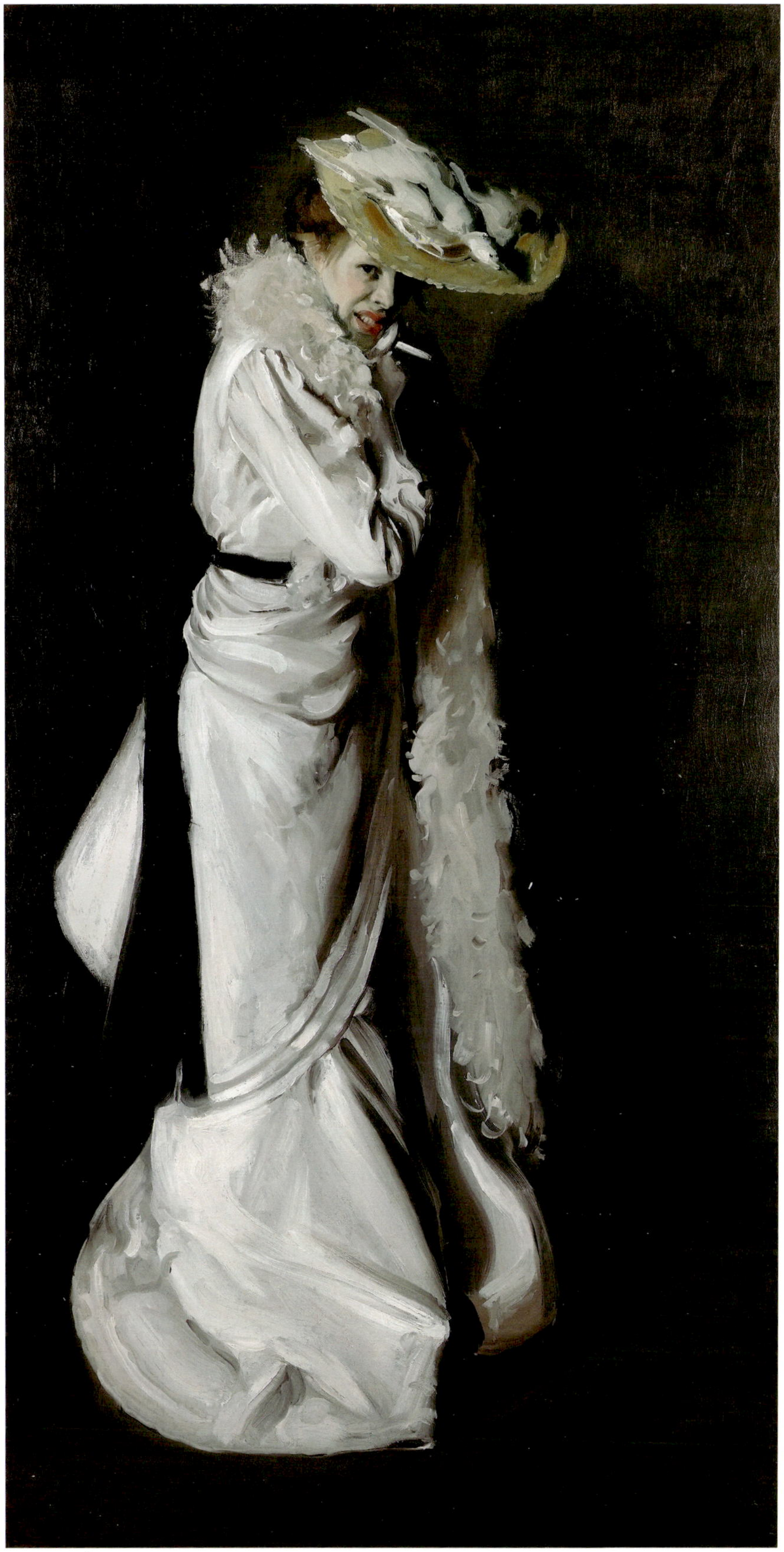

THOMAS WILMER DEWING (1851–1938)

The Fortune Teller

ca. 1904–5
Oil on panel
15¾ × 19⅞ in. (40 × 50.5 cm)

The critic Christian Brinton might have had *The Fortune Teller* in mind when he described Thomas Wilmer Dewing's "specialty" as "amber-toned interiors with here and there an attenuated, highly finished female figure."[1] In telling ways, however, the painting does not conform to Dewing's own conventions. Like his mentor James McNeill Whistler, Dewing often named paintings to emphasize their formal elements, but here the title identifies the subject of the picture and hints at the narratives it might contain—the tale of two women, quite different in demeanor, and the story of a future life conveyed through clairvoyance. The panel is also uncommonly small for a composition containing two figures, as if to draw us close to the picture to decipher its secrets.

Dewing perfected his "specialty" in the 1890s and continued to paint scenes of women in austere interiors, or outdoors in verdant landscape settings, for another twenty years. His finely crafted works, often favorably compared with old master paintings, attracted the patronage of such prominent collectors as New Yorker John Gellatly and Charles Lang Freer of Detroit, who built the premier collection of Dewing's art. It was Freer who recommended Dewing to his business associate William K. Bixby of St. Louis; Bixby purchased *The Fortune Teller* directly from the artist in 1905, soon after it made its public debut at a New York exhibition of the Ten American Painters. Baffled by its enigmatic atmosphere, one critic remarked that *The Fortune Teller* was "happier in its two graceful women and beautiful brush work than in either its composition or clarity of meaning."[2]

Although it has a long history in Western art, Dewing's rendition of the fortune-telling theme lacks the traditional gypsy woman and her nefarious accomplice who dupe an unsuspecting client. Indeed, this more serious scene may have been inspired by a contemporary phenomenon: in the decades following the Civil War, fascination with the occult became so pervasive in American society that a folklorist remarked in 1895 that "clairvoyance might be included in the list of occupations open to women."[3] By the time Dewing painted *The Fortune Teller*, the practice was open even to amateurs. One journalist described the art of reading fortunes in cards as "jolly sport for a winter evening," which any "sharp-witted girl with a keen sense of humor" could master.[4]

In *The Fortune Teller*, two mature women in evening dresses occupy a dimly lit and sparsely furnished room. They sit at a polished wood table adorned with a modest vase of flowers. The central figure's chair is pushed back, as if she was about to rise when the cards lined up along the table's edge riveted her attention. The seer's left hand holds the rest of the deck and drapes across the back of her chair; her right arm extends in the opposite direction so that her form commands the composition. Her companion seems to shrink from that powerful aura: pinned in place by the table, her oddly shadowed head rests against the wall, heavy with dread or with relief. And although the women's eyes do not meet, their fingers nearly touch on the tabletop, as if to convey the telepathic message without words.

LM

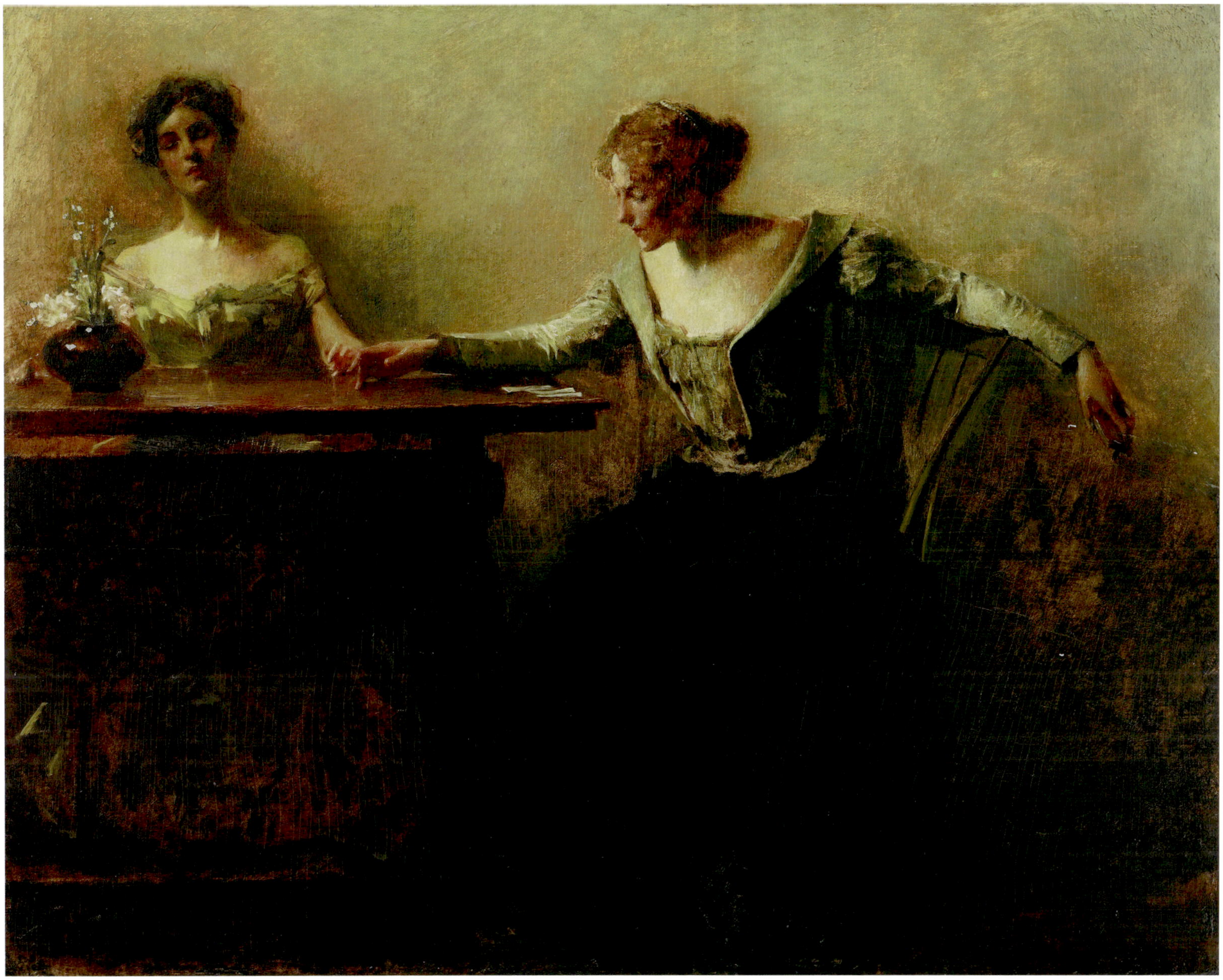

EVERETT SHINN (1876–1953)

A French Music Hall

1906
Oil on canvas
24 × 29½ in. (61 × 74.9 cm)

In 1893, seventeen-year-old Everett Shinn joined the staff of the *Philadelphia Press*. He also entered the Pennsylvania Academy of the Fine Arts and the circle of artists who met at Robert Henri's weekly studio open houses. Shinn's experience as a newspaper illustrator accustomed him to regard the contemporary scene as a worthy subject. The precocious student learned European conventions for depicting modern life subjects from mentors like Henri, John Sloan, George Luks, and William Glackens years before he himself went abroad. In 1897 Shinn, like his Philadelphia colleagues, moved to New York City, working first as a newspaper artist and then for illustrated magazines. In 1899 he was tapped to illustrate William Dean Howells's novel "New York by Night." The book was never published, but Shinn's exciting pastels of nocturnal city life launched his career.[1]

When the Macbeth Gallery exhibition of 1908 made The Eight famous a decade later, Shinn was already a well-known pastelist, oil painter, and muralist. The world of the theater was a critical element in the artist's work in all of these arenas, providing both a source of inspiration and a social and professional milieu from which to obtain patronage. Of course Henri, Sloan, Luks, and Glackens also treated the spectacle of performance and dance. Shinn, however, was acknowledged early on as the one among the Philadelphia circle who was truly stagestruck. The theater paintings Shinn selected to represent him in the Macbeth Gallery exhibition consolidated his place in American art history as a leading chronicler of the world of the stage. A century later, we recognize that early theater images like *A French Music Hall*, from 1906, represent the peak of his performance as a painter.

The pose and costume of the lead actress, rococo revival garden scenery, and spiral of the fiddlehead silhouetted against the stage light in *A French Music Hall* can all be traced to Shinn's 1903 pastel *Theatre Scene* (unlocated).[2] In the oil, Shinn enriched and expanded the composition by shifting the point of view to the rear of the left balcony and adding a blonde companion as a foil to the brunette performer. We peer over the shoulders of the audience as if attending the performance, while a female spectator turns to confront us.

The visual conventions of theater subjects like *A French Music Hall*, with its unusual perspective, strong contrasts of light and shadow, and sharp character studies, had been established by French realist painters in the 1860s and 1870s. Critics were divided in their interpretation of Shinn's obvious debt to artists like Jean-Louis Forain and Edgar Degas. Albert E. Gallatin greatly admired the theater images, yet he felt that Shinn's adept use of French models sometimes approached derivativeness. Most early critics and patrons, however, accepted these sources as providing a pictorial pedigree for progressive American artists and even took a measure of pride in dubbing Shinn the "American" Degas or Forain.

By 1917, Shinn had begun a second career as an art director in the motion-picture industry while he continued to paint and work as an illustrator. *A French Music Hall* must have been a favorite work, as it remained in the artist's collection for forty years. In 1946, when he became a member of the Lotos Club, Shinn presented the painting to the venerable New York writers and artists' establishment as a gift.[3]

LSF

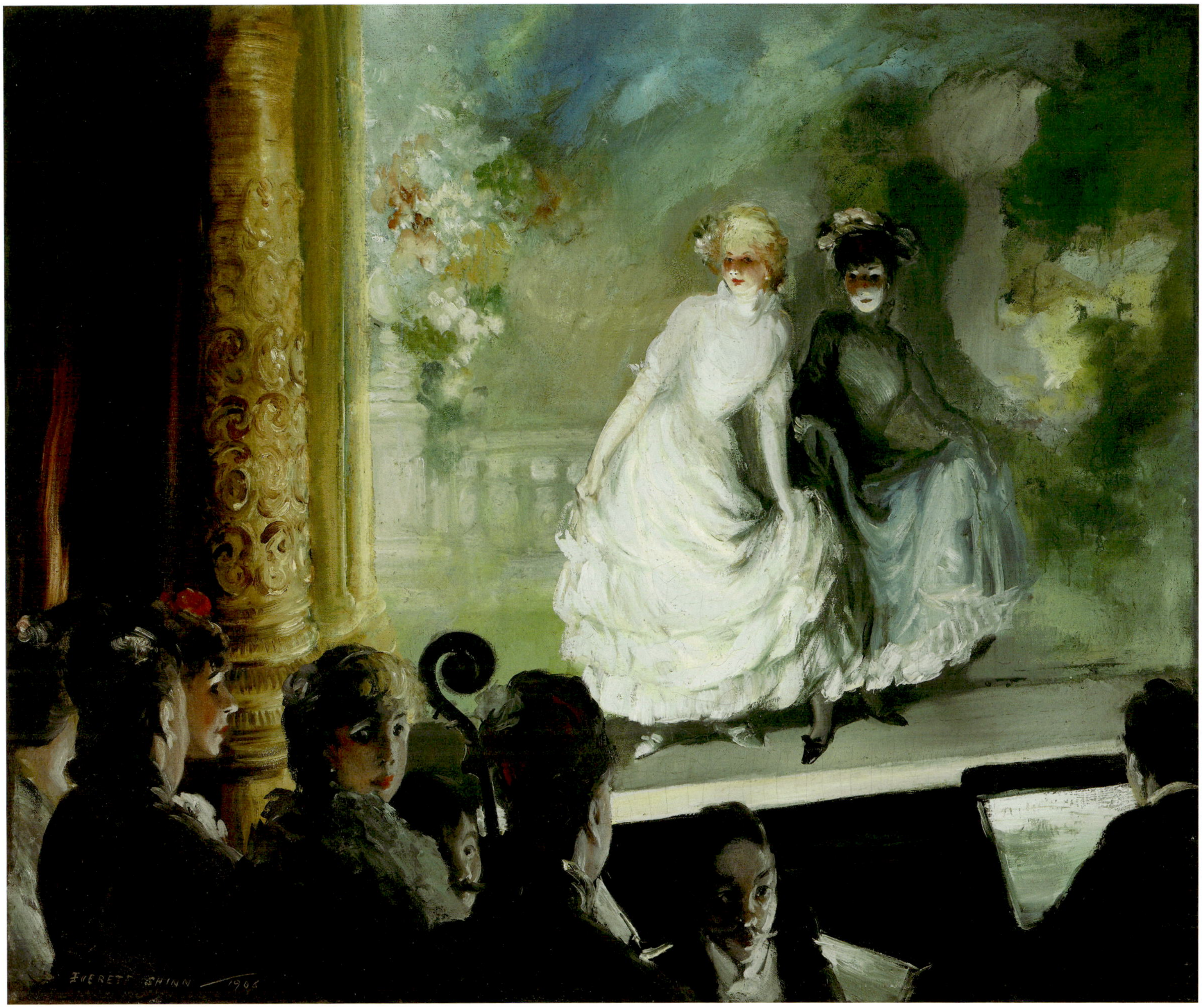
EVERETT SHINN

ROBERT HENRI (1865–1929)

Jessica Penn in Black with White Plumes

1908
Oil on canvas
77 × 38 in. (195.6 × 96.5 cm)

The year 1908 was a landmark for Robert Henri. Under his leadership, a small group of progressive American painters revolted against the conservative tastes and restrictive jury system of New York's powerful National Academy of Design by mounting an independent exhibition at the Macbeth Gallery. This display of work by eight disparate individuals united in their dedication to artistic freedom and their affinity for subjects from modern life captured the attention of Americans nationwide during a twelve-month, multivenue tour. Henri quickly became, in the hyperbolic words of one newspaper, "the most pronounced figure in the art world."[1]

Jessica Penn in Black with White Plumes, painted that year, represents Henri at the height of his powers in his preferred genre: contemporary portraiture. The painter's model, Jesseca Penn (Henri misspelled the model's name in his record book) was a Ziegfeld Follies actress and dancer who made her Broadway debut in 1901. The tall, strikingly beautiful redhead also posed for Henri's friend and fellow Macbeth Gallery exhibitor Arthur Bowen Davies, and appears in a covered wagon in Edwin Howland Blashfield's monumental mural painting *Westward*, at the Iowa State Capitol.[2] Henri had effectively launched his career as a portraitist with a 1902 likeness of Penn (*Young Woman in Black*, Art Institute of Chicago). Inspired by the work of Diego Velázquez and Édouard Manet, Henri's early portraiture introduced American audiences to a radically new mode of representation characterized by a dark palette and spare compositions that focused intensely on the subject's face. "The simpler a background is the better the figure in front of it will be, and . . . the better the figure is the less the observer will need entertainment in the background," explained the painter and esteemed art instructor his 1923 treatise *The Art Spirit*.[3]

Henri's 1902 and 1908 images of Penn were two of a series of full-length portraits of women with monochromatic color schemes that the artist executed during the first decade of the twentieth century.[4] Samuel Isham deemed this series notable enough to include in his influential *History of American Painting* (1905), writing: "The girls in 'white' or 'black' of Henri are modern, complex, and rather mysterious, as they stand slender and graceful with their faces showing bright against the dark background. The workmanship . . . is broad and sure, insistently masterly, with great richness of surface and harmony of tone in the simple schemes of black and white and flesh color."[5]

While *Jessica Penn* postdates Isham's text, his words well describe the Crystal Bridges canvas. Henri's skilled brush deftly manages the challenge of painting black on black, the silk of Penn's gown asserting itself in wrinkles and folds. Henri encouraged budding portraitists to "make the forms of a garment so that a trip through its hills and dales will be delightful," and the "currents" running through Penn's costume subtly remind the viewer that she was a dancer by profession.[6] Yet the main attraction of this image, as in all of Henri's portraits, is the sitter's visage. The light blue ribbon on her sleeves, at her chest, and again at her neck draw the viewer up to the brightly illuminated face of this thoroughly modern woman, who boldly stares back.

EDS

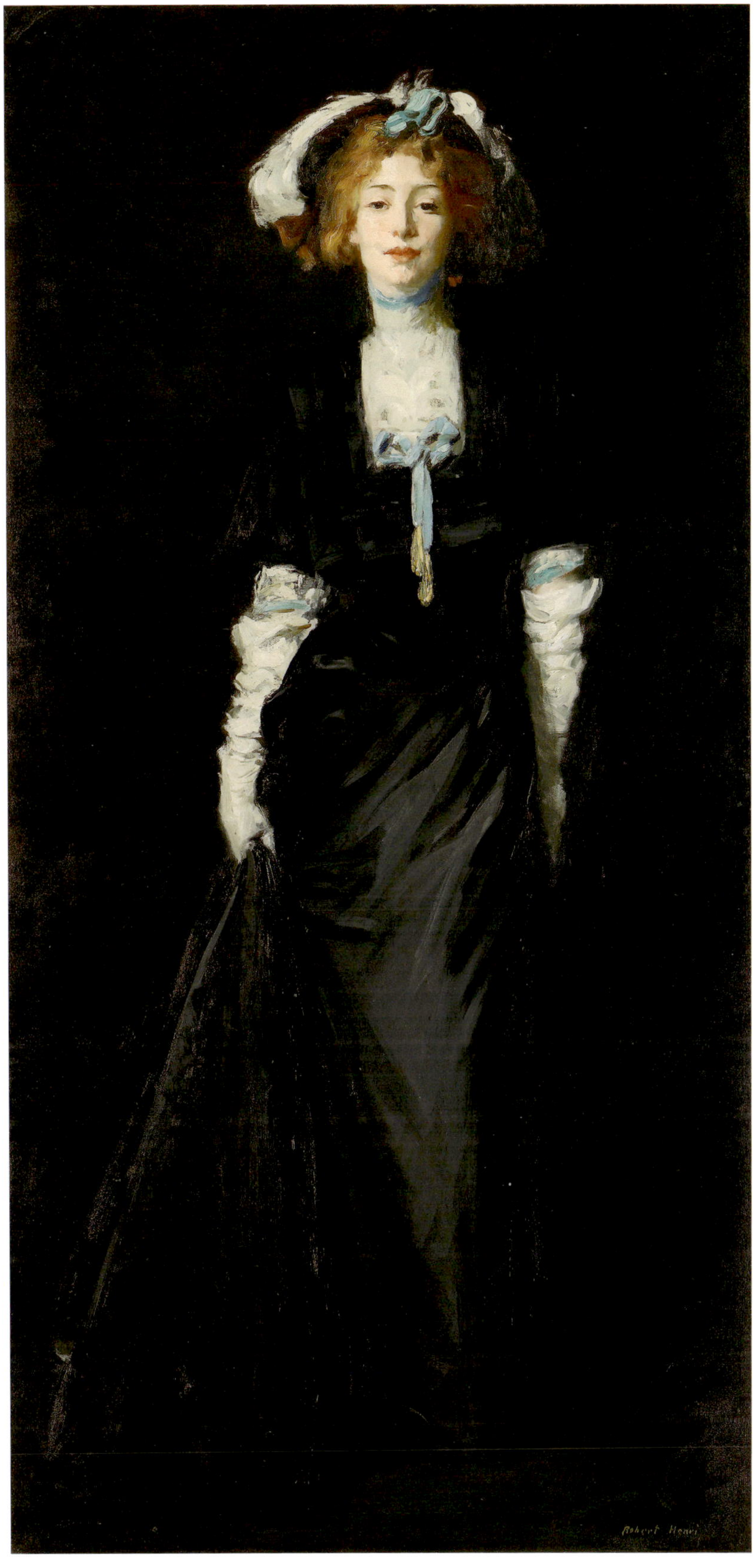
Robert Henri

MAXFIELD PARRISH (1870–1966)

The Lantern Bearers

1908
Oil on canvas on board
40 × 32 in. (101.6 × 81.3 cm)

Even for the untrained eye, there is little doubt when one is in the presence of a work of art by Maxfield Parrish. The combination of Parrish's unmistakable style and legendary fame make him one of the most notable visual artists of early twentieth-century America.

Painted in 1908, *The Lantern Bearers* appeared as the frontispiece in the popular national magazine *Collier's Weekly* on December 10, 1910. *Collier's* pages were larger than most illustrated periodicals of the time, giving Parrish more creative freedom to explore composition and characters.[1] This lively nocturne combines all of the elements of Parrish's most successful works—fantastical characters, luminous color, compositional dynamism, and a sense of mystery. In the fore- and mid-ground, a tightly clustered group of Pierrot-like clowns hang glowing yellow lanterns against a dark, silhouetted tree and a deeply saturated blue sky.[2] In the background, four more golden orbs hover in the sky, leaving the mind and eye to wonder which, if any, is the moon. The clowns pose on a stagelike setting of wide stone steps in keeping with the artist's practice of using classical architectural elements to structure his pictures. Parrish's composition is masterful: with multiple, competing areas of pictorial interest, the viewer's eye dances around the image, eventually settling on the radiant spheres that forestall the advancing darkness.

The jewel-like colors and pristinely smooth surface of *The Lantern Bearers* are the result of an age-old painting technique by which the artist applied layer-upon-layer of thin oil glazes separated by equally thin layers of varnish. Parrish's images were also informed by the distinctively modern medium of photography. Intrigued by fellow Philadelphian and Pennsylvania Academy of the Fine Arts alumnus Thomas Eakins's photographic studies, Parrish cultivated a passion for using the camera.[3] An extant photograph of Parrish's frequent model Sue Lewin posed in the exact position and costume of the seated figure at the far left of *The Lantern Bearers* attests to his use of the relatively new medium in making this work.[4]

Parrish's carefully crafted figure paintings and landscapes reached their largest audience in the form of calendars, advertisements, book illustrations, and magazine covers. The artist created these paintings with their reproduction in mind, knowing that he could reach a broader audience through mass-produced imagery than through the original oils alone. Both a visionary artist and a shrewd businessman, Parrish may have been enchanted by ethereal fantasy but he was also firmly cognizant of economic realities.

One of the leading figures of the so-called Golden Age of American illustration (1880–1920s), Parrish's fame rivaled that enjoyed by Norman Rockwell in the World War II era (p. 244). In 1925, one out of every four American households owned a Parrish print.[5] The artist's success in his era and his continued popularity today remind us that fine art and commercial illustration are not necessarily mutually exclusive. Parrish offers us rich and luxurious visions of places that exist only in our dreams.

NCS

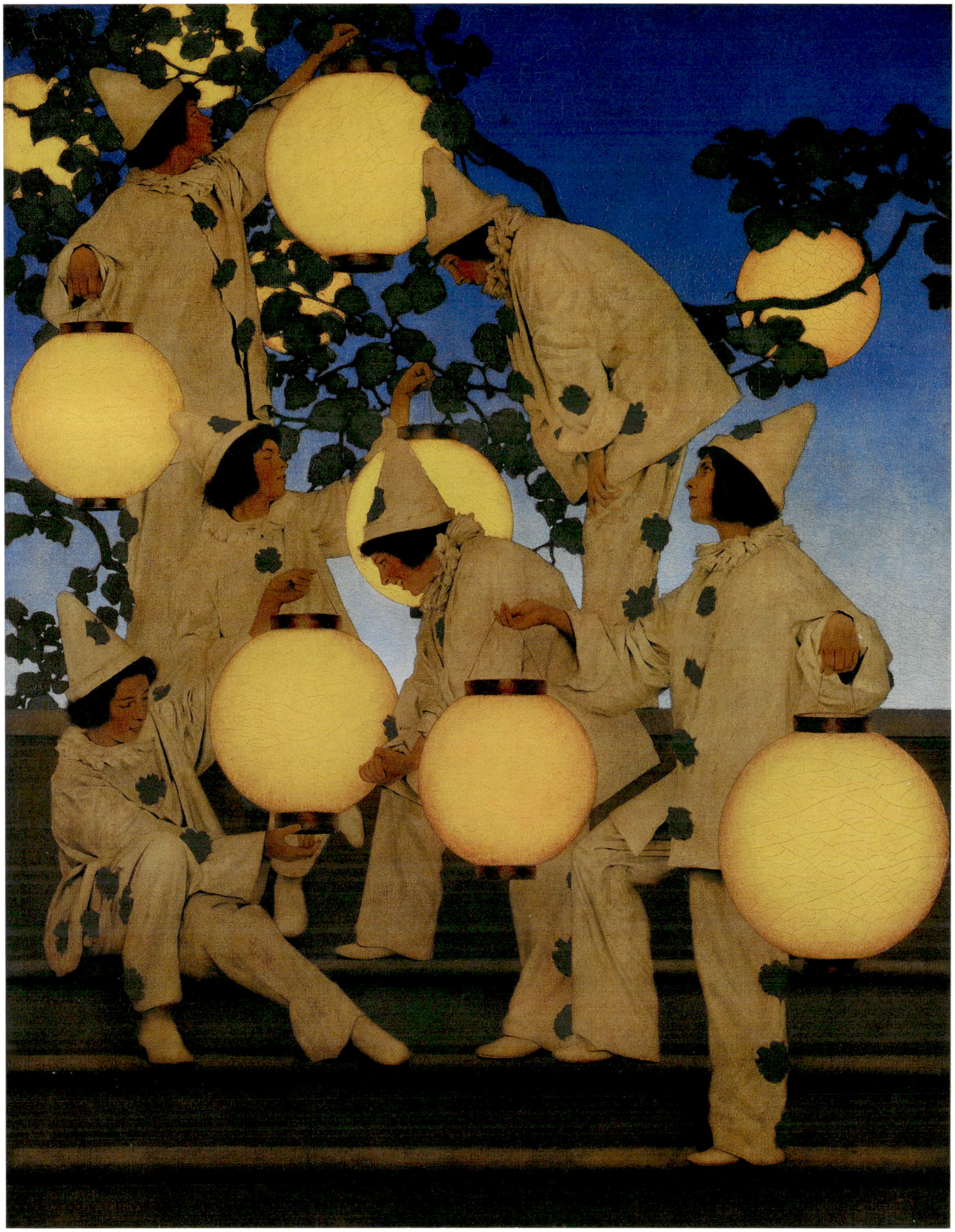

FRANK WESTON BENSON (1862–1951)

Summer Day

1911
Oil on canvas
36⅛ × 32⅛ in. (91.8 × 81.6 cm)

Summer Day, painted in 1911 by Frank Weston Benson, exemplifies a late flowering of American impressionism. It is also a highly personal expression of a time, place, and quality of life that only existed for a passing moment and for a privileged few. The painting portrays a lingering vestige of belle époque luxury, casual elegance, and repose as experienced by a newly prosperous upper-middle class that included the artist. The first decades of the twentieth century were a time shaped by the rising aspirations of a nation that had achieved mercantile and industrial preeminence, a fragile optimism that would be shattered by the outbreak of World War I in Europe in 1914. In Benson's painting, however, it is still high summer in Maine, and for America.

"Summer people," as they are still called by natives and year-round residents of Maine, began populating the mid-coast region of the state in the last decades of the nineteenth century, building enormous "cottages" to house extended families, relatives, visitors and, of course, servants. In 1901 the Salem, Massachusetts-based Benson began renting and in 1906 purchased Wooster Farm, a house and property on North Haven Island in Maine's Penobscot Bay set high on a meadow with vistas to the sea. Unable not to paint, even on holiday, Benson's summer pictures evoke a private world full of quiet, simple pleasures, whether reading, picnicking, hiking, or, as in *Summer Day*, watching casual, often impromptu boat races among rival summer residents and neighboring boat clubs.

Summer Day is a sunny outdoor scene depicting Benson's two youngest daughters—Elisabeth, age eighteen, and Sylvia, age thirteen—casting their eyes toward the high horizon line where the boundary between sea and sky nearly dissolves. An earlier version of the composition included a third female figure—Benson's eldest daughter, Eleanor—holding an umbrella to block the sun, and an additional wooden railing behind the group. Apparently the artist reworked the painting to simplify and open the composition, thereby allowing him to focus more intently on the visual effects of Maine's flickering light radiating off the sea, sky, and figures.[1] Removing the third figure also concentrates attention on Benson's two youngest daughters absorbed in a moment of wordless communion as they watch the passing sailboats.

The soft, billowing sails on and just below the horizon reinforce a sense of gentle movement, as do the girls' cascading gowns, loosely arranged hair, and decorative ribbons, all of which are enveloped by soft ocean breezes. The painting can be seen as Benson's affectionate comparison of his young daughters' radiance and beauty to that of nature itself; an assertion of their essential equivalence. Benson's soft, broken brushwork appears lightly but quickly stroked, and his high-keyed palette of whites and white-inflected blues glinting off the summer sea is a ravishing display of impressionist technique perfectly tuned to his ephemeral, sun-shot subject. *Summer Day* is more than a record of a passing moment; it is a memory lingering in the modern imagination of a younger, more innocent, and altogether idyllic time and place.

CBC

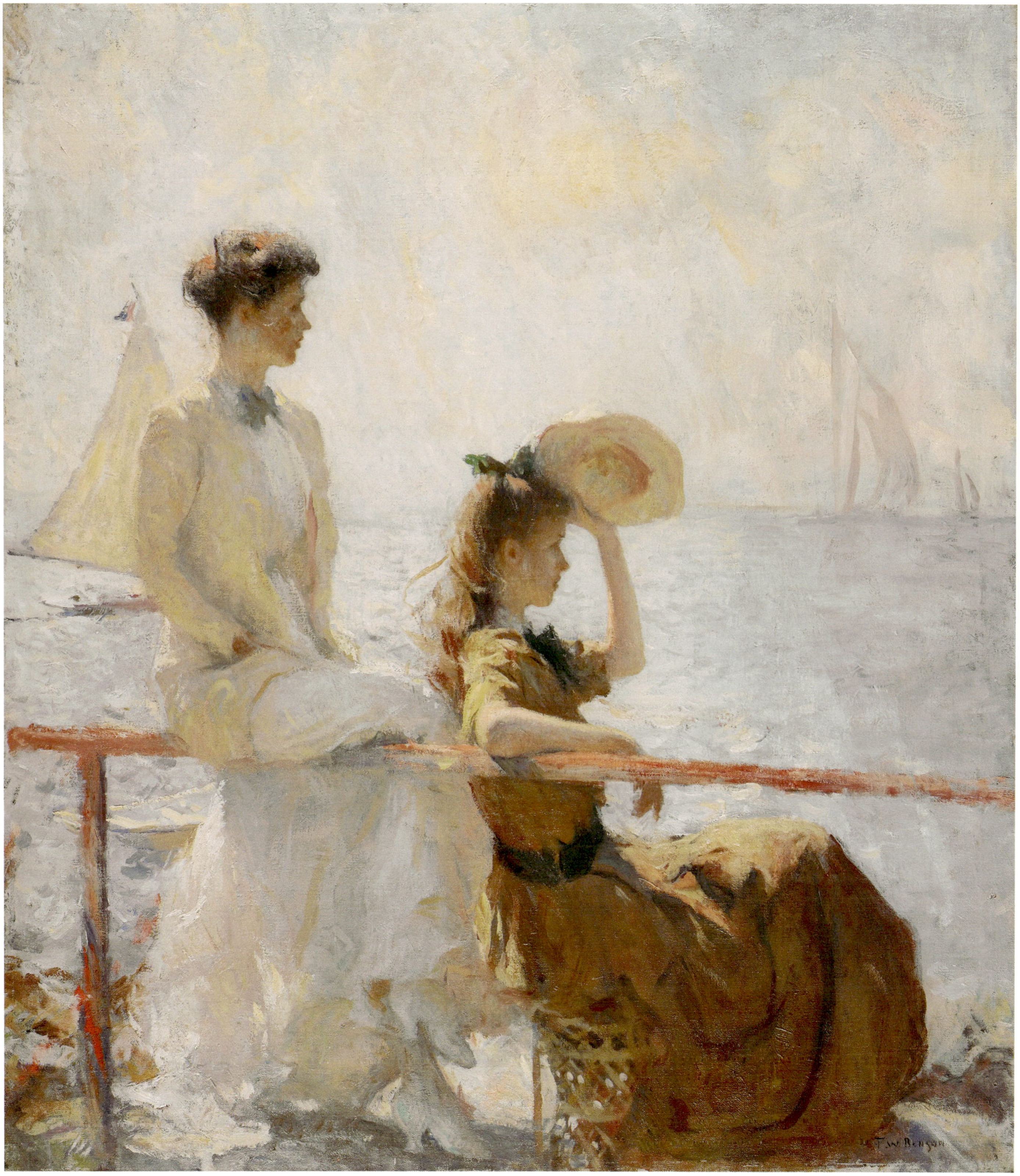
F.W. Benson

GEORGE WESLEY BELLOWS (1882–1925)

Excavation at Night

1908
Oil on canvas
34 × 44 in. (86.4 × 111.8 cm)

George Wesley Bellows is best known for his carefully observed working-class genre scenes, dynamic boxing subjects, and gritty cityscapes. Bellows's astute observations of a modern urban culture characterized by overcrowding, lewd entertainment, and technological innovation vividly captured the rapid pulse of life in early twentieth-century New York City. The artist's commitment to representing human conditions and activities within the urban setting stemmed from his instructor Robert Henri, the charismatic leader of the anti-academic art movement known as the Ashcan School.

One of Bellows's most significant subjects was the excavation site for the ambitious Pennsylvania Station, a Beaux-Arts style building designed by the lauded American architectural firm McKim, Mead & White. Modeled after the Gare d'Orsay in central Paris, the station was commissioned by Pennsylvania Railroad president Alexander Cassatt (brother of artist Mary Cassatt) in 1901.[1] In preparation for building the structure, which was to be the largest indoor space in New York City as well as one of the largest public spaces in the world, over 6,600 feet of tunnels were mined under the Hudson River and over 500 existing buildings demolished.[2] Between 1907 and 1909, Bellows produced four paintings inspired by the ambitious excavation and construction campaign.[3]

Capturing a cold December evening view near the intersection of Thirty-Third Street and Ninth Avenue, *Excavation at Night* was Bellows's second rendition of the railway station's early structural development. In contrast to the first work in this series (the 1907 painting *Pennsylvania Excavation*, Smith College Museum of Art), which provides an expansive daytime prospect of the four city blocks being unearthed to make way for the new station, *Excavation at Night* narrowly focuses on a specific location deep in the bowels of the menacing crater. Intentionally emphasizing activity below the composition's horizon, the painting's low vantage point highlights the sheer enormity of the chasm while adding a human element in the form of graveyard shift laborers gathered around a bonfire. Bellows's coarse painting style—unrefined, gestural, and abstract—well matches his subject, his aggressive brushstrokes evoking the brutal and intensely physical act of excavation.

The artificial glow of city lampposts in the upper third of the composition and the flames from the workmen's bonfire at lower right serve as dramatic light sources, attracting the viewer's eye and leading him or her to explore the dark recesses and crevasses of the shadow-laden site. Bellows's masterful balance of cool and warm colors, the highlighted surfaces and textures of the freshly cut stone walls, and the haunting exteriors of the row of buildings in the background of the image jointly serve to convey an eerie and disruptive mood. "Those tenement houses behind the excavation always give me the creeps," Bellows once remarked, "They're just ordinary houses—but there is something about them that gets me."[4]

The lives of both Bellows and the original Pennsylvania Station were cut short. Bellows died at the age of forty-two following complications from appendicitis. Built to last for centuries, the massive New York rail station that had so captivated the artist was demolished in 1963 to make way for the $116 million sports arena and entertainment complex known as Madison Square Garden.[5] AWJ

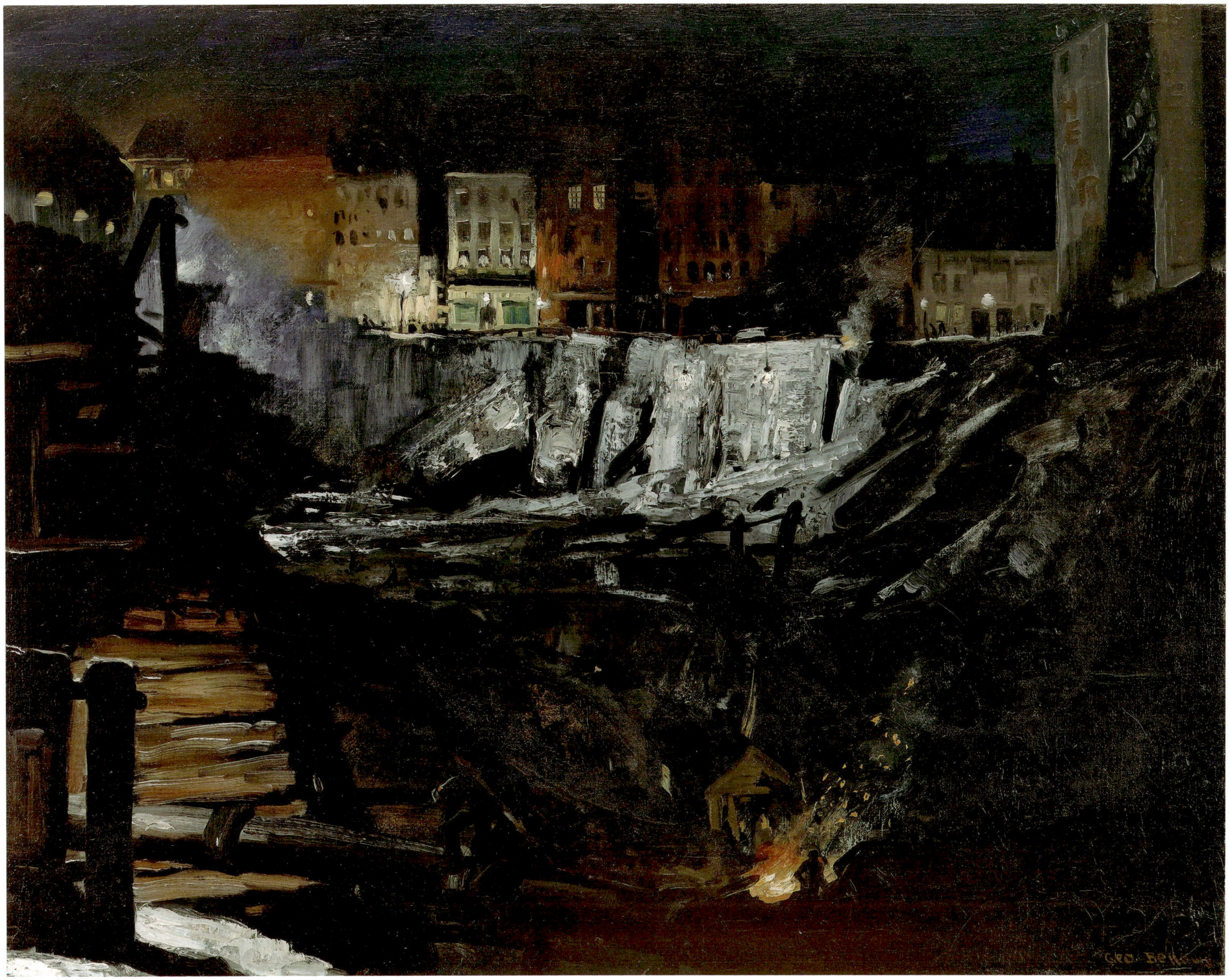

GEORGE WESLEY BELLOWS (1882–1925)

Return of the Useless

1918
Oil on canvas
59 × 66 in. (149.9 × 167.6 cm)

George Wesley Bellows's *Return of the Useless* is the final painting in what has come to be described as the artist's War Series of 1918, a group of drawings, prints, and, finally, painted reprisals of these works on paper.[1] Bellows's powerful, prophetic, doppelgänger of a painting, while less violent and overtly propagandistic than most of the works in the War Series, presents a haunted and haunting image of brutalized civilians returning in boxcars from their forced labor, a horrific vision now forever associated with Nazi Germany and the Holocaust.

The War Series derives from two published sources describing atrocities committed by German troops against Belgian civilians during World War I. The first of these was the Bryce Report, penned in 1915 by Lord James Bryce, former British ambassador to the United States. Published in abbreviated form in the *New York Times*, this report presented eyewitness accounts of the chaotic early days of the German invasion.[2] Bellows's second inspiration was a series of articles by Brand Whitlock, former American ambassador to Belgium, published in the socially progressive journal *Everybody's Magazine* in 1918.[3] An Ohio native like Bellows, Whitlock was a well-known sports writer with whom the artist would have been familiar from his own youthful athletic enterprises. *Return of the Useless* first appeared in print as an illustration for one of Whitlock's articles on the violence in war-torn Belgium.

Bellows initially opposed the United States' involvement in World War I. The artist's political views were socialist leaning, as evidenced by his longtime involvement as editor and contributing artist for the radical magazine *The Masses*. The publication was adamantly antiwar, a sentiment graphically expressed in Bellows's strident illustrations protesting what he saw as pro–British and French government policies. As the war progressed, however, the public became increasingly outraged over civilian casualties such as the 1915 sinking by German U-boats of the ocean liner the *Lusitania*, which resulted in the loss of over 1,100 private citizens, including over 100 Americans. By 1917 Bellows, like most Americans, supported his country's entry into World War I, volunteering for military service and adding his own voice against atrocities suffered by civilians, if not the conflict itself.

In some ways, Bellows's propagandistic war prints are more successful than their painted counterparts. His boldly graphic, black-and-white lithographs powerfully convey the metaphoric struggle between light and darkness that his subjects describe. Moreover, the medium of printmaking allowed Bellows opportunities for mass dissemination of his images in magazines and newspapers. On the other hand, Bellows's paintings benefit from a nearly life-size scale that places the viewer within a few feet of the action, and from the addition of color. By applying a wash of red pigment over the entire boxcar in *Return of the Useless*, Bellows suggested the blood-soaked history of its returning human cargo.

The woman in the center of the composition, who descends from the railcar on stacked crates, draws the viewer's eye toward the dark interior behind her and the human suffering contained therein, while her outstretched arms gesture to the broken and breaking bodies to her either side. Gestures are emphatic, and the action is tightly compressed into a shallow space with intense lighting that evokes theatrical productions and stagecraft. Indeed, despite—or perhaps because of—the painting's horrific content, it is characterized by a heightened sense of unreality. Heartbreakingly, the stage where Bellows set his story was neither fiction nor the final act.

CBC

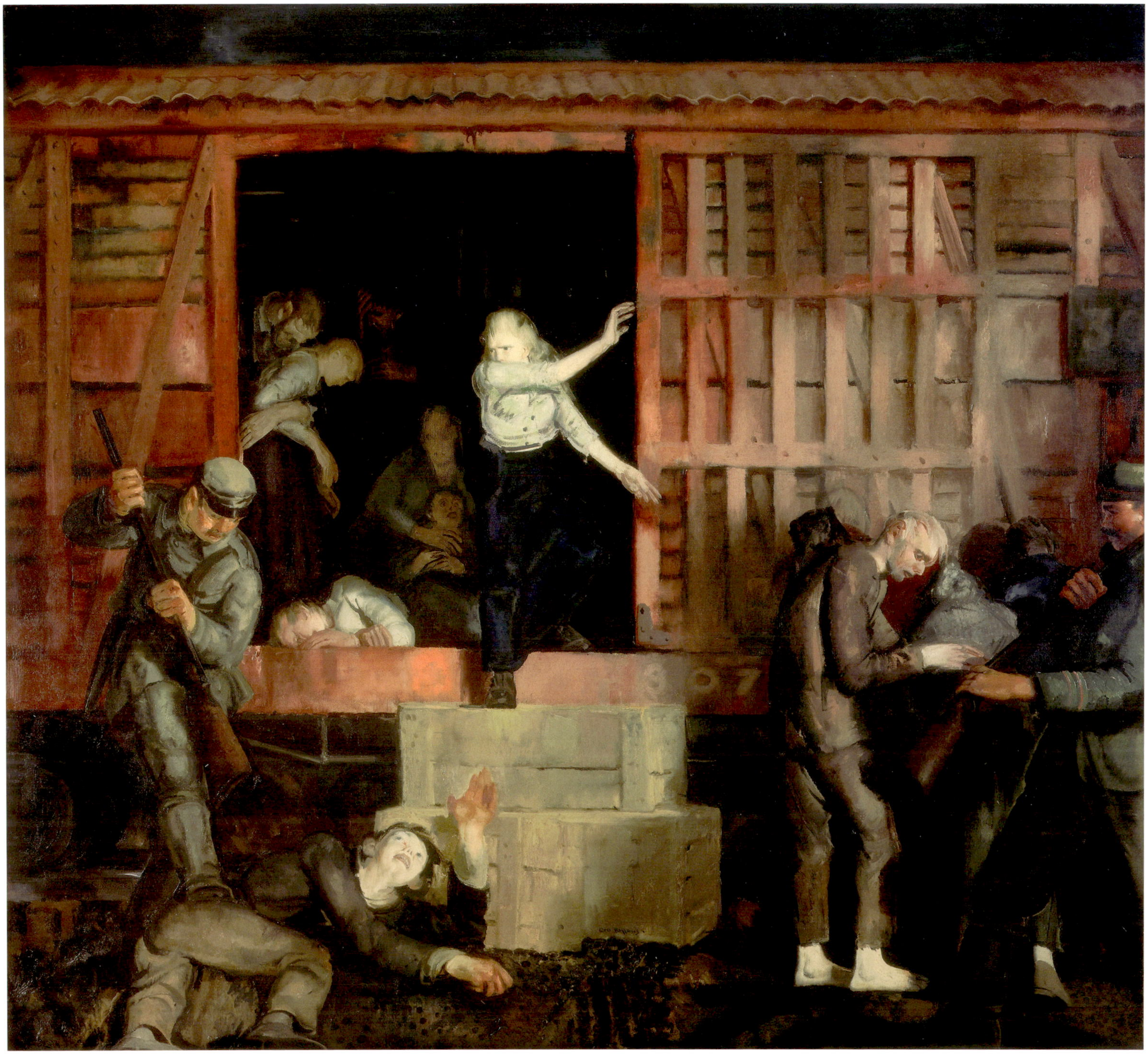

JOHN SLOAN (1871–1951)

Bleecker Street, Saturday Night

1918
Oil on canvas
26 × 32 in. (66 × 81.3 cm)

By the time John Sloan moved from Philadelphia to New York City in 1904, he had already established his reputation as a painter of urban life. The process of conceptualizing his subject matter began while he explored the city on foot. Sloan was not an intrepid wanderer; he preferred investigating his own or adjacent neighborhoods, public places where he could experience the slippery duality of being both a part of and separate from the daily routines of his working-class neighbors. If the canvases that resulted from Sloan's urban excursions present a curious mixture of intimacy and detachment, they also reflect changes in his personal life and outlook, as well as his growing interests and maturity as an artist.

As numerous scholars have noted, Sloan's pictures fall into two phases. The paintings executed between 1904 and 1914 reveal a trenchant interest in the social dynamics of the urban condition. The later, so-called post-Armory pictures betray the influence of the modernist aesthetics on display at the exhibition held in 1913 at the Sixty-Ninth Regiment Armory in New York. As Sloan became increasingly preoccupied with the abstract problems of picture making, his attentiveness to anecdotal details diminished.

Sloan finished *Bleecker Street, Saturday Night* in time to include it in his second solo show at Kraushaar Galleries, in March 1918. His *Notes* document the painting's genesis as an exercise in "building up the picture through the palette."[1] Sloan's challenge was to convincingly illuminate the scene; to set the acid tones of the artificial lighting against the cooler colors of the sky and the inky darkness enveloping the intersection, architecture, and pedestrians. Sloan did not model forms and figures by blending pigments together on the surface of the canvas, but rather by laying thick strokes of carefully modulated color next to and on top of one another. The narrative arc prevalent in his earlier urban paintings has been subordinated to spatial concerns. Here the evening shoppers and strollers play a role, but they are secondary to the diagrammatic arrangement of horizontal and vertical elements.

Sloan did not banish sentiment completely. By giving *Bleecker Street, Saturday Night* a title that specifies the subject's location and the time of day, his audience is able to identify with a familiar activity. The street-level format reinforces the viewer's sense of being present at the scene, of re-experiencing a chance encounter with a stranger or an unexpected meeting with a friend. So, too, Sloan embellished the subject with his uncanny ability to choose the telling detail, in this case the "amputated" building, a victim of New York's ambitious civic improvement project to construct the Seventh Avenue subway and widen and extend both Sixth and Seventh Avenues southward through Greenwich Village.[2] Since Sloan had relocated both his apartment and studio from Chelsea to the Village in 1912, just as the city began demolition, he was directly affected by the plans for urban renewal. Given the recent shift to modernism in his own work, the subjects of transformation and progress were fitting themes for the artist. REL

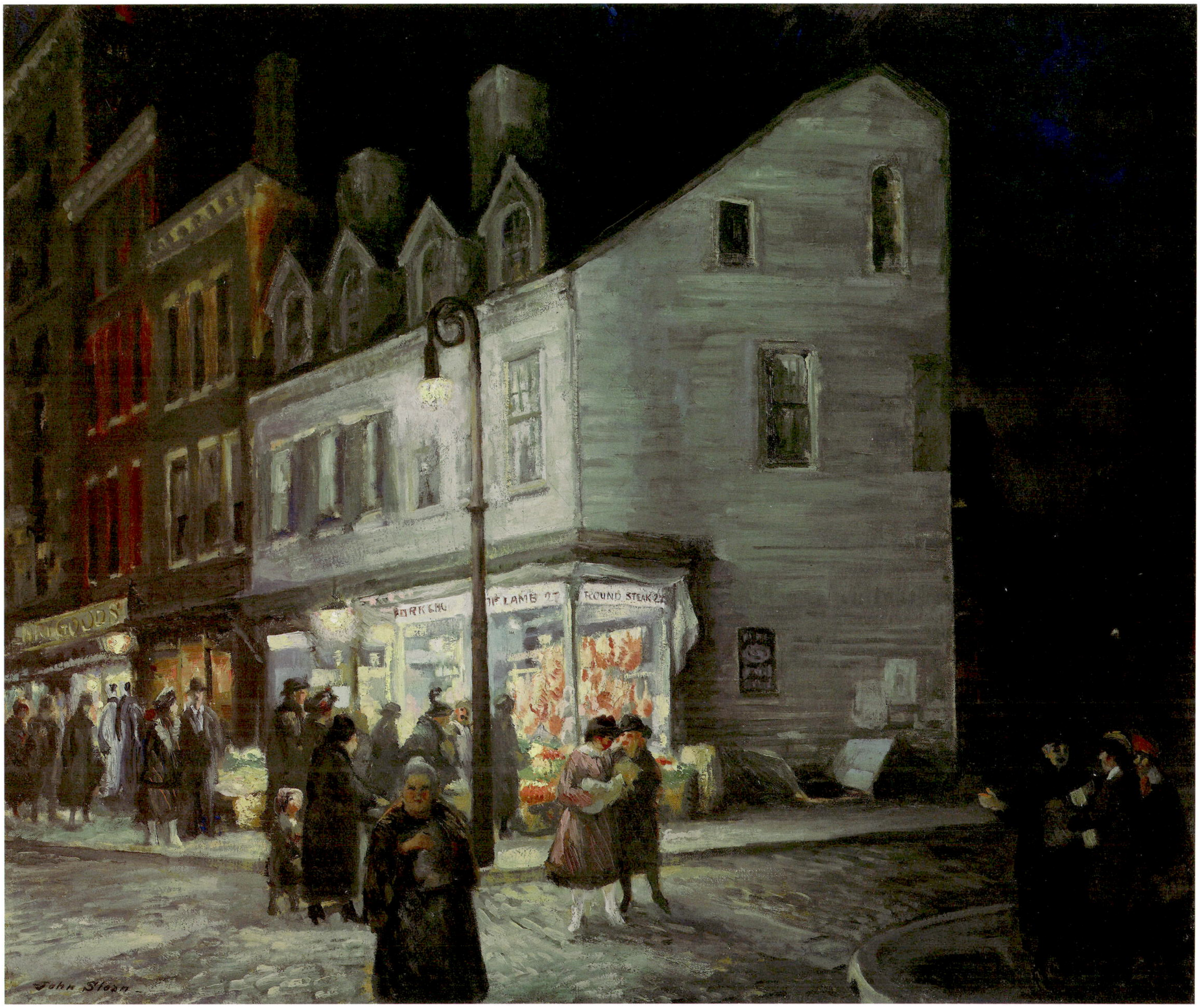
ROUND STEAK
John Sloan

ALFRED HENRY MAURER (1868–1932)

Fauve Landscape with Red and Blue

ca. 1909
Oil on board
22 × 18½ in. (55.9 × 47 cm)
Promised Gift

Upon initial examination, Alfred Henry Maurer's *Fauve Landscape with Red and Blue* appears quiltlike in its abstract patchwork of flat, nearly pure colors held together by thin lines of gray. One must intensely concentrate to apprehend the blue at the painting's center as a pond seen from above, with a small white house with a black roof off to the middle left and, to the right, a serpentine, ashen trail disappearing into a density of trees. Indeed, while this domesticated landscape provides a framework for the composition, for Maurer the painting was ultimately a skillful organization of color and rhythm independent of mimetic representation. This was a startling achievement for an artist born a scant few years after the end of the Civil War.

Maurer's arrival at abstraction was an exception to the rule of his era. In 1897, the artist traveled to Paris for advanced study with the intention of developing a fashionable figurative style in the manner of compatriots James McNeill Whistler and William Merritt Chase. He found early success with traditional figure painting, but his direct encounters with the increasingly abstract art being made around him proved life changing. In 1905, Maurer saw the work of Henri Matisse and the fauves (French for "wild beasts") in the collection of American expatriates Gertrude and Leo Stein, and in 1907 the artist visited the vastly influential Paul Cézanne retrospective exhibition.[1] Maurer immersed himself in the radical new art being pioneered in Paris, and instead of becoming yet another competent society portraitist, emerged as one of America's first modern painters.

Fully embracing and exploiting fauvism's high-keyed color, early in his French tenure Maurer began to layer his work with highly saturated hues. From Cézanne, he learned the immeasurable value of shifting between colors by way of blurred, vibrating edges suffused with empty space. Maurer first exhibited his abstracted landscapes in 1907, in Paris, and in 1909 he was part of a two-person exhibition with John Marin at Alfred Stieglitz's New York gallery, 291. His pioneering work was included in the legendary 1913 Armory Show, which introduced modernism to a broad American public, as well as in the 1916 *Forum Exhibition of Modern American Painters*, the first large-scale display of the American avant-garde.

Maurer electrified the painting *Fauve Landscape with Red and Blue* by employing his power of imagination to create a surface charged with purely intuitive color. The shimmering stretches of green in the upper left stem from Cézanne and the flat blue pool is indebted to Matisse, but the combination of the two is pure Maurer. This approach stood in dramatic contrast to the dominant American aesthetic of impressionism, which emphasized fluid but descriptive color. In choosing intuition over measurable accuracy, Maurer joined the ranks of those artists who staked a philosophical claim for the preeminence of creation over mere transcription. When the New York critic J. F. Chamberlain saw Maurer's work at 291 in 1909 he wrote, "But his pictures! There is no understanding them. Two or three, indeed possess strong indications of internal feeling for the beauty of dazzling light, and for big, splendid forms in nature. But here is one which has in the foreground a great glob of color; what is it? A bursted tomato? A fireman's hat? A red rock?"[2] Given the dramatic stretch of red in *Fauve Landscape with Red and Blue*, one wonders if Chamberlain was reacting to this very painting.

WS

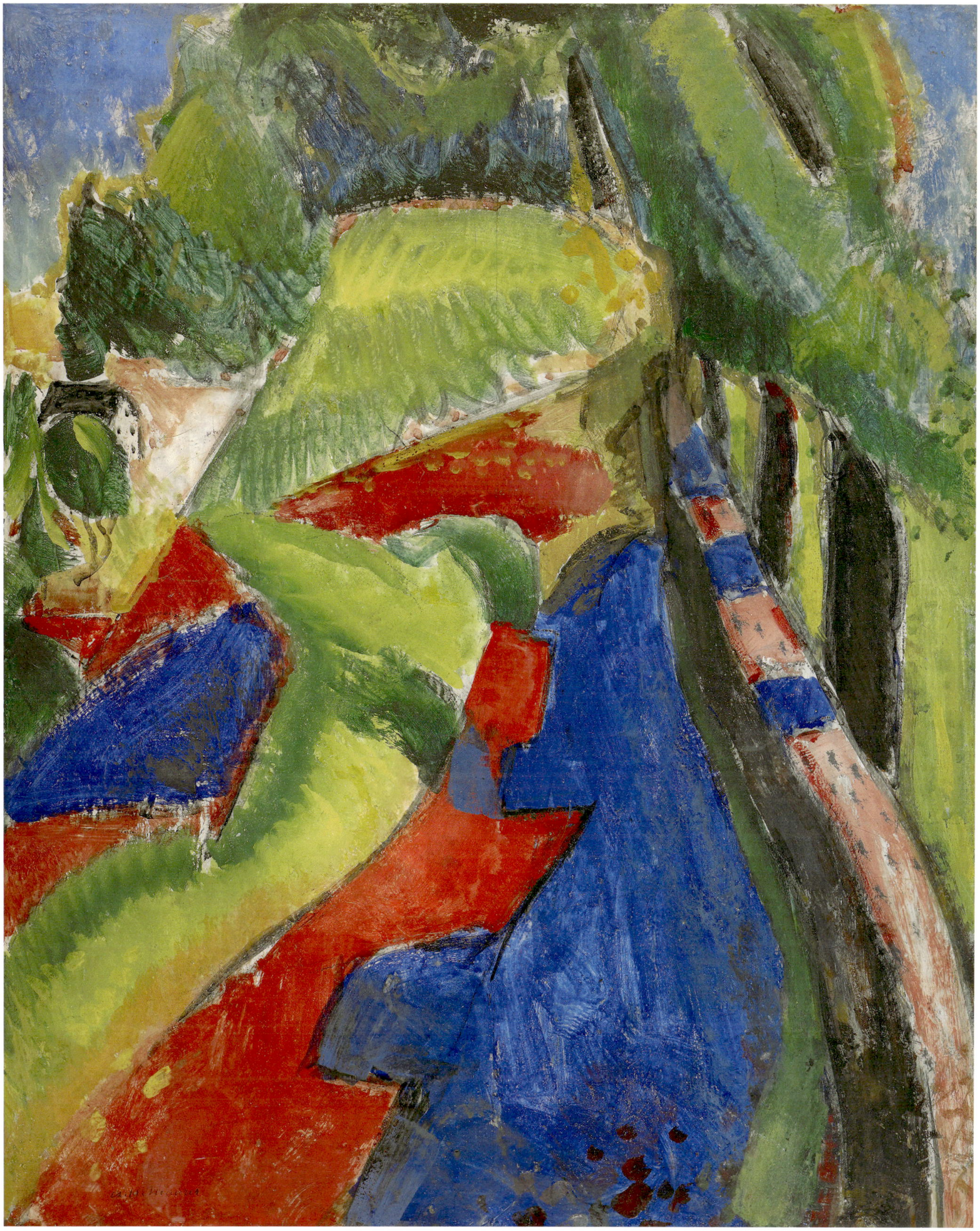

JOHN MARIN (1870–1953)

Grain Elevator (Weehawken Sequence)

ca. 1910–15
Oil on canvas
16⅜ × 19⅜ in. (41.6 × 49.2 cm)
Promised Gift

Between 1910 and 1916, John Marin painted nearly one hundred works in oil and watercolor depicting views from Weehawken, New Jersey, a riverside city located at the southern tip of the Palisade cliffs and directly across the Hudson River from midtown Manhattan. Later known as the Weehawken Sequence, this loosely conceived series occasionally includes scenic vistas up the river or glimpses of the New York skyline through a veil of trees.[1] More often than not, however, Marin focused on Weehawken's industrial waterfront—the busy cargo port, the West Shore Railroad yard and, almost unfailingly, the pier's soaring grain elevator.

The massive brick and steel West Shore granary features prominently in *Grain Elevator*, its rust-colored facade a bold contrast to the patchwork of pale blues, whites, and grays that dominate the composition. The towering new (1905) structure, capable of storing over two hundred million barrels of grain, could not have escaped the artist's notice.[2] Having grown up only a few miles inland from Weehawken, in Rutherford, New Jersey, Marin must have passed the site countless times en route to New York. Though he was in Europe when construction was completed, Marin began painting the grain elevator immediately upon his return to the United States in 1910.[3]

After depicting picturesque settings such as the mountains of the Tyrol and the historic monuments of Paris during his five years abroad, New York's ever-changing urban landscape must have seemed, in contrast, a suitably American subject for the pioneering artist. The grain elevator was among a number of colossal industrial structures sprouting up across the country. Indeed, the United States was emerging as the "Motherland of Industry," as the German Bauhaus architect Walter Gropius wrote in 1913. While American exceptionalism had been rooted in nature in the nineteenth century, in the early twentieth century the machine took center stage. Marin's focus on American industry in the Weehawken Sequence placed him at the forefront of establishing this new national point of view.[4]

Although he embraced native subjects upon his return from Europe, Marin represented them in a manner influenced by the avant-garde art he had seen abroad. The subtle coloration and reduction of forms to near abstractions in *Grain Elevator* suggest the work of Pablo Picasso, Georges Braque, and especially Paul Cézanne. Yet Marin's experimental technique of dragging, rubbing, and generally (as Marin described it) "playing around" with paint was an approach utterly his own.[5] Critics took notice of the painter's experimental methods, though they struggled to characterize his unique aesthetic. Regardless of stylistic lineage, Marin's early abstractions were shocking to the American eye. As one critic acknowledged in 1912, his works "repel or attract according to the imaginative power of the spectator."[6]

As the century progressed, public opinion shifted. By the time of his death in 1953, Marin was considered among America's most important painters—one whose progressive techniques inspired a new generation of artists including the abstract expressionists Mark Rothko and Jackson Pollock. In 1948, the influential critic and modern art champion Clement Greenberg declared: "If it is not beyond all doubt that [Marin] is the best painter alive in America at this moment, he assuredly has to be taken into consideration when we ask who is."[7]

SMH

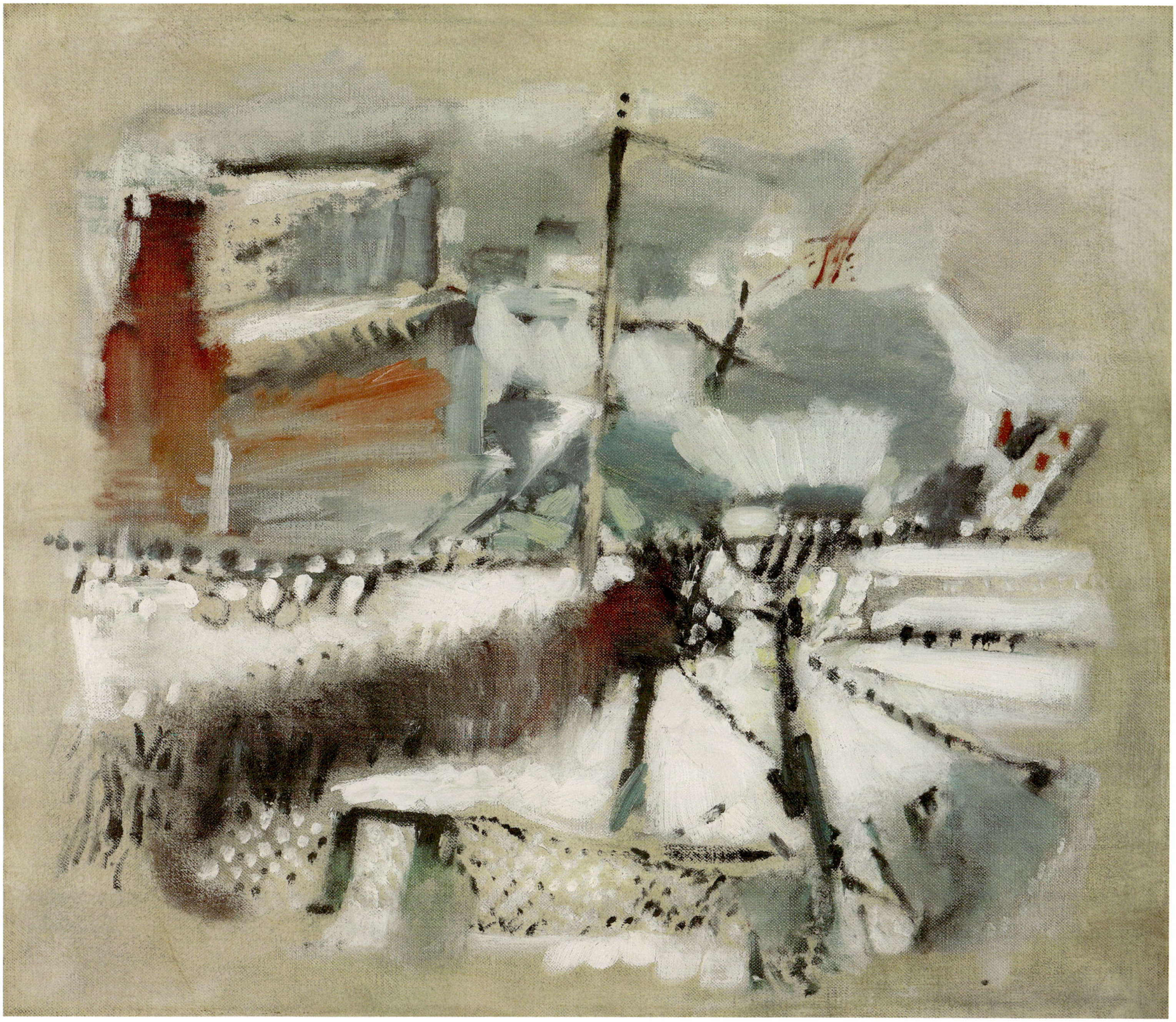

JOHN MARIN (1870–1953)

Telephone Building, Lower New York

1926
Watercolor, graphite, and charcoal on paper
27 × 21 in. (68.6 × 53.3 cm)
Promised Gift

In 1910, John Marin returned from six years in Europe to a New York transformed. New bridges spanned the rivers, cars and electric trolleys had replaced horses and buggies, and construction was well under way on the Woolworth Building, the world's tallest skyscraper.[1] Around this time Marin developed his annual routine of spending summers painting nature in the Berkshires, Adirondacks, and, by 1914, Maine; and devoting his attention to New York City's urban landscape in the winter months.[2]

New York's architecture provided the most salient subject for Marin's city views. He often oriented these compositions vertically to capture the impressive heights of the evolving urban environment. In *Telephone Building, Lower New York*, however, Marin pressed the composition both upward and outward. The massive New York Telephone Building, a new skyscraper completed just months before Marin painted this work, was idiosyncratically designed to accommodate its unusual plot on West Street in lower Manhattan. The structure's seventeen-story base aligns with the obtuse and acute angles of the parallelogram-shaped block upon which it sits. A series of setback levels lead inward to the central tower, which rotates forty-five degrees to stand square with the nearby skyscrapers on Broadway, including the landmark Woolworth Building.[3] In Marin's depiction of this dynamic edifice, angles meet and collide, the building's surface further distorted by the artist's unexpected placement of shadows on the buff brick-and-limestone facade.

A daring and accomplished watercolorist, Marin was a central force in claiming the aqueous art form as a tool for modernist expression. Between the late 1910s and 1928, watercolor was his exclusive medium.[4] The often-unpredictable effects of wet washes of translucent pigment on an absorptive paper ground promoted a spontaneity, freshness, and experimentation that suited his spirited subject matter. Once applied to the paper, Marin manipulated the paint in all manner of ways, often incorporating unconventional media.[5] In *Telephone Building*, the artist's addition of quick, gestural lines made of graphite and charcoal enhances the movement and flow of the composition, guiding the viewer's eye through the design.

Marin's contemporaries often used musical metaphors to describe his pulsating watercolors. According to one Chicago critic, the artist was "the Strawinsky [*sic*] of modern color," capable of composing powerful visual works that expressed aural sensations.[6] Painted with quick, improvisational brushstrokes, *Telephone Building* vibrates with a rhythmic beat. The windows on the building's facade form a staccato procession of squares that is interrupted at seemingly random intervals by blank walls and amorphous splotches of color. The building appears to sway and twist to the noises of the city, revealing an artist thoroughly entranced by modern America.

SMH

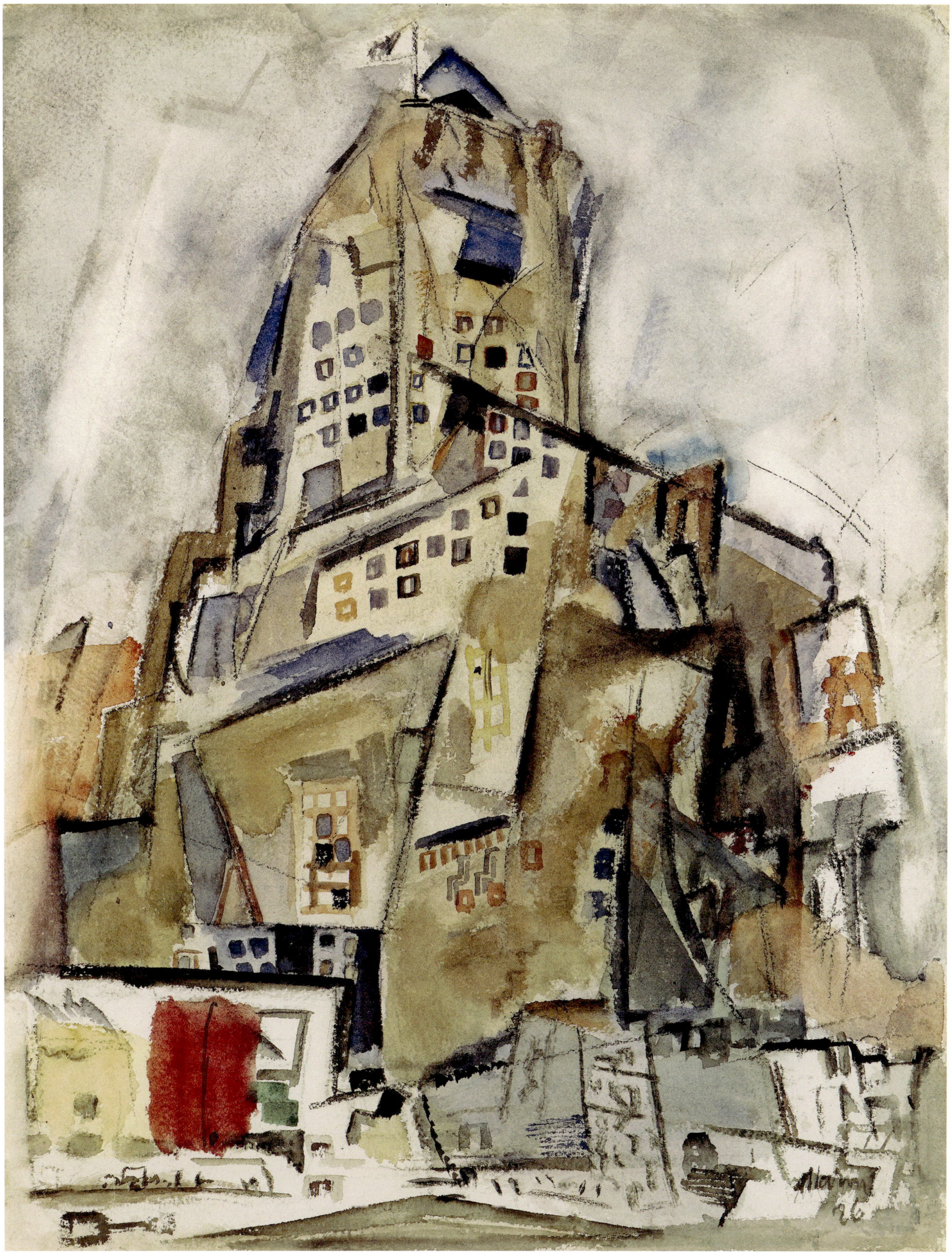

MARSDEN HARTLEY (1877–1943)

Hall of the Mountain King

ca. 1908–9
Oil on canvas
30⅛ × 30 in. (76.5 × 76.2 cm)

In 1908, with funds supplied by an early admirer of his work, Marsden Hartley traveled to his native state, Maine, to steep himself in the art of landscape painting. He settled in North Lovell, a rural village situated within the rugged hills of Stoneham Valley, near the New Hampshire border. The neo-impressionist landscapes he produced there over the course of the late summer and fall reveal a newly confident painting style and a vision of nature that is both jarring and sublimely majestic.

Sustained by long hikes through the heavily forested terrain, Hartley quickly fell in love with the region around Kezar Lake, and especially with the contours of mountains rising up from its banks. He rhapsodized to a friend that he had "now come back I think to the original child within me namely the romanticist, albeit not perhaps a romance of love as of madness for the mountain madness is on me, and the bizarrerie [*sic*] of the hills gives me stronger thoughts than ever."[1] Over the next several months, Hartley painted a series of seasonal views of the mountains near North Lovell that reflected the influence of the Swiss-born artist Giovanni Segantini as much as they also revealed an artist on the cusp of developing his own unique vision. Hartley had first encountered Segantini's work through reproduction in 1903.[2] He immediately adopted the Swiss painter's distinctive, stitchlike brush stroke and later credited Segantini with providing the insight he needed to "begin painting my own mountains."[3]

Hall of the Mountain King is among the most accomplished of the Stoneham Valley paintings. Disregarding the conventions of Western landscape painting, Hartley chose a square format rather than a rectangular one. Instead of rendering perspective through the gradual recession of space, he compressed the foreground and background into a single, continuous plane. The artist's palette of bright pastel colors and his emphasis on the physicality of the paint resulted in an overall decorative quality that many scholars have noted resembles that of a woven tapestry. Hartley's reduction of the mountains into elemental waves and his sculptural treatment of the clouds point to a vision of nature that is less concerned with representing objective reality than it is with expressing the sensory experience of the wilderness.

The titles Hartley ascribed to some of the Maine landscapes underscored his interest in mysticism and spiritualist philosophies, as well as in music. *Hall of the Mountain King* likely refers to the piece of orchestral music written by the Norwegian romantic composer Edvard Grieg for Henrik Ibsen's 1867 fantasy play *Peer Gynt*. When *Peer Gynt* ran on Broadway in early 1907, it was hailed by critics for its innovative, if bewildering, blend of drama and pictures. It is unlikely that either the play or Grieg's score would have escaped Hartley's attention, and although there is no documentation to prove so, it is certainly possible that he attended a performance. Regardless, with *Hall of the Mountain King* Hartley positioned his art as abstract and tonal, visually equivalent to musical sound.

In March 1909, Hartley showed the Maine landscape series to Alfred Stieglitz at the dealer's New York gallery, 291. Impressed by the work, that May Stieglitz opened Hartley's first solo exhibition, which included *Hall of the Mountain King*. It was a pivotal moment for both men; the bond they established would withstand many trials and last until the late 1930s. REL

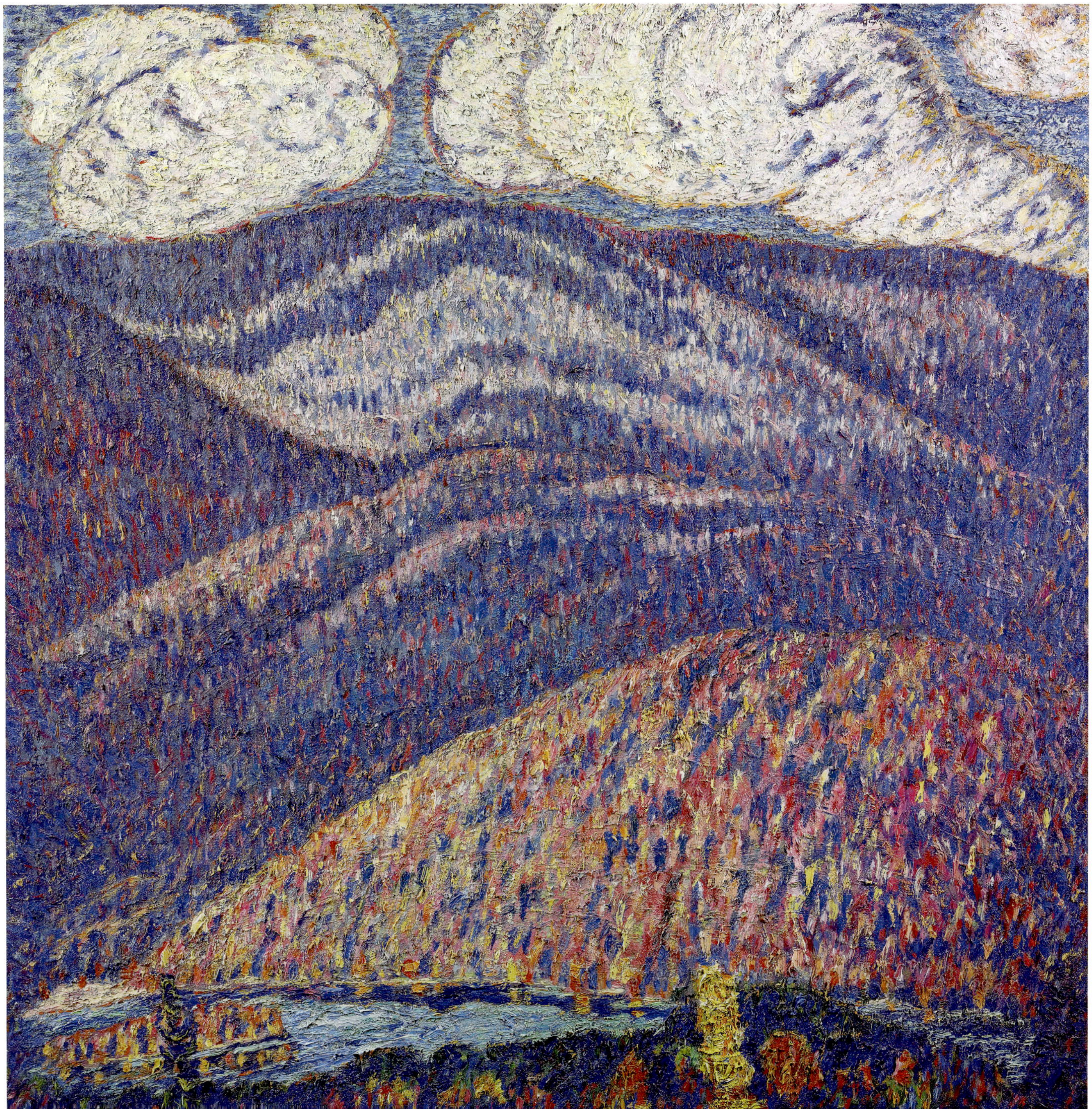

MARSDEN HARTLEY (1877–1943)

Mountains No. 22

1930
Oil on canvas
30 × 36 in. (76.2 × 91.4 cm)
Promised Gift

After living abroad for several years, Marsden Hartley returned to the United States in March 1930. At the suggestion of friends, he traveled to the White Mountains of New Hampshire, settling near Franconia, just across the border from Maine and the Stoneham Valley region he had painted in 1908–9 (p. 198). When Hartley arrived in New Hampshire, his finances were precarious and his spirits exceedingly low. The dire economic conditions of the Great Depression were not the only factors contributing to his anxiety about the future. The large exhibition of his experimental adaptations of Paul Cézanne's techniques, which his longtime dealer, Alfred Stieglitz, had mounted in New York in January 1929, had done little to enhance his reputation. Critics roundly dismissed the showing, but it was Stieglitz's disappointment in the work that must have wounded Hartley most: "You have really made no 'practical' contact in Europe, and you are really without contact in your own country."[1] In his paintings of the French countryside surrounding Aix-en-Provence, Hartley had not achieved "contact," a direct reference to the nationalist rhetoric of the poet William Carlos Williams and his associates, who argued that in order to develop a true American art form artists had to cast aside European influences and root their work in personal experience.

Hartley's move to the White Mountains was thus a deliberate attempt to regain lost ground by immersing himself in a familiar native landscape. The Franconia Valley offered stimulating, unexplored terrain: the western face of the mountains he had known since childhood. Once situated in the town of Sugar Hill, he wrote to his friend Rebecca Strand, "I am alive and established in the wilds of New England—almost as if I had never been away—living exactly as I lived over 20 yrs ago up at North Lovell in the better end of a deserted farm house."[2] Hartley resumed his practice of taking strenuous hikes through the woods, tramping about the Lost River region of Beaver Lake and Franconia Notch, sometimes with his paint kit or a sketchbook in hand.

Mountains No. 22, with its high-keyed palette of vibrant reds, oranges, greens, and blues and its vigorous, parallel brushstrokes, honors Cézanne's precepts. But contrary to Hartley's Provençal paintings, which the critics had decried as derivative, the New Hampshire paintings are characteristically Hartley. He set the mountain against a clear, uniformly blue sky, with a dramatic arrangement of white cloud formations hovering overhead. The mass of the mountain is close to the picture plane and sharply defined, making it seem monumental and majestic.

Perhaps as a visual manifestation of his state of agitation, Hartley chose to dispense with the foreground, preventing the viewer from establishing a resting point. The painting depicts a transitional time of year when the verdant greens of summer give way to the fiery colors of autumn. Shadows play throughout the composition, reinforcing the painting's elegiac, end-of-season mood.

By late October 1930, Hartley determined that the New Hampshire landscape would not provide the artistic breakthrough he had been looking for and returned to Brooklyn feeling both physically and psychologically depleted. Yet the trip to New England had allowed Hartley to reconnect with his native terrain and rediscover the mountain as a protean force within his art. REL

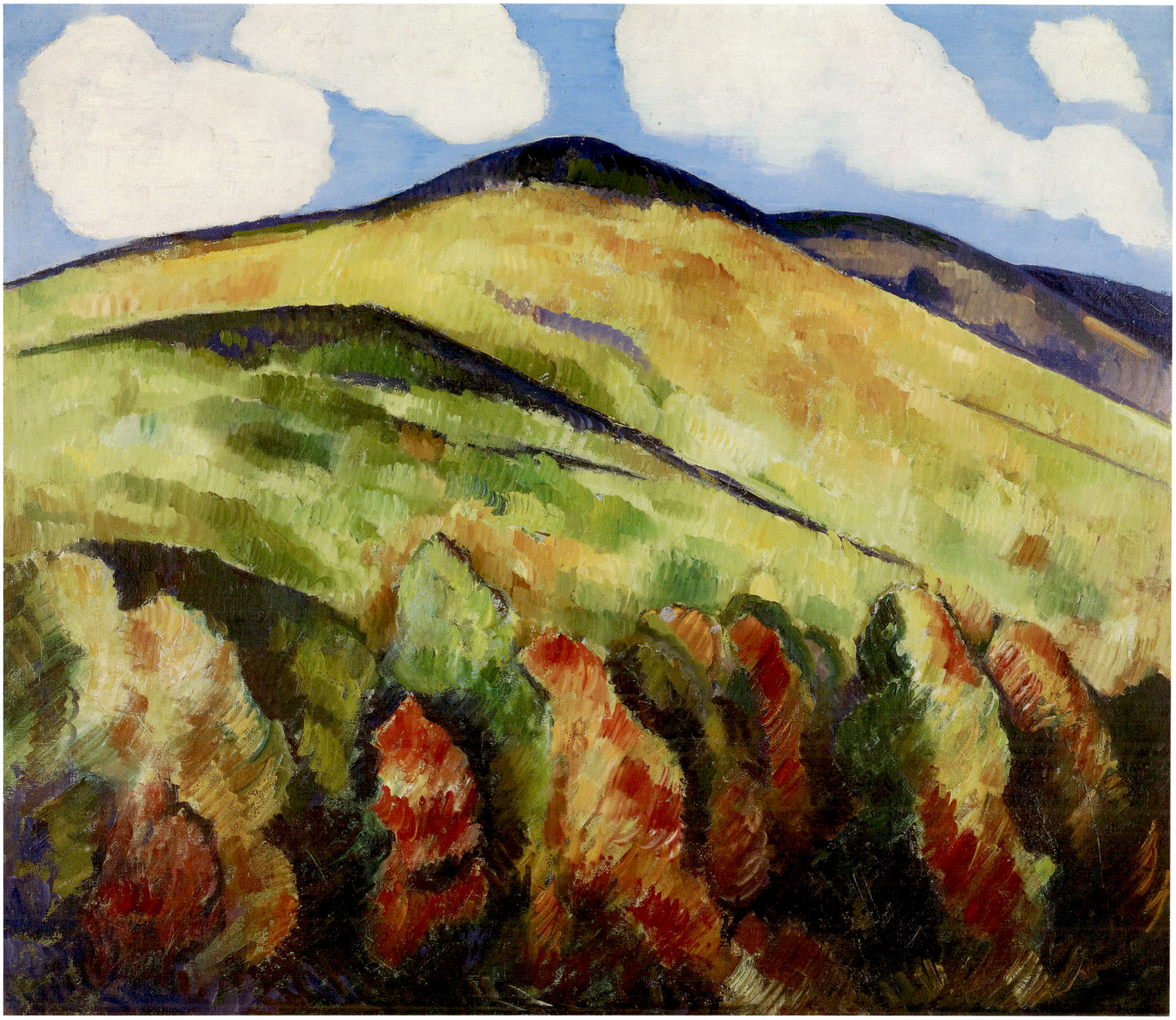

LYONEL FEININGER (1871–1956)

Schlossgasse

1915
Oil on canvas
39½ × 31¼ in. (100.3 × 79.4 cm)

The American modernist Lyonel Feininger, who spent much of his early career in Europe, was an influential member of Germany's avant-garde in the early twentieth century and taught at the innovative art school known as the Bauhaus from 1919 to 1926. Born in New York City to German parents, as a teenager Feininger studied music and drawing at the General Vocational School in Hamburg and painting at the Royal Academy of Art in Berlin. Although Feininger made his name as a painter and printmaker, music was a major source of inspiration for the artist throughout his career. An accomplished pianist and composer of fugues, he believed that music and art were intimately connected. Like musical compositions, Feininger's cubist-inspired images explore interrelationships and synchronization while creating an overall sense of order. In 1913, just two years before painting *Schlossgasse*, the artist boasted, "My pictures are ever nearing closer the Synthesis of the fugue."[1]

Feininger first established his professional reputation as a newspaper cartoonist and illustrator of children's books.[2] Germany's urban architecture became the focus of his work in the fine arts. Feininger's participation in a 1911 exhibition at the Salon des Indépendants in Paris marked a critical moment in the painter's artistic development. There he encountered cubism for the first time and became friends with the French artist Robert Delaunay, a leading proponent of orphism, a related art movement that explored the optical and aesthetic effects of contrasting hues.[3] In a radical departure from his early paintings, which were characterized by the expressive use of color and cartoonlike figuration, Feininger increasingly devoted his attention to the fragmentation of form and a rigorous, nearly scientific study of light and color values.

Concerns of volume and space dominated the painting style Feininger cultivated in the early teens. Beginning in 1912, the artist's architectural motifs became monumental: he shifted from painting broad urban scenes inhabited by multiple figures to close-up views of building facades rendered as near abstractions. *Schlossgasse*, which depicts a blind alleyway leading to the castle in Weimar, epitomizes Feininger's new aesthetic interests. The houses are composed of sharply defined forms and compressed interstices. Manifold perspectives appear simultaneously and numerous planes coexist, overlapping and intersecting. The artist ably created the illusion of volume in a fantastic space of sensitively shaded geometric facets and crystalline forms.[4] The painting's surface serves as a translucent layer through which light seems to shine: it does not infiltrate from the outside, but originates from within the picture itself, adding a dramatic effect to the composition. *Schlossgasse* expresses the artist's formal determination to achieve a firmly structured, glasslike transparency.[5]

As Feininger became increasingly preoccupied with formal issues, the human figure, which had once been a central theme in his work, gradually receded. The two persons in the lower foreground of *Schlossgasse*, who are schematically rendered in a few strokes of black paint, almost disappear in the artist's ambitious exploration of three-dimensional form and prismatic light. MW

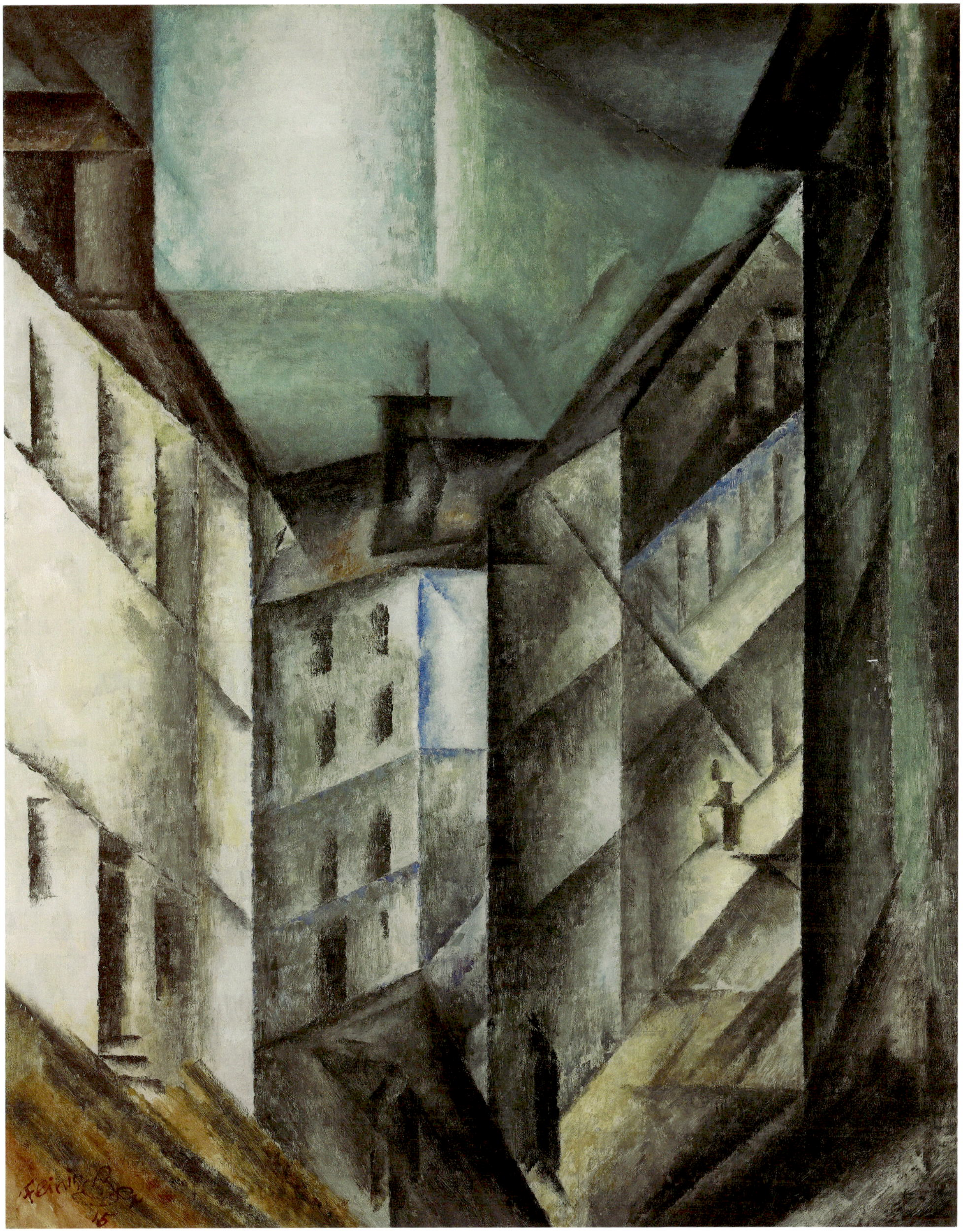

GEORGIA O'KEEFFE (1887–1986)

Evening Star No. II

1917
Watercolor on paper
8¾ × 12 in. (22.2 × 30.5 cm)
Promised Gift

Within the context of her long and productive career, the time Georgia O'Keeffe spent in Texas was relatively brief. Nonetheless, it marked a period of tremendous growth and innovation. O'Keeffe developed a passion for the West Texas landscape while living in Amarillo, where she worked as a public school teacher between 1912 and 1914. When she returned to Texas in the fall of 1916—this time to teach at West Texas State Normal College, located in Canyon, twenty miles south of Amarillo—she was a credentialed art instructor but still a fledgling artist. Her correspondence reveals her enthusiasm for living on the broad expanse of the western prairie, but also her struggle to achieve a personal, expressive imagery within it. Writing to the photographer Paul Strand in November 1917, she enthused: "The plains are wonderful—mellow looking—dry grass the quiet and the bigness of it—anything that makes you feel quiet and bigness like that is marvelous—wouldnt [*sic*] it be great in a person —why cant [*sic*] I make it into shapes—I wish I could want to try."[1] Ironically, at the time O'Keeffe wrote these words, she had already begun to formulate the strategies that would help give "shape" to her art. In 1915, she had achieved an aesthetic breakthrough with a remarkable series of charcoal drawings that revealed her ability to express an interior world of thoughts and feelings through abstract forms.[2]

The vastness of the Texas Panhandle inspired O'Keeffe to shift her focus to the exterior world. The stark, planar geography of the region offered a suitable landscape for her to pursue the advanced techniques of abstract picture making. O'Keeffe's increasing fascination with the "soil and spirit" aestheticism espoused by photographer and gallerist Alfred Stieglitz and his modernist associates compelled her to search for personal metaphors within the "terrible winds" and "wonderful emptiness" of the American West.[3] Moreover, the aridity of the plains, which made the region prone to optically brilliant sunrises and sunsets, facilitated her experiments with the psychic effects of color, a concept that had intrigued her ever since reading Wassily Kandinsky's *The Art of Spiritual Harmony* in 1915.[4] Given her affinity for stargazing, it is not surprising that O'Keeffe focused on the radiance of the evening star rising above the earth's thin crust. She turned the star's effervescence into a series of small, utterly radical watercolors that capture its monumentality and rhythmic movement across the sky.

Eight of the *Evening Star* watercolors are known.[5] Elegant, but also exuberant, the series shows O'Keeffe's technical command of the medium. She brushed her watercolors directly onto the paper without the aid of graphite underdrawing. As evident by the controlled puddling and pooling of the pigments, she had developed an exceptional facility for hand-eye coordination. The graphic power of these watercolors comes from an exquisite combination of fluid yet restrained brushwork, as well as the sharp contrast of pure, saturated colors against white paper. With only a few expressive movements, O'Keeffe captured a specific, if fleeting, moment when the chromatic brilliance of the sky envelops the individual in a wealth of sensations.

REL

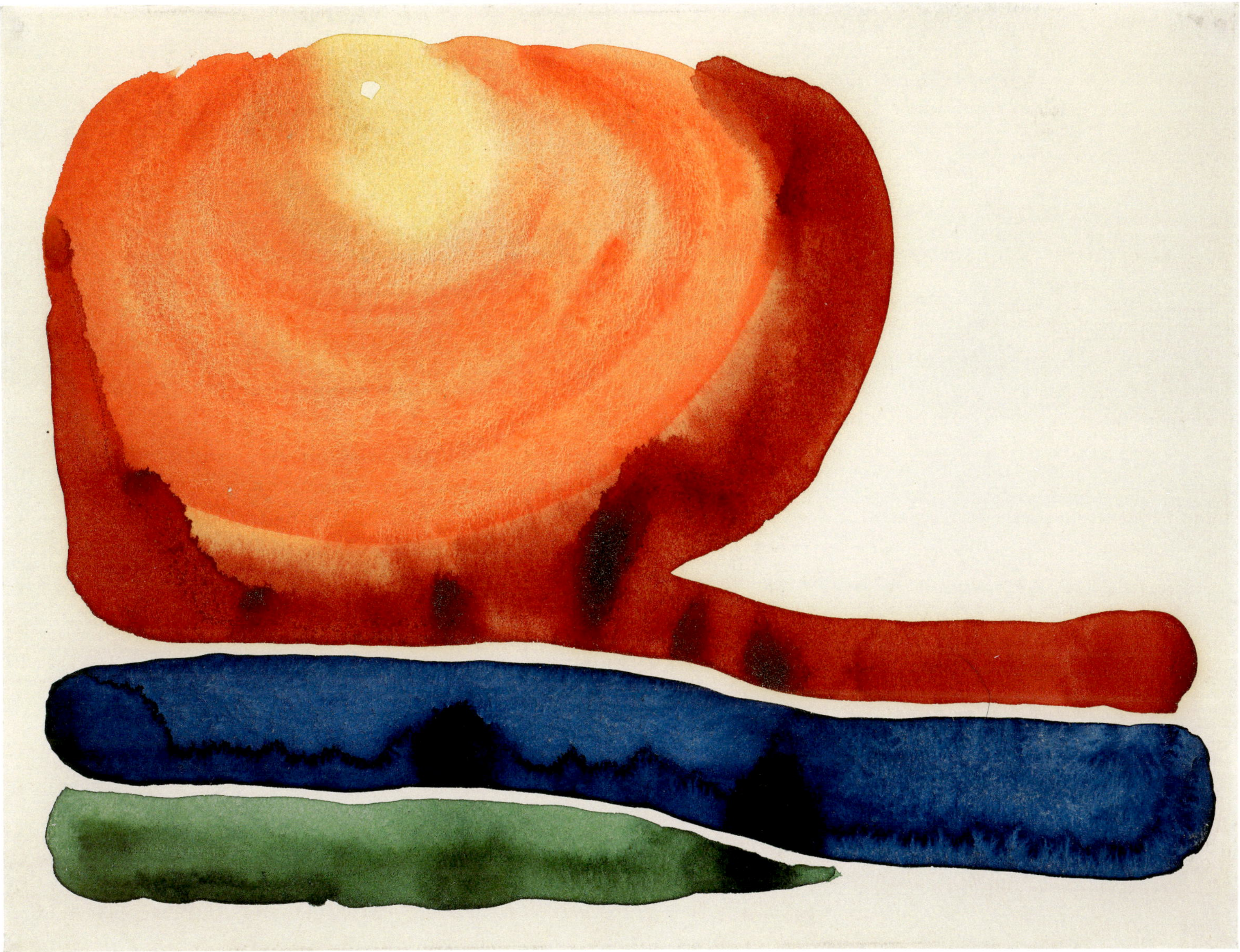

GEORGIA O'KEEFFE (1887–1986)

Mask with Golden Apple

1923
Oil on canvas
9 × 16 in. (22.9 × 40.6 cm)
Promised Gift

Georgia O'Keeffe painted *Mask with Golden Apple* at the point in her career when her personal and professional relationship with her dealer and soon-to-be husband, the photographer Alfred Stieglitz, had reached its apogee. O'Keeffe and Stieglitz had begun working and living together in 1918. By 1920, their shared artistic ambitions had gestated long enough to settle into a mutually satisfying, if at times competitive, collaboration in which each compelled and propelled the other to formulate a new visual language within their respective media. The apple figured prominently in their shared repertoire of images. In the early 1920s, while Stieglitz made photographic portraits of O'Keeffe and his friends holding apples, O'Keeffe obsessively painted the fruit. In these paintings the apple becomes a talisman and a personal identifier, as well as a metaphor for American culture.

The tabletop still life *Mask with Golden Apple* unites two seemingly disparate objects: an African mask belonging to the Ivory Coast's Baule people and the golden apple of the painting's title. It is a curious pairing, a handcrafted wooden mask with a piece of cultivated fruit. Aside from the visual analogy of the rounded form of the apple with the mask's crescent-shaped arcs, there is little else in the composition linking the two elements. Stieglitz had shown the Baule mask at his gallery, 291, in 1914, in the exhibition *Statuary in Wood by African Savages*.[1] This groundbreaking display was intended to underscore the seminal influence of African art on the European avant-garde. After the exhibition closed Stieglitz kept the mask for his personal collection, and following his death O'Keeffe donated it to Fisk University Galleries in Nashville, Tennessee.

O'Keeffe scholar Sarah Whitaker Peters has astutely noted that *Mask with Golden Apple* is the only one of the artist's paintings to include an African mask, and that the collapsed space of the image "possess[es] a distinctly photographic quality."[2] What is also remarkable about the work is O'Keeffe's placement of the mask horizontally within the composition: the spirit is thus presented recumbent. By decontextualizing the sculpture from its intended expressive function, it is rendered powerless. Even more striking, O'Keeffe placed the apple in front of the mask, directly in line with the figure's cheek. Charles C. Eldredge has speculated that O'Keeffe's golden apple may relate to the ancient myths of the Judgment of Paris and the Garden of the Hesperides.[3] Might O'Keeffe have intended the apple as a sly reference to the well-known fable of the golden egg and, if the fruit represents the artist herself, a pun on her stature as the golden girl of Stieglitz's artistic stable? Regardless, it seems clear that in her juxtaposition of these disparate objects, O'Keeffe alluded to the fact that the period for experimenting with European modern primitivism had ended, replaced by a distinctly American idiom symbolized by the apple.

REL

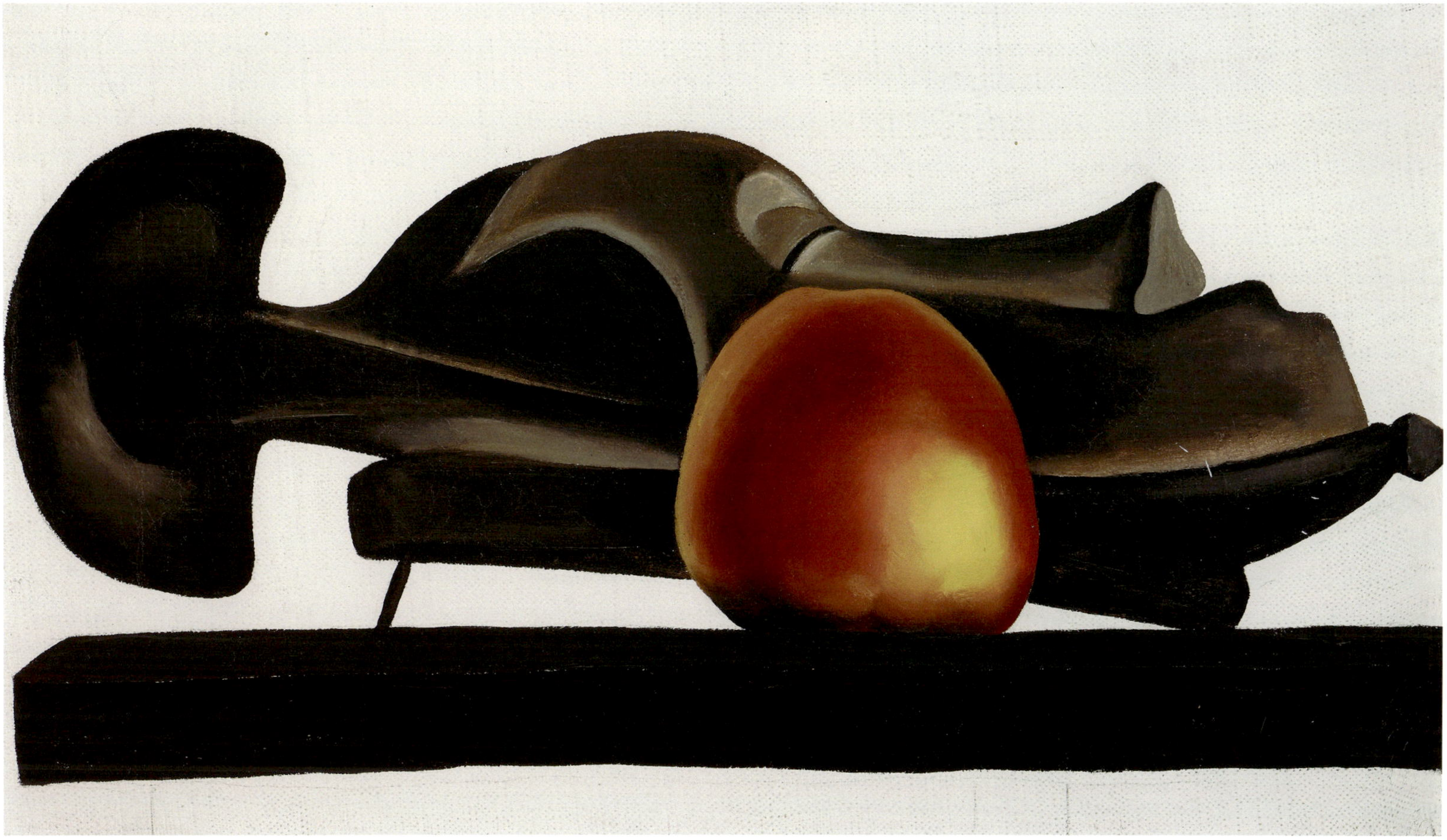

OSCAR BLUEMNER (1867–1938)

Motive of Space and Form— A New Jersey Village (Montville)

1915
Oil on canvas
30 × 40 in. (76.2 × 101.6 cm)

In a 1915 journal entry, the German-born American artist Oscar Bluemner described a winter walk "through the gray morning landscape under a cloudy February sky." The painter remarked of the monochromatic setting "how nice, enchanting, exciting, exhilarating would a sudden transformation of this scene into a May day be with bold colors, blue sky, green ground, red houses, and the contrast of light and shade and clear forms."[1] *Motive of Space and Form—A New Jersey Village (Montville)*, which depicts homes along a canal in the industrial town of Montville, New Jersey, is Bluemner's imaginative execution of this chromatic transformation.

Motive of Space and Form epitomizes Bluemner's distinctive aesthetic, which rendered basic architectonic forms and simplified landscape motifs in a vibrant, expressive color palette. The formal, emotional, and spiritual qualities of color fascinated the artist. He was so intent on selecting the right hues for his paintings that he labored over preparatory sketches and developed his own color theories. Bluemner painted the large house in the center of this picture in his signature vermillion red, a color that earned him the nickname "Vermillionaire."[2] His passion for red and his affection for places where industry and nature converge may have been influenced by his time as a student in the German town of Elberfeld, on the Wupper River.[3] The fabrics and yarns produced in Elberfeld's linen and silk manufactories were dyed with a special "Turkish red" pigment that was the town's trademark.[4] Like the expressionist artists Franz Marc and Wassily Kandinsky, Bluemner assigned emotional meanings to the colors he used in his work. He described red as "chief color and maximum of everything artistic; the strongest attraction, signal, warning, symbol of power, vitality, energy, life."[5]

Bluemner organized his landscape as a grid of color planes, the spatial geometry of which reflects his previous career in architecture as well as his knowledge of contemporary artistic trends.[6] The painter's prismatic rendering of the Montville canal betrays the influence of early cubism, while his iridescent colors evoke the luminous palettes of American synchromists such as Stanton Macdonald-Wright (p. 210).[7] The backlit appearance of the picture's darker, jewel-toned elements create an effect similar to viewing sunlit, stained glass cathedral windows.[8] Bluemner's dynamic composition is characterized by opposing forces: the light blue and white of the sky and waterfall contrast with the dark greens of trees and bushes, while the hard-edged, rectangular buildings counter the curves of the dense vegetation.

Although human figures rarely appear in Bluemner's work, the chromatic vibrancy and strong physical presence of his buildings gives them the appearance of human protagonists. The absence of figures in Bluemner's paintings, his interest in urban architecture, and his flat, geometric schematizations anticipated the precisionist compositions of influential artists such as Charles Demuth (p. 212) and Charles Sheeler (p. 252).

MW

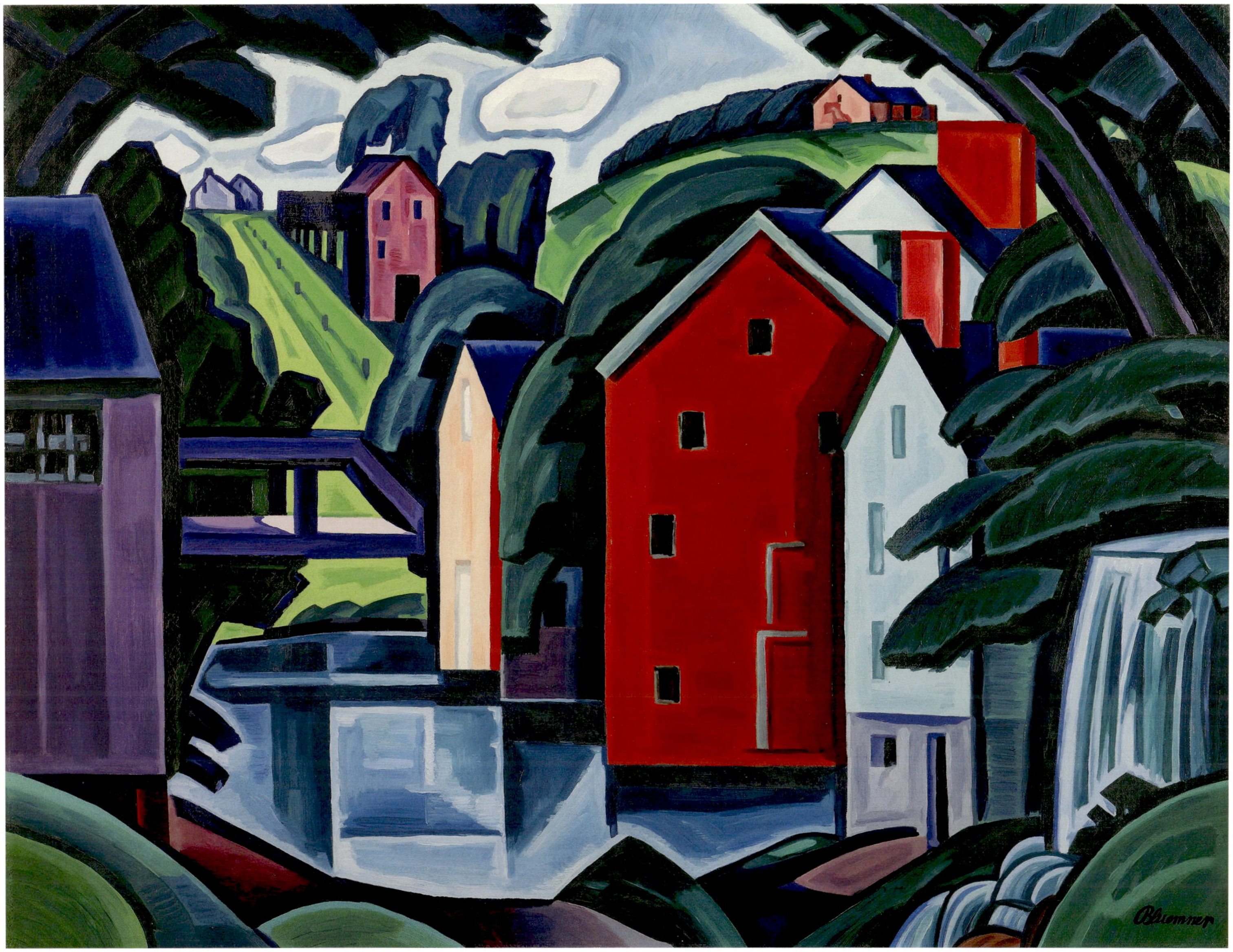
Bluemner

STANTON MACDONALD-WRIGHT (1890–1973)

Au Café (Synchromy)

1918
Oil on canvas
50 × 28 in. (127 × 71.1 cm)
Promised Gift

A perfect green circle appears at the center of *Au Café (Synchromy)*, amidst overlapping wedges of color in what at first appears to be a pure abstraction. From contemplation of this circle, however, two figures begin to emerge. At left, a woman raises a glass toward her lips, while a man sits in the foreground at lower right, his profile a sequence of triangles nearly lost in this prismatically intense yet carefully orchestrated symphony of color.

The artist of this visually dazzling image, Stanton Macdonald-Wright, was clearly well acquainted with the extraordinary advances in painting that marked the first years of the twentieth century—innovations to which he ultimately contributed. Macdonald-Wright arrived in Paris in the fall of 1909, a most opportune historical moment for a young and emerging modernist. Cubism had opened the door to a radical rethinking of the representation of space; fauvism declared the use of color arbitrary; and Wassily Kandinsky equated painting with the evocation of spirit itself. It was within this richly experimental environment that Macdonald-Wright met compatriot Morgan Russell, with whom he founded synchromism—the only recognized pre–World War I vanguard art movement established by Americans.

Macdonald-Wright and his constant companion Russell desired to move away from the achromatic palette of cubism though neither wished to repeat the color work of fauvism, which they perceived as merely decorative. Together, the two Americans sought a more elemental use of chroma, a method that would reveal its basic expressive powers. In an era of "isms," they named their movement synchromism, a word meaning "with color," just as symphony means "with sound." As Macdonald-Wright and Russell developed it, synchromism was a method of painting based on color scales that were made in ways analogous to musical scales. Just as Western music has a twelve-tone system, so the conventional color wheel has twelve colors. In music, it is the intervals (spaces) between notes that establish the harmony of a chord and the character of a scale, and Macdonald-Wright and Russell believed that intervals between colors could be similarly expressive.[1]

Au Café, painted in 1918, summarizes the primary ambitions of synchromism and ably represents Macdonald-Wright's mature aesthetic. The image is based on the regular rhythms of everyday life (a woman and man enjoying coffee at a café), but the composition is a visual improvisation. Macdonald-Wright arranged the brilliant, jewel-like color in staggered blocks and as prismatic shapes, as if to mimic sequences of musical chords. The artist strove to express profound emotion in a manner similar to music. He painted *Au Café* in the "scale" of yellow-green: "This scale," the artist wrote, "is like a spring landscape, freshly washed by rain, delicate and adolescent."[2] Yellow-green was, for Macdonald-Wright, the appropriate scale in which to compose an outdoor scene of a man and woman seated at a sidewalk table (signaling pleasant weather) and enjoying a drink together (portending the birth of romance). Judging from photographs of the period and a lifelong record of self-portraiture, the male figure with his high forehead and hair combed straight back is probably the artist himself.

WS

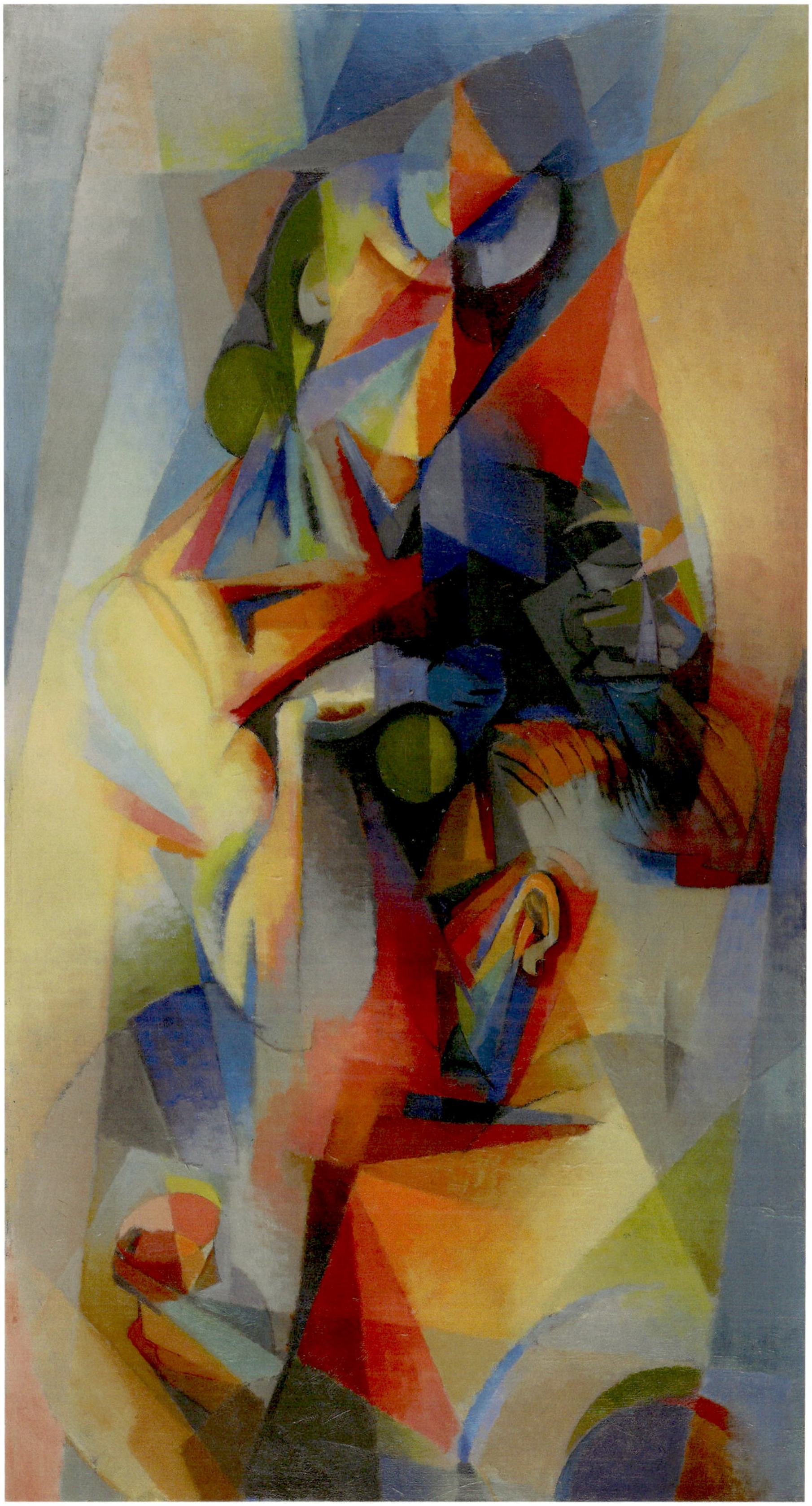

CHARLES DEMUTH (1883–1935)

Sail: In Two Movements

1919
Tempera, watercolor, and pencil on paperboard
16 × 20 in. (40.6 × 50.8 cm)
Promised Gift

One of America's most prominent modernists and a founder of the precisionist movement, Charles Demuth was a master watercolorist who fully understood the subtlety and nuances of the medium.[1] Demuth was born to a prosperous family in Lancaster, Pennsylvania. Although plagued by ill health for most of his life, he traveled extensively in search of artistic inspiration.[2] In 1912, on his third trip to Europe, he studied drawing and watercolor at the Académie Moderne in Paris.[3] Upon returning to the United States in 1914, Demuth began associating with America's artistic and intellectual elite, including Marsden Hartley, Charles Sheeler, and Marcel Duchamp. Demuth divided his time between New York City and Lancaster, spending his summers in Provincetown or Gloucester, Massachusetts, painting the local architecture and sailboats in the bays.[4] In 1915, a solo exhibition at the George Daniel Gallery firmly established his reputation in the artistic vanguard. Shortly thereafter, the influential art impresario Alfred Stieglitz took Demuth under his wing.

Around 1919, Demuth's pictures began to show characteristics of the emerging precisionist aesthetic. His tempera and watercolor *Sail: In Two Movements* from that year is a transitional image that combines the fragmented forms and simultaneity of European avant-garde art with a new representational clarity and exactitude. The painting depicts a sailboat at sea "floating" in a light-colored, prismatic space structured by Demuth's precise pencil lines. The boat is composed of abstract geometric elements rendered from various perspectives. He developed each individual form separately, yet considered each essential to the whole composition. These forms overlap, often creating interesting optical effects. The triangular shapes of the sails and the diagonal lines of the masts imbue the picture with a dynamism that recalls Duchamp's pioneering oil *Nude Descending a Staircase (No. 2)* (1912, Philadelphia Museum of Art) as well as work by the Italian futurists. The diagonal orientation of the masts and their pronounced extension into space enlivens the composition with an overall rhythm, while traces of faded color on the periphery suggest the echoes of past movement.

In keeping with the traditions of analytical cubism, Demuth utilized color only sparingly, to modify his complex of overlaid and intersecting structural planes. He blotted or scored subdued tints of blue, purple, or yellow onto the paperboard, perhaps with the point of a palette knife or the end of a brush handle. The artist applied his colors in various gradations to define the shape of the sails and give the impression of volume. Eye-catching red and brown accents skip from the stern of the boat to the lower half of the second mast.

Demuth painted *Sail: In Two Movements* during a period when he was experimenting with tempera, a medium that allowed him greater control and precision when painting small geometric shapes than did watercolor alone.[5] The artist first mapped out the design in pencil and then applied his pigment in short, curved strokes to describe water and long, straight strokes to model the sails. He applied his paint lightly, allowing areas of the paperboard to show through.

In 1920, the artist learned that he was seriously ill with diabetes.[6] Because he had so little energy, Demuth henceforth restricted himself mostly to painting in watercolor, on small-format papers.[7] MW

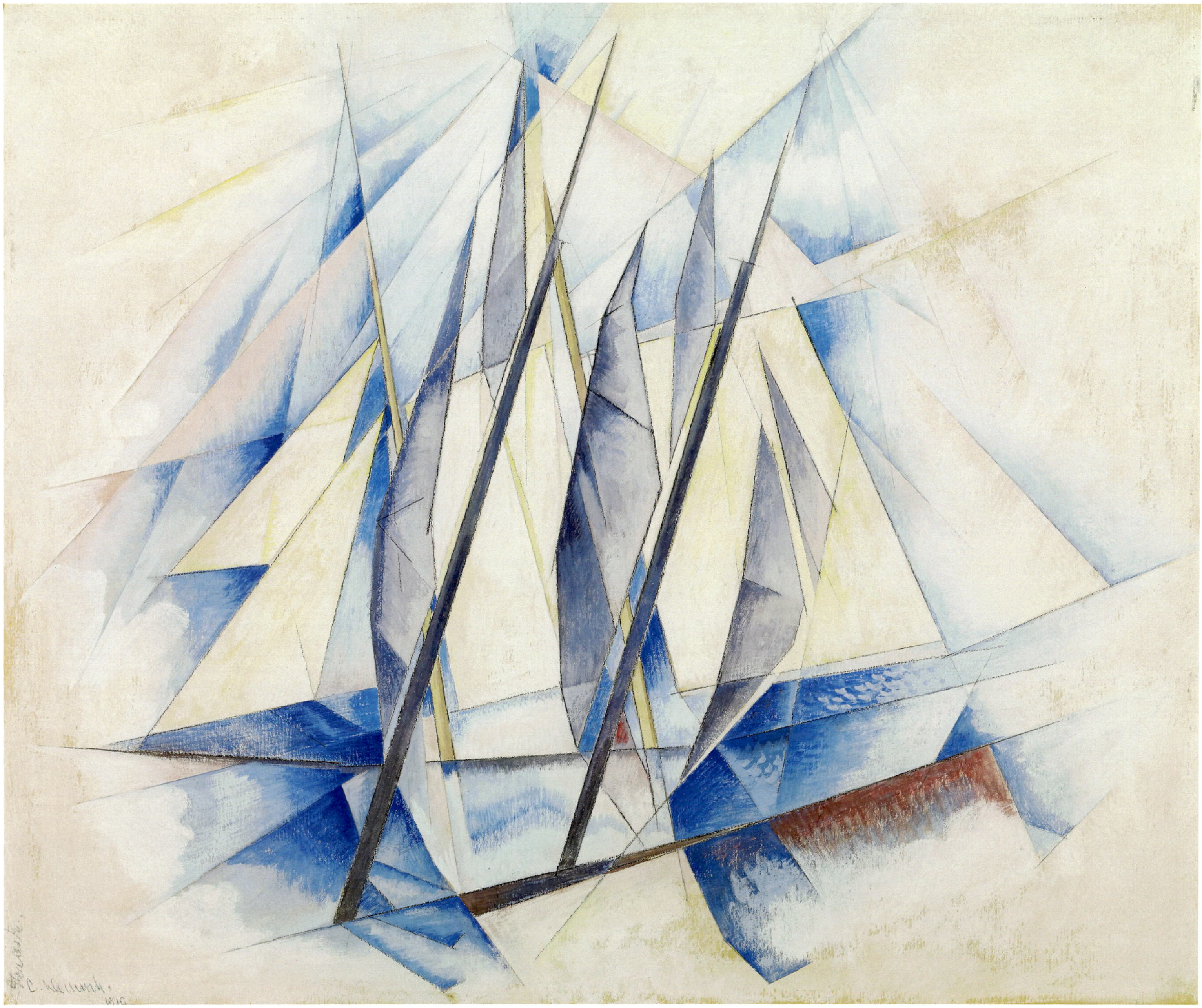

ARTHUR GARFIELD DOVE (1880–1946)

Moon and Sea II

1923
Oil and metallic paint on canvas
24 × 18 in. (61 × 45.7 cm)
Promised Gift

This small painting marks a turning point in the art and life of Arthur Garfield Dove, one of the country's best and most beloved modernists.[1] Dove made the painting in the late fall of 1923, shortly, if not immediately, after a fierce gale had passed over the waters of Long Island Sound.[2] Dove and his new companion, the artist Helen "Reds" Torr, had weathered the storm on their new boat, the Mona, while moored in Manhasset Bay after a perilous journey from the Hudson River. The artist vividly recorded the event in a letter to his mentor and champion, Alfred Stieglitz. Dove related to Stieglitz that he had been "trying to memorize this storm all day so that I can paint it. Storm green and storm grey." He added a postscript: "Storm breaks. . . . What a relief."[3] It is precisely that "relief" and its aftermath that Dove painted, rather than the storm itself.

The painting exudes a calm and serenity that speak volumes about Dove. He had long sought his independence—first from critical and unsupportive parents; then from the backbreaking labor of trying to run a farm in Westport, Connecticut; and, finally, from an unhappy marriage. Life on the water, which he had always loved, seemed to be the answer to weathering his personal struggles, "the storm," one might say, but only after the final test of a storm itself. Dove, the boat, and his relationship with Reds seemed to have passed with flying colors; he could now look forward to calm sailing, as the mood of the painting seems to suggest. So the artist thought, but his life was never to be without hardship and struggle.

Moon and Sea II marks the passing of another storm: the crisis over Dove's productive life as an artist.After an initial surge of important and original work from 1906 through 1912 he had done little for almost ten years, and even Stieglitz wondered if he would ever paint again. Dove was so determined to establish his independence, both financial and artistic, that he had little time or energy left for art. He started again, fitfully, in 1922, but it was really with *Moon and Sea II* that Dove resumed painting, fully committed and fully believing in himself.[4]

There is a new confidence in the work, and its open, asymmetrical composition possesses a lyrical simplicity that marks the best of Dove's art. It is like a private icon, a personal altar before the vastness of nature, the cosmos itself, with which Dove felt a new "unity of interest."[5] While it is virtually a private journal, the image of the moon over the water also relates to the history of romanticism, from the contemplative landscapes of Caspar David Friedrich; to the sun and moon images of Vincent van Gogh, an artist Dove deeply loved; to the seascapes of Albert Pinkham Ryder (p. 116). Dove's exploration of higher realms also parallels Stieglitz's famous cloud-and-sky photographs, the *Equivalents*, begun the same year. The centralized moon and beautiful, subtle coloration look ahead to the circle paintings of Kenneth Noland (p. 268), which are also filled with cosmic references.[6]

WCA

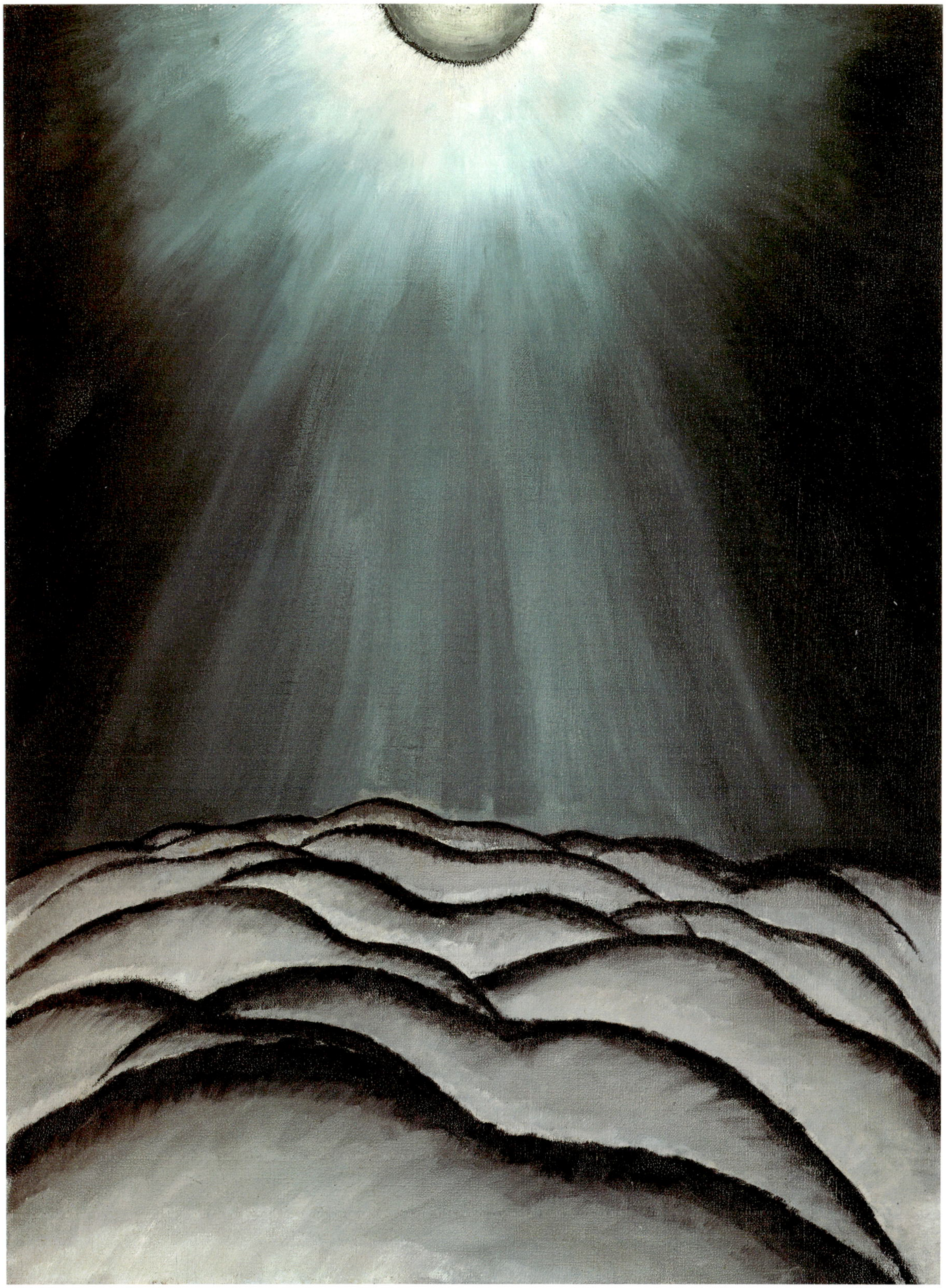

ARTHUR GARFIELD DOVE (1880–1946)

Two Forms

1931
Oil on fiberboard
33⅜ × 24½ in. (84.8 × 62.2 cm)

Arthur Garfield Dove's 1931 exhibition at Alfred Stieglitz's gallery An American Place was a critical triumph. Murdock Pemberton, the first art critic for the *New Yorker*, declared him "One of the country's greatest serious painters," adding enthusiastically that the "reduction to the elemental forms and accepted lines of beauty can be a lovely thing in the hands of such a thorough painter as Dove."[1] In the *New York Times*, Edward Alden Jewell attributed a new "expansiveness" in the paintings to more spacious living quarters. In 1929 Dove and his companion, Helen "Reds" Torr, had moved from their cramped forty-two-foot yawl, the Mona, to the Ketewomoke Yacht Club in Halesite, a waterfront hamlet on Huntington Harbor, off of Long Island Sound. Jewell described the new works as "more commodious than any from his brush," suggesting, "Maybe this betokens the evolution of a 'minor' poet into a 'major.'"[2]

As was typical of the artist's working methods, in the months leading up to his much-lauded 1931 exhibition Dove went out into the community to make "drawings," or "sketches," terms he applied indiscriminately to any small study but that from 1930 forward generally took the form of watercolors. He and Torr periodically reviewed these studies, selecting promising examples to enlarge onto canvas or board. Life in a nautical community offered continual inspiration in the forms of watercraft, industrial buildings, and machinery lining the shore—as well as the celestial phenomena that was a consistent theme for the artist. Dove's life's work ranged from experimental abstractions and assemblages to nature-inspired imagery, and in the early 1930s he navigated between these two poles with facility.

Two Forms was among the last paintings he completed prior to the American Place exhibition. On February 16, 1931, Torr noted in the artists' joint diary: "Both out riding around in afternoon. . . . Arthur made a beautiful drawing from two shapes outside—'Pyramid.'"[3] The following day, Torr recorded that "he cut a panel and mounted it, drew 'Two Forms' on with pantograph [an instrument for copying an image to a desired scale]." Dove continued working on the painting until February 22, when he wrote in the diary, "Finished 'Two Forms.'"[4]

Monumental in presence, if not in size, Dove executed *Two Forms* in a limited palette of gold and gray. A radiant central shape with two rooflike projections at its peak partially obscures an elliptical dark gray mass, resembling a sun in eclipse. Surrounded by a golden halo, the celestial body pulsates with energy, as does the abstracted form that stands before it, like an afterimage resulting from staring for too long at a bright light. The intense, generative vitality evident here, made even more emphatic by the artist's characteristic use of concentric bands of paint radiating outward, demonstrates the primacy for Dove of the sensory experience, which he first described in 1916. "I should like to enjoy life by choosing all its highest instances, to give back in my means of expression all that it gives to me: to give in form and color the reaction that plastic objects and sensations of light from within and without have reflected from my inner consciousness. Theories have been outgrown, the means is disappearing, the reality of the sensation alone remains."[5]

ACDP

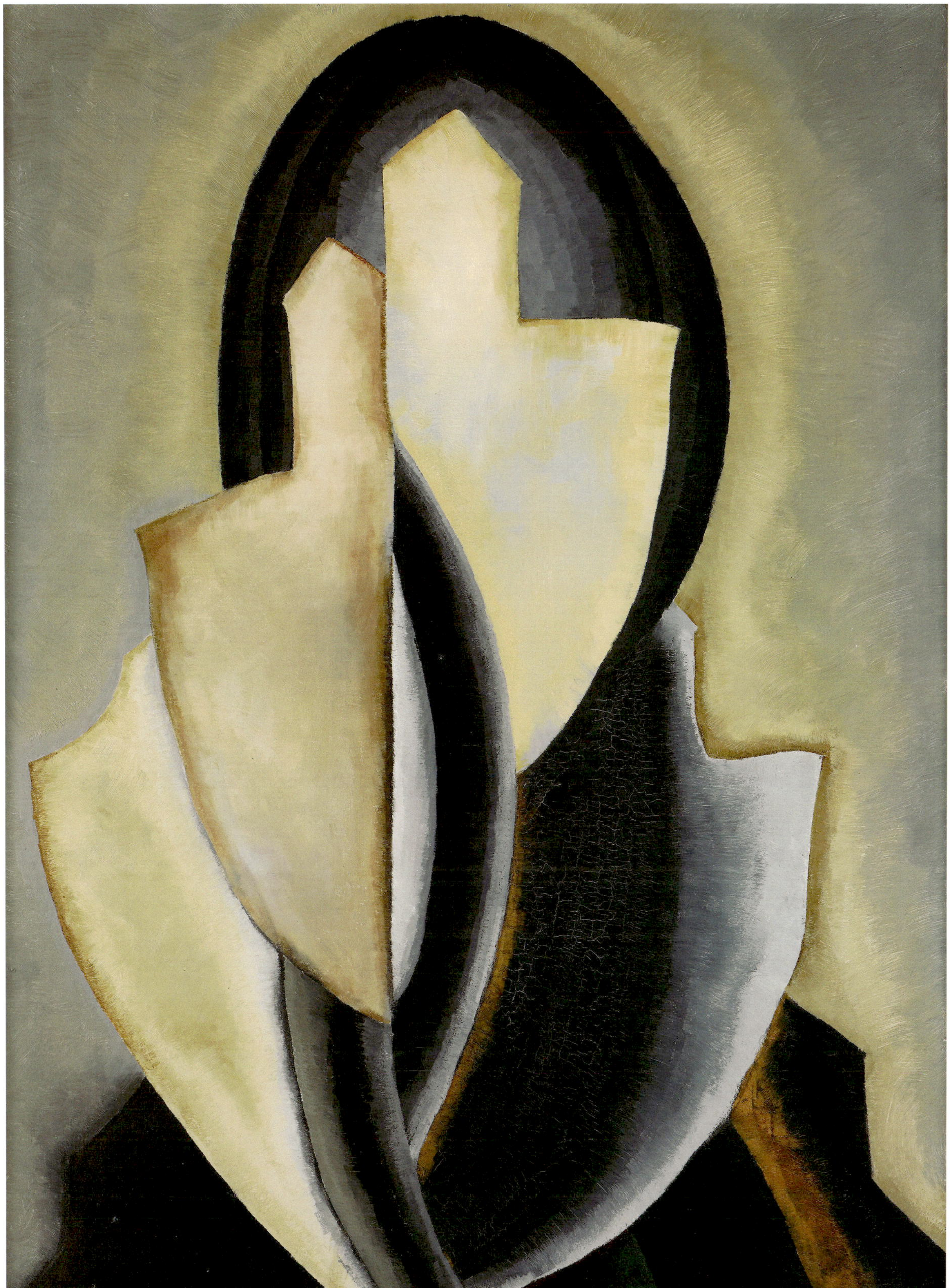

JOSEPH STELLA (1877–1946)

Red Flower

1929
Oil on canvas
57½ × 38¼ in. (146.1 × 97.2 cm)

It is difficult to neatly summarize the life and career of Joseph Stella. The Italian-born painter made some of the most riveting pictures of early twentieth-century America produced by an artist of any nationality. His aesthetic fluctuated between an organic, expressive figuration and a hard-edged abstraction. He devoted his brush with equal zeal to modern subjects like skyscrapers and age-old themes such as flower painting.

Stella immigrated to the United States in 1896 to study medicine and pharmacology, but within a year he had enrolled in classes at New York's Art Students League. He returned to Europe in 1909 for almost four years to view examples of the most advanced art. Most influential was the work of the Italian futurists, whose vigorous embrace of modernity led the painter, upon returning to the United States, to create a series of vibrant, kaleidoscopic images of iconic New York landmarks including Coney Island and the Brooklyn Bridge.[1]

By 1929, Stella had largely abandoned the dynamics of futurism in favor of more static and symbolic compositions. His new body of work included a group of paintings of tropical flowers characterized by vibrant color, extreme symmetry, and a distinct air of mystery. In many of these images, a single blossom placed along a central axis forms the main motif, dividing the canvas into two nearly identical halves. An immense red amaryllis with widely spread petals dominates *Red Flower*.[2] Two exotic birds resembling peacocks flank the flower, raising their elegant heads to its blossom in a reverential gesture. In the background, a dark, brooding palette, heavily encrusted paint, and richly patterned foliage add to the enigmatic atmosphere.

Stella's *Red Flower* reflects a wide range of influences. The painter often visited his home country of Italy during the 1920s and was particularly impressed by Neapolitan peasant textiles and embroidery, which were typically characterized by vibrant colors, symmetrical patterns, and schematic renderings of organic forms.[3] His fanciful flowers and birds suggest the impact of surrealism and symbolism in their emphasis on inner vision and fantasy. Stella may also have been influenced by mystical and ornamental motifs introduced to him by the South Asian art scholar Ananda Coomaraswamy.[4] Visits to North Africa, Barbados, and, more locally, to the Bronx Botanical Gardens and New York Zoological Gardens, gave life to the tropical paintings that exemplified the artist's "everlasting celebration of the joy of living."[5]

Stella was raised by a conservative Catholic family in Naples, a part of Italy deeply rooted in Christian as well as pagan traditions. *Red Flower*'s tripartite composition and its fully frontal view evoke religious paintings of the enthroned Christ or Mary flanked by saints, and also recall the Italian folk custom of creating floral arrangements for religious holidays.[6] The flamelike outlines of the amaryllis petals further imbue the composition with a spiritual aura. Stella's flower paintings followed on a series of Madonna images that he had embellished with floral motifs. *Red Flower* and related works broadened the artist's spiritual discourse from a strictly Christian tradition to a more pantheistic creed that alludes to the sacred and mysterious powers of nature.[7]

MW

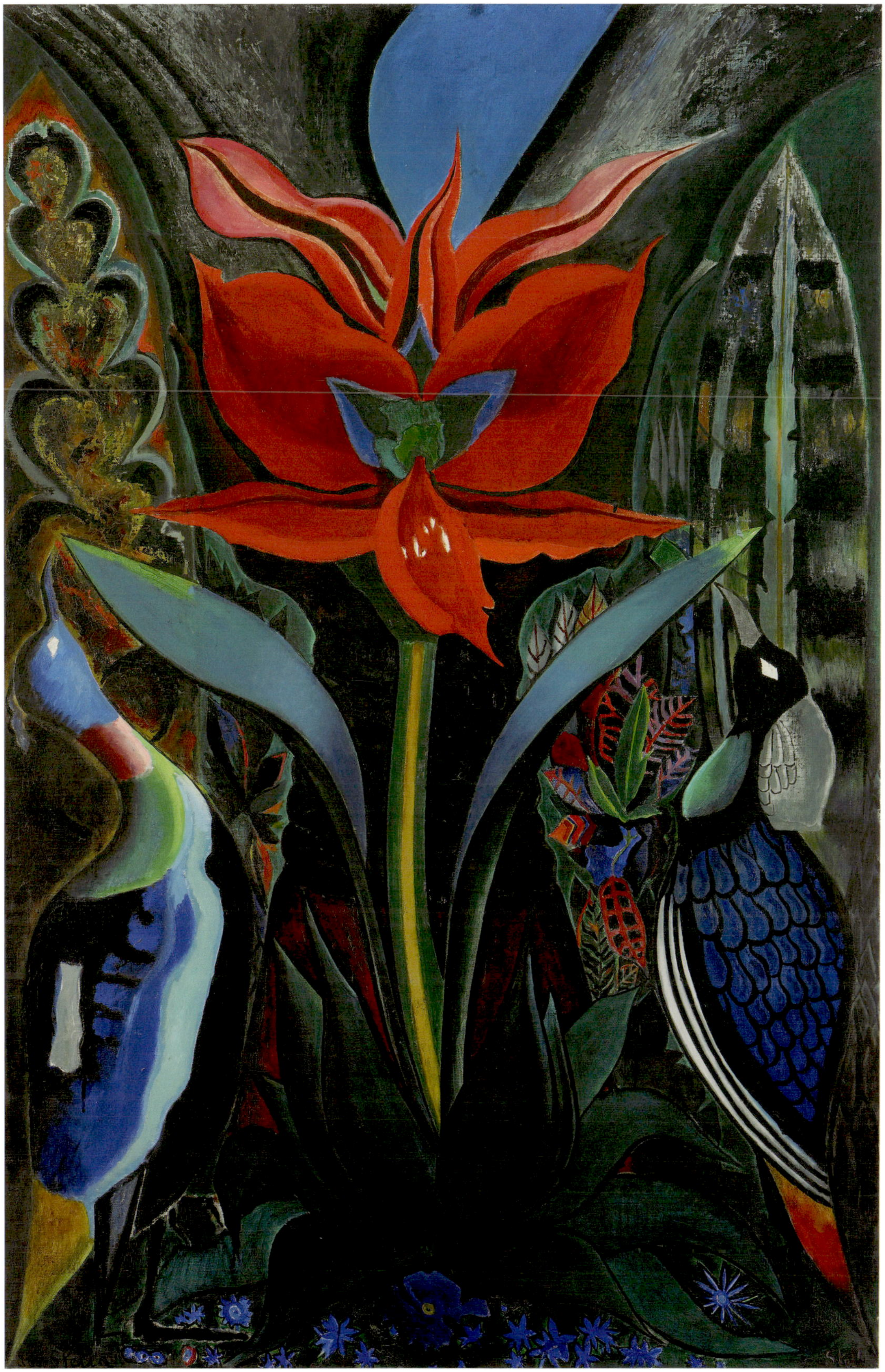

YASUO KUNIYOSHI (1889–1953)

Little Joe with Cow

1923
Oil on canvas
28 × 42 in. (71.1 × 106.7 cm)

In the early 1920s, at the invitation of his patron Hamilton Easter Field, the Japanese-born American painter Yasuo Kuniyoshi spent several formative summers in the rustic community of Ogunquit, Maine, a popular artist's colony on the state's southern coast. During this time Kuniyoshi developed an idiosyncratic style of landscape painting that combined acute observations of his natural surroundings; the visual languages of American folk art, European modernism, and traditional Japanese art; and his rich inner life of fantasy.

The 1923 painting *Little Joe with Cow* depicts a small boy and large yoked cow in a rural setting complete with trees, plants, and a farmhouse. Yet the canvas is anything but a straightforward view of agrarian life. In the service of his highly personal vision, Kuniyoshi distorted traditional linear perspective such that it looks like objects are layered one on top of another. No distance seems to exist between the boy and the cow, for example, and, in a touch of whimsy, an orange-and-brown plant with large slender leaves appears directly above the animal's head as if it wears a headdress. The artist's rejection of conventional modeling in favor of flat planes of color further collapsed the space of the image.

Kuniyoshi also revised naturalistic scale relationships in the service of symbolic meaning in *Little Joe with Cow*. The outsized bovine, which dwarfs the sparsely foliated tree to its immediate left and the white house at the upper left, rises to monumental importance. Indeed, the triangular form of the cow's mountainous back slopes dramatically, seemingly abutting the modest hill in the upper right. Kuniyoshi's rejection of linear perspective and naturalistic scale were informed by the European avant-garde as well as by American folk art, the latter of which the artist collected during the early 1920s.[1] The painting's unconventional, even surreal, portrayal of space and scale might also be seen to evoke a child's eye view of the world.[2]

Children and wide-eyed cows are frequent subjects in Kuniyoshi's work from this period. The cow, which features prominently in nearly sixty of his early paintings, held personal meaning for the artist. According to the Japanese calendar, Kuniyoshi was born in the Year of the Cow, and the painter believed that his fate was guided in part by this animal. He was also drawn to the bovine's unique aesthetic qualities: "I thought it was decorative as well as ugly and so I painted cows constantly until I was exhausted," he explained.[3] Kuniyoshi approached the subject of children with the same enthusiasm for unconventional—even unattractive—forms: "People think that babies are beautiful, but I thought otherwise and so I painted babies and babies."[4] In a nod to his personal biography, Kuniyoshi's children—including Little Joe—typically feature a distinctive combination of almond-shaped Asian eyes and Western apparel.

Little Joe with Cow demonstrates Kuniyoshi's skill at blending disparate Western artistic influences with elements from Eastern culture. The artist's appreciation for all forms of nature is reflected in his detailed depiction of trees, grass, and weeds. The soft shades of gray and brown that surround these botanical forms and the artist's distant views of floating houses and mountains conjure traditional Japanese ink-and-wash landscapes from the Edo Period (1603–1867).[5] The painting's eschewal of linear perspective in favor of a decorative, surface flatness also may derive from the traditional landscape arts of Kuniyoshi's country of birth. MW

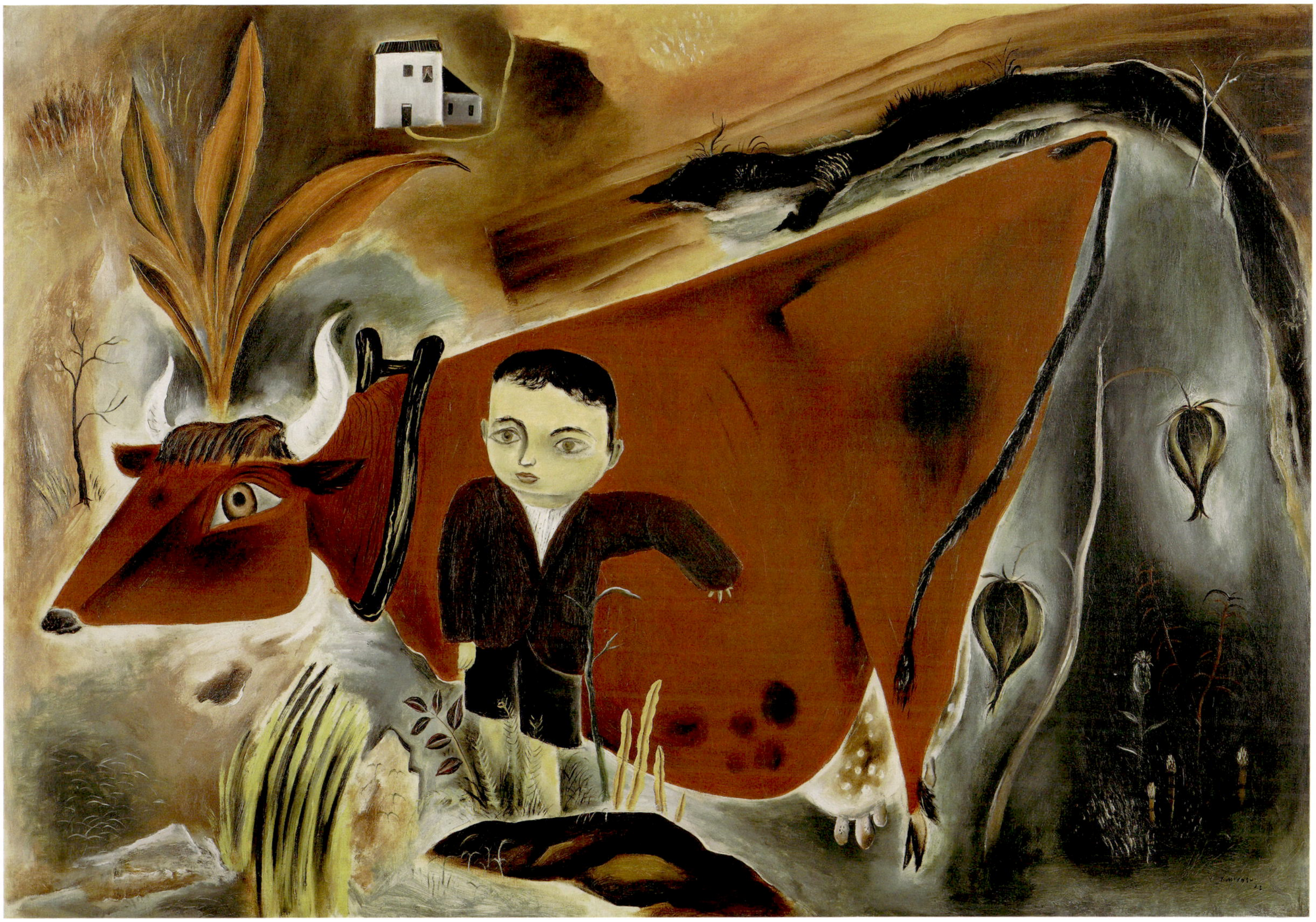

STUART DAVIS (1892–1964)

Rue de l'Echaudé

1928
Oil and sand on canvas
$23\frac{3}{4} \times 36\frac{1}{4}$ in. (60.3 × 92.1 cm)
Promised Gift

In Stuart Davis's 1928 painting of a Paris street, tilting trapezoids of flat, clear color punctuated by rectangles, circles, and dashes play against a cool green field where street and sky are indistinguishable. By the late 1920s Davis had been absorbing the kaleidoscopic variety of aesthetic possibilities offered by the modern world for nearly two decades, and in *Rue de l'Echaudé* the artist's diverse influences—from Robert Henri to jazz music to Pablo Picasso—meld into an inimitable style.

It was no doubt Henri, one of Davis's instructors at the New York School of Art, who first encouraged him to observe and paint contemporary urban life as experienced on the streets. The abstractions of European modernists such as Fernand Léger and Pablo Picasso, which Davis encountered at the famed Armory Show in 1913, showed the painter that he could effectively engage the everyday world around him without resorting to literal representation. These artists proved that it was the unique energies and intellect of the maker that determined the strength of a picture, not his or her slavish imitation of nature.

Yet unlike many of his contemporaries, Davis's aesthetic was largely homegrown. By 1928, when he visited Paris for the first time, the artist was already a confirmed modernist, his style informed by the speed, lights, and sounds of life in New York City as much as it was by the art of the Armory Show. Once in Paris, Davis applied his already years-long investigation of cubist space to the city's inspiring network of narrow streets. *Rue de l'Echaudé* is one of a series of richly textured and rhythmic compositions based on this urban landscape, like jazz variants on a theme. The artist wrote to his father early in his French sojourn, "I am primarily interested in the streets. There is great variety, from the most commonplace to the unique."[1] Davis's canvas incorporates the formal properties found in his famed eggbeater paintings of the previous year: hard-edged shapes align with each other and are split by clean, colored lines constrained to the forms in which they appear.

During his one brief year in Paris, Davis met and received criticism from Léger; visited with famed American expatriate Gertrude Stein; and befriended numerous advanced painters of various nationalities. When he left France to return to the United States, however, it was free from the concern that American art was in the shadow of Europe. The innovative painting style Davis had developed on his native soil—a distinctive aesthetic characterized by a rigorous mix of imagination and formal objectivity—rivaled anything he had seen abroad.

WS

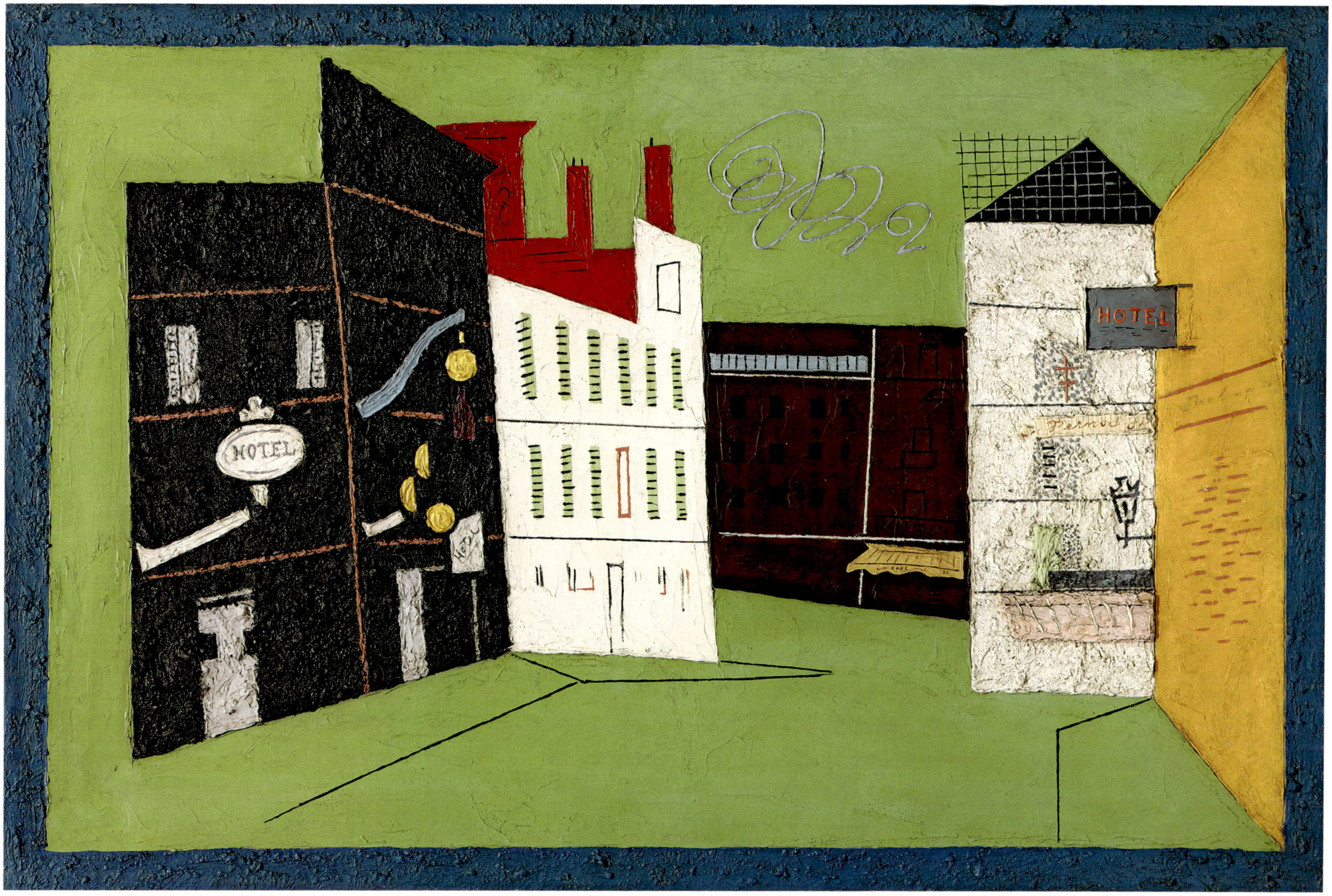
HOTEL
HOTEL

STUART DAVIS (1892–1964)

Still Life with Flowers

1930
Oil on canvas
40 × 32 in. (101.6 × 81.3 cm)

> *For a number of years jazz had a tremendous influence on my thoughts about art and life. For me—I had jazz all my life—I almost breathed it like the air . . . I think all my paintings, at least in part, come from this influence.* —STUART DAVIS[1]

In Paris, in 1928, Stuart Davis's compatriot, friend, and fellow artist Hilaire Hiler introduced him to the music of jazz pianist Earl Hines. It was in that very year in Chicago that Hines, along with Louis Armstrong, made some of the most moving recordings of jazz's golden age, including "Weather Bird," "West End Blues," and "Muggles." Following Davis's return to New York in late 1929, jazz music remained central to his aesthetic experience and his large, complex painting *Still Life with Flowers* may well pay homage to Hines.

The 1930 canvas is classic Davis in construction: an amalgam of geometric and anthropomorphic shapes painted with bright, unmodulated color upon which appear curved and straight lines as well as letters and numbers. For Davis, the words "hotel" and "café," inscribed on the yellow facade at far right, have an identity as shapes in addition to their conventional linguistic signification. The number 9, at lower left, likely refers to the game of golf, an identification that renders the oblong red form upon which the still life rests a golf course of sorts, the looping black line a visual record of the ball's surreal trajectory. The red pennant at lower left adorned with an H represents Harvard, while the blue pennant emblazoned with a Y in the upper center emblematizes Yale. The Y can also be read as a visual pun regarding the painting's dense symbolism: "Why?"

Other recognizable symbols include musical notes on the inverted blue-green chevron that may be a leaf, and, on the floating yellow shape at the far left, the dark outline of a tiny heart. Upon close examination the abstract yellow shape becomes a piano, as seen from the air. Directly above the piano is a white dot, where a musician's head would be, and, underneath it, two black lines that suggest hands on a keyboard. With these abstract elements interpreted thusly, the heart becomes a sign of affection and admiration for the piano and its player. The large "floral" still life at the center of the image might be seen as a whimsical take on the phonograph: the black shape a vinyl record with its (off) center hole painted yellow, and the white flower an amplifier with musical notes shooting out as pistil and stamen. A black arrow extending from the yellow form/piano at the far left, through the still life, and touching the facade of the hotel and café seems to indicate that music is being made there.

It is this bold combination of fragmented, syncopated shapes—the symbolic meanings of which are suggested, but elusive—that made Davis's work so advanced in its time and so influential on subsequent art, and that sustains our interest today. *Still Life with Flowers* is a not-so-still still life and a fitting tribute to Earl Hines, the quintessential piano jazzman. WS

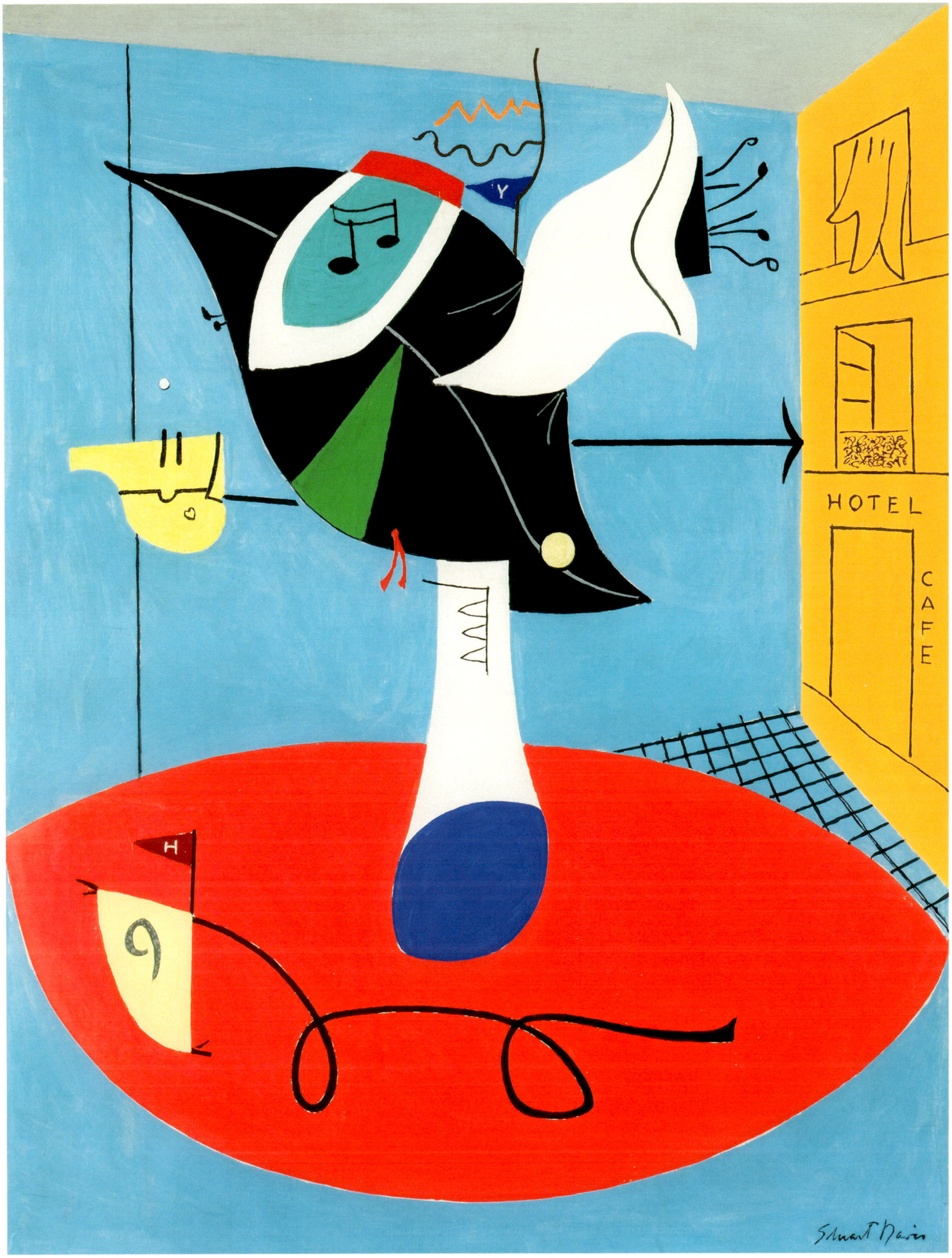
HOTEL
CAFE
Y
H

EDWARD HOPPER (1882–1967)

Roofs of the Cobb Barn

1931
Watercolor on paper
19 15/16 × 27 7/8 in. (50.6 × 70.8 cm)
Promised Gift

One of the most celebrated painters of the twentieth century, Edward Hopper was driven by his intensely personal aesthetic vision together with an insatiable desire to capture the truth. He once declared, "My aim in painting has always been the most exact transcription possible of my most intimate impressions of nature."[1] Accordingly, Hopper's images often appear simultaneously realistic and fantastical, familiar and strange. *Roofs of the Cobb Barn* marries the familiarity of a New England coastal landscape with a surprising element of abstraction—the clean geometric forms and white planes of barn roofs.

Having spent previous summers in small coastal towns around Gloucester, Massachusetts, Hopper visited Cape Cod for the first time in 1930. From this point forward the artist and his wife, Josephine (Jo), returned each summer to paint, building a modest house in the coastal village of South Truro in 1934. This change of locale prompted subtle yet important shifts in Hopper's motifs and the way he handled shape and form. The relative solitude and starkness of the Cape Cod landscape inspired the painter to refine and simplify his compositions. In a nod to modernist aesthetics, he began to eliminate unnecessary pictorial details to reveal the essence of a scene.

Roofs of the Cobb Barn provides an elevated view of postmaster A. B. Burleigh Cobb's barns in South Truro.[2] With its rolling hills in the distance, densely foliated tree at left, and tall grass and bushes in the foreground, the watercolor celebrates the quiet beauty of Cape Cod's topography. Yet the focus of the image is the simple forms of the sun-washed barn roofs. In her husband's record book, Jo Hopper noted her assessment of this remarkable watercolor: "Dark red in shadow all the barn structures. Bright light on tarred roofs at various angles. One of his best this summer. Interesting for planes."[3] Intrigued by the contrast between organic and inorganic forms, Hopper rendered the rigid geometry of the barn buildings in perfect harmony with the natural environment. The composition delivers an unexpectedly modern statement in the context of a realist landscape.[4]

Roofs of the Cobb Barn also explores the effects of light and shade on architecture. The reflected sunlight enhances the buildings' austere forms, transforming them into near abstractions.[5] The gray-white color of the roofs contrasts with the green dune grass and the deep red of the barns' shaded exteriors, creating a balanced design of subtle and bold hues. The passages of watercolor pigment are by turn sheer and sumptuous. Both of these dynamics add complexity and rhythm to the composition.

Through his color choices and skilled brushwork, Hopper convincingly captured the atmospheric haze of this Cape Cod summer scene, with its cloudless, gray sky and windswept grass. The artist's coastal landscapes notably convey a mood very different from the psychologically charged urban scenes for which he is best known. Even though *Roofs of the Cobb Barn* and the painter's other rural watercolors are devoid of human presence, they do not convey isolation, loneliness, and anonymity. Rather, Hopper used light, color, and form to create a peaceful solitude and meditative quiet, suggesting consonance between the natural environment and a human presence. MW

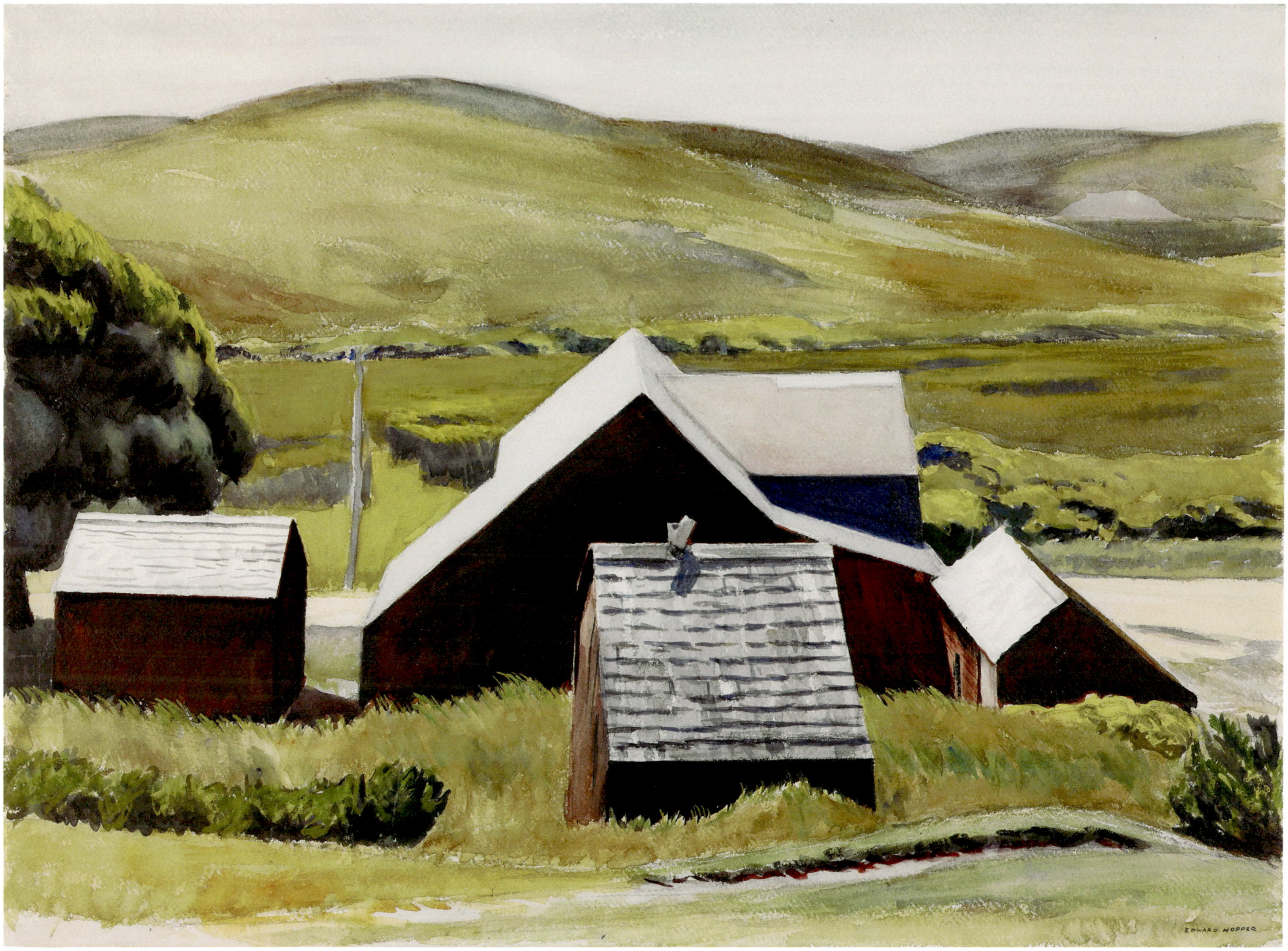
EDWARD HOPPER

GEORGIA O'KEEFFE (1887–1986)

Small Purple Hills

1934
Oil on board
16 × 19¾ in. (40.6 × 50.2 cm)

The early 1930s were especially difficult for Georgia O'Keeffe. The Great Depression curtailed sales of her work, while crises in both her personal life and professional career led to a nervous collapse in early 1933 and a hiatus from painting that lasted over a year. To restore her health and rejuvenate her spirit, O'Keeffe decided to return to New Mexico, departing from New York in June 1934.

Within months of her first extended stay in New Mexico five years earlier, in 1929, O'Keeffe had realized that the high desert plateau of the Piedra Lumbre basin was an ideal location to escape the distractions that plagued her in the Northeast. That summer, O'Keeffe had learned to drive, purchased a Model A Ford, and ventured far into New Mexico's unspoiled wilderness to work in solitude. Inspired by the clarity of the light and the unique geological features of the region, O'Keeffe began painting the landscape to the south and west of Taos, concentrating on the elegant contours of the softly eroded cliffs and sandstone hills. As she explored the area with a painter's eye for color, she devised new strategies for embedding personal symbolism within the breathtaking simplicity of the natural forms, much as she had done in her imaginative abstractions from the teens and 1920s.

Shortly after arriving in New Mexico in 1934, O'Keeffe made her first visit to Ghost Ranch, a 21,000-acre dude ranch on the eastern edge of the Jemez mountain range, directly southwest of Taos. Once settled in one of the guesthouses, O'Keeffe promptly turned her attention to the stability and solidity of the landscape surrounding the property. She painted a series of views of the low, barren hills behind her residence as a way of grounding herself, of regaining the equilibrium she had lost in New York.

In *Small Purple Hills*, O'Keeffe presents a single, isolated land mass silhouetted sharply against the crystalline sky. The massive forms of the hills nearly fill the entire canvas, lending a sense of monumentality that defies their relatively slight stature. The extraordinary clarity and evenness of the light emphasizes the sculptural quality of the rounded slopes, which had collapsed and compressed through millions of years of erosion into fissures and furrowed channels.

As was often her practice, O'Keeffe likely began this composition out of doors and returned to the studio to complete it, relying on notes, as well as memory, to replicate the earth's rich textures and amazing range of colors.[1] This process allowed her to come to terms with her emotional response to the experience of nature through the act of painting. O'Keeffe gently worked dry, matte pigments and blended brushstrokes into the surface of the board to model the reddish-purple hills, as if mimicking the natural rhythms that had shaped them into dusty, striated formations of geologic history. In a remarkable demonstration of technical skill, she presented the hills as both hard and soft, durable and tender, recognizable but also otherworldly. They appear physically close to the viewer yet beyond reach. As she did in many of her works, O'Keeffe further challenged landscape conventions by painting the thin strip frame surrounding *Small Purple Hills*. The painted frame extends the vista beyond the canvas's edge, accentuating the expansiveness of a view the artist sensed could not be contained within the parameters of an easel-size composition.

REL

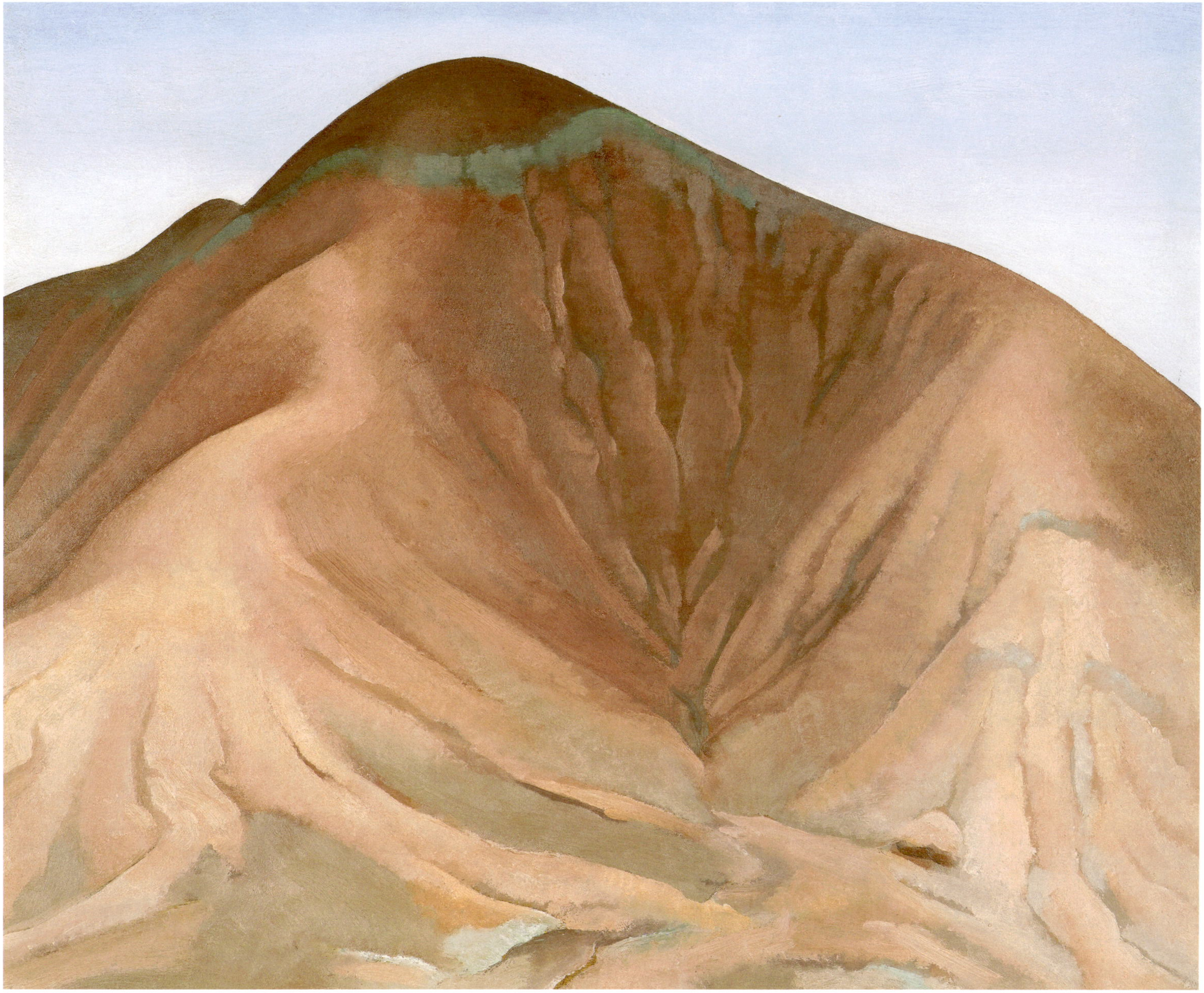

THOMAS HART BENTON (1889–1975)

Ploughing It Under

1934; reworked 1964[1]
Oil on canvas
20¼ × 24¼ in. (51.4 × 61.6 cm)

Thomas Hart Benton, along with Grant Wood and John Steuart Curry, formed the triumvirate of artists known as the regionalists, who flourished in the 1930s and remain best known for their identifiably American subject matter painted in a representational style. Born in Neosho, Missouri, Benton was named for his great uncle, the famous Democratic senator Thomas Hart Benton. His father, Maecenas Eason Benton, was a Democratic member of the United States House of Representatives who represented southwest Missouri for five terms. Although he rejected his family's occupational calling, Benton was nonetheless the inheritor of the populist ideologies of his forebears; he was something of a "politician in paint," as an art historian once described him.[2] Indeed, Benton used his murals, paintings, and prints to document, celebrate, and critique the folkways of ordinary Americans, which, for the artist, increasingly meant those individuals living outside the northeastern seaboard.

Benton's engagement with contemporary politics is strikingly apparent in *Ploughing It Under*. Equally apparent is his commitment to producerism, the belief that progress and national welfare are most effectively realized through labor.[3] By proclaiming a farmer worthy subject matter, the artist joined his father and great uncle in recognizing the primacy of the worker in contemporary American life. With the contours of the mule's muscular body repeating the undulating forms of the earth and clouds, and the farmer leaning forward, exerting his strength, literally "plowing it under," Benton's painting is a symbolic paean to work as a panacea for the ills of the Great Depression.

It is a paean not without irony. The title and subject matter of *Ploughing It Under* refer to the response of farmers to the establishment of the Agricultural Adjustment Act and the Agricultural Adjustment Administration (A.A.A.) in 1933. This early New Deal legislation aimed to increase the prices of staple crops and livestock —thereby giving farmers greater spending power—by reducing agricultural production. Compliant farmers received subsidies and, by 1934, a tax penalized those whose yield exceeded their quota. The latter individuals were forced to bury—or "plow under"—their crop in order to collect A.A.A. monies.[4]

The legislation and ensuing plowing under gained great notoriety. In 1936, the Federal Theater Project produced the play *Triple A—Plowed Under*, the title of which referred to the Supreme Court decision earlier that year that deemed the punitive tax unconstitutional.[5] The A.A.A. facilitated an upward surge in prices for farm-produced staples, yielding farmers a net income of $5 billion in 1936, up from $1.8 billion in 1932. But the economic recovery was largely limited to white commercial landowners; 77 percent of African American beneficiaries were tenant farmers who had to pay off landlords with their profits or subsidies.[6] In choosing an African American laborer for his subject, Benton exposed the flipside of New Deal reform, its often cruel sacrifices and selective rewards.

In a larger sense, Benton contributed to the regionalist mission of rethinking just what counts as fine art in the first place. A sense of restitution—giving someone their due—underscores his project, and *Ploughing It Under* emphasizes the critical importance of worker, mule, and plow alike in American cultural history. This pro-labor sentiment seems to have resonated with a number of the artist's contemporaries: the lithographic version of *Ploughing It Under* became the first work Benton sold through the subscription print firm Associated American Artists, and the edition of 250 quickly sold out.[7]

LGM

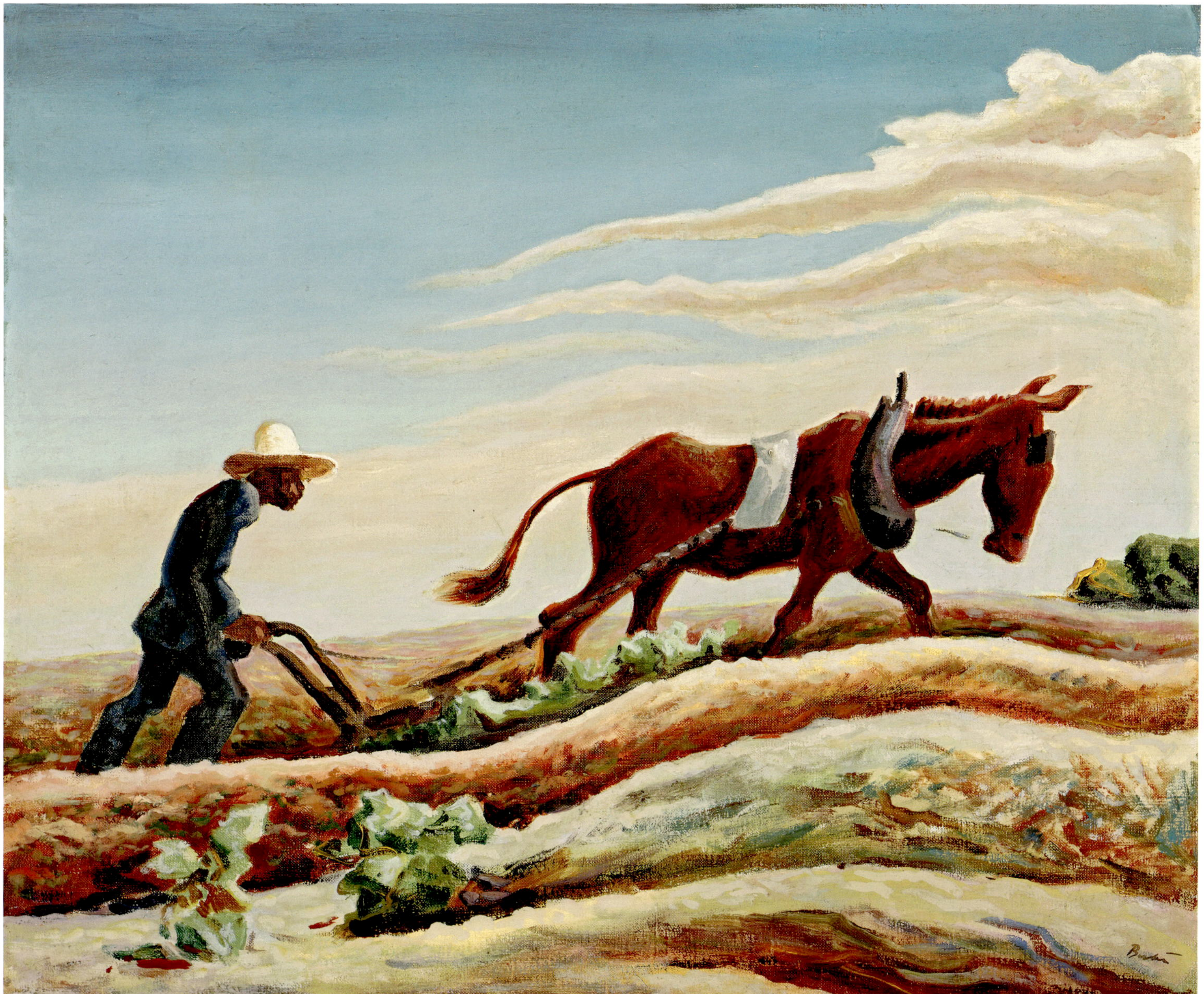

MARSDEN HARTLEY (1877–1943)

Red Flowers and Sailboat

ca. 1935–36
Oil on board
24¼ × 18¼ in. (61.6 × 46.4 cm)

Marsden Hartley lived life in a state of near constant flux. The dozens of physical moves he made throughout his career were triggered as much by the practical need to live cheaply as by an incessant craving for the stimulation of new environments in order to work. For the peripatetic Hartley, the genre of still life offered a kind of perceptual stasis, as well as a way to ground his identity in each new locale. By mining a repertoire of personal belongings, borrowed items, and locally found natural specimens, Hartley gave shape to the psychological currents of his life.

Hartley had painted tabletop still lifes since his early days as an art student, learning the genre's conventions from American masters including William Merritt Chase. His exposure to the spatially complex works of European modernists such as Paul Cézanne, Pablo Picasso, and Henri Matisse during the early 1910s further piqued his interest in the subject.[1] Inspired by the open window pictures of Matisse and André Derain, which integrated landscape elements with still-life objects, Hartley began to employ the motif while residing in Bermuda during the winter of 1916–17.[2] The open window was a formal device that allowed the artist to investigate pictorial space while at the same time exploring the dichotomy between his inner life and external reality. As scholars have frequently noted, Hartley often returned to the open window theme during times of emotional turmoil.[3]

In the mid-1930s Hartley was in perpetual motion, traveling between New York, Bermuda, and Nova Scotia, where he resided happily with a French-Canadian fishing family called the Masons. The Masons, according to Hartley, were "a most amazing family . . . the like of which I have never in my life seen—veritable rocks of Gibraltar in appearance the very salt of salt."[4] With its rich, sensuous surface and deep, contrasting colors, *Red Flowers and Sailboat* displays a decorative vitality that belies its formal complexity. The bouquet, a riotous arrangement of flattened forms, dominates the composition, overpowering and nearly obscuring the harbor view at lower left. The spatial ambiguity and lack of a visible framing device surrounding the window deny the viewer an illusionistic reading. The placement of the vase, which rests either on a tabletop or a windowsill, accentuates the viewer's sense of dislocation.

Hartley rendered the bouquet on a continuous plane with the dark, patterned curtain at right but halted its exuberant progression of floral forms at left, just short of obliterating the seascape. The artist's pronounced use of red in the composition conveys emotion, and, perhaps, spirituality, as evoked by the cruciform shape of the flower at center. The lobster claw positioned beside the vase in the lower right alludes to the painting's coastal setting, but the rosy pink shell's jagged pincer is also clearly sexualized.

Painted as he neared the age of sixty, *Red Flowers and Sailboat* signals Hartley's renewed vigor for life. In both conception and execution, the picture resonates with the aesthetic inspiration he felt within his coastal surroundings and suggests an inflamed passion for someone (perhaps the adored Mason family?) who had recently entered his world.

REL

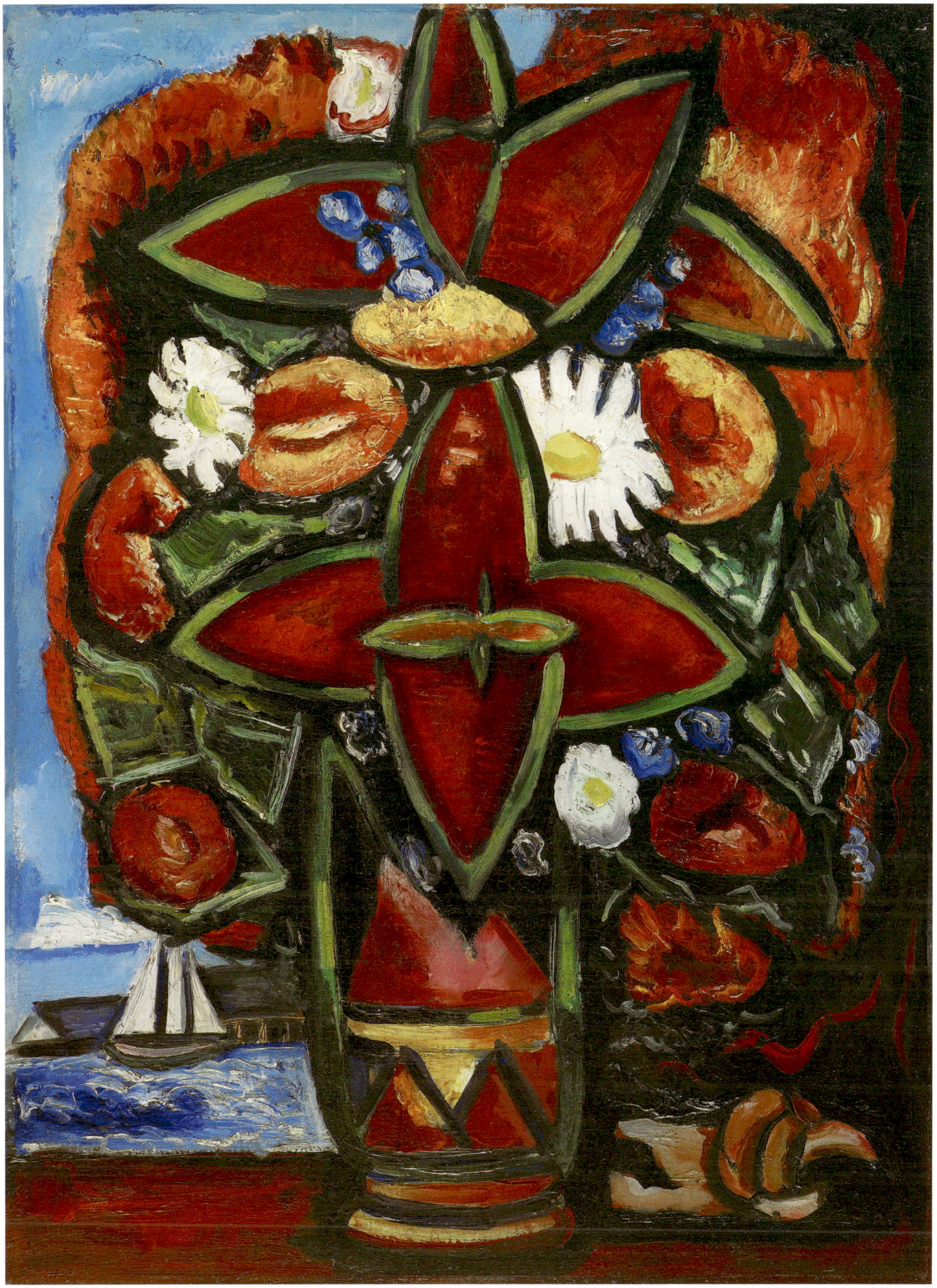

ARSHILE GORKY (ca. 1902–1948)

Composition (Still Life)

1936–37
Oil on canvas
34 × 26 in. (86.4 × 66 cm)
Promised Gift

The vibrant colors and abstracted forms of Arshile Gorky's *Composition (Still Life)* emerged from a time in the immigrant artist's life during which he was engaged in a disciplined and intense study of avant-garde European art. Influenced by a childhood of struggle and loss, and bursting with excitement over modern painting techniques, Gorky's 1936–37 image simultaneously reveals the artist's strong ties to the past and declares his commitment to stylistic innovation.

Born Vosdanig Adoian in the Armenian village of Khorkom, on the eastern border of Ottoman Turkey, as a teenager the artist survived the horror of a massive ethnic genocide. In 1916 Vosdanig, his sister, and his mother fled their homeland to escape the Turkish government's increasing persecution of Armenians. The long journey to the United States was difficult, ultimately claiming his mother's life. The two siblings persevered, however, arriving on Ellis Island in 1920. In a symbolic gesture that asserted his desire to start a new life while acknowledging his difficult past, Vosdanig renamed himself Arshile Gorky: Arshile, a Russian derivative of Achilles, and Gorky, inspired by the Russian writer Maxim Gorky, whose moniker means "the bitter one."[1]

The largely self-taught Gorky found inspiration in art history books, on museum walls, and in the contemporary art around him. The work of modern masters such as Paul Cézanne, Henri Matisse, and Pablo Picasso opened up a new world to the young painter. Gorky believed that true understanding was derived through replication, and set out to learn from these artists by copying their styles. This period of intense, self-directed study continued through the early 1940s.[2]

Drawing from his cubist and fauve idols, Gorky deployed the traditional genre of still life to distinctively modern ends in *Composition (Still Life)*. This masterful work uses arresting color to grab the viewer's attention and a combination of organic and geometric shapes to move his or her eye around the canvas. Bold, black lines hold the eye in place for an extra moment, while the white space at the top and right edges of the composition seem to give permission to wander away from the work, onto the wall. Vibrant, vigorous brushstrokes are left raw, adding movement and life to something that, by its very name, sits still.

The act of searching out recognizable objects transforms the viewing experience from a passive to an active one. One begins to discern a tall vase of flowers on the right side of a table, while a gold, green, and white apple with a thick black stem that recalls the fruit in a Cézanne still life makes its presence known in the lower center. Conversely, some objects flatten and otherwise morph under close examination, leaving the viewer to wonder where the still life begins and ends.

While *Composition (Still Life)* is progressive in its use of color and form, its subject matter is quite conventional. Still life paintings typically depict a fleeting moment in time and often allude to memory and mortality. Following these traditions, Gorky's abstracted composition offers blooming flowers and a ripe apple, both of which will remain fresh long after their models have turned. By choosing an age-old theme and portraying it in an innovative style, Gorky established his place in a lineage of distinguished modern artists who preceded him and emerged as a leader of the next generation. NCS

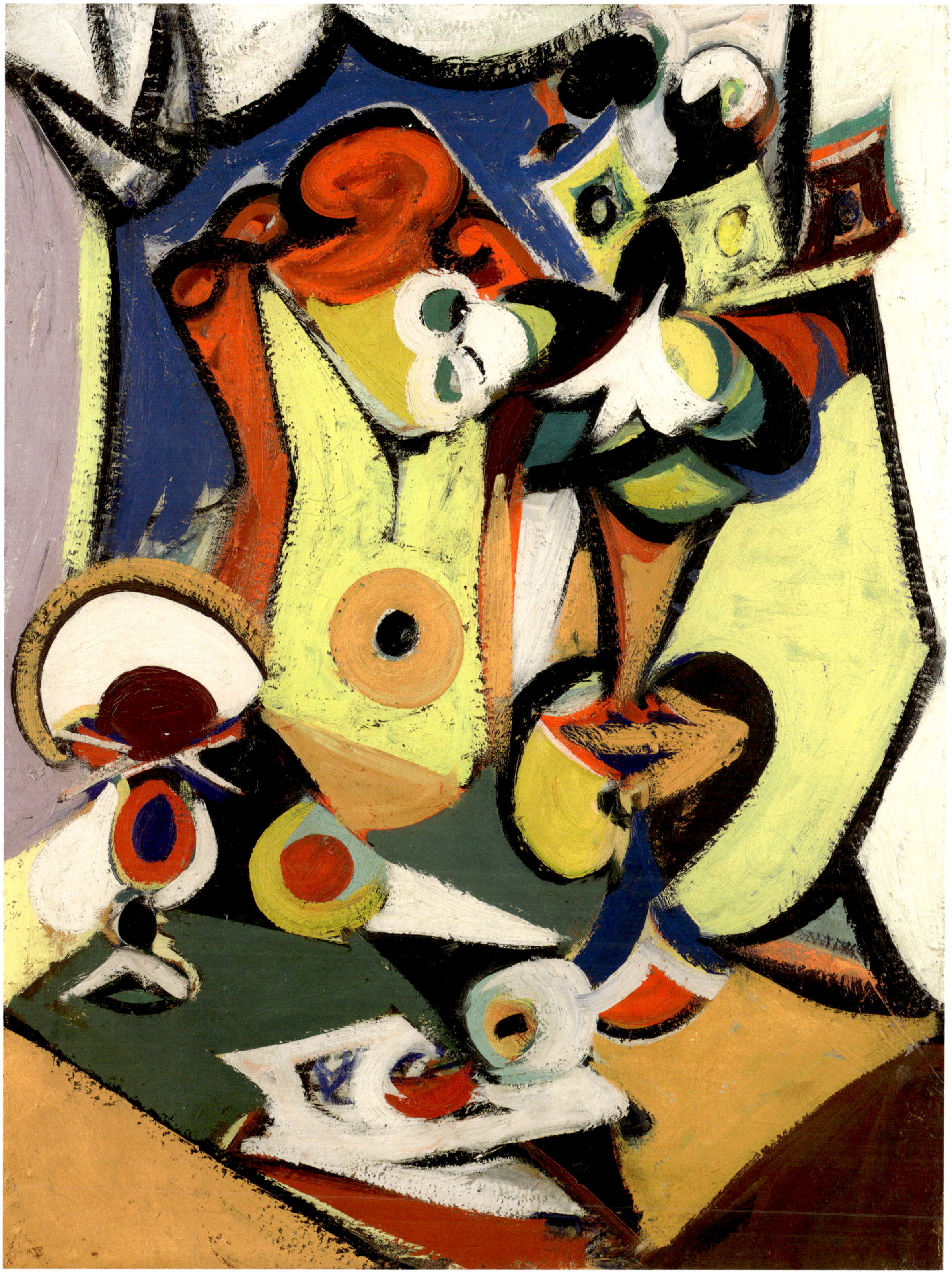

JACKSON POLLOCK (1912–1956)

Reclining Woman

ca. 1938–41
Oil on canvas
10¾ × 21½ in. (27.3 × 54.6 cm)
Promised Gift

Nicknamed "Jack the Dripper" for his signature technique of dripping, flinging, and pouring paint onto his canvases, Cody, Wyoming, native Jackson Pollock was the undisputed leader of the revolutionary art movement known as abstract expressionism.[1] The innovative painting methods Pollock developed in the late 1940s fundamentally changed the face of modern art in the United States and internationally. His bold canvas *Reclining Woman*, dating from about 1940, reveals a painter engaging with art history and contemporary avant-garde styles on his way to developing his own pioneering aesthetic.

Pollock studied at the Art Students League in New York with Thomas Hart Benton, an artist known for depicting everyday American life in a representational style (p. 230). Although the painter began to free himself from Benton's regionalist aesthetic during the late 1930s, his old teacher's rhythmic application of color and fiercely independent spirit were enduring influences. During this period Pollock also began investigating the pictorial and expressive opportunities provided by cubism and surrealism, as well as the emotional symbolism developed by Mexican muralists José Clemente Orozco and David Alfaro Siqueiros.

In *Reclining Woman*, Pollock fundamentally transformed the traditional subject of the recumbent female nude, eschewing beauty and sensuousness in favor of fragmentary form and psychological intensity. Rendered nearly unrecognizable, the woman's elongated head hosts an oversized eye and grotesque mouth; one clawlike and one flower-shaped hand punctuate her attenuated arms; and her breasts are enlarged and distorted. Her left claw and her animal-like legs, one of which resembles a turkey and the other a dog, give the woman the appearance of a wild beast. The red paint covering what at first looked to be the figure's left leg transforms this body part into one half of a uterus. Her right "leg" also resembles a belly with navel that has been separated from the rest of the body. During the late 1930s and the 1940s, Pollock was heavily influenced by the radical formal innovations of Pablo Picasso, who exhibited a series of paintings of sleeping women in his 1939 retrospective at the Museum of Modern Art.[2] Picasso's 1933 *Reclining Nude (Nu Couché)* (private collection) may have been a source for *Reclining Woman*'s diagonal and vertical patterning, heavy black contour lines, and stark coloration, including the figure's red-colored abdomen.[3]

Pollock's nude is monstrous and unsettling in her violent anatomical distortions and dislocations. Painted in energetic, frenetic brushstrokes, *Reclining Woman* imparts an overall mood of conflict, ambiguity, and anxiety. A troubled personality who struggled throughout his adult life with alcoholism and depression, Pollock began undergoing Jungian psychoanalysis in 1938.[4] The drawings Pollock created as part of his treatment often served as source material for his paintings. *Reclining Woman* may reference the artist's conflicted relationship with women: the figure's clawlike left hand enacts a grabbing motion, while the flower-shaped right hand suggests openness and generosity.[5] Pollock's interest in psychologically charged themes and fantastic imagery were also inspired by the surrealists' exploration of the unconscious mind, as well as by Orozco's and Siqueiros's embrace of ancient symbolism and their expressive, bold, and densely layered compositions.

In its gestural brushwork, move toward abstraction, and deeply psychological undercurrents, *Reclining Woman* anticipated the emotionally wrenching, visually stunning, and peerless abstractions with which Pollock would shock and delight the art world later in the decade.

MW

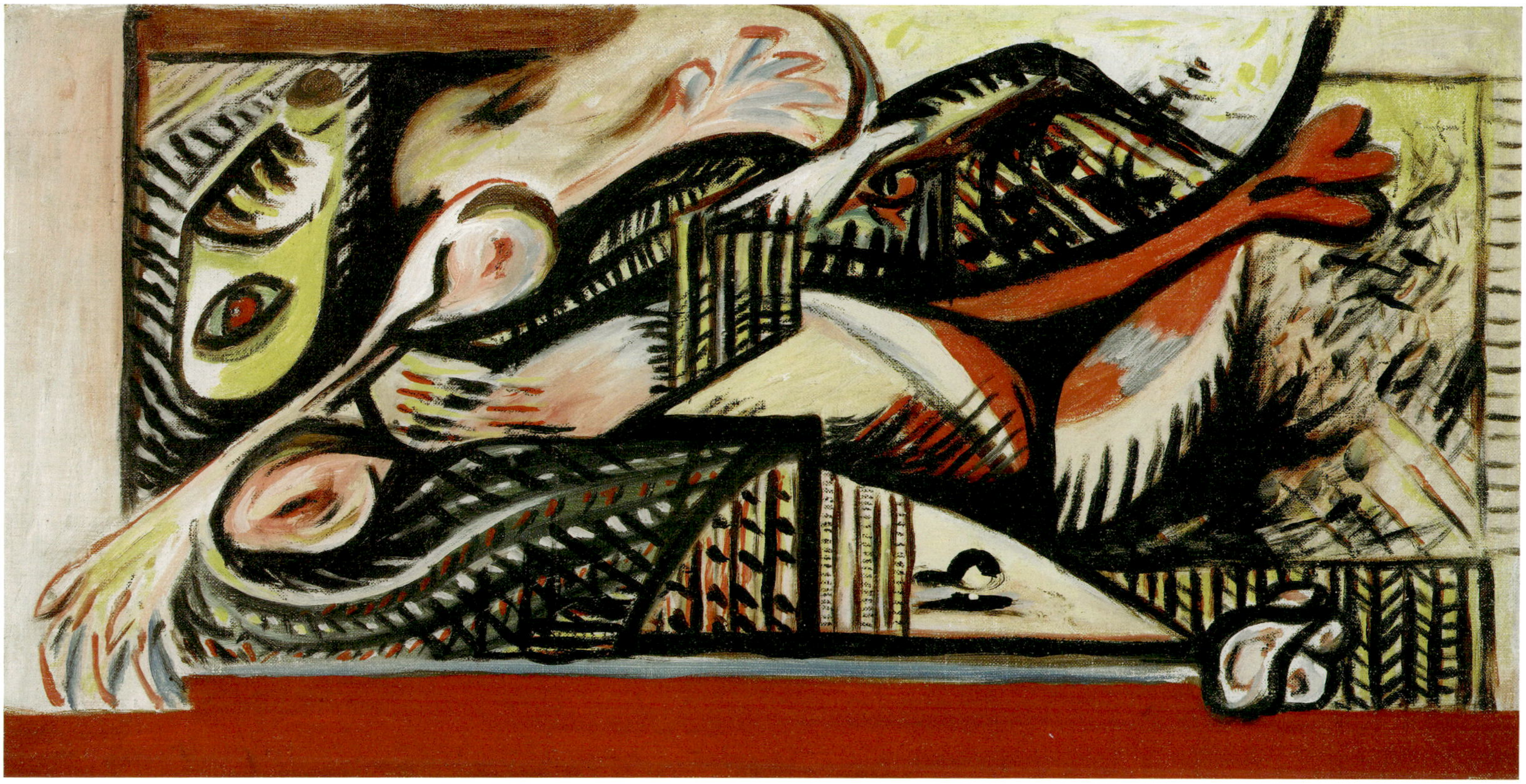

ROMARE BEARDEN (1911–1988)

Sacrifice

1941
Gouache and casein on paper
31¼ × 47 in. (79.4 × 119.4 cm)

Influential American modernist Romare Bearden created a unique visual language and iconography that powerfully conveyed the complexities of African American life. The Charlotte, North Carolina, native and his family moved to New York City when Bearden was a young child to escape the segregationist Jim Crow laws of the South.[1] Bearden's rich family life and friendships with prominent artists, reformers, and activists played a foundational role in the development of his aesthetic sensibility as well as his political and social consciousness.[2] He grew up in the midst of the Harlem Renaissance, a high point of African American cultural expression that saw the rise of such talented painters and musicians as Aaron Douglas and Duke Ellington. During the mid-1930s, Bearden studied with the social realist painter George Grosz at the Art Students League and served as an editorial cartoonist for the *Baltimore Afro-American*. From 1938 through the 1960s he was intermittently employed as a caseworker for the New York City Department of Social Services, a job that gave him piercing insight into the struggles of his fellow New Yorkers, particularly those of the city's minority populations.[3]

Bearden's 1941 gouache and casein painting *Sacrifice* is a visually dynamic and politically charged image informed by varied sources, including art history, religion, and contemporary African American experience. The painting depicts four highly abstracted figures in a fragmented composition, the central one of whom holds a knife at the throat of the figure at the far right. The famed Italian baroque artist Caravaggio's dramatic 1603 painting *The Sacrifice of Isaac* (Uffizi Gallery) seems to have been a source for Bearden's work.[4] The position of Abraham's hand holding the knife at Isaac's throat and the diagonal trajectory of the golden light that illuminates the center of Caravaggio's painting appear nearly verbatim in Bearden's composition.

Among modern influences, Bearden's painting was likely informed by Mexican artist Rufino Tamayo's figurative abstraction, which is characterized by interlocking areas of flat color.[5] The disjointed and dislocated human forms in *Sacrifice* were surely also inspired by Pablo Picasso's 1937 masterwork *Guernica*, which Bearden knew and likely had seen on view at the Museum of Modern Art.[6] Picasso's painting depicts the despair and anguish war inflicts upon individuals, particularly innocent civilians; Bearden's work perhaps represents contemporary African Americans' struggles with segregation, discrimination, and racial violence.[7] Indeed, it might be construed as a representation of self-sacrifice in the service of social justice.

Sacrifice's religiously inspired iconography anticipated Bearden's 1945 series *The Passion of Christ*, the group of twenty-four abstract oils and watercolors with which the artist established his reputation as a modernist of note. For Bearden, biblical themes offered a poignant way of addressing the human condition. "I don't believe that he was essentially a religious person in the sense of doctrinaire," a friend of the artist explained. "It was more of a poetic and a spiritual conception of religion and the Bible. . . . So when he did the biblical scenes it was inevitable that they would not be conventional paintings."[8]

In its compositional structure, *Sacrifice* anticipated the work for which Bearden is most famous today. The painting's collapse of space as well as its overlapping forms and vibrant blocks of color and pattern are pictorial elements that resurfaced in Bearden's richly textured collages. So, too, did the artist's multivalent iconography.

MW

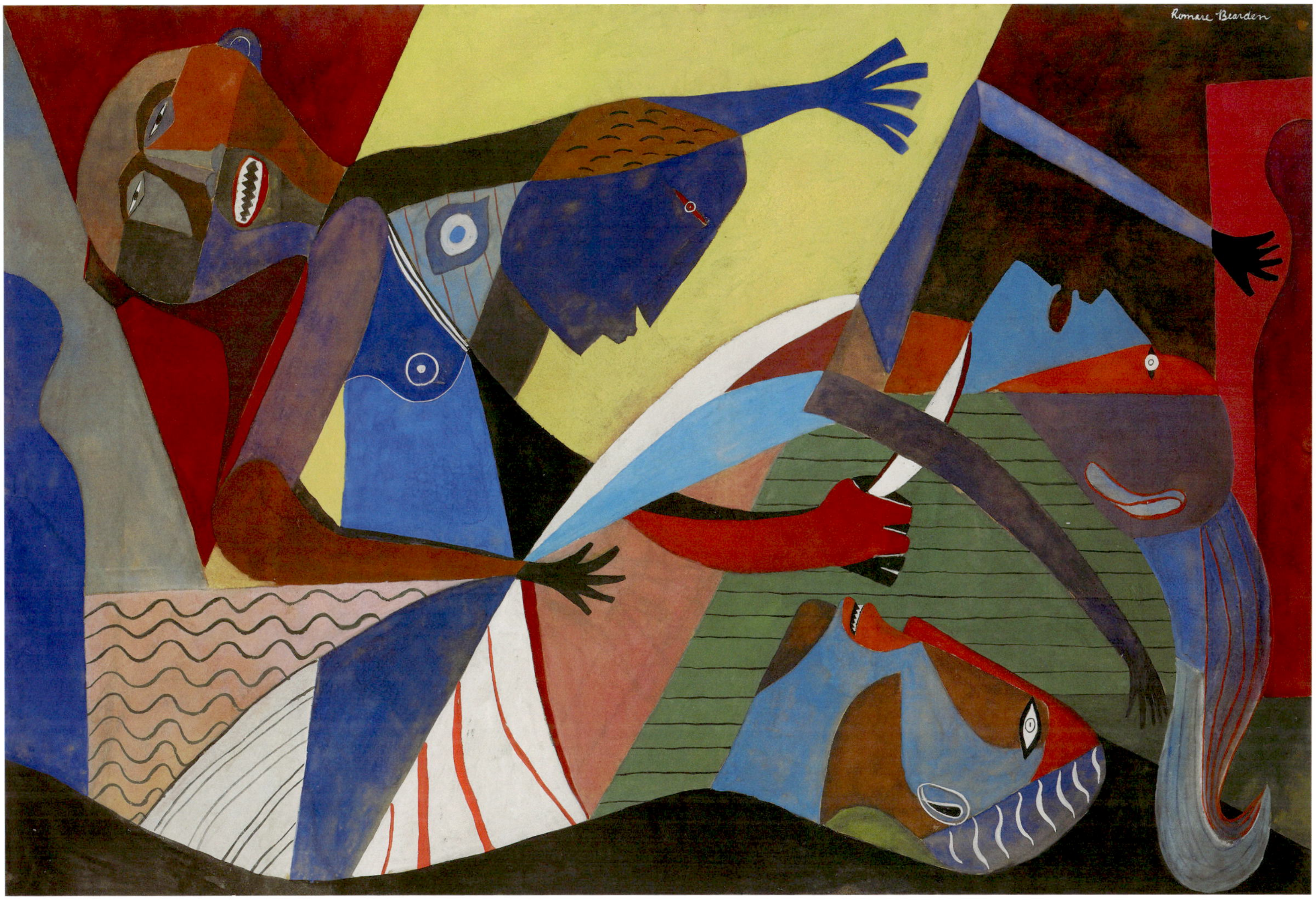
Romare Bearden

DAVID SMITH (1906–1965)

Cello Player

ca. 1946
Oil on board
22 11/16 × 30½ in. (57.6 × 77.5 cm)
Promised Gift

Long celebrated as one of America's greatest sculptors, audiences have increasingly come to appreciate David Smith's important contributions in other media, including photography, drawing, and painting. Smith made *Cello Player* in the later 1940s, during a period of intense creativity influenced by cubism and surrealism.[1] The oil's abstract forms, fantastical imagery, and dramatic yet elegant composition typify Smith's artistic production from this important phase in his career, a decade during which he created some of his most disturbing—and lyrical—works.[2]

The musician and his instrument in *Cello Player* are portrayed in an absurd, dreamlike manner, stretched out and distorted. Interwoven and intertwined, the two become one. The figure's head assumes the shape of a cello bridge fixed with interlocking pegs. His right thumb transforms into the instrument's fingerboard, and his left arm transmutes into strings, which in turn morph into spidery fingers. In fusing the physical forms of the musician and his instrument, Smith posits their perfect harmony. Moreover, the artist's merging of angular, pronged, and curved shapes evokes the intense, often dramatic poses of a performing cellist.

The divergent angles and directional lines of the musician's body and his instrument create a dynamic composition. The pink-colored, chevron-shaped cello strings at center point to the image's upper edge, while the instrument's blue neck reaches straight down and the diagonal lines of the blue bow point to the lower right. Smith visually balanced the active image by juxtaposing geometric and biomorphic forms and evenly distributing color. The blue of the spiral-shaped scroll on the right is repeated on the left in the cello's neck, for example, and the green of the musician's pointy elbow echoes that of his massive green hand.

Widely reproduced images of the much-lauded cello masters Emanuel Feuermann and Gregor Piatigorsky posing with their long, strong fingers on their instruments likely inspired *Cello Player* and two closely related works dating from 1946.[3] *Cello Player* is more abstract and stylized than the tempera painting *Piat* (Estate of David Smith), a portrait of a musician above a landscape composed of bridgelike cellos. The steel sculpture *Cello Player* (collection of David Mirvish), a hybrid of the two paintings, retains the grace of its painted counterparts but elaborates on their exploration of positive and negative space with its open construction and play of varied silhouettes. All three works possess fantastic anatomical imagery and a lively interaction between geometric and organic elements.

When Smith painted *Cello Player* around 1946, steel and iron were scarce due to the high demand for metals within the defense industries. Although he did not abandon sculpture altogether during this period, Smith turned the challenge of limited materials into an opportunity for creative growth, intensely pursuing painting and drawing and exploring his formal and symbolic interests in unprecedented depth. The constant exchange between brush and welding torch seems to have enhanced his artistic vision.[4] Indeed, this surreal fantasy of a musician suggests a painting of a sculpture. The cello's end pin in the lower left, a part of the instrument that is typically narrow and pointed to allow for easy maneuvering on the part of the player, appears wide and flat, like a sculptural base. The practice of making paintings of three-dimensional forms was not unusual for Smith. He often created preparatory drawings for new sculptures, studies for sculptures he never realized, and paintings and drawings after finished sculptural works.[5] MW

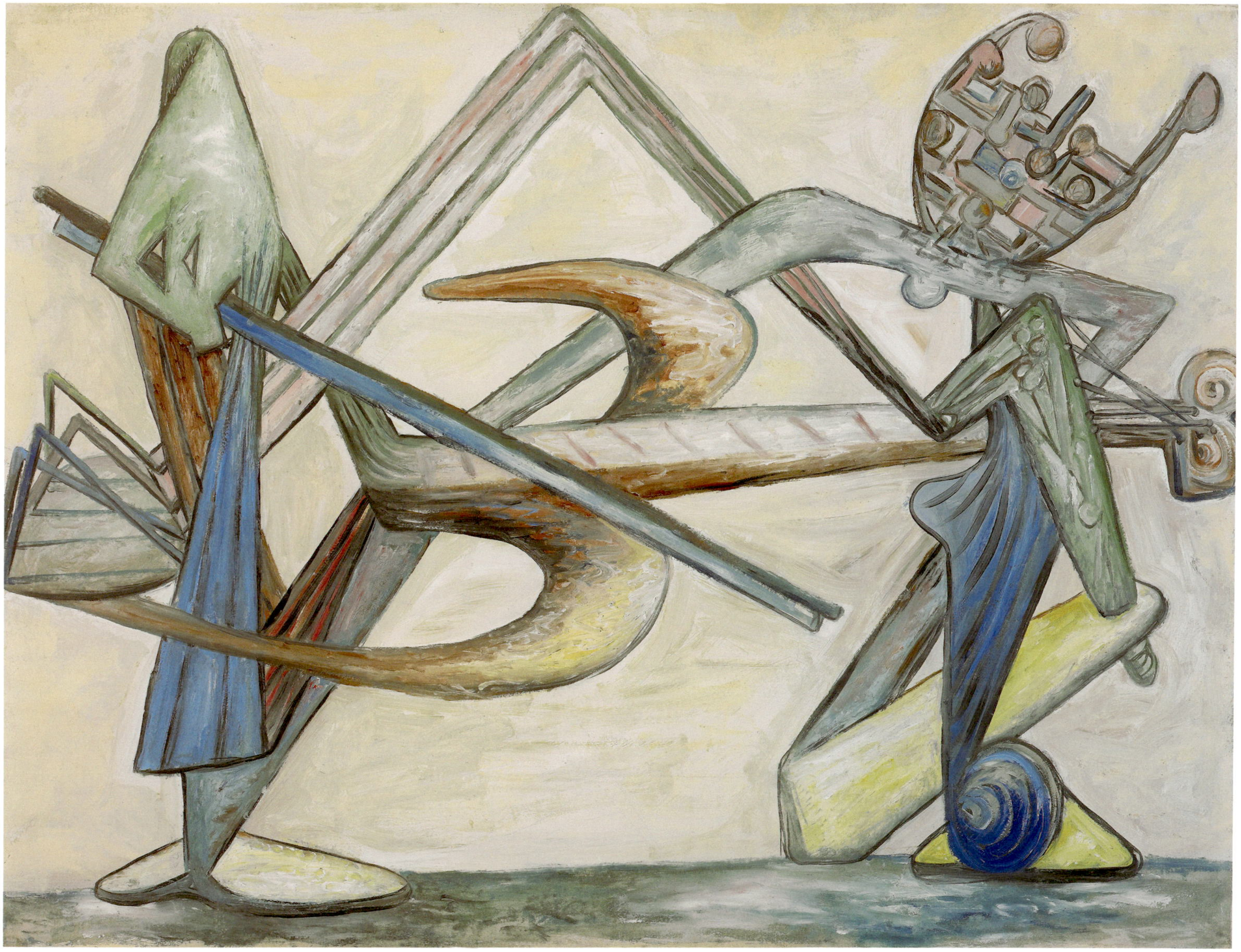

MARSDEN HARTLEY (1877–1943)

Madawaska—Acadian Light—Heavy

1940
Oil on board
40 × 30 in. (101.6 × 76.2 cm)
Promised Gift

Marsden Hartley knew from a young age that he wanted to be an artist. Hartley found himself isolated and unhappy as a boy, both by reason of difficult family circumstances including his mother's death when he was just eight years old, and, as he grew older, as a homosexual living during a fundamentally repressive era in a small New England manufacturing town.[1] Hartley's identity as a gay man coming of age at the turn of a new, transformative century was present in his art from the outset and manifest itself as an artistic restlessness characterized by aesthetic invention, independence, isolation, and introspection.

As a young artist living in the urban centers of New York, Paris, and Berlin, Hartley found social acceptance and an exhilarating sense of creative freedom. This was especially true in Berlin, where the artist fell in love with a young German officer. When the officer was killed early in World War I, Hartley produced a series of abstract, symbolic homages to his friend that are among the most startlingly advanced paintings of their time. When he returned to New York from Europe in 1916, Hartley was at the forefront of the American avant-garde.

In his later years, Hartley once again painted in northern New England and Maine, and eventually ventured to Nova Scotia. The artist's works from this period are among his most deeply personal and expressive. The 1940 canvas *Madawaska—Acadian Light—Heavy* openly confirms what Hartley had theretofore voiced only indirectly, as his "desirous heart."[2] It is one of two very similar versions of the subject: a young boxer from the town of Madawaska, Maine, in the Saint John River Valley, on the border between Maine and French Canada.[3] These paintings reveal Hartley's full-blooded embrace of homosexual desires that up to this point had remained hidden in stylized imagery, encoded in mystical symbols, or subsumed in representations of nature's heaving rhythms.

Thought to be the earlier of the two versions of the theme (the other is in the collection of the Art Institute of Chicago), the painting at Crystal Bridges is comparatively chaste, the figure's stance slightly less frontal and the forms broader, with less closely modeled musculature.[4] The unidentified boxer's neck is a cylindrical, stump-like slab rising out of his mountainous, triangular deltoids, a body shaped by and representative of a harsh, northern environment where until recently even indoor water turned hard for more than half the year and wood splitting is still a survival skill and daily necessity. The athlete's body is backlit from one side, as if he has just exited or is about to enter a floodlit sports arena. He stands in an indeterminate, shallow space, his face and body partially hidden in shadow against a blood-red ground. The portrait conveys a psychological tension that is immediate and direct, true to the blunt grace of the subject, as well as an affecting distance—a quality of incipience and possibility. In late-career images of the idealized male form such as this one, Hartley found a vehicle to effectively carry his cumulative sense of self—of consolation and acceptance, desire and regret—into paintings as brutally honest as they are from the heart.

CBC

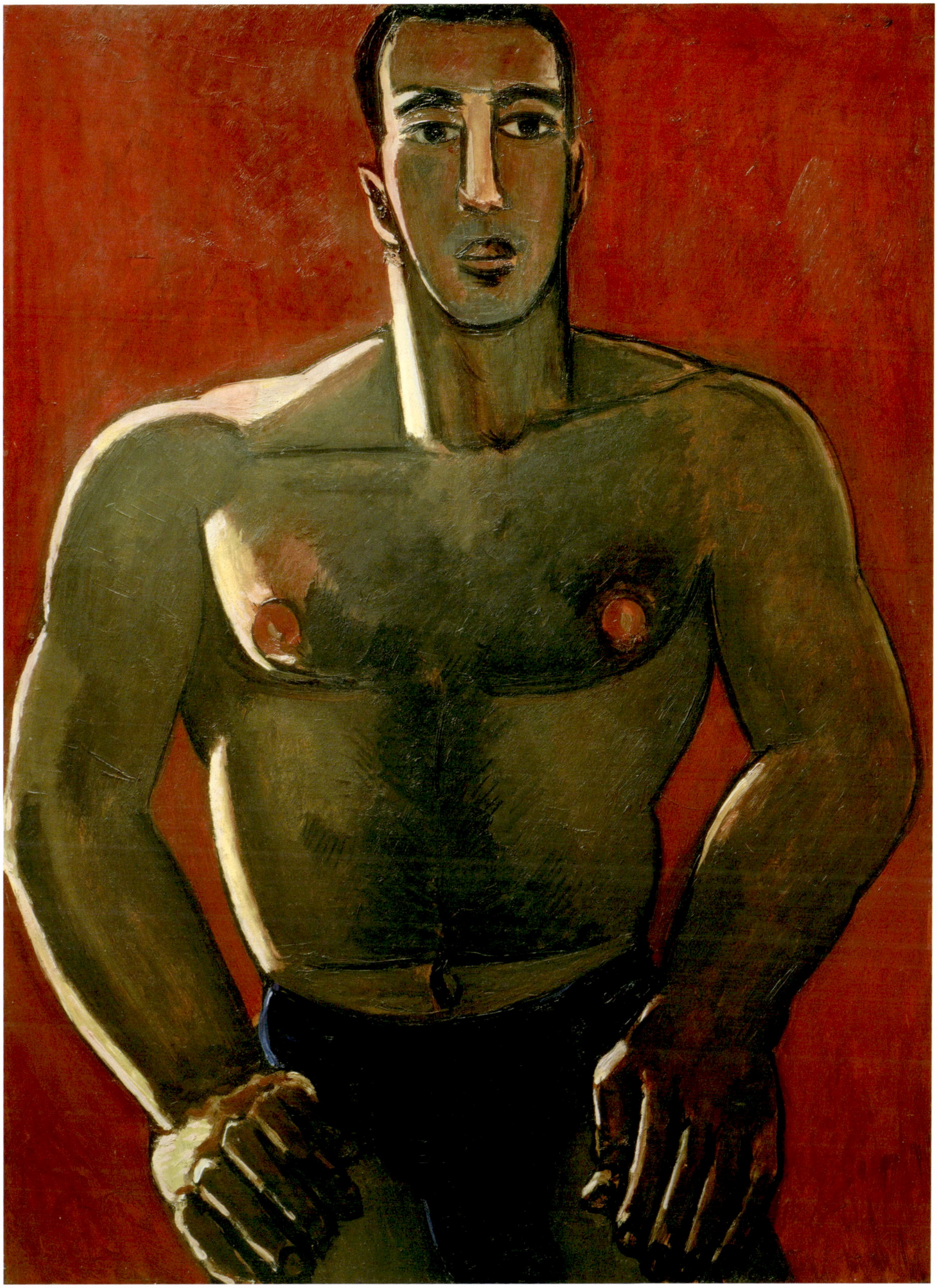

NORMAN ROCKWELL (1894–1978)

Rosie the Riveter

1943
Oil on canvas
52 × 40 in. (132.1 × 101.6 cm)

On May 2, 1943, the cover of the immensely popular illustrated magazine the *Saturday Evening Post* featured a curious new American character: a muscular young woman dressed in shirtsleeves and overalls and brandishing a large riveting gun. Of the 332 magazine covers that Norman Rockwell produced for the *Post* over a span of forty-seven years, none had the immediate impact nor enjoys the enduring influence of this image. Today, Rockwell's *Rosie the Riveter* serves as a powerful reminder of American women's critical contribution to victory during World War II as well as a transcendent symbol of their capabilities, strength, and determination.

The United States' entry into World War II in 1941 prompted a fundamental shift in the composition of the home front workforce. As large numbers of men deployed overseas, traditionally male jobs in manufacturing and other industries were left vacant. Rockwell's magazine cover depicting an American woman employed in the production of military hardware was part of the Office of War Information's wide-reaching "Women in Necessary Services" campaign aimed at enlisting female workers to fill these crucial positions. The artist's protagonist was the first widely publicized pictorial representation of this heroic new type of American woman.[1]

Rosie represents a distinctive melding of wartime American life and art historical tradition. Rockwell's model was a nineteen-year-old telephone operator from the painter's hometown of Arlington, Vermont. Posed before a waving American flag and dressed in red, white, and blue, Rosie proudly displays a series of patriotic badges across the bib of her overalls, including a Red Cross volunteer pin; the Victory pin; the Army-Navy "E" Award for Excellence in War Production; and an employee badge complete with photographic identification. She wears brown loafers, a reminder that metal-toed safety shoes were not manufactured for women until later in 1943.[2] If there is any question about the cause Rosie is serving with her labors, the tattered copy of Adolf Hitler's *Mein Kampf* upon which she tramples immediately brings clarity.

Saturday Evening Post readers were instantly taken with Rosie's homegrown charms. They also may have recognized the distinguished artistic origins of Rockwell's statuesque subject: Michelangelo's painting of the prophet Isaiah on the ceiling of the Sistine Chapel. In July 1943, the *Art Digest* explained: "Rockwell followed Isaiah's pose and proportions as thoroughly as possible in building Rosie up to the great hulk of a war working woman she is. He gave her a ham sandwich instead of a godly gesture; rows of merit buttons and industrial identification tags across her chest where Isaiah's drapers flutter."[3] A magisterial figure posed like a prophet yet represented as a begrimed manual laborer engaged in the mundane activity of eating a sandwich, Rosie is simultaneously lofty and grounded, idealized and accessible. Rockwell was careful to include anecdotal details in his picture that affirmed for uneasy audiences his pioneering subject's enduring femininity: Rosie wears lipstick and painted nails, and a compact and handkerchief peek out of her pocket.[4]

Rosie the Riveter did double duty in supporting the war effort. The magazine cover illustration extolled the virtues of the nation's female defense workers for the *Saturday Evening Post*'s over three million largely middle-class subscribers, while the original painting traveled on a nationwide tour to generate publicity for the United States Treasury Department's War Loan Drives. EDS

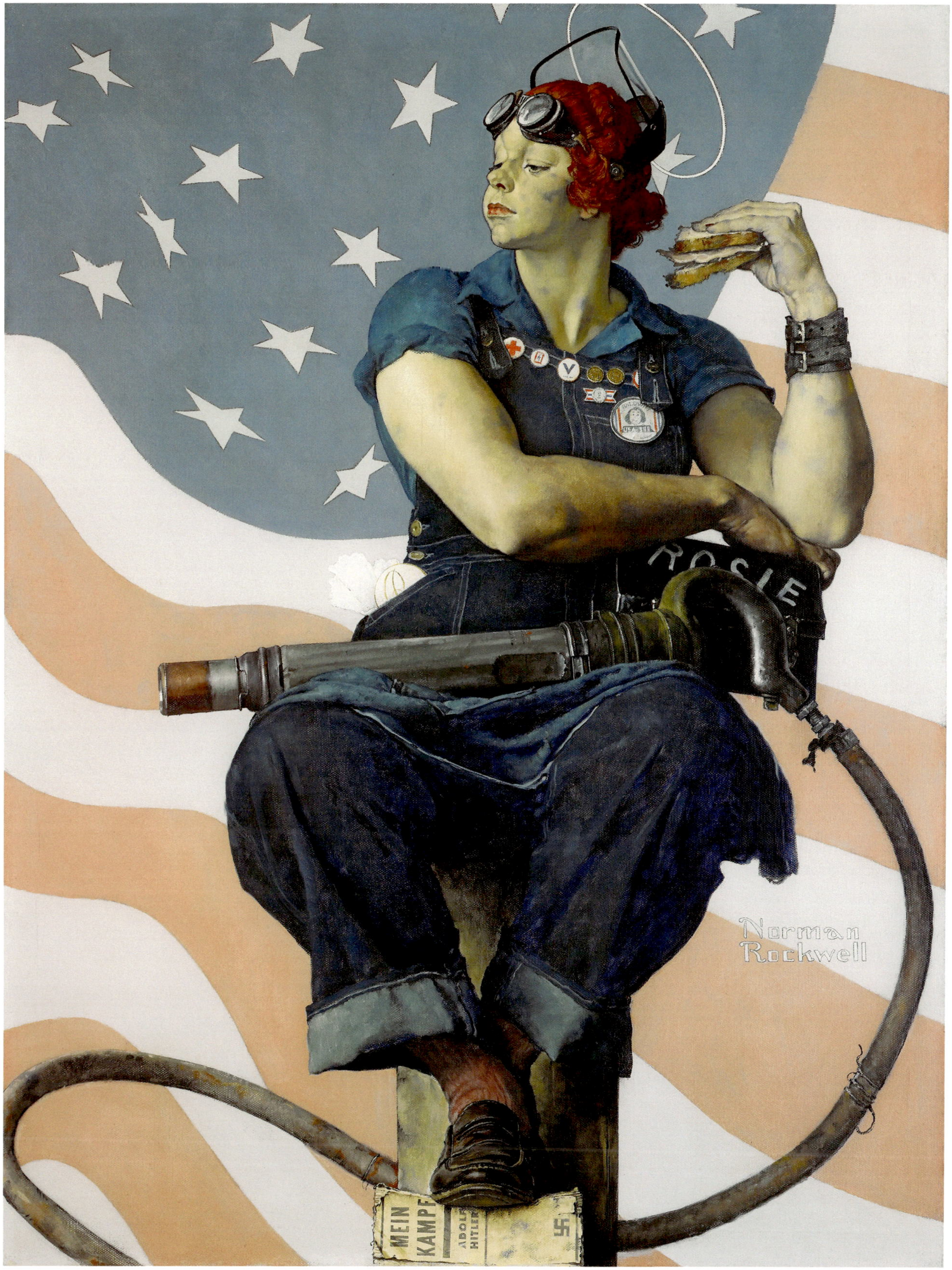
ROSIE
Norman
Rockwell
MEIN
KAMPF

CHARLES EPHRAIM BURCHFIELD (1893–1967)

Dawn in Hemlock Woods

1946; reworked 1961
Watercolor on paper
39 × 60 in. (99.1 × 152.4 cm)

Charles Ephraim Burchfield's late watercolor *Dawn in Hemlock Woods* epitomizes the final, transcendental phase of his work. The artist initially conceived and completed the image in 1946. As ill health prevented him from painting directly from nature during his later years, in 1961 Burchfield modified the watercolor, increasing its size by attaching additional paper strips with nearly invisible seams to the edges of the original. It is an unusual technique that perhaps derived from the artist's early career as a wallpaper designer for the M. H. Birge Company in Buffalo, New York. More than a mere technical conceit, however, this enlargement and revision of an earlier image reflected Burchfield's desire to literally build on and expand his artistic vision. Indeed, the monumentality of mature works like *Dawn in Hemlock Woods* exceeds sheer size. These images, which vibrate with a surging, rhythmic energy, powerfully convey the inner beating heart of nature.

Weather and seasonal change informed the artist's highly individual approach to landscape. *Dawn in Hemlock Woods* evokes the dense, swampy forests of northeast Ohio and upstate New York, where he was born and spent his adult life, respectively. In a journal entry dated March 12, 1922, Burchfield vividly described the spontaneous fires that occasionally erupted in the sulfurous bogs of these northern forests: "The roar of the rapids—it holds me spellbound—thought ceases & yet is scattered to the far horizons where the white flames of March fires are burning. The white flames of March fire[s] flicker like lightning over the black wastes of winter—The side of the hillside is warm like a grate fire."[1] Persephone returning from Hades could not have presented a more compelling, primal vision of spring's fraught arrival in a forsaken land.

Burchfield remains a somewhat isolated figure in art history whose work oscillates between regionalism and modernism, description and dream. Interest in the painter among contemporary artists, however, seems to be on the upswing. In 2010, the sculptor Robert Gober organized an exhibition surveying Burchfield's career for the Hammer Museum at the University of California, Los Angeles.[2] Undoubtedly inspired by Burchfield, Wisconsin-based painter Tom Uttech, who is also represented in the Crystal Bridges collection (p. 308), creates ecstatic visions of the natural abundance and fecundity found in the remote, pristine boundary waters of northern Minnesota and southern Ontario. In addition to Burchfield's unmistakable style and visual inventiveness, contemporary artists also respond positively to his fierce independence and resolute, unwavering belief in his own work. In 1938 he wrote in his journal, "I think of myself—as an artist—as being in a nondescript swamp, up to my knees in mire, painting the vital beauty I see there, in my own way, not caring a damn about tradition, or anyone's opinion."[3]

CBC

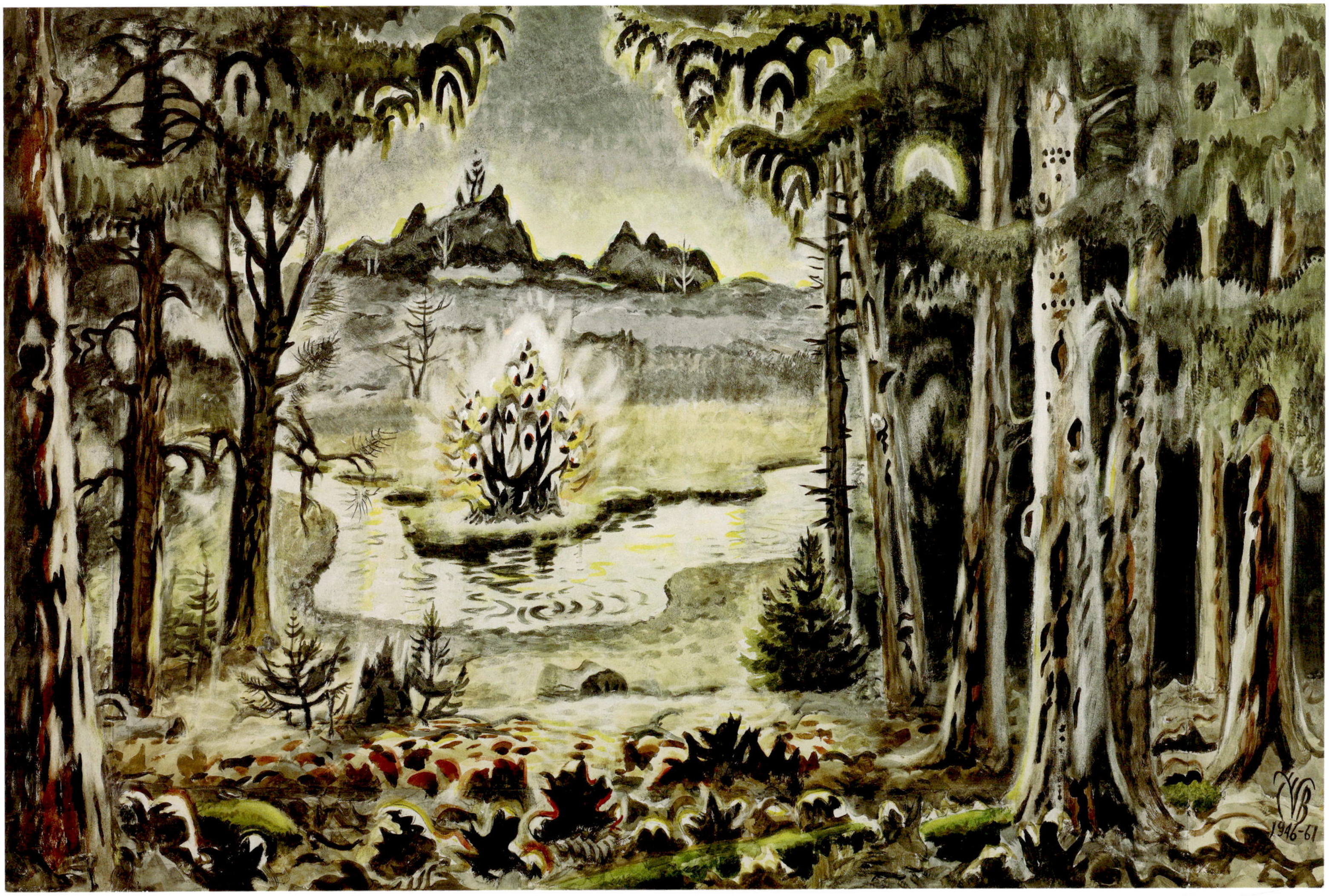

MILTON AVERY (1885–1965)

Nudes

1948
Oil on canvas
48 × 32 in. (121.9 × 81.3 cm)
Promised Gift

The two figures in Milton Avery's *Nudes* are defined by shape, not by form: there is but a hint of shadow (and thus three-dimensionality) in the left leg of the rear figure, and likewise a vague sense of curvature in the left foot of the front figure. In both nudes, the color is flat and arbitrary; the outlines relentlessly clear, as if the shapes are puzzle pieces; and everywhere details are dispensed with. The room these two bodies occupy is likewise incongruously colored: a strong red floor, a pale blue wall. Clearly, Avery was not interested in academic realism, but nor was his ambition complete abstraction. His compromise position—a simplified figuration—emphasized one pursuit over all others: pure painting.

Avery arrived in New York City in 1925, at a time when American political isolationism in reaction to World War I discouraged the embrace of European modernism. Nevertheless, the disciplined yet independent Avery remained open to the lesson of Henri Matisse: that spare and simple compositions animated by subtle and sophisticated color could convey complex, sensual stimulation. Indeed, color became his central aesthetic concern. In 1926 Avery married Sally Michel, a fellow artist whose financial support allowed him to concentrate his full time and energies on painting—devouring art magazines, visiting galleries and museums, and pursuing a personal vision of color that, while influenced by Matisse and modernism, became a highly individual response to the world around him.[1]

Throughout the 1930s and into the 1940s, Avery perfected a style that joined traditional subject matter—portraiture, still life, figure painting, and landscape—with broad areas of clearly defined shapes filled in with thin, flat color. The range of values in his pictures tightened while the colors became increasingly arbitrary, a direct effect of his affinity for Matisse. As mainstream American art grew more narrative and explicit, Avery's work became more aesthetic and equivocal. His ability to remain aloof from prevailing trends and to follow his own instincts was influential on younger modernists. The abstract expressionist Adolph Gottlieb recalled, "When social realism and the American scene were considered the important thing, he took an aesthetic stand as opposed to regional subject matter. His attitude helped reinforce me in my chosen direction. I always regarded him as a brilliant colorist and draftsman, a solitary figure working against the stream."[2]

Nudes dates from 1948, when Avery's decades-long pursuit of sophisticated color harmonies finally came to fruition. He had responded to Matisse and also to Picasso's classical nudes but was a slavish follower of neither, creating his own figural style characterized by calm, order, and monumental repose. In *Nudes*, the painter achieved the quiet stillness that is a hallmark of his work along with an active interplay of color that simultaneously suggests intensity and restraint, austerity and daring. Avery's emphasis on art before biography or politics reminds us of how powerful the intelligent orchestration of color can be. WS

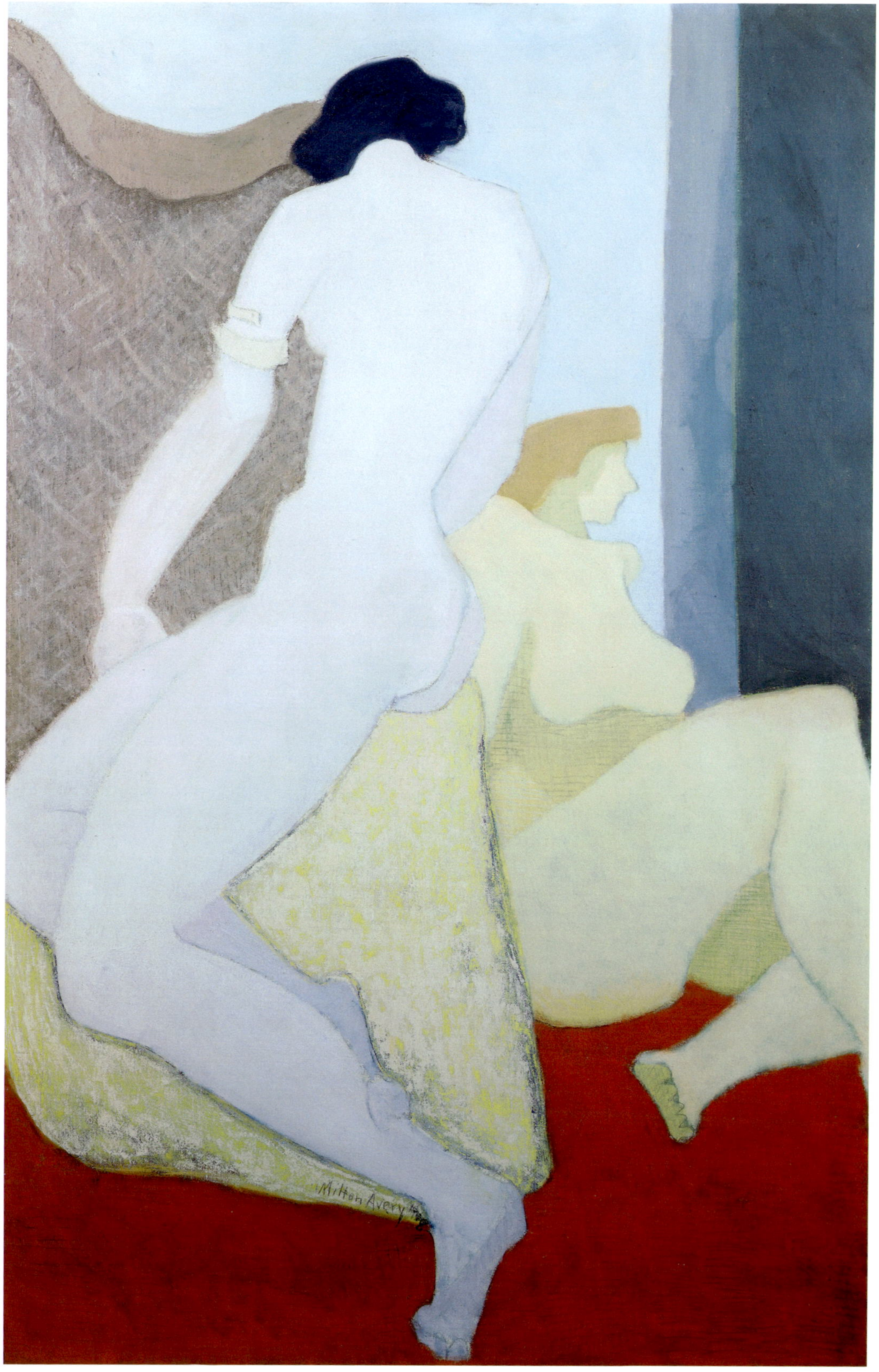
Milton Avery

JACOB LAWRENCE (1917–2000)

Ambulance Call

1948
Egg tempera on board
24 × 20 in. (61 × 50.8 cm)
Promised Gift

In Jacob Lawrence's 1948 Harlem street scene *Ambulance Call*, two ambulance attendants dressed in blue uniforms lift a stretcher carrying an ailing figure covered in white sheets. The patient's head is visible, his mouth open wide in agony. A paramedic with a stethoscope in his pocket stands by, closely monitoring the victim. Surrounding this trio of figures is a densely packed crowd of spectators, whose downcast eyes and sad facial expressions suggest that this is not an anonymous crowd of ghoulish onlookers but a close-knit community of neighbors, friends, and family.[1] On a ledge in the background, a black-and-white cat with a dead bird in its mouth adds to the tragedy of the poignant image.

In the early 1940s, Lawrence—the son of southern black migrants—established his reputation as the prevailing visual chronicler of African American life and a gifted modernist painter. Lawrence's tempera on board *Ambulance Call* exemplifies his expressive melding of traditional narrative subjects and the visual language of modernism. The painting is a tour de force of pure color and form. Schematically rendered figures dressed in bright, monochromatic clothing fill the composition from edge to edge. Lawrence distributed passages of red, blue, yellow, green, and black pigment throughout the picture in a lively, rhythmic pattern. He rendered the figures' facial details as yellow lines that appear to be incised, giving them the ornamental character of filigree. The black zigzag pattern on a male figure's straw hat at middle right and the string of golden circles that form the necklace worn by the woman directly to his left further draw in the viewer. While Lawrence's composition is largely flat and decorative in design, the artist juxtaposed passages of thinly applied color and paint-laden brushstrokes of the same hue to create subtle three-dimensional effects such as folds and creases in the figures' clothing.[2]

Thematically, *Ambulance Call* addresses the struggles and accomplishments of African Americans in Harlem as well as Lawrence's own experience with medical care while living in a culture rife with racial prejudice.[3] In the 1940s, the Harlem Hospital was the only facility in New York City that admitted black patients; consequently, it was the most congested in the city and ailing blacks waited significantly longer to get medical treatment than did their white counterparts. Lawrence's related painting *Free Clinic* (1937, Art Institute of Chicago) depicts sick and injured African Americans in a densely packed waiting room. Historian Nat Brandt has described the case of a black patient who "lay critically ill in an ambulance for more than an hour while officials of Knickerbocker Hospital discussed whether to admit her."[4]

Lawrence portrayed his subjects in *Ambulance Call* with a dignity and humanity that defied their challenging circumstances. The quiet compassion of his painted protagonists mirrored the artist's own approach to political activism. Lawrence carefully avoided the label "protest artist," instead describing himself more broadly as a humanist.[5] Nevertheless, through his commitment to social themes and his illumination of little-known realities the painter raised social consciousness about racial injustice and discrimination. He once stated, humbly: "My pictures express my life and experience. I paint the things I know about and the things I have experienced. The things I have experienced extend into my national, racial, and class group. So I paint the American scene."[6]

MW

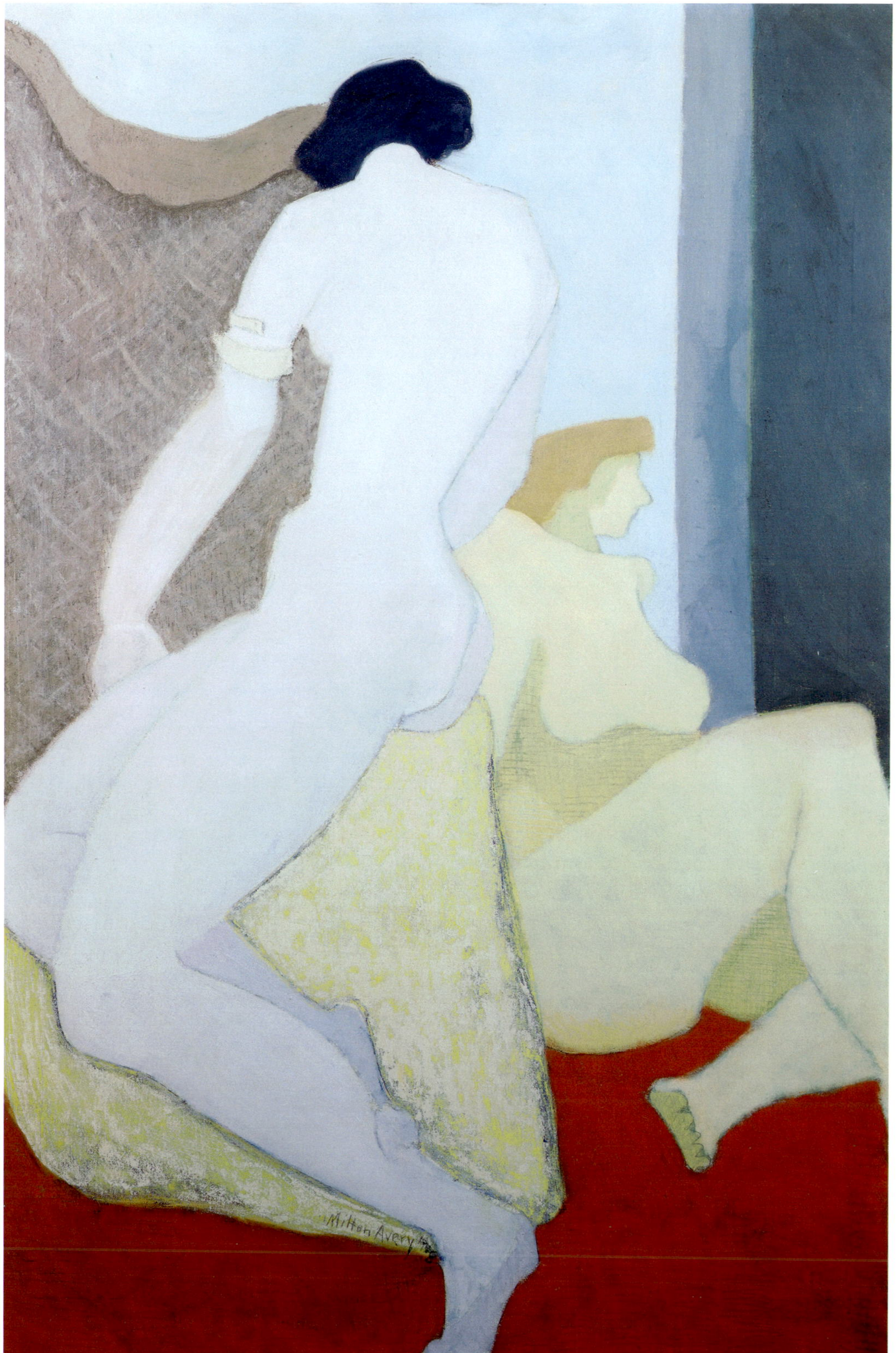
Milton Avery

JACOB LAWRENCE (1917–2000)

Ambulance Call

1948
Egg tempera on board
24 × 20 in. (61 × 50.8 cm)
Promised Gift

In Jacob Lawrence's 1948 Harlem street scene *Ambulance Call*, two ambulance attendants dressed in blue uniforms lift a stretcher carrying an ailing figure covered in white sheets. The patient's head is visible, his mouth open wide in agony. A paramedic with a stethoscope in his pocket stands by, closely monitoring the victim. Surrounding this trio of figures is a densely packed crowd of spectators, whose downcast eyes and sad facial expressions suggest that this is not an anonymous crowd of ghoulish onlookers but a close-knit community of neighbors, friends, and family.[1] On a ledge in the background, a black-and-white cat with a dead bird in its mouth adds to the tragedy of the poignant image.

In the early 1940s, Lawrence—the son of southern black migrants—established his reputation as the prevailing visual chronicler of African American life and a gifted modernist painter. Lawrence's tempera on board *Ambulance Call* exemplifies his expressive melding of traditional narrative subjects and the visual language of modernism. The painting is a tour de force of pure color and form. Schematically rendered figures dressed in bright, monochromatic clothing fill the composition from edge to edge. Lawrence distributed passages of red, blue, yellow, green, and black pigment throughout the picture in a lively, rhythmic pattern. He rendered the figures' facial details as yellow lines that appear to be incised, giving them the ornamental character of filigree. The black zigzag pattern on a male figure's straw hat at middle right and the string of golden circles that form the necklace worn by the woman directly to his left further draw in the viewer. While Lawrence's composition is largely flat and decorative in design, the artist juxtaposed passages of thinly applied color and paint-laden brushstrokes of the same hue to create subtle three-dimensional effects such as folds and creases in the figures' clothing.[2]

Thematically, *Ambulance Call* addresses the struggles and accomplishments of African Americans in Harlem as well as Lawrence's own experience with medical care while living in a culture rife with racial prejudice.[3] In the 1940s, the Harlem Hospital was the only facility in New York City that admitted black patients; consequently, it was the most congested in the city and ailing blacks waited significantly longer to get medical treatment than did their white counterparts. Lawrence's related painting *Free Clinic* (1937, Art Institute of Chicago) depicts sick and injured African Americans in a densely packed waiting room. Historian Nat Brandt has described the case of a black patient who "lay critically ill in an ambulance for more than an hour while officials of Knickerbocker Hospital discussed whether to admit her."[4]

Lawrence portrayed his subjects in *Ambulance Call* with a dignity and humanity that defied their challenging circumstances. The quiet compassion of his painted protagonists mirrored the artist's own approach to political activism. Lawrence carefully avoided the label "protest artist," instead describing himself more broadly as a humanist.[5] Nevertheless, through his commitment to social themes and his illumination of little-known realities the painter raised social consciousness about racial injustice and discrimination. He once stated, humbly: "My pictures express my life and experience. I paint the things I know about and the things I have experienced. The things I have experienced extend into my national, racial, and class group. So I paint the American scene."[6]

MW

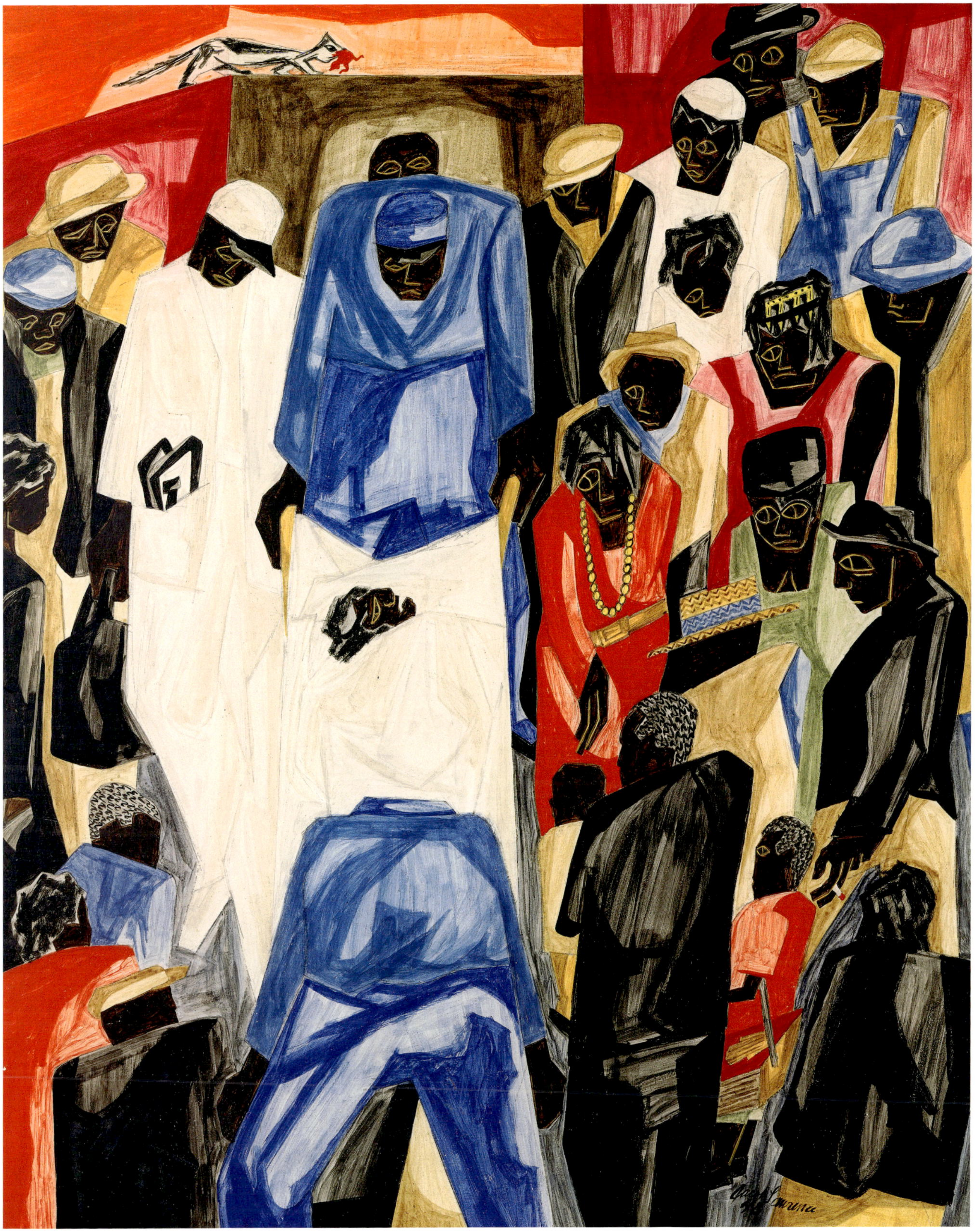

CHARLES SHEELER (1883–1965)

Amoskeag Mills #2

1948
Oil on canvas
28½ × 24 in. (72.4 × 61 cm)
Promised Gift

In 1948, the Currier Gallery of Art (now the Currier Museum of Art) in Manchester, New Hampshire, invited the noted painter and photographer Charles Sheeler to serve as an artist-in-residence. He was to produce two tempera studies on a theme of his choice, one of which the museum trustees and staff would select to be executed as a large oil painting.[1] Sheeler chose as his subject Manchester's historic Amoskeag Mills, a defunct manufacturing facility that had been the largest cotton textile plant in the world at the turn of the twentieth century.[2]

The spare geometry of Amoskeag Mills was well suited to Sheeler's meticulous, hard-edged realism. Influenced by the simplified, geometric compositions of cubism as well as the sharp focus and unconventional cropping of photography, Sheeler and other early American modernists such as Charles Demuth (p. 212) had developed a highly influential new aesthetic, commonly known as precisionism, in the 1920s. Over the course of his lengthy career, Sheeler applied the precisionist style to numerous and varied subjects, but urban and industrial themes like Amoskeag dominated his work.

Sheeler photographed the New Hampshire site extensively during his residency at the Currier and then completed the tempera studies in his studio in Irvington-on-Hudson, New York. Anticipating that the Currier trustees would desire a conventional rendering of the mill yard, both of his preliminary sketches were relatively straightforward descriptions.[3] In the finished oil painting *Amoskeag Mills #2*, however, Sheeler realized his personal vision of the mill. As was typical of his image-making process during the 1940s, the artist combined elements from several different photographic negatives to create a photomontage that was used, along with the tempera study, as a model for his final composition.[4] Like the preparatory photomontage, *Amoskeag Mills #2* synthesizes multiple views. With the exception of the bright red brick of the five-story Waumbec Mill at left, the buildings are a product of the artist's imagination, composed of fragments of several other mill structures. The buildings appear as crystalline masses delineated by dramatic contrasts of light and shadow. Especially on the darker, right side of the painting, it is difficult to identify where one building starts and another begins. Sheeler's merging of abstract form and realistic detail invites viewers to contemplate the often-complex relationship between fact and fiction, present and past.

Although he was more interested in the formal, aesthetic aspects of the mills' architecture than he was in their social and economic history, Sheeler's strangely sterile, uninhabited image reflects the precipitous decline of the New England textile industry beginning in the 1920s. Manchester's Amoskeag Mills permanently closed in 1935, the victim of a combination of mismanagement, strikes, a flood, and the nation's general economic downturn.[5] Sheeler's impersonal painting style, exemplified by *Amoskeag Mills #2*, was a perfect match for a highly mechanized age. Indeed, Sheeler even painted himself out of the work: the canvas's utterly smooth, flawless finish offers almost no evidence of the artist's significant labors. "I just don't want to see any more than is absolutely necessary of the physical materials that go into a picture," he explained.[6] MW

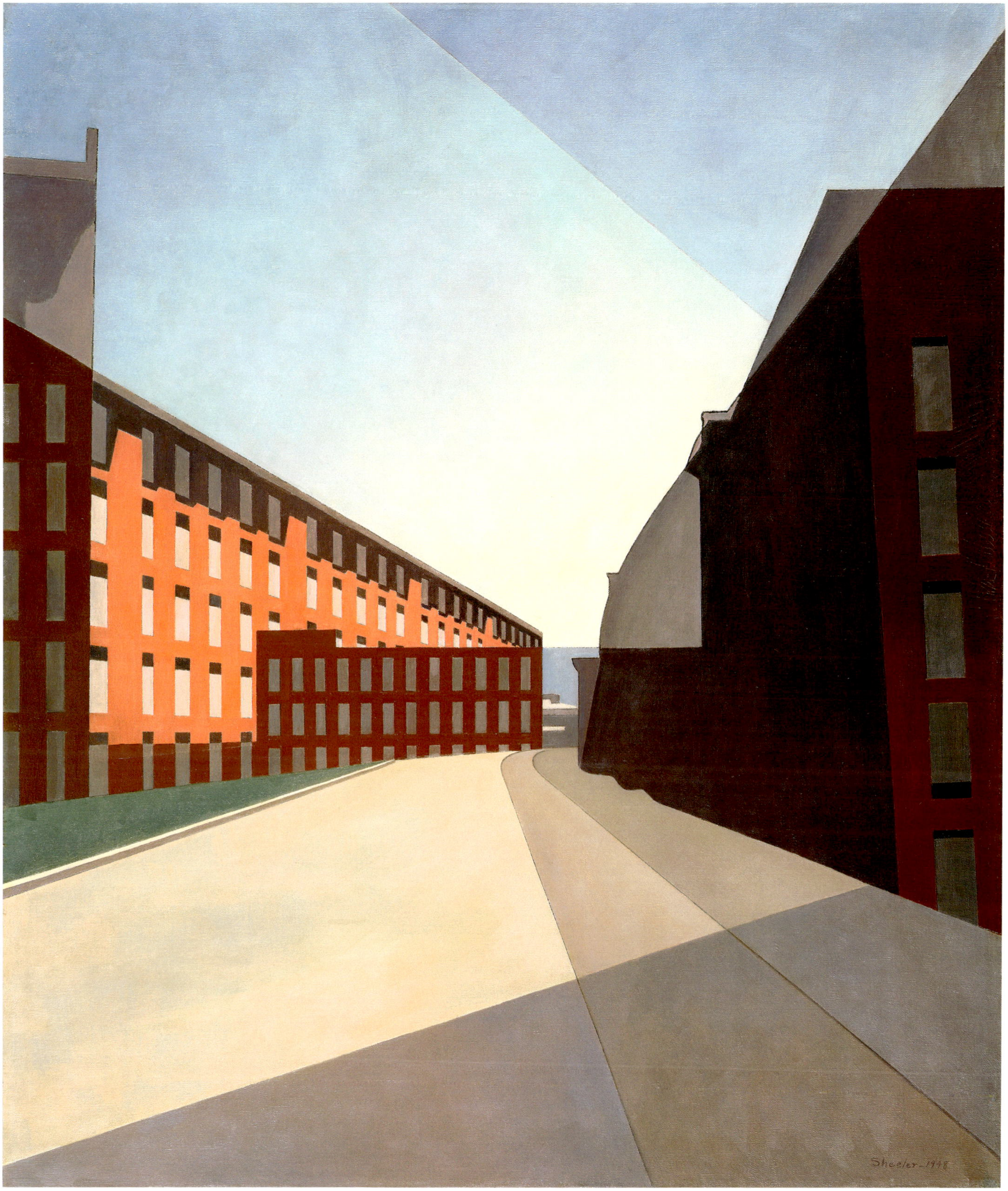
Sheeler

WILL BARNET (B. 1911)

Family and Pink Table (Mary and Sons)

1948
Oil on canvas
36 × 28 in. (91.4 × 71.1 cm)
Promised Gift

Will Barnet has been a professional artist for eight decades. Approaching his one-hundredth year, he continues to work every day. Throughout his long and distinguished career, Barnet has paired humanistic sentiment and personal experience—especially family life—with a formal aesthetic founded in order, balance, and clarity. It is this rare combination of passion and serenity that gives his work its distinctive character.

The Beverly, Massachusetts-born artist studied at the School of the Museum of Fine Arts, Boston, in the late 1920s. When he moved to New York City in 1931, Barnet stepped into the gaping maw and teeth of the Great Depression and dim prospects for a young artist just out of school. Yet by 1948, when Barnet painted *Family and Pink Table (Mary and Sons)*, he had established himself as a respected teacher at the Art Students League and begun to win serious critical attention for his increasingly abstract paintings.[1]

Family and Pink Table presents Barnet's young family gathered around a simple rectangular table inset with checkerboard squares that is reminiscent of colonial New England game tables.[2] Barnet's first wife, Mary Sinclair, who was also an artist, sits in a high-backed chair at the center of the composition flanked by the couple's older sons, Peter and Richard. Peter wears a billed cap and holds a baseball glove in one hand and a ball in the other, while Richard applies a firm grasp to a squirmy cat whose splayed legs suggest displeasure at being held up for inspection. The couple's youngest child, Todd, who is on the floor below or just in front of the table, lies atop a brightly patterned rug, his legs contorted in a vigorous kicking motion.

The painting's rosy-cheeked family group and its vibrant palette convey whimsy and good cheer. Yet the composition's tight cropping and exaggerated spatial compression suggest a closeness verging on unease. While the sense of claustrophobia in *Family and Pink Table* may reference Barnet's struggle to balance his growing family's needs with increasing professional obligations, the formal tensions are fundamentally a function of the artist's ongoing attempts to reconcile abstraction and figuration, form and space. The painting presents a veritable catalogue of his varied visual

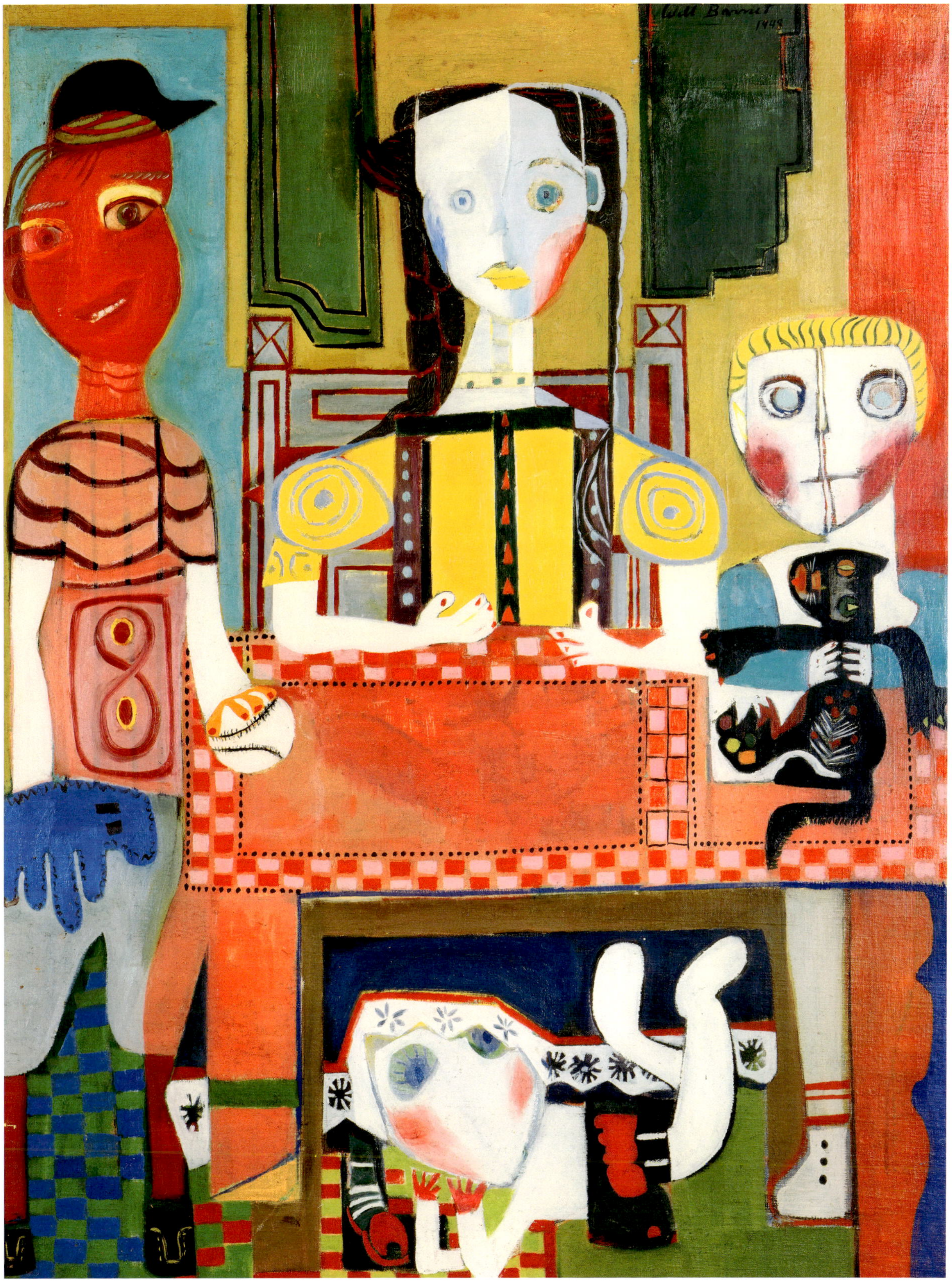
Will Barnet
1948

WILL BARNET (B. 1911)

Woman Reading

1965
Oil on canvas
44 × 35 in. (111.8 × 88.9 cm)
Promised Gift

sources: his own children's artwork, American folk portraits, forms and motifs from Native American cultures, and European cubism and surrealism, especially the work of Paul Klee, Joan Miró, and longtime friend Arshile Gorky (p. 234).

In the 1965 painting *Woman Reading*, completed nearly two decades after *Family and Pink Table*, Barnet reduced the theme of family to a single human figure: his second and present wife of nearly sixty years, Elena, who sits in bed reading accompanied by the couple's cat, Madame Butterfly. While the subject of the picture is intensely personal to the artist, he painted it using a highly controlled aesthetic. Barnet rendered Elena and the cat with a sureness, clarity, and grace of line that even the great French neoclassical painter Jean-Auguste-Dominique Ingres might envy.[3] The simplified and symmetrical composition, with its carefully weighted planes of flat color—red blanket, brown wall, white bedding, blue book—is nearly as minimal as contemporaneous color field paintings by Kenneth Noland (p. 268), Frank Stella, and Ellsworth Kelly. Stylistic associations aside, *Woman Reading* asserts the beauty and warmth inherent in simple forms and quiet pleasures. CBC

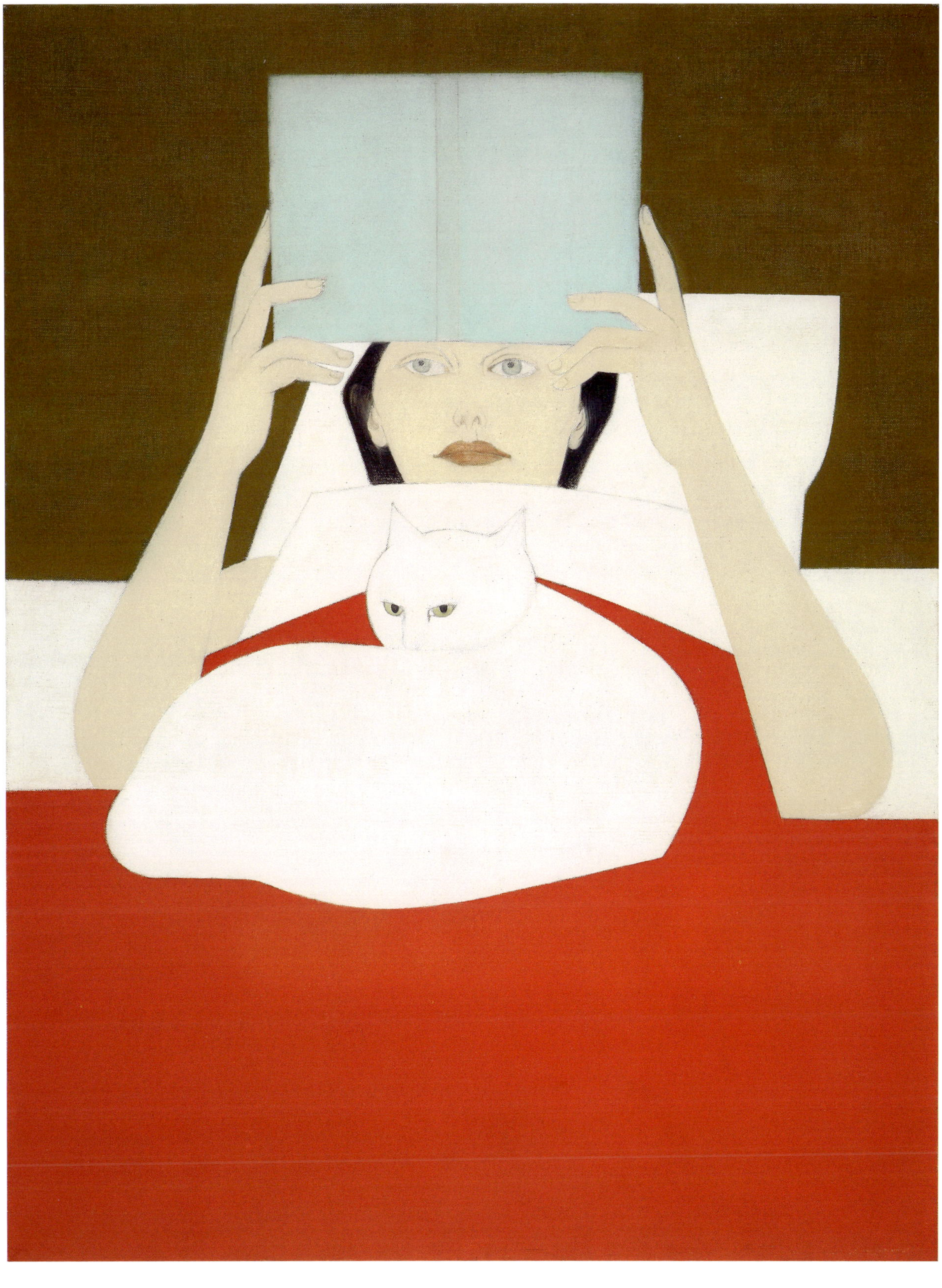

HANS HOFMANN (1880–1966)

Visione Nobilissima

1951
Oil on canvas
38 × 30 in. (96.5 × 76.2 cm)
Promised Gift

Hans Hofmann's *Visione Nobilissima* and *Sun at the Wall* (p. 261) are kindred images. Both are later works by the artist that display his full integration of seeming polar opposites: carefully designed, interlocking geometric shapes and thick swaths of forcefully applied, gestural color. These paintings exemplify Hofmann's belief that things acquire their identity by way of contrast; that is, in relation to their total environment. The artist conceived of painting as an arena in which some areas move forward in space while others retreat (the "push and pull" so common to color theory), and where energy is generated through the competing forces of accident and plan. Hofmann's ability to convey to generations of students a holistic and intellectual as well as a deeply spiritual approach to painting made him one of the most influential teachers in the history of American art.

Born and raised in Germany, Hofmann first encountered modern art in Paris during the years before World War I. Among the numerous and crucial influences of that period was the Paul Cézanne retrospective in 1907, an exhibition that demonstrated how color could provide the basis for creating form and space. A number of artists seized upon this essential observation, including the French abstract painters Robert and Sonia Delaunay, who befriended Hofmann and whose vibrant canvases had an impact on his work. The artist also embraced Wassily Kandinsky's mystical association of color with emotion, music, and other realms of reality. Indeed, color became the centrifugal force in Hofmann's mind and thus in his painting, as he moved from a brightly colored yet still representational style to one completely liberated from the constraints of depicting the natural world.

In 1915, Hofmann founded the Hans Hofmann School of Fine Arts in Munich, where he attracted his first American students. One of these students invited Hofmann to the United States in 1930

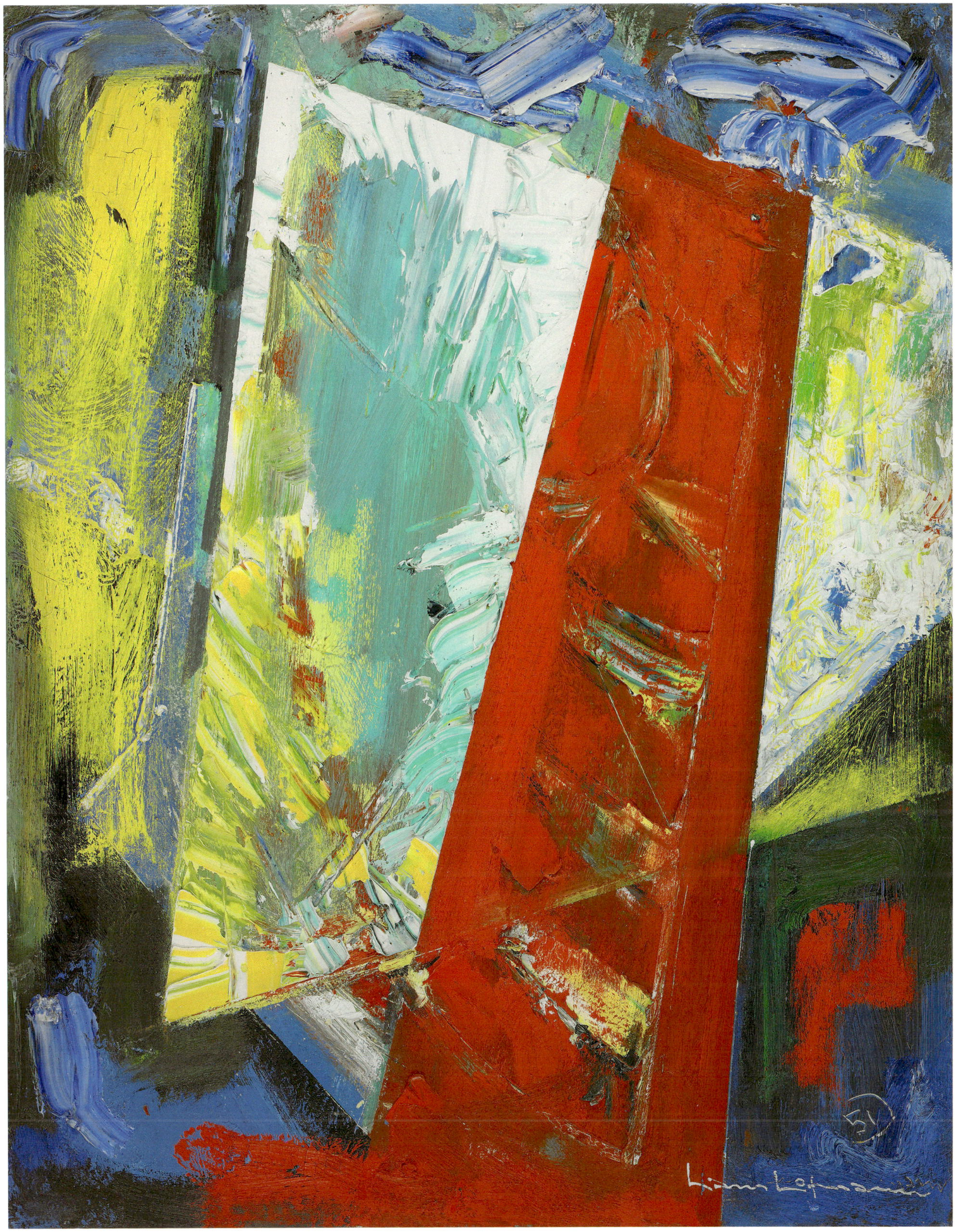

HANS HOFMANN (1880–1966)

Sun at the Wall

1962
Oil on canvas
48 × 36¼ in. (121.9 × 92.1 cm)
Promised Gift

to teach a summer session at the University of California, Berkeley, and, in the face of the rise of fascism in Germany, Hofmann remained in the States permanently, settling in New York City. There he established another school, where he taught advanced thinking about color to a new generation of American painters that included Lee Krasner, Helen Frankenthaler, Red Grooms, and Larry Rivers. His ideas thus came to pervade the work of the New York School and rippled out to the artists they in turn influenced. All the while, Hofmann relentlessly pursued his own experiments on the surface of the canvas, the space where he believed that all energies would ultimately find equilibrium.

In 1951, at age seventy-one, Hofmann painted *Visione Nobilissima*, the title of which refers to a ballet by the German composer Paul Hindemith. Hofmann retained a career-long fascination with the relationship between color and music, and surely the dark, pensive mood of Hindemith's ballet score informed the strident interactions of red, yellow, and blue within and against the picture's dark background. In 1962 Hofmann created his formidable visual poem *Sun at the Wall*. In this work he continued to explore the expressive potential of primary colors and shifting geometries, striving to achieve the balance of forces he believed could exist in a universe driven by opposites. Painted when the artist was eighty-two years old, *Sun at the Wall* is a testament to Hofmann's enduring creative power.

WS

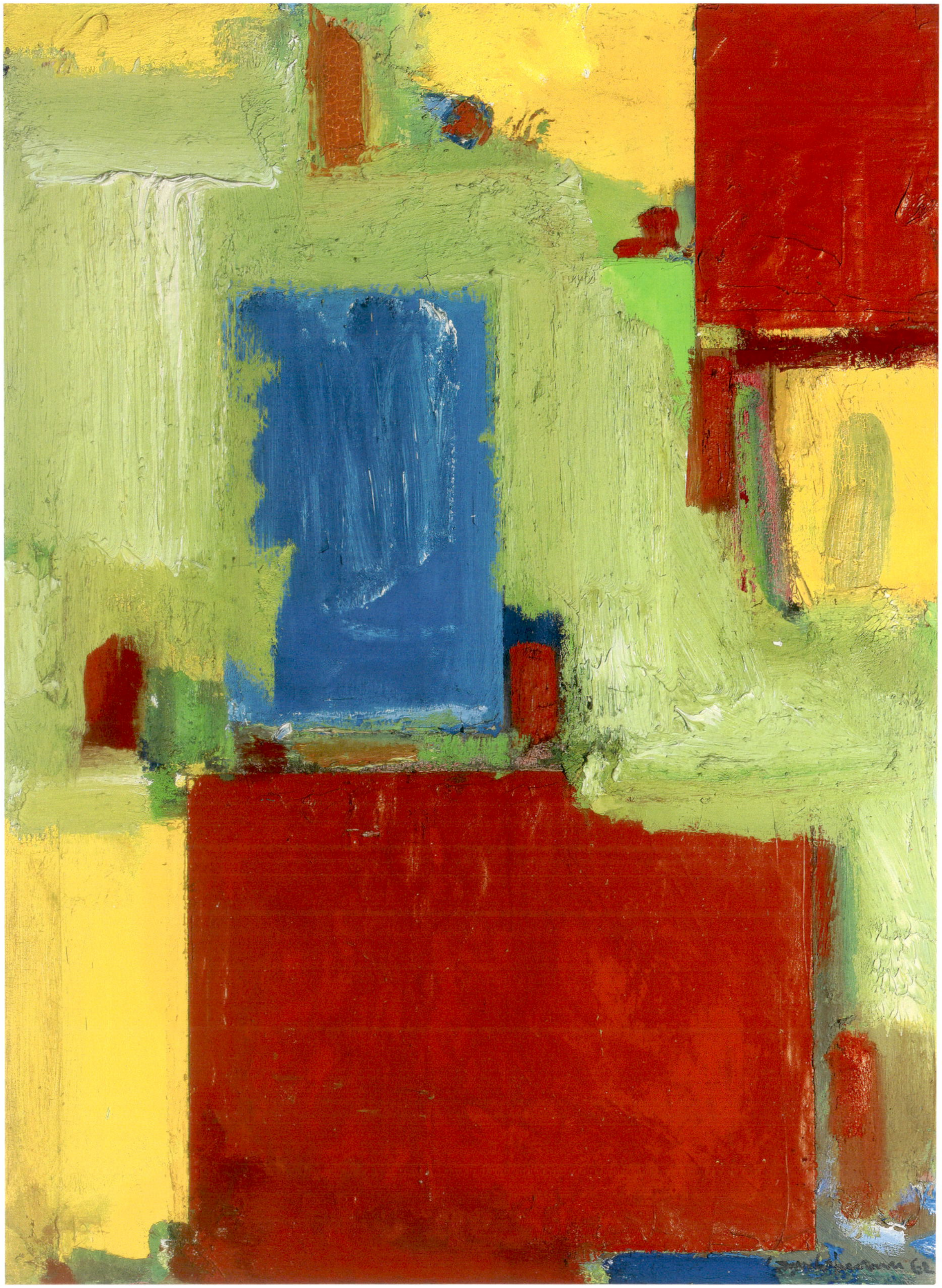

JOAN MITCHELL (1925–1992)

Untitled

1952–53
Oil on canvas
77½ × 71½ in. (196.9 × 181.6 cm)
Promised Gift

From their brazen refusal of harmonious resolution rises their blazing glory. —LINDA NOCHLIN[1]

Joan Mitchell's untitled painting of 1952–53 is an astonishingly mature example of abstract expressionism by an artist whose first exposure to the work of Jackson Pollock, Willem de Kooning, Franz Kline, and other leading members of the movement was just two years earlier. The Chicagoan arrived in New York in 1950 fresh from formal instruction at the Art Institute in her hometown as well as informal study in France, where she had spent as much time as possible looking at the cubists, especially Pablo Picasso, as well as Vincent van Gogh, Henri Matisse, and other School of Paris masters. An outsider by virtue of her Midwestern origins and (young) age as well as her gender, Mitchell's almost immediate acceptance into the abstract expressionists' inner circle was a measure of her precocious talent and fierce determination. Less than three years after arriving in New York she had earned a solo exhibition at the groundbreaking Stable Gallery; it was there that she debuted *Untitled*.[2]

Untitled insistently asserts its physicality as paint on canvas. Its meaning is located in manifold tensions held in uneasy equilibrium, a balance that is all the more compelling for its tenacious grace and sense of imminent dissolution. Whiteness is a crucial element in the composition. For Mitchell, the white of the thinly applied preparatory ground and the variety of white pigments applied to the canvas provided a neutral arena in which color and gesture could perform. Critics at the time associated these predominantly white abstractions marked by slashing and curvilinear gestures with Mitchell's involvement as a youth in competitive ice skating, a connection the painter found irrelevant.[3] The artist herself cited Piet Mondrian's early "plus-and-minus" renderings of trees and piers as precedents for her far more aggressive and irregular intersecting vertical and horizontal mark making.[4]

Beyond any biographical or art historical references, *Untitled* is a record of its facture. Thin dribbles of paint attest to the natural force of gravity as thinned pigment is applied to an upright canvas. Swathes of impasto (thick paint) create dams that retain passages of fluid pigment in some areas and release it in others. While the overall thrust of the canvas is vertical, emphasizing the orientation of the canvas, diagonal strokes and broad, horizontal slathers of paint push back or quietly meander into dissolution. Centripetal forces vie with overallness in a way that typifies Mitchell's mature work. The remarkably open feeling of the large painting is utterly at odds with its dense grid of surface incident, in which color, line, and gesture often collide with or meld into one another. From this moment forward, Mitchell's paintings staked out a territory of instability and immanence, of rage and lyricism, which was held not so much in balance but in an uneasy truce.

While her art is vehemently abstract, as it undoubtedly needed to be in the heady, early days of male-dominated abstract expressionism, Mitchell's work is never completely divorced from the natural world. In 1958, a few years after painting the Crystal Bridges canvas, Mitchell explained, "I paint from remembered landscapes that I carry with me—and remembered feelings of them, which of course become transformed. I could certainly never mirror nature. I would like more to paint what it leaves me with."[5] CBC

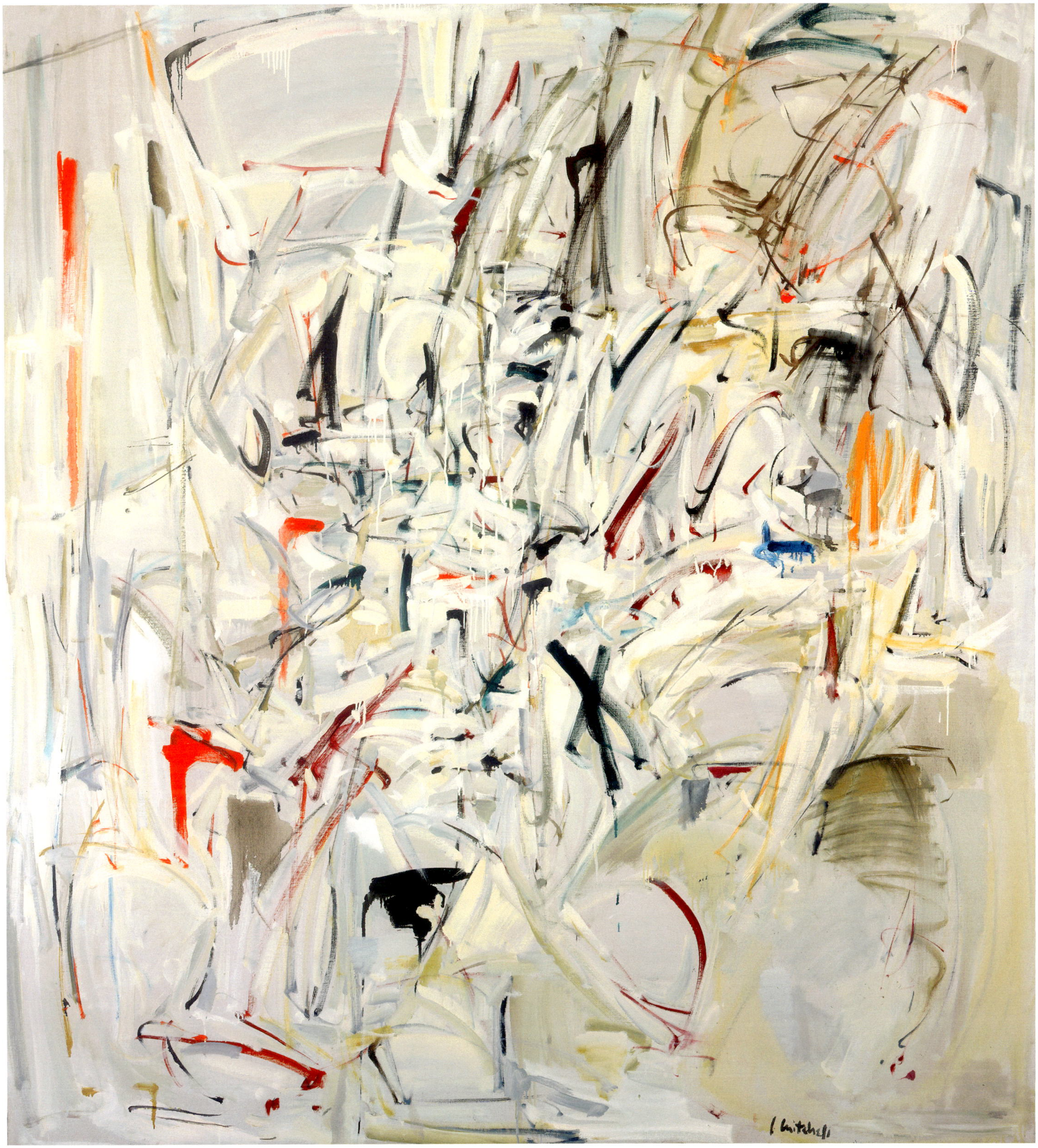

GRACE HARTIGAN (1922–2008)

Rough, Ain't It

1949
Oil and mixed media on canvas
40 × 54 in. (109.7 × 144.3 cm)
Promised Gift

Rough, Ain't It is among Grace Hartigan's earliest mature works in the style that has come to be known as abstract expressionism. Indeed, the painting and collage techniques in this densely layered image not only anticipate the early torn cardboard "combines" of proto-pop pioneer Robert Rauschenberg, but also pay homage to Jackson Pollock and Willem de Kooning, whom the young artist befriended shortly after her move to New York City in 1946. In retrospect, the painting appears to be a kind of Rosetta Stone of the varied styles and technical approaches adopted by the abstract expressionists in creating their new visual language. *Rough, Ain't It* synthesizes surrealist automatism with cubist collage, among other sources. For example, Hartigan applied sand to the painted canvas creating a physical "roughness" of surface, a play on the title of her work and a practice that both the cubist Georges Braque and the surrealist Andre Masson had earlier experimented with in their own paintings.[1] The skeins of cream-colored pigment in the upper third of the canvas suggest the pouring technique with which Pollock was then experimenting, while the vertical drips at the lower edge allude to De Kooning's contemporary canvases, which explore notions of chance and the gravitational pull of thinly applied paint on an upright canvas. *Rough, Ain't It* is as gritty, urban, and full of explosive creative energy as any work from this landmark period in the history of American art.

Until 1948, Hartigan signed her work "George Hartigan." She inscribed *Rough, Ain't It* with a more confident "Hartigan," still a hedging acknowledgment that dealers and critics would likely pay little attention to a fledgling female artist in a milieu dominated by older men. The painting suggests a variety of possible readings, but points most obviously to Hartigan's nearly isolated position as a young woman working in New York's nearly exclusively male art world. Hartigan deftly navigated the obstacles in her way: in 1950, the noted critics Meyer Shapiro and Clement Greenberg included

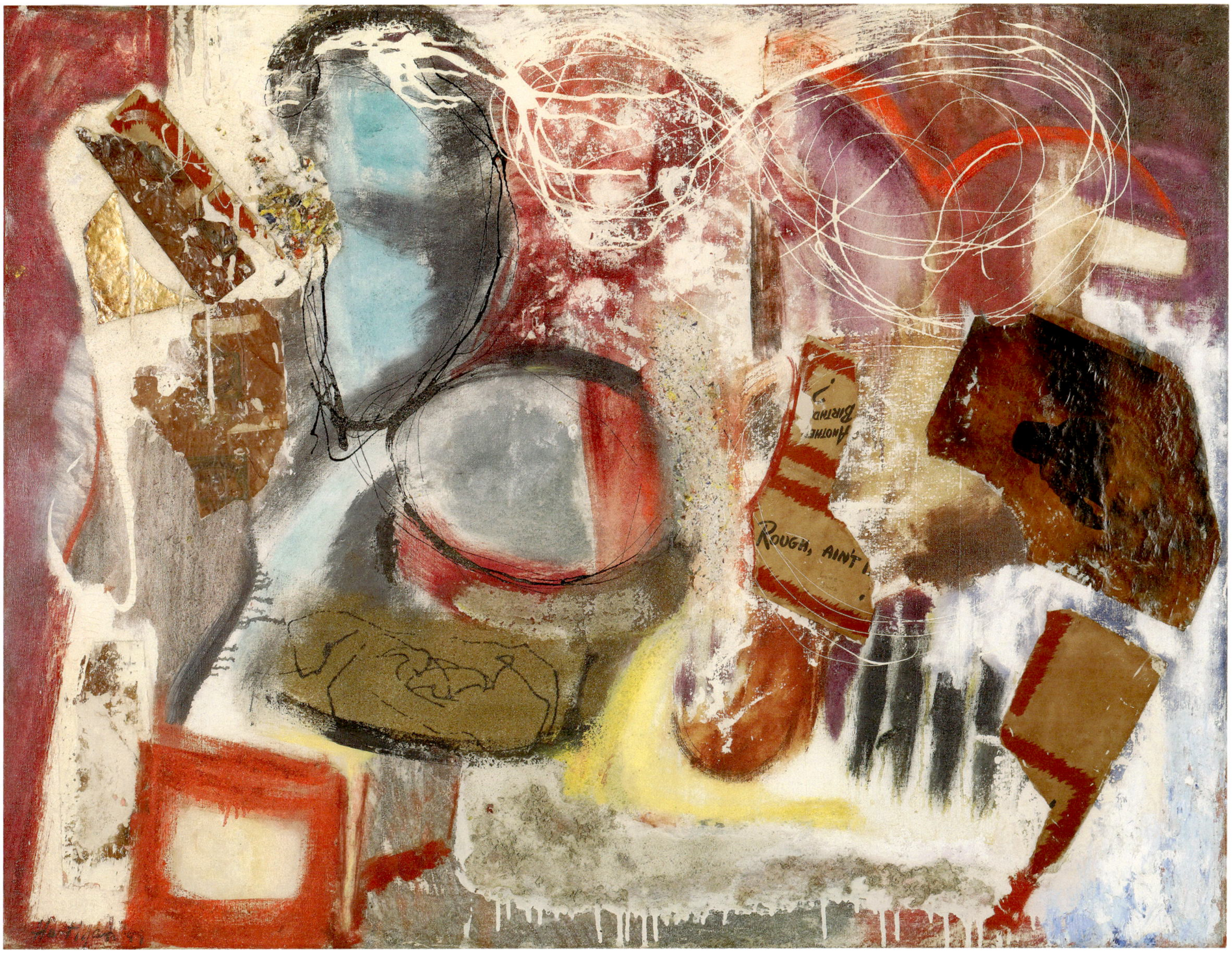
ROUGH, AINT

GRACE HARTIGAN (1922–2008)

Clark's Cove

1962
Oil on canvas
63½ × 71½ in. (161.3 × 181.6 cm)
Promised Gift

examples of her work in the important exhibition *New Talent* at the progressive Kootz Gallery in New York, and in 1958–59, Hartigan was the only female artist featured in the international touring exhibition *The New American Painting*, which introduced abstract expressionism to European audiences.

Synthesizing a specific landscape location with her early interest in the work of Henri Matisse and Milton Avery, Hartigan's 1962 canvas *Clark's Cove* is among the artist's most lyrical paintings of this period, when representation blended seamlessly with abstraction. The seclusion and natural beauty of Clark's Cove, today a popular wedding and honeymoon retreat near Boothbay, Maine, is celebrated in vibrant colors that capture the suddenness of the Maine spring. Indeed, the ecstatic, quivering blue lupine in the upper right quadrant seems to proclaim a rising, new vitality in Hartigan's art. The painting—intensely personal, as was all of her best work—may have reflected recent life changes, most significantly the troubled painter's fourth, last, and most successful marriage, in 1960 to Johns Hopkins University research scientist Winston Price. Although the couple's subsequent move to Baltimore distanced Hartigan from the New York art world, she found professional satisfaction as a beloved teacher at the Maryland Institute College of Art, where she founded the graduate school of painting in 1965. CBC

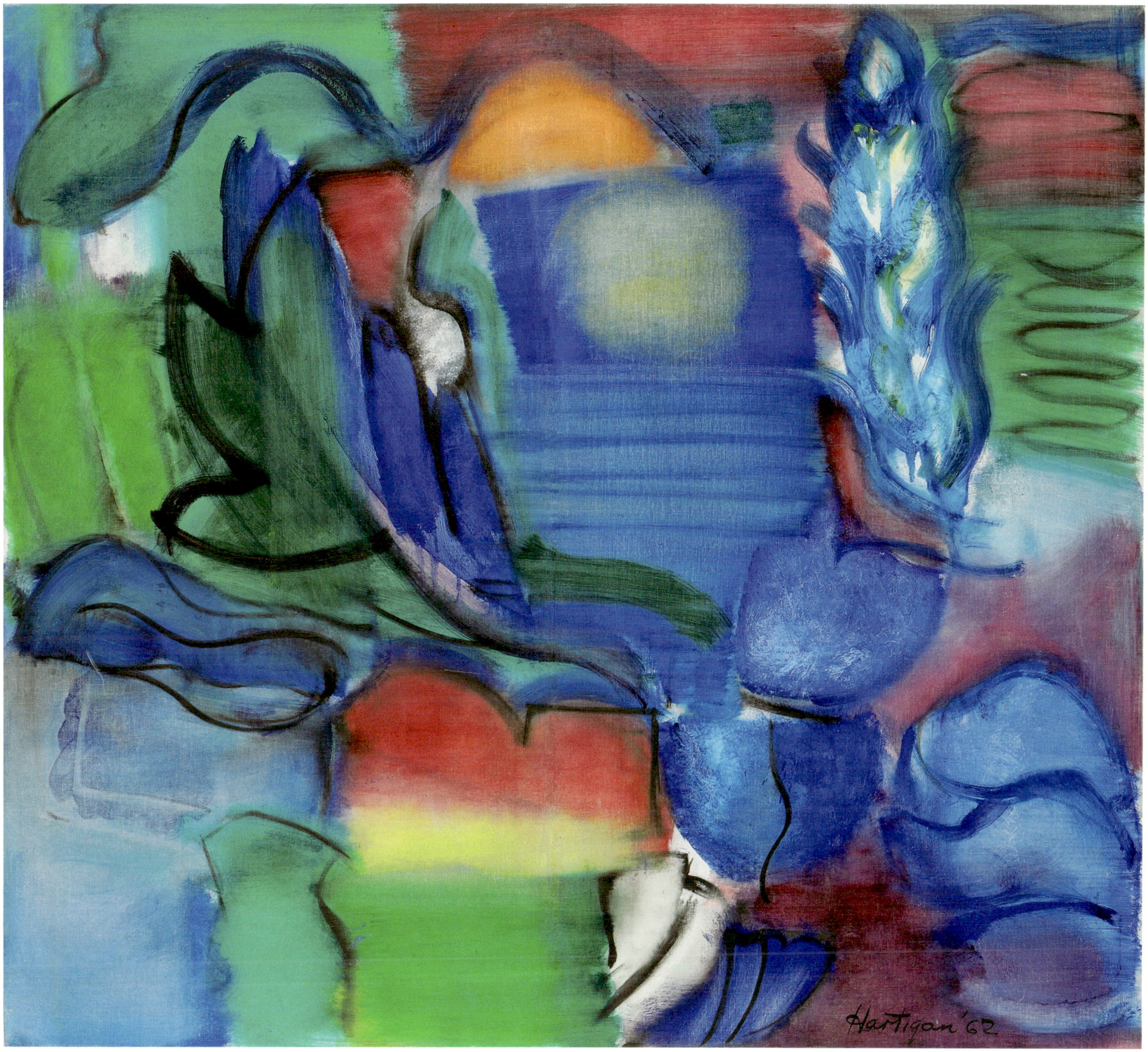
Hartigan '62

KENNETH NOLAND (1924–2010)

Round

1959
Acrylic on canvas
92 × 92 in. (233.7 × 233.7 cm)

Kenneth Noland's *Round* is one of a group of breakthrough paintings the artist created between 1956 and 1962. In this initial series of circle paintings, Noland rejected the work of his predecessors, the abstract expressionists, whose images he felt placed undue emphasis on the artist's persona as revealed by his or her hand and touch. In 1953, the prominent art critic Clement Greenberg had introduced Noland and his close friend Morris Louis to the painter Helen Frankenthaler, who often applied thin washes of pigment directly onto unprimed (bare) canvas. Noland and Louis found that Frankenthaler's innovative staining technique suited their cooler and more purely sensual aesthetic as well as provided the means to unify figure and ground, as color seeps into the very weave of the canvas.[1] A consummate craftsman, Noland was among the first artists to use the new acrylic-based pigments for staining, a technique that opened utterly new coloristic possibilities for large-scale abstract painting.[2]

Round is a transitional image that contains vestiges of abstract expressionist painterliness but also looks toward a new, more reticent style that celebrated color and nonreferential geometric form for their own sake. Here, as in many of his early circle paintings, Noland looked to reinvent the hedonism of Henri Matisse's color through geometry stripped to its bare essentials. The penumbras are painted with a kind of loose urgency, as if the spinning perimeter was brought to a sudden stop. Yet the highly circumscribed, circle-in-a-square format that Noland used for *Round* and other paintings of this period reflects his deepening desire to eliminate evidence of his own hand, focusing instead on simple shapes or forms and especially drawing attention to color as its own reason for existing.

Throughout his long career, Noland worked in series: circles, chevrons, horizontal stripes, plaids, and a variety of shaped-canvas formats with eccentric geometries that emphasized physicality and variability. In the circles (sometimes referred to as targets)—the first of these series—Noland experimented with how color seemed to breathe, expanding and contracting depending on size and placement as well as in relation to other canvases. Many of Noland's early circles are loosely painted images with swirling splotches of color that only approximate geometric figuration. The Crystal Bridges work, with its self-descriptive title, is among the first circles to truly be "round." Noland married his early art education with Josef Albers (p. 270) and especially Ilya Bolotowsky at Black Mountain College with his own highly intuitive but precisely measured shape-to-color calibrations. The artist's keen understanding of the effects of pure color and how physical size controls and directs peripheral vision is unsurpassed in the realm of pure, abstract painting.

A more poetic but not inconsistent view of his artistic contributions is offered by Jamaica Kincaid, one of Noland's close friends and admirers: "If on seeing the shape of an Orb, with its suggestion of the uncontrollable forced into stillness inside borders, we think of a creation narrative, our creation narrative, we are not entirely mistaken. . . . What is the nature of color? What is it that you see when color is forced to represent itself and not a likeness, when color is placed on a naked space, a space whose boundaries are determined by the imagination of the painter?"[3] CBC

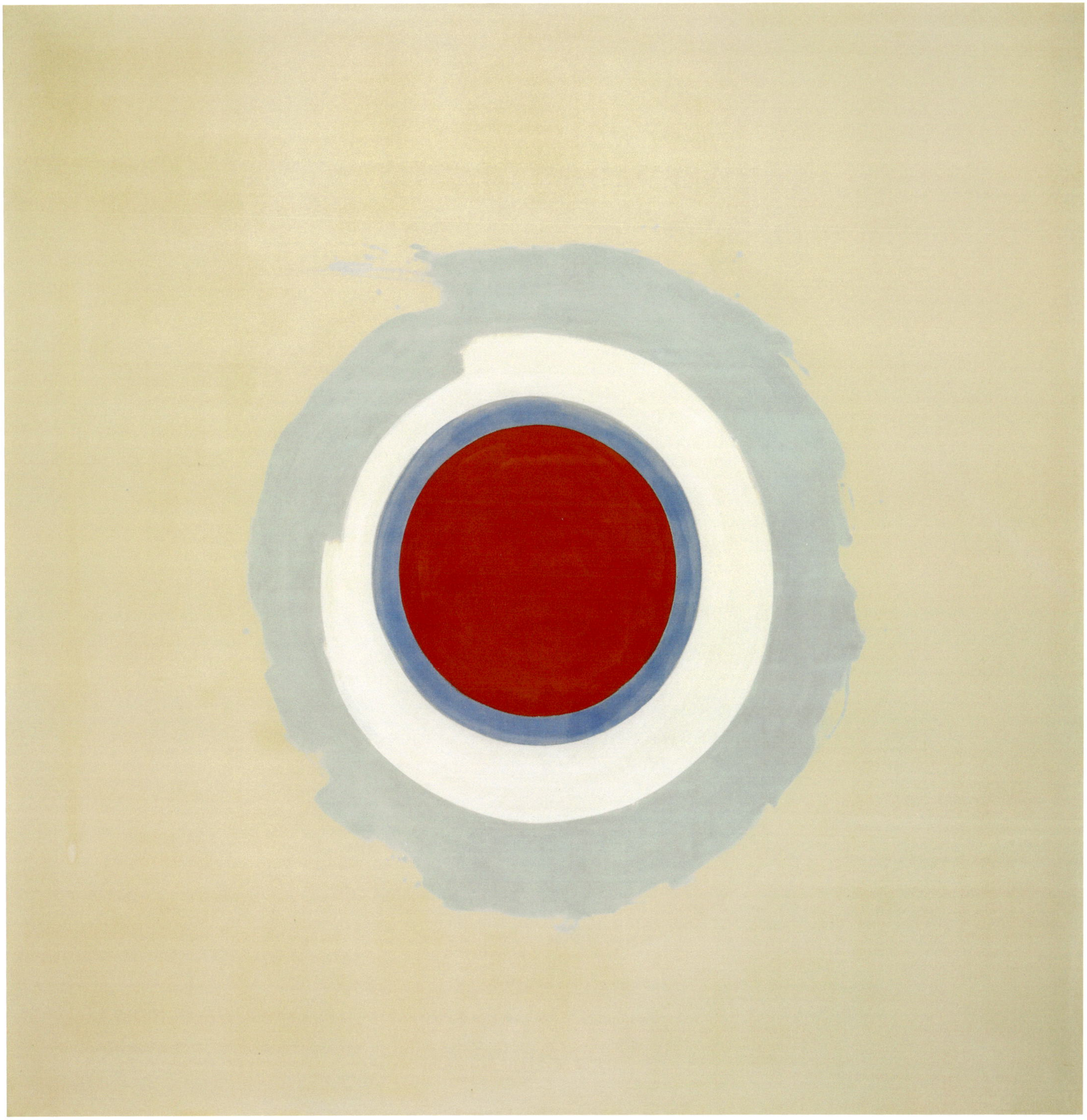

JOSEF ALBERS (1888–1976)

Homage to the Square: Joy

1964
Oil on board
48 × 48 in. (121.9 × 121.9 cm)
Promised Gift

Why paint a square? Because, for Josef Albers, the square is completely nonreferential. No one would confuse it with something in the natural world—a tree, a flower, or a cloud, for example. The square is neutral, depicting nothing but a mathematical relationship (four equal sides). However, the square shape can be a field of color, and squares nesting inside of one another create the possibility for colors to interact. Throughout his career, Albers's subject was simple yet infinitely complex: the act of seeing.

In 1950, Albers began a now famous series entitled *Homage to the Square*. He would ultimately make over a thousand of these works, none smaller than twelve-by-twelve inches and none larger than four-by-four feet. Each image repeated one of the artist's very few regular and strict formats. One might think this was a limiting and sterile approach, but the opposite was true for Albers. By using the same format over and over, he was liberated from concocting new compositions or conceiving new themes; his subject was always the complexities of color and our own shifting perceptions of it. The square-within-a-square-within-a-square format may appear overly mathematical, but Albers's choice of color within it was purely intuitive. As he explained in his influential 1963 book *The Interaction of Color*, an experimental teaching aid for students, artists, and designers, "What counts here—first and last—is not so-called knowledge of so-called facts, but vision—seeing."[1] For Albers, the faculty of sight was in constant need of exercise and examination, which in turn led to deeper understandings of relationships of all kinds.

Albers had always been an educator. The German-born artist taught at the Bauhaus, in Dessau, from 1925 until 1933, when Adolf Hitler's National Socialist Party closed the school. He then came to America, where he first taught at the experimental college in Black Mountain, North Carolina, and subsequently at Yale University, where he was chair of the department of design. Albers wrote of teaching, "Making ourselves and others grow . . . is one of the highest human tasks."[2]

Homage to the Square: Joy is a testament to Albers's austere but effective didactic methods in that it faithfully manifests his dictum: "Do less in order to get more."[3] Each color in the composition is flat and smooth, each touches another yet remains clearly distinct, and each is affected by the order in which the artist placed it. The innermost square is a vibrant yellow; the square that encloses it a slightly darker value; the third square significantly darker, but still a relatively light brown; and, finally, the outermost square is a deep, rusty orange. The only color here that appears to be purely saturated is the innermost yellow; all the others are tonalities (mixtures of primary colors). The principal purpose of these outer tonalities is to amplify and reinforce the lightness and autonomy of the central yellow square, by way of contrast.

The subtitle of this painting, *Joy*, may relate to the unfettered beauty of yellow in its primary state, which we recognize most fully in relation to the shifting variants near it. Indeed, yellow may have been for Albers the chromatic equivalent of happiness, as seeing was, for him, coupled with fantasy and imagination in addition to artistry and optics. WS

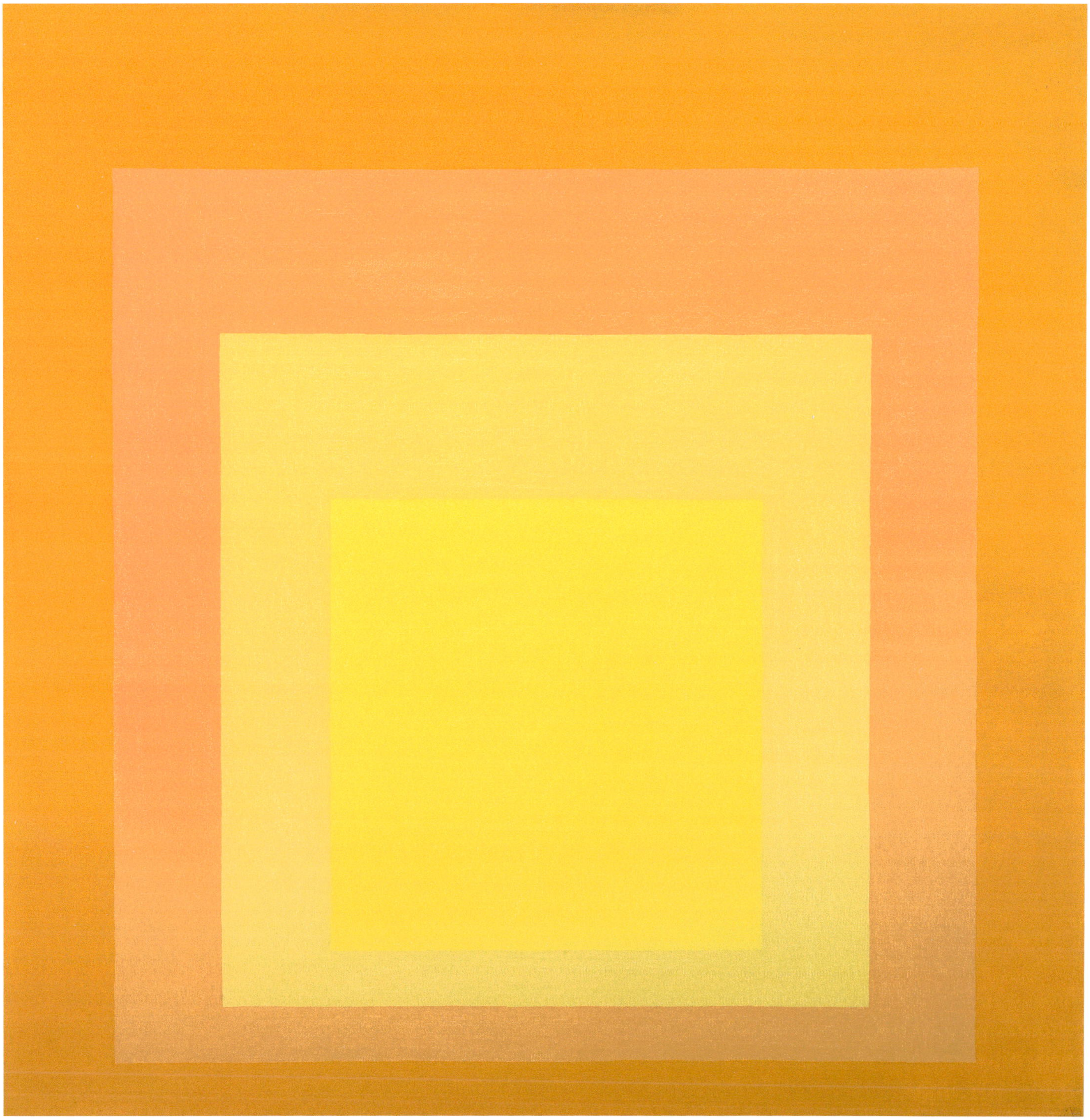

JOHN KOCH (1909–1978)

Studio—End of Day

1961
Oil on canvas
60 × 60 in. (152.4 × 152.4 cm)

John Koch's work does not fit comfortably into the usual, sequential narratives of post–World War II American art, where abstract expressionism begat pop, which begat minimalism, which begat the next great thing. Instead, Koch traveled his own, private path, parallel to yet distinct from that of the nation's artistic mainstream. The painter's first and only major retrospective exhibition was mounted nearly a quarter century after his death, not by an art museum but by the New-York Historical Society.[1] In a way, that makes perfect sense. Koch's work documents an era of intellectual life on the Upper West Side of Manhattan that was exquisitely inhabited by his closest friends and associates. These individuals were mostly writers, musicians, and poets. Many of them were well known, and all of them were artistically literate and consummate craftspeople in their chosen fields. In his numerous paintings of gatherings in the elegant apartments of these members of the New York cognoscenti, Koch vividly captured the tinkling sparkle of fine crystal and the soft evanescence of urbane small talk.

An important subgenre of Koch's work focuses on the artist's own creative endeavors. In *Studio—End of Day,* the artist painted his self-portrait at left, and, at right, the likeness of a striking African American woman recently identified as Rosetta Brooks, an actress and model who posed for Koch and several of his contemporaries.[2] Brooks is the subject of the large painting and related small drawing on Koch's easel. By depicting her in the intimate, workaday activity of getting dressed after a modeling session, Koch draws attention to Brooks as an individual as well as a professional. He also implies that making a painting is an open-ended process that involves collaboration between artist and subject. Yet another implied relationship is that between the artist and his audience. While Koch does not greet the viewer directly, he turns his body outward in a subtle invitation to enter his private world.

Koch often references art historical antecedents, from Rembrandt van Rijn to Diego Velázquez to Édouard Manet. Many of his paintings, perhaps most especially *Studio—End of Day*, are clearly indebted to the seventeenth-century Dutch master Jan Vermeer. The canvas's immaculate brushwork leaves no trace of the artist's hand. Light appears to emanate from deep within the image, a phenomenon that owes much to Koch's laborious technique of building up many layers of paint. Koch was keenly interested in the varied sources and qualities of light. The window on the far left admits a cool, white, natural light that rhymes with the warm, yellow, artificial glow coming through the open door at the far right.

Koch was a representational painter, but his was a selective realism that subordinated transcriptive accuracy to compositional needs, mood, and poetic content. For example, the dog looking out of the window and, perhaps, forward to its late afternoon walk—a touch of domestic routine familiar to many New Yorkers—is fiction; Koch did not have a dog. The position of the bed and the artist's easel, moreover, presents a visual conundrum. In order to see and accurately record his model, the easel would have had to be placed much farther away. And do women normally begin dressing with their shoes? Heels and the male gaze are perhaps another story embedded in Koch's elegant, deceptively real world of art that is also the painter's deft illusion of "how life should be lived."[3] CBC

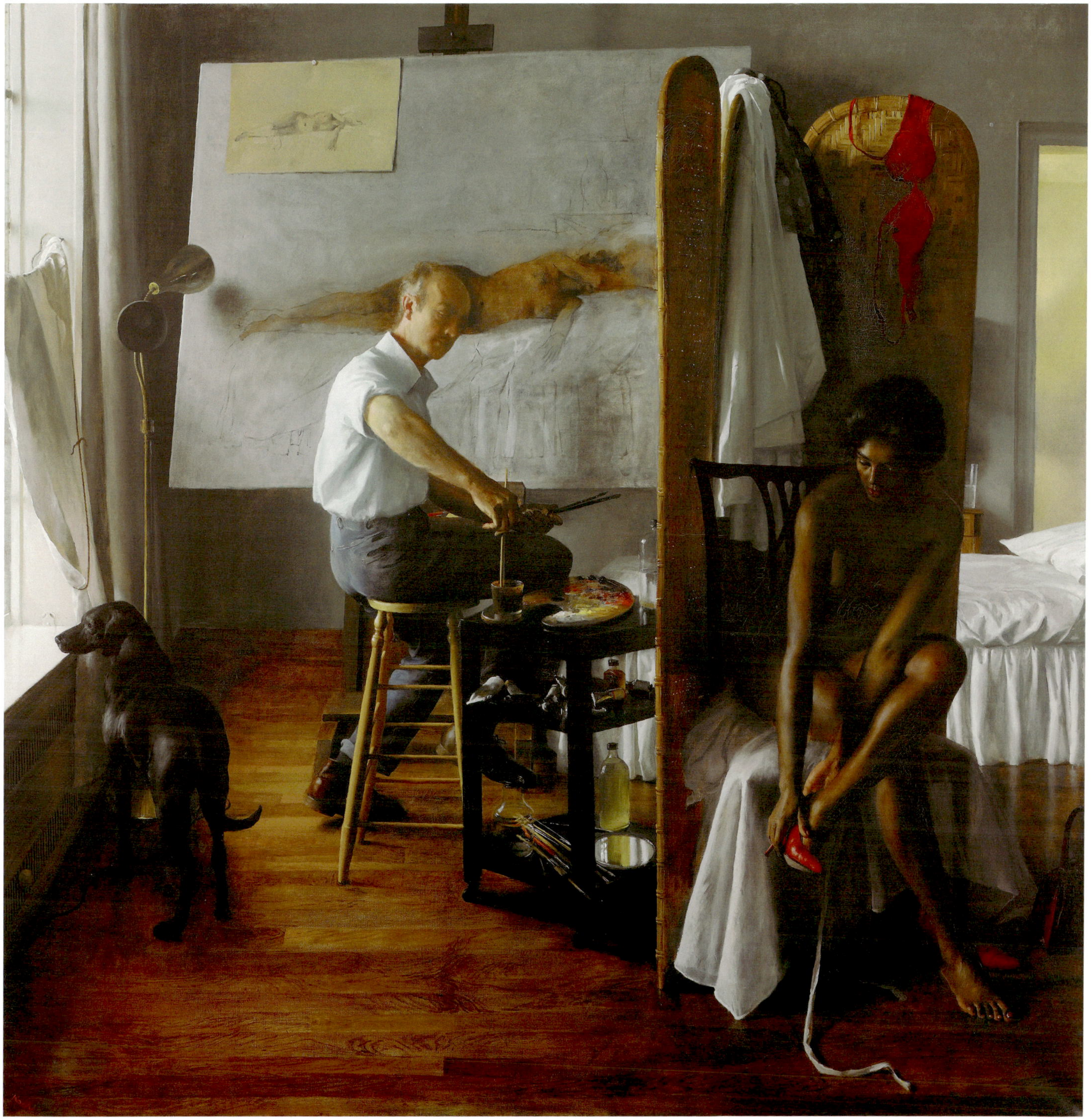

FAIRFIELD PORTER (1907–1975)

October Interior

1963
Oil on canvas
56 × 72 in. (142.2 × 182.9 cm)

On clear, bright afternoons in the village of Southampton, New York—the sort of afternoons one frequently experiences in October—the elm and maple leaves that fill the streets and yards become beautifully translucent. Even as the days grow shorter and the sun sinks southward in the sky, the sharply slanting light suggests something so beautiful as to be eternal.

The noted American realist painter Fairfield Porter's 1963 *October Interior* is set in the sparsely furnished sunroom of the artist's Federal-era home at 49 South Main Street, in Southampton. Porter faced directly into the light to paint his picture. His older daughter, Katie, sits to the right, turning outward to watch her father work, while in the left background, across the narrow lawn outside, Porter's younger daughter, Liz, plays by the swing set. In the center of the sunroom between two patio chairs is a low, square table topped with potted houseplants, and before it a child's rocking horse.

The brilliant, highly keyed marine light of Southampton, reflected and refracted by the nearby ocean and salt pond, permeates the trees, shrubs, and grasses outside, washing through windows and doorways and spreading warmly over the sunroom floor. In his rendering of the houseplants and foliage, Porter's brushwork verges on painterly abstraction. Yet these vibrant, nearly chaotic passages of color are held firmly in check by the ordering symmetry of the three vertical windows and the alternating patches of light and shadow on the stabilizing monochrome of the floor. The lower portion of the far wall, meanwhile, again presents a series of variations of colored light—from hot pink to lilac to yellow ochre—that describe the adjustments the eye makes as it negotiates sunlight head-on. In painting this particular room at a particular time of day Porter challenged the boundary between abstraction and representation, but he did so in a way that seems entirely lyrical and natural.

Katie's languid pose—perhaps she is bored?—contrasts sharply with the upright form of the wooden rocking horse, which—with its bright white body and its shiny carmine bridle and saddle—claims pride of place in the room in a way that seems to suggest that this painting is as much about the absence of children as it is about light and space. Yet little Liz, out of doors in the distance, is almost abstractly rendered. Although the two girls appear in the painting, they are hardly its focus. Porter seems more interested in color harmonies, the interplay of interior and exterior sensation, and the telling nature of the domestic space itself. All here is warm and still, in contrast to the sharply flickering, folial sunlight outside.

In its exploration of interior and exterior realities, and in its oblique, elegiac reference to home, family relationships, and the passing of time, this daring painting takes the colorful, intimate interiors of the French post-impressionist Pierre Bonnard as a starting point. But Porter expands this aesthetic outward into the larger, airier, more gestural visual explorations of the abstract expressionist Willem de Kooning. The result is a distinctly American painting firmly rooted in place, poetic and vibrantly alive in its expressive rendering of space, color, and light.

JDS

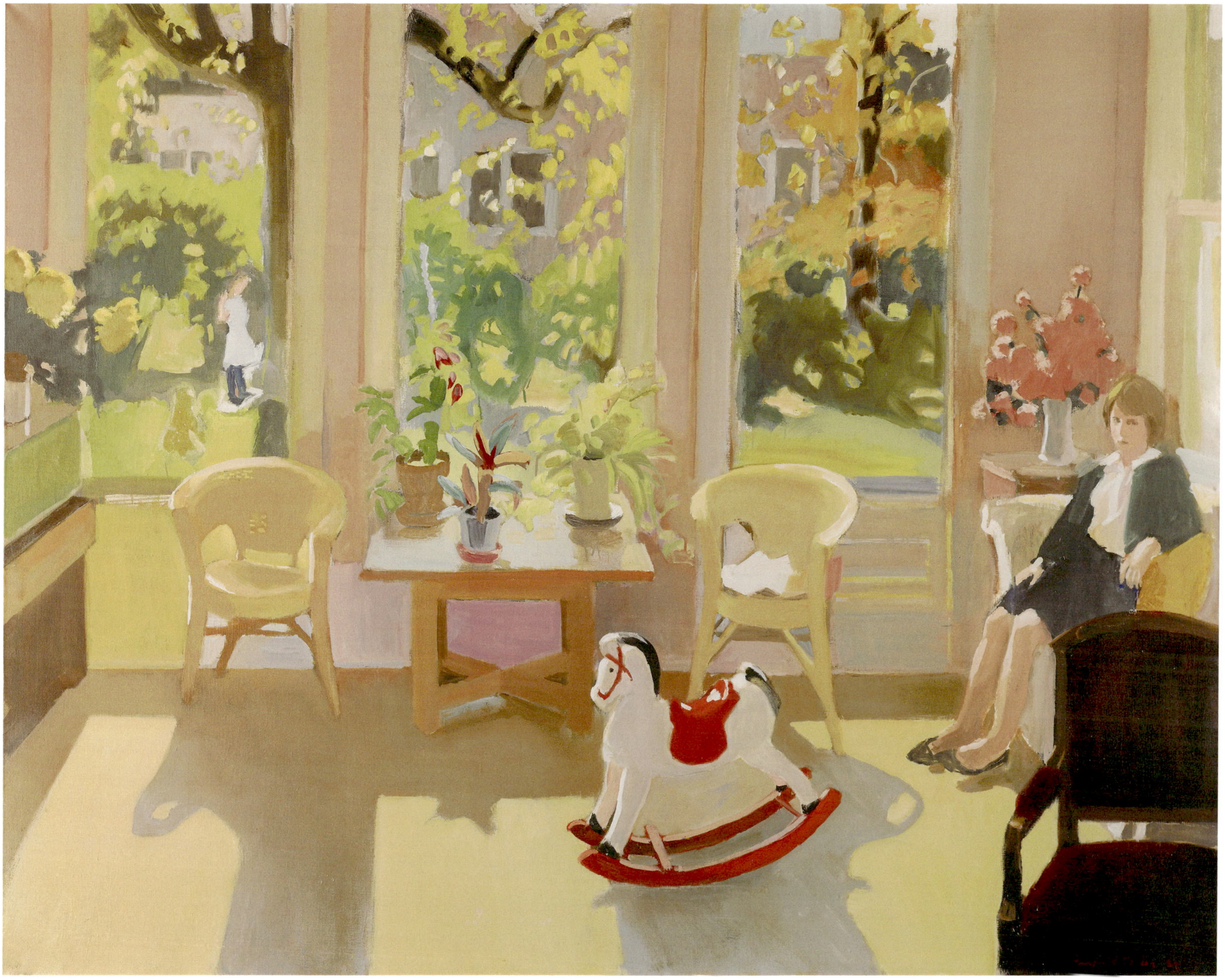

ROBERT RAUSCHENBERG (1925–2008)

Untitled

1963
Oil, graphite, and silkscreen ink on canvas
40½ × 52 in. (102.9 × 132.1 cm)

Painting relates to both art and life. . . . I try to act in that gap between the two. —ROBERT RAUSCHENBERG[1]

Robert Rauschenberg played a pivotal role in the development of American art after World War II. The art world of the late 1940s and early 1950s had been dominated by the grand gestures and larger-than-life personas of the abstract expressionists. Artists such as Jackson Pollock and Willem de Kooning created images in which their bold, expressive marks were understood to be records of their inner lives—painting as revelation. Younger artists like Rauschenberg and Jasper Johns attacked the cult of personality promulgated by the New York School. Juxtaposing the highly lauded gestural brushstroke with modes of representation drawn from mass culture, they challenged viewers to assess which manner of image making more effectively conveyed meaning.[2] Rauschenberg and Johns are credited with both reviving an interest in dada and surrealism and with paving the way for the development of pop art in the 1960s.

Rauschenberg spent the 1950s experimenting with novel ways to narrow the gap between art and life, bringing commonplace images and materials into his work through methods including collage, assemblage, and transfer drawing. In 1962, he began to silkscreen photographic images into his compositions.[3] The following year he produced *Untitled*, a painting dominated by an anonymous photograph of a contemporary urban street scene. Unlike Rauschenberg's earlier assemblages and "combines," in which the artist assembled multiple small images and objects into larger, fragmentary wholes, here a single black-and-white candid shot occupies the entire canvas. In contrast to Rauschenberg's earlier picture-making techniques, silkscreen allowed the artist to render any given image in any given scale.

In *Untitled*, the enlarged, silkscreened snapshot serves as the ground onto which Rauschenberg applied additional layers of signification, including discrete passages of dripping paint, scumbled washes, stenciled letters of various sizes, and some apparent rubbings or erasures. Photographic and hand-drawn images become nearly indistinguishable. A "one way" street sign that is part of the photograph points at and is balanced by an upside-down cruciform shape drawn in graphite across the painted surface. A rectangular Coca-Cola sign in the upper right of the photograph is mirrored at left by an array of applied uppercase letters that suggest words ("Strange" or "X-change" or even "Sex Change").

Confronted with the large, sign-filled photograph and hints of readable language, the viewer cannot help but search for narrative meaning. Yet the sheer number and diversity of marks and signs in the picture frustrate this enterprise, leading the viewer down a series of interpretive dead ends. A restless and prolific image maker, Rauschenberg created pleasingly composed and visually enticing works that rarely cohered into a traditional meaning or story. Ultimately, Rauschenberg succeeded in focusing his viewers' attention on the complex interplay between art and life, opening up myriad possibilities for future generations of artists. DB

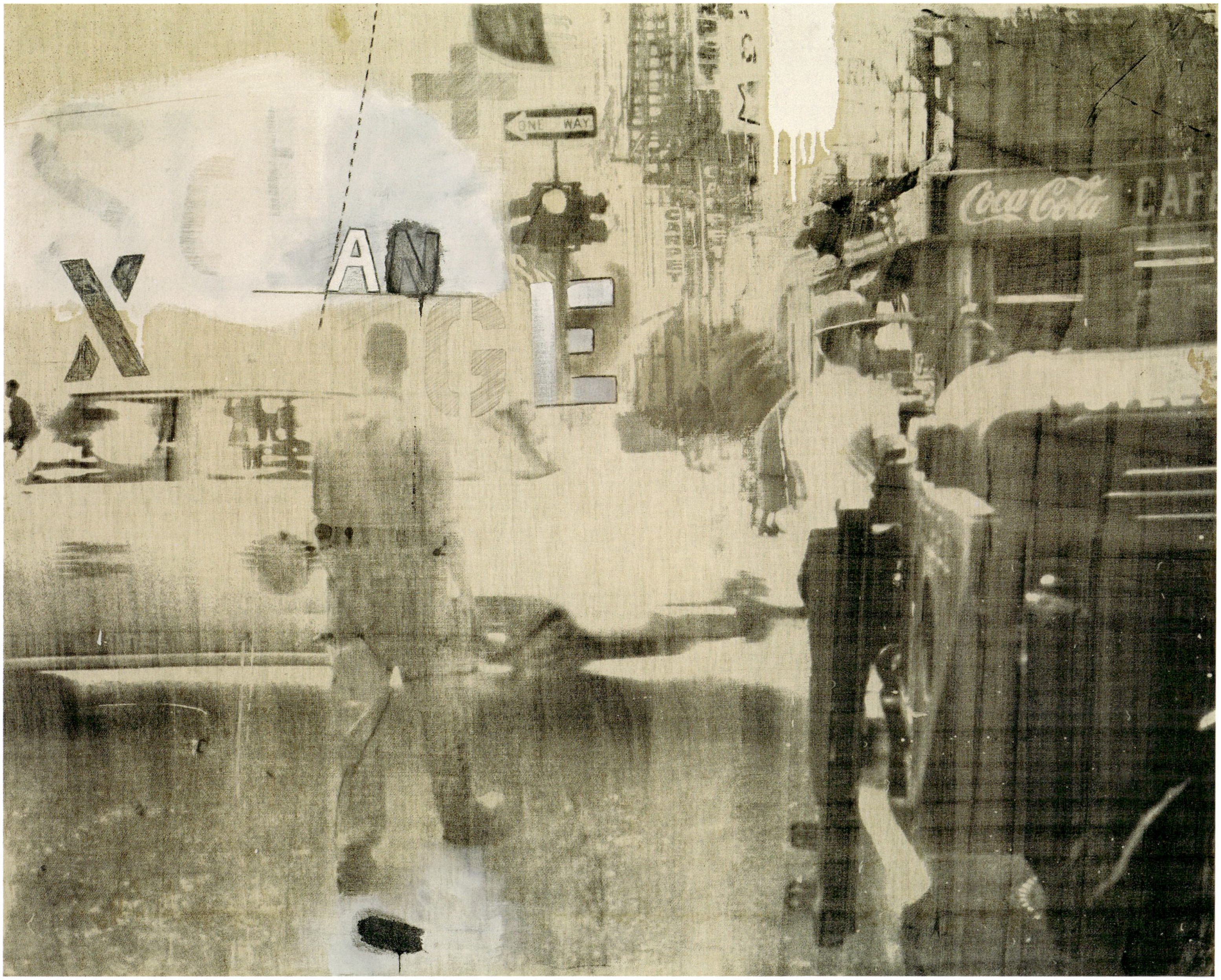
ONE WAY
Coca-Cola

WAYNE THIEBAUD (B. 1920)

Supine Woman

1963
Oil on canvas
36 × 72 in. (91.4 × 182.9 cm)

On the occasion of the artist's earliest exhibition, in 1961, the critic Alfred Frankenstein surmised that Wayne Thiebaud must be "the hungriest artist in California," alluding not to the painter's ambitions but rather to his favored choice of subject matter—delectable prepared foods, especially sweet and decorated desserts.[1] While his early fame depended on these iconic treats, Thiebaud has constantly—if sporadically—pursued other subjects throughout his half-century career. He has long been devoted to the California landscape, for example, especially in its steep hillside terrains, and, from 1962 forward, to the human figure.

In approaching the figure, Thiebaud often chooses subjects attired provocatively or placed in social situations considered titillating or scandalous. Raised as a Mormon, perhaps it was the scantily clad, body-obsessed types that stood out to the young artist in his early years in Southern California. However, Thiebaud drains these subjects of any trace of sensuality or sexuality, instead focusing on them as purely objective forms. The figure is isolated on a simple, unarticulated ground. He or she makes no readable facial expression or bodily gesture. Devoid of personal idiosyncrasy or identifiable likeness, the figure is a subject simply to be observed and painted.

In *Supine Woman*, one of Thiebaud's earliest figural works, the title subject lies stiffly on a blank field of white paint. She stares straight up with an uninflected gaze, and her white dress—while modern and fashionable—reveals little of the body beneath it. Thiebaud upends a centuries-old tradition of painting the reclining female by not subjecting his subject to any of the trappings of art history. She is not identified as an individual, goddess, or mythological being. She is not naked, nor does she present her body or herself for the viewer's appraisal. She reveals nothing of her emotional or psychic state. This *Supine Woman* simply *is*, on canvas at least. Thiebaud describes "a kind of existential tradition" that he seeks to follow. He rejects a history of figure painting wherein "[the] figures seem to have a reason for looking the way they do and acting the way they do . . . they're either posing for their portrait or they're making love or making war or doing something specific." He prefers painting a "direct encounter with the figure as it exists," without allusion to the subject's life beyond the present moment.[2]

As in all of Thiebaud's most accomplished works, the surface of *Supine Woman* is dazzlingly rich with thickly applied paint and features his signature "halation" (brightly colored and contrasting halos surrounding the figure). Often associated with Bay Area figurative painters like Richard Diebenkorn, Thiebaud's approach to his subjects is both masterful and uniquely his own. DB

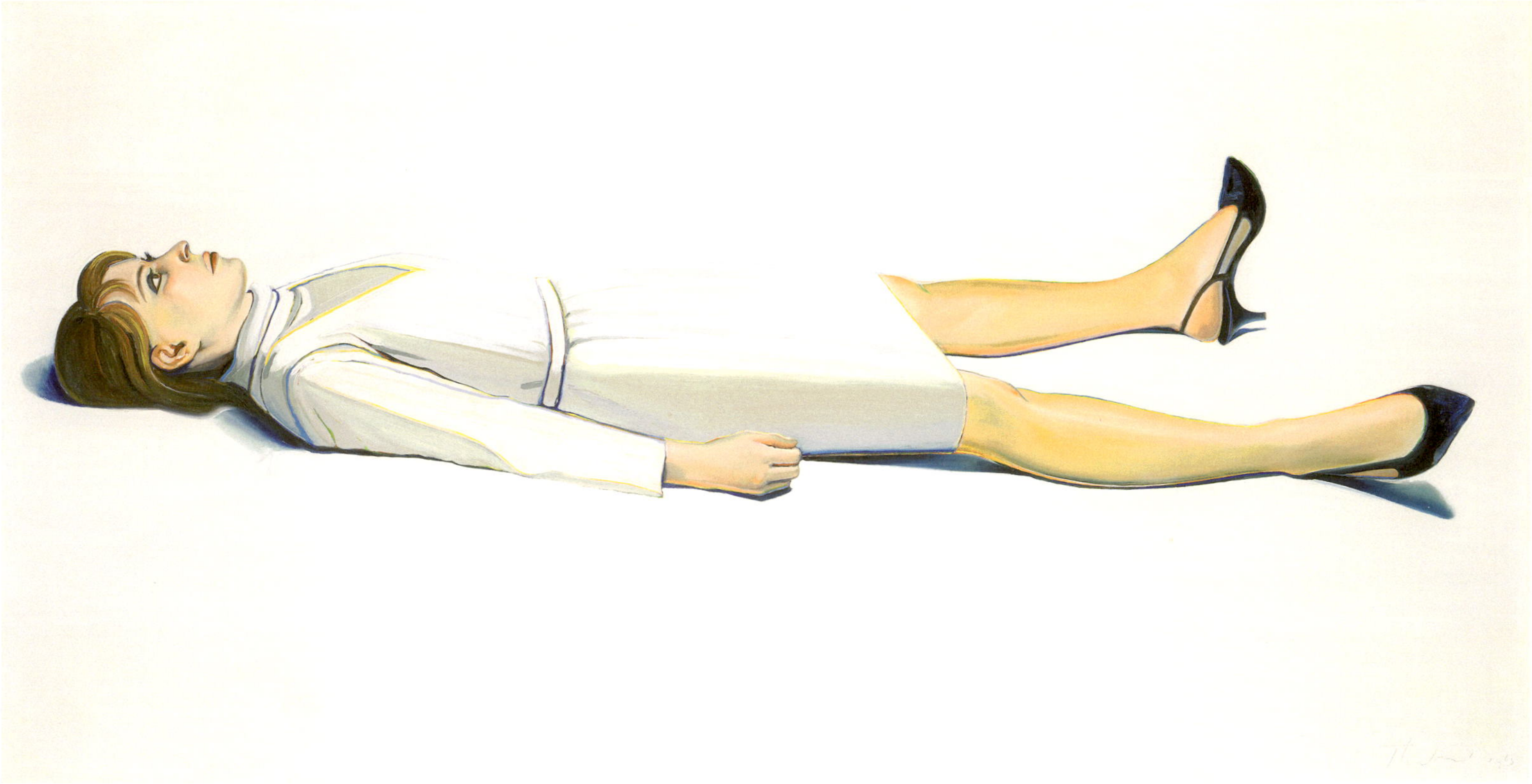

ANDY WARHOL (1928–1987)

Dolly Parton

1985
Synthetic polymer paint and silkscreen ink on canvas
42 × 42 in. (106.7 × 106.7 cm)

A central figure in the pop art movement and one of the most recognized artists of the twentieth century, Andy Warhol captivated the public with his unabashed embrace of commercialism, the media, and celebrity. Using a distinctive painting style that drew from and emulated the look of mass-market imagery, Warhol depicted a wide range of subjects that reflected postwar America's economic prosperity and vibrant consumer culture, from Campbell's soup cans to supermarket tabloids to popular culture icons such as the country music star Dolly Parton.

Warhol began his professional career as an illustrator and graphic artist working for magazines and department stores. During the early 1960s, he developed a pioneering painting technique derived from silkscreen printing that challenged the distinctions between commercially produced images and fine art. An alternative to the gestural brushwork and emotional intensity of abstract expressionism, Warhol's depersonalized, reproductive method of image making, combined with his appropriation of iconography from mass culture, resulted in a novel manifestation of art as commodity.

Warhol began painting commissioned portraits in the mid-1960s. Portraiture quickly became a central theme of his work, and by the mid-1970s, Warhol's clientele included an exclusive list of internationally recognized celebrities. The process of making these iconic likenesses began with a photograph. From 1970 until his unexpected death in 1987, Warhol photographed hundreds of people, both famous and anonymous. His camera of choice was the Polaroid SX-70 Big Shot, a model that was designed to create highly focused, close-up portraits. The artist would conduct an unstructured photo shoot, taking numerous pictures of his sitter, which he called his "sketches." Warhol would eventually select one of these exposures as the basis for his portrait, enlarging the photographic image to the dimensions of a pre-painted, monochromatic canvas and transferring it to the canvas by means of silkscreen (a commercial printing technique that involves pressing ink through a fine screen with areas blocked off by a stencil).[1] The artist's standardized portrait format and highly regimented image-making process resulted in a series of likenesses that simultaneously deified their diverse subjects and rendered them all equivalent.

Dolly Parton is an unexpected and unforgettable portrait of one of America's queens of country music.[2] A teased halo of silver locks and a pair of gold, teardrop-shaped earrings frame the angelic face of America's favorite female country-and-western songwriter and performer. Perhaps in a nod to Byzantine religious icons crafted of precious metals, Warhol extended the silvery color field beyond the natural boundaries of Parton's features, elevating her status to that of an idol. The painting's surface flatness and its palette of cool colors reconfigure her relaxed gaze as a glamorous stare. Indeed, the luscious red of Parton's well-defined lips and the vibrant green that sharply delineates her eyebrows and irises draw attention to the highly constructed nature of a public persona.

Immortalized on canvas among an international company of superstars, Warhol's *Dolly Parton* inaugurates the "Dogpatch Diva" into The Factory hall of fame.[3] What distinguished Warhol from his artistic peers was the connection his mass culture–informed pictures made with the general public. He offered his viewers accessible, widely recognizable subject matter and provoked them to ask the difficult questions: What is art? Who is an artist?

AWJ

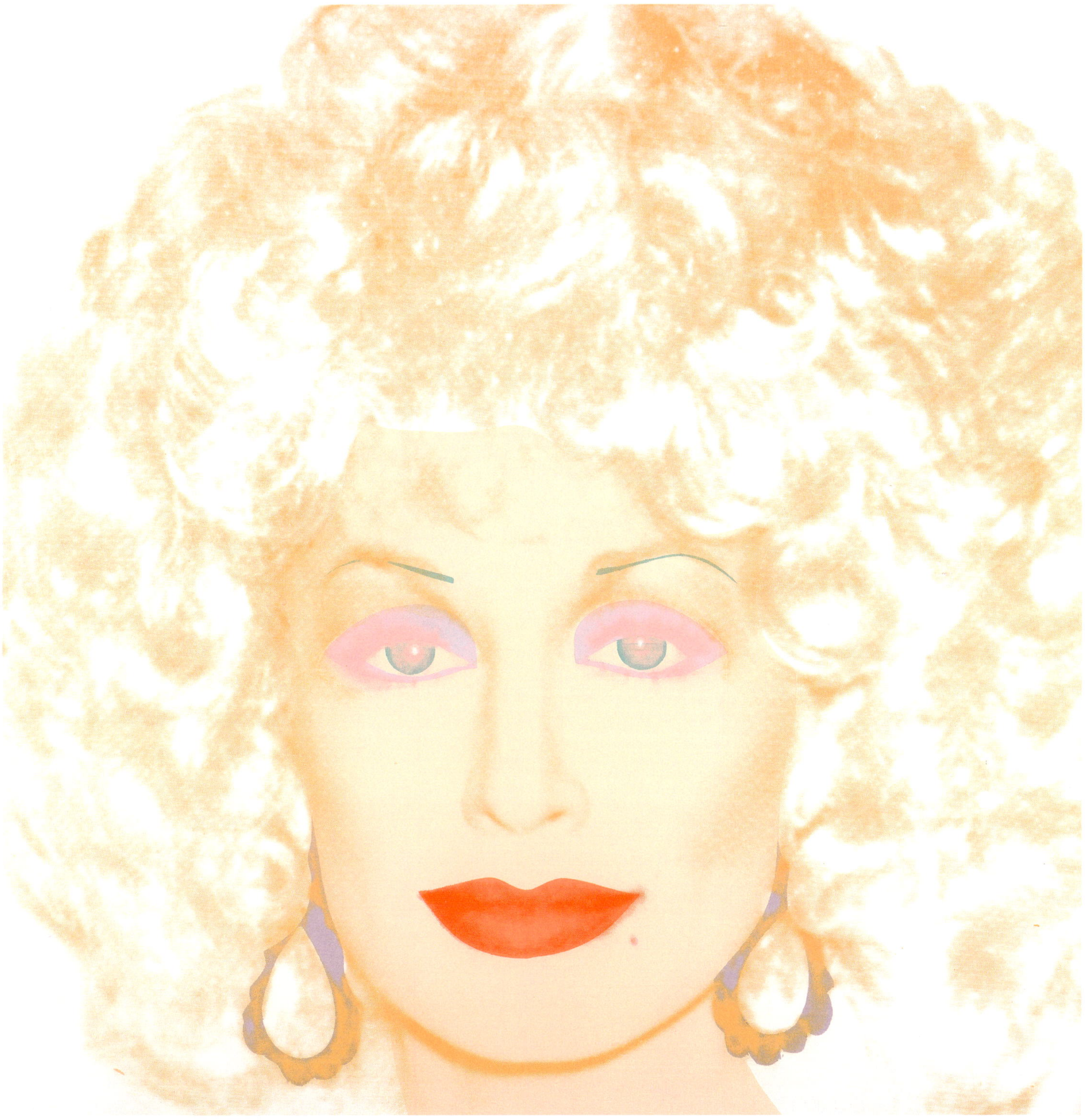

TOM WESSELMANN (1931–2004)

Smoker #9

1973
Oil and Liquitex gesso on linen
83 × 89½ in. (210.8 × 227.3 cm)

> *A major addition to his imagery occurred in 1973. Wesselmann had considered the Mouth series finished when he suddenly thought to include the hand. This greatly enhanced the complexity of the image and renewed his excitement.*
>
> –TOM WESSELMANN, writing as SLIM STEALINGWORTH[1]

What prompted the artist's sudden inspiration? As he sketched the mouth of a favorite model, Peggy Sarno, she took a break to light a cigarette. Sarno's long, elegant fingers, glossy red nails, and burning cigarette heightened the eroticism of the painter's ostensible subject, and his interest was renewed. This episode, as the story goes, stimulated an entirely new series of pictures that would become one of Tom Wesselmann's largest and most compelling.

Wesselmann first discovered his talents as a draftsman while enlisted in the Army during the Korean War, at which time he began drawing cartoons. In 1956, after earning a degree in psychology from the University of Cincinnati and pursuing additional instruction at the Art Academy there, he moved to New York City to study at the Cooper Union School of Art and absorb the energies of the young and thriving downtown art scene. Wesselmann initially earned his living as a cartoonist, publishing in notable magazines including *The New Yorker*. The economy of line required by cartooning would serve to great effect in his burgeoning painting career.[2]

One of the preeminent pop artists of the 1960s, Wesselmann established his repertoire of subject matter early on. Focusing on traditional subjects—still life, landscape, and the nude—he often incorporated consumer items designed for the marketplace as collage or assemblage elements. In 1961, the year that Andy Warhol and Roy Lichtenstein debuted their pop art productions, Wesselmann began his first important series: the *Great American Nude*. In these images, the painter rendered the female figure's most sensual body parts—breasts, mouth, and genitals—with intense attention and focus.[3] In his subsequent *Mouth* and *Smoker* series, Wesselmann refined and expanded this focused attention, often eliminating all excess visual information in order to emphasize the eroticism of his subject. While he had previously dabbled in scale shifts, Wesselmann gave these new works monumental proportions, offering lipstick-clad orifices rendered on an architectural scale.

In addition to editing unnecessary details from his depictions of the human body, the artist soon began to experiment with shaped canvases and negative space in his compositions, perhaps under the influence of the painter Alex Katz.[4] In the case of *Smoker #9*, a grand-scale shaped canvas, this method serves to completely decontextualize the model's sensual mouth, isolating it from a social context and even from its attendant body. The painting's oversized, slick surface reads as a billboard sign or synecdoche of desire. *Smoker #9* features many of the hallmarks of Wesselmann's most accomplished works: evocations of Hollywood glamour, the eroticized body (part), and the fetishized act of smoking. DB

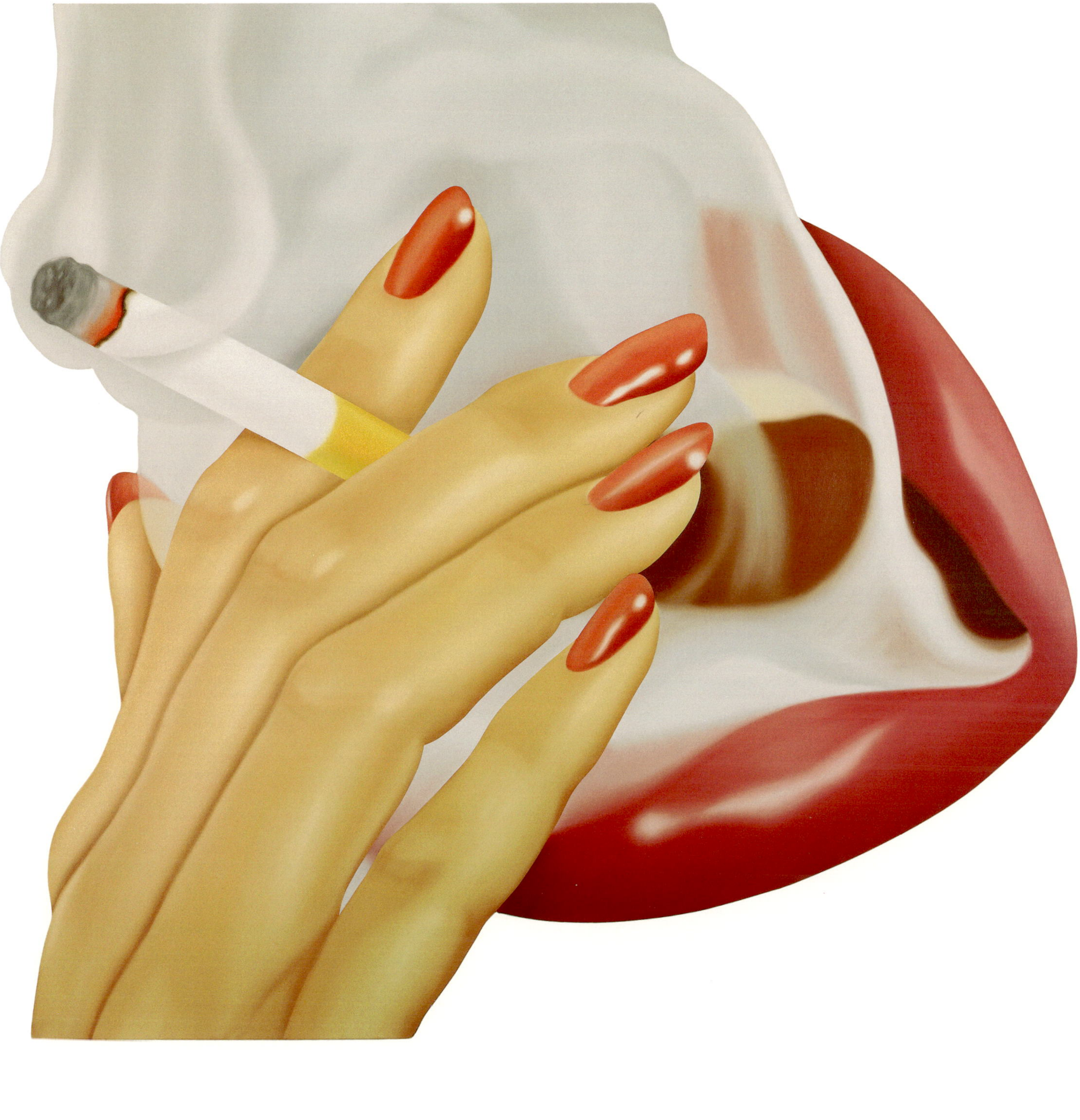

GEORGE TOOKER (1920–2011)

Ward

1971
Egg tempera on gesso panel
20 × 30 in. (50.8 × 76.2 cm)
Promised Gift

In 1971, at the height of the Vietnam War, George Tooker painted *Ward* in his painstaking egg tempera technique. As in so many of the artist's works, the subject of this picture is both recognizable and mysterious. Symbolic readings suggest a Kafkaesque dystopia beneath the painting's carefully crafted surface. Tooker said that he intended the outwardly quiet and calm work "to shock and jolt people."[1]

Ward depicts the interior of an unspecified institution, densely packed with row upon row of beds occupied by the sick, dying, or dead. The specter of death is heightened by the gravestonelike configuration of the metal headboards; the funereal presence of vertically hung American flags in the background; and a closed-off, curtained space at the center of the composition. The cylindrical form of the white sheets covering the recumbent figures evokes caskets, while the painting's pallid palette appears bloodless. The anonymous, undifferentiated bedridden appear to be young victims. By contrast, the four upright figures all seem to be aged. The elderly characters face away from the bedridden (as well as from one another) and out of the picture plane. A somber tone of isolation and disillusionment prevails.

Discussing his so-called public paintings of this period, the artist said, "These were all paintings of protest. I think the rebellion in everyone is at its apex during one's younger years. I painted the world as I saw it, and in many cases I didn't like what I saw."[2] In this context one might interpret *Ward* as a harsh commentary on the Vietnam War, a lament that the nation's youthful soldiers were dying in droves while their forebears, who were approaching the same fate, turn a blind eye to the tragedy.

Tooker, who received the National Medal of the Arts in 2007, began his long career as the protégé of a circle of intellectual sophisticates including Paul Cadmus, Jared French, and Lincoln Kirstein. Under Cadmus's and French's influence, Tooker learned the technique of egg tempera painting, then considered somewhat antiquated, as well as an approach to figuration often described as "magic realism." By the 1950s, perhaps inspired by another teacher, Reginald Marsh, Tooker's work began to address the themes of social injustice and the alienation of modern urban life. In his best-known works, such as *Government Bureau* (1956, The Metropolitan Museum of Art), *The Waiting Room* (1959, Smithsonian American Art Museum), and *Ward*, large groups of people are trapped in mundane, bureaucratic nightmares. In other works from the 1950s to the 1970s, individual figures are isolated in confined architectural spaces, often pressed uncomfortably against the picture plane and seemingly struggling for space and air.

A quiet but influential presence in American art, Tooker's paintings poignantly address the alienating and troubling aspects of modern life. Against the backdrop of abstract expressionism and other experimental idioms, Tooker remained constant in his distinctive painting technique and style while adapting his subject matter to address the complex social and political issues of his time. DB

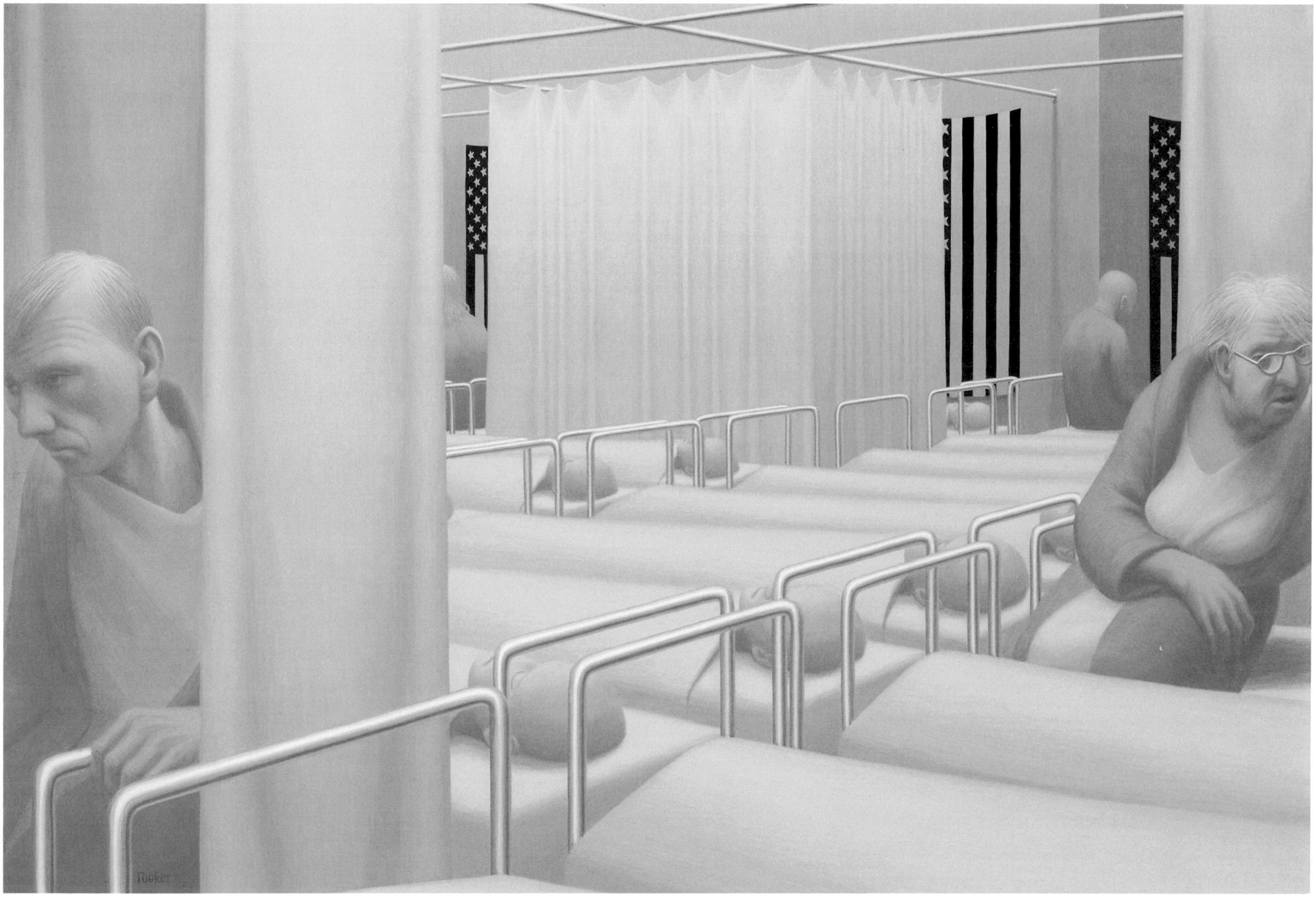
Tooker

NEIL G. WELLIVER (1929–2005)

Snow on Alden Brook

1983
Oil on canvas
96 × 96 in. (243.8 × 243.8 cm)

Neil G. Welliver's methodical, nearly mechanical method of painting produced some of the most lyrical and individual landscapes in contemporary art. *Snow on Alden Brook* is surely among these. Welliver's artistic training under Josef Albers, the German émigré and champion of color abstraction with whom the landscape painter later taught at Yale, provided many critical lessons that he carried with him to the end of his life. Not the least of these was a thorough understanding of the shifting, amorphous relationship between realism and abstraction.

Welliver worked up his wall-size landscape paintings from smaller drawings and oil sketches made directly from nature. Produced outdoors in all conditions and seasons, one imagines the artist cursing the prickly bushes and branches, foul weather, and black flies that were his frequent companions in the field. Resolute in his singular purpose—to make works of art through intense physical effort—Welliver then transferred these studies, often with substantial changes, to large rolls of brown paper that he pricked full of holes with a tailor's wheel, sprinkling charcoal dust through the brown paper onto the primed canvas. Finally, he laid in the paint on the charcoal pattern, beginning at the top left corner and moving down and across the canvas to the lower right. Welliver's laborious, highly systematic image-making technique prompted one critic to describe him as a human laser printer.[1] The result of physically demanding work, his images represent a kind of self-denying discipline and craft that even Albers would likely have approved, landscape imagery notwithstanding.

Welliver's snow pictures, such as *Snow on Alden Brook*, present the most compelling evidence of how the artist synthesized representation and abstraction. The painting clearly and convincingly reads as a record of a light snowfall on an utterly still winter day. Here is the *real* Maine wood, complete with uprooted trees, rock-strewn creek banks, dense thickets of saplings, and a fast-moving stream. If the jabbing, barren branches in the foreground formally balance the composition by providing horizontal relief from the vertical trees receding into the distance, the artist only painted them because they happened to be there. But Welliver's vision of unkempt nature is also about making the viewer aware of the physical facts of paint and canvas. The scrim of lightly falling snow on the surface of the image underscores its identity as a flat piece of cloth covered with myriad flecks of paint.

It is tempting to read something of the artist's tragic personal life into these cool, elegant paintings of a chaotic natural world that is both obdurate and cleansing. Welliver and his work can be said to come from places that are hard and unyielding. And, yet, the paintings have a redemptive quality, suggesting that nature in all its seeming randomness and disarray is finally about renewal and continuity. Few have endured so much loss: in 1975 nearly all of Welliver's life's work up to that time burned in a studio fire; a year later his infant child and young wife died suddenly in quick succession; and in the final decades of his life, he suffered the loss of two grown sons, one dying of natural causes and the other murdered while traveling abroad. He rarely spoke of such things but was honest enough to admit that it affected his work. He just could not say how.[2]

CBC

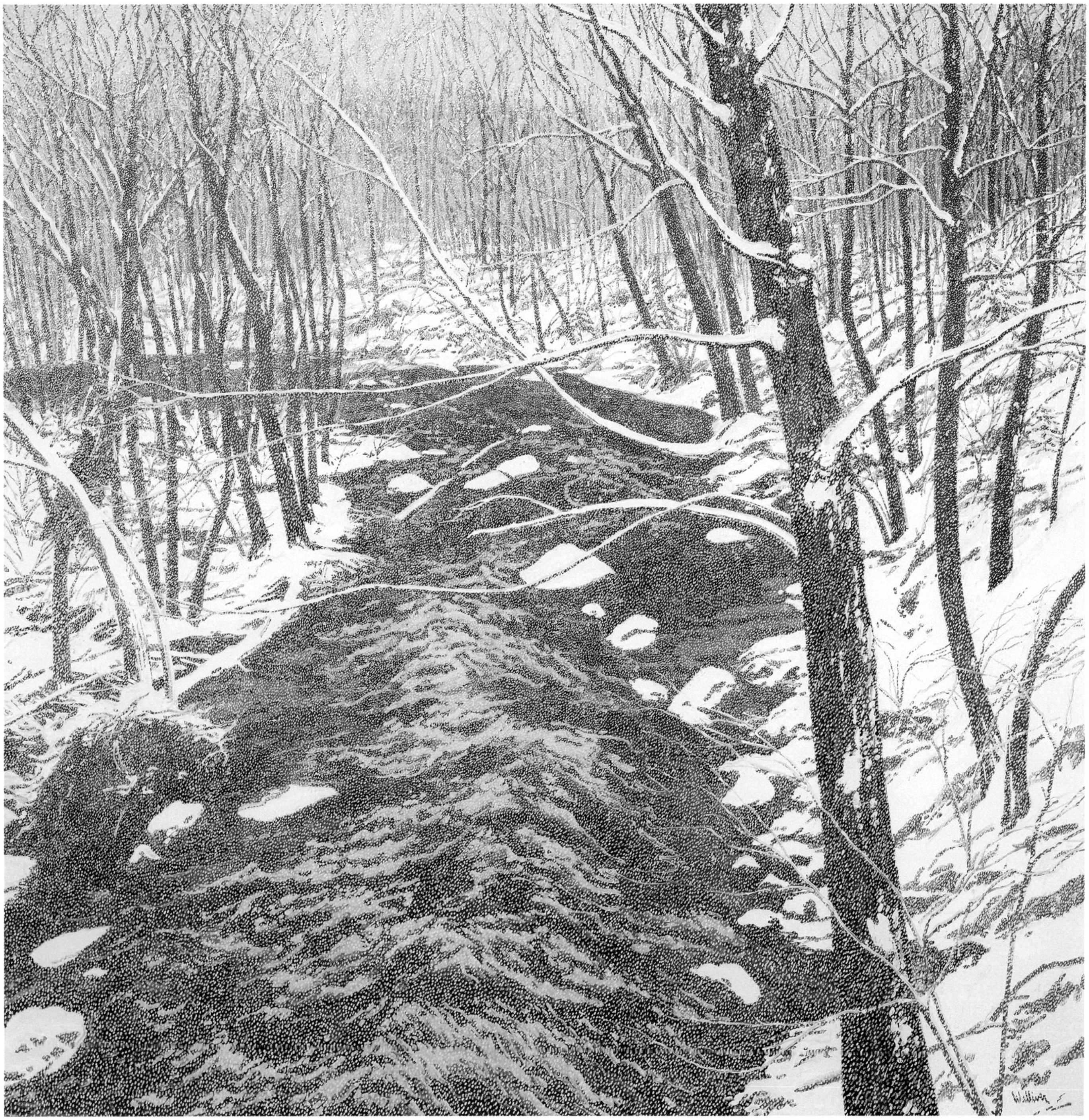

ANDREW WYETH (1917–2009)

Airborne

1996
Egg tempera on panel
40 × 48 in. (101.6 × 121.9 cm)
Promised Gift

A sense of unease in an immaculate world pervades Andrew Wyeth's *Airborne.* One of the artist's most compelling late paintings, the airy and expansive image represents a phase in Wyeth's work during which he infused his precisely detailed, layered temperas with the freedom and energy of watercolor. Some passages in *Airborne*—most notably in the sky and water—recall the dashing bravura of the watercolors that brought Wyeth national acclaim when he was still a teenager. At the same time, a meticulous attention to minute detail harkens to razor-sharp memories and potent personal associations as layered as the process of building up a tempera painting, one brushstroke at a time.

Airborne depicts the artist and his wife Betsy's home on Benner Island, Maine, seven miles out to sea from the nearest mainland town and even further removed from contemporary life. In the upper right of the image across the narrow channel is Allen Island, originally called Pentecost Island by the English adventurer and explorer George Weymouth, who made landfall there on Pentecost Sunday, 1605. Thus, "the whisper of history," as Betsy often says—a history that is both personal and public—inhabits the islands and Wyeth's thoughts about them.[1]

The traditional New England Cape Cod–style house was assembled from salvaged and antique building materials. Designed by Betsy, the house seems to have been modeled on the ancestral residence of the reclusive fisherman Henry Teel, the last descendent of a family that for generations lived on nearby Teel's Island. The oar atop the house that serves as a weather vane originally belonged to Teel, a lanky, laconic Yankee who was the subject of many of Wyeth's earliest watercolors and temperas. One might thus view the painting as a surrogate portrait of the artist's old friend, worn by time and tides. Teel was the male counterpart of Wyeth's model Christina Olson, whose own pride, resilience, and endurance of hardship are poignantly represented in the 1948 painting *Christina's World* (Museum of Modern Art).

In his later years, Wyeth introduced brighter, even jarring, color into his work. Here, a high-keyed, spring-green lawn leads from the foreground to the weathered gray clapboard house and the gunmetal sky. This contrasting palette of bright greens and dull grays vividly conveys the site's weather, tides, and seasonal rhythms. What is unexpected and unnatural is the scrim of floating feathers in the foreground.[2] The suggestion here, as in many of Wyeth's paintings, is that something is taking place just beyond the frame. We can speculate and wonder: might it be a sudden attack on the geese and ducks who summer on the pond next to the house by one of the island's resident bald eagles? Or, more mundanely, might the floating foliage simply be the molting feathers of seagulls? The intimation of violence, overhead and unseen, seems more germane. Unexpected, sudden violence has haunted Wyeth since 1945, when his father was killed as his car stalled on the tracks at a rail crossing in Chadds Ford, Pennsylvania.[3]

Wyeth's son Jamie came closest to defining the painter's art: "His world was a magically airless, crystal-lit microcosm, of which he was the sole inhabitant, and his art will forever remain, by his own design, elusive."[4] In Wyeth's world, reality is always mysterious and illusory: like feathers on a breeze, only momentarily—and perhaps never—there.

CBC

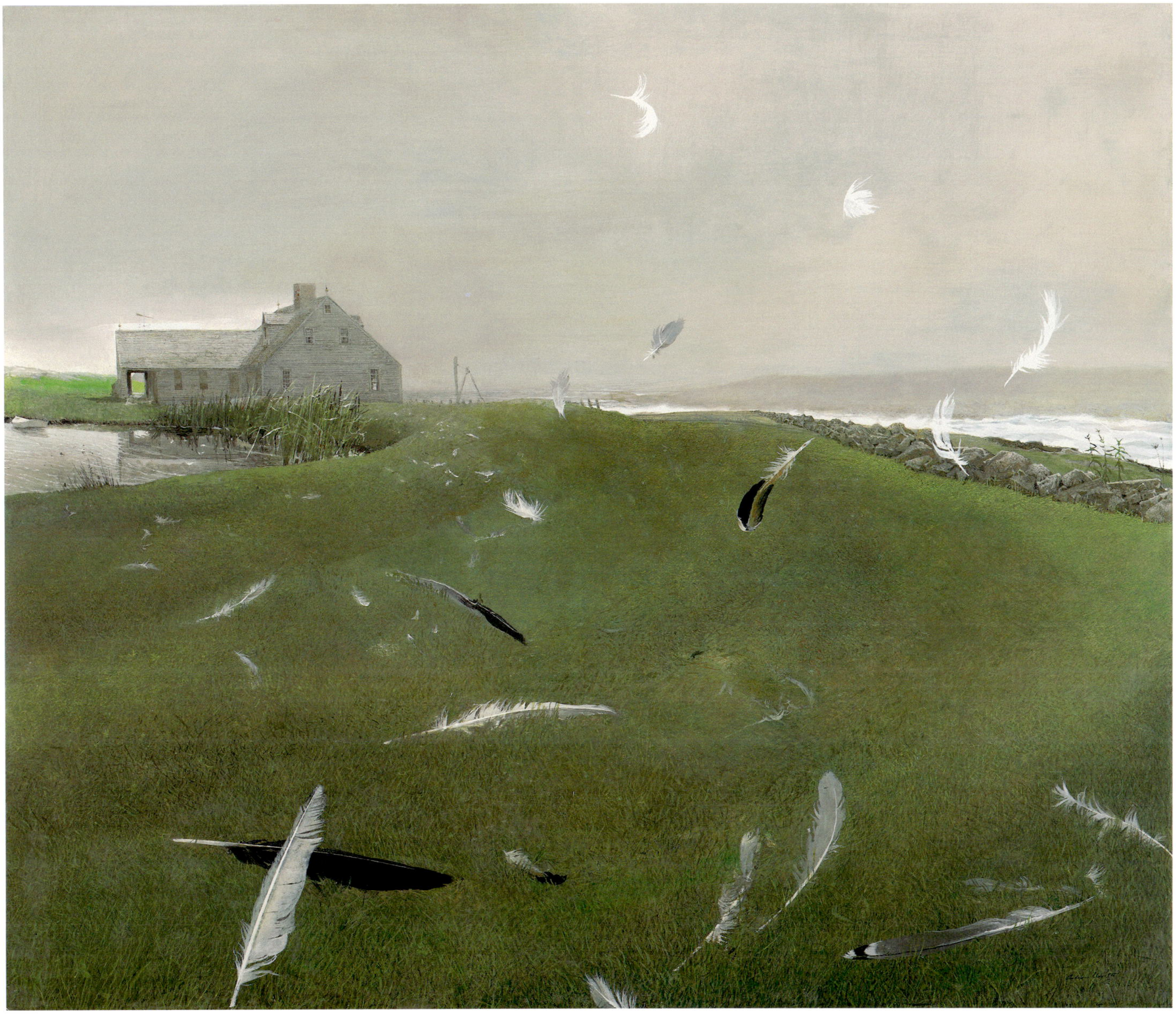

JAMIE WYETH (B. 1946)

Orca Bates

1990
Oil on panel
40 × 40 in. (101.6 × 101.6 cm)
Promised Gift

Orca Bates, a painting of a boy raised on Monhegan Island, Maine, is among Jamie Wyeth's most enigmatic, visually seductive, and emotionally charged portraits. It belongs to a series of paintings of Orca that Wyeth began in late 1989 and continued for five years that chronicles the boy's journey from childhood to adolescence. On Monhegan Island adolescence ends at eighth grade, as teenagers of high school age must leave their homes and their families to complete their education at a state-subsidized boarding school on the mainland. "There his understanding of the ways of seagulls and fishermen," art historian Richard McClanathan has observed of Monhegan youth, "doesn't count for much."[1]

At Wyeth's insistence Orca himself signed *Orca Bates*, at the lower left of the image in red block letters. It is the "signature" painting from the series, a portrait that the artist feels was created in equal measure by the sitter, so naturally does he occupy the imagined space. Orca's youthful, naked vulnerability plays against the massive, tooth-studded whale jawbone, its whiteness and associations with a mythic, distant past a stark contrast to the youthful glow that seems to emanate from within the boy's wet, shimmering body. Sitting on an antique sea chest, Orca is a young Jonah, or Herman Melville's Ishmael, freshly plucked from the sea. His digital watch, an intentional reference to the present, pulls the painting back from historical and literary references that Orca himself would likely find mystifying, if not laughable.

Upon seeing the completed painting, Orca complained that Wyeth distorted the size of his feet. An artist who gained an understanding of anatomy at the level of sinew and bone through field studies with a surgeon at a New York hospital morgue, Wyeth exaggerated his model's feet to suggest the way young men sometimes grow into their bodies in fits and starts. It is, to say the least, an awkward age for boys, harder still, perhaps, for those stepping from a nineteenth-century way of life into the late twentieth.

Wyeth is a master at rendering natural textures, whether molting seagull feathers, aged wood, or new flesh. His technique, practiced since early boyhood, is fluent and sure; surfaces are built over time and paintings can take many weeks to complete. The final results have both solidity and supple freshness. In *Orca Bates* the painter's brushwork is vigorous, with quick, gliding strokes that blend optically to create complex spatial and light effects. The warm earth tones, creamy yellows, and sunburnt reds in the whalebone and Orca's flesh contrast with the cool violets, purples, and blue-grays in the background clapboards and sea chest. The entire surface is alive with activity and painterly touch. Wyeth is a physical painter and loves the feel, smell, and texture of oil paint; generous amounts of it often end up on his clothes, the studio floor, and more or less permanently under his nails.

Naked, a creature of primal nature, Orca is literally in a state of becoming. His world of timelessness and immediacy, of valued traditions colliding with contemporary culture, of lost innocence and bright promise, are all present in Wyeth's remarkable portrait. CBC

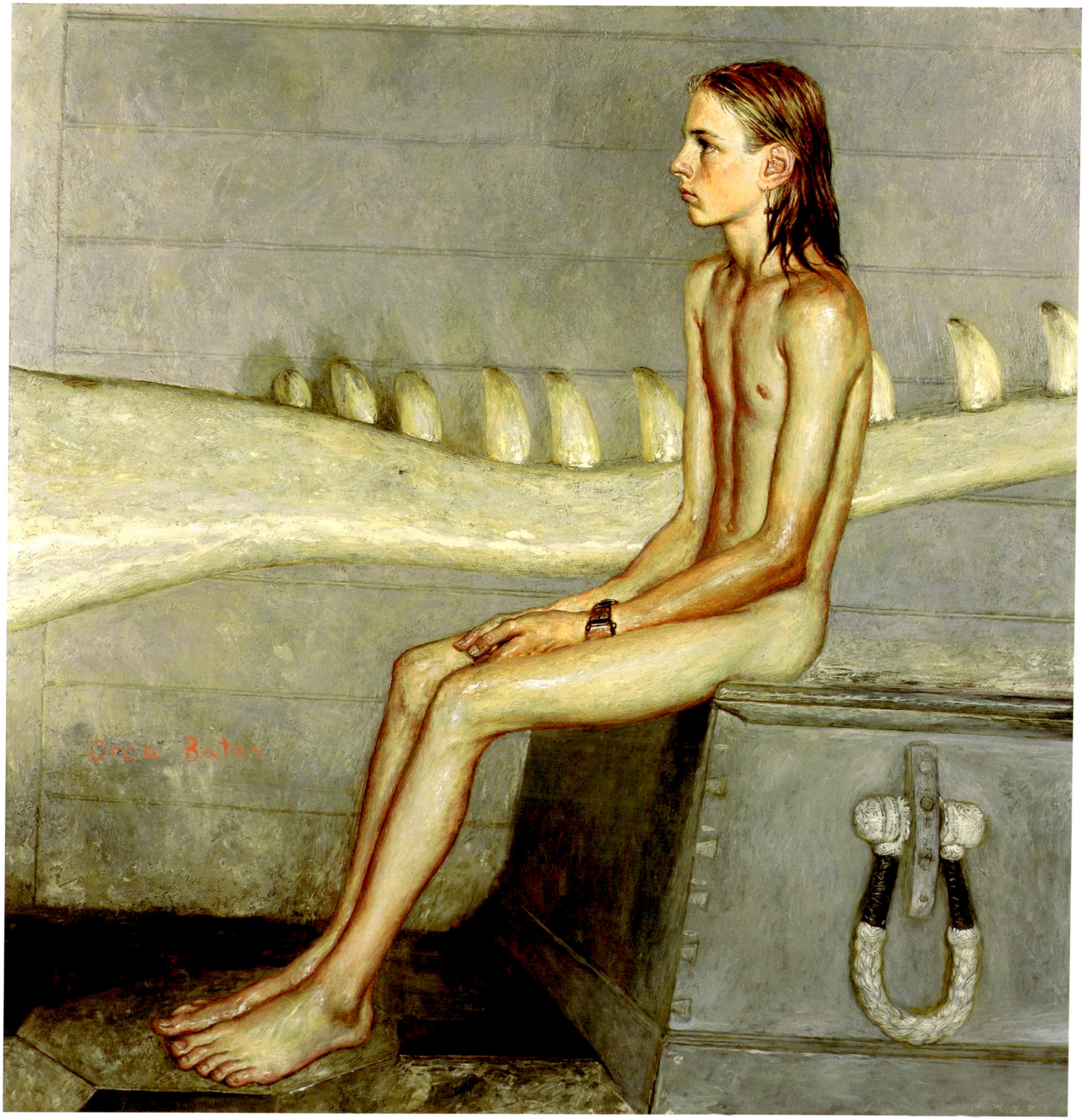
Orca Bates

RICHARD ESTES (B. 1932)

Reflections of the Woolworth Building

2006
Oil on board
18¾ × 12¼ in. (47.6 × 31.1 cm)
Promised Gift

Richard Estes is best known for his immaculate, photorealist paintings of New York City. While he works from photographs, his process is not one of straightforward transcription: Estes often incorporates perspectives and focal points from multiple images into a single composition. In Estes's signature urban views—of windows, stainless steel cladding on high-rise buildings, and other reflective surfaces—what is reflected, the surface on which it appears, and what lies behind the reflection (in the case of widows) are all in sharp focus simultaneously, a perceptual impossibility for the human or camera eye. Estes's 2006 painting *Reflections of the Woolworth Building* epitomizes the artist's unique point of view.

Estes's urban work has been linked to Edward Hopper's renderings of all-but-empty urban streetscapes and rooftops. But Estes's images are far more clinical and detached than those of his predecessor. It is the difference between Hopper's isolated figures in the window of a coffee shop and Estes's pastries in a bakery window competing for attention with signs and buildings mirrored in the glass; between the well-worn and the not-yet-used; shadowy ambiguity and bright, disorienting reflections. Estes renders complex visual information with absolute precision and clarity to create a thoroughly contemporary urban vision—one that offers a multiplicity of undifferentiated, equally weighted choices, whether to satisfy or confound.

A world traveler and longtime summer resident of Mount Desert Island, near Acadia National Park in Maine, Estes's attention in recent years has increasingly turned to nature. His multi-focal-point wizardry and photolike realism inform these landscape paintings, although they evoke surface and spatial dynamics more subtly than do their urban counterparts. In *Antarctica* (p. 295), Estes's 2007 view from a cruise vessel, the artist presents the ice-laden Antarctic shoreline with steep mountains rising from the depths of the sea to the lacy clouds overhead. An expanse of dark ocean, which occupies

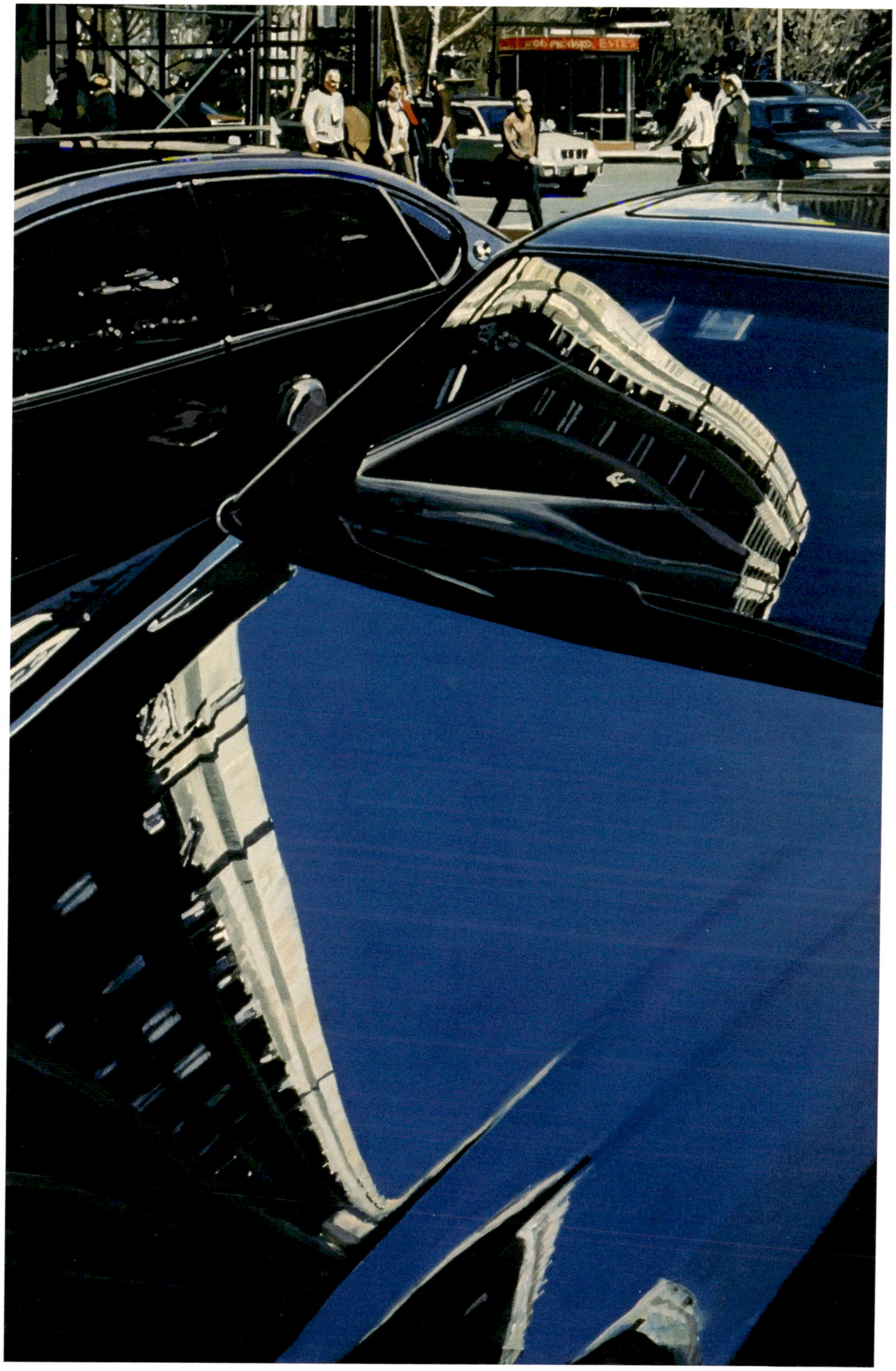

RICHARD ESTES (B. 1932)

Antarctica

2007
Oil on canvas
38 × 66 in. (96.5 × 167.6 cm)
Promised Gift

more than half of the painted surface, contains murky reflections of both landscape and clouds. The rippling wake of the boat at the far right creates a sense of passage along the majestic, uninhabited shoreline, and the overall composition is one that Estes often uses in his cityscapes: a plunging diagonal framed at one edge by a nearly abstract wedge of geometric structure, opening onto an expansive view of what lies beyond.

The contrast between near and far in *Antarctica* amplifies both, and the artist's wide-angle format underscores the vastness of the scene. On close inspection, the blue-white wake alongside the boat's hull becomes entirely abstract, composed of painterly strokes and patterns. Perhaps such bravura passages of pure, painterly delight are both homage and gestural "gotcha" to the abstract expressionists who dominated the New York art scene as Estes was coming of age in the 1950s in Chicago, in what was then viewed as the hinterlands. A New Yorker for nearly his entire adult life, Estes is now as closely associated with his adopted city as any artist since Robert Henri or even Hopper.

Looking at Estes's long career and varied subjects, John Wilmerding, Estes's Maine neighbor and author of a recent monograph on the artist, succinctly articulates what distinguishes his work from both precursors and contemporaries. "Estes brings two consummate talents to his art," Wilmerding explains, "the ability to select out of the random chaos and imperfections of the world around him something worth looking at, and the rarified craftsmanship to transform that view into something cleansed and purified, orderly and even harmonious."[1]

CBC

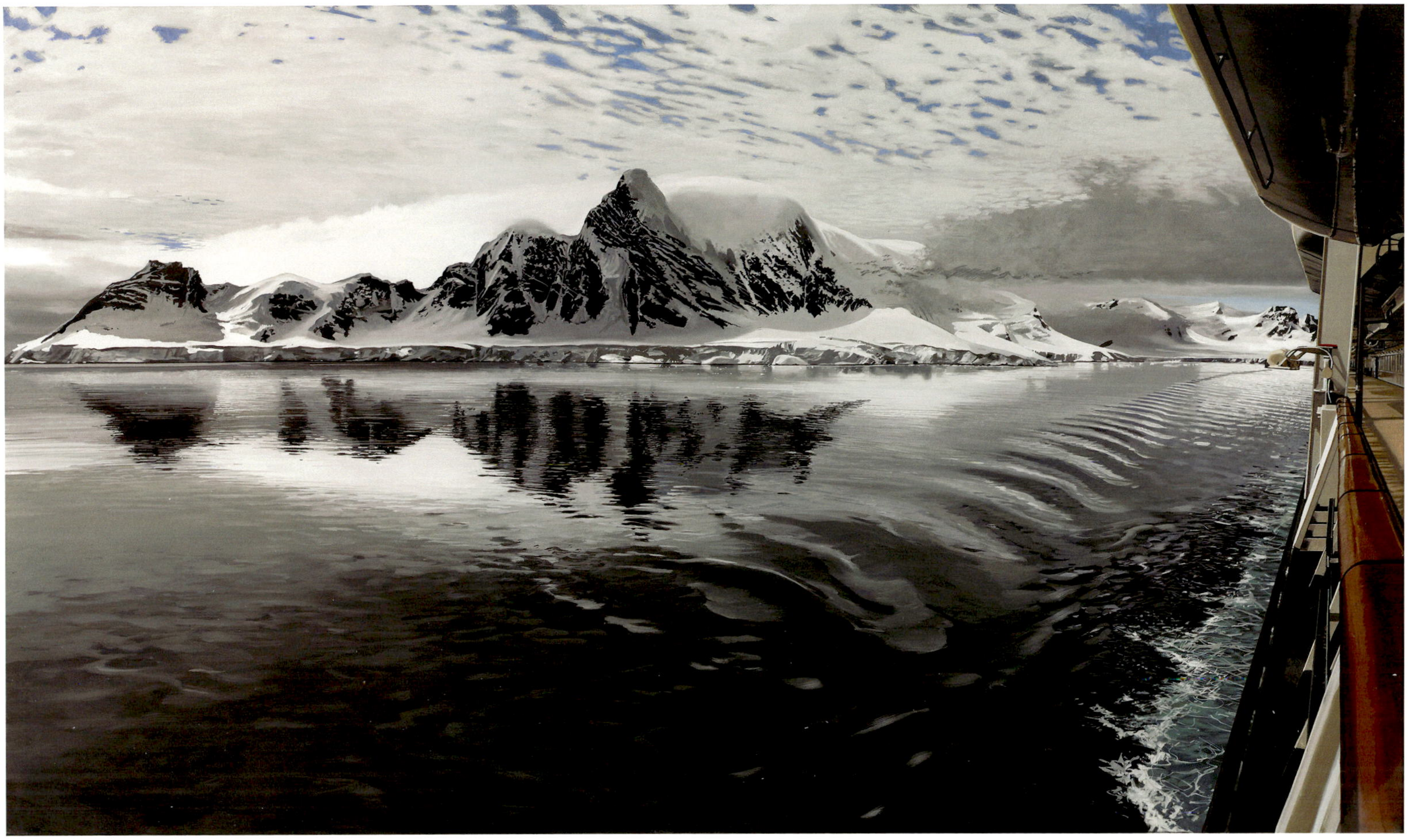

BO BARTLETT (B. 1955)

The Lobster Wars

2007
Oil on linen
80 × 112 in. (203.2 × 284.5 cm)

Life imitates art. Or so it might seem with Bo Bartlett's monumental painting *The Lobster Wars*, completed in 2007. Two years later, in the summer of 2009, stories appeared in the national press about a territorial dispute over the right to set lobster traps in waters just off Matinicus, Maine's most remote inhabited island.[1] One man was shot in the neck on the town dock in front of numerous witnesses; he survived, but was seriously injured. The parties involved were rival families, well known to each other (in fact, related by marriage) as well as to the subject of Bartlett's painting, Ronnie, or "R. K.," Ames. Ames and his family have lived on and fished off of Matinicus for generations. Although Bartlett's painting predates the events of that fateful day in 2009, the artist was keenly aware of the "lobster wars" being fought up and down the Maine coast, especially in recent years as diminishing catches strain wallets and fray nerves.

The Lobster Wars fits squarely into a long tradition of American history and narrative painting. Bartlett's nearly seven-by-ten-foot canvas betrays the legacy of heroic images by such nineteenth-century luminaries as Benjamin West, John Trumbull, and John Singleton Copley. Bartlett cites other sources of inspiration, including the accomplished narrative painter Thomas Eakins and the popular illustrators Howard Pyle and N. C. Wyeth, all figures closely associated with Philadelphia, where Bartlett studied at the Pennsylvania Academy of the Fine Arts. Bartlett is a gifted filmmaker, and cinematic scale and content is central to how the artist conceives and executes his massive narrative paintings.[2]

Although *The Lobster Wars* addresses contemporary, topical issues in a way that is more direct than many of Bartlett's other recent large-scale works, it is pure invention in its details. The slatted wooden lobster trap on the stern of the boat is an antique, a type now obsolete in the trade and recycled (or purpose built) for college dorms and suburban coffee tables. Ames may have a red staysail to help steer his vessel in choppy seas and may even have adorned it with a skull and crossbones like a modern incarnation of Long John Silver from N. C. Wyeth's *Treasure Island*. But it is also possible that Bartlett invented this element of the composition as a wry commentary on Ames's and his trade's tenuous relationship to authority, including their self-imposed territorial rules governing Maine lobstering. That Ames might choose to fly the flag to entertain (or startle) tourists and well-heeled yachtsmen venturing out to Matinicus to find "the real Maine" is an equally plausible explanation for its presence.

Perhaps the most telling detail of the composition is the plume of smoke on the horizon at lower left. The artist seems to be comparing the gravitas of Maine's lobster wars on the fringes of the North Atlantic to important historical naval battles from Actium to Trafalgar to the Battle of Midway. And for lobstermen in waters off Matinicus and neighboring coastal communities, where the underlying conflict between nature and culture imperils a treasured way of life, this analogy resonates. Bartlett's heroic painting plays at the edges of fiction and humor to convey more fundamental, and deadly serious, truths affecting real lives.

CBC

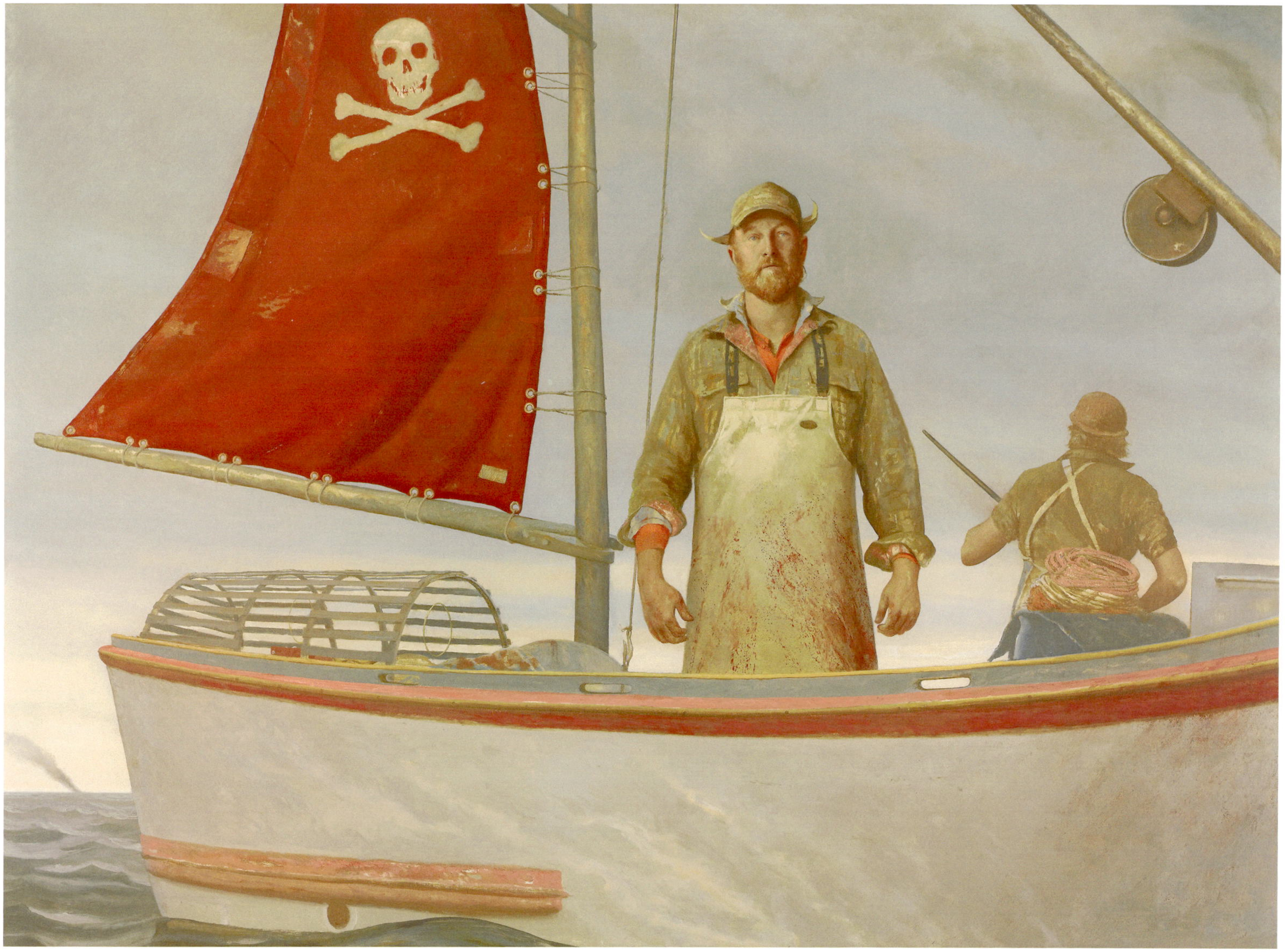

MARY MCCLEARY (B. 1951)

The Falcon Cannot Hear the Falconer

2008
Mixed media collage on paper
39½ × 50¾ in. (100.3 × 128.9 cm)

> *My aim is that the obsessive images that result from this method of working convey an intensity which the viewer finds compelling. . . . I like the irony of using materials that are often trivial, foolish, and temporal to express ideas of what is significant, timeless, and transcendent.* —MARY MCCLEARY[1]

Texas artist Mary McCleary has spent decades inventing and refining her own distinctive art-making technique, one that combines collage, assemblage, and handmade craft to create startlingly realistic and dramatic images. Hovering between painting and relief sculpture, these works utilize commonplace items and materials to convey potent allegories borne of historical, literary, and biblical sources. McCleary's affinity for rough-hewn and hand-fashioned materials—twigs, string, and nails; handmade papers, toys, and ornaments—speaks to her belief in the potency of craft. Indeed, the artist has said, "I've always been drawn to well-crafted, handmade objects . . . to all kinds of folk art. The women in my family were serious collectors of the decorative arts. . . . These were big influences."[2]

William Butler Yeats's 1919 poem "The Second Coming," written in the aftermath of World War I, provides both the title of this work and the two lines of text that are collaged on its lowermost register in small strips of type.[3] Here McCleary depicts a suburban drama—the catastrophic burning of a home—and the rallying assistance and spectatorship of a group of neighbors. In its densely packed, illusionistic surface, cotton batting becomes finely detailed articles of clothing; painted twigs become trees illuminated by nearby flames; twisted bits of multicolored paper become a conflagration worthy of Vincent van Gogh's *The Starry Night* (1889, Museum of Modern Art). Standing apart from the anonymous crowd, a shirtless witness looks outward, confronting the viewer, his face marked with a patterned arrangement of vibrant pigments that approximate war paint. Isolated figures such as this one appear in several of McCleary's works, providing silent commentary and a mysterious presence beyond the familiar, if dramatic, scene.[4]

The first four lines of Yeats's dark, complex poem describe an apocalyptic present:

> Turning and turning in the widening gyre
> The falcon cannot hear the falconer;
> Things fall apart; the centre cannot hold;
> Mere anarchy is loosed upon the world.

McCleary renders the "anarchy" in Yeats's work as a suburban disaster. The white bird circling above the flames may allude to the poet's belief in the cyclical nature of history, offering a glimmer of hope in its prophesy of the Second Coming and the (violent) birth of a new age—a chance to start anew. McCleary has consistently tackled lofty themes, juxtaposing historic and Christian sources with contemporary, everyday imagery and settings. Her technique is a kind of modern alchemy, in which incidental and insignificant materials come together to create richly meaningful works of art. DB

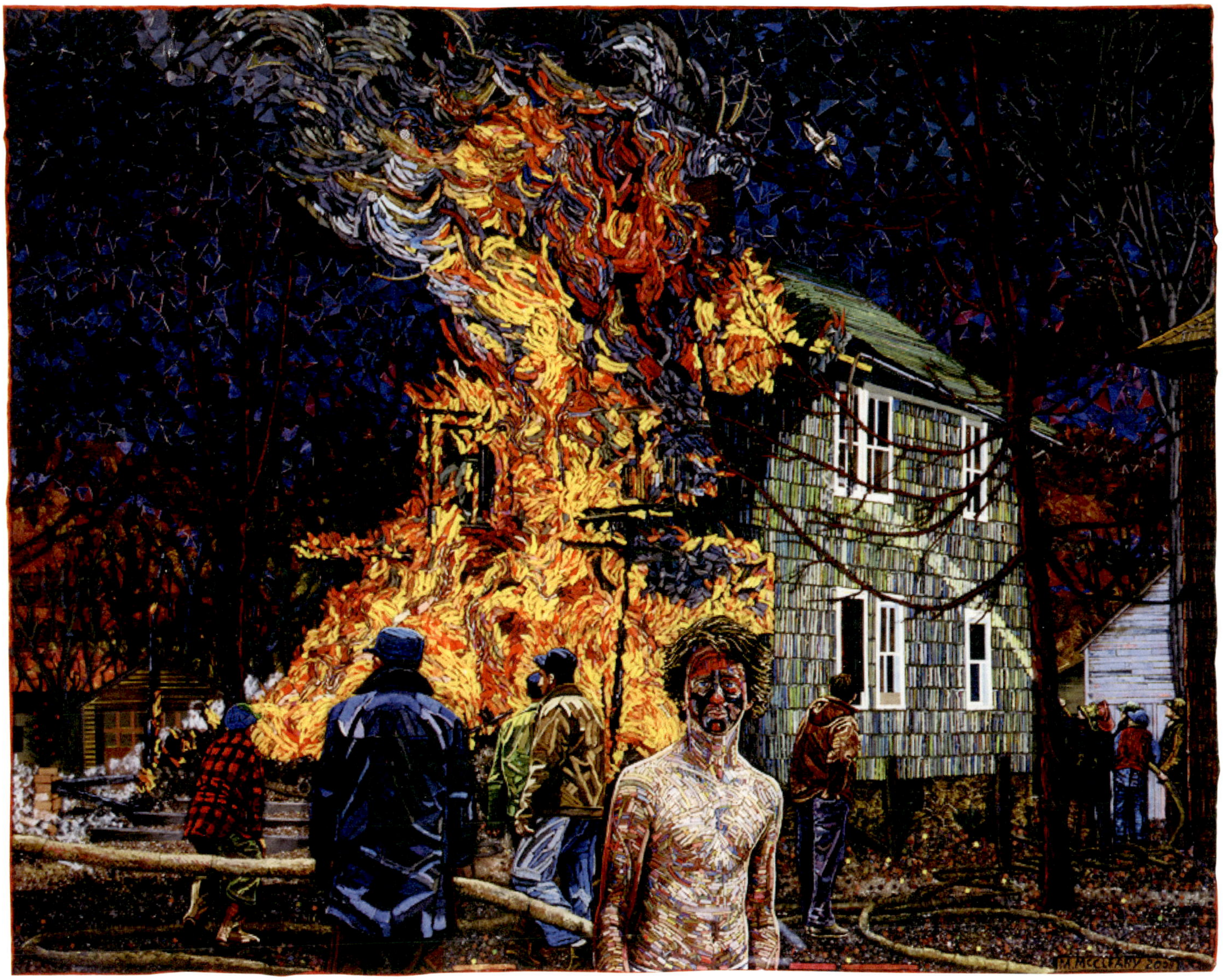

KERRY JAMES MARSHALL (B. 1955)

Our Town

1995
Acrylic and printed-paper collage on canvas
100 × 142 in. (254 × 360.7 cm)

> *You can't be born in Birmingham, Alabama, in 1955 and not feel like you've got some kind of social responsibility. You can't move to Watts in '63, and grow up in South Central near the Black Panthers headquarters and see the kinds of things I saw in my developmental years and not speak about it.*
>
> –KERRY JAMES MARSHALL[1]

In 1997, Kerry James Marshall received the prestigious MacArthur Fellowship (the so-called Genius Award) and was included in both the Whitney Biennial and documenta X, a kind of trifecta for a visual artist. These honors followed Marshall's completion of his *Garden Project*, a series of grand paintings that address the dashed hopes of an earlier era—the urban renewal movement of the 1960s—and cemented the artist's reputation as a major talent.

Marshall was raised in a time and in places defined by issues of race and social justice. As an artist, he came of age as minimalism and conceptual art took their last gasps. Trained at Otis College under Charles White, an important African American painter of social realist subjects, Marshall emerged as part of a new generation of artists that included Julian Schnabel and David Salle. These post-modernists revived grand-scale painting, invested in figuration, and liberally mined historical imagery and styles, effectively challenging modernism's indiscriminate rejection of tradition and restrictive emphasis on novelty and originality.

In the 1995 painting *Our Town* from the *Garden Project*, completed just two years before Marshall received the MacArthur Fellowship, the artist evokes the classic Thornton Wilder play from which he borrows his title. The scene is a familiar one: Dick and Jane-like children play on a suburban street, the family dog in tow, while an apron-clad mom watches from the well-manicured lawn of their perfect colonial house, complete with a swing set and pool in the yard. The painting's title is proudly emblazoned at the upper center of the work. Rendered in a palette dominated by red, white, and blue, Marshall's vibrant image of suburban family life at first appears to be a joyous celebration of the American Dream.

However, numerous disruptions and defacements mar the idyllic scene. Thought bubbles have been emptied, or whited out; cheerful Disneyesque bluebirds carry banners without messages; tree trunks are crudely whitewashed or adorned with yellow ribbons (a display associated with remembrance of an absent loved one, especially in wartime); and the two children seem to be hurtling toward an unresolved and messy patch of lawn. Indeed, upon closer examination the children's facial expressions are enigmatic at best, and the raised right fist of the pigtailed young girl suggests the Black Power gesture most widely associated with the radical Black Panther party of the 1960s.

Like many artists of his generation, Marshall is deeply invested in probing issues of racial and national identity. Exploring the themes of race, class, community, and belonging—subjects that inform his entire *Garden Project*—*Our Town* calls into question the inclusiveness and contemporary relevance of the American social ideal embodied by suburban existence. Marshall poses the question: for whom does "Our Town" really exist? His enigmatic, multilayered work might even be seen to challenge the desirability of this ideal—to suggest that there is something deeply troubling behind the pristine facade.

DB

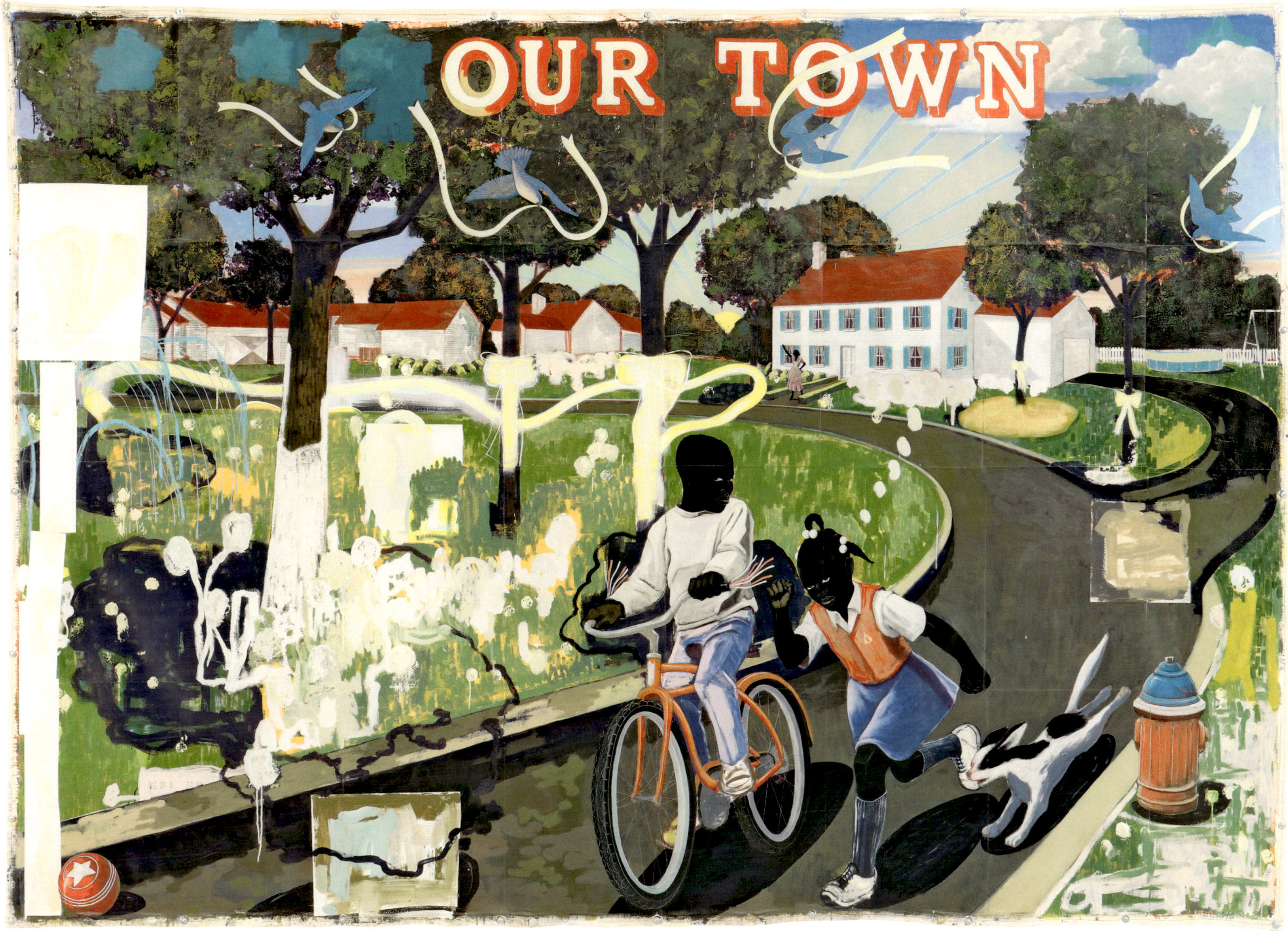
OUR TOWN

KARA WALKER (B. 1969)

A Warm Summer Evening in 1863

2008
Wool tapestry and hand-cut felt silhouette figure
69 × 98 in. (175.3 × 248.9 cm)

In July 1863, New York City witnessed the largest public protest against the Civil War in the northern states. Vehemently objecting to the newly established draft, an angry mob burned buildings, looted goods, and attacked and murdered both black and white Americans. The most brutal assaults, however, were inflicted upon blacks. The draft riots were born from a complex set of political, racial, and class tensions. Working-class immigrants, particularly the Irish, could not afford to buy their way out of the draft, and were forced to fight for a cause they perceived would result in an influx of newly emancipated African Americans with whom they would have to compete for jobs. In their effort to derail Abraham Lincoln's Democratic agenda, many Republican leaders reinforced lower-class white Americans' fears in their political rhetoric.

History is typically told from the perspective of the politically empowered, and rarely accounts for the diversity of individual experience. Kara Walker's large-scale silhouettes critique such official histories by punctuating textbook versions of the past with fantastical visual interventions rooted in the artist's research and vivid imagination. *A Warm Summer Evening in 1863* takes as its subject the 1863 draft riots, reproducing a wood engraving from *Harper's Pictorial History of the Civil War* (1866) in the warp and woof of the textile's silk thread weave. On a tapestry nearly six feet in height, Walker dramatically enlarged the scene from the original *Harper's* print—a throng of protestors attacking the Colored Orphan Asylum located on the corner of Fifth Avenue and Forty-Sixth Street. Rioters wield clubs, victims shield themselves, and a conflagration consumes the orphanage.

Departing from the original engraving, Walker affixed to the tapestry a felt silhouette of a woman lynched by, perhaps, the very bow that previously adorned her dress. We might conclude that the woman is white and well-to-do from her tightly corseted figure. But her wavy hairline resembles that of the stereotyped pickaninnies and negresses in other of Walker's works, a conjecture reinforced by the art form of the silhouette itself, which literally depicts all figures as black. The woman's displaced head, contorted arm, and mangled fingers pointing to the looted orphanage highlight the disquieting forms of lynched and otherwise violated bodies.[1] The most violated bodies are those of black children, attacked and left homeless as their orphanage, established and largely funded by white, upper-class women, burns to the ground. The image depicts rage directed at both black Americans and wealthy white ones. And it demonstrates the potential of people to commit atrocities without discrimination when they perceive power relationships to be unbalanced.

For Walker, the past provides rich material for making art. Yet she describes her work as "all about the now," adding, "I approach this work the same way a Harlequin romance novelist might approach it, all the history, the petticoats—it's all artifice, just a ruse to tantalize the viewer."[2] If we assume her work solely to be about slavery, then we play into a narrowly defined historical position about race: "that 'blackness' is only visible in and against the 'whiteness' of its containing ground."[3] Instead, Walker gives us images that are as much about desire as pain, and as much about gender, sexuality, and class as they are about race. As the critic Jerry Saltz once stated of her work, "No one gets out of Kara Walker's world alive, not even the artist."[4]

AWM

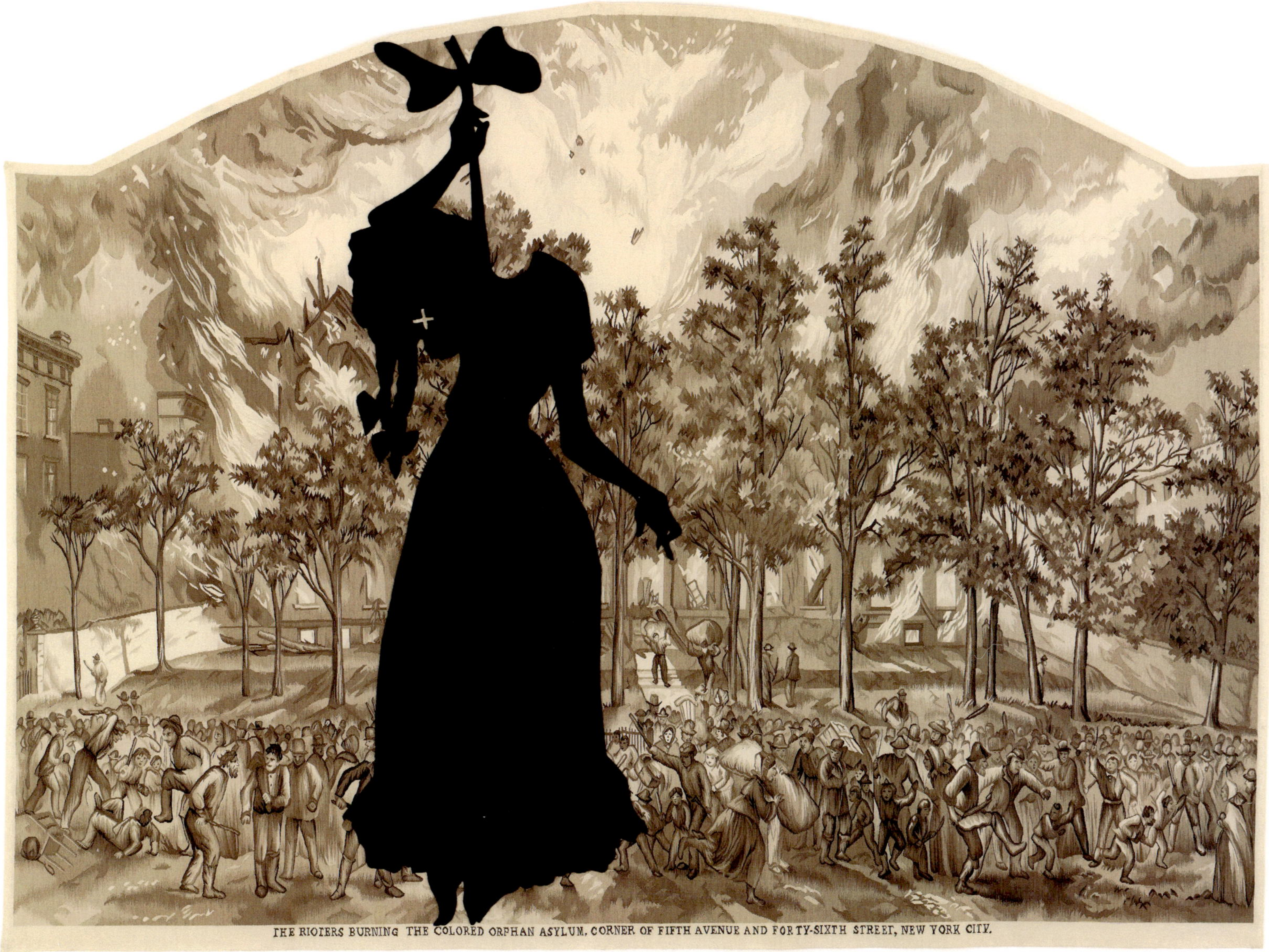
THE RIOTERS BURNING THE COLORED ORPHAN ASYLUM, CORNER OF FIFTH AVENUE AND FORTY-SIXTH STREET, NEW YORK CITY.

JIM HODGES (B. 1957)

When We Stay

1997
Silk, cotton, polyester, and thread
240 × 191¾ in. (609.6 × 487 cm)

Over three hundred square feet of yellow silk flowers, punctuated with reds and pinks, oranges and greens, cascade down to embrace viewers like morning sunshine on a warm spring day in Jim Hodges's *When We Stay*. Sewn together with care, Hodges's suspended floral curtain recalls such diverse art forms as Renaissance tapestries, folk art quilts, and decorative lace and metalwork.[1] Critics typically situate the artist's work within the pop art tradition of Andy Warhol, as well as the more contemplative practices of contemporary artists Felix Gonzalez-Torres and Roni Horn.[2] In using silk rather than actual flowers, Hodges's work invests itself in consumer goods and mechanically reproduced nature, recalling the artificiality that Warhol excavated from and bestowed upon many of his subjects, from his red-and-white Campbell's soup cans to his brightly colored, silkscreened poppies. His work also mediates on life and loss like that of the late Gonzalez-Torres, whose elegiac creations have been associated with the AIDS epidemic; and in the manner of Horn, whose close-up photographs of the ocean's undulating surface suggest parallels between shifting currents and life's own ebbs and flows.

There is something refreshingly open and honest about *When We Stay*, with its brilliant color spectrum and simple pattern of petals and leaves that allows viewers to gaze through it. As Hodges has said, "I've always tried to be transparent and reflective, and never attempted to conceal anything in my practice."[3] The critic Martin Herbert has argued that Hodges's accessible approach speaks to "Marcel Duchamp's dictum that 'the viewer completes the work.'" Indeed, Hodges enthusiastically encourages his audience to read his creations as they like. As Herbert has observed, "[Hodges's art] reframes the Duchampian permission to participate as a warmly human relationship between artist and viewer."[4]

The element of warmth and personal connection in Hodges's work has not been lost on art historians and critics. One writer called the artist's project a discourse into the "phenomenology of love."[5] This love is welcoming, safe, and dependable, and viewers will no doubt find themselves returning again and again to observe, reflect on, and imagine the soft floral fields that Hodges depicts and evokes in *When We Stay*. Without irony, Hodges magically transforms artificial flowers into a meditation on nature, as well as on the often subtle and sweet moments people share in life. For Hodges, to witness and meditate means to connect to the wider world in which we live, to notice that which we so often overlook. As he has said, "We share everything and we are all connected. No one is outside the field [of art and life], though divisions are created and reinforced to undermine our connectedness . . . art has taught me to work toward and for liberation."[6] AWM

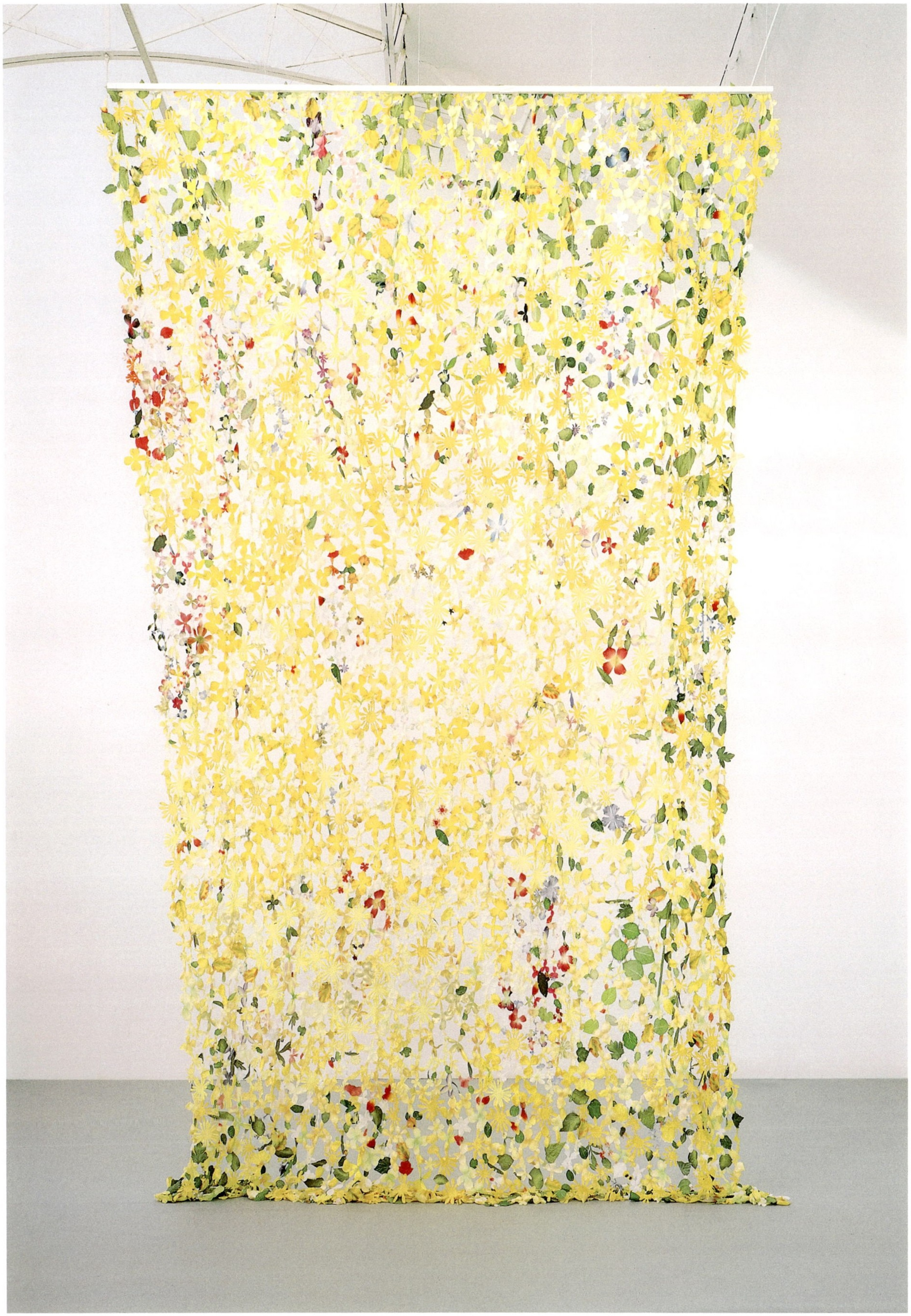

WALTON FORD (B. 1960)

The Island

2009
Watercolor, gouache, pencil, and ink on paper
Panel 1: 95½ × 36 in. (242.6 × 91.4 cm), Panel 2: 95½ × 60 in. (242.6 × 152.4 cm), Panel 3: 95½ × 36 in. (242.6 × 91.4 cm)

Walton Ford's monumental watercolor triptych *The Island* is among his largest and most complex paintings to date.[1] The approximately eight-by-twelve-foot painting depicts dozens of thylacine marsupials, also known as Tasmanian wolves or, more commonly, Tasmanian tigers (because of their distinctive striped fur). Extinct in their native Australia for a thousand years, the species lived on in Tasmania until the mid-1930s, when they fell victim to human predators who mistakenly believed the animals were a threat to sheep herds and therefore to people.

In an image perhaps best described as hallucinatory, Ford depicts the animals as forming a living island sinking into the sea off a barren shoreline. With their bodies piled upon one another as well as among the assorted sheep and sheep parts that are the focus of many of the thylacines' ravenous attention, the creatures are oblivious to their fate. As in other of the artist's large-format watercolors, Ford merges historical truth with a strange, fictional narrative drawn from his thoroughly subjective and sociopolitically charged imagination. He describes the painting as a "sort of cultural history of the way animals live in the human imagination," explaining, "I want it to be a brutal picture of thylacine bloodlust, a blame-the-victim picture, a sort of fever dream of the Tasmanian settler alone in the bush with these animals, although there was never any evidence of one killing a human being, and very little evidence of their eating sheep."[2]

Ford makes reference to early natural history book illustration in his work by artificially aging his paper with utterly convincing faux stains, foxing, and other indications of wear. He freely talks about his attraction to the work of wildlife illustrators and animal painters, including but not limited to John James Audubon, whose iconic folio *The Birds of North America* was first published in 1838. A New York native, Ford had likely seen Audubon's original large-scale watercolors for the book, which are periodically on view at the New-York Historical Society. Along with providing a kind of historical reference point for and a way into his own work, Ford appreciates Audubon and other natural history illustrators—especially the diorama painters employed by the Museum of Natural History in New York in the early twentieth century—for their technical facility and seamless blending of animal taxidermy specimens and painted environments. Notwithstanding the antiquarian look and feel of his watercolors, Ford's triptych also betrays his exploration of more modern art forms including magic realist film and literature, defined by one scholar as "what happens when a highly detailed, realistic setting is invaded by something 'too strange to be believed.'"[3]

An unlikely historical reference cited by Ford himself is Théodore Géricault's *The Raft of the Medusa* (1819, Louvre Museum), a painting depicting the wreck of a French frigate off the coast of Senegal in 1816.[4] This work not only provides a compositional precedent for the writhing, wet, overlapping figures in various states of physical and emotional distress in *The Island*, but also exemplifies the potential of art as a form of cultural critique and accusation. Ford's painting laments humankind's ageless and seemingly limitless capacity for inflicting irrevocable harm and misery on all forms of nature—most bizarrely and blindly, Ford seems to suggest, on ourselves.

CBC

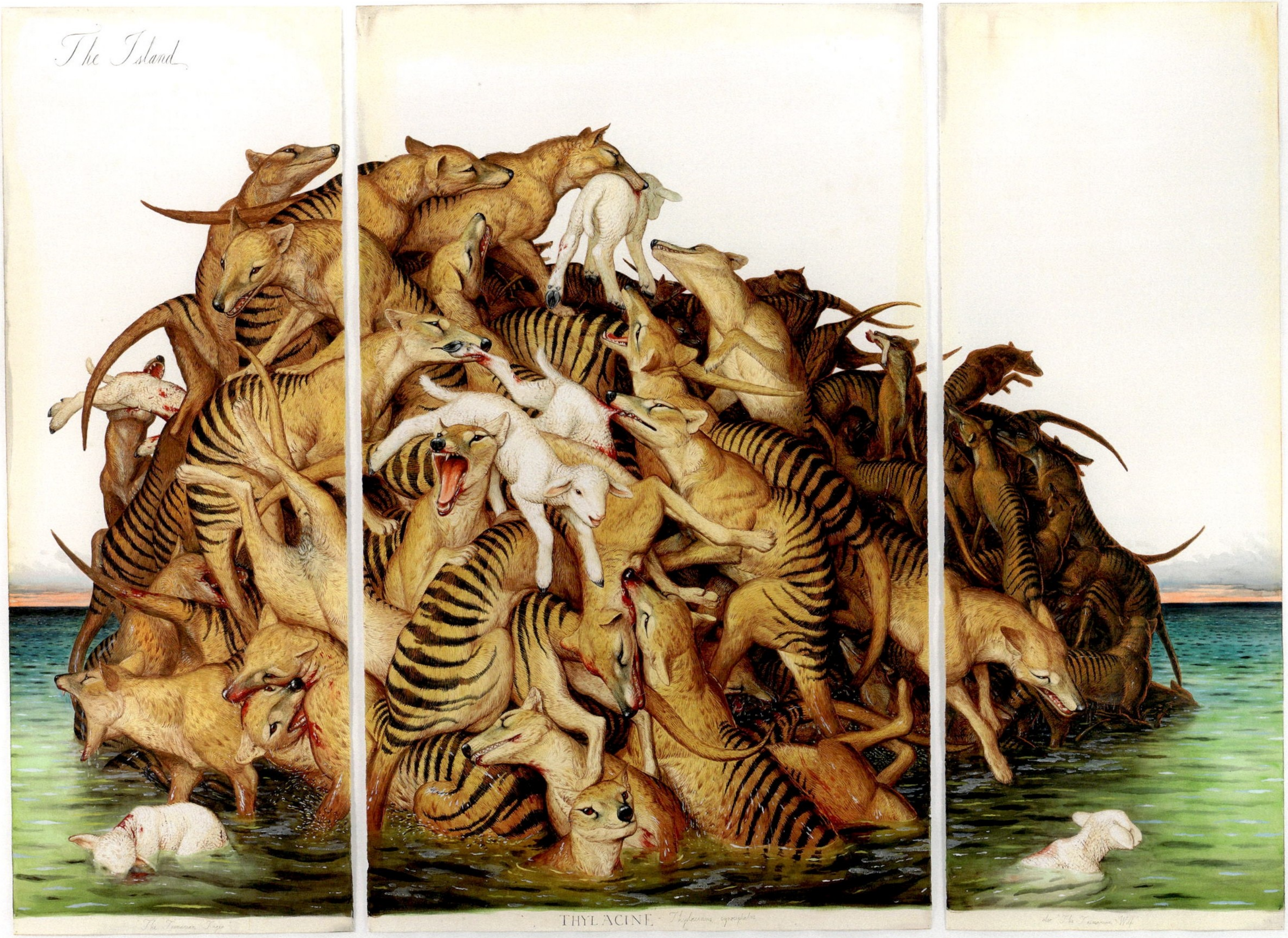
The Island
THYLACINE - Thylacinus cynocephalus

TOM UTTECH (B. 1942)

Enassamishhinjijweian

2009
Oil on linen
103 × 112 in. (261.6 × 284.5 cm)

> *What I'm yearning for is to be the thing, to stop being myself in this body and stop being aware of my life and just be that thing. That's why I paint the stuff. When I'm painting it I can actually be it, because it's my own product. I think that's the closest I'll ever come in my life to being that place.*
>
> –TOM UTTECH[1]

Like a latter-day Charles Burchfield (p. 246), Tom Uttech imbues his grand-scale landscape paintings with a sense of mystery and awe—a pulsating, almost palpable spirituality. Uttech frequently travels to Quetico Provincial Park in Ontario, Canada, just across the United States border from his native northern woods of Wisconsin. There he makes black-and-white photographs featuring carefully observed details of landscape—rocks, trees, roots, and moving water.[2] His final paintings, however, are created completely from memory in the studio. "I sit down, stare at the blank canvas, and start to draw a place where I'd like to be," Uttech explains. "It's in my body, that image, what's up there."[3] The artist's magisterial landscapes evidence a deep understanding and appreciation for the particulars of these special places.

As in the case of many of his paintings, Uttech provided *Enassamishhinjijweian* with a title inspired by the language of the Anishinabe (Ojibwe) Indian tribe. In English, its meaning approximates "hope of good things to come." The picture's artist-made frame alludes to the long tradition of woodcarving and craftsmanship among the Anishinabe. In the lower center of the composition, a lone young bear—a stand-in for the viewer—is witness to the dazzling phenomena before him (and us). A Technicolor sunset pulsates over a distant horizon partly occluded by dozens of flying creatures that fill nearly every inch of the painting's almost nine-foot-square dimensions.

Uttech achieves a satisfying balance of the real and imagined, a measure of his careful observation of nature and his keen knowledge of art history. Each animal and tree is articulated and well defined, while the painting's compositional structure is precise in its geometries and perspective. The horizon line neatly bisects the nature-filled image. In the foreground, fallen trees take the form of converging diagonal lines in a nod to early Renaissance artists' experiments with single-point linear perspective. Placing the diminutive bear before a grand and glorious sunset, Uttech manages to evoke both the Romantic tradition of nineteenth-century German landscape painters such as Casper David Friedrich and the vast, sublime views of Hudson River School artists including Albert Bierstadt. Like many artists working in the twenty-first century, Uttech mines the past to produce iconic images for the present and future.

DB

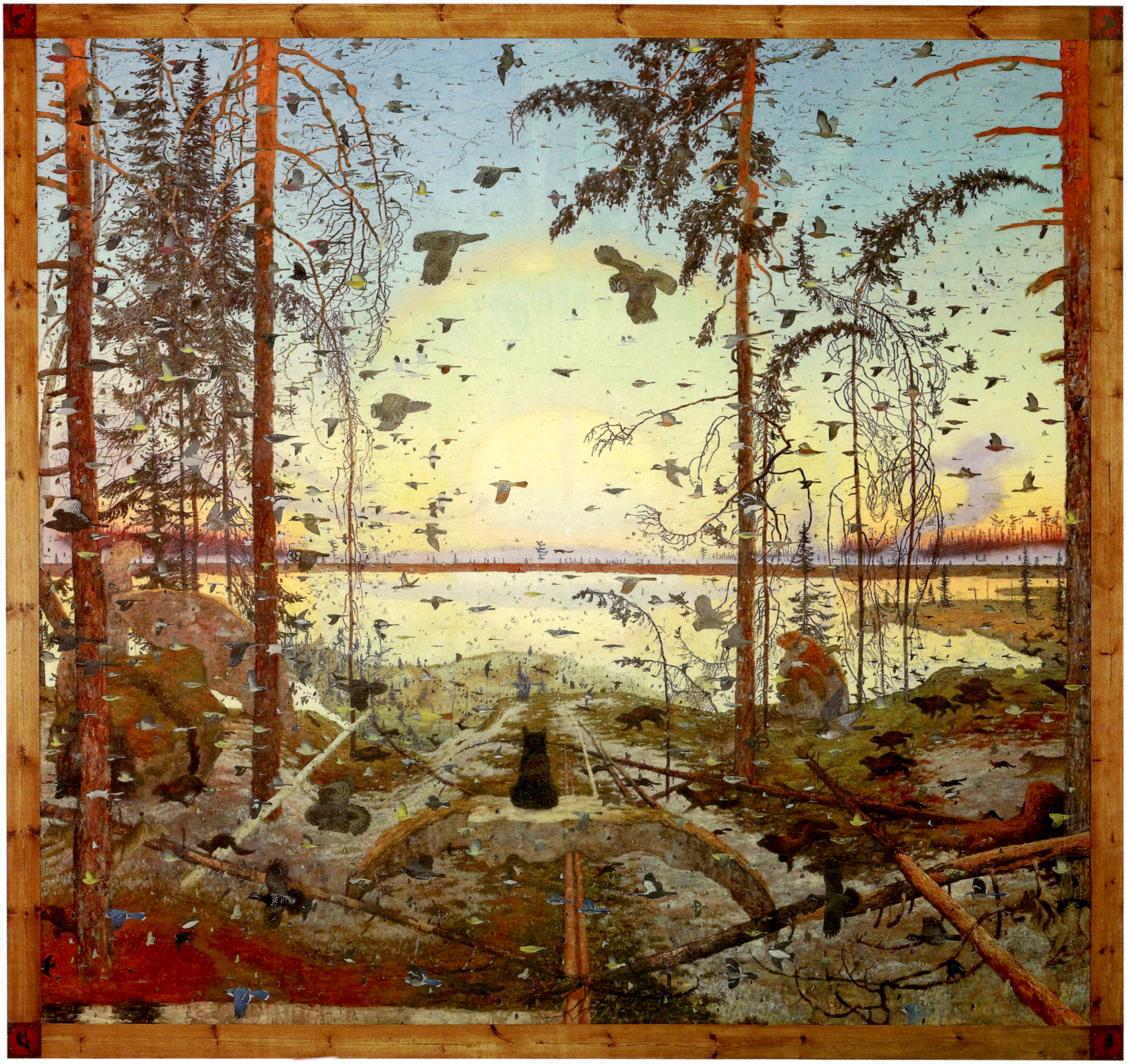

JAMES WOOLDRIDGE

Indians of Virginia (p. 22)

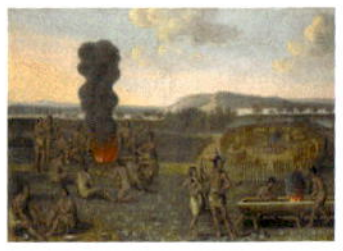

1. Kim Sloan, "First Images of the New World," *American Heritage* 58, no. 5 (Fall 2008): 50–51.
2. John White's watercolors are housed at the British Museum, London. De Bry's engravings after them appear in Thomas Harriot, *A Briefe and True Report of the New Found Land of Virginia* [also known as *Grand Voyages*, volume 1] (Frankfurt: Typis Ioannis Wecheli, 1590). On the history of these images' engraving and publication, see Paul Hulton, *America 1585: The Complete Drawings of John White* (Chapel Hill: University of North Carolina Press, 1984).
3. William Reese Company, "A Major Discovery in Early Paintings of American Indians" (unpublished manuscript, n.d. [ca. 2005], Crystal Bridges curatorial files).
4. Snead and Eastman v. James Wooldridge, October 28, 1680, C6 244 16; and Newman v. Wooldridge, February 15, 1694–95, C10 242 36, National Archives, Richmond, England. Court documents, baptism records, and marriage records for the painter were uncovered by William C. Wooldridge, Suffolk, Va., in the Latter Day Saints Library, Salt Lake City, and the National Archives, Richmond, England, in 2006–8. I am indebted to Wooldridge's research for this account of the artist. For transcripts of court documents made by William C. Wooldridge in 2008, along with a summary of his research, see Crystal Bridges curatorial files.
5. Newman v. Wooldridge, February 15, 1694–95, National Archives, Richmond, England. Transcription courtesy of William C. Wooldridge, Suffolk, Va.
6. William Reese Company, "A Major Discovery."
7. Lance Mayer, "Condition Report" (unpublished technical examination, August 18, 2005, Crystal Bridges curatorial files).
8. Russell Quandt, "Condition Report" (unpublished technical examination, November 21, 1958, Crystal Bridges curatorial files); and William Reese Company, "A Major Discovery."

GERARDUS DUYCKINCK I [ATTRIBUTED TO]

Abigaill Levy Franks, Jacob Franks, Franks Children with Lamb, Moses Levy, Richa Franks, and *Franks Children with Bird* (p. 24)

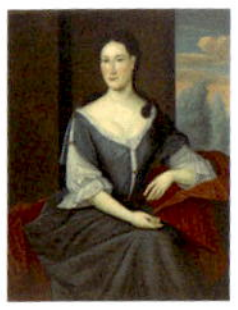

1. For a complete bibliography on the scholarship, see Erica A. Hirshler, "The Levy-Franks Family Portraits," *Magazine Antiques* 138, no. 5 (November 1990): 1020–29; and Paul Needham, *The Celebrated Franks Family Portraits* (New York: Sotheby's Publications, in association with Crystal Bridges Museum of [American] Art, 2008).
2. Hirshler, "The Levy-Franks Family Portraits," 1022.
3. Abigaill Levy Franks to Naphtali Franks, July 9, 1733, and June 9, 1734, in *Letters of the Franks Family, 1733–1748*, ed. Leo Hershkowitz and Isidora S. Meyer (Waltham, Mass.: American Jewish Historical Society, 1968), quoted in Needham, *The Celebrated Franks Family Portraits*, 27.
4. Waldron Phoenix Belknap, *American Colonial Painting* (Cambridge, Mass.: Harvard University Press, 1959), 312–13.

JOHN SINGLETON COPLEY

Mrs. Theodore Atkinson Jr. (Frances Deering Wentworth) (p. 28)

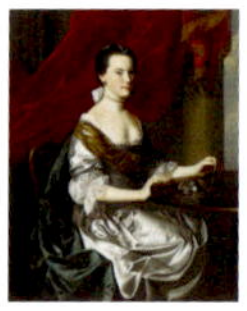

1. For further information on Copley's biography and early career, see Carrie Rebora Barratt and Paul Staiti, *John Singleton Copley in America* (New York: The Metropolitan Museum of Art, 1995).
2. Adding to the scandal surrounding Copley's sitter, Frances married her second suitor, John Wentworth, just days after Theodore Atkinson's death in 1769. See Charles W. Brewster, "Ramble 19," in *Brewster's Rambles about Portsmouth: Sketches of Persons, Localities, and Incidents of Two Centuries* (Portsmouth, N.H.: C. W. Brewster and Son, 1859), 109.

JAMES PEALE SR.

The Ramsay-Polk Family at Carpenter's Point, Cecil County, Maryland (p. 30)

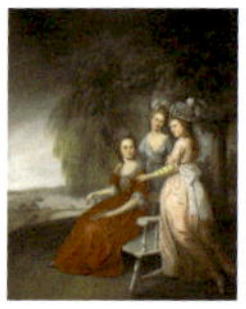

1. Charles Coleman Sellers, *Charles Willson Peale: Later Life, 1790–1827* (Philadelphia: American Philosophical Society, 1947), 54, in Hirschl & Adler Galleries, "James Peale (1749–1831): The Ramsay-Polk Portrait at Carpenter's Point, Cecil County, Maryland" (unpublished manuscript, n.d., Crystal Bridges curatorial files), 7, 8.
2. Frederick Fairchild Sherman, "Two Recently Discovered Portraits in Oils by James Peale," *Art in America* 21 (October 1933): 114–21.

BENJAMIN WEST

Cupid and Psyche (p. 32)

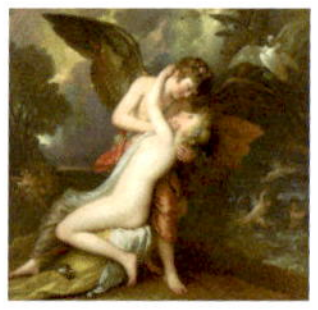

1. Lucius Apuleius, *The Golden Ass*, quoted in cat. entry for *Cupid and Psyche*, in Helmut von Erffa and Allen Staley, *The Paintings of Benjamin West* (New Haven: Yale University Press, 1986), 243.
2. Cat. entry for *Cupid and Psyche*, in von Erffa and Staley, *The Paintings of Benjamin West*, 243.
3. Ibid. West was one of the original subscribers to *The Antiquities of Herculaneum*, a source that provided him with mythological subject matter as well as compositional models.
4. The lions in *Cupid and Psyche* may also refer to *The Antiquities of Herculaneum*, as Hercules's attributes include a lion-skin robe. Alternatively, or in addition, the lions and playful putti may allude to the beneficent role of Britain as the Napoleonic Wars raged throughout continental Europe and beyond.
5. See von Erffa and Staley, *The Paintings of Benjamin West*, 150. Crystal Bridges' painting was among a group of 150 works that West's two sons, Benjamin and Raphael, offered for sale to the United States government, an offer Congress declined.

CHARLES WILLSON PEALE

George Washington (p. 34)

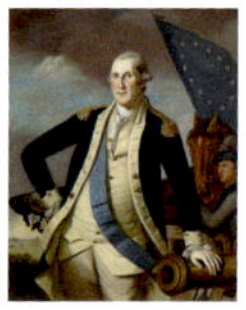

1. On Peale's portraits of Washington, see Charles Coleman Sellers, *Charles Willson Peale* (New York: Scribners, 1969), 225–33; and Sellers, "Charles Willson Peale's Portraits of Washington," *Metropolitan Museum of Art Bulletin*, n.s., 9, no. 6 (February 1951): 147–55.

2. Marquis de Chastellux, *Travels in North America, In the Years 1780–81–82*, trans. “An English Gentleman” (New York: White, Gallaher, and White, 1827), 109.
3. On June 18, 1780, three stars on each epaulette replaced the blue sash depicted in this portrait as the marker of Washington’s status as commander in chief. See Graham Hood, “Easy, Erect, and Noble,” *Colonial Williamsburg Journal* (Summer 2002), http://www.history.org/foundation/journal/summer02/peale.cfm (accessed January 11, 2011).
4. *Important American Paintings, Drawings, and Sculpture* (auction cat. Sotheby’s, New York, May 18, 2004), lot 18.

GILBERT STUART

George Washington [The Constable-Hamilton Portrait] (p. 36)

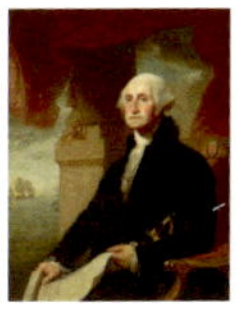

1. For a discussion of the distinct types of portraits of Washington by Stuart, see Ellen G. Miles, “Stuart in Philadelphia,” in Carrie Rebora Barratt and Miles, *Gilbert Stuart* (New York: The Metropolitan Museum of Art, in association with Yale University Press, New Haven, 2004), 133–90.
2. Miles, cat. entry for *George Washington (The Constable-Hamilton Portrait)*, in Barratt and Miles, *Gilbert Stuart*, 184.
3. Ibid., 183.

GILBERT STUART

William Smith (p. 38)

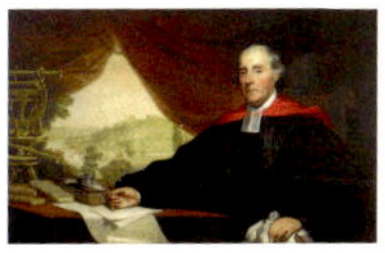

1. Stuart to Joseph Anthony, November 2, 1794 (photostat of original), Massachusetts Historical Society, Boston, quoted in “Stuart in Philadelphia,” in Carrie Rebora Barratt and Ellen Miles, *Gilbert Stuart* (New York: The Metropolitan Museum of Art, in association with Yale University Press, New Haven, 2004), 129.
2. Miles, cat. entry for *William Smith*, in Barratt and Miles, *Gilbert Stuart*, 227.
3. Ibid. The engraving appears in volume one of *The Works of William Smith, D.D., Late Provost of the College and Academy of Philadelphia*, 2 vols. (Philadelphia: Hugh Maxwell and William Fry, 1803).
4. Standard-size canvases in Stuart’s day were either 30 × 25 in. or 50 × 40 in.
5. William R. Smith to John A. McAllister, November 24, 1858, McAllister Manuscripts, Library Company of Philadelphia.
6. Miles, cat. entry for *William Smith*, in Barratt and Miles, *Gilbert Stuart*, 230.

THOMAS SULLY

Colonel Samuel Boyer Davis (p. 40)

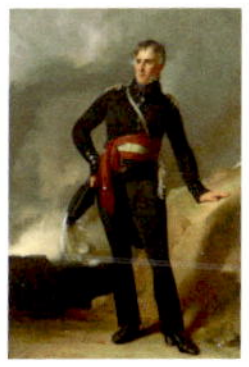

1. On Sully, see Monroe Fabian, *Mr. Sully, Portrait Painter: The Works of Thomas Sully (1783–1872)* (Washington: National Portrait Gallery, 1983).
2. Edward Biddle and Mantle Fielding, *The Life and Works of Thomas Sully (1783–1872)* (Philadelphia: Wickersham Press, 1921), 136.
3. *The Biography and Genealogical History of the State of Delaware* (Chambersburg, Pa.: J. M. Runk and Company, 1899), 2:1359.

RAPHAELLE PEALE

Corn and Cantaloupe (p. 42)

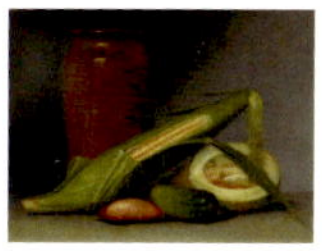

1. Phoebe Lloyd, “Raphaelle Peale’s Anne-Arundel Still Life: A Local Treasure Lost and Found,” *Maryland Historical Magazine* 87, no. 1 (Spring 1992): 5.
2. Ibid.
3. Alexander Nemerov, *The Body of Raphaelle Peale* (Berkeley: University of California Press, 2001), 154.
4. Lloyd, “Raphaelle Peale’s Anne-Arundel Still Life,” 5.
5. Maryland State Archives, Inventories; Prince George’s County, Liber W.A.J. 3, p. 127, cited in Lloyd, “Raphaelle Peale’s Anne-Arundel Still Life,” 4, 8 n. 9. *Corn and Cantaloupe* was valued at a modest $1.50, in accordance with prices for still life in the period. Lloyd notes that the painting was recorded as hanging in the dining room of the Lee estate into the twentieth century.
6. Lloyd, “Raphaelle Peale’s Anne-Arundel Still Life,” 6–7.

JOHN L. KRIMMEL

The Village Politicians (p. 44)

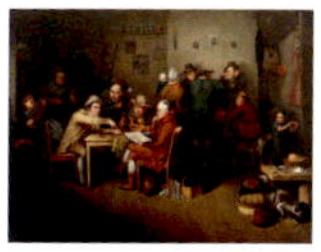

1. Wilkie’s version of *The Village Politicians* (ca. 1806) is owned by the Earl of Mansfield.
2. “Pennsylvania Academy of the Fine Arts Annual Exhibition of 1821,” *Literary Gazette; or Journal of Criticism, Science, and the Arts*, June 30, 1821, 401. For biographical information and a discussion of Wilkie’s influence on Krimmel, see William Dunlap, *The History of the Rise and Progress of the Fine Arts* (New York: George P. Scott, 1834), 2:234–38.
3. *The Jew’s Harp* (ca. 1808, Sudley House, National Museums, Liverpool) and *The Blind Fiddler* (1806, Tate). See Anneliese Harding, “British and Scottish Models for the American Genre Paintings of John Lewis Krimmel,” *Winterthur Portfolio* 38, no. 4 (Winter 2003): 223, 226, 227–28.
4. Ibid., 230, 238–40.
5. Allan Cunningham, *The Life of Sir David Wilkie* (London: J. Murray, 1843), 1:112–13, cited in Harding, “British and Scottish Models,” 236.
6. *The Quilting Frolic* (1813, Winterthur Museum) and *Country Wedding: Bishop White Officiating* (1814, Pennsylvania Academy of the Fine Arts). See “Krimmel’s Picture—Return from Boarding School,” *Analectic Magazine* 2, no. 6 (December 1820): 508.

JOHN VANDERLYN

Niagara and the Rapids (p. 46)

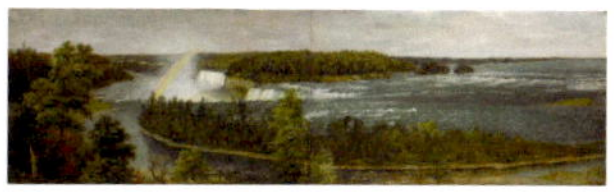

1. Kenneth C. Lindsay, *The Works of John Vanderlyn: From Tammany to the Capitol* (Binghamton: University Art Gallery, State University of New York, 1970), 8, 9. Vanderlyn was the first American artist to study in the French capital.
2. Elizabeth McKinsey, *Niagara Falls: Icon of the American Sublime* (Cambridge: Cambridge University Press, 1985), 57.
3. Ibid., 56–57.
4. Vanderlyn made additional painting trips to Niagara Falls in 1827 and 1837; this oil sketch could date from one of these later visits.
5. Some scholars believe that Vanderlyn planned to create a series of panoramic views of the American landscape similar to his 1818–19 panorama of Versailles, currently housed at the Metropolitan Museum of Art. This enterprise never came to pass. See Lindsay, *The Works of John Vanderlyn*, 3–4; and McKinsey, *Niagara Falls*, 64–73.

6. McKinsey, *Niagara Falls*, 289.
7. *A Distant View of the Falls of Niagara, Including Both Branches with the Island, and Adjacent Shores, Taken from the Vicinity of the Indian Ladder* (ca. 1802–3, Albany Institute of History and Art) and *A View of the Western Branch of the Falls of Niagara, Taken From the Table Rock, Looking up the River, over the Rapids* (1803, probably the painting now in the collection of the Society for the Preservation of New England Antiquities). See Franklin Kelly, cat. entry for "A Distant View of the Falls of Niagara," in *Albany Institute of History and Art: 200 Years of Collecting*, ed. Tammis K. Groft and Mary Alice Mackay (New York: Hudson Hills Press, 1998), 76.

FRANCIS GUY

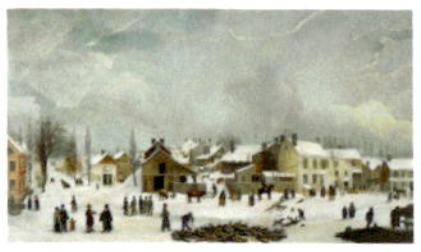

Winter Scene in Brooklyn (p. 48)

1. For more information on the four other versions, see Stiles Tuttle Colwill, *Francis Guy 1760–1820: American Landscape Painter* (Baltimore: Maryland Historical Society, 1981), 68–72; and Teresa A. Carbone, ed., *American Paintings in the Brooklyn Museum* (Brooklyn: Brooklyn Museum, in association with D Giles Limited., London, 2006), 1:571–73.
2. The location, structures, and figures in *Winter Scene in Brooklyn* are identified in a legend on an engraving after the painting by Petrie & Pels of New York, "Brooklyn in 1816: From the Original Painting by F. Guy," published by E. M. Smith, 114 Livingston Street, New York, sometime between 1881 and 1896.
3. William Dunlap, *A History of the Rise and Progress of the Arts of Design in the United States* (1834; repr., New York: Dover Publications, 1969), 149.
4. Rembrandt Peale, "Reminiscences," *Crayon* 3 (1856): 5, quoted in Colwill, *Francis Guy*, 20.
5. Henry R. Stiles, *History of the City of Brooklyn* (1867–72; repr., Westminster, Md.: Heritage Books, 2007), 2:103.
6. Colwill, *Francis Guy*, 70. *Brooklyn Snow Piece* was originally about 58¾ × 95 in., but roughly 18 in. were removed from the left side of the canvas in 1884 following damage by fire. *Winter Scene in Brooklyn* was about 5 in. taller (63 × 106 in.) than its current dimensions before removal of the lower edge. See Colwill, *Francis Guy*, 68–70. The painting underwent another conservation treatment in 1989, during which overpainting in the sky and clouds was removed. The present volume is the first publication to depict the painting in its post-treatment condition.
7. "Guy's Landscape Painting," *Washington Gazette*, June 1, 1820, as reprinted in Colwill, *Francis Guy*, 40. Concluding his discussion of *Brooklyn Snow Piece*, the Washington reviewer wrote, "N.B. The picture of the same description for Baltimore is not yet finished by reason of the painter's indisposition."

CHARLES BIRD KING

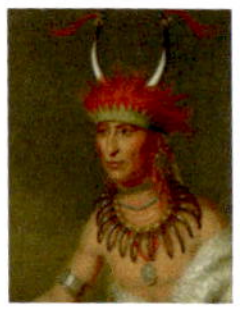

Ottoe Half Chief, Husband of Eagle of Delight (p. 50)

1. Andrew J. Cosentino, *The Paintings of Charles Bird King (1785–1862)* (Washington: Smithsonian Institution Press, 1977), 41.
2. For more on this and other Indian delegations in Washington in the 1820s and 1830s, see Herman J. Viola, *Diplomats in Buckskins: A History of Indian Delegations in Washington City* (Washington: Smithsonian Institution Press, 1981).
3. Ibid., 24–25.
4. The full inscription on the reverse of the painting reads, "Ottoe Half Chief/Husband of Eagle of Delight/by C. B. King/no. 2."
5. Cosentino, *The Paintings of Charles Bird King*, 69–70.
6. Replicas also exist in the collections of the Danish National Museum, the Gulf States Paper Corporation, the Joslyn Art Museum, and the White House. For detailed information and reproductions of these other known versions, see Cosentino, *The Paintings of Charles Bird King*, 181–83.
7. Thomas Loraine McKenney and James Hall, *History of the Indian Tribes of North America, with Biographical Sketches and Anecdotes of the Principal Chief. Embellished with One Hundred and Twenty Portraits, from the Indian Gallery in the Department of War, at Washington* (Philadelphia: F. W. Greenough, 1838–44). These lithographs were based on paintings after the King originals painted by the artist Henry Inman in the early 1830s. Crystal Bridges owns a copy of McKenney and Hall's publication.
8. Ibid., 372.
9. Viola, *Diplomats in Buckskins*, 120.

SAMUEL FINLEY BREESE MORSE

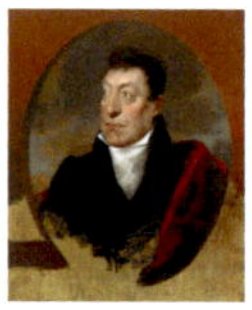

Marquis de Lafayette (p. 52)

1. Stanley J. Idzerda, Anne C. Loveland, and Marc H. Miller, *Lafayette, Hero of Two Worlds: The Life and Pageantry of His Farewell Tour of America, 1824–1825* (Flushing, N.Y.: Queens Museum, 1989).
2. On the portrait commission and Morse's work, see Paul J. Staiti, *Samuel F. B. Morse* (Cambridge: Cambridge University Press, 1989).
3. Morse, *Samuel F. B. Morse: His Letters and Journals*, ed. Edward Lind Morse (Boston: Houghton Mifflin, 1914), 1:262.

EDWARD DALTON MARCHANT

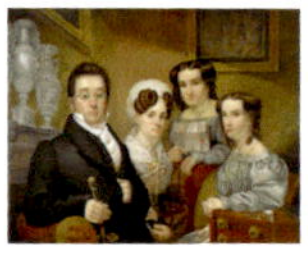

Samuel Beals Thomas, with His Wife, Sarah Kellogg Thomas, and Their Two Daughters, Abigail and Pauline (p. 54)

1. On Marchant, see Andrew L. Thomas, "The Flight from Folk to Fine Art: The Plain Portraits of Edward Dalton Marchant (1806–1887), A.N.A." (master's thesis, George Washington University, 1995).
2. Gregory A. Kuharic, "The Samuel B. Thomas Family" (unpublished manuscript, 1988, Hirschl & Adler Galleries Archives, New York).

LEON POMAREDE

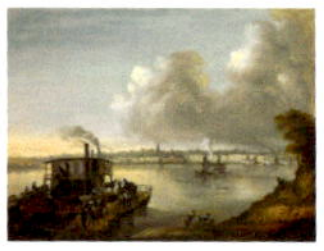

View of St. Louis (p. 56)

1. Judith A. Barter and Lynn E. Springer, *Currents of Expansion: Painting in the Midwest, 1820–1940* (St. Louis: Saint Louis Art Museum, 1977), 49.
2. "Physical Growth of the City of Saint Louis," http://stlouis.missouri.org/heritiage69 (accessed August 11, 2010).
3. Joseph A. Dacus and James William Buell, *A Tour of Saint Louis: The Inside Life of a Great City* (Saint Louis: Western Publishing Company, Jones & Griffin, 1878), 16; and Richard J. Compton, ed., *Pictorial Saint Louis* (St. Louis: R. Compton and Co., 1876), n.p., facing *Saint Louis, 1832*, engraved from the painting by Leon Pomerade [*sic*].
4. Compton, *Pictorial Saint Louis*, n.p.
5. Charles Keemle, *The Saint Louis Directory for the Years 1837–8* (St. Louis: C. Keemle, 1838), iii; Keemle, *The Saint Louis Directory for the Years 1840–1* (St. Louis: C. Keemle, 1841), iii–iv; and Buell, *A Tour of Saint Louis*, 17–18.

THOMAS MORAN

Valley of the Catawissa in Autumn (p. 78)

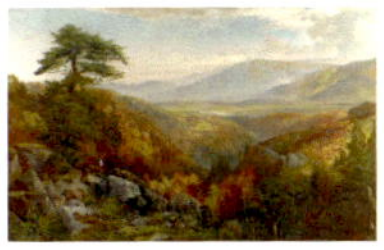

1. For Moran's biography, see Nancy K. Anderson et al., *Thomas Moran* (New Haven: Yale University Press, in association with the National Gallery of Art, Washington, 1997); and Anne Morand, *Thomas Moran: The Field Sketches, 1856–1923* (Norman: University of Oklahoma Press, in association with the Thomas Gilcrease Institute of American History and Art, Tulsa, 1996).
2. H. D. Mears, "The Catawissa Railroad," *Harper's New Monthly* 25, no. 145 (June 1862): 20–28.
3. Ibid., 26–27.
4. Ibid., 27.

ALBERT BIERSTADT

Indian Encampment (p. 80)

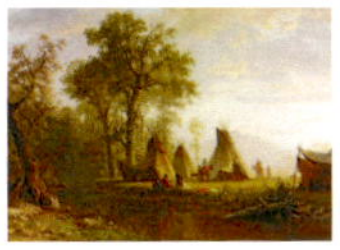

1. Bierstadt, letter to *The Crayon*, July 10, 1859, quoted in John C. Ewers, *Artists of the Old West* (Garden City, N.Y.: Double Day & Company, 1965), 182.
2. Bierstadt traveled with Colonel Frederick W. Lander's 1859 survey party as a private citizen. It is not known how the artist gained permission to join the expedition. See Nancy K. Anderson, "'Wondrously Full of Invention': The Western Landscapes of Albert Bierstadt," in *Albert Bierstadt: Art and Enterprise*, ed. Anderson and Linda S. Ferber (Brooklyn: Brooklyn Museum of Art, 1990), 71, 106 n. 7.

WILLIAM TROST RICHARDS

Landscape (p. 82)

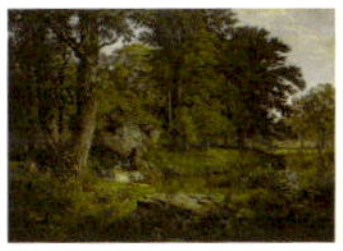

1. For Richards's biography, see Linda S. Ferber, *William Trost Richards (1833–1905): American Landscape and Marine Painter* (New York: Garland Publishing, 1980).
2. For Richards as an American Pre-Raphaelite, see Linda S. Ferber and William H. Gerdts, *The New Path: Ruskin and the American Pre-Raphaelites* (New York: Brooklyn Museum, 1985); and Ferber, "A Philadelphia Pre-Raphaelite in New York: William Trost Richards," *Archives of American Art Journal* 47, nos. 1–2 (Spring 2008): 4–15.
3. Henry T. Tuckerman, *Book of the Artists* (New York: G. P. Putnam and Son, 1867), 524; and Proteus [Eugene Benson], "Concerning a Picture in Goupil's Gallery," *New-York Commercial Advertiser*, February 27, 1862, 2, quoted in Ferber, "A Philadelphia Pre-Raphaelite," 9.
4. L., "Philadelphia Art Notes," *Round Table*, May 14, 1864, 344. I am grateful to Col. Merl M. Moore Jr. for bringing this article to my attention.
5. Ibid.

MARTIN JOHNSON HEADE

The Gems of Brazil: Crimson Topaz, Black-breasted Plovercrest, Amethyst Woodstar, and *The Harbor at Rio de Janeiro* (p. 84)

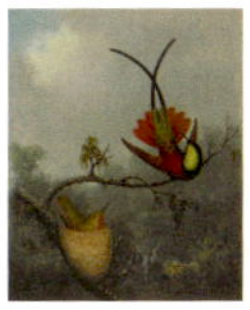

1. *Boston Transcript*, August 12, 1863, quoted in Janet L. Comley, "The Gems of Brazil," in Theodore E. Stebbins Jr. et al., *Martin Johnson Heade* (New Haven: Yale University Press, 1999), 71.
2. In the *Boston Transcript*'s 1863 account of Heade's planned trip to Brazil, for example, the author described the birds as "winged jewels." Heade, quoted in Comley, "Tropical Landscapes," in Stebbins, *Martin Johnson Heade*, 49.
3. On Church and Heade, see Stebbins, *The Life and Work of Martin Johnson Heade: A Critical Analysis and Catalogue Raisonné* (New Haven: Yale University Press, 2000), 21–24, 80–84.
4. In recognition of Heade's achievement, the Emperor of Brazil, Dom Pedro II, distinguished the artist with a high state honor, naming him Knight of the Order of the Rose. The emperor's remarks about *The Gems* are, in part, quoted in Theodore E. Stebbins Jr., *The Life and Works of Martin Johnson Heade* (New Haven: Yale University Press, 1975), 131. It is unclear whether or not *The Harbor at Rio de Janeiro* appeared in this exhibition.
5. On Heade's social and professional barriers, see Stebbins, *The Life and Works*, 101–5. In his astute analysis of *The Gems*, Franklin Kelly describes the failure of the project as a metaphor for the artist's largely frustrated career. See Kelly, cat. entry for *The Gems of Brazil*, in *American Paintings from the Manoogian Collection* (Washington: National Gallery of Art, 1989), 116.
6. Ibid., 120.
7. Only one confirmed painting from the group of twelve *Gems* that Heade exhibited at the Academy of Fine Arts in Rio is known to exist today (private collection). Stebbins asserts that the Crystal Bridges paintings have the polished appearance of the works Heade produced in London after returning from Brazil. See Stebbins, *The Life and Works*, 71–72.

MARTIN JOHNSON HEADE

Study of Pink Roses, Leaves, Heliotrope, a Carnation and an Orchid and *Study of Varied Flowers with a Hummingbird* (p. 88)

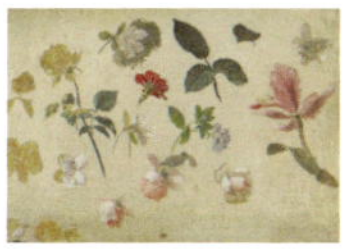

1. One of Heade's distinctly Victorian still-life compositions, *Mixed Flowers with a Box and Pearls* features an abundant array of mid-century bric-a-brac. See Theodore E. Stebbins Jr., *The Life and Work of Martin Johnson Heade: A Critical Analysis and Catalogue Raisonné* (New Haven: Yale University Press, 2000), 129–33. Other works of possible association also appear in Stebbins, *The Life and Work*, 310.
2. Ella M. Foshay, "Charles Darwin and the Development of American Flower Imagery," *Winterthur Portfolio* 15, no. 4 (Winter 1980): 303–5.
3. On Heade and the Victorian taste for orchids, see Stebbins, *The Life and Work*, 91–94.
4. Heade gave twenty-four oil sketches to Floridian Wilma E. Davis, whom he met while visiting her parents. In a note to the Saint Augustine Historical Society, where Davis ultimately donated the set, Davis remarked that Heade gave them to her after seeing her work and suggested the studies might help her artistic pursuits. See Daniel Grant, "Heade Sketches Sold Privately," *Maine Antique Digest* (August 2009): 12:A.

MARTIN JOHNSON HEADE

Haystacks (p. 90)

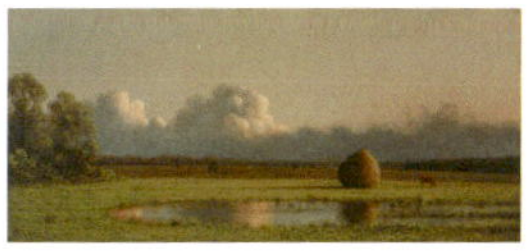

1. Theodore E. Stebbins Jr. has written about the disconnect between Heade's flat, "anti-picturesque" marshland landscapes and his contemporaries' representations of majestic mountains and wooded wilderness, which conformed to picturesque conventions as defined by the eighteenth-century British aesthetic theorist William Gilpin. See Stebbins, *The Life and Work of Martin Johnson Heade: A Critical Analysis and Catalogue Raisonné* (New Haven: Yale University Press, 2000), 115–17.
2. The profile of this landscape, which shows a cluster of trees at left with a slow rise in the distant right, bears a strong resemblance to a number of other

works identified as Newburyport locations. See Stebbins, *The Life and Work*, cat. nos. 210, 215, 252.

3. Stebbins, "Marshes," in Stebbins et al., *Martin Johnson Heade* (New Haven: Yale University Press, 1999), 29. Stebbins discusses the often remarked upon comparison between Heade's and Monet's haystack compositions in *The Life and Work*, 127.
4. Salt marsh hay harvesting was a labor-intensive task. The wet conditions of the marsh made it impossible to take advantage of new harvesting technologies, so much of this crop continued to be hand-harvested. Stebbins credits the great tradition and local history associated with the farming of salt marshes with the survival of these increasingly inefficient farmlands. See Stebbins, *The Life and Work*, 126–27; and Stebbins, *The Life and Works of Martin Johnson Heade* (New Haven: Yale University Press, 1975), 52–53.

EASTMAN JOHNSON

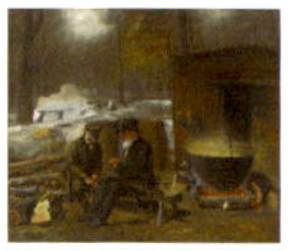

At the Camp—Spinning Yarns and Whittling (p. 92)

1. "American Art," *Knickerbocker* 58, no. 1 (July 1861): 48.
2. The Maine native described his subject as "picturesque and interesting . . . partly on account of its being associated with my pleasantest early recollections." Johnson to John F. Coyle, March 13, 1864, Artists' Correspondence, reel D10, frame 1372, Archives of American Art, Smithsonian Institution, Washington, quoted in Teresa A. Carbone, "The Genius of the Hour: Eastman Johnson in New York, 1860–1880," in Carbone and Patricia Hills, *Eastman Johnson: Painting America* (Brooklyn: Brooklyn Museum of Art, in association with Rizzoli International Publications, 1999), 59.
3. Patricia Hills, "The Genre Painting of Eastman Johnson: The Sources and Development of His Style and Themes" (PhD diss., New York University, 1973), 103.
4. Johnson likely intended *Sugaring Off*, an immense (53¾ × 96½ in.), unfinished oil painting in the collection of the Rhode Island School of Design, to be the culmination of this series. It is not known why he did not finish the work. See Brian T. Allen, *Sugaring Off: The Maple Sugar Paintings of Eastman Johnson* (Williamstown: Sterling and Francine Clark Art Institute, 2004), 9.
5. Carbone has identified the "top-hatted and bearded old-timer" as a recurring theme in Johnson's genre paintings. See "The Genius of the Hour," in Carbone and Hills, *Eastman Johnson*, 50.
6. Jane Weiss, "Home-Loving Sentiments: Domestic Contexts for Eastman Johnson's Paintings," in Carbone and Hills, *Eastman Johnson*, 169.
7. Allen, *Sugaring Off*, 38.
8. The Washington, D.C.-based artist is believed to have followed Union troops on several military campaigns in Virginia. See Carbone, "The Genius of the Hour," in Carbone and Hills, *Eastman Johnson*, 54, 57.
9. Anne C. Rose, "Eastman Johnson and the Culture of American Individualism," in Carbone and Hills, *Eastman Johnson*, 229.

EASTMAN JOHNSON

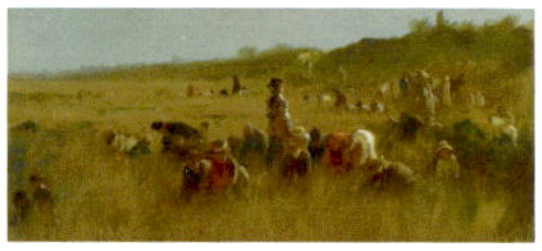

Cranberry Pickers, Nantucket (p. 94)

1. Frank Folwer, quoted in Will H. Low et al., "The Field of Art: Eastman Johnson—His Life and Works," *Scribner's Magazine* 40, no. 2 (August 1906): 256.
2. Johnson to Jarvis McEntee, October 12, 1879, Misc. mss: Jervis McEntee, reel D30, frame 517, Archives of American Art, Smithsonian Institution, Washington, quoted in Marc Simpson, "Taken with a Cranberry Fit: Eastman Johnson on Nantucket," in Simpson, Sally Mills, and Patricia Hills, *Eastman Johnson: The Cranberry Harvest, Island of Nantucket* (San Diego: Timken Art Gallery, 1990), 31. Johnson first visited Nantucket in the summer of 1869 or 1870. From that point forward, he and his wife returned there annually, buying a house and investing in local real estate as the island became a popular tourist destination. Simpson, "Taken with a Cranberry Fit," 33–37.
3. Crystal Bridges' painting contains most of the figures and features of Johnson's final canvas.
4. Simpson, "Taken with a Cranberry Fit," in Simpson, Mills, and Hills, *Eastman Johnson: The Cranberry Harvest*, 31.
5. See Josephine Donovan, *New England Local Color Literature: A Woman's Tradition* (New York: Frederick Ungar, 1983), cited in Teresa A. Carbone and Patricia Hills, *Eastman Johnson: Painting America* (Brooklyn: Brooklyn Museum of Art, in association with Rizzoli International Publications, 1999), 104.
6. Simpson, "Taken with a Cranberry Fit," in Simpson, Mills, and Hills, *Eastman Johnson: The Cranberry Harvest*, 40.
7. For the rest of his career, the artist turned almost exclusively to portraiture.
8. James Carroll Beckwith, quoted in Will H. Low et al., "The Field of Art: Eastman Johnson—His Life and Works," 255.

ALFRED THOMPSON BRICHER

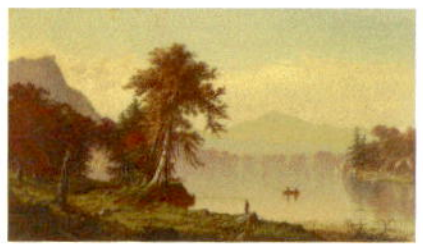

View of Mount Washington (p. 96)

1. For more on Bricher, see Jeffrey E. Brown and Ellen W. Lee, *Alfred Thompson Bricher: 1837–1908* (Indianapolis: Indianapolis Museum of Art, 1973); and Donald E. Keyes, *The White Mountains: Place and Perceptions* (Hanover: University Press of New England, in association with University Art Galleries, University of New Hampshire, 1980), 80–82. For chromolithographs after Bricher's works, see Peter C. Marzio, *The Democratic Art: Pictures for a Nineteenth-Century America: Chromolithography, 1840–1900* (Boston: David R. Godine, in association with the Amon Carter Museum of Western Art, Fort Worth, 1979).

ROBERT SELDON DUNCANSON

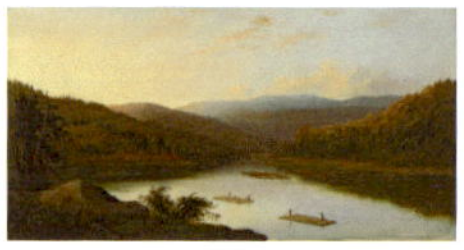

Landscape (p. 98)

1. Joseph D. Ketner II, *The Emergence of the African-American Artist: Robert S. Duncanson, 1821–1872* (Columbia: University of Missouri Press, 1994), 14–15.
2. *Daily Cincinnati Gazette*, May 30, 1861, 2, quoted in Ketner, *The Emergence of the African-American Artist*, 92.
3. *Daily Cincinnati Gazette*, November 24, 1865, 2, quoted in Ketner, *The Emergence of the African-American Artist*, 137.
4. Allan Pringle, "Robert S. Duncanson in Montreal, 1863–1865," *American Art Journal* 17, no. 1 (Autumn 1985): 31.
5. http://www.thecanadianencyclopedia.com/index.cfm?PgNm=TCE&Params=A1ARTA0008014 (accessed August 30, 2010).

WORTHINGTON WHITTREDGE

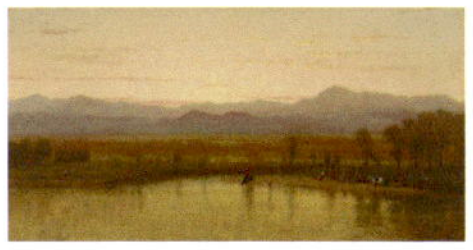

Twilight on the Plains, Platte River, Colorado (p. 100)

1. Peter Hassrick and Patricia Trenton, *The Rocky Mountains: A Vision for Artists in the Nineteenth Century* (Norman: University of Oklahoma Press, 1983), 211.
2. Cheryl A. Cibulka, *Quiet Places: The American Landscapes of Worthington Whittredge* (Washington: Adams Davidson Galleries, 1982), 22.
3. *Rocky Mountain News*, June 26, 1866, quoted in Hassrick and Trenton, *The Rocky Mountains*, 374–75, n. 23.
4. *The Autobiography of Worthington Whittredge, 1820–1910*, ed. John I. H. Baur (1942; repr., New York: Arno Press, 1969), 45–46, quoted in Cibulka, *Quiet Places*, 22.
5. Anthony F. Janson, *Worthington Whittredge* (Cambridge: Cambridge University Press, 1989), 111.

THOMAS MORAN

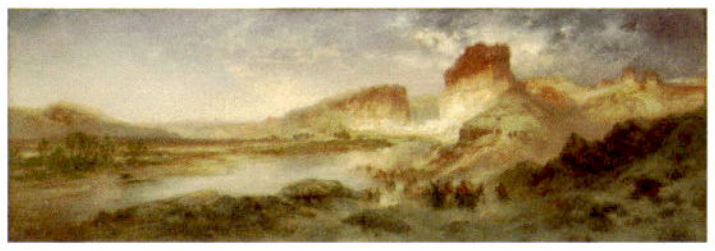

Green River, Wyoming (p. 102)

1. For Moran's Green River paintings, see Nancy K. Anderson et al., *Thomas Moran* (New Haven: Yale University Press, in association with the National Gallery of Art, Washington, 1997); and Joni Louise Kinsey, *Thomas Moran and the Surveying of the American West* (Washington: Smithsonian Institution Press, 1992).

GEORGE INNESS

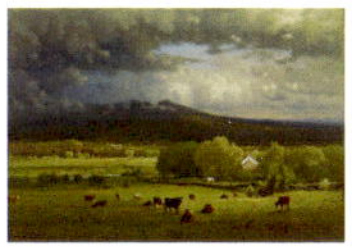

Sunset on the River (p. 104)

1. Beatrice E. Borchardt, "Lady of Utopia: The Story of Marcus and Rebecca Buffum Spring of Eagleswood" (unpublished manuscript, 1973, Raritan Bay Union Papers, New Jersey Historical Society, Newark, N.J.), 10; and Leo G. Mazow, "George Inness: Problems in Antimodernism" (PhD diss., University of North Carolina at Chapel Hill, 1996), 45–64.
2. Michael Quick, *George Inness: A Catalogue Raisonné* (New Brunswick, N.J.: Rutgers University Press, 2007), 1:278–79, 313–14.
3. Sally M. Promey, "The Ribband of Faith: George Inness, Color Theory, and the Swedenborgian Church," *American Art Journal* 26 (1994): 44–65.
4. "Mr. Inness on Art Matters," *Art Journal* [London] n.s. 5 (1879): 377. See also Rachael Ziady DeLue, *George Inness and the Science of Landscape* (Chicago: University of Chicago Press, 2004); and Leo G. Mazow, "Rethinking the Civilized Landscape: George Inness and Evolution in the 1880s and 1890s," in *George Inness: The 1880s and 1890s* (Annville, Pa: Suzanne H. Arnold Art Gallery, Lebanon Valley College, 1999): 6–17.

WINSLOW HOMER

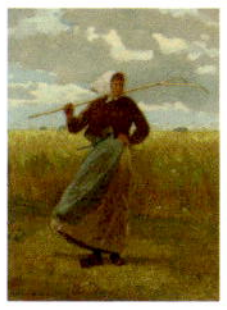

The Return of the Gleaner (p. 106)

1. All of the works are included in Lloyd Goodrich, *Record of Works by Winslow Homer*, ed. Abigail Booth Gerdts (New York: Spanierman Gallery, 2005), 2:38–65. The bibliography on Homer is voluminous; for an overview of Homer's experience in France, see Nicolai Cikovsky Jr. and Franklin Kelly, *Winslow Homer* (Washington: National Gallery of Art, 1995), 27–34.
2. The Civil War and a lack of funds prevented an earlier trip. See Sally Mills, "Chronology," in Marc Simpson, *Winslow Homer: Paintings of the Civil War* (San Francisco: Fine Arts Museums of San Francisco, 1988), 19.
3. Homer's awareness of French art has been often noticed. Recently, Erica Hirshler offered a deeper understanding of Homer's connection to Millet as well as an overview of the American painter's earliest opportunities to view French art in "Pent Fury: Winslow Homer and Jean-François Millet" (lecture, College Art Association, Chicago, Ill., February 2010).
4. For an overview of the rise of the "new" woman in America after the Civil War, see Holly Pyne Connor, ed., *Off the Pedestal: New Women in the Art of Homer, Chase, and Sargent* (Newark: Newark Museum, 2006).

WINSLOW HOMER

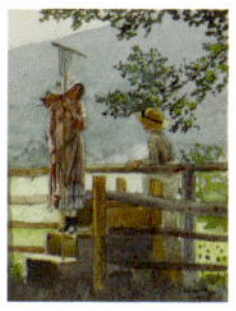

Spring (p. 108)

1. See Lloyd Goodrich, *Record of Works by Winslow Homer*, ed. Abigail Booth Gerdts (New York: Spanierman Gallery, 2008), vol. 3; and John Wilmerding and Linda Ayres, *Winslow Homer in the 1870s: Selections from the Valentine-Pulsifer Collection* (Princeton: Princeton University Press, 1990).
2. Linda Ayres and Jane Myers, *American Paintings, Watercolors, and Drawings from the Collection of Rita and Daniel Fraad* (Fort Worth: Amon Carter Museum of Western Art, 1985), 10.
3. Nicolai Cikovsky Jr. and Franklin Kelly, *Winslow Homer* (Washington: National Gallery of Art, 1995), 163.
4. William Laffan, "The Watercolor Exhibition," *New York Sun*, February 2, 1879, 3, quoted in Margaret C. Conrads, *Winslow Homer and the Critics: Forging a National Art in the 1870s* (Princeton: Princeton University Press, 2001), 151.
5. Kristi Dahm, "Transparent Watercolor and Paper," in Martha Tedeschi with Dahm, *Watercolors by Winslow Homer: The Color of Light* (Chicago: Art Institute of Chicago, 2008), 54; and *Frank Leslie's Illustrated Newspaper*, February 22, 1879, 1–2.
6. William Laffan, "The Watercolor Exhibition," quoted in Conrads, *Winslow Homer*, 150. For the full compliment of positive responses to Homer's watercolor submissions, see Conrads, *Winslow Homer*, 148–55.

WINSLOW HOMER

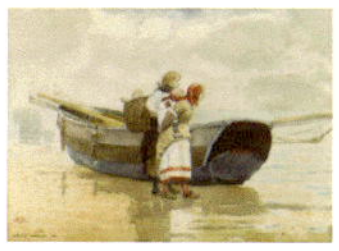

On the Beach, Tynemouth (p. 110)

1. On the critical response to Homer's 1881 watercolors, see Margaret C. Conrads, *Winslow Homer and the Critics: Forging a National Art in the 1870s* (Princeton: Princeton University Press, 2001), 179–95; and Nicolai Cikovsky Jr. and Franklin Kelly, *Winslow Homer* (Washington: National Gallery of Art, 1995), 171–73.
2. For an overview of why Homer may have chosen Cullercoats, and Cullercoats as an art community, see Tony Harrison, *Winslow Homer in England* (Ocean Park, Maine: Hornby Editions, 2004), 11–29; Cikovsky and Kelly, *Winslow Homer*, 173–76; and William H. Gerdts, "Winslow Homer in Cullercoats," *Yale University Art Gallery Bulletin* 36 (Spring 1977): 22, 32–35.
3. Homer also produced one oil painting, and there are thirty-six extant drawing fragments related to this trip (Cooper-Hewitt, National Design Museum, Smithsonian Institution). Abigail Booth Gerdts kindly supplied the numbers of works related to his Cullercoats trip as well as the history of the title variations, provenance, and exhibition history for *On the Beach, Tynemouth*, which will be listed in the forthcoming Homer catalogue raisonné, Lloyd Goodrich, *Record of Works by Winslow Homer*, ed. Abigail Booth Gerdts

(New York: Spanierman Gallery, [2011]), 4:1057. The titling of the watercolor as Tynemouth dates back at least to 1911, when it was exhibited in the *Homer Memorial Exhibition* at the Metropolitan Museum of Art, but it is difficult to definitively locate the scene without any recognizable landmarks. On identifying the location of such scenes, see Gerdts, "Winslow Homer in Cullercoats," 29.

4. Cikovsky and Kelly, *Winslow Homer*, 177; and Judith Walsh, "More Skillful, More Refined, More Delicate: England," in Martha Tedeschi with Kristi Dahm, *Watercolors by Winslow Homer: The Color of Light* (Chicago: Art Institute of Chicago, 2008), 85. The length of Homer's stay in London is unknown.
5. Walsh, "More Skillful, More Refined," 89.
6. On Homer's use of blotting, see Walsh, "More Skillful, More Refined," 78.
7. Gerdts, "Winslow Homer in Cullercoats," 33.

JOSEPH DECKER

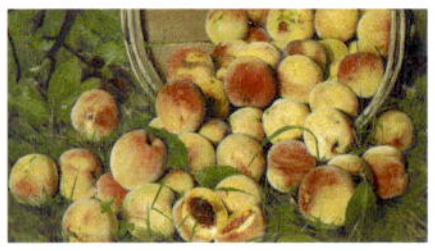

Basket of Peaches (p. 112)

1. Helen A. Cooper, "The Rediscovery of Joseph Decker," *American Art Journal* 10, no. 1 (May 1978): 55–58.
2. "Fifty-Ninth Academy," *Art Interchange* 12 (April 12, 1884): 101; and "The National Academy of Design," *Art Amateur* 12 (December 1884): 4.
3. "The Society of American Artists: Ninth Exhibition," *Studio* 2 (June 1887): 216–17, quoted in William H. Gerdts, *Joseph Decker (1853–1924): Still Lifes, Landscapes, and Images of Youth* (New York: Coe Kerr Gallery, 1988), n.p.
4. "The National Academy of Design, The Sixtieth Annual Exhibition," *Studio*, n.s., 18 (April 11, 1885): 210, quoted in Helen A. Cooper, "The Rediscovery of Joseph Decker," 61.

JOHN HABERLE

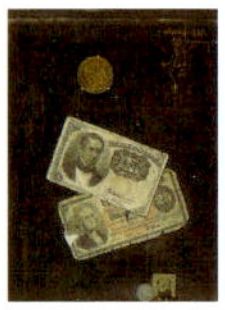

Small Change (p. 114)

1. "Art Institute Pictures," *Chicago Tribune*, June 3, 1888, 26, quoted in William H. Gerdts, "The Artist's Public Face," in Doreen Bolger et al., *William M. Harnett* (New York: The Metropolitan Museum of Art, 1992), 95.
2. For a discussion of the popular appeal of trompe l'oeil painting, see Paul Staiti, "Illusionism, Trompe l'Oeil, and the Perils of Viewership," in Bolger, *William M. Harnett*, 31–47.
3. Paper notes in denominations of five to fifty cents, so-called fractional currency, were issued at the beginning of the Civil War and remained in use until 1876. Considered nearly worthless, the slang term for such bills was "shinplasters," a reference to their use as bandages for superficial cuts and scratches. In 1879, Harnett painted ten-cent fractional currency in *Shinplaster* (private collection) and *Still Life with a Ten-Cent Bill* (Philadelphia Museum of Art). See Bruce W. Chambers, *Old Money: American Trompe L'Oeil Images of Currency* (New York: Berry-Hill Galleries, 1988), 20.
4. Gertrude Grace Sill notes that Thomas B. Clarke acquired *Imitation* in 1887, for $350. See *John Haberle: American Master of Illusion* (New Britain, Conn.: New Britain Museum of Art, 2010), 16.
5. Linda Ayres, *American Paintings from the Manoogian Collection* (Washington: National Gallery of Art, 1989), 112 n. 4.

ALBERT PINKHAM RYDER

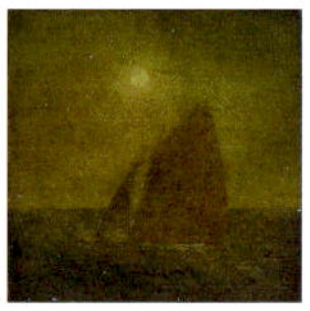

Misty Moonlight (p. 116)

1. Ryder, quoted in Adelaide Louise Samson, "Paragraphs from the Studio of a Recluse," *Broadway Magazine* 14 (September 1905): 10–11, in William Innes Homer and Lloyd Goodrich, *Albert P. Ryder: Painter of Dreams* (New York: Harry N. Abrams, 1989), 186.
2. Lance Mayer and Gay Myers, Lyman Allyn Art Museum, "Report of Examination" (unpublished technical examination, November 20, 2006, Crystal Bridges curatorial files).
3. Elizabeth Broun, *Albert Pinkham Ryder* (Washington: Smithsonian Institution Press, 1989), 2.

GEORGE HENRY SMILLIE

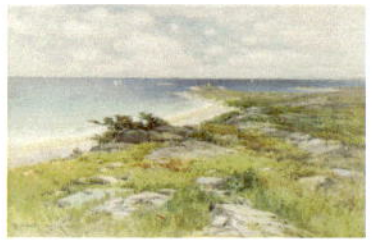

Coastal Scene, New York (p. 118)

1. Donelson F. Hoopes, *American Watercolor Painting* (New York: Galahad Books, 1977), 11.
2. See, for example, "Fine Arts," *Independent*, February 11, 1886, 38; "Water Colors and Etchings," *New York Times*, January 30, 1886, 5; and "The Fine Arts; The Water-Color Society," *Critic: A Weekly Review of Literature and the Arts* 110 (February 6, 1886): 71.
3. Hoopes, *American Watercolor Painting*, 59–60. The name was changed in 1878.
4. "First One Hundred Year Members," americanwatercolorsociety.org http://americanwatercolorsociety.org/a_first_100_years.php?letter=s#list (accessed September 9, 2010).
5. Hoopes, *American Watercolor Painting*, 59.
6. R. R., "Lessons on Trees," *Art Amateur* 27, no. 1 (June 1892): 13.

CHILDE HASSAM

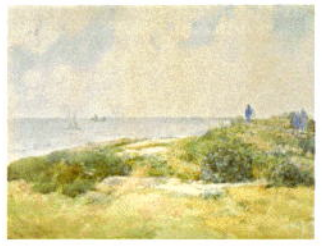

Isles of Shoals and *Paris at Twilight* (p. 120)

1. For more on Celia Thaxter, see Rosamond Thaxter, *Sandpiper: The Life and Letters of Celia Thaxter* (Portsmouth, N.H.: Peter E. Randall, 1963); and Jane Vallier, *Poet on Demand: The Life, Letters, and Work of Celia Thaxter* (Portsmouth, N.H.: Peter E. Randall, 1994).
2. Hassam would later incorporate the horse-drawn carriage, a central element of late nineteenth-century urban street life, into countless scenes of Boston and New York City.
3. In Paris the boulevard system was originally conceived and executed to facilitate troop movements in response to the nearly continuous waves of proletariat street uprisings during the chaotic, post–French Revolutionary decades of the first half of the nineteenth century. Hassam described living in Boston in an interview published in the *Art Amateur* in 1892. "I lived in Columbus Avenue in Boston. The street was all paved in asphalt, and I used to think it very pretty when it was wet and shining, and caught the reflections of passing people and vehicles." Quoted in H. Barbara Weinberg, David Park Curry, and Doreen Bolger, *American Impressionism and Realism: The Painting of Modern Life, 1885–1915* (New York: The Metropolitan Museum of Art, in association with Harry N. Abrams, 1994), 174.

THOMAS EAKINS

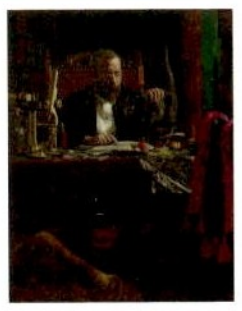

Professor Benjamin Howard Rand and *The Art Student [James Wright]* (p. 124)

1. Sidney D. Kirkpatrick, *The Revenge of Thomas Eakins* (New Haven: Yale University Press, 2006), 44.
2. Elizabeth Johns, *Thomas Eakins: The Heroism of Modern Life* (Princeton: Princeton University Press, 1983), 24.
3. An alternate, but not mutually exclusive, theory is that Eakins painted Rand's likeness as a means of promoting his work to the Jefferson alumni association, which had recently begun to commission portraits. See Ellwood C. Parry III, "The Gross Clinic as Anatomy Lesson and Memorial Portrait," *Art Quarterly* 32, no. 4 (Winter 1969), cited in John Wilmerding, *Thomas Eakins* (Washington: Smithsonian Institution Press, 1993), 78.
4. Marc Simpson, "The 1880s," in *Thomas Eakins*, ed. Darrell Sewell (Philadelphia: Philadelphia Museum of Art, 2001), 118.

CHARLES FREDERIC ULRICH

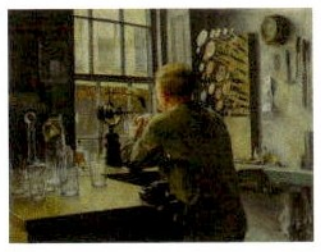

The Glass Engraver (p. 128)

1. Many of Ulrich's craft images are lost and only known today through exhibition reviews or reproductive engravings. Exceptions include *An Amateur Etcher* (1882, private collection) and *The Glassblowers* (1883, Museo de Arte de Ponce, Puerto Rico).
2. Emily D. Shapiro, "Machine Crafted: The Image of the Artisan in American Genre Painting, 1877–1908" (PhD diss., Stanford University, 2003).
3. "The Autumn Exhibition at the Academy," *Critic*, November 4, 1882, 302; and "The Exhibition at the New York Academy," *New York Tribune*, October 20, 1883, Thomas Benedict Clarke Scrapbooks, 1880–1930, reel 598, frame 220, Archives of American Art, Smithsonian Institution, Washington.
4. "Noted American Artists," *New York World*, December 7, 1884, 21. See also Andrea Meislin, "Charles Frederic Ulrich in New York, 1882 to 1884" (master's thesis, University of Arizona, 1996), 41.
5. Thomas Kessner, *The Golden Door: Italian and Jewish Immigrant Mobility in New York City 1880–1915* (New York: Oxford University Press, 1977), 48.

JAMES HENRY BEARD

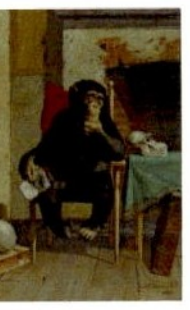

"It is Very Queer, Isn't It?" (p. 130)

1. "James H. Beard," *New York Times*, April 5, 1893, 5.
2. A review published when Beard first exhibited this painting elucidates how its unusual title was understood at the time. The critic narrated the picture's action thusly: "'It is very queer, isn't it,' he [the ape] asks, as he strokes his chin after reading Darwin's *Descent of Man*." See "The Academy Exhibition," *New York Times*, November 29, 1885, 2.
3. "Artist Beard and Crowley," *Current Literature* 1, no. 5 (November 1888): 440.
4. Charles Henry Webb, "Mr. Crowley," *St. Nicholas: An Illustrated Magazine for Young Folks* 15, no. 10 (August 1888): 739, 740. The author counted twenty-three articles on Mr. Crowley in national papers for the years 1887–88, the years of his "marriage" to a chimpanzee named Kittie and his subsequent death from pneumonia.
5. "Artist Beard and Crowley," 440.
6. "The Academy Exhibition," 2.

WILLIAM HOLBROOK BEARD

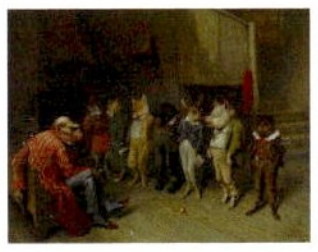

School Rules (p. 132)

1. William H. Gerdts, *William Holbrook Beard: Animals in Fantasy* (New York: Alexander Galleries, 1981), 7–8.
2. For contemporary comparisons to Aesop, see "Humor in Animals," *Literary World* 17, no. 2 (January 23, 1886): 19; and "Aesop of the Brush," *New York Daily Tribune*, February 25, 1900, 3.
3. "Aesop of the Brush," 3.
4. William Holbrook Beard, *Action in Art* (New York: Putnam and Sons, 1893), 246.
5. Robert McCracken Peck, "William Holbrook Beard, 1824–1900," *Magazine Antiques* 146, no. 5 (November 1994): 698, 700.
6. See, for instance, "Death of W. H. Beard: He was Prominent as A Painter of Animals," *Baltimore Sun*, February 21, 1900, 2; "Humor in Animals," 19; and "American Art," *National Repository* 7 (March 1880): 207. See also Gerdts, *William Holbrook Beard*, 19.
7. In classical mythology, Nestor was a wise counselor to younger warriors. *New York World*, December 7, 1884, quoted in Gerdts, *William Holbrook Beard*, 21, 23 n. 66.

JOHN SINGER SARGENT

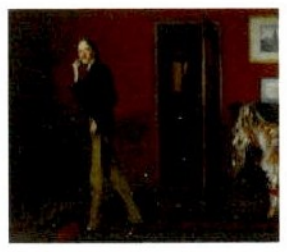

Robert Louis Stevenson and His Wife (p. 134)

1. See for example, Evan Charteris, *John Sargent* (New York: Charles Scribner's Sons, 1927), 79–80; Marc Simpson, *Uncanny Spectacle: The Public Career of the Young John Singer Sargent* (New Haven: Yale University Press, 1997), 124, 147; and Richard Ormond and Elaine Kilmurray, *John Singer Sargent: The Early Portraits* (New Haven: Yale University Press, 1998), 167–69.
2. Sargent's first portrait of Stevenson, painted in 1884, is believed to have been destroyed. His third portrait, painted in 1887, is in the collection of the Taft Museum in Ohio. See Ormond and Kilmurray, eds., *John Singer Sargent* (Washington: National Gallery of Art), 120.
3. Sargent to Henry James, June 29, 1885, quoted in Simpson, *Uncanny Spectacle*, 124.
4. Robert Louis Stevenson to Will H. Low, October 22, 1885, quoted in Ormond and Kilmurray, *John Singer Sargent: The Early Portraits*, 167.
5. Fanny Stevenson to Margaret Isabella Balfour Stevenson, August 13, 1885, quoted in Ormond and Kilmurray, *John Singer Sargent: The Early Portraits*, 167.
6. Sargent to Robert Louis Stevenson, November 1885, quoted in Ormond and Kilmurray, *John Singer Sargent: The Early Portraits*, 168.

GEORGE DE FOREST BRUSH

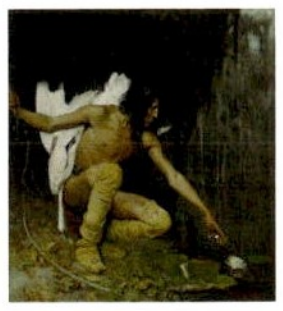

The Indian and the Lily (p. 136)

1. Brush to Charles Erskine Scott Wood, January 2, 1887, Charles Erskine Scott Wood Papers, Bancroft Library, University of California, Berkeley.
2. See Emily Dana Shapiro, "'A Purpose in Every Stroke': Brush's Images of Indian Artisanry," in *George de Forest Brush: The Indian Paintings*, ed. Nancy K. Anderson (Washington: National Gallery of Art, in association with Lund Humphries, London, 2008), 83–100.
3. Judith Walsh, "The Language of Flowers in Nineteenth-Century American Painting," *Antiques* 156, no. 4 (October 1999): 526.

4. Brush, "An Artist Among the Indians," *Century* 30, no. 1 (May 1885): 56–57. Brush's romanticized approach to his subjects in part accounts for the artist's lack of ethnographic accuracy. His hunter dons Apache boot moccasins with toe guards, which were usually worn in cactus country rather than a swamp environment. I thank Crystal Bridges assistant curator Manuela Well-Off-Man for sharing her knowledge of traditional Native American costume.
5. *Brooklyn Eagle*, 1888, quoted in Mary Lublin, "Living for Art: Brush and His Indians," in *George de Forest Brush: The Indian Paintings*, ed. Anderson, 70.
6. http://web1.audubon.org/waterbirds/species.php?speciesCode=rosspo (accessed August 5, 2010).

DENNIS MILLER BUNKER

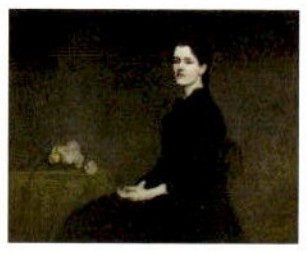

Anne Page (p. 138)

1. Aestheticism was just then being popularized in the United States, where Oscar Wilde was on a speaking tour devoted to interpreting aesthetic ideas of beauty.
2. Crystal Bridges owns a plaster version of Saint-Gaudens's portrait bust of Anne Page.
3. Bunker to Anne Page, September 1, 1886, quoted in Erica E. Hirshler, *Dennis Miller Bunker: American Impressionist* (Boston: Museum of Fine Arts, 1994), 46.
4. Bunker to Page, March 11, 1887, quoted in Michael Quick, *American Portraiture in the Grand Manner, 1720–1920* (Los Angeles: Los Angeles County Museum of Art, 1981), 216.

GARI MELCHERS

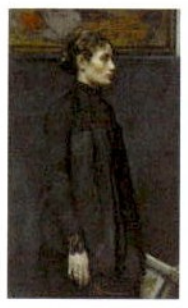

The Embroideress [Portrait of Mrs. Hitchcock] (p. 140)

1. After Melchers married in 1903, his wife replaced Hitchcock as the artist's primary model. See George Mesman, "Julius Garibaldi Melchers (1860–1932): A Survey of His Dutch Paintings with Emphasis on His Religious Works" (PhD diss., City University of New York, 1990), 131–32.
2. Joseph G. Dreiss, *Gari Melchers: His Works in the Belmont Collection* (Charlottesville: University Press of Virginia, 1984), 105. Other examples include *The Shipbuilder* (ca. 1896, Royal Academy, Dresden); *The Fencer* (ca. 1895, Gari Melchers Home and Studio); and *The Ice Sweeper* (location unknown).
3. Scholars have speculated about whether Mrs. Hitchcock's unconventional garment, which does not gather at the waist but rather hangs loose in folds, might be maternity wear. See Linda Ayres and Jane Myers, *American Paintings, Watercolors, and Drawings from the Collection of Rita and Daniel Fraad* (Fort Worth: Amon Carter Museum, 1985), 26. Mrs. Hitchcock is not known to have ever been pregnant. Alternatively, the garment might be an imaginatively embellished version of an artist's smock. I thank Alden O'Brien, curator of costumes and textiles, DAR Museum; and Jan Glier Reeder, consulting curator, Brooklyn Museum Costume Collection, The Costume Institute, The Metropolitan Museum of Art, for sharing their expertise on late nineteenth-century women's apparel.
4. *Chicago Daily News*, September 23, 1890; *Chicago Tribune*, September 2, 1890; and *New York Evening Post*, February 6, 1890. I thank Joanna D. Catron, curator at the Gari Melchers Home and Studio, for bringing these sources to my attention.
5. Henriette Lewis-Hind, "Foreword," in *Gari Melchers: Painter* (New York: William Edwin Rudge, 1928), n.p.

WILLIAM MERRITT CHASE

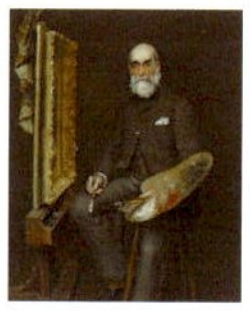

Worthington Whittredge (p. 142)

1. M[ariana] G[riswold] Van Rensselaer, "William Merritt Chase," *American Art Review* 2, no. 3 (January 1881): 92. This group of American artists recently returned from Europe also included John Henry Twachtman, James Carroll Beckwith, Thomas Wilmer Dewing, and John La Farge. The "new men" introduced to America the prevailing styles in Munich (where Chase trained) and Paris. Ultimately Paris's influence would eclipse that of Munich.
2. New rules in 1877 favoring senior academicians over younger artists in the academy's annual exhibitions, and financially driven decisions to reduce spending on studio classes were among the artists' main grievances. See Ronald G. Pisano, *A Leading Spirit in American Art: William Merritt Chase, 1849–1916* (Seattle: University of Washington Press, 1983), 39–40. On the "new movement" and the Society of American Artists, see "Our Art Clubs: Society of American Artists," *Art Union* 2, no. 4 (October 1885): 79; and S[amuel] G[reen] W[heeler] Benjamin, "Society of American Artists: Third Exhibition," *American Art Review* 1 no. 6 (April 1880): 258–62.
3. On Chase's studio, see Nicolai Cikovsky Jr., "William Merritt Chase's Tenth Street Studio," *Archives of American Art* 16, no. 2 (1976): 2–14; and Mary Sayre Haverstock, "The Tenth Street Studio," *Art in America* 54, no. 5 (September/October 1966): 48–57.
4. *New York Times*, April 6, 1891, 6, quoted in Pisano, *William Merritt Chase: Portraits in Oil, The Complete Catalogue of Known and Documented Works by William Merritt Chase (1849–1916)* (New Haven: Yale University Press, 2006), 94.
5. Chase must have presented the portrait to the artist, since it was in the Whittredge family for over a century.
6. *The Autobiography of Worthington Whittredge, 1820–1910*, ed. John I. H. Baur (Brooklyn: Brooklyn Museum Journal, 1942). Chase may have admired Whittredge because of the older artist's openness to the new trends later in life.

JOHN FREDERICK PETO

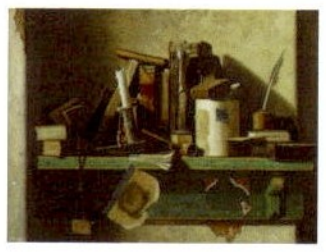

Old Companions (p. 144)

1. Alfred Frankenstein, *After the Hunt: William Harnett and Other American Still Life Painters, 1870–1900*, rev. ed. (Berkeley: University of California Press, 1969), 109.
2. Frankenstein, *The Reality of Appearance: The Trompe L'oeil Tradition in American Painting* (New York: New York Graphic Society, 1970), 104.
3. http://www.hba-llc.com/projects/preservation/petohouse/petohouse.html#nogo (accessed August 29, 2010).
4. John Wilmerding, *Important Information Inside: The Art of John F. Peto and the Idea of Still-Life Painting in Nineteenth-Century America* (New York: Harper & Row, 1983), 137. Other paintings featuring the green bookshelf include *Still Life with Lard Oil Lamp* (ca. 1900, Newark Museum) and *Lamps of Other Days* (1888, Amon Carter Museum of American Art).

JOHN SINGER SARGENT

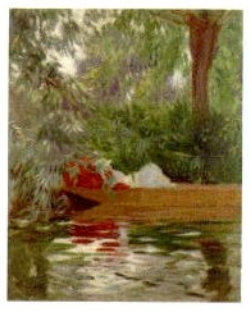

Under the Willows (p. 146)

1. Elaine Kilmurray and Richard Ormond, eds., *John Singer Sargent: Figures and Landscapes, 1883–1889: The Complete Paintings, Volume 5* (New Haven: Yale University Press, 2010), 148.
2. Kilmurray and Ormond, *John Singer Sargent* (Washington: National Gallery of Art, 1999), 120.
3. Kilmurray and Ormond, *John Singer Sargent: Figures and Landscapes*, 148.

DENNIS MILLER BUNKER

Wild Asters (p. 148)

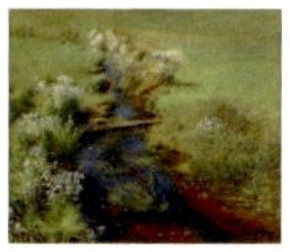

1. *The Brook at Medfield* (Isabella Stewart Gardner Museum); *The Brook: Medfield* (private collection); and *The Pool: Medfield* (Museum of Fine Arts, Boston) are the other three paintings in this series.
2. "Fine Arts," *Boston Herald*, February 2, 1890, 12, quoted in Erica E. Hirshler, *Dennis Miller Bunker and His Circle* (Boston: Isabella Stewart Gardner Museum, 1995), 8.

JOHN LA FARGE

Peonies in a Breeze (p. 150)

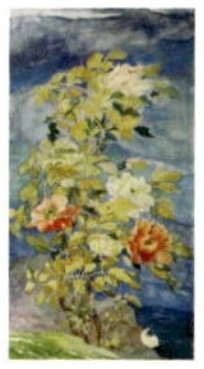

1. Maria Oakey Dewing, "Flower Painters and What the Flower Offers to Art," *Art and Progress* 6 (June 1915): 256–57.
2. Arthur Edwin Bye, *Pots and Pans; or, Studies in Still-Life Painting* (Princeton: Princeton University Press, 1921), 194.
3. *Peonies in the Wind with Kakemono Borders* (Smithsonian American Art Museum).
4. Cecilia Waern, *John La Farge: Artist and Writer* (New York: Macmillan, 1896), 68.

JOHN HENRY TWACHTMAN

September Sunshine (p. 152)

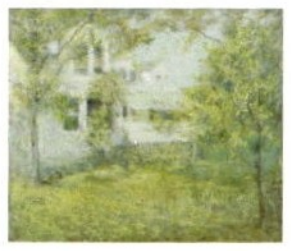

1. John Douglass Hale, "The Life and Creative Development of John H. Twachtman" (PhD diss., Ohio State University, 1957), 70.
2. Warrantee Deeds, Greenwich Town Hall, Book 60:165; and Book 61:488.
3. "The Society of American Artists," *Art Amateur* 32 (May 1895): 158.
4. Twachtman to Julian Alden Weir, ca. spring 1889, J. Alden Weir Papers (WEFA 350), Weir Farm National Historic Site, Wilton, Conn.
5. For a photograph of the house taken about the time Twachtman acquired it, see Lisa N. Peters, *John Henry Twachtman: An American Impressionist* (New York: Hudson Hills Press, 1999), 97.
6. Theodore Robinson, diary entries, May 16 and May 30, 1894, Frick Art Reference Library, N.Y.
7. "Twachtman's Painted Poems: Comparisons with French and Japanese Impressionists," *New York Times*, January 10, 1905, 6. For this reference I am grateful to Lisa N. Peters, coauthor, John Henry Twachtman catalogue raisonné, Spanierman Gallery, LLC, New York (in progress).

THEODORE ROBINSON

World's Columbian Exposition (p. 154)

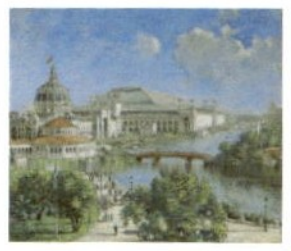

1. Robinson to Claude Monet, March 22, 1892, quoted in Sona Johnston, "Theodore Robinson and Claude Monet," in *In Monet's Light: Theodore Robinson at Giverny* (Baltimore: Baltimore Museum of Art, 2004), 205.
2. Robinson was one of the few American artists in Giverny to develop a close friendship with Monet. See Sona Johnston, *Theodore Robinson, 1852–1896* (Baltimore: Baltimore Museum of Art, 1973).
3. See H. Barbara Weinberg, "Summers in the Country," in Kathleen Adler, Erica E. Hirshler, and Weinberg, *Americans in Paris, 1880–1900* (London: National Gallery, 2006), 142, 145.
4. Johnston, "Theodore Robinson and Claude Monet," in *In Monet's Light*, 70, 186; and Marc Simpson, cat. entry for *World's Columbian Exposition*, in *American Paintings from the Manoogian Collection* (Washington: National Gallery of Art, 1989), 154. The three paintings Robinson exhibited at the exposition were *The Layette* (1892, Corcoran Gallery of Art), *Winter Landscape* (1889, Terra Foundation for American Art), and *Roman Fountain* (ca. 1891, private collection).
5. Crystal Bridges' painting was the second of two Millet commissioned for *The Book of the Builders: Being the Chronicle of the Origin and Plan of the World's Fair . . .* (Springfield, Ohio: Columbian Memorial Publication Society, 1894), which he co-authored with Daniel Burnham. Although works by several other American impressionists are reproduced, neither of Robinson's paintings appeared in the book. See Carol Troyen, cat. entry for *World's Columbian Exposition*, in Theodore E. Stebbins et al., *A New World: Masterpieces of American Painting, 1760–1910* (Boston: Museum of Fine Arts, 1983), 319, 320 n. 2.
6. Simpson, cat. entry for *World's Columbian Exposition* in *American Paintings from the Manoogian Collection*, 154. Charles Dudley Arnold's photograph is found in most standard guides to and histories of the fair, including Norman Bolotin and Christine Laing, *The World's Columbian Exposition: The Chicago World's Fair of 1893* (Urbana: University of Illinois Press, 2002), 50. The buildings are identified in Stebbins, *A New World*, 319.
7. David F. Burg, *Chicago's White City of 1893* (Lexington: University Press of Kentucky, 1976), 144.
8. Bolotin and Laing, *The World's Columbian Exposition*, 44, 89.
9. Robinson to Monet, August 17, 1893, in Johnston, *In Monet's Light*, 205.

MAURICE BRAZIL PRENDERGAST

People on the Beach: Revere Beach (p. 156)

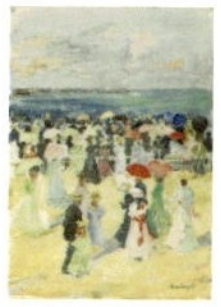

1. For Prendergast's chronology, see Carol Clark, Nancy Mowll Mathews, and Gwendolyn Owens, *Maurice Brazil Prendergast, Charles Prendergast: A Catalogue Raisonné* (Williamstown, Mass.: Williams College Museum of Art, 1990), 726–29.
2. For Prendergast's response to the changes in the parks and beaches of Boston, see Mathews, *The Art of Leisure: Maurice Prendergast in the Williams College Museum of Art* (Williamstown, Mass: Williams College Museum of Art, 1999), especially the chapters "Franklin Park, Boston," and "The South Shore."
3. Arthur Wesley Dow, a friend of Prendergast, recorded these principles in his famous textbook *Composition* (1899), but they were the result of much discussion in Boston, particularly at the Museum of Fine Arts, where Dow served as assistant curator of the Japanese department. See Frederick Moffatt, *Arthur Wesley Dow (1857–1922)* (Washington: Smithsonian Institution Press, 1977), 65–70.

WILLIAM MERRITT CHASE

Seaside Flowers (p. 158)

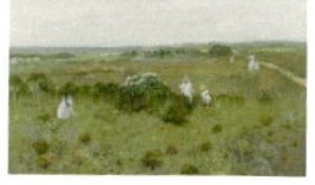

1. See Katherine Metcalf Roof, *The Life and Art of William Merritt Chase* (New York: Scribner and Sons, 1917), 162; and Ronald G. Pisano, *William Merritt Chase: A Leading Spirit in American Art* (Seattle: Henry Art Gallery, 1983), 121–22.
2. Although he sold the Chase School in 1898, Chase continued to teach there after it was renamed the New York School (the school later became Parsons New School of Design). On Chase as a teacher, see June L. Ness, "William Merritt Chase and the Shinnecock Art School," *Archives of American Art Journal* 13, no. 3 (1973): 8–12; and Pisano, *William Merritt Chase: A Leading Spirit*, 87–145.

3. Pisano, *William Merritt Chase, Landscapes in Oil: The Complete Catalogue of Known and Documented Works by William Merritt Chase (1849–1916), Volume 3* (New Haven: Yale University Press, 2009), 125. Chase's eldest son, Robert Stewart Chase, was born in 1898; the artist had lost two infant sons to illness, in 1891 and 1894, respectively.

JAMES MCNEILL WHISTLER

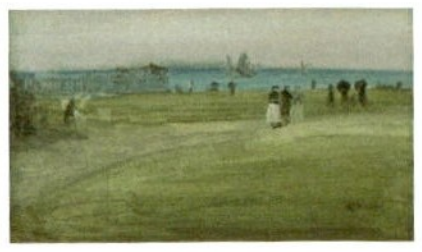

Green and Violet: The Evening Walk (p. 160)

1. This painting has traditionally been dated 1885 and assigned to that earlier trip to Dieppe.
2. D. Croal Thomson, "New Pictures by Mr. Whistler," *Art Journal* 29 (January 1897): 10–11.
3. Elizabeth Pennell, journal entry, March 8, 1921, Pennell-Whistler Collection, box 351, Manuscript Division, Library of Congress, Washington.
4. Whistler to Rosalind Birnie Philip, [September 28, 1896], *The Correspondence of James McNeill Whistler, 1855–1903*, ed. Margaret F. MacDonald, Patricia de Montfort, and Nigel Thorp, online edition, University of Glasgow, http://www.whistler.arts.gla.ac.uk/correspondence (accessed October 19, 2010).

MARIA OAKEY DEWING

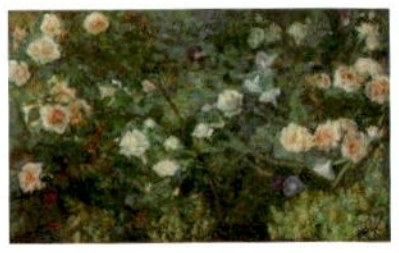

Rose Garden (p. 162)

1. Dewing, "Flower Painters and What the Flower Offers to Art," *Art and Progress* 6 (June 1915): 262.
2. Dewing to Royal Cortissoz, February 20, 1921, quoted in Doreen Bolger et al., *In Pursuit of Beauty: Americans and the Aesthetic Movement* (New York: The Metropolitan Museum of Art, 1986), 420.
3. "Some Lady Artists of New York," *Art Amateur* 3 (July 1880): 27.
4. Susan A. Hobbs, "Maria Oakey Dewing's Flowers and Figures," *Magazine Antiques* 165 (January 2004): 156.
5. Dewing, "Flower Painters," 255.
6. Frances Grimes, "Reminiscences," [1950s], reprinted in Susan Faxon Olney et al., *A Circle of Friends: Art Colonies of Cornish and Dublin* (Durham, N.H.: University Art Galleries, 1985), 64.
7. Dewing to Royal Cortissoz, February 2, 1913, and May 1, 1923, quoted in Jennifer A. Martin, "Royal Cortissoz and Maria Oakey Dewing's 'Rose Garden,'" *Yale University Library Gazette* 52 (October 1977): 86, 87.

WILLARD LEROY METCALF

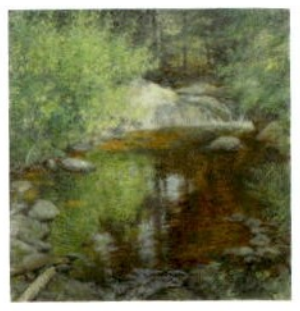

The Pool (p. 164)

1. Francis Murphy, *Willard Leroy Metcalf: A Retrospective* (Springfield, Mass.: Museum of Fine Arts, 1976), xii.
2. Bernard Teevan, "A Painter's Renaissance," *International Studio* 82 (October 1925): 3.
3. Teevan, "A Painter's Renaissance," 3.
4. Royal Cortissoz, "Willard L. Metcalf: An American Landscape Painter," *Appleton's Booklovers Magazine* 6 (October 1905): 510.
5. Ibid., 509.

WILLIAM TROST RICHARDS

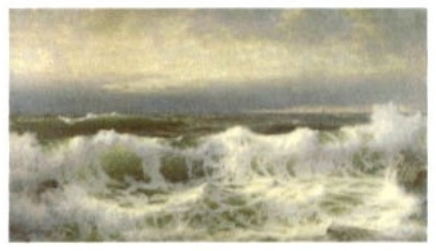

Along the Shore (p. 166)

1. For Richards as a marine painter, see references cited in entry for *Landscape* (p. 82).
2. Clarence Cook, *Art and Artists of Our Time* (New York: S. Hess, 1888), 294, quoted in Linda S. Ferber, *William Trost Richards (1833–1905): American Landscape and Marine Painter* (New York: Garland Publishing, 1980), viii.

EDWARD SHERIFF CURTIS

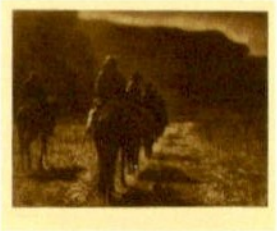

The Vanishing Race—Navaho (p. 168)

1. Photogravure is a photomechanical printing process that utilizes a printing press and a copper plate that has been chemically etched with a photographic image from a positive transparency. A popular method for the mass production of photographs in the late nineteenth and early twentieth century, photogravure was most notably used by Alfred Stieglitz for the publications *Camera Notes* and *Camera Work*. The process produces high-quality, tonally rich images.
2. Theodore Roosevelt wrote the foreword in the first text volume of *The North American Indian*. An ardent supporter of Curtis's work, earlier in the decade Roosevelt had commissioned the photographer to take portraits of his children, and Curtis documented the president's 1905 inauguration. After J. P. Morgan Sr.'s death in 1913, his son took over funding for the project.
3. Mick Gidley, *Edward S. Curtis and the North American Indian Project in the Field* (Lincoln: University of Nebraska Press, 2003), 7. The print run was limited to five hundred copies. Due to a variety of factors, Morgan and Curtis did not succeed in selling all the subscriptions.
4. Curtis's work on the project actually exceeded the publication's twenty-three-year run, as negatives used in the series date as early as 1903.
5. Gidley, *Edward S. Curtis*, 4.
6. Christopher M. Lyman, *The Vanishing Race and Other Illusions: Photographs of Indians by Edward S. Curtis* (Washington: Smithsonian Institution Press, 1982), 17.
7. Curtis, *The North American Indian, Volume 1: The Apache, The Jicarillas, The Navaho* (Cambridge: The University Press, 1907), xiii.
8. Lyman, *The Vanishing Race*, 19.

FREDERIC REMINGTON

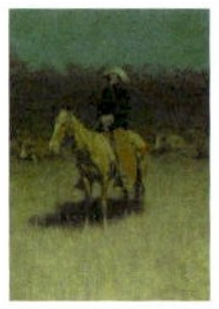

Cowpuncher's Lullaby (p. 170)

1. Andreas Blühm and Louise Lippencott, *Light! The Industrial Age 1750–1900, Art & Science & Technology & Society* (New York: Thames and Hudson, 2001), 25; and William C. Sharpe, "What's Out There," in *Frederic Remington: The Color of Night*, ed. Nancy K. Anderson (Princeton: Princeton University Press, 2003), 19.
2. Alexander Nemerov, *Frederic Remington and Turn-of-the-Century America* (New Haven: Yale University Press, 1995), 45–46.
3. Nancy K. Anderson, "Introduction," in *Frederic Remington: The Color of Night*, 12.
4. William H. Goetzmann and William N. Goetzmann, *The West of the Imagination* (New York: W. W. Norton, 1986), 246.
5. "A Closed Chapter of Life: Paintings of Western Life by Frederic Remington," *New York Times*, December 23, 1906, mag. sec., 4.
6. "Exhibitions Now On," *American Art News*, December 22, 1906, 6; and "Reviews," *Craftsman* (February 1907): 635.
7. "A Closed Chapter of Life," mag. sec., 4.

WILLIAM MERRITT CHASE

The Song (p. 172)

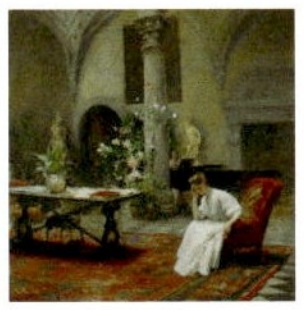

1. See Ronald G. Pisano, "William Merritt Chase: *The Song*" (unpublished manuscript, December 12, 1989, Crystal Bridges curatorial files). I am indebted to the research of Pisano, who published extensively on Chase.
2. N. Otero-Santiago, "William Merritt Chase," in *The Lure of Italy: American Artists and the Italian Experience 1760–1914*, ed. Theodore E. Stebbins Jr. (Boston: Museum of Fine Arts, 1992), 360.
3. On the decorative emphasis in late nineteenth-century painting and the role of women in this context, see Bailey Van Hook, "Decorative Images of American Women: The Aristocratic Aesthetic of the Late Nineteenth Century," *Smithsonian Studies in American Art* 4, no. 1 (Winter 1990): 45–69. James McNeill Whistler and Thomas Wilmer Dewing, both acquaintances of Chase, were two of the most notable American artists to emphasize the decorative over the narrative. Chase also would have known the works of the French impressionists, who regularly utilized the female form for decorative ends.
4. Otero-Santiago, "William Merritt Chase," 360. Chase particularly admired the seventeenth-century Dutch painter Johannes Vermeer, who engaged the theme of music in several of his compositions. Like many of his peers, Chase also admired Vermeer and his contemporaries for their avoidance of overt narrative and storytelling.

ALFRED HENRY MAURER

Jeanne (p. 174)

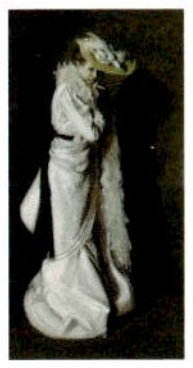

1. Shortly after Maurer completed *Jeanne* it received critical acclaim on both sides of the Atlantic. Between 1906 and 1914, Maurer showed the painting in exhibitions in Berlin, Paris, London, Bremen, Venice, and Philadelphia, and in 1915 it was featured in the landmark Panama-Pacific International Exposition in San Francisco.
2. Mahonri M. Young to Alfred Maurer, n.d., Mahonri M. Young II Archives, N.Y.
3. Crystal Bridges owns a second full-length portrait of Blazy by Maurer: an oil painting entitled *The Midinette (Portrait of a Woman)*, from about 1902.
4. Stacey Epstein, "Alfred H. Maurer: Aestheticism to Modernism 1897–1916" (PhD diss., City University of New York, 2003), chap. 3.
5. Hats decorated with aviary plumage were considered a high fashion statement in the late nineteenth and early twentieth century. Sometimes an entire taxidermied bird would be mounted on springs so that it could move in a naturalistic manner. See http://www.victoriana.com/Victorian-Hats/birdhats.htm (accessed October 21, 2010).
6. H. Barbara Weinberg, Doreen Bolger, and David Park Curry, *American Impressionism and Realism: The Painting of Modern Life, 1885–1915* (New York: The Metropolitan Museum of Art, 1994), 258.
7. Elizabeth McCausland, *A. H. Maurer: A Biography of America's First Modern Painter* (New York: A. A. Wyn, 1951), 83.

THOMAS WILMER DEWING

The Fortune Teller (p. 176)

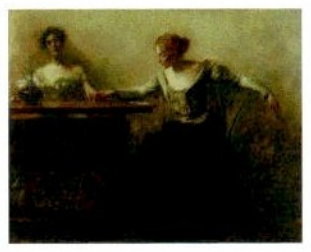

1. Christian Brinton, "The New Spirit in American Painting," *Bookman* 27 (June 1908): 351.
2. "Exhibitions: Past and to Come," *Brush and Pencil* 15 (April 1905): 87.
3. Henry Carrington Bolton, "Fortune-Telling in America To-Day," *Journal of American Folklore* 8 (October–December 1895): 299.
4. "Fortune-Telling by Cards: Jolly Sport for a Winter Evening" *New York Times*, January 11, 1903, SM:5.

EVERETT SHINN

A French Music Hall (p. 178)

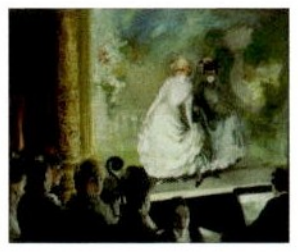

1. The content of this entry is drawn entirely from Linda S. Ferber, "Stagestruck: The Theater Subjects of Everett Shinn," in *American Art around 1900: Lectures in Memory of Daniel Fraad*, ed. Doreen Bolger and Nicolai Cikovsky Jr. (Washington: National Gallery of Art, 1990), 51–67. See also Linda Ayres and Jane Myers, *American Paintings, Watercolors, and Drawings from the Collection of Rita and Daniel Fraad* (Fort Worth: Amon Carter Museum, 1985), 82–83.
2. This work is known through a photograph formerly in the collection of Arthur G. Altschul. See Ferber, "Stagestruck," in Bolger and Cikovsky, *American Art around 1900*, 61, fig. 12.
3. See Ayers and Myers, *American Paintings, Watercolors, and Drawings*, 83.

ROBERT HENRI

Jessica Penn in Black with White Plumes (p. 180)

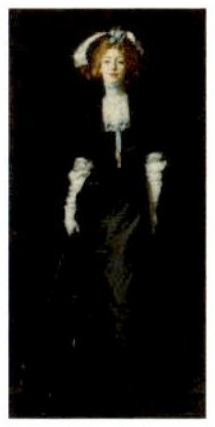

1. *Brooklyn Standard-Union*, May 27, 1908, quoted in Bennard B. Perlman, *Robert Henri: His Life and Art* (New York: Dover Publications, 1991), 85.
2. Bennard B. Perlman, *The Lives, Loves, and Art of Arthur B. Davies* (Albany: State University of New York Press, 1998), 128; and Tom Longden, "Beauty of Model Penn Lives on in Portraits," *Des Moines Register*, July 19, 2010, http://www.desmoinesregister.com/article/99999999/FAMOUSIOWANS/802100338/Penn-Jesseca (accessed August 15, 2010).
3. Henri, *The Art Spirit: 85th Anniversary Edition* (Philadelphia: J. B. Lippincott, 1923; New York: Basic Books, 2007), 38.
4. Valerie Ann Leeds, *My People: The Portraits of Robert Henri* (Seattle: University of Washington Press, 1994), 19.
5. Samuel Isham, *The History of American Painting* (1905; repr., New York: Macmillan Company, 1936), 506.
6. Henri, *The Art Spirit*, 252.

MAXFIELD PARRISH

The Lantern Bearers (p. 182)

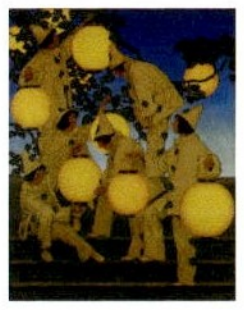

1. Laurence S. Cutler and Judy Goffman Cutler, *Maxfield Parrish: A Retrospective* (San Francisco: Pomegranate Art Books, 1995), 7.
2. At the height of the artist's fame, this vivid cobalt blue color became widely known as "Parrish blue," even receiving mention in F. Scott Fitzgerald's 1920 novelette "May Day": "The great plate-glass front had turned to a deep creamy blue, the color of a Maxfield Parrish moonlight—a blue that seemed to press close upon the pane as if to crowd its way into the restaurant." See Fitzgerald, "May Day," in *The Curious Case of Benjamin Button and Other Jazz Age Stories*, ed. Patrick O'Donnell (New York: Charles Scribner's Sons, 1922 [as *Tales of the Jazz Age*]; Penguin Classics, 2008), 263.
3. Alma Gilbert, *Maxfield Parrish: Master of Make Believe* (London: Philip Wilson Publishers, 2005), 31.

4. Alma Gilbert, *The Make Believe World of Maxfield Parrish and Sue Lewin* (San Francisco: Pomegranate Books, 1990; Berkeley: Ten Speed Press, 1997), 32. Lewin appears to have served as the model for all six of Parrish's identical Pierrots. See Gilbert, *The Make Believe World*, 25.
5. Alma Gilbert, *Maxfield Parrish: The Masterworks*, 2nd ed. (Berkeley: Ten Speed Press, 1995), 164.

FRANK WESTON BENSON

Summer Day (p. 184)

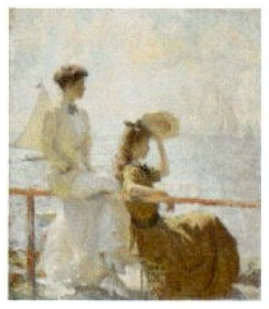

1. Pentimenti of Eleanor's figure and the umbrella are clearly discernible in the painting, as first noted by Faith Andrews Bedford. The sequence of the painting's gestation and final realization is complicated. Benson was known to rework paintings as his thinking about composition changed. Bedford argues that a photograph of *Summer Day* when it contained all three sisters indicates Eleanor was added after the painting was finished with only the two younger sisters. Still later, Benson painted Eleanor out, essentially going back to the original composition. Aside from purely compositional concerns, there was a degree of family tension during the summer of 1911. Eleanor, freshly graduated from Smith College in the summer of 1911, was thought to have returned home that spring "a parlor pink." Her father's disapproval of Eleanor's left-leaning liberal attitudes from Smith extended to the younger girls, who blamed their older sister for "ruining" their own chances for a college education (though Benson did make sure they attended the best girls' boarding schools). See Bedford, Susan C. Faxon, and Bruce W. Chambers, *Frank W. Benson: A Retrospective* (New York: Berry-Hill Galleries, 1989), 75.

GEORGE WESLEY BELLOWS

Excavation at Night (p. 186)

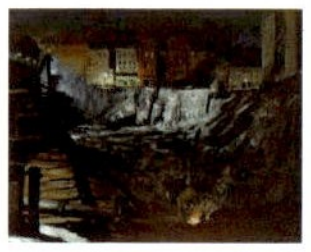

1. Marianne Doezema, *George Bellows and Urban America* (New Haven: Yale University Press, 1992), 19–20.
2. Lorraine B. Diehl, *The Late, Great Pennsylvania Station* (New York: Four Walls Eight Windows, 1996): 57–64.
3. The station was completed in 1910 and opened to the public in 1911. In addition to *Excavation at Night*, these works include *Pennsylvania Excavation* (1907, Smith College Museum of Art); *Pennsylvania Station Excavation* (ca. 1907–8, Brooklyn Museum); and *Blue Morning* (1909, National Gallery of Art, Washington). See Doezema, *George Bellows*, 41.
4. "Began Art Career as Illustrator on Maikio," *Lantern* [Ohio State University], undated clipping in Bellows scrapbook, George Wesley Bellows Papers, Special Collections Department, Amherst College Archives and Special Collections, Amherst College Library, quoted in Doezema, *George Bellows and Urban America*, 44.
5. While the aboveground portions of the original Pennsylvania Station were demolished in 1963, the extensive network of underground tunnels and rails were left intact. A new head house was built for these tunneled tracks in 1968; today, this second incarnation of Pennsylvania Station (commonly known as Penn Station) is New York City's busiest rail depot and a major commuter rail hub.

GEORGE WESLEY BELLOWS

Return of the Useless (p. 188)

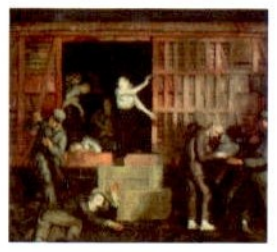

1. Gordon K. Allison and Glenn C. Peck, *George Bellows and the War Series of 1918* (New York: Hirschl & Adler Galleries, 1983), 10.
2. "Bryce Committee's Report on Deliberate Slaughter of Belgium Non-Combatants," *New York Times*, May 13, 1915, 6.
3. Brand Whitlock, "Belgium: The Tightening Grip, Including the Story of Cardinal Mercier's Heroic Stand Against Tyranny," *Everybody's Magazine* 39 (December 1918): 9–17, 68–74.

JOHN SLOAN

Bleecker Street, Saturday Night (p. 190)

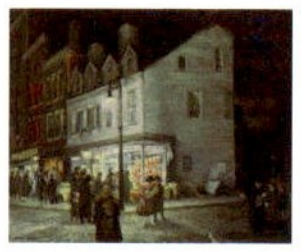

1. John Sloan, *Notes*, John Sloan Trust, Delaware Art Museum, quoted in Rowland Elzea, *John Sloan's Oil Paintings: A Catalogue Raisonné, Part One* (Newark: University of Delaware Press, 1991), 226. In 1909, Sloan became interested in a system of painting based on the ideas of the artist and theoretician Hardesty G. Maratta, who manufactured premixed oil paints. Maratta's system was based on a scale of tonal gradations that uniformly systematize the palette into color triads, with the twelve major color divisions analogous to the twelve halftones of the musical scale. Despite its complexity, Maratta's system was embraced to varying degrees by a number of Sloan's contemporaries, including Robert Henri and George Bellows.
2. John Sloan, *Gist of Art* (New York: American Artists Group, 1939), 255.

ALFRED HENRY MAURER

Fauve Landscape with Red and Blue (p. 192)

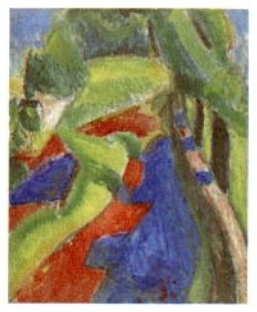

1. According to Stacy Epstein, "Maurer was perhaps the first American artist to see the work of Matisse and that of other advanced modern painters in the Steins' collection." See Epstein, *Alfred H. Maurer: Aestheticism to Modernism* (New York: Hollis Taggart Galleries, 1999), 26.
2. J. F. Chamberlain, *New-York Daily Mail*, April 3, 1909, quoted in Epstein, *Alfred H. Maurer*, 35.

JOHN MARIN

Grain Elevator (Weehawken Sequence) (p. 194)

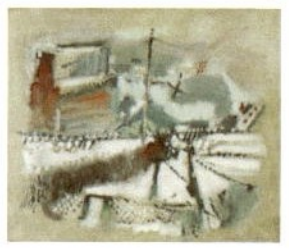

1. MacKinley Helm first described the "Weehawken Sequence," in the catalogue for the 1947 Marin retrospective exhibition organized by the Institute of Modern Art, Boston. For more on the series, see Ruth E. Fine, *John Marin* (New York: Abbeville Press, 1990), 112–19; and Sheldon Reich, *John Marin: A Stylistic Analysis and Catalogue Raisonné, Part II* (Phoenix: University of Arizona Press, 1970), 355–57, 404–5, 424–45.
2. "New York's Improvements at Weehawken," *Railway Age*, August 10, 1900, 114. The structure was demolished in 1968. See also http://american-colossus.blogspot.com/2009/04/grain-elevator-in-weehawken-new-jersey.html (accessed November 21, 2010).
3. The precise dates for many of the works in Marin's Weehawken Sequence, including *Grain Elevator*, are not known. Though Sheldon Reich assigned the work a date of 1915 based on its dark palette, others categorize the painting as

an early image, dating it to 1910. The composition resembles a series of cubist-inspired etchings that Marin produced in 1915.

4. In his widely published and translated 1913 essay "Die Entwicklung moderne Industriebaukunst," Gropius favorably compared the "overwhelmingly monumental power" of the United States' streamlined utilitarian structures to the great architectural achievements of Egypt. On the granary and the influence of industrial forms on American modernism, see Wanda M. Corn, *The Great American Thing: Modern Art and National Identity, 1915–1935* (Berkeley: University of California Press, 1999), 218.
5. Marin, quoted in Kristi Dahm, "Playing Around with Paint: John Marin's Evolving Watercolor Technique," in Martha Tedeschi, *John Marin's Watercolors: A Medium for Modernism* (New Haven: Yale University Press, 2010), 41.
6. J. Nilsen Laurvik, *Camera Work* 39 (July 1912): 38, quoted in Fine, *John Marin*, 104.
7. Clement Greenberg, "Review of an Exhibition of John Marin," in *Clement Greenberg: The Collected Essays and Criticism*, ed. John O'Brien (Chicago: University of Chicago Press, 1986), 2:268, quoted in Fine, *John Marin*, 9.

JOHN MARIN

Telephone Building, Lower New York (p. 196)

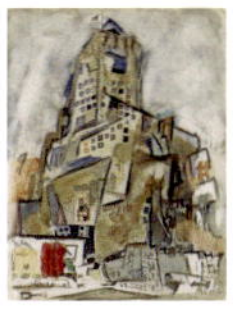

1. Photographer, gallerist, and influential modern art promoter Alfred Stieglitz once claimed that Marin had "fallen in love" with the Woolworth Building. Stieglitz, quoted in Dorothy Norman, *Alfred Stieglitz: An American Seer* (1960), in Martha Tedeschi, *John Marin's Watercolors: A Medium for Modernism* (New Haven: Yale University Press, 2010), 99. On Marin's impressions of New York, see Ruth E. Fine, *John Marin* (New York: Abbeville Press, 1990), 119.
2. For more on Marin's artistic practice between 1910 and 1930, see Fine, *John Marin*, 75–164.
3. On the New York Telephone Building, see Joseph Korom Jr., *The American Skyscraper, 1840–1940: A Celebration of Height* (Boston: Branden Books, 2008), 350–51. For historic photographs of the building by Berenice Abbott, see http://mcny.org/museum-collections/berenice-abbott/a156.htm (accessed November 23, 2010).
4. Ruth Fine, "Prelude: To Paint Disorder Under a Big Order," in Tedeschi, *John Marin's Watercolors*, 16.
5. Kristi Dahm, "Playing Around with Paint," in Tedeschi, *John Marin's Watercolors*, 41.
6. Seymour DeKoven, "John Marin, Whitman of American Painting," *Chicago Evening Post Magazine of the Art World*, June 1, 1926, 5, quoted in Tedeschi, "John Marin's Loaded Brush: Orchestrating the Modern American Watercolor," in Tedeschi, *John Marin's Watercolors*, 21.

MARSDEN HARTLEY

Hall of the Mountain King (p. 198)

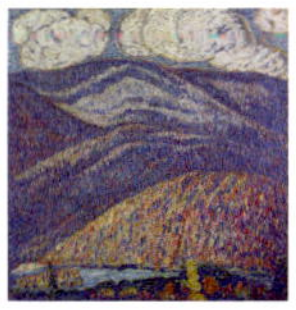

1. Hartley to Shaemas O'Sheel, October 19, 1908, quoted in Townsend Ludington, *Marsden Hartley: The Biography of an American Artist* (Ithaca: Cornell University Press, 1992), 54–55.
2. See Barbara Haskell, *Marsden Hartley* (New York: Whitney Museum of American Art, 1980), 13.
3. *Somehow a Past: The Autobiography of Marsden Hartley*, ed. Susan Elizabeth Ryan (Cambridge: MIT Press, 1997), 186–87; and Haskell, *Marsden Hartley*, 13.

MARSDEN HARTLEY

Mountains No. 22 (p. 200)

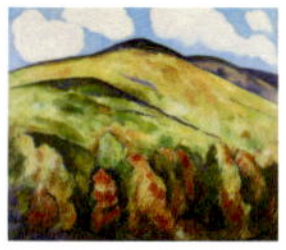

1. Alfred Stieglitz to Marsden Hartley, February 5, 1929, quoted in Townsend Ludington, "Marsden Hartley on Native Ground," in Sarah Greenough et al., *Modern Art and America: Alfred Stieglitz and His New York Galleries* (Washington: National Gallery of Art, 2001), 402.
2. Hartley to Rebecca Strand, July 4, 1930, quoted in Gail R. Scott, cat. entry for *Mountains No. 22*, in *American Paintings, Drawings & Sculpture* (auction cat. Sotheby's, New York, December 3, 2009), lot 21.

LYONEL FEININGER

Schlossgasse (p. 202)

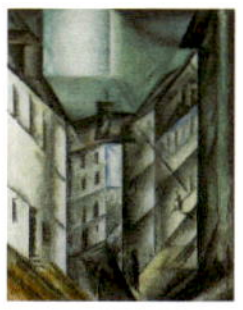

1. Feininger to Alfred Vance Churchill, March 13, 1913, quoted in H. Hess, *Lyonel Feininger* (New York: Harry N. Abrams, 1961), 56.
2. Feininger was best known as creator and illustrator of *The Kin-der-kids* and *Wee Willie Winkie's World* for the *Chicago Tribune*. Early in his career, he drew cartoons for the German satirical magazines *Ulk* and *Lustige Blätter*.
3. Delaunay used color combinations based on Michel-Eugène Chevreul's law of simultaneous contrast of colors. See Gustav Vriesen, *Robert Delaunay: Light and Color* (New York: H. N. Abrams, 1957), 44.
4. A highly finished charcoal study for *Schlossgasse* dated May 11, 1915 (location unknown) reveals the intense concentration with which the artist worked to create the convincing impression of volume. Feininger also created a pen-and-ink drawing of the subject, which was published in the German periodical *Zeit-Echo* in 1915 (location unknown), and created several etchings on the motif in 1914 and 1916. See *Zeit-Echo* 2, no. 5 (1915–16): 72; and Leona E. Prasse, *Lyonel Feininger: A Definitive Catalogue of His Graphic Work: Etchings, Lithographs, Woodcuts* (Cleveland: Cleveland Museum of Art, 1972), 87, 252.
5. Feininger wrote about the glasslike quality of his painting style in a 1913 letter: "My 'Cubism,' call it rather, if it must have a name, 'prism-ism.'" Feininger to Churchill, March 13, 1913, quoted in Hess, *Lyonel Feininger*, 56.

GEORGIA O'KEEFFE

Evening Star No. II (p. 204)

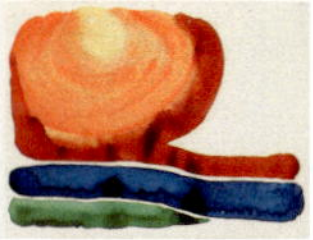

1. O'Keeffe to Paul Strand, November 12, 1917, quoted in Sarah Whitaker Peters, *Becoming O'Keeffe: The Early Years* (New York: Abbeville Press, 2001), 188.
2. Barbara Haskell, "Georgia O'Keeffe: Making the Unknown—Known," in *Georgia O'Keeffe: Abstraction* (New Haven: Yale University Press, 2009), 8–10.
3. O'Keeffe, quoted in Anita Pollitzer, "That's Georgia," *Saturday Review*, November 4, 1950, reprinted in *Lovingly Georgia: The Complete Correspondence of Georgia O'Keeffe and Anita Pollitzer*, ed. Clive Giboire (New York: Simon and Schuster, 1990), 291.
4. Peters, *Becoming O'Keeffe*, 13.
5. O'Keeffe recalled that she made ten watercolors of the evening star in *Georgia O'Keeffe* (New York: Viking Press, 1976), n.p. Barbara Buhler Lynes records eight extant watercolors in *Georgia O'Keeffe: Catalogue Raisonné* (New Haven: Yale University Press, 1999), 1:115–18.

GEORGIA O'KEEFFE

Mask with Golden Apple (p. 206)

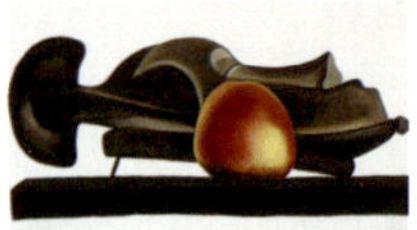

1. The mask is illustrated in Helen M. Shannon, "African Art, 1914: The Root of Modern Art," in Sarah Greenough et al., *Modern Art and America: Alfred Stieglitz and His New York Galleries* (Washington: National Gallery of Art, 2001), 180.
2. Sarah Whitaker Peters, *Becoming O'Keeffe: The Early Years* (New York: Abbeville Press, 2001), 274.
3. See Charles C. Eldredge's illuminating discussion of O'Keeffe's apple paintings in *Georgia O'Keeffe: American and Modern* (New Haven: Yale University Press, 1993), 182–87.

OSCAR BLUEMNER

Motive of Space and Form—A New Jersey Village (Montville) (p. 208)

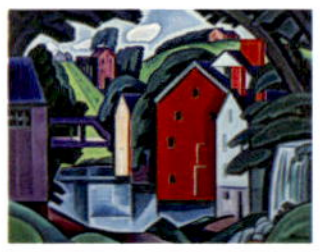

1. Bluemner, journal entry, February 12, 1915, Oscar Bluemner Papers, 1886–1939, 1960, Series 3: Painting & Theory Diaries, 1912–15, box 1, folder 34, Archives of American Art, Smithsonian Institution, Washington. Trans. Manuela Well-Off-Man. Bluemner analyzed the pictorial effects of color, light, and form in additional journal entries about *Motive of Space and Form*.
2. Debra Force, *Oscar Bluemner: Visions of the Modern Landscape* (New York: Debra Force Fine Art, 2004), 3.
3. Bluemner was attracted to the "intimate landscape of our common surroundings, where town and country mingle." Bluemner, quoted in Barbara Haskell, *Oscar Bluemner: A Passion for Color* (New York: Whitney Museum of American Art, 2005), 44–45.
4. Force, *Oscar Bluemner*, 3.
5. Bluemner, quoted in Jeffrey R. Hayes, *Oscar Bluemner* (Cambridge: Cambridge University Press, 1991), 91–92.
6. Bluemner studied architecture and painting at the Royal Academy of Design in Berlin. Upon immigrating to the United States in 1892, he initially worked as an architectural draftsman, creating the winning design for the Bronx borough courthouse in 1903. Haskell, *Oscar Bluemner*, 25.
7. Bluemner regarded color as a universal language akin to music that touches all areas of the psyche when properly orchestrated, and he often gave his works musical titles.
8. The artist wrote about his early influences: "In my native city, Elberfeld-Darmen, the splendor of the colors in the local silk industries . . . made an indelible impression that compensated me for the eternally gray, rainy city sky. The colorfully glowing stained glass windows of the old cathedrals of the Rhineland were also part of it." See "Bluemner, seine Ziele, sein Werk.—Interessantes Interview," *New-Yorker Staats-Zeitung (Abendblatt)*, November 19, 1915, n.p.

STANTON MACDONALD-WRIGHT

Au Café (Synchromy) (p. 210)

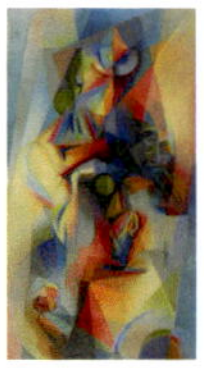

1. On color scales as used by the synchromists, see Will South, *Color, Myth & Music: Stanton Macdonald-Wright and Synchromism* (Raleigh: North Carolina Museum of Art, 2001).
2. Macdonald-Wright, *A Treatise on Color* (Los Angeles: privately printed, 1924), 25.

CHARLES DEMUTH

Sail: In Two Movements (p. 212)

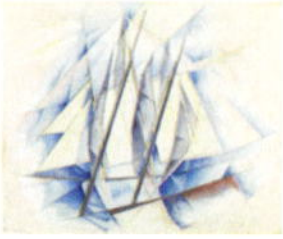

1. Wolfgang Born, who coined the word "precisionism," identified Demuth "as the artist who had paved the way for a style appropriate to the new industrial reality." Born, quoted in Barbara Haskell, *Charles Demuth* (New York: Whitney Museum of American Art, 1987), 134.
2. At age four or five Demuth contracted Perthes, a disease that left him with one short leg due to deformation of the hip joint. Haskell, *Charles Demuth*, 12.
3. Demuth also attended the Académie Julian and Académie Colarossi. See Haskell, *Charles Demuth*, 28.
4. Demuth summered in Provincetown in 1915, 1916, 1918, and 1920; and in Gloucester in 1917 and 1919. See Haskell, *Charles Demuth*, 127.
5. Emily Farnham, *Charles Demuth: Behind a Laughing Mask* (Norman: University of Oklahoma Press, 1971), 147; and Haskell, *Charles Demuth*, 130.
6. Farnham, *Charles Demuth*, 147. Demuth is believed to be one of the first persons in the United States to have received insulin to treat diabetes.
7. Demuth ultimately found watercolor easiest to work with. He explained, "I don't have to return and fuss if it goes bad as one always does in oil or tempera." Demuth, quoted in Farnham, *Charles Demuth*, 147.

ARTHUR GARFIELD DOVE

Moon and Sea II (p. 214)

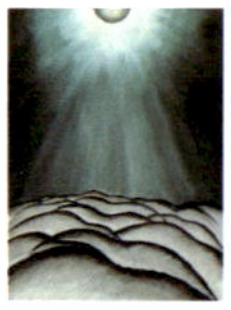

1. The text of this entry is drawn entirely from William C. Agee, "Arthur Dove: *Moon and Sea II*," in *Villa America: American Moderns, 1900–1950*, ed. Elizabeth Armstrong (Newport Beach, Calif.: Orange County Museum of Art, 2005), 55–56.
2. *After the Storm, Silver and Green (Vault Sky)* (State Museum of New Jersey), an almost identical version of the theme, bears a title perhaps more descriptive of the force and the essence of the work.
3. Dove to Alfred Stieglitz, October 24, 1923, quoted in *Dear Stieglitz, Dear Dove*, ed. Ann Morgan (Newark: University of Delaware Press, 1988), 97–98.
4. If there was a first version of this painting, its location is not known.
5. Dove to Stieglitz, October 24, 1923, quoted in *Dear Stieglitz*, ed. Morgan, 97–98.
6. For the Dove/Noland connection, see William C. Agee, *Kenneth Noland: The Circle Paintings* (Houston: Museum of Fine Arts, 1996).

ARTHUR GARFIELD DOVE

Two Forms (p. 216)

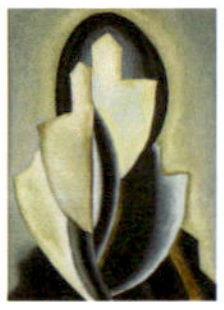

1. Murdock Pemberton, "The Art Galleries," *New Yorker*, March 21, 1931, 68–70.
2. Edward Alden Jewell, "Dove Again: A Movement Toward Larger Design," *New York Times*, March 15, 1931, Arthur and Helen Torr Dove Papers, Series 4, box 3, folder 30, Archives of American Art, Smithsonian Institution, Washington.
3. Helen Torr Dove, unpublished diary entries, February 16–22, 1931, Arthur and Helen Torr Dove Papers, Series 3, box 2, folder 4, Archives of American Art.
4. In his card catalogue of paintings, Dove recorded that *Two Forms* was painted on beaverboard [fiberboard] coated with white lead paint mixed with oil and turpentine. See Arthur and Helen Torr Dove Papers, Reel 2803, frame 741, Archives of American Art.
5. Arthur Dove, "Explanatory Note," in *Forum Exhibition of Modern American Painters* (New York: Anderson Galleries, 1916; repr., New York: Arno Press, 1968), n.p.

JOSEPH STELLA

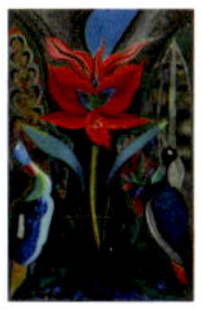

Red Flower (p. 218)

1. Barbara Haskell, *Joseph Stella* (New York: Whitney Museum of American Art, 1994), 225–28.
2. In Greek mythology, Amaryllis is a nymph bestowed with the attributes of determination, pride, and radiant beauty. Stella's knowledge of the specific symbolic meanings of flowers is not known, but it is clear that flowers served as a means for the artist to express his sensual nature and drive for spiritual transcendence. See Joann Moser, *Visual Poetry: The Drawings of Joseph Stella* (Washington: National Museum of American Art, 1990), 113; and Paolo Mantegazza, *The Legend of Flowers* (London: Hesperides Press, 2006), 131–38.
3. Barbara Rose, *Flora: The Flower Paintings by Joseph Stella* (West Palm Beach: Eaton Fine Arts, 1998), 18.
4. For Stella's Asian influences, see Haskell, *Joseph Stella*, 184; and Irma B. Jaffe, *Joseph Stella: The Tropics* (New York: Richard York Gallery, 1988), 107.
5. Jaffe, *Joseph Stella*, 10.
6. Rose, *Flora*, 17.
7. Haskell, *Joseph Stella*, 151.

YASUO KUNIYOSHI

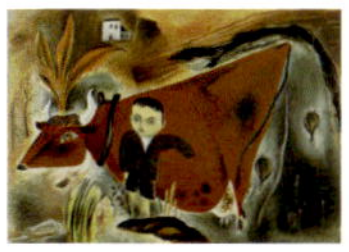

Little Joe with Cow (p. 220)

1. Kuniyoshi was familiar with works by French modernists like Paul Cézanne through museum visits and his studies at the Art Students League. See Donald B. Goodall, *Yasuo Kuniyoshi, 1889–1953* (Austin: The University Art Museum, 1975), 27. The popularity of American folk art amongst Kuniyoshi and his artist friends is described in Lloyd Goodrich, *Yasuo Kuniyoshi* (New York: Whitney Museum of American Art, 1948), 17.
2. Goodall, *Yasuo Kuniyoshi, 1889–1953*, 42.
3. Kuniyoshi, "East to West," *Magazine of Art* 33 (February 1940): 72–83, quoted in Goodrich, *Yasuo Kuniyoshi,* 13.
4. Kuniyoshi, "East to West," 17.
5. Goodrich, *Yasuo Kuniyoshi*, 13. For more information on Edo-period landscape paintings, see Calvin L. French, *The Poet Painters: Buson and His Followers* (Ann Arbor: University of Michigan Museum of Art, 1974), 18; and Christine Guth, *Japanese Art of the Edo Period* (London: Weidenfeld & Nicolson, 1995).

STUART DAVIS

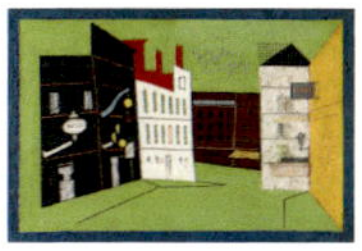

Rue de l'Echaudé (p. 222)

1. Davis, quoted in Lowery Stokes Sims, *Stuart Davis: American Painter* (New York: Metropolitan Museum of Art, 1991), 33.

STUART DAVIS

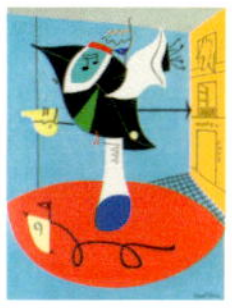

Still Life with Flowers (p. 224)

1. Davis, quoted in Katharine Kuh, *The Artist's Voice: Talks with Seventeen Modern Artists* (Harper and Row, 1962 [as *The Artist's Voice: Talks with Seventeen Artists*]; rev. ed. New York: Da Capo Press, 1990), 53.

EDWARD HOPPER

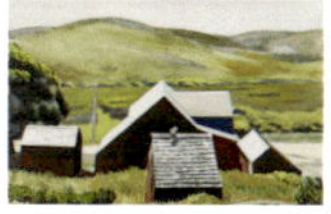

Roofs of the Cobb Barn (p. 226)

1. Hopper, quoted in *Edward Hopper*, ed. Sheena Wagstaff (London: Tate Publishing, 2004), 15.
2. Josephine Hopper listed the postman's name as "Burly" in Hopper's record book. See Virginia Mecklenburg, *Edward Hopper: The Watercolors* (Washington: National Museum of American Art, 1999), 97.
3. Gail Levin, *Edward Hopper: A Catalogue Raisonné* (New York: Whitney Museum of American Art, 1995), vol. 4, CD-ROM.
4. If one compares this painting with Hopper's unfinished watercolor *Cobb's Barn and Distant Houses* (1931, Whitney Museum of American Art), which shows the same buildings from a different perspective, it becomes clear that the artist chose the bird's-eye view for *Roofs of the Cobb Barn* as a means of emphasizing the geometric elements in the landscape. See Mecklenburg, *Edward Hopper*, 110, 111.
5. Hopper's preference for structural clarity distinguished him from artists of the American Scene movement such as Thomas Hart Benton, with whom he is often associated. The exactness with which Hopper painted the rural architecture and the extent to which the barns approach geometric abstraction link the painter to the precisionists Charles Sheeler and Charles Demuth.

GEORGIA O'KEEFFE

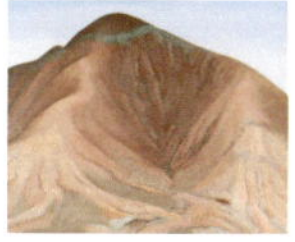

Small Purple Hills (p. 228)

1. See Bruce Robertson, "Useable Form: O'Keeffe's Materials, Methods, and Motifs," in *Georgia O'Keeffe: Abstraction*, ed. Barbara Haskell (New Haven: Yale University Press, 2009), 125–33.

THOMAS HART BENTON

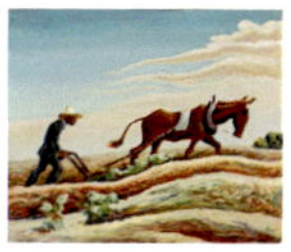

Ploughing It Under (p. 230)

1. Benton's 1964 reworking of *Ploughing It Under* seems to have been intended to brighten the colors of portions of the painting, most especially the sky, which had darkened over time. See Elise Effmann, assistant conservator of paintings, Kimbell Art Museum, "Examination Report" (unpublished technical examination, May 24, 2006, Crystal Bridges curatorial files).
2. Elizabeth Broun, "Thomas Hart Benton: A Politician in Paint," *Smithsonian Studies in American Art* 1 (Spring 1987): 58–77.
3. On Benton's emphasis on producerism, see Erika Doss, *Benton, Pollock, and the Politics of Modernism: From Regionalism to Abstract Expressionism* (Chicago: University of Chicago Press, 1991), 67–138.
4. Leon F. Litwack et al., *The United States: Becoming a World Power*, 2nd ed. (Englewood Cliffs, N.J.: Prentice-Hall, 1987), 2:637, 639. In 1933 alone, 10.4 million acres of cotton were plowed under. See J. Richard Gruber, *Thomas Hart Benton and the American South* (Augusta, Ga.: Morris Museum of Art, 1998), 48.
5. David Eldridge, *American Culture in the 1930s* (Edinburgh: Edinburgh University Press, 2008), 65, 160.
6. Litwack et al., *The United States*, 2:639–40.
7. Creekmore Fath, ed., *The Lithographs of Thomas Hart Benton* (1969; repr., Austin: University of Texas Press, 1979), 36; and Doss, *Benton, Pollock, and the Politics of Modernism*, 164.

MARSDEN HARTLEY

Red Flowers and Sailboat (p. 232)

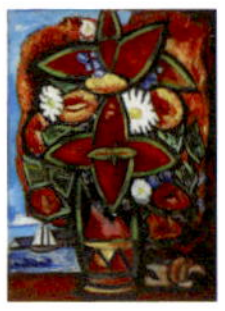

1. Bruce Weber, *The Heart of the Matter: The Still Lifes of Marsden Hartley* (New York: Berry-Hill Galleries, 2003), 16–22.
2. Ibid., 36.
3. See, for example, ibid., 35; and, more recently, Heather Hole, *Marsden Hartley and the West: The Search for an American Modernism* (New Haven: Yale University Press, 2007), 86–88.
4. Hartley to Adelaide Kuntz, November 1935, quoted in Townsend Ludington, *Marsden Hartley: The Biography of an American Artist* (Ithaca: Cornell University Press, 1998), 244.

ARSHILE GORKY

Composition (Still Life) (p. 234)

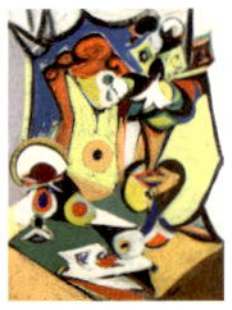

1. The information about Gorky's biography in this text derives from Melissa Kerr, "Chronology," in *Arshile Gorky: A Retrospective*, ed. Michael R. Taylor (Philadelphia: Philadelphia Museum of Art, 2009), 354–69.
2. Ibid., 359.

JACKSON POLLOCK

Reclining Woman (p. 236)

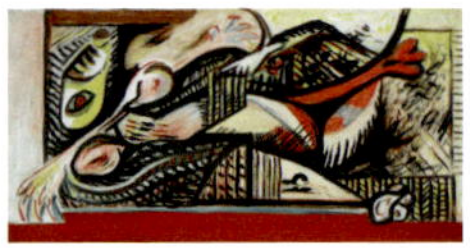

1. "Art: The Wild Ones," *Time Magazine*, February 20, 1956, 75.
2. Pollock owned a copy of the exhibition's catalogue. See Ellen Landau, *Jackson Pollock* (New York: Harry N. Abrams, 1989), 106.
3. Pollock may have been aware of this work through his friendship with artist-critic John Graham, who wrote an article entitled "Primitive Art and Picasso" for the April 30, 1937 issue of the *Magazine of Art*. Another work that may have inspired *Reclining Woman* is the painted-bronze sculpture *Reclining Woman Who Dreams* (1929, Hirshhorn Museum and Sculpture Garden), by the Swiss surrealist sculptor Alberto Giacometti. The most striking similarity between these two compositions is the series of parallel lines protruding from the center of the reclining women's bodies. Pollock knew Giacometti through his artist friend Mercedes Matter. See Ellen Landau, *Mercedes Matter* (New York: MB Art Publishing, 2010), 20.
4. Pollock began visiting the Jungian analyst Dr. Joseph L. Henderson in 1939. The artist believed in the psychological relevance of visual symbols. Susan Davidson, *No Limits, Just Edges: Jackson Pollock Paintings on Paper* (New York: Guggenheim Publications, 2005), 12, 13.
5. Landau argues, "Pollock's conflicted feelings about women were traceable to unresolved emotions toward his own mother," who is often described as having been domineering. According to Landau, Pollock's emotions toward his mother "rang[ed] from guilt to contempt." See *Jackson Pollock*, 109–10.

ROMARE BEARDEN

Sacrifice (p. 238)

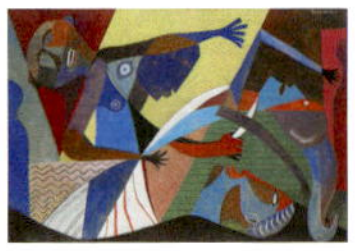

1. Ruth Fine, "Romare Bearden: The Spaces Between," in Fine, *The Art of Romare Bearden* (Washington: National Gallery of Art, in association with Harry N. Abrams, New York, 2003), 6.
2. Bearden's mother was a prominent Harlem civic and social leader. See Myron Schwartzman, "The Eagle Flies on Friday: Harlem in the 1930s," in Fine, *The Art of Romare Bearden*, 67–70. Bearden was an active member of the Harlem Artists Guild, which worked to increase the number of black artists in the Works Progress Administration's Federal Art Project, as well as of the 306 studio, a guildlike assembly of African American artists, writers, and musicians in Harlem.
3. Ibid., 92.
4. Bearden's *The Painter's Mind* (1969) demonstrates how thoroughly the artist had studied the old masters of the Italian baroque, including Caravaggio. See Nathan A. Scott, "Romare Bearden," *Callaloo* 36 (Summer 1988): 421.
5. The numerous reproductions of Tamayo's work among Bearden's papers seem to confirm his admiration for the Mexican artist's work. See Fine, "Romare Bearden: The Spaces Between," in Fine, *The Art of Romare Bearden*, 11.
6. Bearden mentions *Guernica* in one of his manuscripts. See Series 3: Writings By and About Bearden, ca. 1950s–1980s, Romare Bearden Papers, 1937–1982, box 3, folder 2, p. 4, Archives of American Art, Washington.
7. See Stetson Kennedy, *Jim Crow Guide: The Way It Was* (Boca Raton: Florida Atlantic University Press, 1990), 216–17; and Joseph Boskin, ed., *Urban Racial Violence in the Twentieth Century* (Beverly Hills: Glencoe Press, 1976), 14–15. In 1941, the year that Bearden painted *Sacrifice*, the March on Washington Movement was established to hold the Fair Employment Practices Committee (FEPC) to its mission of desegregating the armed forces and to agitate for civil rights more generally.
8. Maxwell T. Cohen, quoted in Schwartzman, "The Eagle Flies," 130.

DAVID SMITH

Cello Player (p. 240)

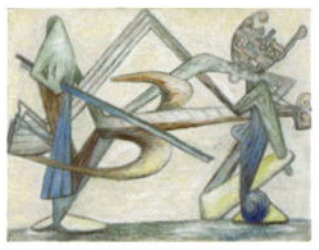

1. A major inspiration for David Smith's art from this period was the Museum of Modern Art's 1936–37 exhibition *Fantastic Art, Dada, Surrealism*, which he is known to have visited. See Edward F. Fry and Miranda McClintic, *David Smith: Painter, Sculptor and Draftsman* (New York: George Braziller, 1982), 12.
2. In his day Smith was often linked to the abstract expressionists, many of whom were intensely interested in exploring surrealism and the subconscious.
3. There are a number of newspaper photographs of string musicians, many of them dating to the late 1930s and early 1940s, among Smith's personal papers. See Fry and McClintic, *David Smith*, 134.
4. Smith explained, "I do not recognize the limits where painting ends and sculpture begins," asserting, "I never conceived of myself as anything other than a painter because my work came right through the raised surface, and color and objects applied to the surface . . . if I'm having trouble with a sculpture I always paint my troubles out." Quoted in Trinkett Clark, *The Drawings of David Smith* (Washington: International Exhibitions Foundation, 1985), 18, 25.
5. Allyn Shepard, researcher, Estate of David Smith, e-mail message to author, September 20, 2010. Since the Crystal Bridges painting is not dated, it is difficult to determine whether Smith made it before or after his 1946 sculpture *Cello Player*. Although the painting very closely resembles the sculpture, it is not an exact copy of the three-dimensional work.

MARSDEN HARTLEY

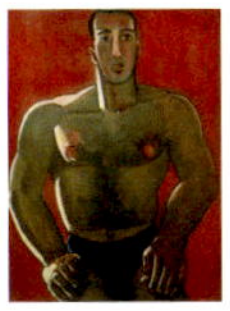

Madawaska—Acadian Light—Heavy (p. 242)

1. During Hartley's childhood, Lewiston saw a large influx of French-Canadian immigrants seeking work in the textile mills, a population defined by language and religion and largely separate from and discriminated against by the town's original Protestant, Yankee settlers. Whether or not Hartley identified with the outsider status of his French-Canadian neighbors on some level of memory or his subconscious is not known.
2. Hartley, quoted in Bruce Robertson, *Marsden Hartley* (New York: Harry N. Abrams, in association with the National Museum of American Art, Smithsonian Institution, Washington, 1995), 43.
3. The St. John River Valley is the traditional home of Acadian settlers who fled there between 1755 and 1763 when the British "Great Expulsion" forced the removal of the original French population from the Maritime Provinces of Eastern Canada.
4. The Art Institute of Chicago's version of *Madawaska* is identical to Crystal Bridges' painting in title, size, and date. Bram Dijkstra, cat. entry for *Madawaska—Acadian Light—Heavy*, in *Villa America: American Moderns, 1900–1950*, ed. Elizabeth Armstrong (Newport Beach, Calif.: Orange County Museum of Art, 2005), 90–92.

NORMAN ROCKWELL

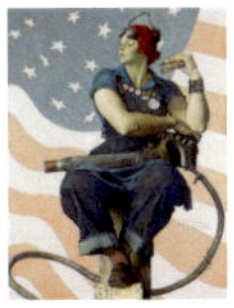

Rosie the Riveter (p. 244)

1. Maureen Honey, *Creating Rosie the Riveter: Class, Gender, and Propaganda during World War II* (Amherst: University of Massachusetts Press, 1984). Crystal Bridges also owns *Day Shift*, an undated oil painting by Francis Criss that depicts a very similar image of a World War II–era female industrial worker.
2. Allison L. Hepler, "'And We Want Steel Toes Like the Men': Gender and Occupational Health during World War II," *Bulletin of the History of Medicine* 72, no. 4 (Winter 1998): 689–713.
3. *Art Digest* 17, no. 18 (July 1, 1943): 14.
4. Melissa Dabakis, "Norman Rockwell's *Rosie the Riveter* and the Discourses of Wartime Womanhood," in *Gender and American History Since 1890*, ed. Barbara Melosh (New York: Routledge, 1992), 182–206.

CHARLES EPHRAIM BURCHFIELD

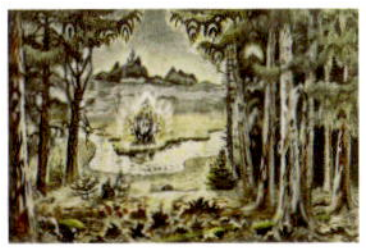

Dawn in Hemlock Woods (p. 246)

1. Burchfield, *Charles Burchfield's Journals: The Poetry of Place*, ed. J. Benjamin Townsend (Albany: SUNY Press, 1993), 357.
2. The 2009–10 exhibition *Heat Waves in a Swamp* was curated by Robert Gober for the Hammer Museum, in association with the Burchfield Penney Art Center at Buffalo State College, Buffalo, N.Y., and also traveled to the Whitney Museum of American Art. See Cynthia Burlingham et al., *Heat Waves in a Swamp: The Paintings of Charles Burchfield* (Los Angeles: Hammer Museum, in association with DelMonico Books/Prestel, 2009).
3. Burchfield, quoted in Robert Gober, "The Paintings of Charles Burchfield," *American Art Review* 22, no. 2 (2010): 125.

MILTON AVERY

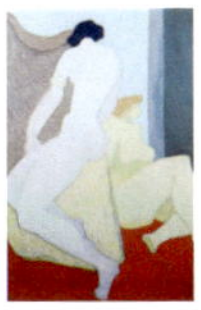

Nudes (p. 248)

1. Barbara Haskell, *Milton Avery* (New York: Whitney Museum of American Art, in association with Harper & Row, 1982), 26. Matisse had a one-person show at the Museum of Modern Art in New York in 1931, a prominent art world event that Avery surely attended.
2. Adolph Gottlieb, quoted in Charlotte Willard, "In the Art Galleries," *New York Post*, January 10, 1965, in Haskell, *Milton Avery*, 56.

JACOB LAWRENCE

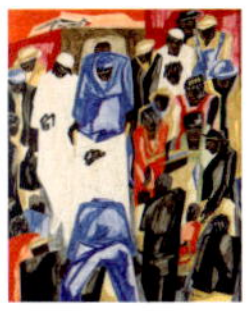

Ambulance Call (p. 250)

1. Lawrence described the closeness of his Harlem neighborhood in an interview: "It was a very cohesive community. You knew people. You didn't know their names, but you'd pass people on the street and see the face[s] over and over again." Interview by James Buell and David Driskell, February 4, 1982, transcript, Amistad Research Center, Museum Services Files, Tulane University, quoted in Patricia Hills, *Painting Harlem Modern: The Art of Jacob Lawrence* (Berkeley: University of California Press, 2009), 11.
2. Early in his career Lawrence was fascinated by the patterns he saw in his everyday life, and these visual recollections contributed to the strength of his compositions. "Our homes were very decorative, full of pattern, like inexpensive throw rugs, all around the house. It must have had some influence, all this color and everything." Lawrence, quoted in Leslie King-Hammond, "Inside-Outside, Uptown-Downtown: Jacob Lawrence and the Aesthetic Ethos of the Harlem Working-Class Community," in *Over the Line: The Art and Life of Jacob Lawrence*, ed. Peter T. Nesbett and Michelle Dubois (Seattle: University of Washington Press, 2001), 73. Lawrence's rigorous attention to the effect of color on shape, form, and space in *Ambulance Call* may derive in part from his 1946 experience teaching alongside the artist and color theorist Josef Albers at Black Mountain College, an experimental art school near Asheville, North Carolina.
3. See Romare Bearden and Harry Henderson, *A History of African-American Artists: From 1792 to the Present* (New York: Pantheon Books, 1993), 296. The year after he completed *Ambulance Call*, Lawrence created the *Hillside Hospital* series—eleven paintings based on his stay in the Queens hospital's psychiatric ward that focus on the patients' daily routines. See Ellen Harkins Wheat, *Jacob Lawrence: American Painter* (Seattle: Seattle Art Museum, 1986), 101, 102.
4. Nat Brandt, *Harlem at War: The Black Experience in WWII* (New York: Alfred A. Knopf, 1996), 42.
5. Wheat, *Jacob Lawrence*, 114.
6. Ibid., 192.

CHARLES SHEELER

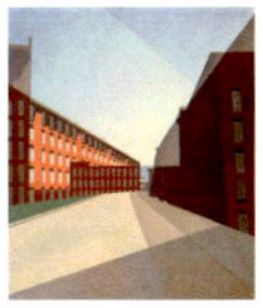

Amoskeag Mills #2 (p. 252)

1. The Currier Museum of Art's board of trustees selected the tempera study *Amoskeag Canal* to be executed in oil (Currier Museum of Art). The rejected study, *Amoskeag Mill Yard #1*, was also purchased by the Currier and later translated into the Crystal Bridges' painting. Another major oil that resulted from Sheeler's residency was the 1949 painting *Manchester* (Baltimore Museum of Art). See

Charles Brock, *Charles Sheeler: Across Media* (Berkeley: University of California Press, 2006), 151.
2. Tamara K. Hareven and Randolph Langenbach, *Amoskeag: Life and Work in an American Factory City* (New York: Pantheon Books, 1978), 10, 94.
3. See Brock, *Charles Sheeler*, 128.
4. The photomontage Sheeler used as study for *Amoskeag Mills #2* is titled *Millyard Passage* (Museum of Fine Arts, Boston). The artist created his montages by "sandwiching two or three negatives into his enlarger. He then exposed the composite image and printed the result." See http://www.artic.edu/aic/exhibitions/sheeler/themes.html (accessed October 5, 2010).
5. See Hareven and Langenbach, *Amoskeag*, 119, 293–359.
6. Sheeler, quoted in Martin Friedman, *Charles Sheeler* (New York: Watson-Guptill, 1975), 13.

WILL BARNET

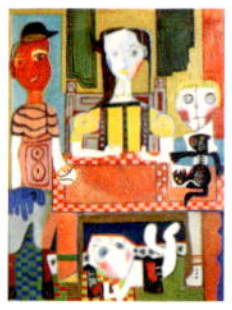

Family and Pink Table (Mary and Sons) and *Woman Reading* (p. 254)

1. Barnet's first solo museum show was held in 1942, at the Virginia Museum of Fine Arts, Richmond. In 1946, both the Smithsonian Institution in Washington and the Bertha Schaefer Gallery in New York City mounted Barnet exhibitions. See Gail Stavitsky, *Will Barnet: A Timeless World* (Montclair, N.J.: Montclair Art Museum, 2000), 112–14.
2. Barnet was likely familiar with colonial American furniture forms from the time he spent studying at the School of the Museum of Fine Arts, Boston. The artist's portraits of his grandchildren often feature games and sports.
3. Barnet has called Ingres "one of the greatest abstract painters of all time." Quoted in Stavitsky, *Will Barnet*, 35.

JOAN MITCHELL

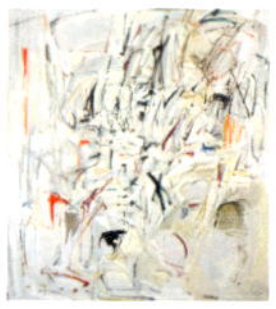

Untitled (p. 262)

1. Linda Nochlin, "A Rage to Paint," in *The Paintings of Joan Mitchell*, ed. Jane Livingston (New York: Whitney Museum of American Art, 2002), 58.
2. Mitchell's friend Tom Hess, an art critic and former director of the Guggenheim Museum, recalled years later that "one of the Abstract Expressionist elders proclaimed ruefully that it had taken him eighteen years to get to where Joan Mitchell was in as many months." Quoted in Livingston, *The Paintings of Joan Mitchell*, 22.
3. Judith E. Bernstock, *Joan Mitchell* (New York: Hudson Hills Press, 1988), 28.
4. Ibid., 29.
5. Ibid., 31.

GRACE HARTIGAN

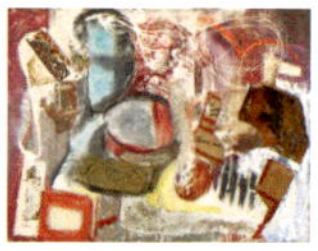

Rough, Ain't It and *Clark's Cove* (p. 264)

1. The origins and sources of Hartigan's interest in collage betray a general interest in the collages of Braque and Pablo Picasso. See Robert Saltonstall Mattison, *Grace Hartigan: A Painter's World* (New York: Hudson Hills Press, 1990), 43. Braque's later still-life paintings include sand mixed with oil paint, although there is no indication that Hartigan saw these. Masson's use of glue and sand in his paintings attracted the attention of many artists in New York during the 1940s, including Jackson Pollock. See Henry Adams, *Tom and Jack: The Intertwined Lives of Thomas Hart Benton and Jackson Pollock* (New York: Bloomsbury Press, 2009), 259.

KENNETH NOLAND

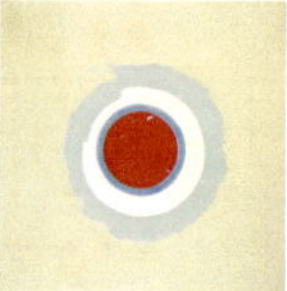

Round (p. 268)

1. Terry Fenton, "Morris Louis," http://www.sharecom.ca/fenton/louis.html. At the end of Fenton's brief article on Louis the author includes a 1983 comment by Clement Greenberg, who states, "I'm glad you gave Ken some of the credit, which belongs properly only to his leading Morris to NY, Frankenthaler, & me in the first place in 1953."
2. Acrylic paints, unlike oils, dry quickly and do not rot canvas. The development of water-based acrylics and gels in the mid-1960s greatly expanded the possibilities for achieving variation in color intensity, suspension, luminescence, and degrees of translucency. See Terry Fenton, "Appreciating Noland," in *Kenneth Noland: Themes and Variations, 1958–2000* (Rockland, Maine: Farnsworth Art Museum, 2002), 14–16.
3. Jamaica Kincaid, "A Way to Begin," in *Kenneth Noland*, 8–9.

JOSEF ALBERS

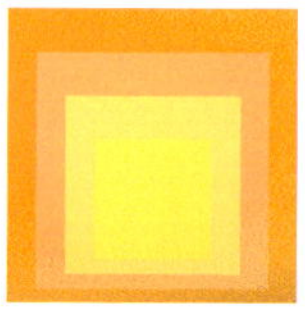

Homage to the Square: Joy (p. 270)

1. Albers, *The Interaction of Color* (New Haven: Yale University Press, 1963), 2.
2. Albers (unpublished lecture, Black Mountain College Meeting at the Museum of Modern Art, New York, January 9, 1941, Josef Albers Papers, Yale University Library).
3. Albers, quoted in Katharine Kuh, *The Artist's Voice: Talks with Seventeen Modern Artists* (Harper and Row, 1962 [as *The Artist's Voice: Talks with Seventeen Artists*]; rev. ed. New York: Da Capo Press, 1990), 20.

JOHN KOCH

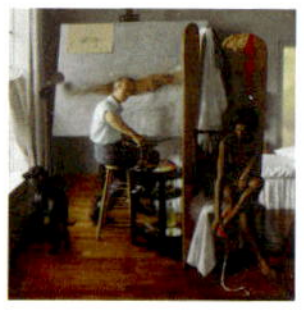

Studio—End of Day (p. 272)

1. Philip Lopate et al., *John Koch: Painting a New York Life* (New York: New-York Historical Society, in association with Scala Publishers, 2001).
2. See Susan Dodge-Peters Daiss, "John Koch: *Interlude*, 1963," in *Seeing America: Painting and Sculpture from the Collection of the Memorial Art Gallery of the University of Rochester*, ed. Marjorie B. Searl (Rochester, N.Y.: University of Rochester Press, 2006), 275–77, 321 n. 6.
3. Grady T. Turner, "Enigmatic Intimacy: The Interior World of John Koch," in Lopate et al., *John Koch*, 33.

ROBERT RAUSCHENBERG

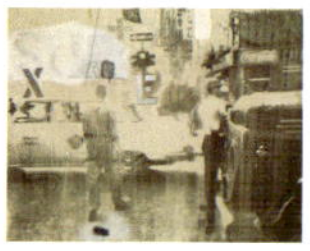

Untitled (p. 276)

1. Rauschenberg, quoted in Alan R. Solomon, *Robert Rauschenberg* (New York: Jewish Museum, 1963), n.p.
2. In 1953, Rauschenberg famously acquired and then erased a drawing by de Kooning, retitling the work *Erased de Kooning Drawing* (San Francisco Museum of Modern Art).
3. Andy Warhol began using silkscreened photographic imagery in his paintings at exactly the same time.

WAYNE THIEBAUD

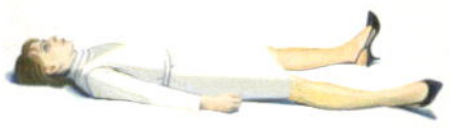

Supine Woman (p. 278)

1. Alfred Frankenstein, quoted in Steven A. Nash, *Wayne Thiebaud: A Paintings Retrospective* (San Francisco: Fine Arts Museums of San Francisco, 2000), 199.
2. "Interview with Wayne Thiebaud," in Stephen C. McGough, *Thiebaud Selects Thiebaud: A Forty-Year Survey from Private Collections* (Sacramento: Crocker Art Museum, 1996), 8.

ANDY WARHOL

Dolly Parton (p. 280)

1. See Tony Shafrazi, "Andy Warhol: Portraits," 12; and Carter Ratcliff, "Looking Good: Andy Warhol's Utopian Portraiture," 18, in *Andy Warhol Portraits*, ed. Shafrazi (New York: Phaidon Press, 2009).
2. Soon after the work's completion in 1985, Parton's theme park, Dollywood, located in the foothills of the Great Smoky Mountains in her home state of Tennessee, opened to the public as a vacation destination. It was a fitting and appropriate canonization of the country music legend as a popular culture icon and entertainment sensation.
3. The term "Dogpatch Diva" associates Parton with the blond, buxom Daisy Mae Scraggs, a fictional character from Al Capp's national syndicated comic strip *Li'l Abner*. The satirical comic lampooned the hillbilly culture and politics of Appalachia. The Factory was the name of Warhol's studio, which served as a popular meeting place for artists, musicians, and celebrities.

TOM WESSELMANN

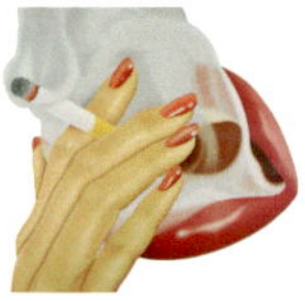

Smoker #9 (p. 282)

1. Slim Stealingworth [pseudonym of Tom Wesselmann], *Tom Wesselmann* (New York: Harry N. Abrams, 1980), 66.
2. For more on Wesselmann's biography, see John Wilmerding, *Tom Wesselmann: His Voice and Vision* (New York: Rizzoli, 2008).
3. The *Great American Nude* series began with *Great American Nude #1* in 1961 and includes one hundred works spanning most of the decade.
4. Alex Katz, who had been making cutout figure paintings for some time, gave Wesselmann his first one-person exhibition at the Tanager Gallery in 1961.

GEORGE TOOKER

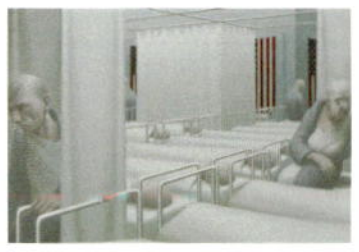

Ward (p. 284)

1. Tooker, quoted in Thomas H. Garver, *George Tooker* (New York: Clarkson N. Potter, 1985), 45.
2. Tooker, interview by David Tunkl, n.d., David Tunkl Fine Art, Los Angeles.

NEIL G. WELLIVER

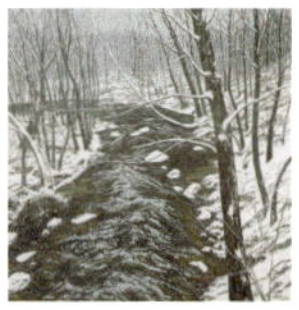

Snow on Alden Brook (p. 286)

1. Jeremy Sigler, "Neil Welliver: The Absent Painter," *Brooklyn Rail* (December 2006/January 2007): 42.
2. Edgar Allen Beem, "The Landscape of Loss," *Boston Globe Magazine*, March 19, 1995, 22–23; 31–35.

ANDREW WYETH

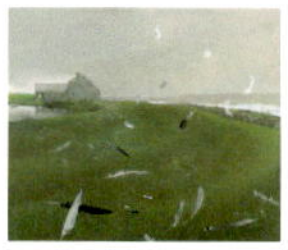

Airborne (p. 288)

1. Conversation with the author, 2004.
2. Before Crystal Bridges purchased the painting from the artist, *Airborne* was among a relatively small group of pictures that Wyeth and his wife retained as representative of his strongest work. Although it was on loan to the Farnsworth Museum in Rockland, Maine, during the winter months, each summer for several years the painting returned to Benner Island. Wyeth would occasionally add a feather to the composition, as if to test whether his viewers were looking "deep," as he felt was necessary to know any work of art. Conversations with the author.
3. Richard Meryman, *Andrew Wyeth: A Secret Life* (New York: Harper Collins, 1996).
4. Jamie Wyeth, "Fond Farewells: Andrew Wyeth," *TIME Magazine* 147, no. 25, December 28, 2009, 175.

JAMIE WYETH

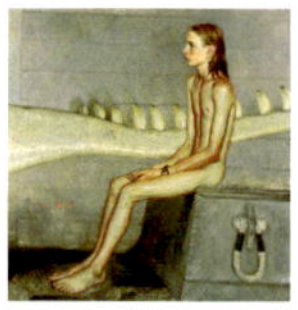

Orca Bates (p. 290)

1. Richard McClanathan, "Jamie Wyeth on Monhegan," *Island Journal* [Rockland, Maine] 8 (1991): 42.

RICHARD ESTES

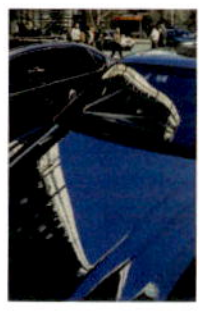

Reflections of the Woolworth Building and *Antarctica* (p. 292)

1. John Wilmerding, *Richard Estes* (New York: Rizzoli, 2006), 219.

BO BARTLETT

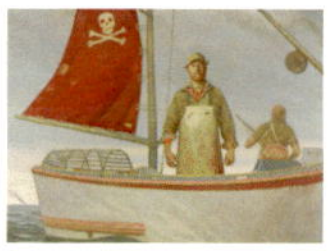

The Lobster Wars (p. 296)

1. Matinicus Island is twenty miles out to sea from the mainland and the nearest commercial port in Rockland. It has a year-round population of fewer than two dozen families, all of whom are involved in one way or another in the Maine lobster industry. There are no legally sanctioned lobstering territories in Maine, but generations of fisherman have abided by unwritten "understandings" that occasionally erupt in violence, although only rarely in shootings.
2. Bartlett's award-winning 1995 documentary film on the artist Andrew Wyeth, *Snow Hill*, provides insight into his approach to portraiture in the context of composition, structure, symbolism, and storytelling on a grand scale.

MARY MCCLEARY

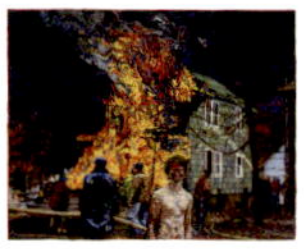

The Falcon Cannot Hear the Falconer (p. 298)

1. McCleary, quoted in marymccleary.com/Statement/html (accessed September 28, 2010).
2. McCleary, *Beginning with the Word: Constructed Narratives, 1985–2000* (Galveston, Tex.: Galveston Art Center, 2000), 4.
3. Yeats's poem has provided inspiration and titles for artists ranging from Chinua Achebe to Joan Didion to Joni Mitchell.
4. See, for example, McCleary's mixed-media collage *Jerusalem, Athens, Alexandria, Vienna, London* (2003, El Paso Museum of Art).

KERRY JAMES MARSHALL

Our Town (p. 300)

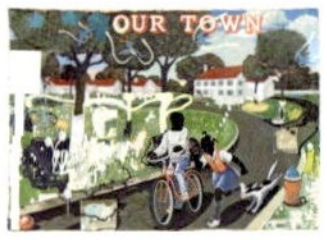

1. Marshall, interview by Calvin Reid, *Bomb* 62 (Winter 1998): 45.

KARA WALKER

A Warm Summer Evening in 1863 (p. 302)

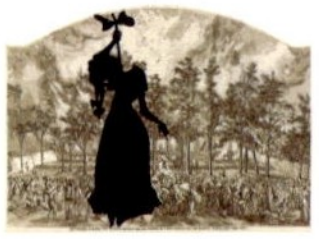

1. Michele Wallace, "The Enigma of the Negress Kara Walker," in *Kara Walker: Narratives of a Negress*, ed. Ian Berry et al. (Cambridge, Mass.: MIT Press, 2003), 177. "This work is as much about gender and sexual violation as it is about race and racial boundaries," Wallace argues.
2. "Thelma Golden/Kara Walker: A Dialogue," in *Kara Walker: Pictures from Another Time*, ed. Annette Dixon (Ann Arbor: University of Michigan Museum of Art, 2002), 46.
3. Anne M. Wagner, "The Black-White Relation," in *Kara Walker: Narratives of a Negress*, 96. See also Hamza Walker, "A Mind Is a Terrible Thing to Waste," in *Witness to Her Art*, ed. Rhea Anastas, with Michael Brenson (Annandale-on-Hudson, N.Y.: Bard College, 2006), 278–79. Hamza Walker describes the tendency to associate Walker's work with slavery as "a willful projection on the viewer's part," calling this sentiment "symptomatic of the segregation we all muster an overwhelming earnestness to ignore, i.e. repress."
4. Jerry Saltz, "Making the Cut," *Village Voice,* November 24, 1998, 135.

JIM HODGES

When We Stay (p. 304)

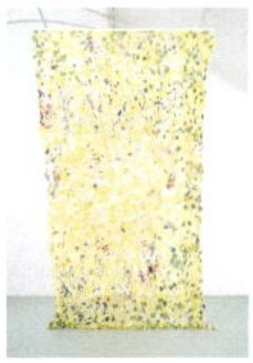

1. Dana Self, "Jim Hodges: *Welcome*" (press release, Kemper Museum of Contemporary Art, Kansas City, Mo., 1998).
2. See Cate Marquis, "'I Remember Heaven' Offers Intriguing Pairing of Artists," *Frieze* no. 116 (June 18, 2008); and Marco Tagliafierro, "Jim Hodges: Fondazione Bevilacqua la Masa," trans. Marguerite Shore, *Artforum International* 48 no. 10 (Summer 2010): 372.
3. Hodges, quoted in Mark Rappolt, "Generator," *Art Review* no. 29 (2009): 44–45.
4. Martin Herbert, "Jim Hodges" (press release, Camden Arts Centre, London, 2010).
5. Tagliafierro, "Jim Hodges: Fondazione Bevilacqua la Masa," 372.
6. Rappolt, "Generator," 44–45.

WALTON FORD

The Island (p. 306)

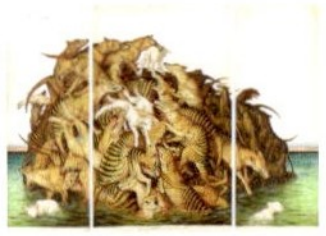

1. Ford's use of the triptych format for this massive watercolor was partly a function of its size and medium. Watercolors are generally glazed for protection, but the lightweight plexiglass sheets (instead of glass) used to facilitate portability tend to flex into the artwork if they are too large. Triptych formats inevitably are associated with the multipanel religious altarpieces commissioned for major churches and cathedrals during the Renaissance and Baroque periods. Among the most common subjects for these works were Last Judgment scenes, which often include writhing bodies in an indeterminate, otherworldly space.
2. Ford, quoted in Calvin Tompkins, "Man and Beast: The Narrative Art of Walton Ford," *New Yorker*, January 26, 2009, 51.
3. Matthew C. Stretcher, "Magical Realism in the Search for Identity in the Fiction of Murakami Haruki," *Journal of Japanese Studies* 25 (Summer 1999): 267.
4. Tompkins, "Man and Beast," 52; confirmed in conversation with the author, October 2009.

TOM UTTECH

Enassamishhinjijweian (p. 308)

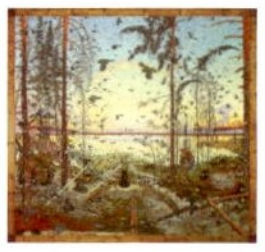

1. Uttech, quoted in Margaret Andera, *Magnetic North: The Landscapes of Tom Uttech* (Milwaukee: Milwaukee Art Museum, 2004), 27.
2. Ibid., 11.
3. Lucy R. Lippard, "Bringing to Life: Tom Uttech's Paintings—2009," http://www.alexandregallery.com/artists/viewPress/179 (accessed September 28, 2010).

SCULPTURE at CRYSTAL BRIDGES

Christopher B. Crosman

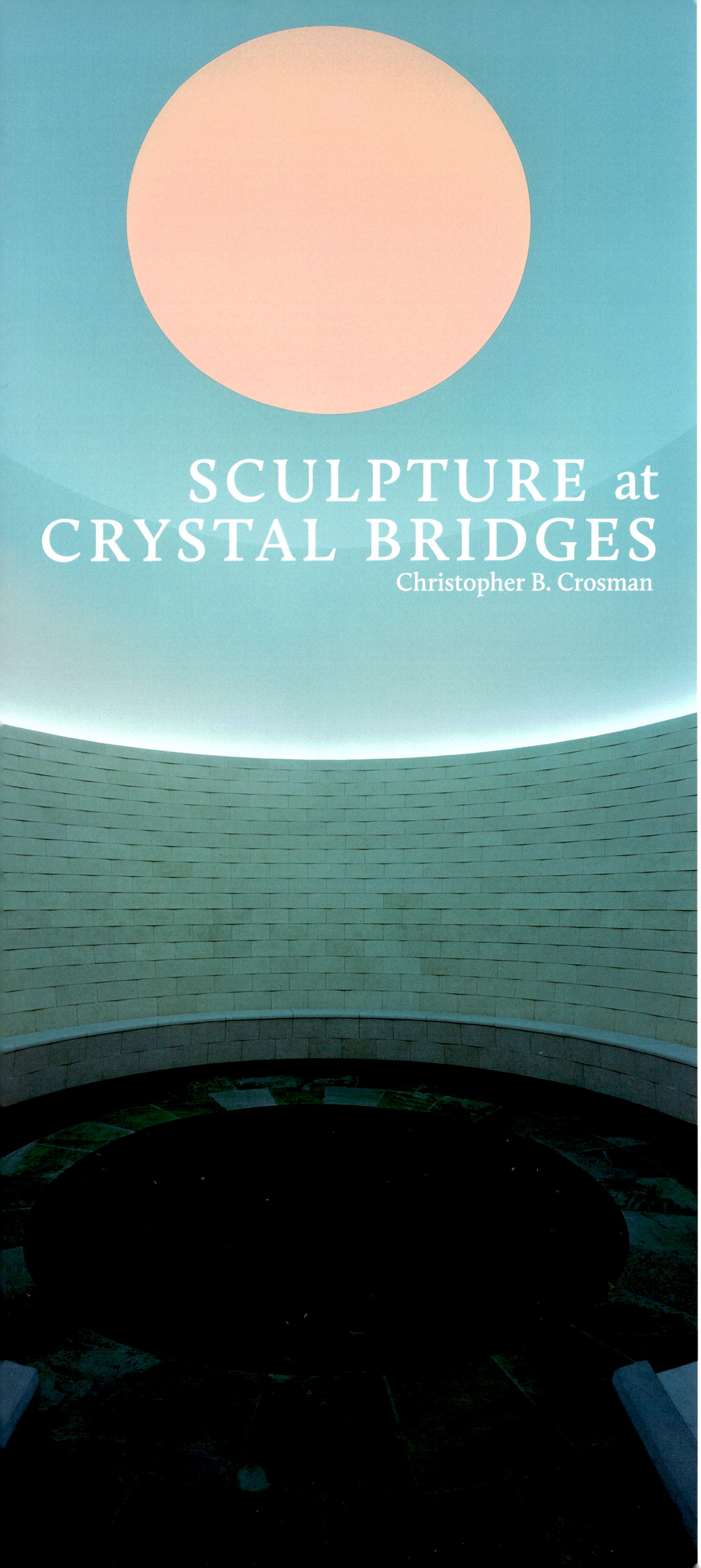

At this time, Crystal Bridges' sculpture holdings consist of a relatively small but widely varied group of works. These objects were chosen first and foremost for their individual merits, but also with an eye toward aesthetic and contextual relationships within the overall collection. Harriet Whitney Frishmuth's exuberant, erotically charged bronze *The Bubble* (1928, fig. 1), an over life-size sculpture of a leaping woman holding an iridescent glass ball, may at first seem to have little to do with Maxfield Parrish's oil painting of festive though chaste lantern bearers (1908, p. 182). But viewed together, the two joyous works' spherical shapes and dance-like rhythms seem to bounce back and forth. Likewise, Augustus Saint-Gaudens's plaster bust of Anne Page (1895) is pleasing on its own, but truly comes alive in proximity to Dennis Miller Bunker's elegant painted portrait of the stately Boston beauty (1887, p. 138).[1]

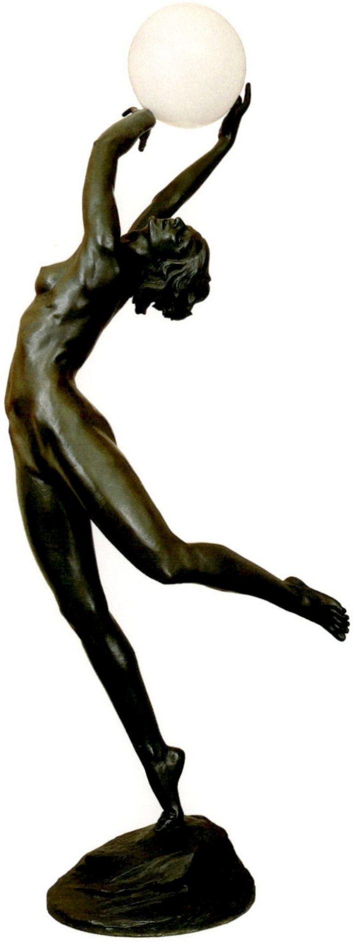

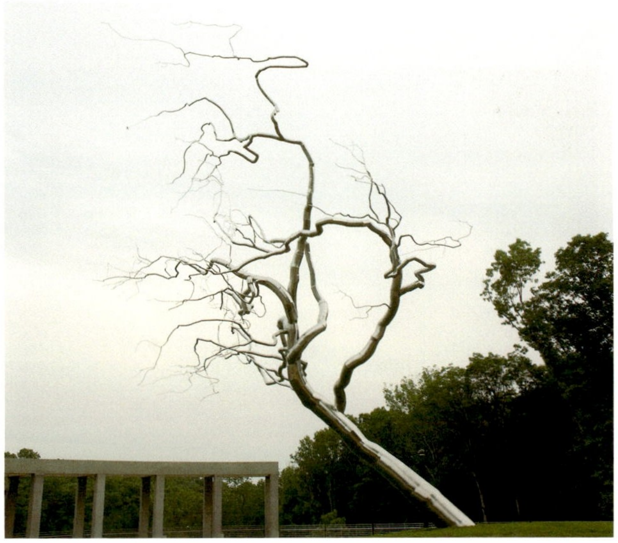

Outdoor sculpture is an integral part of the Crystal Bridges experience. Roxy Paine's *Yield* (2011, fig. 2) is the first work of art visitors see when arriving from the main vehicular drive, while James Turrell's *The Way of Color* Skyspace (2009, fig. 3) greets those approaching the museum on the walking trail from downtown Bentonville, and visitors coming from the north initially encounter Mark di Suvero's monumental *Lowell's Ocean* (2005–8; fig. 4). These three diverse works created by innovative American artists with international reputations serve as physical and theoretical anchors for the museum's broader holdings, introducing the collection's recurrent themes of nature; resourcefulness and invention; and American art on the world stage. The trio of physically imposing and visually striking contemporary works herald an extraordinary art experience throughout the museum complex and grounds.

Set on a teardrop-shaped island at the museum's entrance, the sinuous branches of Paine's soaring Dendroid reach out naturalistically toward the building, the downward-sloping hillside, and the streambed below.[2] Made of welded stainless steel plate, pipe, and rod, *Yield* conflates natural forms with industrial and technological engineering. Paine is known for precisely replicating the shape and dimensions of real trees but fabricating their gleaming trunks and limbs by means of resolutely inorganic materials and processes. The artist has called attention to the "transformative aspect" of these hybrid constructions, "an alchemical transformation that is a potential symbol of the positive and negative consequences of technology."[3] For Paine, the same stainless steel structures that facilitate the production of life-saving pharmaceuticals also raise the specter of chemical pipeline catastrophes.

Turrell's *The Way of Color* offers a circular chamber sixteen feet in diameter within which seated viewers are encouraged to contemplate light as a phenomenon that is governed by time and place, infinitely changeable, and impossible to hold in memory.[4] The artist programmed the 396 LED (light-emitting diode) light sources in the chamber to adjust to subtle changes in the appearance of dawn and dusk over the course of a year. Like Josef Albers's *Homage to the Square* paintings (p. 270), these

FIG 1 Harriet Whitney Frishmuth (1880–1980), *The Bubble*, 1928. Bronze with iridescent glass ball, 94 × 38¾ × 26 in. (238.8 × 98.4 × 66 cm) (without ball). Fractional Gift of Frank L. Hohmann, III

FIG 2 Roxy Paine (b. 1966), *Yield*, 2011. Stainless steel, 47½ × 45 ft. (14.5 × 13.7 m)

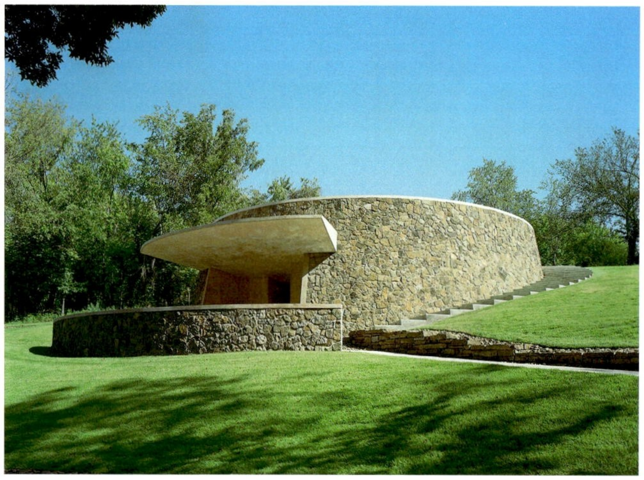

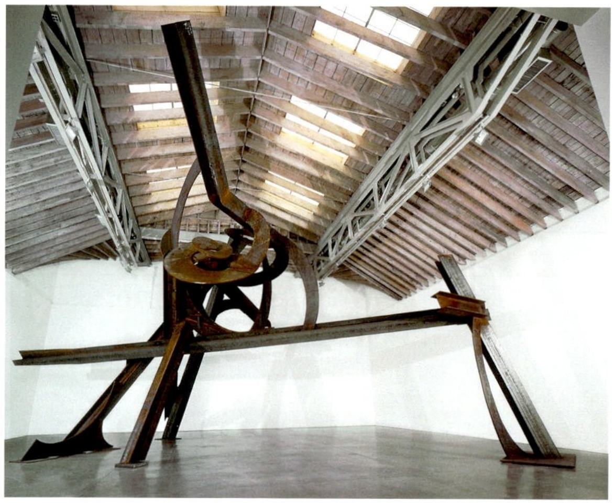

"light shows" demonstrate how the perception of color changes in relation to its context. Inside Turrell's Skyspace, colored artificial light dramatically alters the appearance of the firmament visible through the open oculus overhead. A gray-blue sky might look black, mauve, or even pink through the circular opening, depending on the relationship between the natural light in the sky and the hues reflected on the interior walls and ceiling. Indeed, visitors often feel compelled to check the sky's true color by stepping outside of Turrell's constructed environments.

Di Suvero's *Lowell's Ocean* directly addresses basic sculptural concerns, including weight, balance, and gravity; the relationship of parts to a whole; and the interaction between a three-dimensional work of art and the space that surrounds it. The four-legged structure asserts its industrial origins through its materials, which include unpainted steel I-beams and rough-cut sheet metal. Topping the elegantly balanced composition is a massive, inch-thick steel plate that di Suvero torqued and sheered into the clockwork-like spring that gives the sculpture its powerful sense of pressure and release, movement and stasis. Yet even this dramatic monument to an urban-industrial landscape fits seamlessly into the museum site, with its ever-encroaching forests, steeply rising hillsides, and water flowing through the North Bridge weir system to rejoin the ancient streambed.

The sculpture trail leading from downtown Bentonville to the museum was conceived as an informal setting for not only monumental works of art but also more intimately scaled and accessibly themed objects that engage a wide range of ages and interests. Sculptural surprises were carefully planned throughout the heavily forested terrain. And because this locale was the Walton family's childhood escape—their private Sherwood Forest of the imagination—several of the sculptures that punctuate the landscape were specifically selected with playfulness in mind. In Dan Ostermiller's bronze *Shore Lunch* (1999), a stylized and rather pudgy bronze bear gnaws on perhaps the largest trout ever caught in the Ozarks, or at least from the nearby stream. A few steps further one finds André Harvey's life-size bronze *Stella* (2009), a smiling, friendlier porcine relative of the ubiquitous "Razorback" mascot of the University of Arkansas in neighboring Fayetteville. Visitors from New England may recognize Nancy Schön's lethargic hare being overtaken by a high-stepping tortoise (2009) from the cast of this sculpture installed at the finish line of the Boston Marathon.

Regional artists were commissioned to create sculptures for the museum grounds. George Dombek's bronze *Tour de Apple Tree* (2010), which depicts a bicycle made of twigs hiding in the branches of a fruit tree, is located where the bike trail veers north. Pat Musick and Jerry Carr's *A Place Where They Cried* (2010), in which several dozen upright, native stone plinths cross

FIG 3 James Turrell (b. 1941), *The Way of Color*, 2009. Stone, concrete, stainless steel, and LED lighting, 228 × 652 in. (579.1 × 1656.1 cm)

FIG 4 Mark di Suvero (b. 1933), *Lowell's Ocean*, 2005–8. Steel, 256 × 366 × 532 in. (650.2 × 929.6 × 1351.3 cm)

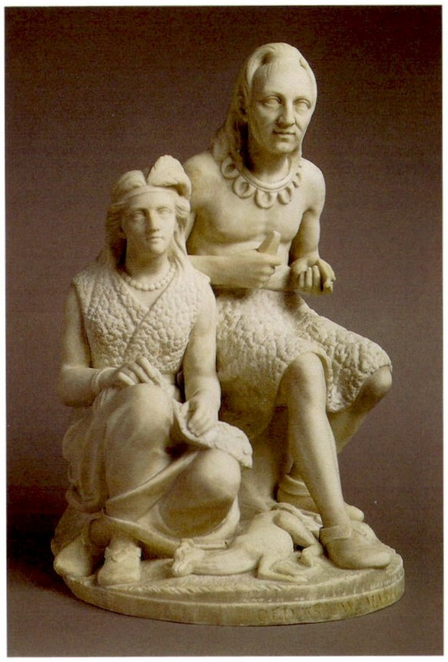

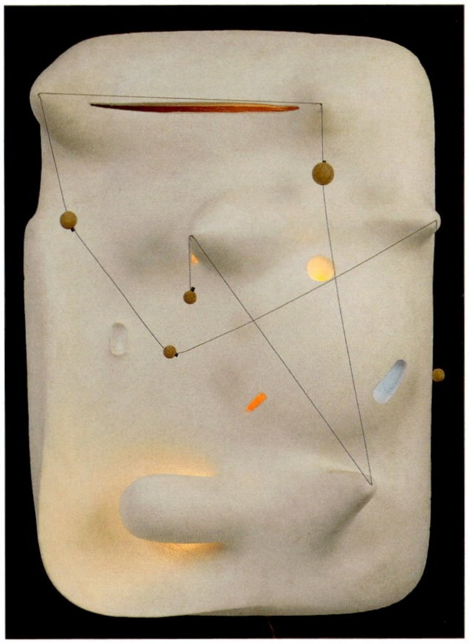

a streambed, memorializes Cherokee Indians who endured the Trail of Tears, a section of which passed through Bentonville.

Much of the land around Crystal Bridges remains undeveloped and available for future projects. While the dense woodlands and steep terrain may prove inhospitable to more traditional outdoor sculpture, there is ample space for site-specific work and temporary installations. The grounds are a part of the museum canvas that is meant to remain unfinished, available to subsequent generations for continual reconsideration and reinvention.

Sculpture also appears throughout the interconnected museum buildings and, when appropriate, is integrated thematically or chronologically with work in other art forms. For example, Giuseppe Ceracchi's marble portrait of Alexander Hamilton, the first United States Secretary of the Treasury (1794), appears near a roughly contemporary painted likeness of George Washington by Gilbert Stuart commissioned by a prominent New York merchant as a gift to Hamilton (1797, p. 36).[5] Hiram Powers's neoclassical marble bust of the Roman goddess Proserpine (ca. 1840) is mounted in proximity to Benjamin West's romantic painting *Cupid and Psyche* (1808, p. 32). Edmonia Lewis's marble parlor sculpture *The Old Arrow Maker* (1866–72, fig. 5) was inspired by Henry Wadsworth Longfellow's 1855 poem *The Song of Hiawatha*, which is also the subject of N. C. Wyeth's painting *Hiawatha Fishing* (1907) in the collection.

The American Renaissance and its lingering influence through the first half of the twentieth century are ably represented with bronzes by Frederick William MacMonnies, Alexander Stirling Calder (father of mobile inventor, Alexander Calder) and, as noted above, Harriet Whitney Frishmuth. Modernist sculpture in the collection ranges from John Bradley Storrs's life-size, allegorical bronze figures *Night* and *Day* (1929) to Isamu Noguchi's visionary *Lunar Landscape* (1943, fig. 6), a cast Magnasite composite relief articulated with cork, string, and internal electric lights visible through slits and apertures in the white surface. Alexander Calder's monumental freestanding mobile *Trois noirs sur un rouge* (1968) is a kinetic marvel that betrays the artist's early career as a mechanical engineer as well as his sophisticated understanding of contemporary trends in European avant-garde art.

Sculpture dating from the mid-twentieth century to the present is an ongoing focus of Crystal Bridges' collecting. Commanding metal sculptures by Seymour Lipton (*Spring Ceremonial*, 1951, and *Angel*, 1975) reflect post–World War II intellectual currents in art and philosophy that probed dreams, myth, and the unconscious. Similar ideas and imagery appear in paintings in the collection by Jackson Pollock (p. 236), Mark Rothko, Theodoros Stamos, and David Smith (p. 240). A metal screen punctuated by circular holes that allude to the benday dots found in commercial printing serves as the backdrop for pop artist Roy

FIG 5 Edmonia Lewis (1844–after 1911), *The Old Arrow Maker*, 1866–72. White marble, 20 × 14 × 14 in. (50.8 × 35.6 × 35.6 cm)

FIG 6 Isamu Noguchi (1904–1988), *Lunar Landscape*, 1943. Magnasite, cork, string, and electric lights, approx. 35 × 25¼ × 7 in. (88.9 × 64.1 × 17.8 cm)

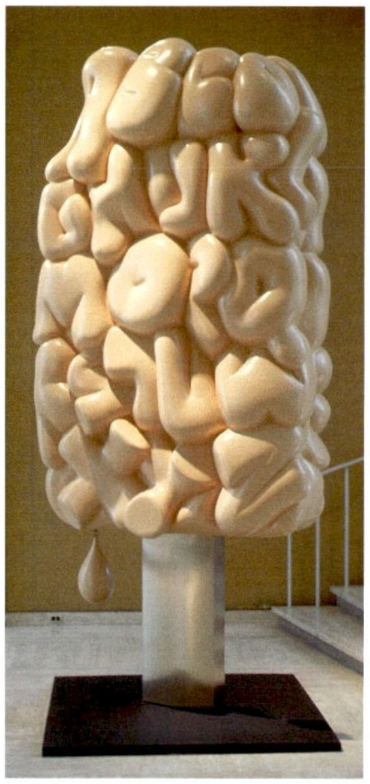

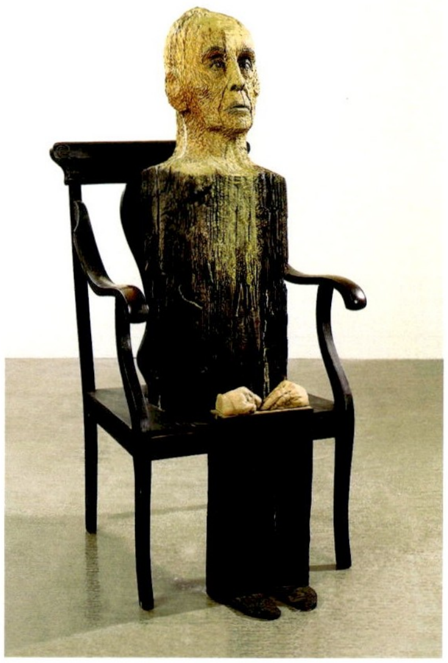

Lichtenstein's enamel-painted steel *Standing Explosion (Red)* (1966, fig. 3 in Introduction). The juxtaposition between the three-dimensional sculpture and its source in mass-produced print media such as comic books is a knowing sight gag. Moreover, the "explosion" that neither moves nor makes any sound, simply sitting on its pedestal of high art, underscores the pop aesthetic of distancing "coolness" and emotional detachment. Claes Oldenburg's twelve-foot-high by five-and-a-half-foot-wide fiberglass and bronze *Alphabet/Good Humor* (1975, fig. 7) is a monument to a fleeting moment in the transitory life of a melting confection. As was typical of the sculptor's artistic practice, Oldenburg transformed an ordinary object through dramatic alterations of scale, material, and surface detail. The flesh-colored forms that comprise the frozen treat read simultaneously as letters of the alphabet and as body parts. Sex and consumerism happily cohabitate in this orgiastic alphabet.

Marisol, another artist sometimes linked to pop art, draws from her aristocratic South American roots as well as more than half a century at the center of the post–World War II New York avant-garde. Marisol was the only woman widely accepted by the male-dominated pop art movement. In *Portrait of Martha Graham* (1977, fig. 8), the subject's blocklike, static figure seems to run counter to her pioneering role in the history of modern dance, but the sculpture's solidity and brutal honesty celebrate an aging doyenne whose reputation is as secure as it is immutable. The gouges, indentations, and heavily worked pencil drawing that mark the surface of the wood-and-plaster figure recall Marisol's early involvement with abstract expressionism as well as her recollection of the often crudely carved and highly expressive religious sculpture that adorned the Spanish colonial churches of her youth.

Another strong female artist in the collection and one of the very few post–World War II American women sculptors to achieve international acclaim, Louise Nevelson was sixty years old when she first gained significant attention from critics, collectors, and museums. Crystal Bridges' *Night Zag Wall* (1969–74, fig. 10 in Introduction) is a prime example of the walls of stacked boxes filled with found objects and painted a uniform black (or occasionally white or gold) for which Nevelson is best known. *Night Zag Wall*'s sense of mystery, ritual, and dream are the result of the sculptor's keen understanding of formal arrangement and visual rhythm. Nevelson's Russian-Jewish heritage, along with a relatively isolated youth in the rural fishing village of Rockland, Maine, where her father supported the family with his salvage lumber business, undoubtedly affected her artistic development.

Eat Meat (1969; cast in aluminum 1975, fig. 9), by Louisiana native Lynda Benglis, is nearly contemporaneous with Nevelson's *Night Zag Wall*. Although Nevelson can be credited with opening the door to younger female sculptors like Benglis, the two artists' objectives are generations apart. *Eat Meat* typifies

FIG 7 Claes Oldenburg (b. 1929), *Alphabet/Good Humor*, 1975. Painted fiberglass and bronze, 142 × 68 × 28 in. (360.7 × 172.7 × 71.1 cm)

FIG 8 Marisol (b. 1930), *Portrait of Martha Graham*, 1977. Oil and pencil on wood and plaster, 53 × 25½ × 32½ in. (134.6 × 64.8 × 82.6 cm)

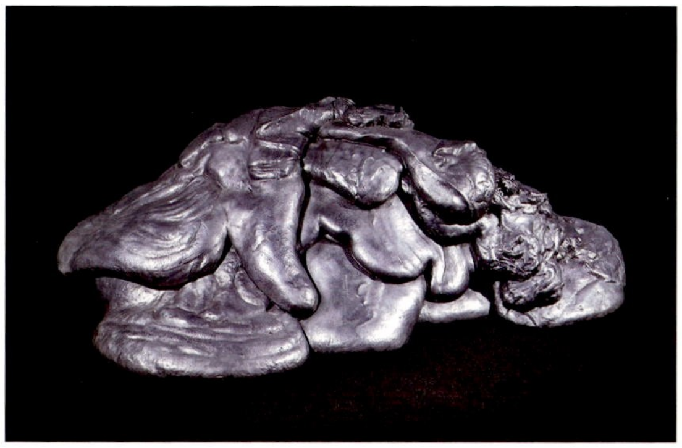

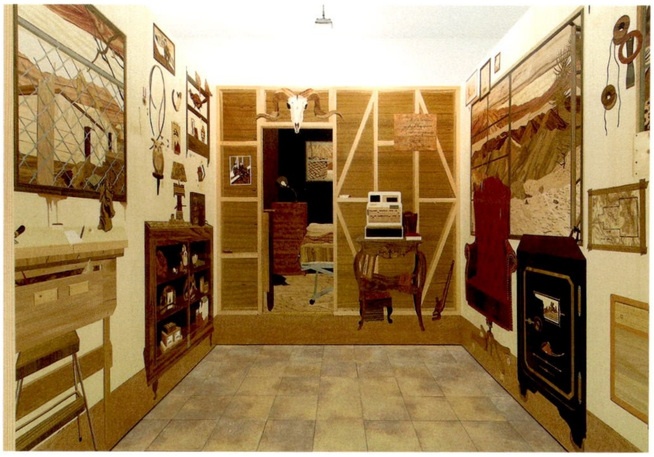

Benglis's "anti-form" sculptures, which are cast from blobs of polyurethane foam that ooze and flow of their own accord. The sculptor initially intended these works to chide the poured, dripped, and seemingly unpredictable paintings of Pollock and his mostly male abstract expressionist colleagues. Benglis's work from this period also registered the artist's dissatisfaction with what she considered the muscular, male-oriented world of the then emerging minimalist movement, which relied on geometric form, repetition, massive weight, hard edges, and industrial materials. Using "softer" materials and forms, Benglis developed a new, feminist aesthetic grounded in indeterminacy, fluidity, and contour. An artist as daring as any of the post–World War II era, Benglis's best work hovers on the knife-edge between consequence and outrage.

A gathering strength in the collection is work that blurs traditional boundaries between media. In her marquetry *Room* (2007–8, fig. 10), Alison Elizabeth Taylor created a built environment that literally turns sculpture inside out. Confounding viewer expectations, the furniture, shelves, and decorative items in the space take the form of two-dimensional illusions of three-dimensional forms achieved through the meticulous inlay of varying types of wood. Taylor and Jim Hodges (p. 304) are two among a group of tremendously talented contemporary artists who are successfully challenging the long-held but increasingly arbitrary divisions between craft and fine art.

Crystal Bridges' collection includes a number of examples by contemporary sculptors whose work demonstrates an extraordinary—even obsessive—dedication to craft and workmanship. Karen LaMonte's life-size, cast glass dresses are tours de force of sensuality and manual skill. The eminent art critic Arthur C. Danto, nearly overwhelmed by her artistry, reached deep into his considerable erudition to invoke an Elizabethan sonnet by Robert Herrick in response. So perfectly does the poem capture the radiance of LaMonte's *Dress Impression with Wrinkled Cowl* (2007, fig. 11) that the text bears repeating here:

> Whenas in silks my Julia goes,
> Then, then, methinks, how sweetly flows
> That liquefaction of her clothes!
>
> Next, when I cast mine eyes and see
> That brave vibration each way free,
> —O how that glittering taketh me![6]

Nick Cave's carefully crafted Soundsuits have been compared to the purposefully outré drag queen costumes of London's underground performance scene, the fashions worn by African American Mardi Gras Indians in New Orleans, and even German conceptual artist Joseph Beuys's "social sculptures."[7] An Alvin Ailey–trained dancer, Cave originally conceived the Soundsuits

FIG 9 Lynda Benglis (b. 1941), *Eat Meat*, 1969/75. Cast aluminum, 24 × 80 × 54 in. (61 × 203.2 × 137.2 cm)

FIG 10 Alison Elizabeth Taylor (b. 1973), *Room*, 2007–8. Wood veneer, pyrography, shellac, 96 × 120 × 96 in. (243.8 × 304.8 × 243.8 cm)

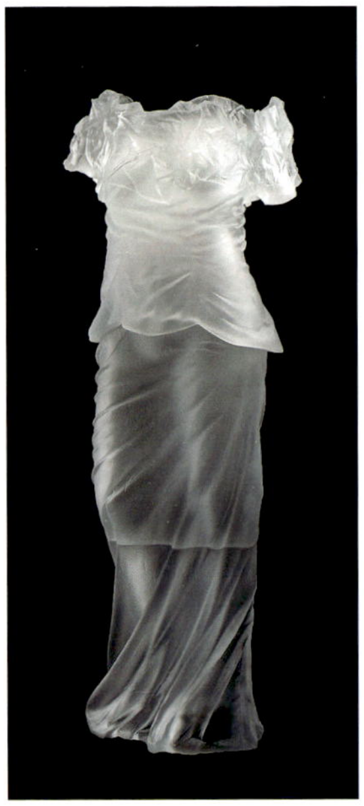

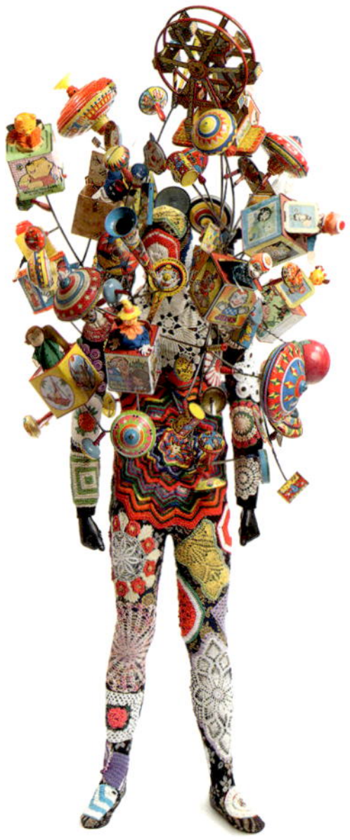

as costumes for performances. When worn by dancers, the head-to-toe outfits make sounds ranging from the rhythmic swish of long, brightly colored clumps of hair to the lively jangle of metal components sewn into the garments. Whether installed in a museum as sculpture or seen in performance, the Soundsuits gain potency as an ensemble; dancers, after all, need partners. The more traditional of Crystal Bridges' two Soundsuits (2009) utilizes brightly colored crocheted and macramé beads and buttons to form complex circle patterns reminiscent of ritual tattoos and scarification as well as the vibrant, patterned textiles found in many regions of Africa. The other suit (2010, fig. 12) incorporates numerous vintage (ca. 1950–70) mechanical tin toys, including music-playing tops and jack-in-the-boxes. Cross-cultural references aside—or perhaps because of them—Cave's work conveys a joie de vivre that is as infectious as it is wildly, wonderfully exuberant. Truly, his Soundsuits are an American celebration.

NOTES

1. Augustus Saint-Gaudens's bronze bas-relief portraits *Gertrude Vanderbilt at the Age of Seven* (1882) and *Robert Louis Stevenson* (1887) also complement paintings in the collection.
2. I wish to thank Crystal Bridges' landscape architect Scott Eccleston for sharing with me his astute observation about the interaction between Paine's *Yield* and the museum complex.
3. Joao Ribas, "The AI Interview: Roxy Paine," *ARTINFO*, April 10, 2007, quoted in Eleanor Heartney, *Roxy Paine* (New York: Prestel, 2009), 21.
4. The dimensions of Turrell's Skyspace were determined by the approximate space required to seat an average elementary school class of around thirty students.
5. The noted Italian neoclassical sculptor Giuseppe Ceracchi was active elsewhere in Europe and in the United States, where he executed his bust of Alexander Hamilton. Crystal Bridges' collection contains a number of works by non-American artists who treated American subjects or spent considerable time in the United States.
6. Robert Herrick, "Upon Julia's Clothes" (1648), quoted in Arthur C. Danto, "The Poetry and Meaning of Loss: The Glass Dresses of Karen LaMonte," in *Karen LaMonte: Absence Adorned* (Seattle: University of Washington Press, 2005), 13.
7. Jori Finkel, "I Dream the Clothing Electric," *New York Times*, April 5, 2009, http://www.nytimes.com/2009/04/05/arts/design/05fink.html (accessed December 14, 2010).

FIG 11 Karen LaMonte (b. 1967), *Dress Impression with Wrinkled Cowl*, 2007. Cast glass, 56 × 21 × 17 in. (142.2 × 53.3 × 43.2 cm)

FIG 12 Nick Cave (b. 1959), *Soundsuit*, 2010. Appliquéd found knitted and crocheted fabric, metal armature, painted metal and wood toys, 97 × 48 × 42 in. (246.4 × 121.9 × 106.7 cm)

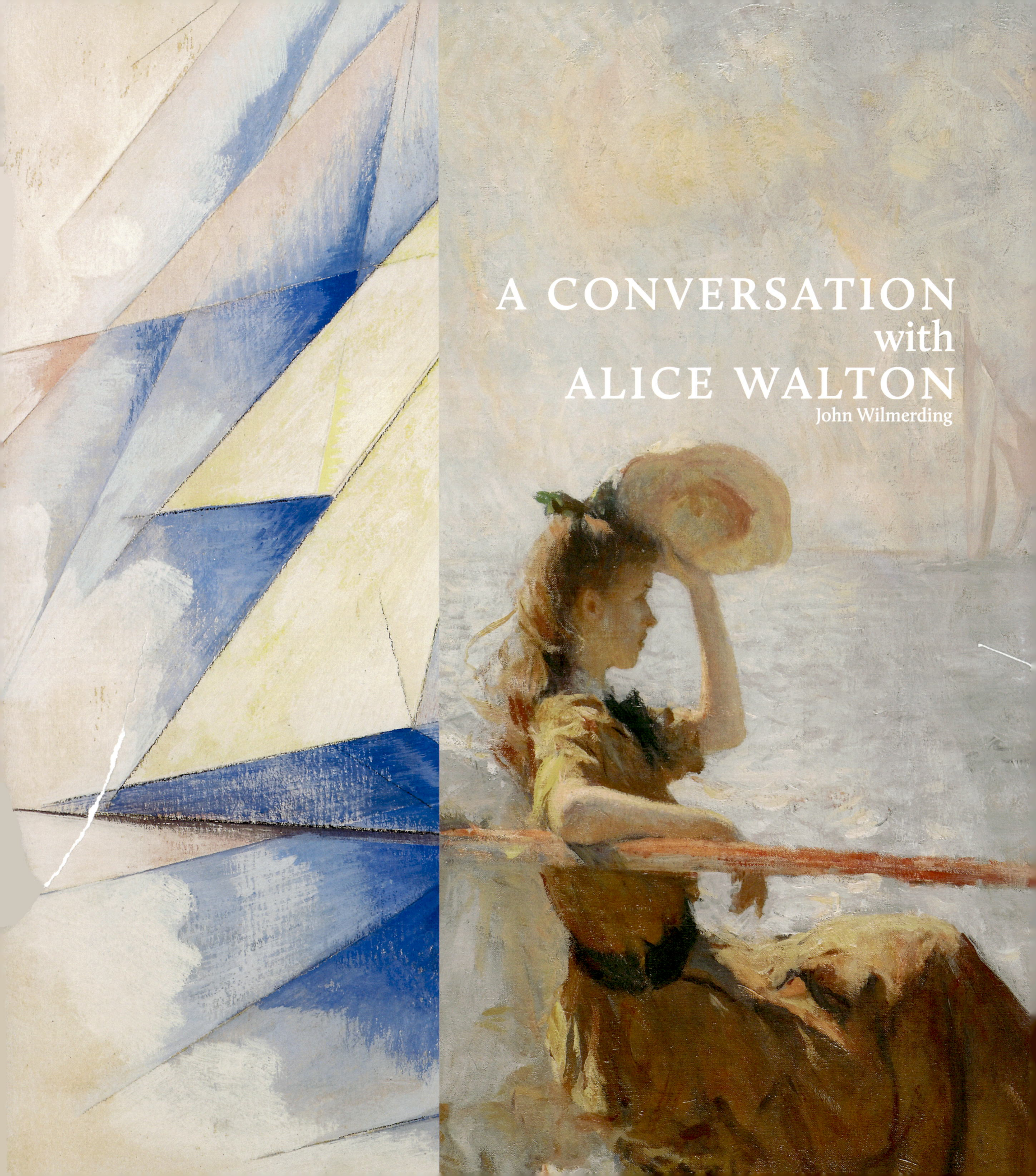
A CONVERSATION
with
ALICE WALTON
John Wilmerding

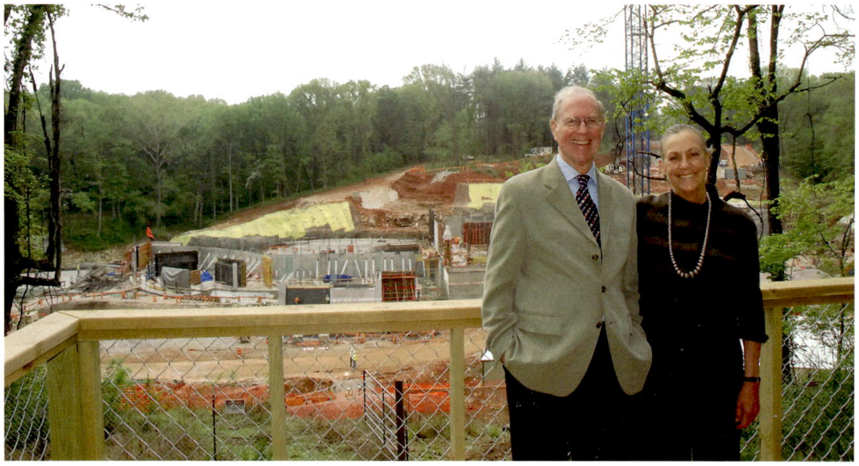

I met Alice Walton in 2004, thanks to the recommendations of colleagues. Shortly thereafter, she invited me to advise on acquisitions for the museum and to help guide development of the collection. I became part of a small team of staff members and outside professionals who worked with Alice in these formative years of the institution. Needless to say, it has been an exciting honor to help bring her conception of Crystal Bridges Museum of American Art into a reality.

The following is excerpted from an interview that took place at Crystal Bridges in August 2009.

John Wilmerding: So, Alice, I'm interested in particular, now that your mother and father are gone, what forces were they in your life growing up? Give us a little bit of a personal biography, where you were born, where you went to school, where you lived?

Alice Walton: I was born in Newport, Arkansas, in 1949, proud of it. We moved to Bentonville when I was less than a year old. My mother's family was in Claremore, Oklahoma, and she wanted us to be a little closer—this [Bentonville] was halfway in between.

My father, one phrase that he used when we were growing up was, "You can be anything you want to be; just think it through first." I've always had this interest in art, which my mother encouraged.

JW: Let's fill in a little bit more. What has educated you beyond family?

AW: I grew [up] with three older brothers—Rob, John, and Jim—in Bentonville. We lived in town until I was in the sixth grade, when we moved to where our present family home is, right above [the site for] Crystal Bridges. So, Crystal Bridges was our backyard growing up. We all attended Bentonville High School and we would walk through the woods to school.

JW: How early did you become aware of your parents' business and philanthropic interests?

AW: Work was always a part of our life, and as a family we did it together; it was just what we did. But community service, and community giving, is a cornerstone of our family. I have always wanted—searched for—a way to give that was truly meaningful.

JW: Now let's turn to your first interest in art. Talk a little about your first inklings in making art and even art as something that appealed to you.

AW: I always drew. Second or third grade is the earliest I remember, because that was when I got in trouble drawing horses in school. But growing up, Dad would take a month off every summer and we would put the canoe on top of the station wagon and trailer behind. We would pick a different part of the country to see and go to the museums and go sightseeing while we

FIG 1 John Wilmerding and Alice Walton at the Crystal Bridges observation deck during construction, May 2009 were camping. That was a special thing. I always wanted to paint landscapes when we were camping.

JW: Did you do that with watercolors?

AW: With watercolor primarily; I was piddling with watercolor all along. I got honorable mention in the fourth grade for the head of an Indian woman. My claim to fame!

JW: I'm interested in the connective tissue between painting watercolors and, at a certain point, becoming aware of others' works of art. I guess I'm asking: Is this the genesis of the collecting instinct?

AW: I never associated my own art with collecting. It was the joy of doing it. I have always loved art. We have great arts and crafts fairs in Northwest Arkansas, and we have a lot of good regional artists and artisans.

JW: How did that phase of collecting, which was essentially regional art, segue into collecting American art?

AW: Both my father and my mother were always so thankful for the opportunities that we have in this country. And how can we say thank you for these opportunities?

JW: Do you remember what some of your early nonregional art purchases were?

AW: Twachtman, John Twachtman—his Yellowstone Falls [*Lower Falls of the Yellowstone*, ca. 1895] was a fairly early one.

I didn't make the leap to national American art with the idea of a museum in mind. The museum idea probably started in the mid-1990s, when I thought about what this part of the world [Northwest Arkansas] is really lacking. I don't know that I even started there. I probably started with what means a lot, what would be meaningful to me and to others that I could give? And nothing else came to mind. Unless they wanted a herd of horses on the [Bentonville town] square![1]

JW: By the end of the 1990s it seems that the idea for an art museum in Bentonville crystallized, so to speak?

AW: I think it was after I moved to Texas and had some time to think about things other than business. That's when I got serious.

JW: It's after that, that our association began and you began to bring in others to help. What does one go through when one moves from an idea and an emotion to actually creating an entity?

AW: Several things came together, and one was my mother's and my brother's efforts to put that land [the Bentonville property where Crystal Bridges is located] together. You have to have a place to put a museum.

JW: As they were preserving that land did they have any particular goal, or was it just to save landscape in their family?

AW: Mother had always said, someday this will be used for something very special. I brought up the idea of the museum and my love of art and my collecting.

JW: The land, you've taken a major step. What did you do next? Who did you call next?

AW: We had a pretty good collection going. I had been visiting museums around the country, methodically meeting with people, including museum directors, and trying to chart our way. Then all of a sudden we made the bid on *Kindred Spirits*.

When I first saw that painting I had goose bumps. That was a big leap. It was scary as far as I was concerned. The painting seemed to epitomize all we were trying to accomplish here, the integration of art and the land.

JW: Looking out over the [Crystal Bridges] construction platform, we're in kind of a *Kindred Spirits* landscape here. In a way, the acquisition of Durand's painting was the first, transformative foundation of the museum coming into its own, taking on an identity nationally.

AW: I remember us sitting in the room there at Sotheby's [in the spring of 2005] when we saw it [*Kindred Spirits*]. It was a transformative moment for me in terms of taking this [museum] from what I perceived of as a gift to the community to what I now think of as a gift to the nation.

JW: Do you have any thoughts about how you might want to use *Kindred Spirits* as an "ambassador"?

AW: I believe that museums need to exchange and share more, and we've tried to make a statement about that. We want to lend and we want to borrow, and I think that is an important part of our philosophy.

JW: How did you go about establishing the scope of the museum and its activities? What did you want to pursue there?

AW: We've always said that we want a very special space for the permanent collection and that it's going to be a significant national collection—not heavily regional or local. And it needs space appropriate to such a collection.

In terms of the temporary exhibitions, we are not limited to American art. I think that is a key role that Crystal Bridges can play as the region's major art museum. It needs to bring things that people don't have access to—that may be European art, it may be Asian art, it may be Mexican art, South American art. I don't want to limit exhibitions because of the role they can play in providing access to art that the community wouldn't otherwise have the opportunity to experience.

JW: You've collected across media in a way that many sister institutions haven't so evenhandedly—sculpture, works on paper, archival materials, illustrated books, etc. But how did that evolve? That is to say, your interest in broader coverage?

AW: When I started collecting in the 1990s, I started reading art history books. And I fell in love with art again.

JW: Had you any art history background before that?

AW: None.

JW: Training?

AW: None! Zero. I just fell in love with learning about art. And, what made it come full circle for me was when we got the opportunity in early 2004 to purchase a great private American art library [approximately twenty-five thousand books and primary research materials dating from the Age of Discovery to the present]. I want people to have the access and the opportunity and the joy that I've had in tying the art into the history of this country.

JW: The notion that this would be a museum for research, as I understand it, wasn't necessarily on your mind until that moment. So again, this was an unusual opportunity that helped refine and clarify the museum's mission, am I right?

AW: Yes, I started thinking about the real joy that I get from collecting, and a key piece of that is learning the history of these artworks and how they relate to our history as a nation. As a family, education has always been our number one focus. For me, this became the cement for the whole project.

JW: Come back to the shaping of the collection. You have been actively buying for a good five years since that moment of the Durand purchase. On one level, it is a survey collection and it stretches from the colonial period to the present. But it is also a very personal collection. It seems to me that, like many single donor museums, it has certain concentrations, certain artists.

AW: First of all there has to be opportunity, because you can't *make* a collection happen, I don't think. And this collection is the result of opportunity available up until now. I can't help but become fascinated with certain artists and attracted to certain artists. I think all of us are that way. We do have several areas of strong depth.

JW: Who are some of those artists?

AW: Martin Johnson Heade, whom I love. And Alfred Maurer comes to mind as a very different kind of painter that I also like very much. Stuart Davis is another. Also, Marsden Hartley. I am a bit fascinated by the early twentieth century, but I started out being most interested in the mid- to late nineteenth century. As

I've learned, as people have opened my eyes to different areas, then what I love expands and grows.

JW: Like contemporary art. When you started, you didn't think of it . . .

AW: Never dreamed of it. And I guess my experience in terms of getting to where we are today is really about growth and development. And it's not gonna quit until I'm not sitting here anymore, I hope! I hope Crystal Bridges gives other people that same opportunity.

I think our museum should be a reflection of today's culture, which is much more casual and much more comfortable and much more connected to the interests and lives of the younger generation.

JW: Have you had any awareness of being in a fairly elite group, at least in the history of American culture? That is, a history of women collectors and museum founders that goes back to Abby Rockefeller, Electra Havemeyer Webb, Isabella Stewart Gardner, Ima Hogg. Has that been on your mind now that the museum is coming to fruition? Are you proud of that? To be in that circle?

AW: I'm proud to be mentioned or thought of anywhere near that circle. It's not been a conscious thing. It's been a learning process, an education process for me.

JW: This brings us to the present, having just toured the site and seen a James Turrell going into the hillside. Elaborate a little bit on the Turrell, because that's going to come as a wonderful surprise to visitors, I think.

AW: There is no more satisfying way to physically and emotionally experience art as nature and nature as art than visiting a Turrell Skyspace. I know people who wouldn't go into the museum probably will after they experience the Turrell.

JW: Finally, future directions for the museum. Once it's open, what kind of things do you want it to be doing?

AW: I hope that we always have a strong focus on community and education. The museum should be a comfortable place for people—for everyone.

NOTE

1. Walton's other great passion is horses. She is a prominent breeder and trainer of cutting horses, and has competed for many years in cutting-horse competitions.

CONTRIBUTORS

WCA William C. Agee is the Evelyn Kranes Kossak Professor of Art History at Hunter College.

DB Don Bacigalupi is the executive director of Crystal Bridges Museum of American Art.

CRB Carrie Rebora Barratt is associate director for collections and administration at The Metropolitan Museum of Art.

MCC Margaret C. Conrads is the Samuel Sosland Senior Curator of American Art at the Nelson-Atkins Museum of Art.

CBC Christopher B. Crosman is founding curator of the collection at Crystal Bridges Museum of American Art.

AD Alison Demorotski is curatorial assistant at Crystal Bridges Museum of American Art.

ACDP Anne Cohen DePietro is director of American art at Doyle New York.

SE Stacey Epstein is director of modernism at Hollis Taggart Galleries.

LSF Linda S. Ferber is vice president and senior art historian at the New-York Historical Society.

SMH Stephanie Mayer Heydt is the Margaret and Terry Stent Curator of American Art at the High Museum of Art.

AWJ Aaron W. Jones is interpretation manager at Crystal Bridges Museum of American Art.

SGL Susan G. Larkin is an independent art historian and curator specializing in late nineteenth- and early twentieth-century American art.

REL Rebecca E. Lawton is curator of paintings and sculpture at the Amon Carter Museum of American Art.

NMM Nancy Mowll Mathews is the Eugénie Prendergast Senior Curator of Nineteenth- and Twentieth-Century Art and Lecturer in Art, Williams College Museum of Art.

AWM Alissa Walls Mazow is assistant professor of contemporary art at the University of Arkansas.

LGM Leo G. Mazow is associate professor of American art at the University of Arkansas.

LM Linda Merrill teaches art history at Emory University and has served as curator of American art at the Freer Gallery of Art and the High Museum of Art.

EDS Emily D. Shapiro is an independent scholar of American art with curatorial experience at the Corcoran Gallery of Art and George Washington's Mount Vernon Estate & Gardens.

WS Will South is chief curator at the Dayton Art Institute and a specialist in American modernism.

JDS Justin D. Spring is a biographer, art historian, and curator specializing in twentieth-century American art and culture.

NCS Niki Ciccotelli Stewart is director of education at Crystal Bridges Museum of American Art.

LS Lisa Strong is manager of curatorial affairs at the Corcoran Gallery of Art.

MW Manuela Well-Off-Man is assistant curator at Crystal Bridges Museum of American Art.

JW John Wilmerding is the Christopher Binyon Sarofim Professor of American Art, emeritus, at Princeton University; chairman of the board of trustees at the National Gallery of Art; and a trustee at Crystal Bridges Museum of American Art.

INDEX

Italicized page references refer to illustrations. Endnotes are indicated with "n" followed by the endnote number.

IMAGE CREDITS

© 2011 The Josef and Anni Albers Foundation/Artists Rights Society (ARS), New York. Photography by Dwight Primiano: 2 (detail), 271

Photography by Amon Carter Museum of American Art: 35, 51, 75, 81, 95, 111, 115, 209, 229

© 2011 Artists Rights Society (ARS), New York/VG Bild-Kunst, Bonn. Photography by Dwight Primiano: 203

© 2011 Milton Avery Trust/Artists Rights Society (ARS), New York: 249

© Will Barnet, courtesy Alexandre Gallery, New York. Photo Courtesy Alexandre Gallery, New York: 255

© Will Barnet, courtesy Alexandre Gallery, New York. Photography by Dwight Primiano: 257

© Bo Bartlett, 2011. Photography by Dwight Primiano: 297

Art © Romare Bearden Foundation/Licensed by VAGA, New York, NY. Photography by Dwight Primiano: 239

Art © Lynda Benglis/Licensed by VAGA, New York, NY. Photo Courtesy of Margo Leavin Gallery, Los Angeles; photo: Michael Tropea: 339 (fig. 9)

© Estate of Frank Weston Benson. Photography by Dwight Primiano: 185, 341 (detail)

Art © T. H. Benton and R. P. Benton Testamentary Trusts/UMB Bank Trustee/Licensed by VAGA, New York, NY: 231

Reproduced with permission of the Charles E. Burchfield Foundation. Photography by Dwight Primiano: 247

© Nick Cave. Photography: James Prinz Images Courtesy of Jack Shainman Gallery, NY: 340 (fig. 12)

© Chuck Close, Courtesy The Pace Gallery. Photography by Steven Watson: 12 (fig. 2)

Photo: Susan A. Cole, Seattle Art Museum: 139, 181

Photography by Douglas Dalton: 189

Art © Estate of Stuart Davis/Licensed by VAGA, New York, NY. Photo: Tim Thayer: 223

Art © Estate of Stuart Davis/Licensed by VAGA, New York, NY. Photo courtesy of the Saint Louis Art Museum: 225

© Delaware Art Museum/Artists Rights Society (ARS), New York. Photography by Dwight Primiano: 191

© Mark di Suvero. Photo Courtesy of the artist and Paula Cooper Gallery, New York; photo: Jeffrey Price: 336 (fig. 4)

© The Estate of Arthur G. Dove, courtesy Terry Dintenfass, Inc. Photo: Robert LaPrelle: 20 (detail), 21 (detail), 215

© The Estate of Arthur G. Dove, courtesy Terry Dintenfass, Inc. Photography by Dwight Primiano: 217

Art © Marisol Escobar/Licensed by VAGA, New York, NY. Photo Courtesy of Sotheby's, Inc. © (2011): 338 (fig. 8)

© Richard Estes, Courtesy of the Marlborough Gallery, New York: 293

© Richard Estes, Courtesy of the Marlborough Gallery, New York. Photography by Dwight Primiano: 10–11 (detail), 295

© Walton Ford. Photo Courtesy the Artist and Paul Kasmin Gallery: 307

© 2011 The Arshile Gorky Foundation/Artists Rights Society (ARS), New York. Photo: Robert LaPrelle: 6 (detail), 235

© Estate of Grace Hartigan, Rex Stevens, executor. Photography by Steven Watson: 265

© Estate of Grace Hartigan, Rex Stevens, executor. Photo © Christie's Images/The Bridgeman Art Library: 267

© Estate of Marsden Hartley, Yale University Committee on Intellectual Property. Photography by Amon Carter Museum of American Art: 199

© Estate of Marsden Hartley, Yale University Committee on Intellectual Property. Photography by Steven Watson: 201

© Estate of Marsden Hartley, Yale University Committee on Intellectual Property. Photography by Dwight Primiano: 233

© Estate of Marsden Hartley, Yale University Committee on Intellectual Property. Photo Courtesy Alexandre Gallery, New York: 243

© Jim Hodges. Photo Courtesy of Sotheby's, Inc. © (2011): 305

© 2011 Renate, Hans and Maria Hofmann Trust/Artists Rights Society (ARS), New York. Photography by Dwight Primiano: 259

© 2011 Renate, Hans and Maria Hofmann Trust/Artists Rights Society (ARS), New York. Photo © Christie's Images/The Bridgeman Art Library: 261

Photography by John Horner: 8 (fig. 2), 9 (fig. 3)

© Estate of John Koch, Courtesy Kraushaar Galleries. Photography by Dwight Primiano: 273

Art © Estate of Yasuo Kuniyoshi/Licensed by VAGA, New York, NY. Photography by Amon Carter Museum of American Art: 221

Photograph by John Lamberton, courtesy of The Nelson-Atkins Museum of Art, Kansas City, Missouri: 18 (fig. 11), 77

© Karen LaMonte 2008. Photography by Martin Polak: 340 (fig. 11)

Photo: Robert LaPrelle: 1 (detail), 33, 103, 147, 175

© 2011 The Jacob and Gwendolyn Lawrence Foundation, Seattle/Artists Rights Society (ARS), New York. Photo: Tim Thayer: 251

© Estate of Blanche Lazzell. Photography by Steven Watson: 16 (fig. 9)

© Estate of Roy Lichtenstein. Photo © Christie's Images/The Bridgeman Art Library: 13 (fig. 3)

Charles Deering McCormick Library of Special Collections, Northwestern University Library: 169

Copyrighted by the Estate of Stanton & Jean Macdonald-Wright, 2011. Photography by Dwight Primiano: 211

© 2011 Estate of John Marin/Artists Rights Society (ARS), New York. Photography by Dwight Primiano: 195

© 2011 Estate of John Marin/Artists Rights Society (ARS), New York. Photo: Tim Thayer: 197

© Kerry James Marshall. Photography by Vancouver Art Gallery: 18 (fig. 12), 301

© Mary McCleary. Photo courtesy of the artist and the Moody Gallery, Houston, TX: 299

Photography by The Metropolitan Museum of Art: 14 (fig. 5), 65

© Estate of Joan Mitchell. Photo Courtesy of the Joan Mitchell Foundation: 263

Photograph courtesy of The Museum of Fine Arts, Houston: 37

Photograph courtesy of The National Gallery of Art, Washington: 67

© 2011 Estate of Louise Nevelson/Artists Rights Society (ARS), New York. Photo Courtesy of Sotheby's, Inc. © (2011): 17 (fig. 10)

© 2011 The Isamu Noguchi Foundation and Garden Museum, New York/Artists Rights Society (ARS), New York. Photography by Dwight Primiano: 337 (fig. 6)

Art © Estate of Kenneth Noland/Licensed by VAGA, New York, NY. Photography by Dwight Primiano: 269

© 2011 Georgia O'Keeffe Museum/Artists Rights Society (ARS), New York. Photography by Dwight Primiano: 205, 207

© Claes Oldenburg. Photo courtesy of the Oldenburg van Bruggen Studio: 338 (fig. 7)

© Roxy Paine. Courtesy James Cohan Gallery, New York/Shanghai: 335 (fig. 2)

Photo Courtesy of Philadelphia Museum of Art: 125

© 2011 Pollock-Krasner Foundation/Artists Rights Society (ARS), New York. Photography by Dwight Primiano: 237

© Estate of Fairfield Porter. Photography by Dwight Primiano: 275

Photography by Dwight Primiano: 1 (detail), 3 (detail), 4 (detail), 6 (detail), 16 (fig. 8), 23, 25, 26, 27, 29, 31, 39, 41, 43, 47, 49, 53, 55, 57, 59, 61, 63, 71, 73, 83, 85, 86, 87, 89, 91, 93, 97, 99, 101, 109, 113, 117, 119, 121, 123, 127, 129, 131, 135, 137, 141, 143, 145, 153, 155, 157, 159, 165, 171, 173, 177, 179, 183, 193, 219, 227

Art © Estate of Robert Rauschenberg/Licensed by VAGA, New York, NY. Photography by Steven Watson: 277

Printed by permission of the Norman Rockwell Family Agency, Book Rights Copyright © 1943 The Norman Family Entities. Photography by Dwight Primiano: 15 (fig. 6), 245

Art © Estate of David Smith/Licensed by VAGA, New York, NY. Photography by Dwight Primiano: 241

Photograph Courtesy of Sotheby's, Inc. © (2011): 107, 337 (fig. 5)

Photography by Lee Stalsworth: 163

© Alison Elizabeth Taylor. Courtesy James Cohan Gallery, New York/Shanghai. Photo: Jason Mandella: 339 (fig. 10)

Art © Wayne Thiebaud/Licensed by VAGA, New York, NY. Photo: Robert LaPrelle: 279

© George Tooker. Photography by Dwight Primiano: 285

© James Turrell, Courtesy The Pace Gallery. Photography by Timothy Hursley: 334 (detail), 336 (fig. 3)

© Tom Uttech, courtesy Alexandre Gallery, New York. Photography by Steven Watson: 309

© Ursula von Rydingsvard, Courtesy Galerie Lelong, New York. Photo Courtesy Galerie Lelong, New York: 13 (fig. 4)

© Kara Walker. Courtesy of Sikkema Jenkins & Co., New York. Photo Courtesy of Sikkema Jenkins & Co., Inc.: 303

© 2011 The Andy Warhol Foundation for the Visual Arts/Artists Rights Society (ARS), New York. Photo: Robert LaPrelle: 15 (fig. 7), 281

Photography by Steven Watson: 10 (detail), 20 (detail), 69, 79, 105, 133, 167, 213, 341 (detail)

© Neil Welliver, courtesy Alexandre Gallery, New York. Photo Courtesy Alexandre Gallery, New York: 287

Art © Estate of Tom Wesselmann/Licensed by VAGA, New York, NY. Photography by Dwight Primiano: 283

© Estate of Andrew Wyeth. Photo: Robert LaPrelle: 289

© Jamie Wyeth: 291

Third printing, 2012

CRYSTAL BRIDGES
MUSEUM OF AMERICAN ART

Published in association with
Hudson Hills Press LLC
3556 Main Street, Manchester,
Vermont 05254.

Distributed in the United States, its territories and possessions, and Canada by National Book Network, Inc. Distributed outside North America by Antique Collectors' Club, Ltd.

Produced by Marquand Books, Inc., Seattle
www.marquand.com

General Editor: Christopher B. Crosman
Managing Editor: Emily D. Shapiro
Copyeditor: Emily D. Shapiro
Proofreader: Carrie Wicks
Designer: Zach Hooker
iamabookdesigner.com
Typeset by Brynn Warriner in Calluna
Color management by iocolor, Seattle
Printed and bound in China by Artron Color Printing, Ltd.

Library of Congress Cataloging-in-Publication Data
Crystal Bridges Museum of American Art.
Celebrating the American spirit: masterworks from Crystal Bridges Museum of American Art/foreword by Don Bacigalupi; Christopher B. Crosman, general editor; Emily D. Shapiro, managing editor; with contributions by William C. Agee...[et al.].—1st ed.
p. cm.
ISBN 978-1-55595-371-3 (hardcover : alk. paper)—ISBN 978-1-55595-372-0 (softcover : alk. paper)
1. Art, American—Catalogs. 2. Art—Arkansas—Bentonville—Catalogs. 3. Crystal Bridges Museum of American Art—Catalogs. I. Crosman, Christopher B. II. Shapiro, Emily D. III. Agee, William C. IV. Title. V. Title: Masterworks from Crystal Bridges Museum of American Art.
N6505.C79 2011
708.167'13—dc23 2011025279

Page 1: John Singer Sargent, *Under the Willows*, detail, 147; Alfred Thompson Bricher, *View of Mount Washington*, detail, 97

Pages 2–3: Josef Albers, *Homage to the Square: Joy*, detail, 271; Childe Hassam, *Isles of Shoals*, detail, 121

Pages 4–5: Francis Guy, *Winter Scene in Brooklyn*, detail, 49; Charles Sheeler, *Amoskeag Mills #2*, detail, 253

Page 6: Joseph Decker, *Basket of Peaches*, detail, 113; Arshile Gorky, *Composition (Still Life)*, detail, 235

Pages 10–11: Thomas Moran, *Valley of the Catawissa in Autumn*, detail, 79; Richard Estes, *Antarctica*, detail, 295

Pages 20–21: William Trost Richards, *Along the Shore*, detail, 167; Arthur Garfield Dove, *Moon and Sea II*, detail, 215

Page 334: James Turrell, *The Way of Color*, detail

Page 341: Charles Demuth, *Sail: In Two Movements*, detail, 213; Frank Weston Benson, *Summer Day*, detail, 185